Audi A3 Diesel
Owners Workshop Manual

Peter T Gill and John S Mead

Models covered

(5912 - 368)

Hatchback (3-door) & Sportback (5-door)
Turbo-Diesel: 1.6 litre (1599cc), 1.9 litre (1896cc) & 2.0 litre (1968cc)

Does NOT cover petrol models, Quattro or Cabriolet
Does NOT cover new Audi A3 range introduced September 2012

© Haynes Group Limited 2015

ABCDE
FGHIJ
KLMNO
PQ

A book in the **Haynes Owners Workshop Manual Series**

All rights reserved. No part of this book may be reproduced or transmitted in any form or by any means, electronic or mechanical, including photocopying, recording or by any information storage or retrieval system, without permission in writing from the copyright holder.

ISBN **978 0 85733 912 6**

British Library Cataloguing in Publication Data
A catalogue record for this book is available from the British Library.

Printed in India

Haynes Group Limited
Sparkford, Yeovil, Somerset BA22 7JJ, England

Haynes North America, Inc
2801 Townsgate Road, Suite 340, Thousand Oaks, CA 91361

Disclaimer

There are risks associated with automotive repairs. The ability to make repairs depends on the individual's skill, experience and proper tools. Individuals should act with due care and acknowledge and assume the risk of performing automotive repairs.

The purpose of this manual is to provide comprehensive, useful and accessible automotive repair information, to help you get the best value from your vehicle. However, this manual is not a substitute for a professional certified technician or mechanic.

This repair manual is produced by a third party and is not associated with an individual vehicle manufacturer. If there is any doubt or discrepancy between this manual and the owner's manual or the factory service manual, please refer to the factory service manual or seek assistance from a professional certified technician or mechanic.

Even though we have prepared this manual with extreme care and every attempt is made to ensure that the information in this manual is correct, neither the publisher nor the author can accept responsibility for loss, damage or injury caused by any errors in, or omissions from, the information given.

Contents

Illegal Copying

It is the policy of the Publisher to actively protect its Copyrights and Trade Marks. Legal action will be taken against anyone who unlawfully copies the cover or contents of this Manual. This includes all forms of unauthorised copying including digital, mechanical, and electronic in any form. Authorisation from the Publisher will only be provided expressly and in writing. Illegal copying will also be reported to the appropriate statutory authorities.

Contents

The Audi A3 models covered by this manual date from April 2008 to September 2012 and are available in 3-door Hatchback and 5-door Sportback bodystyles.

A wide variety of engine sizes are available but this manual covers the 4-cylinder turbocharged diesel engine models of 1.6, 1.9 and 2.0 litre capacity, with SOHC 8v or DOHC 16v cylinder heads. 1.9 litre engines are equipped with unit injectors, utilising a rocker shaft and arm assembly with a second set of camshaft lobes to compress each unit injector in turn to provide higher injection pressures, and increased accuracy of injection timing. 1.6 and 2.0 litre engines utilise conventional common rail fuel injection.

Fully-independent front and rear suspension is fitted, with the components attached to a subframe assembly; the rear suspension uses trailing arms together with multi-link transverse arms.

A 5- or 6-speed manual gearbox is fitted as standard to all models, with a 6- or 7-speed DSG (Direct Shift Gearbox) automatic transmission available as an option on 1.6 and 2.0 litre models.

The dual-circuit, servo-assisted braking system has discs all round, with ABS, Electronic Differential Lock (EDL) Electronic Stability Program (ESP) Emergency Brake Assist (EBA) and Electronic Brakeforce Distribution (EBD) either fitted as standard, or optionally available, for extra safety when braking in emergency situations.

A wide range of standard and optional equipment is available within the A3 range, including power steering, air conditioning, remote central locking, electric windows, electronic engine immobiliser and supplemental restraint systems.

For the home mechanic, the A3 models are straightforward vehicles to maintain, and most of the items requiring frequent attention are easily accessible.

Your Audi A3 Manual

The aim of this manual is to help you get the best value from your vehicle. It can do so in several ways. It can help you decide what work must be done (even should you choose to get it done by a garage). It will also provide information on routine maintenance and servicing, and give a logical course of action and diagnosis when random faults occur. However, it is hoped that you will use the manual by tackling the work yourself. On simpler jobs it may even be quicker than booking the car into a garage and going there twice, to leave and collect it. Perhaps most important, a lot of money can be saved by avoiding the costs a garage must charge to cover its labour and overheads.

The manual has drawings and descriptions to show the function of the various components so that their layout can be understood. Tasks are described and photographed in a clear step-by-step sequence.

References to the 'left' and 'right' of the vehicle are in the sense of a person in the driver's seat facing forward.

Acknowledgements

Thanks are due to Draper Tools Limited, who provided some of the workshop tools, and to all those people at Sparkford who helped in the production of this manual.

This manual is not a direct reproduction of the vehicle manufacturer's data, and its publication should not be taken as implying any technical approval by the vehicle manufacturers or importers.

We take great pride in the accuracy of information given in this manual, but vehicle manufacturers make alterations and design changes during the production run of a particular vehicle of which they do not inform us. No liability can be accepted by the authors or publishers for loss, damage or injury caused by any errors in, or omissions from, the information given.

Working on your car can be dangerous. This page shows just some of the potential risks and hazards, with the aim of creating a safety-conscious attitude.

General hazards

Scalding

• Don't remove the radiator or expansion tank cap while the engine is hot.

• Engine oil, transmission fluid or power steering fluid may also be dangerously hot if the engine has recently been running.

Burning

• Beware of burns from the exhaust system and from any part of the engine. Brake discs and drums can also be extremely hot immediately after use.

Crushing

• When working under or near a raised vehicle, always supplement the jack with axle stands, or use drive-on ramps.

Never venture under a car which is only supported by a jack.

• Take care if loosening or tightening high- torque nuts when the vehicle is on stands. Initial loosening and final tightening should be done with the wheels on the ground.

Fire

• Fuel is highly flammable; fuel vapour is explosive.

• Don't let fuel spill onto a hot engine.

• Do not smoke or allow naked lights (including pilot lights) anywhere near a vehicle being worked on. Also beware of creating sparks (electrically or by use of tools).

• Fuel vapour is heavier than air, so don't work on the fuel system with the vehicle over an inspection pit.

• Another cause of fire is an electrical overload or short-circuit. Take care when repairing or modifying the vehicle wiring.

• Keep a fire extinguisher handy, of a type suitable for use on fuel and electrical fires.

Electric shock

• Ignition HT and Xenon headlight voltages can be dangerous, especially to people with heart problems or a pacemaker. Don't work on or near these systems with the engine running or the ignition switched on.

• Mains voltage is also dangerous. Make sure that any mains-operated equipment is correctly earthed. Mains power points should be protected by a residual current device (RCD) circuit breaker.

Fume or gas intoxication

• Exhaust fumes are poisonous; they can contain carbon monoxide, which is rapidly fatal if inhaled. Never run the engine in a confined space such as a garage with the doors shut.

• Fuel vapour is also poisonous, as are the vapours from some cleaning solvents and paint thinners.

Poisonous or irritant substances

• Avoid skin contact with battery acid and with any fuel, fluid or lubricant, especially antifreeze, brake hydraulic fluid and Diesel fuel. Don't syphon them by mouth. If such a substance is swallowed or gets into the eyes, seek medical advice.

• Prolonged contact with used engine oil can cause skin cancer. Wear gloves or use a barrier cream if necessary. Change out of oil-soaked clothes and do not keep oily rags in your pocket.

• Air conditioning refrigerant forms a poisonous gas if exposed to a naked flame (including a cigarette). It can also cause skin burns on contact.

Asbestos

• Asbestos dust can cause cancer if inhaled or swallowed. Asbestos may be found in gaskets and in brake and clutch linings. When dealing with such components it is safest to assume that they contain asbestos.

Special hazards

Hydrofluoric acid

• This extremely corrosive acid is formed when certain types of synthetic rubber, found in some O-rings, oil seals, fuel hoses etc, are exposed to temperatures above 4000C. The rubber changes into a charred or sticky substance containing the acid. *Once formed, the acid remains dangerous for years. If it gets onto the skin, it may be necessary to amputate the limb concerned.*

• When dealing with a vehicle which has suffered a fire, or with components salvaged from such a vehicle, wear protective gloves and discard them after use.

The battery

• Batteries contain sulphuric acid, which attacks clothing, eyes and skin. Take care when topping-up or carrying the battery.

• The hydrogen gas given off by the battery is highly explosive. Never cause a spark or allow a naked light nearby. Be careful when connecting and disconnecting battery chargers or jump leads.

Air bags

• Air bags can cause injury if they go off accidentally. Take care when removing the steering wheel and trim panels. Special storage instructions may apply.

Diesel injection equipment

• Diesel injection pumps supply fuel at very high pressure. Take care when working on the fuel injectors and fuel pipes.

⚠️ *Warning: Never expose the hands, face or any other part of the body to injector spray; the fuel can penetrate the skin with potentially fatal results.*

Remember...

DO

• Do use eye protection when using power tools, and when working under the vehicle.

• Do wear gloves or use barrier cream to protect your hands when necessary.

• Do get someone to check periodically that all is well when working alone on the vehicle.

• Do keep loose clothing and long hair well out of the way of moving mechanical parts.

• Do remove rings, wristwatch etc, before working on the vehicle – especially the electrical system.

• Do ensure that any lifting or jacking equipment has a safe working load rating adequate for the job.

DON'T

• Don't attempt to lift a heavy component which may be beyond your capability – get assistance.

• Don't rush to finish a job, or take unverified short cuts.

• Don't use ill-fitting tools which may slip and cause injury.

• Don't leave tools or parts lying around where someone can trip over them. Mop up oil and fuel spills at once.

• Don't allow children or pets to play in or near a vehicle being worked on.

The following pages are intended to help in dealing with common roadside emergencies and breakdowns. You will find more detailed fault finding information at the back of the manual, and repair information in the main chapters.

If your car won't start and the starter motor doesn't turn

- ☐ If it's a model with automatic transmission, make sure the selector is in P or N.
- ☐ Open the bonnet and make sure that the battery terminals are clean and tight.
- ☐ Switch on the headlights and try to start the engine. If the headlights go very dim when you're trying to start, the battery is probably flat. Get out of trouble by jump starting (see next page) using a friend's car.

If your car won't start even though the starter motor turns as normal

- ☐ Is there fuel in the tank?
- ☐ Is there moisture on electrical components under the bonnet? Switch off the ignition, then wipe off any obvious dampness with a dry cloth. Spray a water-repellent aerosol product (WD-40 or equivalent) on ignition and fuel system electrical connectors like those shown in the photos. (Note that diesel engines don't usually suffer from damp).

A Check the condition and security of the battery connections

B Check the fuses in the fusebox located on the left-hand side of the engine compartment

C Check the wiring to the air mass meter

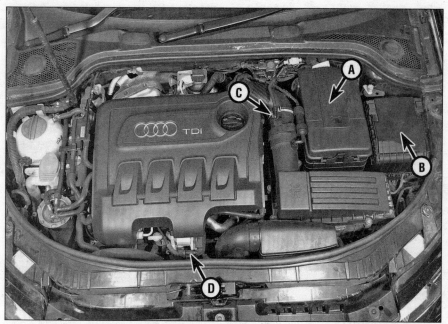

Check that electrical connections are secure (with the ignition switched off) and spray them with a water-dispersantspray like WD-40 if you suspect a problem due to damp

D Check that the throttle valve housing wiring is secure

Jump starting

When jump-starting a car using a booster battery, observe the following precautions:

✓ Before connecting the booster battery, make sure that the ignition is switched off.
✓ Remove the ignition key in case the central locking engages when the jump leads are connected.
✓ Ensure that all electrical equipment (lights, heater, wipers, etc) is switched off.
✓ Take note of any special precautions printed on the battery case.

✓ Make sure that the booster battery is the same voltage as the discharged one in the vehicle.
✓ If the battery is being jump-started from the battery in another vehicle, the two vehicles MUST NOT TOUCH each other.
✓ Make sure that the transmission is in neutral (or PARK, in the case of automatic transmission).

> **HAYNES HiNT**
>
> *Jump starting will get you out of trouble, but you must correct whatever made the battery go flat in the first place. There are three possibilities:*
>
> **1** *The battery has been drained by repeated attempts to start, or by leaving the lights on.*
>
> **2** *The charging system is not working properly (alternator drivebelt slack or broken, alternator wiring fault or alternator itself faulty).*
>
> **3** *The battery itself is at fault (electrolyte low, or battery worn out).*

1 Connect one end of the red jump lead to the positive (+) terminal of the flat battery.

2 Connect the other end of the red jump lead to the positive (+) terminal of the booster battery.

3 Connect one end of the black jump lead to the negative (-) terminal of the booster battery.

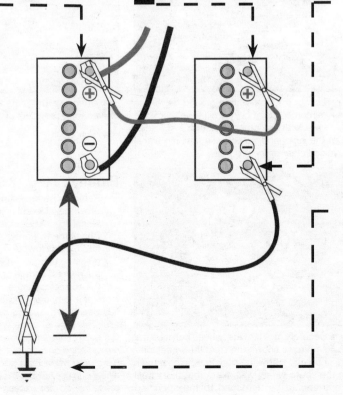

4 Connect the other end of the black jump lead to the earth stud on the left-hand side of the engine compartment.

5 Make sure that the jump leads will not come into contact with the fan, drivebelts or other moving parts of the engine. Start the engine using the booster battery and run it at idle speed. Switch on the lights, rear window demister and heater blower motor, then disconnect the jump leads in the reverse order of connection. Turn off the lights etc.

Wheel changing

Some of the details shown here will vary according to model

⚠️ **Warning: Do not change a wheel in a situation where you risk being hit by other traffic. On busy roads, try to stop in a lay-by or a gateway. Be wary of passing traffic while changing the wheel – it is easy to become distracted by the job in hand.**

Preparation

- ☐ When a puncture occurs, stop as soon as it is safe to do so.
- ☐ Park on firm level ground, if possible, and well out of the way of other traffic.
- ☐ Use hazard warning lights if necessary.
- ☐ If you have one, use a warning triangle to alert other drivers of your presence.
- ☐ Apply the handbrake and engage first or reverse gear (or P on models with automatic transmission).
- ☐ Chock the wheel diagonally opposite the one being removed – a couple of large stones will do for this.
- ☐ If the ground is soft, use a flat piece of wood to spread the load under the jack.

Changing the wheel

1 The spare wheel and tools are stored in the luggage compartment. Raise the floor covering, and lift out the jack and wheel changing tools from the centre of the wheel.

2 Use the wire hook to remove the wheel bolt caps.

3 Use the wheel brace to slacken each wheel bolt by half a turn.

4 Use the special adapter when slackening the locking wheel bolt.

5 Locate the jack on firm ground below the reinforced point on the sill (don't jack the vehicle at any other point of the sill), then turn the jack handle clockwise until the wheel is raised clear of the ground.

6 Unscrew the wheel bolts (using the adapter provided) and remove the wheel.

7 Fit the spare wheel, and screw in the bolts. Lightly tighten the bolts with the wheelbrace then lower the vehicle to the ground.

8 Securely tighten the wheel bolts in the sequence shown then refit the wheel trim/ hub cap. Stow the punctured wheel back in the spare wheel well. Note that the wheel bolts should be tightened to the specified torque at the earliest possible opportunity.

Finally . . .

- ☐ Remove the wheel chocks.
- ☐ Stow the jack and tools in the spare wheel.
- ☐ Check the tyre pressure on the wheel just fitted. If it is low, or if you don't have a pressure gauge with you, drive slowly to the nearest garage and inflate the tyre to the correct pressure.

Note: *If a temporary 'space-saver' spare wheel has been fitted, special conditions apply to its use. This type of spare wheel is only intended for use in an emergency, and should not remain fitted any longer than it takes to get the punctured wheel repaired. While the temporary wheel is in use, ensure it is inflated to the correct pressure, do not exceed 50 mph, and avoid harsh acceleration, braking or cornering.*

Identifying leaks

Puddles on the garage floor or drive, or obvious wetness under the bonnet or underneath the car, suggest a leak that needs investigating. It can sometimes be difficult to decide where the leak is coming from, especially if an engine undershield is fitted. Leaking oil or fluid can also be blown rearwards by the passage of air under the car, giving a false impression of where the problem lies.

 Warning: Most automotive oils and fluids are poisonous. Wash them off skin, and change out of contaminated clothing, without delay.

 The smell of a fluid leaking from the car may provide a clue to what's leaking. Some fluids are distinctively coloured. It may help to remove the engine undershield, clean the car carefully and to park it over some clean paper overnight as an aid to locating the source of the leak. Remember that some leaks may only occur while the engine is running.

Sump oil

Engine oil may leak from the drain plug...

Oil from filter

...or from the base of the oil filter.

Gearbox oil

Gearbox oil can leak from the seals at the inboard ends of the driveshafts.

Antifreeze

Leaking antifreeze often leaves a crystalline deposit like this.

Brake fluid

A leak occurring at a wheel is almost certainly brake fluid.

Towing

When all else fails, you may find yourself having to get a tow home – or of course you may be helping somebody else. Long-distance recovery should only be done by a garage or breakdown service. For shorter distances, DIY towing using another car is easy enough, but observe the following points:

☐ Use a proper tow-rope – they are not expensive. The vehicle being towed must display an ON TOW sign in its rear window.

☐ Always turn the ignition key to the 'on' position when the vehicle is being towed, so that the steering lock is released, and that the direction indicator and brake lights will work.

☐ Only attach the tow-rope to the towing eyes provided.

☐ Before being towed, release the handbrake and select neutral on the transmission.

☐ Note that greater-than-usual pedal pressure will be required to operate the brakes, since the vacuum servo unit is only operational with the engine running.

☐ The driver of the car being towed must keep the tow-rope taut at all times to avoid snatching.

☐ Make sure that both drivers know the route before setting off.

☐ Only drive at moderate speeds and keep the distance towed to a minimum. Drive smoothly and allow plenty of time for slowing down at junctions.

Introduction

There are some very simple checks which need only take a few minutes to carry out, but which could save you a lot of inconvenience and expense.

These checks require no great skill or special tools, and the small amount of time they take to perform could prove to be very well spent, for example:

☐ Keeping an eye on tyre condition and pressures will not only help to stop them wearing out completely, but could also save your life.

☐ Many breakdowns are caused by electrical problems. Battery-related faults are particularly common, and a quick check on a regular basis will often prevent the majority of these.

☐ If your car develops a break fluid leak, the first time you might know about it is when your brakes don't work properly. Checking the level regularly will give advance warning of this kind of problem.

☐ If the oil or coolant levels run low, the cost of repairing any engine damage will be far greater than fixing the leak, for example.

Underbonnet check points

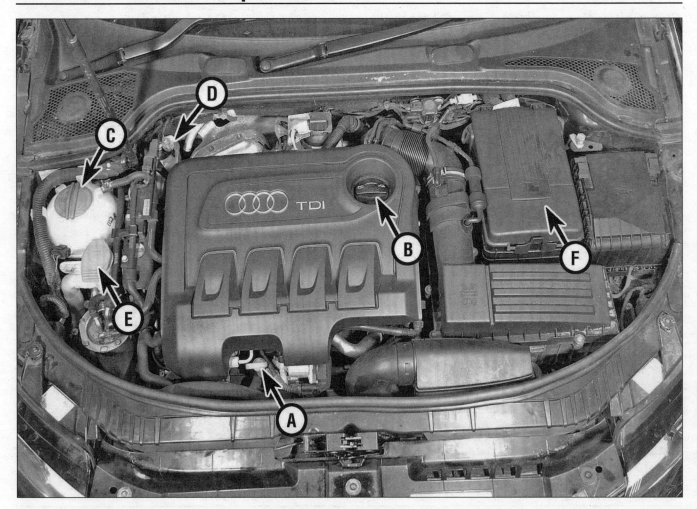

▲ 2.0 litre engine (others similar)

A *Engine oil level dipstick*
B *Engine oil filler cap*

C *Coolant expansion tank*
D *Brake (and clutch) fluid reservoir*

E *Screen washer fluid reservoir*
F *Battery*

Engine oil level

Before you start

✔ Make sure that the car is on level ground.
✔ Check the oil level before the car is driven, or at least 5 minutes after the engine has been switched off.

 HAYNES HiNT *If the oil is checked immediately after driving the vehicle, some of the oil will remain in the upper engine components, resulting in an inaccurate reading on the dipstick.*

The correct oil

Modern engines place great demands on their oil. It is very important that the correct oil for your car is used (see *Lubricants and fluids*).

Car care

● If you have to add oil frequently, you should check whether you have any oil leaks. Place some clean paper under the car overnight, and check for stains in the morning. If there are no leaks, then the engine may be burning oil.
● Always maintain the level between the upper and lower dipstick marks. If the level is too low, severe engine damage may occur. Oil seal failure may result if the engine is overfilled by adding too much oil.

1 The dipstick is often brightly coloured for easy identification (see *Underbonnet check points* for exact location). Withdraw the dipstick.

2 Using a clean rag or paper towel, wipe all the oil from the dipstick. Insert the clean dipstick into the tube as far as it will go, then withdraw it again.

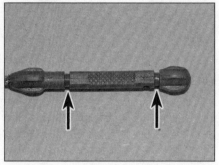

3 Note the level on the end of the dipstick, which should be between the upper (MAX) and lower (MIN) mark.

4 Oil is added through the filler cap aperture. Unscrew the cap.

5 Place some cloth rags around the filler cap aperture, then top-up the level. A funnel may help to reduce spillage. Add the oil slowly, checking the level on the dipstick frequently. Avoid overfilling (see Car care).

Coolant level

 Warning: Do not attempt to remove the expansion tank pressure cap when the engine is hot, as there is a very great risk of scalding. Do not leave open containers of coolant about, as it is poisonous.

Car Care

● With a sealed-type cooling system, adding coolant should not be necessary on a regular basis. If frequent topping-up is required, it is likely there is a leak. Check the radiator, all hoses and joint faces for signs of staining or wetness, and rectify as necessary.

● It is important that antifreeze is used in the cooling system all year round, not just during the winter months. Don't top up with water alone, as the antifreeze will become diluted.

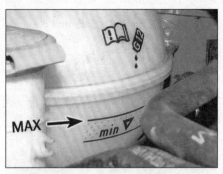

1 The coolant level varies with the temperature of the engine. When the engine is cold, the coolant level should be between the MIN and MAX marks.

2 If topping-up is necessary, wait until the engine is cold. Slowly unscrew the cap to release any pressure present in the cooling system, and remove the cap.

3 Add a mixture of water and the specified antifreeze (see *Lubricants and fluids*) to the expansion tank until the coolant level is halfway between the level marks. Refit the cap and tighten it securely.

Brake (and clutch) fluid level

Note: *On manual transmission models, the fluid reservoir also supplies the clutch master cylinder with fluid*

Before you start

✔ Make sure that the car is on level ground.
✔ Cleanliness is of great importance when dealing with the braking system, so take care to clean around the reservoir cap before topping-up. Use only clean brake fluid.

Safety first!

● If the reservoir requires repeated topping-up, this is an indication of a fluid leak somewhere in the system, which should be investigated immediately. Note that the level will drop naturally as the brake pad linings wear, but must never be allowed to fall below the MIN mark.
● If a leak is suspected, the car should not be driven until the braking system has been checked. Never take any risks where brakes are concerned.

 Warning: Brake fluid can harm your eyes and damage painted surfaces, so use extreme caution when handling and pouring it. Do not use fluid which has been standing open for some time, as it absorbs moisture from the air, which can cause a dangerous loss of braking effectiveness.

1 The MIN and MAX marks are indicated on the reservoir. The fluid level must be kept between the marks at all times. If topping-up is necessary, first wipe clean the area around the filler cap to prevent dirt entering the hydraulic system.

2 Unscrew and remove the reservoir cap.

3 Carefully add fluid, taking care not to spill it onto the surrounding components (use a funnel). Use only the specified fluid (see *Lubricants and fluids*); mixing different types can cause damage to the system. On completion, securely refit the cap and wipe away any spilt fluid.

Tyre condition and pressure

It is very important that tyres are in good condition, and at the correct pressure – having a tyre failure at any speed is highly dangerous. Tyre wear is influenced by driving style – harsh braking and acceleration, or fast cornering, will all produce more rapid tyre wear. As a general rule, the front tyres wear out faster the the rears. Interchanging the tyres from front to rear ("rotating" the tyres) may result in more even wear. However, if this is completely effective, you may have the expense of replacing all four tyres at once!

Remove any nails or stones embedded in the tread before they penetrate the tyre to cause deflation. If removal of a nail does reveal that the tyre has been punctured, refit the nail so that its point of penetration is marked. Then immediately change the wheel, and have the tyre repaired by a tyre dealer.

Regularly check the tyres for damage in the form of cuts or bulges, especially in the side walls. Periodically remove the wheels, and clean any dirt or mud from the inside and outside surfaces. Examine the wheel rims for signs of rusting, corrosion or other damage. Light alloy wheels are easily damaged by "kerbing" whilst parking; steel wheels may also become dented or buckled. A new wheel is very often the only way to overcome severe damage.

New tyres should be balanced when they are fitted, but it may become necessary to re-balance them as they ear, or if the balance weights fitted to the wheel rim should fall off. Unbalanced tyres will wear more quickly, as will the steering and suspension components. Wheel imbalance is normally signified by vibration, particularly at t certain speed (typically around 50 mph). If this vibration is felt only through the steering wheel, then it is likely that just the front wheels need balancing. If, however, the vibration is felt through the whole car, the rear wheels could be out of balance. Wheel balancing should be carried out by a tyre dealer or garage.

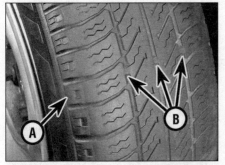

1 Tread Depth - visual check
The original tyres have tread wear safety bands (B), which will appear when the trad depth reaches approximately 1.6 mm. The band positions are indicated by a triangular mark on the tyre sidewall (A)

2 Tread Depth - manual check
Alternatively, tread wear can be monitored with a simple, inexpensive device known as a tread depth indicator gauge

3 Tyre Pressure Check
Check the tyre pressures regularly with the tyres cold. Do not adjust the tyre pressures immediately after the vehicle has been used, or an inaccurate setting will result

Tyre tread wear patterns

Shoulder Wear

Underinflation (wear on both sides)
Under-inflation will cause overheating of the tyre, because the tyre will flex too much, and the tread will not sit correctly on the road surface. This will cause a loss of grip and excessive wear, not to mention the danger of sudden tyre failure due to heat build-up.
Check and adjust pressures
Incorrect wheel camber (wear on one side)
Repair or renew suspension parts
Hard cornering
Reduce speed!

Centre Wear

Overinflation
Over-inflation will cause rapid wear of the centre part of the tyre tread, coupled with reduced grip, harsher ride, and the danger of shock damage occurring in the tyre casing.
Check and adjust pressures

If you sometimes have to inflate your car's tyres to the higher pressures specified for maximum load or sustained high speed, don't forget to reduce the pressures to normal afterwards.

Uneven Wear

Front tyres may wear unevenly as a result of wheel misalignment. Most tyre dealers and garages can check and adjust the wheel alignment (or "tracking") for a modest charge.
Incorrect camber or castor
Repair or renew suspension parts
Malfunctioning suspension
Repair or renew suspension parts
Unbalanced wheel
Balance tyres
Incorrect toe setting
Adjust front wheel alignment
Note: The feathered edge of the tread which typifies toe wear is best checked by feel.

Washer fluid level

● Screenwash additives not only keep the windscreen clean during bad weather, they also prevent the washer system freezing in cold weather – which is when you are likely to need it most. Don't top-up using plain water, as the screenwash will become diluted, and will freeze in cold weather.

 Warning: On no account use engine coolant antifreeze in the screen washer system – this may damage the paintwork.

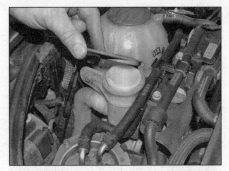

1 The screenwash fluid reservoir is located on the right-hand side of the engine compartment, behind the headlight. Pull up the filler cap to release it from the reservoir.

2 When topping-up the reservoir, a screenwash additive should be added in the quantities recommended on the bottle.

Battery

Caution: Before carrying out any work on the vehicle battery, read the precautions given in 'Safety first!' at the start of this manual.

✔ Make sure that the battery tray is in good condition, and that the clamp is tight. Corrosion on the tray, retaining clamp and the battery itself can be removed with a solution of water and baking soda. Thoroughly rinse all cleaned areas with water. Any metal parts damaged by corrosion should be covered with a zinc-based primer, then painted.

✔ Periodically (approximately every three months), check the charge condition of the battery as described in Chapter 5. A 'magic eye' charge indicator is fitted to the standard battery – if the indicator is green in colour, the battery is fully-charged, however, if it is colourless, it should be recharged. If it is yellow in colour, the battery should be renewed.

✔ If the battery is flat, and you need to jump start your vehicle, see *Jump starting*.

1 The battery is located on the left-hand side of the engine compartment, next to the fuse and relay box. Lift the cover from the insulation box to gain access to the battery terminals.

2 Check the security and condition of all the battery and fuse connections. The exterior of the battery should be inspected periodically for damage such as a cracked case or cover.

3 If corrosion (white, fluffy deposits) is evident, remove the cables from the battery terminals (refer to Disconnecting the battery in Reference), clean them with a small wire brush, then refit them. Automotive stores sell a tool for cleaning the battery post...

4 ...as well as the battery cable clamps.

Electrical systems

✔ Check all external lights and the horn. Refer to the appropriate Sections of Chapter 12 for details if any of the circuits are found to be inoperative.

✔ Visually check all accessible wiring connectors, harnesses and retaining clips for security, and for signs of chafing or damage.

 HAYNES HiNT *If you need to check your brake lights and indicators unaided, back up to a wall or garage door and operate the lights. The reflected light should show if they are working properly.*

1 If a single indicator light, brake light or headlight has failed, it is likely that a bulb has blown and will need to be renewed. Refer to Chapter 12 for details. If both brake lights have failed, it is possible that the brake light switch operated by the brake pedal has failed. Refer to Chapter 9 for details.

2 If more than one indicator light or headlight has failed, it is likely that either a fuse has blown or that there is a fault in the circuit (see *Electrical fault finding* in Chapter 12). The main fuses are in the fusebox beneath a cover on the right-hand end of the facia panel. Use a small screwdriver to prise off the cover. The circuits protected by the fuses are shown on the inside of the cover. Additional fuses and fusible links are in the fusebox located on the left-hand side of the engine compartment.

3 To renew a blown fuse, pull it from its location in the fusebox, using the plastic pliers provided. Fit a new fuse of the same rating, available from car accessory shops. It is important that you find the reason that the fuse blew (see *Electrical fault finding* in Chapter 12).

Wiper blades

Note: *It is possible to park the wipers in a Service/Winter position with both wipers pointing upwards to allow unrestricted removal of the blades. To do this, operate the wipers within 10 seconds of switching off the ignition. The wiper arms can now be lifted away from the windscreen.*

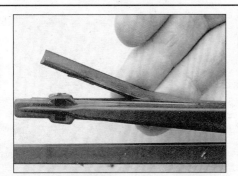

1 Check the condition of the wiper blades; if they are cracked or show any signs of deterioration, or if the glass swept area is smeared, renew them. For maximum clarity of vision, wiper blades should be renewed annually, as a matter of course.

2 To remove a windscreen wiper blade, pull the arm fully away from the screen until it locks. On standard wipers, swivel the blade through 90°, press the locking tab with your fingers, and slide the blade out of the hooked end of the arm.

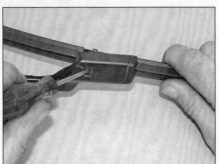

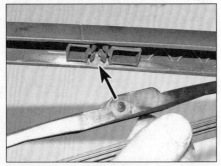

3 On aerodynamic wipers, depress the catch with a screwdriver, and pull the blade from the arm.

4 Where applicable, don't forget to check the tailgate wiper blade as well. To remove the blade, depress the retaining tab and slide the blade out of the hooked end of the arm.

Lubricants and fluids

Note: *Using lubricants and fluids which do not meet the VAG standard may invalidate the warranty*

Engine

Standard (distance/time) service interval	Multigrade engine oil, viscosity SAE 5W/40 to 20W/50
Engines without particulate filter	VW 505 01 or better
Engines with particulate filter	VW 507 00 or better
LongLife (variable) service interval	VAG LongLife engine oil
Engines without particulate filter	VW 506 01, 507 00 or better
Engines with particulate filter	VW 507 00 or better

Cooling system	Mixture of 40% VW coolant G12 plus-plus (TL-VW 774 G) or G12 plus (TL-VW 774 F) and 60% water
Manual transmission	Synthetic gear oil, viscosity SAE 75W/90 VW G50
DSG semi-automatic transmission	G 052 145
Braking system	Hydraulic fluid to SAE J1703F or DOT 4

Tyre pressures

Note: *Always refer to the tyre pressure data sticker on the edge of the driver's side front door for the correct tyre pressures for your particular vehicle(see illustration). Pressures apply only to original-equipment tyres, and may vary if any other make or type is fitted; check with the tyre manufacturer or supplier for correct pressures if necessary.*

Tyre pressure readings on driver's door

Chapter 1
Routine maintenance and servicing

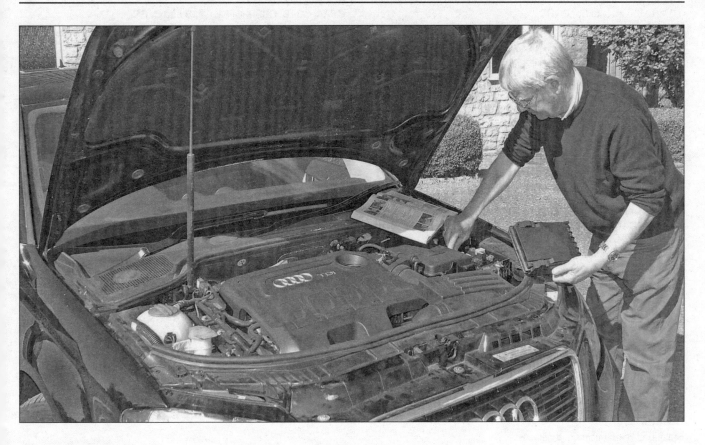

Contents

Degrees of difficulty

| **Easy,** suitable for novice with little experience | | **Fairly easy,** suitable for beginner with some experience | | **Fairly difficult,** suitable for competent DIY mechanic | | **Difficult,** suitable for experienced DIY mechanic | | **Very difficult,** suitable for expert DIY or professional | |

Lubricants and fluids

Refer to the end of *Weekly Checks*

Engine codes

1.6 litre, 16-valve, turbo, DOHC...............................	CAYB and CAYC
1.9 litre, 8-valve, turbo, SOHC...............................	BLS and BXE
2.0 litre, 16-valve, turbo, DOHC...............................	CBAA, CBAB, CBBB, CFFA, CFFB and CFGB

Note: *See 'Vehicle identification' at the end of this manual for the location of engine code markings.*

Capacities

Engine oil (including filter)

1.6 and 2.0 litre engines.....................................	4.3 litres
1.9 litre engines	4.0 litres

Cooling system

All engines	8.0 litres

Transmission

Manual transmission:

1.6 litre engines (type 0A4 transmission)	1.7 litres
1.9 litre engines (type 0AF transmission)	2.0 litres
2.0 litre engines (type 02Q transmission)	2.3 litres

DSG transmission:

1.6 litre engines (type 0AM transmission)......................	1.7 litres
2.0 litre engines (type 02E transmission)	5.2 litres

Fuel tank (approximate)

All models...	55 litres

Washer reservoirs

Models with headlight washers	5.5 litres
Models without headlight washers.............................	3.0 litres
Models with auxiliary heaters.................................	4.0 litres

Cooling system

Antifreeze mixture:

40% antifreeze	Protection down to -25°C
50% antifreeze	Protection down to -35°C

Note: *Refer to antifreeze manufacturer for latest recommendations.*

Brakes

Brake pad lining minimum thickness:

Front	2.0 mm
Rear	2.0 mm

Torque wrench settings

	Nm	lbf ft
Manual transmission drain plug (0A4 transmission)................	35	25
Manual transmission filler/level plug:		
0AF transmission	30	22
02Q transmission:		
Multi-point socket head	30	22
Hexagon socket head.................................	45	31
Manual transmission pivot pin retaining bolt (0A4 transmission)......	25	18
Oil filter cap	25	18
Reversing light switch (0A4 transmission)	20	15
Roadwheel bolts...	120	89
Sump drain plug...	30	22

The maintenance intervals in this manual are provided with the assumption that you, not the dealer, will be carrying out the work. These are the minimum intervals recommended by us for vehicles driven daily. If you wish to keep your vehicle in peak condition at all times, you may wish to perform some of these procedures more often. We encourage frequent maintenance, since it enhances the efficiency, performance and resale value of your vehicle.

When the vehicle is new, it should be serviced by a dealer service department (or other workshop recognised by the vehicle manufacturer as providing the same standard of service) in order to preserve the warranty. The vehicle manufacturer may reject warranty claims if you are unable to prove that servicing has been carried out as and when specified, using only original equipment parts or parts certified to be of equivalent quality.

All Audi models are equipped with a service interval display indicator in the instrument panel. Every time the engine is started the panel will illuminate for approximately 20 seconds with service information. With the standard non-variable display, the service intervals are in accordance with specific distances and time periods. With the LongLife display, the service interval is variable according to the number of starts, length of journeys, vehicle speeds, brake pad wear, bonnet opening frequency, fuel consumption, oil level and oil temperature, however the vehicle must be serviced at least every two years. At a certain mileage before the next service is due, 'Service in XXXX miles, XXX days' or 'Oil change in XXXX miles, XXX days' will appear at the bottom of the speedometer. Once the service interval has been reached, the message SERVICE DUE! will be shown together with an acoustic signal. Note that if the variable (LongLife) service interval is being used, the engine must only be filled with the recommended Longlife engine oil (see *Lubricants and fluids*).

After completing a service, Audi technicians use a special instrument to reset the service display to the next service interval, and a print-out is put in the vehicle service record. The display can be reset by the owner as described in Section 5, but note that for models using the 'LongLife' interval, the procedure will automatically reset the display to the 10 000 miles 'distance' interval. To have the display reset to the 'variable' (LongLife) interval, it is necessary to take the vehicle to an Audi dealer who will use a special instrument to encode the on-board computer.

Every 250 miles
- [ ] Refer to *Weekly checks*

Every OIL service
- [ ] Renew the engine oil and filter (Section 3)

Note: *Frequent oil and filter changes are good for the engine. We recommend changing the oil at least once a year.*

- [ ] Check the front and rear brake pad thickness (Section 4)
- [ ] Reset the service interval display (Section 5)

Every SERVICE
In addition to the items listed above, carry out the following:

- [ ] Check the condition of the exhaust system and its mountings (Section 6)
- [ ] Check all underbonnet components and hoses for fluid and oil leaks (Section 7)
- [ ] Renew the fuel filter (Section 8)
- [ ] Check the condition of the auxiliary drivebelt (Section 9)
- [ ] Check the coolant antifreeze concentration (Section 10)

Every SERVICE (continued)
- [ ] Check the brake hydraulic circuit for leaks and damage (Section 11)
- [ ] Check the headlight beam adjustment (Section 12)
- [ ] Renew the pollen filter element (Section 13)
- [ ] Check the manual transmission oil level (Section 14)
- [ ] Check the underbody protection for damage (Section 15)
- [ ] Check the condition of the driveshaft gaiters (Section 16)
- [ ] Check the steering and suspension components for condition and security (Section 17)
- [ ] Check the battery condition, security and electrolyte level (Section 18)
- [ ] Lubricate all hinges and locks (Section 19)
- [ ] Check the condition of the airbag unit(s) (Section 20)
- [ ] Check the operation of the windscreen/tailgate/ headlight washer system(s) (as applicable) (Section 21)
- [ ] Check the engine management self-diagnosis memory for faults (Section 22)
- [ ] Check the operation of the sunroof and lubricate the guide rails (Section 23)
- [ ] Carry out a road test and check exhaust emissions (Section 24)

Every 40 000 miles or 4 years, whichever comes first
Note: *Most dealers perform these tasks every second SERVICE.*

In addition to the items listed above, carry out the following:
- [ ] Renew the DSG transmission oil (Section 25)
- [ ] Renew the air filter element (Section 26)
- [ ] Renew the auxiliary drivebelt (Section 27)

Every 60 000 miles
- [ ] Renew the timing belt and tensioner roller (Section 28)

Note: *Audi specify a timing belt renewal interval of 75 000 miles for models manufactured up to MY 2006, and 95 000 miles for models manufactured from MY 2007-on. They specify a tensioner roller renewal interval of 150 000 miles for models manufactured up to MY 2006, and 190 000 miles for models manufactured from MY 2007-on. However, if the vehicle is used mainly for short journeys, we recommend that this shorter renewal interval be adhered to. The belt and tensioner renewal interval is very much up to the individual owner but, bearing in mind that severe engine damage will result if the belt breaks in use, we recommend the shorter interval.*

Every 95 000 miles, then every 19 000 miles
- [ ] Check the particulate filter ash deposit mass (Section 29)

Every 2 years
- [ ] Renew the brake (and clutch) fluid (Section 30)
- [ ] Renew the coolant (Section 31)

Note: *This work is not included in the Audi schedule and should not be required if the recommended VAG G12 LongLife coolant antifreeze/inhibitor is used.*

Underbonnet view of a 2.0 litre model

1 Engine oil filler cap	5 Fuel filter	8 Master cylinder brake fluid
2 Engine oil dipstick	6 Windscreen/headlight	reservoir
3 Oil filter	washer fluid reservoir	9 Battery
4 Coolant expansion	7 Particulate filter	10 Fusebox
tank		11 Air cleaner housing

Front underbody view

1 Brake caliper
2 Lower arm
3 Engine oil drain plug
4 Intercooler hoses
5 Steering track rod
6 Driveshaft
7 Coolant circulation pump
8 Subframe
9 Air conditioning compressor

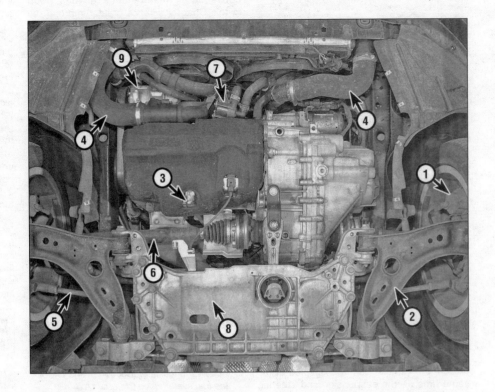

Rear underbody view

1 Exhaust silencer
2 Rear track control lower arm
3 Rear anti-roll bar
4 Rear suspension transverse link
5 Spare wheel well
6 Rear suspension subframe beam
7 Rear trailing arm and cover
8 Fuel tank

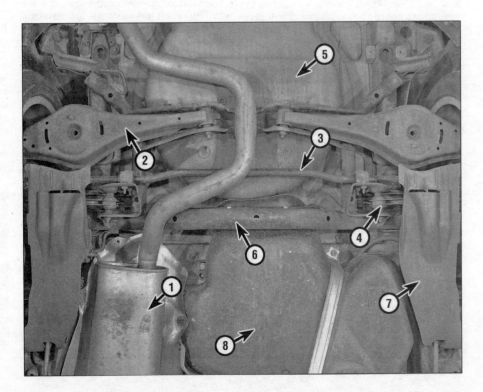

1 Introduction

1 This Chapter is designed to help the home mechanic maintain his/her vehicle for safety, economy, long life and peak performance.
2 The Chapter contains a master maintenance schedule, followed by Sections dealing specifically with each task in the schedule. Visual checks, adjustments, component renewal and other helpful items are included. Refer to the accompanying illustrations of the engine compartment and the underside of the vehicle for the locations of the various components.
3 Servicing your vehicle will provide a planned maintenance programme, which should result in a long and reliable service life. This is a comprehensive plan, so maintaining some items but not others will not produce the same results.
4 As you service your vehicle, you will discover that many of the procedures can – and should – be grouped together, because of the particular procedure being performed, or because of the proximity of two otherwise unrelated components to one another. For example, if the vehicle is raised for any reason, the exhaust can be inspected at the same time as the suspension and steering components.
5 The first step in this maintenance programme is to prepare yourself before the actual work begins. Read through all the Sections relevant to the work to be carried out, then make a list and gather all the parts and tools required. If a problem is encountered, seek advice from a parts specialist, or a dealer service department.

2 Regular maintenance

1 If, from the time the vehicle is new, the routine maintenance schedule is followed closely, and frequent checks are made of fluid levels and high-wear items, as suggested throughout this manual, the engine will be kept in relatively good running condition, and the need for additional work will be minimised.
2 It is possible that there will be times when the engine is running poorly due to the lack of regular maintenance. This is even more likely if a used vehicle, which has not received regular and frequent maintenance checks, is purchased. In such cases, additional work may need to be carried out, outside of the regular maintenance intervals.
3 If engine wear is suspected, a compression test will provide valuable information regarding the overall performance of the main internal components. Such a test can be used as a basis to decide on the extent of the work to be carried out. If, for example, a compression

test indicates serious internal engine wear, conventional maintenance as described in this Chapter will not greatly improve the performance of the engine, and may prove a waste of time and money, unless extensive overhaul work is carried out first.
4 The following series of operations are those most often required to improve the performance of a generally poor-running engine:

Primary operations

a) Clean, inspect and test the battery (See 'Weekly checks').
b) Check all the engine-related fluids (See 'Weekly checks').
c) Check the condition and tension of the auxiliary drivebelt (Section 9).
d) Check the condition of the air filter, and renew if necessary (Section 26).
e) Check the condition of all hoses, and check for fluid leaks (Section 7).

5 If the above operations do not prove fully effective, carry out the following secondary operations:

Secondary operations

6 All items listed under Primary operations, plus the following:
a) Check the charging system (see Chapter 5).
b) Check the preheating system (see Chapter 5).
c) Renew the fuel filter (Section 8) and check the fuel system (see Chapter 4A or 4B).

3 Engine oil and filter renewal

1 Frequent oil and filter changes are the most important preventative maintenance procedures, which can be undertaken by the DIY owner. As engine oil ages, it becomes diluted and contaminated, which leads to premature engine wear.
2 Before starting this procedure, gather all the necessary tools and materials. Also make sure that you have plenty of clean rags and newspapers handy, to mop-up any spills. Ideally, the engine oil should be warm, as it will drain better, and more built-up sludge will be removed with it. Take care, however, not to touch the exhaust or any other hot

parts of the engine when working under the vehicle. To avoid any possibility of scalding, and to protect yourself from possible skin irritants and other harmful contaminants in used engine oils, it is advisable to wear gloves when carrying out this work. Access to the underside of the vehicle will be greatly improved if it can be raised on a lift, driven onto ramps, or jacked up and supported on axle stands (see *Jacking and vehicle support*). Whichever method is chosen, make sure that the vehicle remains level, or if it is at an angle, that the drain plug is at the lowest point. Undo the retaining screws and remove the engine undertray, then also remove the engine top cover.
3 Slacken the sump drain plug about half a turn. Position the draining container under the drain plug, then remove the plug completely **(see illustration)**. Recover the sealing ring from the drain plug. To drain all oil from the engine, loosen the cap from the top of the oil filter housing using a socket or spanner – this will allow the oil to drain from the filter housing into the sump.

> **HAYNES HiNT** *Keep the drain plug pressed into the sump while unscrewing it by hand the last couple of turns. As the plug releases, move it away sharply so the stream of oil issuing from the sump runs into the container, not up your sleeve.*

4 Allow some time for the old oil to drain, noting that it may be necessary to reposition the container as the oil flow slows to a trickle.
5 After all the oil has drained, wipe off the drain plug with a clean rag, and fit a new sealing washer. Clean the area around the drain plug opening, and refit the plug. Tighten the plug securely. **Note:** *On some engines, the sealing washer is integral with the drain plug. On these engines, the drain plug must be renewed.*
6 Place absorbent cloths around the oil filter housing to catch any spilt oil. Where necessary, unbolt the bracket and unclip the wiring loom from over the oil filter, or unclip the solenoid valve from above the filter **(see illustration)**.

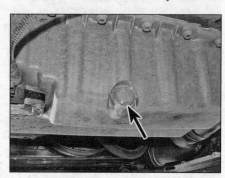

3.3 Sump drain plug (arrowed)

3.6 Where necessary, unclip the solenoid valve (arrowed) for access to the filter.

3.7a Use a 32 mm socket to unscrew the filter cap...

3.7b...withdraw the filter and cap...

3.7c...then slide the old filter from the cap

7 Fully unscrew the cap from the top of the oil filter and remove it together with the filter element. Recover the large sealing ring from the cap, and the small sealing ring from the centre rod. Unclip the filter element from the cap and dispose of it **(see illustrations)**.

8 Using a clean rag, wipe all oil and sludge from the inside of the filter housing and cap.

9 Fit new sealing rings, then refit the assembly and tighten to the specified torque. Make sure the filter element is engaged with the cap and the correct way up **(see illustrations)**. Wipe up any spilt oil before refitting the engine top cover.

10 Remove the old oil and all tools from under the car then refit the undertray and lower the car to the ground. Also refit the engine top cover.

11 Remove the dipstick, and then unscrew the oil filler cap from the cylinder head cover. Fill the engine, using the correct grade and type of oil (see *Lubricants and fluids*). An oilcan spout or funnel may help to reduce spillage. Pour in half the specified quantity of oil first, and then wait a few minutes for the oil to run to the sump (see *Weekly checks*). Continue adding oil a small quantity at a time until the level is up to the maximum mark on the dipstick. Refit the filler cap.

12 Start the engine and run it for a few minutes; check for leaks around the oil filter cap and the sump drain plug. Note that there may be a few seconds delay before the oil pressure warning light goes out when the engine is started, as the oil circulates through the engine oil galleries and the new oil filter before the pressure builds-up.

⚠️ *Warning: Warning: Do not increase the engine speed above idling while the oil pressure light is illuminated, as considerable damage can be caused to the turbocharger.*

13 Switch off the engine, and wait a few minutes for the oil to settle in the sump once more. With the new oil circulated and the filter completely full, recheck the level on the dipstick, and add more oil as necessary.

14 Dispose of the used engine oil safely, with reference to *General repair procedures* in the Reference section of this manual.

3.9a The new oil filter comes with large and small O-ring seals

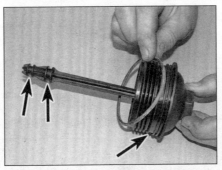

3.9b Fit the three seals to the oil filter cap in the positions shown...

3.9c...then slide the new filter to the cap...

3.9d...noting 'TOP' on the filter for correct fitting

3.9e Lubricate the O-ring seals with clean engine oil...

3.9f...then refit to the filter housing

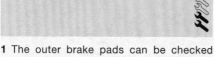

4 Brake pad check

1 The outer brake pads can be checked without removing the wheels, by observing the brake pads through the holes in the wheels **(see illustration)**. If necessary, remove the wheel trim. The thickness of the pad lining must not be less than the dimension given in the Specifications.
2 If the outer pads are worn near their limits, it is worthwhile checking the inner pads as well. Apply the handbrake then jack up vehicle and support it on axle stands (see *Jacking and vehicle support*). Remove the roadwheels.
3 Use a steel rule to check the thickness of the brake pads, and compare with the minimum thickness given in the Specifications **(see illustration)**.
4 For a comprehensive check, the brake pads should be removed and cleaned. The operation of the caliper can then also be checked, and the condition of the brake disc itself can be fully examined on both sides. Refer to Chapter 9.
5 If any pad's friction material is worn to the specified minimum thickness or less, all four pads at the front or rear, as applicable, must be renewed as a set.
6 On completion of the check, refit the roadwheels and lower the vehicle to the ground.

5 Resetting the service interval display

1 After all necessary maintenance work has been completed, the service interval display must be reset. Audi technicians use a special dedicated instrument to do this, and a print-out is then put in the vehicle service record. It is possible for the owner to reset the display as described in the following paragraphs, but note that the procedure will automatically reset the display to a 10 000 mile interval. To continue with the 'variable' intervals which take into consideration the number of starts, length of journeys, vehicle speeds, brake pad wear, bonnet opening frequency, fuel consumption, oil level and oil temperature, the display must be reset by a Audi dealership using the special dedicated instrument.

Vehicles with driver information system (DIS)

2 To reset the standard display manually, switch on the ignition, and then pull out the reset button (lower left of speedometer). With the reset button out, SERVICE DUE! will appear in the display screen (between the speedometer and the rev. counter). Pull the button again until OIL CHANGE IN – – – – MILES – – – DAYS is shown on the display screen. **Note:** *If you do not pull the reset button within 5 seconds, the display screen will switch out of reset mode and revert back to normal display.*

Vehicles without driver information system (DIS)

3 To reset the standard display manually, switch on the ignition, and a spanner symbol will appear in the display screen (in the speedometer). Pull out the reset button (lower left of speedometer) to activate the reset mode. Pull the button out once more until '– – –' is shown on the display screen. **Note:** *If you do not pull the reset button within 5 seconds, the display screen will switch out of reset mode and revert back to normal display.*

6 Exhaust system check

1 With the engine cold (at least an hour after the vehicle has been driven), check the complete exhaust system from the engine to the end of the tailpipe. The exhaust system is most easily checked with the vehicle raised on a hoist, or suitably supported on axle stands, so that the exhaust components are readily visible and accessible (see *Jacking and vehicle support*).
2 Check the exhaust pipes and connections for evidence of leaks, severe corrosion and damage. Make sure that all brackets and mountings are in good condition, and that all relevant nuts and bolts are tight. Leakage at any of the joints or in other parts of the system will usually show up as a black sooty stain in the vicinity of the leak.
3 Rattles and other noises can often be traced to the exhaust system, especially the brackets and mountings. Try to move the pipes and silencers. If the components are able to come into contact with the body or suspension parts, secure the system with new mountings. Otherwise separate the joints (if possible) and twist the pipes as necessary to provide additional clearance.

7 Hose and fluid leak check

Note: *Also refer to Section 11.*
1 Visually inspect the engine joint faces, gaskets and seals for any signs of water or oil leaks. Pay particular attention to the areas around the camshaft cover, cylinder head, oil filter and sump joint faces. Bear in mind that, over a period of time, some very slight seepage from these areas is to be expected – what you are really looking for is any indication of a serious leak. Should a leak be found, renew the offending gasket or oil seal by referring to the appropriate Chapters in this manual.
2 Also check the security and condition of all the engine-related pipes and hoses. Ensure that all cable-ties or securing clips are in place and in good condition. Clips which are broken

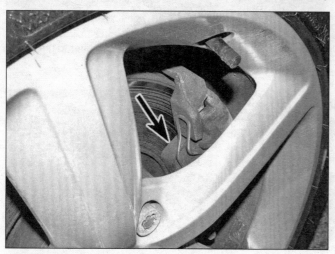

4.1 The outer brake pads can be observed through the holes in the wheels

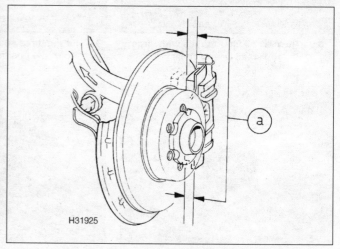

4.3 The thickness (a) of the brake pad linings must not be less than the specified amount

8.2a Undo the screws...

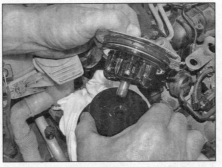

8.2b...and remove the top of the filter housing

8.3a Remove the cover seal...

or missing can lead to chafing of the hoses, pipes or wiring, which could cause more serious problems in the future.

3 Carefully check the radiator hoses and heater hoses along their entire length. Renew any hose, which is cracked, swollen or deteriorated. Cracks will show up better if the hose is squeezed. Pay close attention to the hose clips that secure the hoses to the cooling system components. Hose clips can pinch and puncture hoses, resulting in cooling system leaks.

4 Inspect all the cooling system components (hoses, joint faces, etc) for leaks (see Haynes Hint). Where any problems of this nature are found on system components, renew the component or gasket with reference to Chapter 3.

 HAYNES HINT *A leak in the cooling system will usually show up as white- or antifreeze coloured deposits on the area adjoining the leak.*

5 Where applicable, inspect the DSG transmission fluid cooler hoses for leaks or deterioration.

6 With the vehicle raised, inspect the fuel tank and filler neck for punctures, cracks and other damage. The connection between the filler neck and tank is especially critical. Sometimes a rubber filler neck or connecting hose will leak due to loose retaining clamps or deteriorated rubber.

7 Carefully check all rubber hoses and metal fuel lines leading away from the tank. Check for loose connections, deteriorated hoses, crimped lines, and other damage. Pay particular attention to the vent pipes and hoses, which often loop up around the filler neck and can become blocked or crimped. Follow the lines to the front of the vehicle, carefully inspecting them all the way. Renew damaged sections as necessary.

8 From within the engine compartment, check the security of all fuel hose attachments and pipe unions, and inspect the fuel hoses and vacuum hoses for kinks, chafing and deterioration.

8 Fuel filter renewal

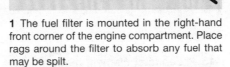

1 The fuel filter is mounted in the right-hand front corner of the engine compartment. Place rags around the filter to absorb any fuel that may be spilt.

2 Undo the screws from around the top of the filter housing and lift the cover from the top of the housing **(see illustrations)**.

3 Remove the seal and discard, as a new one must be used on refitting. Also, on 1.9 litre engines, remove the inner seal from the top of the filter element centre pillar **(see illustrations)**.

4 Withdraw the old filter element from the housing and discard **(see illustration)**.

5 Use a pipette/syringe to draw out the

dirty fuel and water residue from inside the fuel filter lower housing. Then insert the new filter element, pressing it down fully into position **(see illustration)**.

6 On 1.9 litre engines, locate a new inner seal on the top of the filter element.

7 To help the engine start easier (to prevent having to bleed the system), top up the lower filter housing with clean diesel, making sure that no dirt or water enters the system.

8 Fit a new seal to the cover, then refit to the housing. Insert the screws and tighten securely.

9 Start and run the engine at idle, then check around the fuel filter for fuel leaks. **Note:** *It may take a few seconds of cranking before the engine starts.*

9 Auxiliary drivebelt check

1 Apply the handbrake, then jack up the front of the vehicle and support it on axle stands (see *Jacking and vehicle support*).

2 Using a socket on the crankshaft pulley bolt, turn the engine slowly clockwise so that the full length of the auxiliary drivebelt can be examined. Look for cracks, splitting and fraying on the surface of the belt; check also for signs of glazing (shiny patches) and separation of the belt plies. If damage or wear is visible, or if there are traces of oil or grease on it, the belt should be renewed (see Section 27).

8.3b...and on 1.9 litre engines, the centre seal

8.4 Removing the old filter element

8.5 Inserting the new filter element

10 Antifreeze check

1 The cooling system should be filled with the recommended G12 antifreeze and corrosion protection fluid – do not mix this antifreeze with any other type. Over a period of time, the concentration of fluid may be reduced due to topping-up with water (this can be avoided by topping-up with the correct antifreeze mixture – see Specifications) or fluid loss. If loss of coolant has been evident, it is important to make the necessary repair before adding fresh fluid.

2 With the engine cold, carefully remove the cap from the expansion tank. If the engine is not completely cold, place a cloth rag over the cap before removing it, and remove it slowly to allow any pressure to escape.

3 Antifreeze checkers are available from car accessory shops. Draw some coolant from the expansion tank and observe how many plastic balls are floating in the checker. Usually, 2 or 3 balls must be floating for the correct concentration of antifreeze, but follow the manufacturer's instructions.

4 If the concentration is incorrect, it will be necessary to either withdraw some coolant and add antifreeze, or alternatively drain

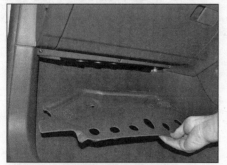

13.2 Removing the facia lower trim from beneath the glovebox

the old coolant and add fresh coolant of the correct concentration (see Section 31).

11 Brake hydraulic circuit check

1 Check the entire brake hydraulic circuit for leaks and damage. Start by checking the master cylinder in the engine compartment. At the same time, check the vacuum servo unit and ABS units for signs of fluid leakage.

2 Raise the front and rear of the vehicle and support it on axle stands (see *Jacking and vehicle support*). Check the rigid hydraulic brake lines for corrosion and damage.

3 At the front of the vehicle, check that the flexible hydraulic hoses to the calipers are not twisted or chafing on any of the surrounding suspension components. Turn the steering on full lock to make this check. Also check that the hoses are not brittle or cracked.

4 Lower the vehicle to the ground after making the checks.

12 Headlight beam adjustment

1 Accurate adjustment of the headlight beam is only possible using optical beam-setting equipment, and this work should therefore be carried out by an Audi dealer or service station with the necessary facilities.

2 Basic adjustments can be carried out in an emergency, and further details are given in Chapter 12.

13 Pollen filter element renewal

1 The pollen filter is located in the heater unit and is accessed from inside the car, on the passenger's side.

2 Remove the clips and withdraw the facia lower trim from beneath the glovebox **(see illustration)**.

3 Slide the access cover to the left (arrow on cover) to remove **(see illustration)**. **Note:** *On some models, there may be a retaining screw in the cover to prevent it from moving.*

4 Slide out the pollen filter element downwards from the heater unit **(see illustration)**.

5 Fit the new element then refit the access cover.

6 Refit the facia lower trim beneath the glovebox.

14 Manual transmission oil level check

1 Park the car on a level surface. For improved access to the filler/level plug, apply the handbrake, then jack up the front of the vehicle and support it on axle stands (see *Jacking and vehicle support*), but note that the rear of the vehicle should also be raised to ensure an accurate level check. The oil level must be checked before the car is driven, or at least 5 minutes after the engine has been switched off. If the oil is checked immediately after driving the car, some of the oil will remain distributed around the transmission components, resulting in an inaccurate level reading.

0AF and 02Q transmissions

2 Undo the retaining screws and remove the engine undertray. Wipe clean the area around the transmission filler/level plug, which is situated on the front of the transmission casing **(see illustrations)**.

3 The oil level should reach the lower edge of the filler/level hole. A certain amount of oil will have gathered behind the filler/level plug, and will trickle out when it is removed; this does not necessarily indicate that the

13.3 Remove the access cover...

13.4...and slide out the pollen filter element

level is correct. To ensure that a true level is established, wait until the initial trickle has stopped, then add oil as necessary until a trickle of new oil can be seen emerging. The level will be correct when the flow ceases; use only good-quality oil of the specified type.

4 If the transmission has been overfilled so that oil flows out when the filler/level plug is removed, check that the car is completely level (front-to-rear and side-to-side), and allow the surplus to drain off into a suitable container.

5 When the oil level is correct, refit the filler/level plug and tighten it to the specified torque.

6 Wipe off any spilt oil then refit the engine undertray, tighten the retaining screws securely, and lower the car to the ground.

0A4 transmission

7 Undo the retaining screws and remove the engine undertray.

8 On these transmissions, it's impossible to check the level of the oil through the 'filler' plug, due to the engine/transmission installation angle; the level of the fluid is above the lower edge of the filler hole. The only method of ensuring the correct fluid level is to completely drain and refill the transmission.

9 Remove the air cleaner housing as described in Chapter 4A Section 2.

10 In order to drain the transmission, the pivot pin must be removed from the underside of the transmission casing. However, to prevent the position of the selector forks being altered, press the selector shaft down, then turn the angled locking rod upwards, and lock the shaft in position **(see illustration)**.

11 Place a container under the transmission casing.

12 Unscrew the drain plug from the base of the differential housing, and allow the oil to drain **(see illustration)**.

13 Then undo the retaining bolt, pull out the pivot pin nearest the passenger's roadwheel and allow the oil to drain **(see illustration 14.12)**. The pivot pin O-ring seal must be renewed.

14 When the oil has finished draining clean the surrounding area, then refit the pivot pin (with a new O-ring seal), and tighten the retaining bolt to the specified torque.

15 When the oil has finished draining, clean the surrounding area, refit the drain plug and tighten it to the specified torque.

16 Rotate the selector-shaft locking rod to its original position.

17 Unscrew the reversing light switch from the top of the transmission casing.

18 Using a 600 mm length of 10 mm (external) diameter hose, and funnel, add 1.7 litres of fresh oil to the transmission.

19 Refit the reversing light switch, and tighten it to the specified torque.

20 The remainder of refitting is a reversal of removal.

14.2a Transmission filler/level plug location on 0AF transmissions

14.2b Transmission drain plug (A) and filler/level plug (B) locations on 02Q transmissions

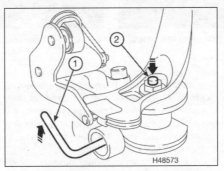

14.10 Press down the selector shaft (2), and rotate the locking rod (1) upwards

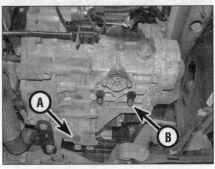

14.12 Oil drain pug (A) and pivot pin (B) on the 0A4 transmission

15 Underbody protection check

1 Raise and support the vehicle on axle stands (see *Jacking and vehicle support*). Using an electric torch or lead light, inspect the entire underside of the vehicle, paying particular attention to the wheel arches. Look for any damage to the flexible underbody coating, which may crack or flake off with age, leading to corrosion. Also check that the wheel arch liners are securely attached with any clips provided – if they come loose, dirt may get in behind the liners and defeat their purpose. If there is any damage to the underseal, or any corrosion, it should be repaired before the damage gets too serious.

16 Driveshaft gaiter check

1 With the vehicle raised and securely supported on stands, slowly rotate the roadwheel. Inspect the condition of the outer constant velocity (CV) joint rubber gaiters, squeezing the gaiters to open out the folds. Check for signs of cracking, splits

or deterioration of the rubber, which may allow the grease to escape, and lead to water and grit entry into the joint. Also check the security and condition of the retaining clips. Repeat these checks on the inner joints **(see illustration)**. If any damage or deterioration is found, the gaiters should be renewed (see Chapter 8 Section 3).

2 At the same time, check the general condition of the CV joints themselves by first holding the driveshaft and attempting to rotate the wheel. Repeat this check by holding the inner joint and attempting to rotate the driveshaft. Any appreciable movement indicates wear in the joints, wear in the driveshaft splines, or a loose driveshaft-retaining bolt.

16.1 Check the condition of the driveshaft gaiters (arrowed)

17.4 Check for wear in the hub bearings by grasping the wheel and trying to rock it

18.1 Battery location beneath the insulation cover

17 Steering and suspension check

1 Raise the front and rear of the vehicle, and securely support it on axle stands (see *Jacking and vehicle support*).

2 Visually inspect the track rod end balljoint dust cover, the lower front suspension balljoint dust cover, and the steering rack-and-pinion gaiters for splits, chafing or deterioration.

3 Any wear of these components will cause loss of lubricant, together with dirt and water entry, resulting in rapid deterioration of the balljoints or steering gear.

4 Grasp the roadwheel at the 12 o'clock and 6 o'clock positions, and try to rock it **(see illustration)**. Very slight free play may be felt, but if the movement is appreciable, further investigation is necessary to determine the source. Continue rocking the wheel while an assistant depresses the footbrake. If the movement is now eliminated or significantly reduced, it is likely that the hub bearings are at fault. If the free play is still evident with the footbrake depressed, then there is wear in the suspension joints or mountings.

5 Now grasp the wheel at the 9 o'clock and 3 o'clock positions, and try to rock it as before. Any movement felt now may again be caused by wear in the hub bearings or the steering track rod balljoints. If the inner or outer balljoint is worn, the visual movement will be obvious.

6 Using a large screwdriver or flat bar, check for wear in the suspension mounting bushes by levering between the relevant suspension component and its attachment point. Some movement is to be expected as the mountings are made of rubber, but excessive wear should be obvious. Also check the condition of any visible rubber bushes, looking for splits, cracks or contamination of the rubber.

7 With the car standing on its wheels, have an assistant turn the steering wheel back-and-forth about an eighth of a turn each way. There should be very little, if any, lost movement between the steering wheel and roadwheels. If this is not the case, closely observe the joints and mountings previously described, but in addition, check the steering column universal joints for wear, and the rack-and-pinion steering gear itself.

8 Check for any signs of fluid leakage around the front suspension struts and rear shock absorbers. Should any fluid be noticed, the suspension strut or shock absorber is defective internally, and should be renewed. **Note:** *Suspension struts/shock absorbers should always be renewed in pairs on the same axle to ensure correct vehicle handling.*

9 The efficiency of the suspension strut/shock absorber may be checked by bouncing the vehicle at each corner. Generally speaking, the body will return to its normal position and stop after being depressed. If it rises and returns on a rebound, the suspension strut/shock absorber is probably suspect. Examine also the suspension strut/shock absorber upper and lower mountings for any signs of wear.

18 Battery check

1 The battery is located on the left-hand side of the engine compartment. Where an insulator cover is fitted, open the cover to gain access to the battery **(see illustration)**.

2 Where necessary, open the fuse holder plastic cover (squeeze together the locking lugs to release the cover) to gain access to the battery positive (+) terminal and fuse holder connections.

3 Check that both battery terminals and all the fuse holder connections are securely attached and are free from corrosion. **Note:** *Before disconnecting the terminals from the battery, refer to 'Disconnecting the battery' in the Reference Chapter at the end of this manual.*

4 Check the battery casing for signs of damage or cracking and check the battery retaining clamp bolt is securely tightened. If the battery casing is damaged in any way the battery must be renewed (see Chapter 5 Section 3).

5 If the vehicle is not fitted with a sealed-for-life maintenance-free battery, check the electrolyte level is between the MAX and MIN level markings on the battery casing. If topping-up is necessary, remove the battery (see Chapter 5 Section 3) from the vehicle then remove the cell caps/cover (as applicable). Using distilled water, top the electrolyte level of each cell up to the MAX level mark then securely refit the cell caps/cover. Ensure the battery has not been overfilled then refit the battery to the vehicle.

6 On completion of the check, clip the cover securely back onto the fuse holder and close up the insulator cover (where fitted).

19 Hinge and lock lubrication

1 Lubricate the hinges of the bonnet, doors and tailgate with light general-purpose oil. Similarly, lubricate all latches, locks and lock strikers. At the same time, check the security and operation of all the locks, adjusting them if necessary (see Chapter 11).

2 Lightly lubricate the bonnet release mechanism and cable with suitable grease.

20 Airbag unit check

1 Inspect the exterior condition of the airbag(s) for signs of damage or deterioration. If an airbag shows signs of damage, it must be renewed (see Chapter 12 Section 26). Note that it is not permissible to attach any stickers to the surface of the airbag, as this may affect the deployment of the unit.

21 Windscreen/tailgate/headlight washer system check

1 Check that each of the washer jet nozzles are clear and that each nozzle provides a strong jet of washer fluid.
2 The tailgate jet should be aimed to spray at the centre of the screen, using a pin.
3 The windscreen washer nozzles should be aimed slightly above the centre of the screen using a small screwdriver to turn the jet eccentric.
4 The headlight inner jet should be aimed slightly above the horizontal centreline of the headlight, and the outer jet should be aimed slightly below the centreline. Audi technicians use a special tool to adjust the headlight jet after pulling the jet out onto its stop.
5 Especially during the winter months, make sure that the washer fluid frost concentration is sufficient.

22 Engine management self-diagnosis memory fault check

1 This work should be carried out by an Audi dealer or diagnostic specialist using special equipment. The diagnostic socket is located at the lower part of the facia on the driver's side, by the bonnet release lever **(see illustration)**.

23 Sunroof check and lubrication

1 Check the operation of the sunroof, and leave it in the fully open position.
2 Wipe clean the guide rails on each side of the sunroof opening, then apply lubricant to them. Audi recommend lubricant spray G 052 778.

24 Road test and exhaust emissions check

Instruments and electrical equipment

1 Check the operation of all instruments and electrical equipment including the air conditioning system.
2 Make sure that all instruments read correctly, and switch on all electrical equipment in turn, to check that it functions properly.

Steering and suspension

3 Check for any abnormalities in the steering, suspension, handling or road 'feel'.
4 Drive the vehicle, and check that there are no unusual vibrations or noises, which

22.1 Diagnostic plug location

may indicate wear in the driveshafts, wheel bearings, etc.
5 Check that the steering feels positive, with no excessive 'sloppiness', or roughness, and check for any suspension noises when cornering and driving over bumps.

Drivetrain

6 Check the performance of the engine, clutch (where applicable), gearbox/transmission and driveshafts.
7 Listen for any unusual noises from the engine, clutch and gearbox/transmission.
8 Make sure the engine runs smoothly at idle, and there is no hesitation on accelerating.
9 Check that, where applicable, the clutch action is smooth and progressive, that the drive is taken up smoothly, and that the pedal travel is not excessive. Also listen for any noises when the clutch pedal is depressed.
10 On manual transmission models, check that all gears can be engaged smoothly without noise, and that the gear lever action is smooth and not abnormally vague or 'notchy'.
11 On automatic transmission models, make sure that all gearchanges occur smoothly, without snatching, and without an increase in engine speed between changes. Check that all the gear positions can be selected with the vehicle at rest. If any problems are found, they should be referred to an Audi dealer.
12 Listen for a metallic clicking sound from the front of the vehicle, as the vehicle is driven slowly in a circle with the steering on full-lock. Carry out this check in both directions. If a clicking noise is heard, this indicates wear in a driveshaft joint, in which case renew the joint if necessary.

Braking system

13 Make sure that the vehicle does not pull to one side when braking, and that the wheels do not lock when braking hard.
14 Check that there is no vibration through the steering when braking.
15 Check that the handbrake operates correctly without excessive movement of the lever, and that it holds the vehicle stationary on a slope.
16 Test the operation of the brake servo unit as follows. With the engine off, depress the footbrake four or five times to exhaust the

vacuum. Hold the brake pedal depressed, and then start the engine. As the engine starts, there should be a noticeable 'give' in the brake pedal as vacuum builds-up. Allow the engine to run for at least two minutes, and then switch it off. If the brake pedal is depressed now, it should be possible to detect a hiss from the servo as the pedal is depressed. After about four or five applications, no further hissing should be heard, and the pedal should feel considerably harder.
17 Under controlled emergency braking, the pulsing of the ABS unit must be felt at the footbrake pedal.

Exhaust emissions check

18 Although not part of the manufacturer's maintenance schedule, this check will normally be carried out on a regular basis according to the country the vehicle is operated in. Currently in the UK, exhaust emissions testing is included as part of the annual MOT test after the vehicle is 3 years old.

25 DSG transmission oil renewal

1 The semi-automatic (DSG) dual shift gearbox is fitted to the following models.
a) *The 1.6 litre engine has the 7-speed dual clutch (0AM) transmission.*
b) *The 2.0 litre engine has the 6-speed dual clutch (02E) transmission.*
2 Both transmissions are filled for life, and are not part of the service schedule. If there has been an oil leak from the transmission, after the leak has been rectified, renew the transmission oil as described in Chapter 7B Section 6.

26 Air filter element renewal

1 The air cleaner is located in front of the battery in the left-hand front corner of the engine compartment **(see illustration)**. First, remove the engine top cover.

26.1 The air cleaner is located in the left-hand front corner of the engine compartment

2 Undo the screws and lift the air cleaner lid complete with air mass meter 10 to 15 cm from the base **(see illustration)**. Take care not to strain the air mass meter wiring and air duct.

3 Lift out the air filter element, noting how it is fitted **(see illustration)**.

4 Remove any debris that may have collected inside the air cleaner.

5 Fit a new air filter element in position, ensuring that the edges are securely seated.

6 Refit the lid and tighten the screws, then refit the engine top cover.

27 Auxiliary drivebelt renewal

1.9 litre engines

1 For improved access, apply the handbrake, and then jack up the front of the vehicle and support it on axle stands (see *Jacking and vehicle support*).

2 Remove the right-hand front roadwheel, then remove the access panel from the inner wheel arch.

3 Use a spanner on the lug provided and then turn the tensioner clockwise. Lock the tensioner in its released position by inserting a drill bit through the lug into the tensioner body **(see illustration)**.

4 Note how the drivebelt is routed, then remove it from the crankshaft pulley, alternator pulley, and air-conditioning compressor pulley.

26.2 Undo the screws and lift the cover from the air cleaner body...

5 Locate the new drivebelt on the pulleys, then remove the drill bit and release the tensioner. Check that the belt is located correctly in the multigrooves in the pulleys.

6 Refit the access panel and roadwheel, and lower the vehicle to the ground.

1.6 and 2.0 litre engines

7 There are two different types of tensioner fitted to these engines; the routing of the belt is the same, although the procedure for belt renewal is different.

8 When the belt is removed, check all pulleys are free from any damage and are secure. Also check that the alternator and air-conditioning compressor are mounted securely.

9 For improved access, apply the handbrake, and then jack up the front of the vehicle and support it on axle stands (see *Jacking and vehicle support*).

26.3...then lift out the air filter element

10 Remove the right-hand front roadwheel, then remove the access panel from the inner wheel arch.

With tensioner spring element

11 Use a spanner on the centre bolt and turn the tensioner clockwise. Lock the tensioner in its released position by inserting a locking pin (Allen key or similar) through the lug into the tensioner body**(see illustrations)**.

12 Note how the drivebelt is routed, then remove it from the crankshaft pulley**(see illustration)**, alternator pulley, and air conditioning compressor pulley.

13 Locate the new drivebelt on the pulleys, then by holding the pressure of the tensioner with a spanner, remove the locking pin. Slowly release the pressure on the spanner **(see illustration)** so that the tensioner takes up the slack in the belt. Check that the belt is located correctly in the multi-grooves in the pulleys.

14 Start the engine and check that the drivebelt runs, as it should over the pulleys. Make sure that all tools and hands are kept clear of the drivebelt with the engine running.

15 With the engine stopped, refit the access panel and roadwheel, and then lower the vehicle to the ground. Refit the engine top cover if removed.

With tensioner roller

16 Undo the tensioner roller retaining bolt, and remove the tensioner roller from the engine. Note the retaining bolt is below the tensioner roller, and goes up through the mounting bracket in a vertical direction **(see**

27.3 Rotate the tensioner and lock it in place with a suitable drill bit (arrowed)

27.11a Turn the tensioner clockwise...

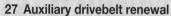

27.11b...and lock the tensioner in position

27.12 Note the fitted position of the belt before removal

27.13 With the locking pin removed, slowly take up the slack in the belt

illustration). Discard the retaining bolt, as a new one will be required for refitting.

17 Note how the drivebelt is routed, then remove it from the crankshaft pulley, alternator pulley, and air-conditioning compressor pulley.

18 Locate the new drivebelt on the pulleys, then fit the tensioner roller, making sure its guide pin is located correctly in the mounting bracket.

19 Fit the new retaining bolt, and then tighten to the following five stages:

a) *Tighten bolt by hand at this point.*
b) *Tighten bolt until it reaches stop.*
c) *Turn bolt back through 90°*
d) *Tighten bolt to 30 Nm.*
e) *Tighten a further 90°*

20 When tensioner roller is fitted and the belt is tensioned, check the tensioner retaining bolt. The part of the bolt that has protruded out through the upper end of the mounting bracket (behind the tensioner roller) must not protrude more than 2.5mm higher than the outer surface of the tensioner roller. This ensures that the bolt has been tightened to its end stop.

21 Start the engine and check that the drivebelt runs, as it should over the pulleys. Make sure that all tools and hands are kept clear of the drivebelt with the engine running.

22 With the engine stopped, refit the access panel and roadwheel, and then lower the vehicle to the ground. Refit the engine top cover if removed.

28 Timing belt and tensioner roller renewal

1 Refer to Chapter 2A for 1.6 litre engines, Chapter 2B for 1.9 litre engines and Chapter 2C for 2.0 litre engines.

29 Particulate filter ash deposit mass check

1 Eventually, the amount of ash deposited in the particle filter by the filtration process will cause a blockage, and engine running problems. Audi state that the maximum amount of ash is 60g. At this point, the particle filter must be renewed. Unfortunately, the mass of the ash can only be established using dedicated Audi diagnostic equipment, connected to the vehicle through the diagnostic plug under the drivers side of the facia. Consequently, we recommend this task is entrusted to a Audi dealer or suitably equipped specialist.

30 Brake (and clutch) fluid renewal

Warning: Brake hydraulic fluid can harm your eyes and damage painted surfaces, so use extreme caution when handling and

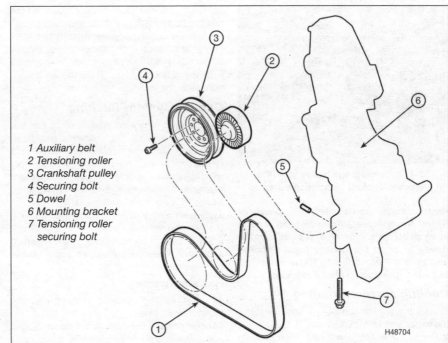

1 Auxiliary belt
2 Tensioning roller
3 Crankshaft pulley
4 Securing bolt
5 Dowel
6 Mounting bracket
7 Tensioning roller
*   securing bolt*

27.16 Auxiliary drivebelt with tensioning roller

pouring it. Do not use fluid that has been standing open for some time, as it absorbs moisture from the air. Excess moisture can cause a dangerous loss of braking effectiveness.

1 The procedure is similar to that for the bleeding of the hydraulic system as described in Chapter 9 Section 2, except that the brake fluid reservoir should be emptied by siphoning, using a clean poultry baster or similar before starting, and allowance should be made for the old fluid to be expelled when bleeding a section of the circuit. Since the clutch hydraulic system also uses fluid from the brake system reservoir, it should also be bled at the same time by referring to Chapter 6, Section 2.

2 Working as described in Chapter 9, open the first bleed screw in the sequence, and pump the brake pedal gently until nearly all the old fluid has been emptied from the master cylinder reservoir.

3 Top-up to the MAX level with new fluid, and continue pumping until only the new fluid remains in the reservoir, and new fluid can be seen emerging from the bleed screw. Tighten the screw, and top the reservoir level up to the MAX level line.

4 Work through all the remaining bleed screws in the sequence until new fluid can be seen at all of them. Be careful to keep the master cylinder reservoir topped-up to above the MIN level at all times, or air may enter the system and greatly increase the length of the task.

5 When the operation is complete, check that all bleed screws are securely tightened, and

that their dust caps are refitted. Wash off all traces of spilt fluid, and recheck the master cylinder reservoir fluid level.

6 On models with a manual transmission unit, once the brake fluid has been changed the clutch fluid should also be renewed. Referring to Chapter 6, bleed the clutch until new fluid is seen to be emerging from the slave cylinder bleed screw, keeping the master cylinder fluid level above the MIN level line at all times to prevent air entering the system. Once the new fluid emerges, securely tighten the bleed screw then disconnect and remove the bleeding equipment. Securely refit the dust cap then wash off all traces of spilt fluid.

7 On all models, ensure the master cylinder fluid level is correct (see *Weekly checks*) and thoroughly check the operation of the brakes and (where necessary) clutch before taking the car on the road.

31 Coolant renewal

Note: *This work is not included in the Audi schedule and should not be required if the recommended VAG G12 LongLife coolant antifreeze/inhibitor is used. However, if standard antifreeze/inhibitor is used, the work should be carried out at the recommended interval.*

Warning: Wait until the engine is cold before starting this procedure. Do not allow antifreeze to come in contact with your skin, or with the painted surfaces of the vehicle.

31.4 Disconnect the hoses from the electric coolant circulation pump

Rinse off spills immediately with plenty of water. Never leave antifreeze lying around in an open container, or in a puddle in the driveway or on the garage floor. Children and pets are attracted by its sweet smell, but antifreeze can be fatal if ingested.

Cooling system draining

1 With the engine completely cold, unscrew the expansion tank cap.

2 Firmly apply the handbrake then jack up the front of the vehicle and support it on axle stands (see *Jacking and vehicle support*). Undo the retaining screws and remove the engine undertray to gain access to the base of the radiator.

3 Position a suitable container beneath the coolant drain outlet, which is fitted to the coolant bottom hose end fitting. Loosen the drain plug (there is no need to remove it completely) and allow the coolant to drain into the container. If desired, a length of tubing can be fitted to the drain outlet to direct the flow of coolant during draining. Where no drain outlet is fitted to the hose end fitting, remove the retaining clip and disconnect the bottom hose from the radiator to drain the coolant (see Chapter 3).

4 On 1.6 and 2.0 litre engines, release the clamps and disconnect the hoses from the electric coolant circulation pump, located at the front side of the cylinder block, below the oil cooler **(see illustration)**.

5 To fully drain the system also disconnect one of the coolant hoses from the oil cooler which is located at the front of the cylinder block.

6 If the coolant has been drained for a reason other than renewal, then provided it is clean, it can be re-used.

7 Once all the coolant has drained, securely

tighten the radiator drain plug or reconnect the bottom hose to the radiator (as applicable). Also reconnect the coolant hose(s) to the oil cooler and electric circulation pump (where applicable) and secure them in position with the retaining clips. Refit the undertray, tightening the retaining screws securely.

Cooling system flushing

8 If the recommended Audi coolant has not been used and coolant renewal has been neglected, or if the antifreeze mixture has become diluted, the cooling system may gradually lose efficiency, as the coolant passages become restricted due to rust, scale deposits, and other sediment. The cooling system efficiency can be restored by flushing the system clean.

9 The radiator should be flushed separately from the engine, to avoid excess contamination.

Radiator flushing

10 To flush the radiator, first tighten the radiator drain plug.

11 Disconnect the top and bottom hoses and any other relevant hoses from the radiator (see Chapter 3).

12 Insert a garden hose into the radiator top inlet. Direct a flow of clean water through the radiator, and continue flushing until clean water emerges from the radiator bottom outlet.

13 If after a reasonable period, the water still does not run clear, the radiator can be flushed with a good proprietary cleaning agent. It is important that their manufacturer's instructions are followed carefully. If the contamination is particularly bad, insert the hose in the radiator bottom outlet, and reverse-flush the radiator.

Engine flushing

14 To flush the engine, remove the thermostat (see Chapter 3, Section 4).

15 With the bottom hose disconnected from the radiator, insert a garden hose into the coolant housing. Direct a clean flow of water through the engine, and continue flushing until clean water emerges from the radiator bottom hose.

16 When flushing is complete, refit the thermostat (see Chapter 3, Section 4) and reconnect the hoses.

Cooling system filling

17 Before attempting to fill the cooling

system, ensure the drain plug is securely closed and make sure that all hoses are connected and are securely retained by their clips. If the recommended Audi coolant is not being used, ensure that a suitable antifreeze mixture is used all year round, to prevent corrosion of the engine components (see following sub-Section).

18 Remove the expansion tank filler cap and slowly fill the system with the coolant. Continue to fill the cooling system until bubbles stop appearing in the expansion tank. Help to bleed the air from the system by repeatedly squeezing the radiator bottom hose.

19 When no more bubbles appear, top the coolant level up to the MAX level mark then securely refit the cap to the expansion tank.

20 Run the engine at a fast idle speed until the cooling fan cuts in. Wait for the fan to stop then switch the engine off and allow the engine to cool.

21 When the engine has cooled, check the coolant level with reference to *Weekly checks*. Top-up the level if necessary, and refit the expansion tank cap.

Antifreeze mixture

22 If the recommended Audi coolant is not being used, the antifreeze should always be renewed at the specified intervals. This is necessary not only to maintain the antifreeze properties, but also to prevent corrosion, which would otherwise occur as the corrosion inhibitors become progressively less effective.

23 Always use an ethylene glycol based antifreeze, which is suitable for use in mixed-metal cooling systems. The quantity of antifreeze and levels of protection are indicated in the Specifications.

24 Before adding antifreeze, the cooling system should be completely drained, preferably flushed, and all hoses checked for condition and security.

25 After filling with antifreeze, a label should be attached to the expansion tank, stating the type and concentration of antifreeze used, and the date installed. Any subsequent topping-up should be made with the same type and concentration of antifreeze.

Caution: Do not use engine antifreeze in the windscreen/tailgate washer system, as it will damage the vehicle paintwork. A screenwash additive should be added to the washer system in the quantities stated on the bottle.

Chapter 2 Part A
1.6 litre engine in-car repair procedures

Contents

Degrees of difficulty

Easy, suitable for novice with little experience | **Fairly easy,** suitable for beginner with some experience | **Fairly difficult,** suitable for competent DIY mechanic | **Difficult,** suitable for experienced DIY mechanic | **Very difficult,** suitable for expert DIY or professional

Specifications

General

Manufacturer's engine codes:
1599 cc (1.6 litre), 16-valve, DOHC .... CAYB and CAYC

Maximum outputs:	Power	Torque
Engine code:		
CAYB	66 kW @ 4200 rpm	230 Nm @ 1500 to 2500 rpm
CAYC	77 kW @ 4400 rpm	250 Nm @ 1500 to 2500 rpm

Bore .... 79.5 mm
Stroke .... 80.5 mm
Compression ratio .... 16.5 : 1
Firing order... 1 – 3 – 4 – 2
No.1 cylinder location...................................... Timing belt end

Note: *See 'Vehicle identification' in Reference chapter for the location of engine code markings.*

Lubrication system

Oil pump type... Gear type, belt-driven from crankshaft
Oil pressure switch (green)................................. 0.5 bar
Oil pressure (oil temperature 80°C):
Minimum @ idling... 0.6 bar
Minimum @ 2000 rpm...................................... 1.0 bar
Maximum @ high rpm...................................... 5.0 bar

Torque wrench settings

	Nm	lbf ft
Ancillary (alternator, etc) bracket mounting bolts*:		
Stage 1 (all six bolts)	40	30
Stage 2 (for two lower bolts)	Angle-tighten a further 45°	
Stage 2 (for four upper bolts)	Angle-tighten a further 90°	
Auxiliary drivebelt tensioner securing bolt:		
Stage 1	20	15
Stage 2	Angle-tighten a further 180°	
Big-end bearing caps bolts*:		
Stage 1	30	22
Stage 2	Angle-tighten a further 90°	
Camshaft retaining frame bolts	10	7
Camshaft cover bolts	10	7
Camshaft sprocket hub centre bolt	100	74
Camshaft sprocket-to-hub bolts	25	18
Common rail bolts	22	16
Coolant pump bolts	15	11
Crankshaft oil seal housing bolts	15	11
Crankshaft pulley-to-sprocket bolts*:		
Stage 1	10	7
Stage 2	Angle-tighten a further 90°	
Crankshaft sprocket bolt*:		
Stage 1	180	133
Stage 2	Angle-tighten a further 90°	
Stage 3	Angle-tighten a further 45°	
Cylinder head bolts*:		
Stage 1	30	22
Stage 2	50	44
Stage 3	Angle-tighten a further 90°	
Stage 4	Angle-tighten a further 90°	
Engine mountings:		
RH engine mounting*:		
Mounting bracket to engine:		
Stage 1	40	30
Stage 2	Angle-tighten a further 180°	
Mounting to body:		
Stage 1	40	30
Stage 2	Angle-tighten a further 90°	
Mounting to bracket:		
Stage 1	60	44
Stage 2	Angle-tighten a further 90°	
LH engine/transmission mounting*:		
Mounting to body:		
Stage 1	40	30
Stage 2	Angle-tighten a further 90°	
Mounting to bracket on transmission:		
Stage 1	60	44
Stage 2	Angle-tighten a further 90°	
Rear mounting link*:		
Link-to-transmission:		
Short (front) bolt:		
Stage 1	40	30
Stage 2	Angle-tighten a further 90°	
Long (rear) bolt:		
Stage 1	60	44
Stage 2	Angle-tighten a further 90°	
Link-to-subframe:		
Stage 1	100	74
Stage 2	Angle-tighten a further 90°	
Flywheel*:		
Stage 1	60	44
Stage 2	Angle-tighten a further 90°	
Fuel pump hub nut	95	70
Fuel pump sprocket bolts*	20	15
Main bearing cap bolts*:		
Stage 1	65	48
Stage 2	Angle-tighten a further 90°	
Oil cooler screws	11	7

Torque wrench settings

	Nm	lbf ft
Oil drain plug*...	30	22
Oil filter housing-to-cylinder block bolts*:		
Stage 1..	14	10
Stage 2..	Angle-tighten a further 180°	
Oil filter cover...	25	18
Oil level/temperature sensor-to-sump bolts.....................	9	7
Oil pick-up pipe securing bolts	9	7
Oil pressure warning light switch	22	16
Oil pump securing bolts...................................	16	11
Piston oil spray jet bolt.................................	27	19
Sump:		
Sump-to-cylinder block bolts........................	13	9
Sump-to-transmission bolts..........................	40	30
Thermostat housing	15	11
Timing belt outer cover bolts	10	7
Timing belt tensioner roller securing nut:		
Stage 1..	20	15
Stage 2..	Angle-tighten a further 45°	
Timing belt idler pulleys:		
Lower idler roller nut................................	20	15
Upper idler roller (small) bolt........................	15	11
Upper idler roller (large) bolt*:		
Stage 1	50	37
Stage 2	Angle-tighten a further 90°	

*Do not re-use fasteners

1 General Information

How to use this Chapter

1 This Part of Chapter 2 describes those repair procedures that can reasonably be carried out on the engine while it remains in the vehicle. If the engine has been removed from the vehicle and is being dismantled as described in Part D, any preliminary dismantling procedures can be ignored.

2 Note that while it may be possible physically to overhaul certain items while the engine is in the vehicle, such tasks are not usually carried out as separate operations, and usually require the execution of several additional procedures (not to mention the cleaning of components and of oilways); for this reason, all such tasks are classed as major overhaul procedures, and are described in Part D of this Chapter.

Engine description

3 Throughout this Chapter, engines are referred to by type, and are identified and referred to by the manufacturer's code letters. A listing of all engines covered, together with their code letters, is given in the Specifications at the start of this Chapter.

4 The engines are water-cooled, double overhead camshafts (DOHC), in-line four-cylinder units, with cast-iron cylinder blocks and aluminium-silicone alloy cylinder heads. All are mounted transversely at the front of the vehicle, with the transmission bolted to the left-hand end of the engine.

5 The crankshaft is of five-bearing type, and thrustwashers are fitted to the centre main bearing (No.3) to control crankshaft endfloat.

6 Drive for the exhaust camshaft is by a toothed timing belt from the crankshaft, with the intake camshaft driven by interlocking gears at the left-hand end of both camshafts. The gears incorporate a toothed backlash compensator element. Each camshaft is mounted at the top of the cylinder head, and is secured by a bearing frame/ladder.

7 The valves are closed by coil springs, and run in guides pressed into the cylinder head. The valves are operated by roller rocker arms incorporating hydraulic tappets.

8 The gear-type oil pump is driven by a belt from the right-hand (timing belt) end of the crankshaft. Oil is drawn from the sump through a strainer, and then forced through an externally mounted, renewable filter. From there, it is distributed to the cylinder head, where it lubricates the camshaft journals and hydraulic tappets, and also to the crankcase, where it lubricates the main bearings, connecting rod big-ends, gudgeon pins and cylinder bores. A coolant-fed oil cooler is fitted to the oil filter housing on all engines. Oil jets are fitted to the base of each cylinder – these spray oil onto the underside of the pistons, to improve cooling.

9 All engines are fitted with a combined brake servo vacuum pump, driven by the camshaft on the transmission end of the cylinder head.

10 On all engines, engine coolant is circulated by a pump, driven by the timing belt. For details of the cooling system, refer to Chapter 3.

Operations with engine in car

11 The following operations can be performed without removing the engine:

a) Compression pressure – testing.
b) Camshaft cover – removal and refitting.
c) Crankshaft pulley – removal and refitting.
d) Timing belt covers – removal and refitting.
e) Timing belt – removal, refitting and adjustment.
f) Timing belt tensioner and sprockets – removal and refitting.
g) Camshaft oil seals – renewal.
h) Camshafts and hydraulic tappets – removal, inspection and refitting.
i) Cylinder head – removal and refitting.
j) Cylinder head and pistons – decarbonising.
k) Sump – removal and refitting.
l) Oil pump – removal, overhaul and refitting.
m) Crankshaft oil seals – renewal.
n) Engine/transmission mountings – inspection and renewal.
o) Flywheel – removal, inspection and refitting.

Note: It is possible to remove the pistons and connecting rods (after removing the cylinder head and sump) without removing the engine. However, this is not recommended. Work of this nature is more easily and thoroughly completed with the engine on the bench, as described in Chapter 2D.

2 Compression and leakdown tests – description and interpretation

Compression test

Note: *A compression tester suitable for use with diesel engines will be required for this test.*

1 When engine performance is down, or if misfiring occurs which cannot be attributed to the ignition or fuel systems, a compression test can provide diagnostic clues as to the engine's condition. If the test is performed regularly, it can give warning of trouble before any other symptoms become apparent.

2 The engine must be fully warmed-up to normal operating temperature, the battery must be fully charged, and you will require the aid of an assistant.

3 Remove the glow plugs as described in Chapter 5, Section 11, and then fit a compression tester to the No.1 cylinder glow plug hole. The type of tester that screws into the plug thread is preferred.

Note: *Part of the glow plug removal procedure is to disconnect the fuel injector wiring plugs. As a result of the plugs being disconnected and the engine cranked, faults may be stored in the ECU memory. These must be erased after the compression test.*

4 Have your assistant crank the engine for several seconds on the starter motor. After one or two revolutions, the compression pressure should build-up to a maximum figure and then stabilise. Record the highest reading obtained.

5 Repeat the test on the remaining cylinders, recording the pressure in each.

6 The cause of poor compression is less easy to establish on a diesel engine than on a petrol engine. The effect of introducing oil into the cylinders (wet testing) is not conclusive, because there is a risk that the oil will sit in the recess on the piston crown, instead of passing to the rings. However, the following can be used as a rough guide to diagnosis.

7 All cylinders should produce very similar pressures. Any difference greater than that specified indicates the existence of a fault. Note that the compression should build-up quickly in a healthy engine. Low compression on the first stroke, followed by gradually increasing pressure on successive strokes, indicates worn piston rings. A low compression reading on the first stroke, which does not build-up during successive strokes, indicates leaking valves or a blown head gasket (a cracked head could also be the cause).

8 A low reading from two adjacent cylinders is almost certainly due to the head gasket having blown between them and the presence of coolant in the engine oil will confirm this.

9 On completion, remove the compression tester, and refit the glow plugs, with reference to Chapter 5, Section 11.

10 Reconnect the wiring to the injector solenoids. Finally, have an Audi dealer or suitably equipped specialist erase any fault codes from the ECU memory.

Leakdown test

11 A leakdown test measures the rate at which compressed air fed into the cylinder is lost. It is an alternative to a compression test, and in many ways it is better, since the escaping air provides easy identification of where pressure loss is occurring (piston rings, valves or head gasket).

12 The equipment required for leakdown testing is unlikely to be available to the home mechanic. If poor compression is suspected, have the test performed by a suitably equipped garage.

3 Engine assembly and valve timing marks – general information and usage

General information

1 TDC is the highest point in the cylinder that each piston reaches as it travels up-and-down when the crankshaft turns. Each piston reaches TDC at the end of the compression stroke and again at the end of the exhaust stroke, but TDC generally refers to piston position on the compression stroke. No 1 piston is at the timing belt end of the engine.

2 Positioning No 1 piston at TDC is an essential part of many procedures, such as timing belt removal and camshaft removal.

3 The design of the engines covered in this

3.8 The alignment mark (arrowed) on the crankshaft sprocket should be almost vertical

Chapter is such that piston-to-valve contact may occur if the camshaft or crankshaft is turned with the timing belt removed. For this reason, it is important to ensure that the camshaft and crankshaft do not move in relation to each other once the timing belt has been removed from the engine.

Setting TDC on No 1 cylinder

Note: *VAG special tool T10050 is required to lock the crankshaft sprocket in the TDC position. Alternatively obtain a tool from automotive tool specialists. Try asttools.co.uk.*

4 Raise the front of the vehicle and support it securely on axle stands (see *'Jacking and vehicle support'* in Reference chapter). Remove the front right-hand road wheel, then release the fasteners and remove the lower section of the wheelarch liner.

5 Remove the auxiliary drivebelt as described in Chapter 1, Section 27.

6 Remove the crankshaft pulley/vibration damper as described in Section 5.

7 Remove the timing belt outer covers as described in Section 6.

8 Using a spanner or socket on the crankshaft sprocket bolt, turn the crankshaft in the normal direction of rotation (clockwise) until the alignment mark on the face of the sprocket is almost vertical, and the hole in the camshaft sprocket hub aligns with the hole in the cylinder head **(see illustration)**.

9 While in this position it should be possible to insert the VAG tool T10050 to lock the crankshaft, and a 6 mm diameter rod/drill bit to lock the camshafts **(see illustrations)**.

3.9a Fit the tool to the hole in the oil seal housing (arrowed)…

3.9b …so the marks on the tool and sprocket align (arrowed)

3.9c Insert a 6 mm locking tool into the camshaft hub …

3.9d ...with the arrow almost at the 12 o'clock position

Note: *The mark on the crankshaft sprocket and the mark on the VAG tool must align, whilst at the same time the shaft of tool must engage in the drilling in the crankshaft oil seal housing.*
10 The engine is now set to TDC on No.1 cylinder.

4 Camshaft cover – removal and refitting

Removal

1 Remove the fuel injectors as described in Chapter 4A, Section 4 and fuel rail as described in Chapter 4A, Section 11.
2 Remove the timing belt upper cover as described in Section 6.
3 Note their fitted positions, then disconnect the vacuum hoses from the camshaft cover, and release them, and the wiring loom from the retaining clips at the rear of the cover **(see illustration)**.
4 Squeeze together the sides of the collar, and disconnect the breather hose from the camshaft cover **(see illustration)**.
5 Undo the bolts and move the coolant return pipe and fuel return pipe to one side.
6 Release the wiring from the clips at the rear of the cover, then unscrew the camshaft cover retaining bolts and lift the cover away. If the cover sticks, do not attempt to lever it off – instead free it by working around the cover and tapping it lightly with a soft-faced mallet **(see illustration)**.

4.7a Renew the cover seal if necessary

4.3 Unclip the wiring from the retaining clips

7 Recover the camshaft cover gasket. Inspect the gasket carefully, and renew it if damage or deterioration is evident – note that the retaining bolts and seals must be pushed fully through the cover **(see illustrations)**.
8 Clean the mating surfaces of the cylinder head and camshaft cover thoroughly, removing all traces of oil – take care to avoid damaging the surfaces as you do this.

Refitting

9 Refit the camshaft cover by following the removal procedure in reverse, tightening the cover retaining bolts to the specified torque, starting with the centre bolts and working outwards.

5 Crankshaft pulley – removal and refitting

Removal

1 Switch off the ignition and all electrical consumers and remove the ignition key.
2 Raise the front right-hand side of the vehicle, and support securely on axle stands (see *'Jacking and vehicle support'* in Reference chapter). Remove the roadwheel.
3 Remove the securing fasteners and withdraw the lower section of the front wheel arch liner.
4 Slacken the bolts securing the crankshaft pulley to the sprocket **(see illustration)**. If necessary, the pulley can be prevented from

4.7b Bolts and seals must be pushed fully through the cover before fitting the gasket

4.4 Squeeze together the sides of the collar to disconnect the breather hose

4.6 Undo the bolts and lift away the camshaft cover

turning by counterholding with a spanner or socket on the crankshaft sprocket bolt.
5 Remove the auxiliary drivebelt, as described in Chapter 1, Section 27.
6 Unscrew the bolts securing the pulley to the sprocket, and remove the pulley. Discard the bolts – new ones must be fitted.

Refitting

7 Refit the pulley over the locating peg on the crankshaft sprocket, then fit the new pulley securing bolts.
8 Refit the auxiliary drivebelt as described in Chapter 1, Section 27.
9 Prevent the crankshaft from turning as during removal, then fit the pulley securing bolts, and tighten to the specified torque.
10 Refit the wheel arch liner.
11 Refit the roadwheel and lower the vehicle to the ground.

5.4 Undo the pulley bolts, counterholding it with a socket on the centre sprocket bolt

6.1 Pull the plastic cover upwards from the mountings

6.2 Unclip the hoses from the retaining clips

6.3a Disconnect the wiring connector...

6.3b ...undo the two retaining bolts...

6.3c ...and withdraw the mounting bracket

6 Timing belt covers – removal and refitting

Upper outer cover

1 Pull the engine top cover upwards to release the mountings (see illustration).

2 Release the hoses from the retaining clips on the right-hand side of the cylinder head and move them to one side (see illustration).

3 Disconnect the wiring plug, undo the retaining bolts, and remove the pressure differential sender (for particulate filter) including bracket from the top of the engine mounting and move it to one side (see illustrations).

4 Undo the retaining bolt, then twist the washer reservoir filler neck to remove it from engine compartment (see illustration).

5 Undo the retaining bolts and nut, then remove the fuel filter from the engine mounting and move it to one side (see illustrations). The fuel hoses do not need to be disconnected from the filter.

6 To make access easier, undo the retaining bolt, disconnect the wiring connector and move the coolant reservoir to one side (see illustration).

7 Disconnect the radiator outlet temperature sensor wiring plug (see illustration).

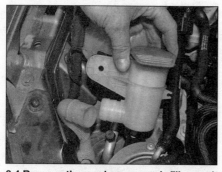

6.4 Remove the washer reservoir filler neck

6.5a Undo the filter retaining bolts/nut (arrowed)...

6.5b ...and release the fuel pipe retaining clip

6.6 Move the coolant reservoir to one side

6.7 Disconnect the temperature sensor wiring connector

6.8a Release the rear lower clip (arrowed)…

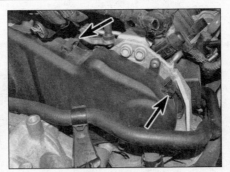

6.8b …the two upper front clips (arrowed)…

6.8c …and manoeuvre the upper cover from place

8 Release the 3 clips and remove the timing belt upper cover **(see illustrations)**.
9 Refitting is a reversal of removal, noting that the lower edge of the upper cover engages with the lower cover.

Lower outer cover

10 Remove the upper cover as described previously.
11 If not already done, remove the crankshaft pulley as described in Section 5.
12 Unscrew the five bolts securing the lower cover, and remove it **(see illustrations)**.
13 Refitting is a reversal of removal; noting that the upper edge of the lower cover engages with the upper cover.

Rear cover

14 Remove the timing belt, tensioner and sprockets as described in Section 7 and Section 8.

15 Undo the retaining bolt and remove the rear hub cover from the end of the camshaft.
16 Slacken and withdraw the retaining bolts and lift the timing belt inner cover from the studs on the end of the engine, and remove it from the engine compartment**(see illustrations)**. It may be required to remove the coolant pump (Chapter 3), before the rear cover can be removed.
17 Refitting is a reversal of removal.

---

7 Timing belt – removal, inspection and refitting

Note: *There are two types of tensioner fitted to this engine and they are not interchangeable* **(see illustration)**. *Check to see which type is fitted before removing the timing belt.*

Type A tensioner requires a locking pin for installation and it tensions the belt by rotating clockwise. Type B tensioner does not require a locking pin for installation and it tensions the belt by rotating anti-clockwise. See text.

Removal

1 The primary function of the toothed timing belt is to drive the camshaft, but it also drives the coolant pump and high-pressure fuel pump. Should the belt slip or break in service, the valve timing will be disturbed and piston-to-valve contact may occur, resulting in serious engine damage. For this reason, it is important that the timing belt is tensioned correctly, and inspected regularly for signs of wear or deterioration.
2 Switch off the ignition and all electrical consumers and remove the ignition key.

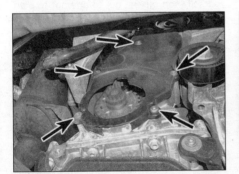

6.12a Undo the lower cover retaining bolts (arrowed)…

6.12b …and manoeuvre the lower cover from place

6.16a Remove the retaining bolts…

6.16b …and remove the rear cover

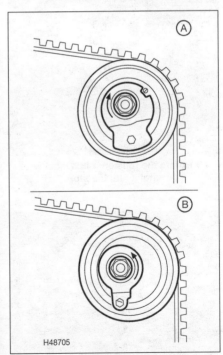

7.0 Two types of tensioner type (A) and (B)

A Roller tensions clockwise
B Roller tensions anti-clockwise

7.4 Slacken the sprocket-to-hub bolts (arrowed)

7.5 Slacken the high-pressure fuel pump sprocket bolts (arrowed)

7.6 Insert an Allen key, slacken the nut, and rotate the hub anti-clockwise until a 2 mm rod/drill bit (arrowed) can be inserted to lock the hub to the pulley

3 Set the engine to TDC on No. 1 cylinder as described in Section 3.

4 Slacken the three bolts securing the sprocket to the camshaft hub by 90° **(see illustration)**.

5 Slacken the three bolts securing the sprocket to the high-pressure fuel pump by 90° **(see illustration)**.

Type A tensioner

6 Insert a suitable Allen key into the tensioner hub, then slacken the retaining nut and rotate the tensioner hub anti-clockwise until it can be locked in place using a 2.0 mm pin/drill bit **(see illustration)**.

7 Leaving the pin in place, now rotate the tensioner hub clockwise to the stop, and hand-tighten the retaining nut **(see illustration)**.

Type B tensioner

8 Insert a suitable Allen key into the tensioner hub, then slacken the retaining nut and rotate the tensioner hub clockwise, until the tensioner hub is loosened. When in position hand-tighten the retaining nut.

All engines

9 If the original timing belt is to be refitted, mark the running direction of the belt, to ensure correct refitting.

Caution: If the belt appears to be in good condition and can be re-used, it is essential that it is refitted the same way around, otherwise accelerated wear will result, leading to premature failure.

10 Slide the belt from the sprockets, taking care not to twist or kink the belt excessively if it is to be re-used.

Inspection

11 Examine the belt for evidence of contamination by coolant or lubricant. If this is the case, find the source of the contamination before progressing any further. Check the belt for signs of wear or damage, particularly around the leading edges of the belt teeth. Renew the belt if its condition is in doubt; the cost of belt renewal is negligible compared with potential cost of the engine repairs, should the belt fail in service. The belt must be renewed if it has covered the mileage given in Chapter 1, however, if it has covered less, it is prudent to renew it regardless of condition, as a precautionary measure.

12 If the timing belt is not going to be refitted for some time, it is a wise precaution to hang a warning label on the steering wheel, to remind yourself (and others) not to attempt to start the engine. Have the battery disconnected to prevent any engine damage.

13 If the tensioner roller is to be renewed, the engine mounting will also need to be removed, as described in Section 16. Then the tensioner removed as described in Section 8.

Refitting

14 Ensure that the crankshaft and camshaft are still set to TDC on No 1 cylinder, as described in Section 3. The camshaft sprocket bolts should be renewed, and slackened at this point.

15 Renew the high-pressure fuel pump sprocket bolts one at a time. They should also be slackened.

16 Using a screwdriver on the bolts heads, rotate the high-pressure fuel pump clockwise until a 6.0 mm locking pin/drill bit can be inserted into the housing adjacent to the sprocket, locking the pump in place **(see illustration)**.

17 Rotate the camshaft sprocket and high-pressure fuel pump sprocket fully clockwise so that the securing bolts are at the end of the elongated holes **(see illustrations)**.

18 Loop the timing belt loosely under the crankshaft sprocket.

Note: *Observe any direction of rotation markings on the belt.*

19 Fit the belt around the tensioner pulley,

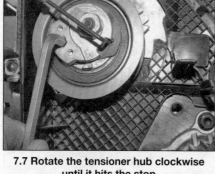

7.7 Rotate the tensioner hub clockwise until it hits the stop

7.16 Rotate the high-pressure fuel pump clockwise until a 6 mm drill bit/rod can be inserted into the housing and hub(arrowed)

7.17a Rotate the sprockets fully clockwise until the fuel pump sprocket...

7.17b ...and camshaft sprocket bolts are at the end of the elongated holes

7.20 Timing belt routing

7.21a Rotate the tensioner clockwise…

engage the timing belt teeth with the camshaft sprockets, then manoeuvre it into position around the coolant pump sprocket and the fuel pump sprocket. Make sure that the belt teeth seat correctly on the sprockets.

Note: *Slight adjustment to the position of the camshaft sprocket may be necessary to achieve this. Avoid bending the belt back on itself or twisting it excessively as you do this.*

20 Finally, fit the belt around the idler roller **(see illustration)**. Ensure that any slack in the belt is in the section of belt that passes over the tensioner roller.

Type A tensioner

21 Loosen the timing belt tensioner securing nut, and pull out the tensioner locking pin. Turn the tensioner clockwise with an Allen key until the pointer is just past the middle of the gap in the tensioner base plate **(see illustrations)**. With the tensioner held in this position, tighten the securing nut to the specified torque and angle.

Type B tensioner

22 Loosen the timing belt tensioner securing nut, and turn the tensioner anti-clockwise with an Allen key until the pointer is just past the

middle of the gap in the tensioner base plate **(see illustration)**. With the tensioner held in this position, tighten the securing nut to the specified torque and angle.

All engines

23 Counterhold the camshaft sprocket and fuel pump sprocket with a home made tool to prevent any rotation, and then tighten the camshaft sprocket and fuel pump sprocket bolts to 20 Nm **(see illustrations)**.

24 Remove the sprockets' locking tools and the crankshaft locking tool **(see illustrations)**.

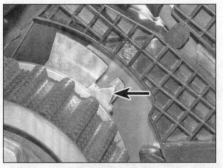

7.21b …until the pointer (arrowed) is just past the gap in the base plate

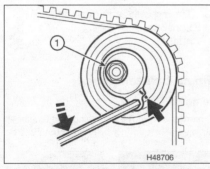

7.22 Turn the tensioner anti-clockwise and secure the retaining nut (1)

7.23a Counterhold the camshaft sprocket…

7.23b …and the pump sprocket, while the bolts are tightened

7.24a Remove the upper locking pins…

7.24b …and crankshaft locking tool

7.26 Check the pointer (arrowed) is centred or within 5mm to the right of the gap in the base plate

7.27 Slight misalignment of the pump sprocket timing hole (arrowed) is acceptable

8.4 Coolant pipe upper mounting bolt and lower mounting nut (arrowed)

25 Using a spanner or wrench and socket on the crankshaft pulley centre bolt, rotate the crankshaft clockwise through two complete revolutions. Reset the engine to TDC on No.1 cylinder, with reference to Section 3 and refit the crankshaft locking tool.

26 Check that the tensioner roller indicator arm is centred, or within a maximum of 5 mm to the right of the notch in the base plate **(see illustration)**. If not, hold the tensioner hub stationary with an Allen key, slacken the retaining nut and position the arm in the centre of the notch. Tighten the retaining nut to the specified torque. Remove the Allen key.

27 Check that the camshaft sprocket locking pin can still be inserted.

Note: *It's very difficult to align the locking point of the fuel pump hub again (see illustration). However, a slight misalignment of holes will not affect engine performance.*

28 If the camshaft sprocket locking pin cannot be inserted, pull the crankshaft locking tool slight away from the engine, and rotate the crankshaft anti-clockwise slightly past TDC. Now slowly rotate the crankshaft clockwise until the camshaft sprocket locking tool can be inserted.

29 If the locating pin of the crankshaft locking tool is to the left of the corresponding hole, slacken the camshaft sprocket bolts,

slowly rotate the crankshaft clockwise until the locking tool can be fully inserted. Tighten the camshaft sprocket bolts to 20 Nm.

30 If the locating pin of the crankshaft locking tool is to the right of the corresponding hole, slacken the camshaft sprocket bolts, rotate the crankshaft anti-clockwise slightly until the pin is to the left of the hole, then slowly rotate it clockwise until the lock tool can be fully inserted. Tighten the camshaft sprocket bolts to 20 Nm.

31 Remove the crankshaft and camshaft locking tools, then rotate the crankshaft 2 complete revolutions clockwise and check the locking tools can be reinserted. If necessary, repeat the adjustment procedure described previously.

32 Tighten the camshaft and fuel pump sprocket bolts to the specified torque.

33 The remainder of refitting is a reversal of removal.

---

8   Timing belt tensioner and sprockets – removal and refitting

Timing belt tensioner

Removal

1 In order to remove the timing belt tensioner, the engine mounting bracket must first be

removed. Either support the engine from above using a crossbeam or an engine hoist or support if from underneath with a trolley jack and block of wood.

2 Remove the timing belt as described in Section 7.

3 Undo the bolts and remove the right-hand engine mounting.

4 Undo the bolt securing the coolant pipe to the mounting bracket **(see illustration)**.

5 Working in the wheelarch area, undo the nut securing the lower end of the coolant pipe.

6 Undo the 3 retaining bolts and remove the engine mounting bracket **(see illustration)**.

7 Unscrew the timing belt tensioner nut, and remove the tensioner from the engine.

Refitting

8 When refitting the tensioner to the engine, ensure that the lug on the tensioner backplate engages with the corresponding cut-out in the rear timing belt cover, then refit the tensioner nut **(see illustration)**.

9 The remainder of refitting is a reversal of removal.

Idler pulleys

Removal

10 Remove the timing belt as described in Section 7.

11 Unscrew the relevant idler pulley/roller

8.6 Engine mounting bracket bolts (arrowed)

8.8 Ensure the lug on the backplate engages with the cut-out in the timing belt cover (arrowed)

8.11 Timing belt idler pulleys

8.17 Using a puller to remove the crankshaft sprocket

securing bolt/nut, and then withdraw the pulley **(see illustration)**.

Refitting

12 Refit the pulley and tighten the securing bolt or nut to the specified torque.

Note: *Renew the large roller/pulley retaining bolt (where applicable).*

13 Refit and tension the timing belt as described in Section 7.

Crankshaft sprocket

Note: *A new crankshaft sprocket securing bolt must be used on refitting.*

Removal

14 Remove the timing belt as described in Section 7.

15 The sprocket securing bolt must now be slackened, and the crankshaft must be prevented from turning as the sprocket bolt is unscrewed. To hold the sprocket, make up a suitable tool, and screw it to the sprocket using a two bolts screwed into two of the crankshaft pulley bolt holes.

16 Hold the sprocket using the tool, then slacken the sprocket securing bolt. Take care, as the bolt is very tight. Do not allow the crankshaft to turn as the bolt is slackened.

17 Unscrew the bolt, and slide the sprocket from the end of the crankshaft, noting which

way round the sprocket's raised boss is fitted. If required, use a puller to withdraw the sprocket from the end of the crankshaft **(see illustration)**.

Refitting

18 Commence refitting by positioning the sprocket on the end of the crankshaft.

19 Fit a new sprocket securing bolt, then counterhold the sprocket using the method employed on removal, and tighten the bolt to the specified torque in the three stages given in the Specifications.

20 Refit the timing belt as described in Section 7.

Camshaft sprocket

Removal

21 Remove the timing belt as described in Section 7, then rotate the crankshaft 90° anti-clockwise to prevent any accidental piston-to-valve contact.

22 Unscrew and remove the three retaining bolts and remove the camshaft sprocket from the camshaft hub.

Refitting

23 Refit the sprocket ensuring that it is fitted the correct way round, as noted before removal, then insert the new sprocket bolts, and tighten by hand only at this stage.

24 If the crankshaft has been turned, turn the crankshaft clockwise 90° back to TDC.

25 Refit and tension the timing belt as described in Section 7.

Camshaft hub

Note: *VAG technicians use special tool T10051 to counterhold the hub, however it is possible to fabricate a suitable alternative.*

Removal

26 Remove the camshaft sprocket as described previously in this Section.

27 Engage special tool T10051 with the three locating holes in the face of the hub to prevent the hub from turning. If this tool is not available, fabricate a suitable alternative. Whilst holding the tool, undo the central hub retaining bolt about two turns **(see illustration)**.

28 Slide the hub from the camshaft. If necessary, attach special tool T10052 (or a similar three-legged puller) to the hub, and evenly tighten the puller until the hub is free of the camshaft taper **(see illustration)**.

Refitting

29 Ensure that the camshaft taper and the hub centre is clean and dry, locate the hub on the taper, noting that the built-in key in the hub taper must align with the keyway in the camshaft taper **(see illustration)**.

8.27 Fabricate a home made tool to counterhold the hub. Undo the bolt...

8.28 ...and slide the hub from the camshaft

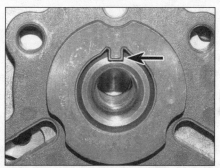

8.29 Ensure the integral key aligns with the keyway in the camshaft (arrowed)

9.4a Using flat metal bar and cable ties to secure the camshafts...

9.4b ...to the upper ladder frame for removal

30 Hold the hub in this position with tool T10051 (or similar home-made tool), and tighten the central bolt to the specified torque.
31 Refit the camshaft sprocket as described previously in this Section.

Coolant pump sprocket

32 The coolant pump sprocket is integral with the coolant pump. Refer to Chapter 3 for details of coolant pump removal.

9 Camshaft and hydraulic tappets – removal, inspection and refitting

Note: *A new camshaft oil seal(s) will be required on refitting. VAG removal tool T40094 (or similar tool) will be required to refit the camshafts – this is necessary to prevent damage to the retaining frame and cylinder head as the camshafts are refitted.*

Removal

1 With the timing set at TDC, remove the camshaft hub (see Section 8).
2 Remove the camshaft cover (see Section 4).
3 Remove the brake vacuum pump as described in Chapter 9, Section 21.

9.7 Make alignment marks for the position of the sprockets

4 If the camshafts are not going to be renewed, use two flat pieces of metal flat bar and cable ties and secure the two camshafts to the retaining frame **(see illustrations)**. Progressively unscrew the camshaft retaining frame bolts in the reverse of the sequence shown in **illustration 9.27**, and carefully remove the retaining frame, complete with camshafts. Remove the oil seal from the end of the camshaft and discard it – a new one will be required for refitting.
5 If the camshafts are going to be renewed, progressively unscrew the camshaft retaining frame bolts in the reverse of the sequence shown in **illustration 9.27**, and carefully remove the retaining frame. Then carefully lift the camshafts from the cylinder head, keeping them identified for location. Remove the oil seal from the end of the camshaft and discard it – a new one will be required for refitting.
6 Lift the rocker arms and hydraulic tappets from place. Store the rockers and tappets in a container with numbered compartments to ensure they are refitted to their correct locations. It is recommended that the tappets are kept immersed in oil for the period they are removed from the cylinder head.

Inspection

7 If the camshafts are still secured to the

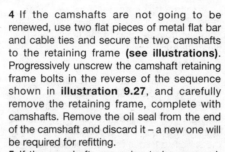

9.10 Check the tappets for wear

retaining frame, mark the two sprockets in relation with each other, then cut the cable ties to remove them from the frame **(see illustration)**. With the camshafts removed, examine the retaining frame and the bearing locations in the cylinder head for signs of obvious wear or pitting. If evident, a new cylinder head will probably be required. Also check that the oil supply holes in the cylinder head are free from obstructions.
8 Visually inspect the camshafts for evidence of wear on the surfaces of the lobes and journals. Normally their surfaces should be smooth and have a dull shine; look for scoring, erosion or pitting and areas that appear highly polished, indicating excessive wear. Accelerated wear will occur once the hardened exterior of the camshaft has been damaged, so always renew worn items.
Note: *If these symptoms are visible on the tips of the camshaft lobes, check the corresponding rocker arm, as it will probably be worn as well.*
9 If the machined surfaces of the camshaft appear discoloured or blued, it is likely that it has been overheated at some point, probably due to inadequate lubrication. This may have distorted the shaft, so have the camshaft runout and endfloat checked by an automotive engine reconditioning specialist.
10 Inspect the hydraulic tappets for obvious signs of wear or damage **(see illustration)**, and renew if necessary. Check that the oil holes in the tappets are free from obstructions.

Refitting

11 Oil the rocker arms and hydraulic tappets, and then refit them to their original positions.

  Warning: After fitting hydraulic tappets, wait a minimum of 30 minutes (or preferably, leave overnight) before starting the engine; to allow the tappets time to settle, otherwise the valve heads will strike the pistons.

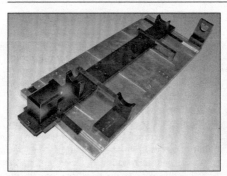

9.12 VAG special tool No. T40094 shown

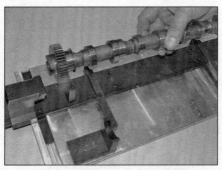

9.13a Position the inlet camshaft on the tool with the head bolt indent facing outwards…

9.13b …then slide the end of the special tool, in to the slot in the end of the camshaft

Using VAG special tool No.T40094

12 If the camshafts were removed from the retaining frame, use the VAG special tool No.T40094, as shown in the following procedures **(see illustration)**.

13 Position the inlet camshaft as shown with the cylinder head bolt indents facing outwards, then slide the end support into the slot in the end of the camshaft **(see illustrations)**.

14 Position the exhaust camshaft on the supports, again with the cylinder head bolt indents facing outwards, and then fit the locating clamp into the slot in the end of the camshaft **(see illustrations)**.

15 Fit the VAG clamping tool No.T40096 to the double gear on the exhaust camshaft, tightening the knurled thumb wheel until the faces of the gear teeth are in alignment **(see illustration)**. Note some camshafts only have a single sprocket, so will not require this procedure.

16 Slide the exhaust camshaft towards the inlet camshaft until the gear teeth engage **(see illustration)**.

17 Ensure the gasket faces of the retaining frame are clean, then apply a smear of clean engine oil to the bearing surfaces and lower the frame into position over the camshafts **(see illustrations)**. Ensure the bearing surfaces locate correctly on the camshafts.

18 Fit the clamping tool No.T40095 over the camshafts and frame, and tighten the thumbwheels to hold the camshafts in position in the frame **(see illustration)**.

9.14a Position the exhaust camshaft on the tool with the head bolt indent facing outwards…

9.14b …then fit special tool clamp into the slot in the end of the exhaust camshaft

9.15 Tighten the thumbwheel to align the gear teeth. Ensure the clamping jaw with the arrow is seated on the wider gear

9.16 Slide the exhaust camshaft to the inlet camshaft until the teeth are in mesh

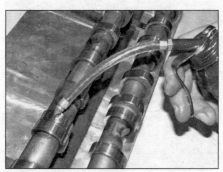

9.17a Lubricate the bearing mountings…

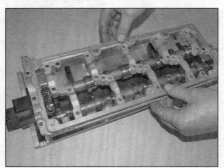

9.17b …and fit the upper ladder frame to the camshafts

9.18 Secure the camshafts in place in the frame using tool No. T40095

9.19a Slide the locking tool out from the end of the inlet camshaft...

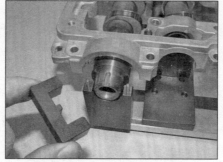

9.19b ...and remove the locking clamp from the end of the exhaust camshaft

19 Slide out locking clamps from each end of the camshafts **(see illustrations)**, and then lift the camshafts, retaining frame and clamping tool from the VAG special tool no. 40094.

Without VAG special tool

20 Ensure the gasket faces of the retaining frame are clean, then apply a smear of clean engine oil to the bearing surfaces and turn it upside down on a clean surface.

21 Position the camshafts on the retaining frame with the cylinder head bolt indents facing outwards. Align the marks made on the camshaft sprockets on removal **(see illustration 9.7)**.

22 If a double gear is fitted to the exhaust camshaft, fit the VAG clamping tool No.T40096 (or similar) to align the faces of the teeth. If the VAG clamping tool is not available use two flat bladed screwdrivers and a pair of pliers, this will need an assistant to keep firm pressure on the camshafts to make sure they locate in the retaining frame correctly **(see illustrations)**. Note some camshafts only have a single sprocket, so will not require this procedure.

23 With the marks on the sprockets aligned and the cylinder head bolt indents facing outwards, the slot in the end of the inlet camshaft (that drives the vacuum pump) should be horizontal and the slot in the end of the exhaust camshaft (that locates the timing belt sprocket) should be at the top when fitted **(see illustrations)**.

24 With the camshafts correctly in position, ensuring the camshafts locate correctly in the bearing surfaces on the retaining frame, use two flat pieces of metal flat bar and cable ties to secure them in position **(see illustration)**.

Caution: Make sure the camshafts are located correctly in the bearing surfaces on the retaining frame, otherwise damage can occur, and this could damage the retaining frame when tightening down onto the cylinder head. The retaining frame is matched to the cylinder head and can only be purchased with a new cylinder head. If there is any doubt, then the VAG special tool should be used, see previous refitting procedure.

All

25 Ensure the sealing surfaces of the cylinder head are clean, and then apply a 2.0 mm wide

9.22a VAG special tool for aligning teeth on sprocket

9.22b Using two flat bladed screwdrivers and a pair of pliers to align teeth

9.23a inlet camshaft slot needs to be horizontal

9.23b Slot in end of exhaust camshaft should be at the 12 o'clock position

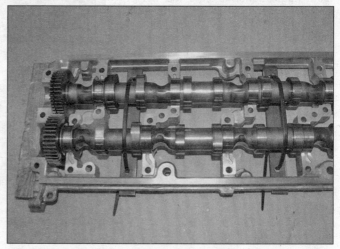

9.24 Camshafts are secured to the ladder frame with two pieces of flat bar and cable ties

9.25a Apply a 2.0 mm thick bead of sealant...

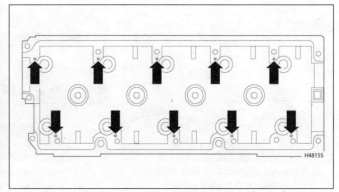

9.25b ...to the area shown by the thick, black line, taking care not to block the oil holes (arrowed)

bead of sealant (D 176 501 A1 or equivalent) as shown. Take care not to apply too much sealant, ensuring the oil holes are not blocked (see illustrations).

26 Fit a new sealing cap to the timing belt end of the cylinder head and make sure the locating dowels are fitted to the cylinder head (see illustrations).

27 Apply a smear of clean engine oil to the bearing surfaces and place the camshafts, frame and clamping tool in place on the cylinder head. Progressively, carefully, hand tighten the frame retaining bolts in the sequence shown (see illustration), until the retaining frame makes contact with the cylinder head over the complete surface, then tighten the bolts to the specified torque, again in the correct sequence.

28 Remove the gear aligning tool (T40096) and the clamping tool (T40095), or the metal flat bars and cable ties from the top of the camshaft retaining frame (see illustration).

29 Renew the camshaft oil seal as described in Section 10.

30 The remainder of refitting is a reversal of removal.

9.26a Fit a new seal/end cap to the cylinder head

9.26b Check that the locating dowels are in place

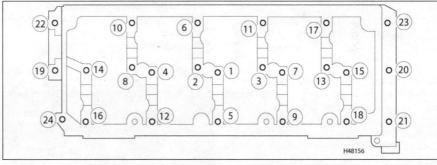

9.27 Camshaft retaining frame bolt tightening sequence

10 Camshaft oil seals – renewal

Right-hand oil seal

1 Remove the camshaft sprocket and hub, as described in Section 8.

2 Drill two small holes into the existing oil seal, diagonally opposite each other. Take great care to avoid drilling through into the seal housing or camshaft sealing surface. Thread two self-tapping screws into the holes, and using a pair of pliers, pull on the heads of the screws to extract the oil seal (see illustration).

3 Clean out the seal housing and the sealing surface of the camshaft by wiping it with a lint-free cloth. Remove any swarf or burrs that may cause the seal to leak.

4 Do not lubricate the lip and outer edge of the new oil seal, push it over the camshaft until it is positioned in place above its housing. To prevent damage to the sealing lips, wrap

9.28 Remove the cable ties and flat bar from the top of the ladder frame

10.2 Screw in a self-tapping screw, then pull the screw and seal from place

10.4 Using a plastic sleeve to slide seal over end of camshaft

10.5 Note some seals have 'OUTSIDE' (arrowed) to show fitted position

some adhesive tape around the end of the camshaft **(see illustration)**.

5 Using a hammer and a socket of suitable diameter, drive the seal squarely into its housing. Make sure the seal is fitted the correct way around, some have 'OUTSIDE' stamped on the seal **(see illustration)**. **Note:** *Select a socket that bears only on the hard outer surface of the seal, not the inner lip that can easily be damaged.*

6 Refit the camshaft sprocket and its hub, as described in Section 8.

Left-hand oil seal

7 The left-hand camshaft oil seal is formed by the brake vacuum pump seal. Refer to Chapter 9, Section 21, for details of brake vacuum pump removal and refitting.

11 Cylinder head – removal, inspection and refitting

Note: *The cylinder head must be removed with the engine cold. New cylinder head bolts and a new cylinder head gasket will be required on refitting, and suitable studs will be required to guide the cylinder head into position – see text.*

Removal

1 Remove the battery as described in Chapter 5, Section 3.

2 Drain the cooling system (Chapter 1, Section 31) and engine oil (Chapter 1, Section 3).

3 Pull the plastic cover on the top of the engine upwards to release it from its mountings.

4 Remove the air cleaner assembly as described in Chapter 4A, Section 2.

5 Undo the bolts and remove the battery tray **(see illustration)**.

6 Remove the radiator cooling fan(s) and shroud as described in Chapter 3, Section 5.

7 Undo the bolts and remove the air hose/duct from the intercooler to the turbocharger. Release the wiring looms from the clips as necessary to enable the duct to be manoeuvred from place.

8 Remove the camshaft cover as described in Section 4.

9 Remove the camshaft sprocket and hub as described in Section 8.

10 Remove the inlet manifold as described in Chapter 4A, Section 5.

11 Undo the retaining bolts, and remove the charge air pipe from the turbocharger **(see illustration)**.

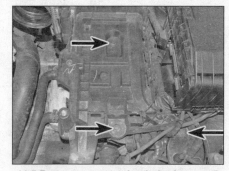

11.5 Battery tray securing bolts (arrowed)

12 Remove the EGR pipes from the cylinder head as described in Chapter 4C, Section 4.

13 Remove the exhaust manifold as described in Chapter 4C, Section 7. There is no need to completely remove the particulate filter from the vehicle. Slacken the Allen bolt and release the clamp securing the diesel particulate filter/catalytic converter to the turbocharger, then undo the bolts/nuts securing the brackets to the cylinder block/head and lay the filter/converter to one side.

14 Apply a little lubrication spray to the rubber sleeve, pull up the pipe from the vacuum pump, then undo the 4 retaining bolts and remove the vacuum pump from the left-hand end of the cylinder head **(see illustration)**. Renew the pump-to-cylinder head seal/gasket as described in Chapter 9, Section 21.

15 Disconnect the coolant temperature sensor wiring plug at the left-hand end of the cylinder head, and release the wiring loom from any retaining clips.

16 Disconnect the gearchange cables from the levers on the transmission as described in Chapter 7A, Section 3 (manual transmission) or Chapter 7B, Section 4 (DSG transmission).

17 Undo the bolts/nut, securing the gearchange bracket to the top of the transmission. Move the bracket and cables to one side.

18 Note their fitted locations, then release the clamps and disconnect the various coolant hoses from the cylinder head.

19 Disconnect the wiring connector from the oil pressure switch, undo the bolt securing the pipe bracket at the left-hand end of the cylinder head **(see illustrations)**, and the bolt

11.11 Remove the charge air pipe from the turbocharger

11.14 Disconnect the vacuum pipe

11.19a Disconnect the oil pressure switch wiring connector

11.19b Undo the retaining bolt/screw and remove the lifting bracket

11.20 Undo the bolt (arrowed) securing the timing belt guard

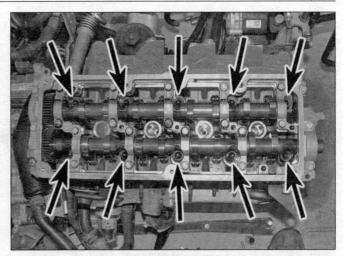

11.21 Undo the cylinder head bolts using a M12 multi-splined (12 pointed star) tool

securing the lifting bracket on the rear of the head.

20 Undo the bolt securing the timing belt guard adjacent to the timing belt tensioner, and the bolt securing the camshaft position sensor, then remove the tensioner retaining nut **(see illustration)**.

21 Using an M12 multi-splined tool (12 pointed star), undo the cylinder head bolts, working from the outside-in, evenly and gradually **(see illustration)**. Remove the bolts and recover the washers. Check that nothing remains connected, and starting at the gearbox side, lift the cylinder head from the engine block, sliding the belt tensioner from the mounting stud as the cylinder head is removed. Seek assistance if possible, as it is a heavy assembly.

22 Remove the gasket from the top of the block, noting the locating dowels. If the dowels are a loose fit, remove them and store them with the head for safekeeping. Do not discard the gasket yet – it will be needed for identification purposes.

Inspection

23 Dismantling and inspection of the cylinder head is covered in Chapter 2D, Section 6.

Cylinder head gasket selection

Note: *A dial test indicator (DTI) will be required for this operation.*

24 Examine the old cylinder head gasket for manufacturer's identification markings **(see illustration)**. These will be in the form of holes, and a part number on the edge of the gasket. Unless new pistons have been fitted, the new cylinder head gasket must be of the same type as the old one.

25 If new piston assemblies have been fitted as part of an engine overhaul, or if a new short engine is to be fitted, the projection of the piston crowns above the cylinder head mating face of the cylinder block at TDC must be measured. This measurement is used to determine the thickness of the new cylinder head gasket required.

26 Anchor a dial test indicator (DTI) to the top face (cylinder head gasket mating face) of the cylinder block, and zero the gauge on the gasket mating face.

27 Rest the gauge probe on No 1 piston crown, and turn the crankshaft slowly by hand until the piston reaches TDC. Measure and record the maximum piston projection at TDC (see illustration).

28 Repeat the measurement for the remaining pistons, and record the results.

29 If the measurements differ from piston-to-piston, take the highest figure, and use this to determine the thickness of the head gasket required as follows:

Piston projection	Gasket identification (number of holes)
0.91 to 1.00 mm	1
1.01 to 1.10 mm	2
1.11 to 1.20 mm	3

30 Purchase a new gasket according to the results of the measurements.

Refitting

31 The mating faces of the cylinder head and block must be perfectly clean before refitting the head. Use a scraper to remove all traces of gasket and carbon, also clean the tops of the pistons. Take particular care with the aluminium surfaces, as the soft metal is easily damaged.

32 Make sure that debris is not allowed to enter the oil and water passages – this is particularly important for the oil circuit, as carbon could block the oil supply to the camshaft and crankshaft bearings. Using adhesive tape and paper, seal the water, oil and bolt holes in the cylinder block.

33 To prevent carbon entering the gap between the pistons and bores, smear a little grease in the gap. After cleaning a piston, rotate the crankshaft to that the piston moves down the bore, and then wipe out the grease and carbon with a cloth rag. Clean the other piston crowns in the same way.

34 Check the head and block for nicks, deep scratches and other damage. If slight, they may be removed carefully with a file. More serious damage may be repaired by machining, but this is a specialist job.

35 If warpage of the cylinder head is suspected, use a straight-edge to check it for distortion, as described in Chapter 2D.

36 Ensure that the cylinder head bolt holes in the crankcase are clean and free of oil. Syringe or soak up any oil left in the bolt holes. This is most important in order that the correct bolt tightening torque can be applied, and to prevent the possibility of the block

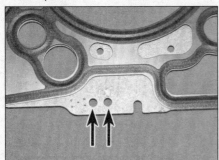

11.24 The holes (arrowed) identify the thickness of the cylinder head gasket

11.27 Measure the piston protrusion using a DTI gauge

11.39 Ensure the dowels are in place, then fit the new gasket with the part number uppermost (arrowed)

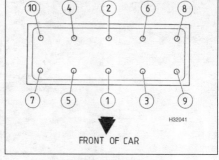

11.42a Cylinder head bolt tightening sequence

11.42b Tighten the cylinder head bolts to the Stage 1 torque

being cracked by hydraulic pressure when the bolts are tightened.

37 Turn the crankshaft anti-clockwise all the pistons at an equal height, approximately half-way down their bores from the TDC position (see Section 3). This will eliminate any risk of piston-to-valve contact as the cylinder head is refitted.

38 Where applicable, refit the manifolds.

39 Ensure that the cylinder head locating dowels are in place in the cylinder block, and then fit the new cylinder head gasket over the dowels, ensuring that the part number is uppermost **(see illustration)**.

Note: *Audi recommend that the gasket is only removed from its packaging immediately prior to fitting.*

40 Lower the cylinder head into position on the gasket, ensuring that it engages correctly

over the dowels. Refit the timing belt tensioner as the cylinder head is refitted.

41 Fit the washers in place then fit the new cylinder head bolts to the locations, and screw them in as far as possible by hand. Do not oil the bolt threads.

42 Working progressively, in sequence, tighten all the cylinder head bolts to the specified Stage 1 torque **(see illustrations)**.

43 Again working progressively, in sequence, tighten all the cylinder head bolts to the specified Stage 2 torque.

44 Tighten all the cylinder head bolts, in sequence, through the specified Stage 3 angle **(see illustration)**.

45 Finally, tighten all the cylinder head bolts, in sequence, through the specified Stage 4 angle.

46 The remainder of the refitting procedure

is a reversal of the removal procedure, noting the following points:

a) *Tighten all fasteners to their specified torque where given.*

b) *Renew all seals and gaskets.*

c) *Refill the cooling system as described in Chapter 1, Section 31.*

d) *Refill the engine oil, as described in Chapter 1, Section 3.*

e) *Ensure all wiring is correctly routed.*

f) *Run the vehicle and make sure the cooling fans operate when the engine gets up to temperature.*

12 Sump – removal and refitting

Removal

1 Apply the handbrake, then jack up the front of the vehicle and support securely on axle stands (see *'Jacking and vehicle support'* in Reference chapter).

2 Remove the securing screws and withdraw the engine undershield(s).

3 Drain the engine oil as described in Chapter 1, Section 3.

4 Release the retaining clips and remove the air hose from the intercooler outlet to the charge air pipe **(see illustration)**.

5 Undo the retaining bolts, release the clamp and move the charger air pipe from the front of the cylinder block **(see illustrations)**.

11.44 Use an angle-tightening gauge

12.4 Slacken the two retaining clips (arrowed)

12.5a Undo the retaining bolt on the end of the sump (arrowed)…

12.5b …and the bolt on the front of the cylinder block…

12.5c …then disconnect the pressure switch wiring connector

12.7a Release the two clips (arrowed) at the rear of the sump

12.7b At the front, prise down the centre pin and pull the clip downwards (arrowed)

12.7c Remove the insulation cover from the around the sump

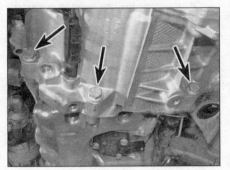

12.8a Undo the three transmission to sump bolts (arrowed)...

12.8b ...and also the four bolts (arrowed), at the transmission end of the sump

12.8c Lower the sump from the cylinder block

Disconnect the charger air pressure sensor wiring plug.

6 Disconnect the wiring connector from the oil level/temperature sender in the sump.

7 Release the retaining clips and remove the sump insulation cover from the sump **(see illustrations)**.

8 Unscrew and remove the bolts securing the sump to the cylinder block, and the bolts securing the sump to the transmission casing, then withdraw the sump **(see illustrations)**. If necessary, release the sump by tapping with a soft-faced hammer.

Refitting

9 Begin refitting by thoroughly cleaning the mating faces of the sump and cylinder block. Ensure that all traces of old sealant are removed.

10 Ensure that the cylinder block mating face of the sump is free from all traces of old sealant, oil and grease, and then apply a 2.0 to 3.0 mm thick bead of silicone sealant (VW D 176 404 A2 or equivalent) to the sump **(see illustration)**.

Note: *The sealant should be run around the inside of the bolt holes in the sump. The sump must be fitted within 5 minutes of applying the sealant.*

11 Offer the sump up to the cylinder block, then refit the sump-to-cylinder block bolts, and lightly tighten them by hand, working progressively in a diagonal sequence.

Note: *If the sump is being refitted with the engine and transmission separated, make sure*

that the sump is flush with the flywheel end of the cylinder block.

12 Refit the sump-to-transmission casing bolts, and tighten them lightly, using a socket.

13 Again working in a diagonal sequence, lightly tighten the sump-to-cylinder block bolts, using a socket.

14 Tighten the sump-to-transmission casing bolts to the specified torque.

15 Working in a diagonal sequence,

12.10 Apply a bead of sealant around the inside of the bolt holes

progressively tighten the sump-to-cylinder block bolts to the specified torque.

16 The remainder of refitting is a reversal of removal, noting to allow at least 30 minutes from the time of refitting the sump for the sealant to dry, then refill the engine with oil, with reference to Chapter 1, Section 3.

13 Oil pump and drive belt – removal, inspection and refitting

Oil pump removal

1 Remove the sump as described in Section 12.

2 Unscrew the flange bolts and remove the oil pick-up pipe/filter from the oil pump **(see illustration)**. Recover the O-ring seal and

13.2 Remove the oil pick-up pipe/filter

13.3 Remove the oil baffle plate bolt (which is also one of the oil pump mounting bolts)

13.4 Oil pump mounting bolts (arrowed)

13.11 Fit a new seal to the end of the oil pick-up pipe

discard, as a new one will be required for refitting.

3 Unscrew the securing bolt, and remove the oil baffle from the cylinder block **(see illustration)**.

4 Unscrew and remove the mounting bolts, and release the oil pump from the dowels in the crankcase **(see illustration)**. Unhook the oil pump drive sprocket from the belt and withdraw the oil pump and oil pick-up pipe from the engine. Note, the bolt holding the baffle plate is also one of the pump mounting bolts.

Oil pump inspection

5 Clean the pump thoroughly, and inspect for signs of damage or wear. If evident, renew the oil pump.

Oil pump refitting

6 Prime the pump with oil by pouring oil into the pick-up pipe aperture while turning the driveshaft.

7 If the drive belt and crankshaft sprocket have been removed, delay refitting them until after the oil pump has been mounted on the cylinder block.

8 Engage the oil pump sprocket with the drive belt, and then locate the oil pump on the dowels. Refit and tighten the mounting bolts to the specified torque.

9 Where applicable, refit the drive belt and crankshaft sprocket using a reversal of the removal procedure.

10 Refit the oil baffle plate, and tighten the securing bolt.

11 Refit the pick-up pipe to the oil pump, using a new O-ring seal, and tighten the securing bolts **(see illustration)**.

12 Refit the sump as described in Section 12.

Oil pump drive belt and sprockets

Note: *VW sealant (D 176 404 A2 or equivalent) will be required to seal the crankshaft oil seal housing on refitting, and it is advisable to fit a new crankshaft oil seal.*

Removal

13 Proceed as described in paragraphs 1 and 2.

14 To remove the belt, remove the timing belt as described in Section 7, then unbolt the crankshaft oil seal housing from the cylinder block, as described in Section 15. Unhook the belt from the sprocket on the end of the crankshaft.

15 The oil pump drive sprocket is a press-fit on the crankshaft, and cannot easily be removed. Consult an Audi dealer for advice if the sprocket is worn or damaged.

Inspection

16 It is wise to renew the belt in any case if the engine is to be overhauled, If there is any doubt as to the condition of the belt, renew it.

Refitting

17 If the oil pump has been removed, refit the oil pump as described previously in this Section before refitting the belt and sprocket.

18 Engage the oil pump sprocket with the

belt, then engage the belt with the crankshaft sprocket.

19 Fit a new crankshaft oil seal to the housing, and refit the housing as described in Section 15.

20 Where applicable, refit the oil baffle and pick-up pipe, and tighten the securing bolts.

21 Refit the sump as described in Section 12.

14 Flywheel – removal, inspection and refitting

Removal

1 On manual gearbox models, remove the gearbox (see Chapter 7A) and clutch (see Chapter 6).

2 On semi-automatic (DSG) transmission models, remove the transmission as described in Chapter 7B.

3 The flywheel can only be fitted in one position due to the offset of the flywheel mounting holes in the end of the crankshaft **(see illustration)**.

Note: *Manual transmission models are fitted with a dual-mass flywheel.*

4 Rotate the outside of the dual-mass flywheel so that the bolts align with the holes (if necessary).

5 Unscrew the bolts and remove the flywheel. Using a locking tool, counter-hold the flywheel to prevent it from turning **(see illustration)**. Discard the bolts, as new ones must be fitted.

Note: *In order not to damage the flywheel, do not allow the bolt heads to make contact with the flywheel during the unscrewing procedure.*

Inspection

6 Check the dual-mass flywheel for wear and damage. Examine the starter ring gear for excessive wear to the teeth. If the driveplate or its ring gear are damaged, the complete driveplate must be renewed. The flywheel ring gear, however, may be renewed separately from the flywheel, but the work should be entrusted to an Audi dealer. If the clutch friction face is discoloured or scored excessively, it may be possible to regrind it, but this work should also be entrusted to an Audi dealer.

7 The following are guidelines only, but should

14.3 Flywheel bolts are offset and can only be fitted in one position – DSG transmission (0AM) shown

14.5 Use a locking tool to counterhold the flywheel

14.8 Flywheel warpage check – see text

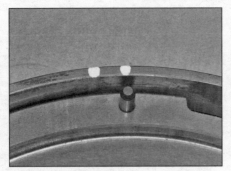

14.9 Flywheel free rotational movement check alignment marks – see text

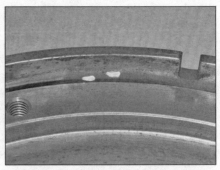

14.11 Flywheel lateral movement check marks – see text

indicate whether professional inspection is necessary. The dual-mass flywheel should be checked as follows:

Warpage

8 Place a straight edge across the face of the drive surface, and check by trying to insert a feeler gauge between the straight edge and the drive surface **(see illustration)**. The flywheel will normally warp like a bowl – ie. Higher on the outer edge. If the warpage is more than 0.40 mm, the flywheel may need replacing.

Free rotational movement

9 This is the distance the drive surface of the flywheel can be turned independently of the flywheel primary element, using finger effort alone. Move the drive surface in one direction and make a mark where the locating pin aligns with the flywheel edge. Move the drive surface in the other direction (finger pressure only) and make another mark **(see illustration)**. The total of free movement should not exceed 20.0 mm. If it's more, the flywheel may need replacing.

Total rotational movement

10 This is the total distance the drive surface can be turned independently of the flywheel primary element. Insert two bolts into the clutch pressure plate/damper unit mounting holes, and with the crankshaft/flywheel held stationary, use a lever/pry bar between the bolts and use some effort to move the drive surface fully in one direction – make a mark where the locating pin aligns with the flywheel edge. Now force the drive surface fully in the opposite direction, and make another mark.

The total rotational movement should not exceed 44.00 mm. If it does, have the flywheel professionally inspected.

Lateral movement

11 The lateral movement (up and down) of the drive surface in relation to the primary element of the flywheel, should not exceed 2.0 mm. If it does, the flywheel may need replacing. This can be checked by pressing the drive surface down on one side into the flywheel (flywheel horizontal) and making an alignment mark between the drive surface and the inner edge of the primary element. Now press down on the opposite side of the drive surface, and make another mark above the original one. The difference between the two marks is the lateral movement **(see illustration)**.

12 There should be no cracks in the drive surface of the flywheel. If cracks are evident, the flywheel may need replacing.

Refitting

13 Refitting is a reversal of removal. Use new bolts when refitting the flywheel or driveplate **(see illustration)**, and coat the threads of the bolts (if not already coated with locking compound) with locking fluid before inserting them. Tighten them to the specified torque.

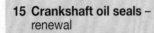

15 Crankshaft oil seals – renewal

Note: *The oil seals are a PTFE (Teflon) type and are fitted dry, without using any grease*

or oil. These have a wider sealing lip and have been introduced instead of the coil spring type oil seal.

Timing belt end oil seal

1 Remove the timing belt as described in Section 7, and the crankshaft sprocket with reference to Section 8.

2 To remove the seal without removing the housing, drill two small holes diagonally opposite each other, insert self-tapping screws, and pull on the heads of the screws with pliers **(see illustration)**.

3 Alternatively, to remove the oil seal complete with its housing, proceed as follows.

a) *Remove the sump as described in Section 12. This is necessary to ensure a satisfactory seal between the sump and oil seal housing on refitting.*

b) *Unbolt and remove the oil seal housing.*

c) *Working on the bench, lever the oil seal from the housing using a suitable screwdriver. Take care not to damage the seal seating in the housing.*

4 Thoroughly clean the oil seal seating in the housing.

5 Wind a length of tape around the end of the crankshaft (or a plastic sleeve) to protect the oil seal lips as the seal (and housing, where applicable) is fitted **(see illustration)**.

6 Fit a new oil seal to the housing, pressing or driving it into position using a socket or tube of suitable diameter. Ensure that the socket or tube bears only on the hard outer ring of the seal, and take care not to damage the seal lips. Press or drive the seal into position until it is seated on the shoulder in the housing **(see**

14.13 Use new bolts when refitting

15.2 Pull the screw and seal from place using pliers

15.5 Using a plastic sleeve to slide the seal over the end of the crankshaft

15.6 Carefully tap the seal into position

15.12a Remove the intermediate plate from the dowels…

15.12b …and from behind the top of the crankshaft seal housing

illustration). Make sure that the closed end of the seal is facing outwards.

7 If the oil seal housing has been removed, proceed as follows, otherwise proceed to paragraph 10.

8 Clean all traces of old sealant from the crankshaft oil seal housing and the cylinder block, then coat the cylinder block mating faces of the oil seal housing with a 2.0 to 3.0 mm thick bead of silicone sealant (VW D 176 404 A2, or equivalent). Note that the seal housing must be refitted within 5 minutes of applying the sealant. *Caution: DO NOT put excessive amounts of sealant onto the housing as it may get into the sump and block the oil pick-up pipe.*

9 Refit the oil seal housing, and tighten the bolts progressively to the specified torque.

10 Refit the sump as described in Section 12.

11 Refit the crankshaft sprocket with reference to Section 8, and the timing belt as described in Section 7.

Flywheel end oil seal

Note: *In these engines, the seal, sealing flange and sender wheel are a complete unit. Special tools are required to refit the sealing flange, and press the sender wheel onto the end of the crankshaft. It is not possible to accurately fit these parts without the tools, which may be available from VAG (part no. T10134) and are available from aftermarket automotive tool specialists. E.g. Laser tools).*

12 Remove the flywheel as described in Section 14, then prise the intermediate plate from the locating dowels on the cylinder block and unhook it from behind the top of the seal housing **(see illustrations)**.

13 Undo the bolt securing the crankshaft speed sensor and remove it from the seal housing, then undo the bolts securing the sealing flange to the cylinder block **(see illustrations)**.

14 Insert three 6 x 35 mm bolts into the threaded holes in the sealing flange. Tighten the bolts gradually and evenly, and press the sealing flange, and sender wheel from the crankshaft/cylinder block **(see illustrations)**. The seal, sender wheel and sealing flange are supplied as a complete unit.

15 Ensure the mating face of the cylinder block is clean and free from debris. The new sealing flange/seal/sender wheel assembly is supplied with a sealing lip support ring, which serves as a fitting sleeve, and must not be removed prior to installation. Equally, the sender wheel must not be separated from the assembly.

16 If using the VAG tool, proceed as follows. If using an aftermarket tool specialist's product, follow the instructions supplied with the tool. Rotate the large spindle nut until it's level with the end of the clamping surface of the spindle, then clamp the spindle in a vice **(see illustrations)**.

15.13a Undo the crankshaft speed sensor retaining bolt – arrowed

15.13b Sealing flange bolts (arrowed)

15.14a Screw in three 6 x 35 mm bolts…

15.14b …and draw the sealing flange and sender wheel from place

15.16a Rotate the nut until its level with the end of the flat clamping surface…

15.16b …then clamp it in a vice

15.17a Rotate the nut until the inner part of the tool…

15.17b …is flush with the flat surface of the housing

15.18a Remove the securing clip…

17 Press the tool housing downwards until it rests on the nut and washer. Rotate the nut until the inner part of the tool is at the same height as the housing **(see illustration)**.

18 Remove the seal securing clip. The hole on the sender wheel must align with the marking on the sealing flange **(see illustrations)**.

19 Place the flange outer side down on a clean, flat surface, then press the seal guide fitting sleeve (supplied ready fitted), housing, and sender wheel downwards until all the components are flat on the surface. In this position the upper edge of the sender wheel should be level with the edge of the sealing flange **(see illustrations)**.

20 Place the sealing flange on the assembly tool, so the pin locates in the hole in the sender wheel **(see illustration)**.

21 Push the sealing flange and guide fitting sleeve against the tool whilst tightening the 3 knurled screws. Ensure the pin is still located in the sender wheel **(see illustration)**.

22 Ensure the end of the crankshaft is clean, and is locked at TDC on No. 1 cylinder as described in Section 3.

23 Unscrew the large nut to the end of the spindle threads, then press the spindle inwards as far as possible **(see illustrations)**.

24 Align the flat side of the assembly with the sump flange, then secure the tool to the

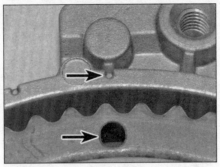

15.18b …the hole in the sender wheel should align with the marking on the flange (arrowed)

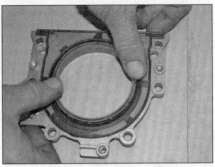

15.19a Press the assembly downwards on a clean, flat surface…

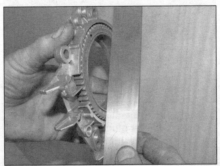

15.19b …so the upper edge of the sender wheel is level with the edge of the flange

15.20 Fit the flange to the tool, ensuring the pin locates in the hole (arrowed)

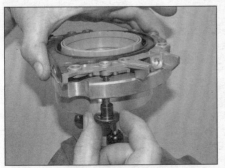

15.21 With the pin engaged in the hole, tighten the 3 knurled screws to secure the flange to the tool

15.23a Unscrew the nut to the end of the thread…

15.23b …and push the spindle in as far as possible

15.24 Hand-tighten the Allen bolts (arrowed), to secure the tool to the crankshaft

15.25 Use two M7 x 35 mm bolts (arrowed) to guide the sealing flange

15.26 Push the black knob into the hole in the crankshaft

crankshaft using the integral Allen bolts **(see illustration)**. Only hand tighten the bolts.

25 Insert two M7 x 35 mm bolts to guide the sealing flange to the cylinder block **(see illustration)**.

26 Using hand pressure alone, push the tool assembly onto the crankshaft until the seal guide fitting sleeve contacts the crankshaft flange, then push the guide pin (black knob) into the hole in the crankshaft. This is to ensure the sender wheel reaches its correct installation position **(see illustration)**.

27 Rotate the large nut until it makes contact with the tool housing, then tighten it to 35 Nm. After tightening this nut, a small air gap must still be present between the sealing flange and cylinder block **(see illustrations)**.

28 Unscrew the large nut; the two M7 x 35 Nm screws, the three knurled screws and the Allen bolts securing the tool to the crankshaft. Remove the tool, and pull the seal guide fitting sleeve from place (if it didn't come out with the tool) **(see illustration)**.

29 Use a vernier caliper or feeler gauge

to measure the fitted depth of the sender wheel in relation to the crankshaft flange **(see illustration)**. The correct depth is 0.5 mm.

30 If the gap is correct, fit the sealing flange bolts and tighten them to the specified torque.

31 If the gap is too small, re-attach the tool to the sealing flange and crankshaft, then refit the two M7 x 35 mm guide bolts to the flange. Tighten the large spindle nut to 40 Nm, remove the tool and re-measure the air gap. If the gap is still too small, re-attach the tool and tighten the spindle nut to 45 Nm. Re-measure the gap. When the gap is correct, refit the flange retaining bolts, and tighten them to the specified torque.

32 The remainder of refitting is a reversal of removal.

16 Engine/transmission mountings – inspection and renewal

Inspection

1 If improved access is required, jack up the front of the vehicle, and support it securely on axle stands (see 'Jacking and vehicle support' in Reference chapter). Remove the engine top cover, then remove the engine undertray.

15.27a After tightening the spindle nut to 35 Nm…

15.27b …there should be an air gap between the sealing flange and the cylinder block (arrowed)

15.28 Remove the tool and seal fitting guide sleeve

15.29 Measure the fitted depth of the sender wheel in relation to the end of the crankshaft

16.8 Undo the filter retaining bolts/nut (arrowed)

16.9 Right-hand engine mounting

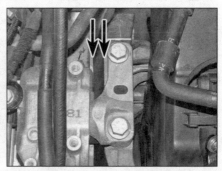

16.10 There must be at least 10 mm between the bracket and the chassis member (arrowed)

2 Check the mounting rubbers to see if they are cracked, hardened or separated from the metal at any point; renew the mounting if any such damage or deterioration is evident.

3 Check that all the mountings are securely tightened; use a torque wrench to check if possible.

4 Using a large screwdriver or a crowbar, check for wear in the mounting by carefully levering against it to check for free play. Where this is not possible, enlist the aid of an assistant to move the engine/transmission back-and-forth, or from side-to-side, whilst you observe the mounting. While some free play is to be expected, even from new components, excessive wear should be obvious. If excessive free play is found, check first that the fasteners are correctly secured, and then renew any worn components as described in the following paragraphs.

Renewal

Right-hand mounting

Note: *New mounting securing bolts will be required on refitting.*

5 Attach a hoist and lifting tackle to the engine lifting brackets on the cylinder head, and raise the hoist to just take the weight of the engine. Alternatively the engine can be supported on a trolley jack under the engine. Use a block of wood between the sump and the head of the jack, to prevent any damage to the sump.

6 For improved access, unscrew the coolant reservoir and move it to one side, leaving the coolant hoses connected.

7 Disconnect the wiring plug, undo the retaining bolts, and remove the pressure differential sender (for particulate filter) including bracket from the top of the engine mounting and move it to one side.

8 Undo the retaining bolts and move the fuel filter to one side **(see illustration)**. Where applicable, move any wiring harnesses, pipes or hoses to one side to enable removal of the engine mounting.

9 Unscrew the bolts securing the mounting to the engine bracket, and then unscrew the bolts securing it to the body **(see illustration)**. Withdraw the mounting from the engine compartment.

10 Refitting is a reversal of removal, bearing in mind the following points.

a) *Use new securing bolts.*
b) *There must be at least 10 mm between the engine mounting bracket and the right-hand side chassis member* **(see illustration)**.
c) *The side of the mounting support arm must be parallel to the side of the engine mounting bracket.*
d) *Tighten all fixings to the specified torque.*

Left-hand mounting

Note: *New mounting bolts will be required on refitting.*

11 Remove the engine top cover.

12 Attach a hoist and lifting tackle to the engine lifting brackets on the cylinder head, and raise the hoist to just take the weight of the engine and transmission. Alternatively the engine can be supported on a trolley jack under the transmission. Use a block of wood between the transmission and the head of the jack, to prevent any damage to the transmission.

13 Remove the battery and battery tray, as described in Chapter 5, Section 3.

14 Unscrew the bolts securing the mounting to the transmission, and the remaining bolts securing the mounting to the body **(see illustration)**, then lift the mounting from the engine compartment.

15 Refitting is a reversal of removal, bearing in mind the following points:

a) *Use new mounting bolts.*
b) *The edges of the mounting support arm must be parallel to the edge of the mounting.*
c) *Tighten all fixings to the specified torque.*

16.14 Left-hand engine/transmission mounting

Rear mounting (torque arm)

Note: *New mounting bolts will be required on refitting.*

16 Apply the handbrake, then jack up the front of the vehicle and support securely on axle stands (see 'Jacking and vehicle support' in Reference chapter). Remove the engine undertray for access to the rear mounting (torque arm).

17 Support the rear of the transmission beneath the final drive housing. To do this, use a trolley jack and block of wood, or alternatively wedge a block of wood between the transmission and the subframe.

18 Working under the vehicle, unscrew and remove the bolt securing the mounting to the subframe.

19 Unscrew the two bolts securing the mounting to the transmission, then withdraw the mounting from under the vehicle **(see illustration)**.

20 Refitting is a reversal of removal, but use new mounting securing bolts, and tighten all fixings to the specified torque.

17 Engine oil cooler/filter housing – removal and refitting

Removal

1 The oil cooler is mounted on the lower part of the oil filter housing on the front of the cylinder block.

2 Position a container beneath the oil filter

16.19 Rear mounting arm-to-transmission bolts

17.4a Undo the engine oil cooler retaining screws

17.4b Renew the seals/gaskets

housing, then undo the retaining bolts and remove the oil filter housing from the cylinder block **(see illustrations)**.

Refitting

6 Refitting is a reversal of removal, bearing in mind the following points:
a) *Use new oil cooler and housing O-rings* **(see illustration)**.
b) *Tighten the oil cooler and filter housing bolts to the correct torque.*
c) *On completion, check and if necessary top-up the oil and coolant levels.*

18 Oil pressure warning light switch – removal and refitting

housing to catch escaping oil and coolant.
3 Clamp the oil cooler coolant hoses to minimise coolant spillage, or drain the cooling system as described in Chapter 1, Section 31.
4 Unscrew the oil cooler retaining screws and remove the oil cooler from the front of the oil

filter housing **(see illustrations)**. Recover the O-rings from between the cooler and the oil filter housing, new ones will be required for refitting.
5 If required, disconnect the coolant hose, unclip the dipstick from the side of the

Removal

1 The oil pressure warning light switch is fitted to the left-hand rear of the cylinder head

17.5a Disconnect the coolant hoses…

17.5b …release the oil dipstick guide tube retaining clip (arrowed)…

17.5c …and undo the filter housing retaining bolts (arrowed)

17.6 Renew the seals/gaskets

18.1 Oil pressure warning light switch location (arrowed)

18.2 Remove the air intake hose

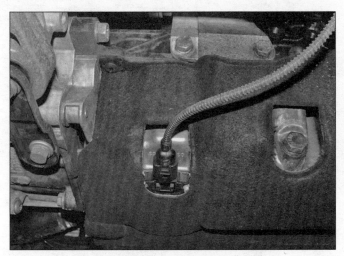

19.1 Oil level/temperature sensor location

19.4 Remove the insulation cover to access the bolts

(see illustration). Remove the engine top cover to gain access to the switch.

2 Slacken the retraining clips and remove the air intake hose from the turbocharger **(see illustration)**.

3 Disconnect the wiring connector and wipe clean the area around the switch.

4 Unscrew the switch and remove it, along with its sealing washer (where fitted). If the switch is to be left removed from the engine for any length of time, plug the aperture in the cylinder head.

Refitting

5 Examine the sealing washer for signs of damage or deterioration and if necessary renew.

6 Refit the switch, complete with washer (where fitted), and tighten it securely.

7 Securely reconnect the wiring connector, refit the air intake hose and then, if necessary, top-up the engine oil as described in *Weekly Checks*. On completion, refit the engine top cover.

19 Oil level/temperature sender
– removal and refitting

Removal

1 The oil level/temperature sender is fitted to bottom of the sump **(see illustration)**.

2 Drain the engine oil as described in Chapter 1, Section 3.

3 Disconnect the wiring connector from the sender.

4 Release the retaining clips and remove the insulation cover from the sump **(see illustration)**.

5 Wipe clean the area around the sender, then undo the three retaining bolts and remove the sender.

Refitting

6 Examine the sealing washer for signs of damage or deterioration and if necessary renew.

7 Refit the switch and tighten the retaining bolts to the specified torque.

8 Refit the insulation cover, then reconnect the wiring connector and refill the engine with oil (refer to Chapter 1, Section 3).

Notes

Chapter 2 Part B
1.9 litre engine in-car repair procedures

Contents

Degrees of difficulty

| **Easy,** suitable for novice with little experience | 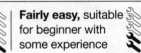 | **Fairly easy,** suitable for beginner with some experience | 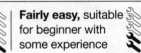 | **Fairly difficult,** suitable for competent DIY mechanic | 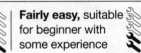 | **Difficult,** suitable for experienced DIY mechanic | 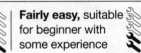 | **Very difficult,** suitable for expert DIY or professional | |

Specifications

General

Manufacturer's engine codes:		
1896 cc (1.9 litre), 8-valve, SOHC	BLS and BXE	
Maximum outputs:	**Power**	**Torque**
All engines	77 kW at 4000 rpm	250 Nm at 1800-2400 rpm
Bore	79.5 mm	
Stroke	95.5 mm	
Compression ratio:		
Engine code BLS	18.5 : 1	
Engine code BXE	19.0 : 1	
Compression pressures:		
Minimum compression pressure	Approximately 19.0 bar	
Maximum difference between cylinders	Approximately 5.0 bar	
Firing order	1 – 3 – 4 – 2	
No 1 cylinder location	Timing belt end	

Note: See 'Vehicle identification' in Reference Chapter for the location of engine code markings.

Camshaft

Camshaft endfloat (maximum)	0.15 mm
Camshaft bearing running clearance (maximum)	0.11 mm
Camshaft run-out (maximum)	0.01 mm

Lubrication system

Oil pump type	Gear type, chain-driven from crankshaft
Oil pressure (oil temperature 80°C) at 2000 rpm	2.0 bar

Torque wrench settings

	Nm	lbf ft
Ancillary (alternator, etc) bracket mounting bolts	45	33
Air conditioning compressor	45	33
Alternator and tensioner	25	18
Auxiliary drivebelt tensioner securing bolt	25	18
Big-end bearing caps bolts: *		
Stage 1	30	22
Stage 2	Angle-tighten a further 90°	
Camshaft bearing cap bolts engines: *		
Stage 1	8	6
Stage 2	Angle-tighten a further 90°	
Camshaft cover nuts/bolts	10	7
Camshaft sprocket hub centre bolt	100	74
Camshaft sprocket-to-hub bolts	25	18
Coolant pump bolts	15	11
Crankshaft oil seal housing bolts	15	11
Crankshaft pulley-to-sprocket bolts:		
Stage 1	10	7
Stage 2	Angle-tighten a further 90°	
Crankshaft sprocket bolt: *		
Stage 1	120	89
Stage 2	Angle-tighten a further 90°	
Cylinder head bolts: *		
Stage 1	35	26
Stage 2	60	44
Stage 3	Angle-tighten a further 90°	
Stage 4	Angle-tighten a further 90°	
Engine mountings:		
RH engine mounting:		
Limiter:		
Stage 1	20	15
Stage 2	Angle-tighten a further 90°	
Mounting to engine:		
Stage 1	60	44
Stage 2	Angle-tighten a further 90°	
Mounting to body:		
Stage 1	40	30
Stage 2	Angle-tighten a further 90°	
LH engine mounting:		
Mounting to body:		
Stage 1	60	44
Stage 2	Angle-tighten a further 90°	
Mounting to transmission:		
Stage 1	40	30
Stage 2	Angle-tighten a further 90°	
Rear mounting link:		
To transmission:		
Stage 1	40	30
Stage 2	Angle-tighten a further 90°	
To subframe:		
Stage 1	100	74
Stage 2	Angle-tighten a further 90°	
Flywheel:		
Stage 1	60	44
Stage 2	Angle-tighten a further 90°	
Main bearing cap bolts: *		
Stage 1	65	48
Stage 2	Angle-tighten a further 90°	
Oil drain plug	30	22
Oil filter housing-to-cylinder block bolts: *		
Stage 1	15	11
Stage 2	Angle-tighten a further 90°	
Oil filter cover	25	18
Oil level/temperature sensor-to-sump bolts	10	7
Oil pick-up pipe securing bolts	15	11
Oil pressure relief valve plug	40	30
Oil pressure warning light switch	20	15
Oil pump chain tensioner bolt	15	11

Torque wrench settings (continued)

	Nm	lbf ft
Oil pump securing bolts	15	11
Oil pump sprocket securing bolt:		
Stage 1	20	15
Stage 2	Angle-tighten a further 90°	
Piston oil spray jet bolt	25	18
Pump injector rocker arm shafts: *		
Stage 1	20	15
Stage 2	Angle-tighten a further 90°	
Sump:		
Sump-to-cylinder block bolts	15	11
Sump-to-transmission bolts	45	33
Tandem pump bolts:		
Upper	20	15
Lower	10	7
Thermostat housing	15	11
Timing belt idler pulley bolt	20	15
Timing belt outer cover bolts	10	7
Timing belt rear cover-to-cylinder head bolt	10	7
Timing belt tensioner roller securing nut:		
Stage 1	20	30
Stage 2	Angle-tighten a further 45°	
Timing belt idler pulleys:		
Lower right-hand idler roller (below coolant pump sprocket) bolt: *		
Stage 1	40	30
Stage 2	Angle-tighten a further 90°	
Upper idler roller bolt	20	15

Do not re-use fasteners

1 General Information

How to use this Chapter

1 This Part of Chapter 2 describes those repair procedures that can reasonably be carried out on the engine while it remains in the vehicle. If the engine has been removed from the vehicle and is being dismantled as described in Part D, any preliminary dismantling procedures can be ignored.

2 Note that while it may be possible physically to overhaul certain items while the engine is in the vehicle, such tasks are not usually carried out as separate operations, and usually require the execution of several additional procedures (not to mention the cleaning of components and of oilways); for this reason, all such tasks are classed as major overhaul procedures, and are described in Part D of this Chapter.

Engine description

3 Throughout this Chapter, engines are referred to by type, and are identified and referred to by the manufacturer's code letters. A listing of all engines covered, together with their code letters, is given in the Specifications at the start of this Chapter.

4 The engines are water-cooled, single overhead camshaft, in-line four-cylinder units, with cast-iron cylinder blocks and aluminium-alloy cylinder heads. All are mounted transversely at the front of the vehicle, with the transmission bolted to the left-hand end of the engine.

5 The crankshaft is of five-bearing type, and thrustwashers are fitted to the centre main bearing to control crankshaft endfloat.

6 Drive for the camshaft is by a toothed timing belt from the crankshaft. The camshaft is mounted at the top of the cylinder head, and is secured by bearing caps.

7 The valves are closed by coil springs, and run in guides pressed into the cylinder head. The camshaft actuates the valves directly, through self-adjusting hydraulic tappets.

8 The gear-type oil pump is driven by a chain from a sprocket on the crankshaft. Oil is drawn from the sump through a strainer, and then forced through an externally-mounted, renewable filter. From there, it is distributed to the cylinder head, where it lubricates the camshaft journals and hydraulic tappets, and also to the crankcase, where it lubricates the main bearings, connecting rod big-ends, gudgeon pins and cylinder bores. A coolant-fed oil cooler is fitted to the oil filter housing on all engines. Oil jets are fitted to the base of each cylinder – these spray oil onto the underside of the pistons, to improve cooling.

9 The engines are fitted with a combined brake servo vacuum pump and fuel lift pump (tandem pump), driven by the camshaft on the transmission end of the cylinder head.

10 Engine coolant is circulated by a pump, driven by the timing belt. For details of the cooling system, refer to Chapter 3.

Operations with engine in car

11 The following operations can be performed without removing the engine:
a) *Compression pressure – testing.*
b) *Camshaft cover – removal and refitting.*
c) *Crankshaft pulley – removal and refitting.*
d) *Timing belt covers – removal and refitting.*
e) *Timing belt – removal, refitting and adjustment.*
f) *Timing belt tensioner and sprockets – removal and refitting.*
g) *Camshaft oil seals – renewal.*
h) *Camshaft and hydraulic tappets – removal, inspection and refitting.*
i) *Cylinder head – removal and refitting.*
j) *Cylinder head and pistons – decarbonising*
k) *Sump – removal and refitting.*
l) *Oil pump – removal, overhaul and refitting.*
m) *Crankshaft oil seals – renewal.*
n) *Engine/transmission mountings – inspection and renewal.*
o) *Flywheel/driveplate – removal, inspection and refitting.*

Note: *It is possible to remove the pistons and connecting rods (after removing the cylinder head and sump) without removing the engine. However, this is not recommended. Work of this nature is more easily and thoroughly completed with the engine on the bench, as described in Chapter 2D.*

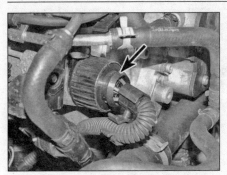

2.3 Disconnect the injector solenoids wiring plug connector (arrowed)

2 Compression and leakdown tests – description and interpretation

Compression test

Note: *A compression tester suitable for use with diesel engines will be required for this test.*

1 When engine performance is down, or if misfiring occurs which cannot be attributed to the ignition or fuel systems, a compression test can provide diagnostic clues as to the engine's condition. If the test is performed regularly, it can give warning of trouble before any other symptoms become apparent.

2 The engine must be fully warmed-up to normal operating temperature, the battery must be fully-charged, and you will require the aid of an assistant.

3 Disconnect the injector solenoids by disconnecting the connector at the end of the cylinder head **(see illustration)**.

Note: *As a result of the wiring being disconnected, faults will be stored in the ECU memory. These must be erased after the compression test.*

4 Remove the glow plugs as described in Chapter 5, Section 11, then fit a compression tester to the No 1 cylinder glow plug hole. The type of tester which screws into the plug thread is preferred.

5 Have your assistant crank the engine for several seconds on the starter motor. After one or two revolutions, the compression pressure should build-up to a maximum figure and then stabilise. Record the highest reading obtained.

6 Repeat the test on the remaining cylinders, recording the pressure in each.

7 The cause of poor compression is less easy to establish on a diesel engine than on a petrol engine. The effect of introducing oil into the cylinders (wet testing) is not conclusive, because there is a risk that the oil will sit in the recess on the piston crown, instead of passing to the rings. However, the following can be used as a rough guide to diagnosis.

8 All cylinders should produce very similar pressures. Any difference greater than that specified indicates the existence of a fault. Note that the compression should build-up quickly in a healthy engine. Low compression on the first stroke, followed by gradually increasing pressure on successive strokes, indicates worn piston rings. A low compression reading on the first stroke, which does not build-up during successive strokes, indicates leaking valves or a blown head gasket (a cracked head could also be the cause).

9 A low reading from two adjacent cylinders is almost certainly due to the head gasket having blown between them and the presence of coolant in the engine oil will confirm this.

10 On completion, remove the compression tester, and refit the glow plugs, with reference to Chapter 5, Section 11.

11 Reconnect the wiring to the injector solenoids. Finally, have an Audi dealer erase the fault codes from the ECU memory.

Leakdown test

12 A leakdown test measures the rate at which compressed air fed into the cylinder is lost. It is an alternative to a compression test, and in many ways it is better, since the escaping air provides easy identification of where pressure loss is occurring (piston rings, valves or head gasket).

13 The equipment required for leakdown testing is unlikely to be available to the home mechanic. If poor compression is suspected, have the test performed by a suitably-equipped garage.

3 Engine assembly and valve timing marks – general information and usage

General information

1 TDC is the highest point in the cylinder that each piston reaches as it travels up-and-down when the crankshaft turns. Each piston reaches TDC at the end of the compression stroke and again at the end of the exhaust stroke, but TDC generally refers to piston position on the compression stroke. No 1 piston is at the timing belt end of the engine.

2 Positioning No 1 piston at TDC is an essential part of many procedures, such as timing belt removal and camshaft removal.

3 The design of the engines covered in this Chapter is such that piston-to-valve contact may occur if the camshaft or crankshaft is turned with the timing belt removed. For this reason, it is important to ensure that the camshaft and crankshaft do not move in relation to each other once the timing belt has been removed from the engine.

Setting TDC on No 1 cylinder

Note: *VAG special tool T10100 is required to lock the crankshaft sprocket in the TDC position.*

4 Remove the auxiliary drivebelt as described in Chapter 1, Section 27.

5 Remove the crankshaft pulley/vibration damper as described in Section 5.

6 Remove the timing belt covers as described in Section 6.

7 Remove the glow plugs, as described in Chapter 5, Section 11, to allow the engine to turn more easily.

8 Using a spanner or socket on the crankshaft sprocket bolt, turn the crankshaft in the normal direction of rotation (clockwise) until the alignment mark on the face of the sprocket is at the 2 o'clock position **(see illustrations)**.

9 The arrow (marked 4Z) on the rear section of the upper timing belt upper cover should

3.8a Position the crankshaft so that the mark on the sprocket (arrowed) is at the 2 o'clock position...

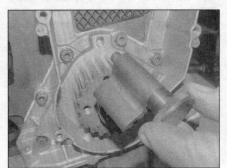

3.8b...then insert the locking tool...

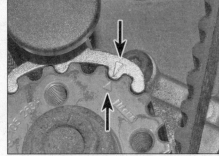

3.8c...and align the marks (arrowed) on the tool and sprocket

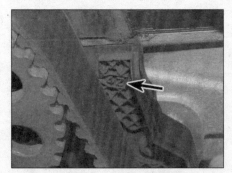

3.9 Align the arrow on the rear of the cover (arrowed) between the lugs on the rear of the camshaft hub sender wheel

3.10 Insert a 6 mm drill bit through the camshaft hub into the cylinder head to lock the camshaft

4.1 One of the cover locating pegs (arrowed) and also the breather pipe (arrowed)

align between the two lugs on the rear of the camshaft hub sender wheel (see illustration).

10 While in this position it should be possible to insert a 6 mm diameter rod to lock the camshaft (see illustration).

Note: *The mark on the crankshaft sprocket and the mark on the VAG tool must align, whilst at the same time the shaft of tool must engage in the drilling in the crankshaft oil seal housing.*

11 The engine is now set to TDC on No 1 cylinder.

4   Camshaft cover – removal and refitting

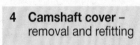

Removal

1 Remove the dipstick and prise off and remove the engine top cover, and then disconnect the breather hose from the camshaft cover (see illustration).

2 Remove the timing belt upper cover as described in Section 6.

3 On engine code BLS, undo the two bolts and detach the inlet manifold flap from the inlet manifold. Release the clamp and detach the inlet hose from the ducting as the flap is removed.

4 Unscrew the camshaft cover retaining bolts and lift the cover away. If it sticks, do not attempt to lever it off – instead free it by working around the cover and tapping it lightly with a soft-faced mallet.

5 Recover the camshaft cover gasket. Inspect the gasket carefully, and renew it if damage or deterioration is evident – note that the retaining bolts must be pushed fully through the gasket before refitting the cover (see illustration).

6 Clean the mating surfaces of the cylinder head and camshaft cover thoroughly, removing all traces of oil and old gasket – take care to avoid damaging the surfaces as you do this.

Refitting

7 Refit the camshaft cover by following the

4.5 Refit the gasket making sure the retaining bolts are pushed fully through the gasket before refitting the cover

removal procedure in reverse, noting the following points:

a) *Apply suitable sealant to the points where the camshaft bearing cap contacts the cylinder head (see illustration).*

b) *Tighten the camshaft cover retaining nuts/bolts progressively to the specified torque in the sequence shown (see illustration).*

4.7a Apply sealant to the points (arrowed) on the cylinder head

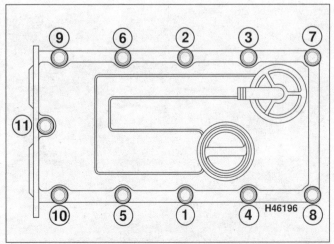

4.7b Camshaft cover tightening sequence

5.3 Prising out the crankshaft pulley centre cap

5.4 Crankshaft pulley retaining bolts (arrowed)

6.1 Removing the air inlet hose from across the top of the timing belt cover

5 Crankshaft pulley – removal and refitting

Removal

1 Switch off the ignition and all electrical consumers and remove the ignition key.
2 Remove the auxiliary drivebelt as described in Chapter 1, Section 27
3 Where applicable, prise the cover from the centre of the pulley to expose the securing bolts **(see illustration)**.
4 Slacken the bolts securing the crankshaft pulley to the sprocket and remove the pulley **(see illustration)**. If necessary, the pulley can be prevented from turning by counterholding with a spanner or socket on the crankshaft sprocket bolt.

Refitting

5 Refit the pulley over the locating peg on the crankshaft sprocket, and then refit the pulley securing bolts.
6 Prevent the crankshaft from turning as during removal, then tighten the retaining bolts to the specified torque.
7 Refit the auxiliary drivebelt as described in Chapter 1, Section 27.

6 Timing belt covers – removal and refitting

Upper outer cover

1 Where applicable, release the retaining clips and remove the air inlet hose from across the top of the timing belt cover **(see illustration)**.
2 Release the uppermost part of the timing belt outer cover by prising open the metal spring clips, then withdraw the cover away from the engine **(see illustrations)**.
3 Refitting is a reversal of removal, noting that the lower edge of the upper cover engages with the centre cover.

Centre outer cover

4 Remove the auxiliary drivebelt as described in Chapter 1, Section 27.
5 Remove the crankshaft pulley as described in Section 5. It is assumed that, if the centre cover is being removed, the lower cover will be also – if not, simply remove the components described in Section 5 for access to the crankshaft pulley, and leave the pulley in position.
6 With the upper cover removed (paragraphs 1 and 2), unscrew and remove the retaining bolts from the centre cover. Withdraw the centre cover from the engine, noting how it fits over the lower cover.
7 Refitting is a reversal of the removal procedure.

Lower outer cover

8 Remove the upper and centre covers as described previously.
9 If not already done, remove the crankshaft pulley as described in Section 5.
10 Unscrew the remaining bolt(s) securing the lower cover, and lift it out.
11 Refitting is a reversal of removal; locate the centre cover in place before fitting the top two bolts.

Rear cover

12 Remove the upper, centre and lower covers as described previously.
13 Remove the timing belt, tensioner and sprockets as described in Section 7 and Section 8.
14 Slacken and withdraw the retaining bolts and lift the timing belt inner cover from the studs on the end of the engine, and remove it from the engine compartment.
15 Refitting is a reversal of removal.

6.2a Release the retaining clips (one arrowed)...

6.2b ...and withdraw the upper cover

7.5a Use a spanner to turn the tensioner clockwise...

7.5b...then lock with a suitable metal rod...

7.22 Position the camshaft sprocket so that the securing bolts are in the centre part of the elongated holes

7 Timing belt – removal, inspection and refitting

Removal

1 The primary function of the toothed timing belt is to drive the camshaft, but it also drives the coolant pump. Should the belt slip or break in service, the valve timing will be disturbed and piston-to-valve contact may occur, resulting in serious engine damage. For this reason, it is important that the timing belt is tensioned correctly, and inspected regularly for signs of wear or deterioration.

2 Switch off the ignition and all electrical consumers and remove the ignition key.

3 Apply the handbrake, then jack up the front of the vehicle and support securely on axle stands (see *Jacking and vehicle support* in Reference chapter

4 Remove the securing screws and withdraw the engine undertray, and the front section of the right-hand wheel arch liner. Also, remove the engine top cover.

5 Remove the auxiliary drivebelt as described in Chapter 1, Section 27, then unbolt and remove the drivebelt tensioner **(see illustrations).**

6 Remove the crankshaft pulley as described in Section 5.

7 Remove the timing belt covers as described in Section 6.

8 Support the engine and remove the right-hand engine mounting as described in Section 18.

9 Remove the fuel filter from its bracket and place to one side.

10 Where necessary, remove the intercooler charge air pipe.

11 Unbolt the filler neck from the screen washer reservoir.

12 Where applicable, unbolt the fuel filter bracket from the engine mounting.

13 Unbolt the coolant expansion tank and position it to one side.

Note: *Do not disconnect the hoses.*

14 Set the engine to TDC on No 1 cylinder as described in Section 3.

15 If the original timing belt is to be refitted, mark the running direction of the belt, to ensure correct refitting.

Caution: If the belt appears to be in good condition and can be re-used, it is essential that it is refitted the same way around, otherwise accelerated wear will result, leading to premature failure.

16 Loosen the bolts securing the sprocket to the camshaft while holding the sprockets with a suitable tool.

17 Loosen the timing belt tensioner securing nut, then use circlip pliers or an Allen key (as applicable) to turn the tensioner anti-clockwise until a suitable pin or drill bit can be inserted through the locking holes. Now, turn the tensioner clockwise to the stop and tighten the securing nut.

18 Slide the belt from the sprockets, taking care not to twist or kink the belt excessively if it is to be re-used.

Inspection

19 Examine the belt for evidence of contamination by coolant or lubricant. If this is the case, find the source of the contamination before progressing any further. Check the belt for signs of wear or damage, particularly around the leading edges of the belt teeth. Renew the belt if its condition is in doubt; the cost of belt renewal is negligible compared with potential cost of the engine repairs, should the belt fail in service. The belt must be renewed if it has covered the mileage given in Chapter 1, however, if it has covered less, it is prudent to renew it regardless of condition, as a precautionary measure.

20 If the timing belt is not going to be refitted for some time, it is a wise precaution to hang a warning label on the steering wheel, to remind yourself (and others) not to attempt to start the engine.

Refitting

21 Ensure that the crankshaft and camshaft are still set to TDC on No 1 cylinder, as described in Section 3.

22 Position the camshaft sprocket(s) so that the securing bolts are in the centre part of the elongated holes **(see illustration).**

23 Loop the timing belt loosely under the crankshaft sprocket.

Note: *Observe any direction of rotation markings on the belt.*

24 Engage the timing belt teeth with the camshaft sprocket(s), then manoeuvre it into position around the tensioning roller, crankshaft sprocket, and finally around the coolant pump sprocket. Make sure that the belt teeth seat correctly on the sprockets.

Note: *Slight adjustment to the position of the camshaft sprocket may be necessary to achieve this. Avoid bending the belt back on itself or twisting it excessively as you do this. Ensure that any slack in the belt is in the section of belt that passes over the tensioner roller.*

25 Loosen the timing belt tensioner securing nut, and turn the tensioner anti-clockwise with the circlip pliers or an Allen key (as applicable) until the locking pin can be removed. Now, turn the tensioner clockwise until the pointer is in the middle of the gap in the tensioner base plate. With the tensioner held in this position, tighten the securing nut to the specified torque and angle.

26 Tighten the camshaft sprocket bolts to the specified torque, remove the sprocket locking pin(s) and the crankshaft locking tool.

27 Using a spanner or wrench and socket on the crankshaft pulley centre bolt, rotate the crankshaft through two complete revolutions. Reset the engine to TDC on No 1 cylinder, with reference to Section 3 and check that the crankshaft and camshaft sprocket locking pins can still be inserted. If the camshaft sprocket locking pin cannot be inserted, slacken the retaining bolts, turn the hub until the pin fits, and tighten the sprocket retaining bolts to the specified torque.

28 Refit the coolant expansion tank.

29 Where applicable, refit the fuel filter bracket to the engine mounting.

30 Refit the screen washer reservoir filler neck.

31 Refit the fuel filter to its mounting bracket, and where necessary reconnect the fuel lines and intercooler charge air pipe.

32 Refit the right-hand engine mounting as described in Section 18.

33 Refit the timing belt covers as described in Section 6.

34 Refit the crankshaft pulley/vibration damper as described in Section 5.

35 Refit the auxiliary drivebelt tensioner, then refit the auxiliary drivebelt with reference to Chapter 1, Section 27.

36 Refit the engine undertray, right-hand wheel arch liner and engine top cover, and lower the vehicle to the ground.

8 Timing belt tensioner and sprockets – removal and refitting

Timing belt tensioner

Removal

1 Remove the timing belt as described in Section 7.

2 Unscrew the timing belt tensioner nut, and remove the tensioner from the engine **(see illustration)**.

Refitting

3 When refitting the tensioner to the engine, ensure that the lug on the tensioner backplate engages with the corresponding cut-out in the rear timing belt cover, then refit the tensioner nut **(see illustration)**.

4 Refit and tension the timing belt as described in Section 7, making sure that the tensioner backplate is correctly engaged with the hole in the cylinder head.

Idler pulleys

Removal

5 Remove the timing belt as described in Section 7.

6 Unscrew the relevant idler pulley securing bolt/nut, and then withdraw the pulley.

Refitting

7 Refit the pulley and tighten the securing bolt or nut to the specified torque. **Note:** *Renew the bolt (where applicable).*

8 Refit and tension the timing belt as described in Section 7.

Crankshaft sprocket

Note: *A new crankshaft sprocket securing bolt must be used on refitting.*

Removal

9 Remove the timing belt as described in Section 7.

8.2 Timing belt tensioner nut

10 The sprocket securing bolt must now be slackened, and the crankshaft must be prevented from turning as the sprocket bolt is unscrewed. To hold the sprocket, make up a suitable tool, and screw it to the sprocket using two bolts screwed into two of the crankshaft pulley bolt holes.

11 Hold the sprocket using the tool, then slacken the sprocket securing bolt. Take care, as the bolt is very tight. Do not allow the crankshaft to turn as the bolt is slackened.

12 Unscrew the bolt, and slide the sprocket from the end of the crankshaft, noting which way round the sprocket's raised boss is fitted.

Refitting

13 Commence refitting by positioning the sprocket on the end of the crankshaft, with the raised boss fitted as noted on removal.

14 Fit a new sprocket securing bolt, then counterhold the sprocket using the method employed on removal, and tighten the bolt to the specified torque in the two stages given in the Specifications **(see illustration)**.

15 Refit the timing belt as described in Section 7.

Camshaft sprocket

Removal

16 Remove the timing belt as described in Section 7.

17 Unscrew and remove the three retaining

8.14 Fitting a new crankshaft sprocket securing bolt

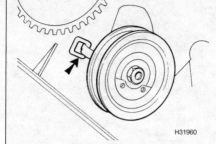

8.3 Ensure that the lug on the tensioner backplate engages with the cut-out in the rear timing belt cover

bolts and remove the camshaft sprocket from the camshaft hub.

Refitting

18 Refit the sprocket ensuring that it is fitted the correct way round, as noted before removal, then insert the sprocket bolts, and tighten by hand only at this stage.

19 If the crankshaft has been turned, turn the crankshaft clockwise 90° back to TDC.

20 Refit and tension the timing belt as described in Section 7.

Camshaft hub

Note: *VAG technicians use special tool T10051 to counterhold the hub, however it is possible to fabricate a suitable alternative – see below.*

Removal

21 Remove the camshaft sprocket as described previously in this Section.

22 Engage special tool T10051 with the three locating holes in the face of the hub to prevent the hub from turning. If this tool is not available, fabricate a suitable alternative. Whilst holding the tool, undo the central hub retaining bolt about two turns **(see illustration)**.

23 Leaving the central hub retaining bolt in place, attach VAG tool T10052 (or a similar three-legged puller) to the hub, and evenly tighten the puller until the hub is free of the camshaft taper **(see illustration)**.

Refitting

24 Ensure that the camshaft taper and the

8.22 Using a fabricated tool to counterhold the camshaft hub

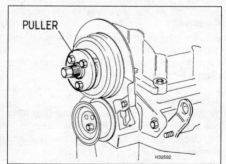

8.23 Attach a three-legged puller to the hub, and evenly tighten the puller until the hub is free of the camshaft taper

hub centre is clean and dry, locate the hub on the taper, noting that the built-in key in the hub taper must align with the keyway in the camshaft taper **(see illustration)**.

25 Hold the hub in this position with tool T10051 (or similar home-made tool), and tighten the central bolt to the specified torque.

26 Refit the camshaft sprocket as described previously in this Section.

Coolant pump sprocket

27 The coolant pump sprocket is integral with the coolant pump. Refer to Chapter 3 for details of coolant pump removal.

9 Pump injector rocker shaft assembly – removal and refitting

8.24 The built in key in the hub taper must align with the keyway in the camshaft taper (arrowed)

Removal

1 Remove the camshaft cover as described in Section 4. In order to ensure that the rocker arms are refitted to their original locations, use a marker pen or paint and number the arms 1 to 4, with No 1 nearest the timing belt end of the engine. If the arms are not fitted to their original locations the injector basic clearance setting procedure must be carried out as described in Chapter 4B, Section 4.

2 Slacken the locknut of the adjustment screw on the end of the rocker arm above the respective injector, and undo the adjustment screw until the rocker arm lies against the plunger pin of the injector. Starting at the outside and working in, gradually and evenly slacken and remove the rocker shaft retaining bolts. Lift off the rocker shaft. Discard the rocker shaft bolts, new ones must be fitted **(see illustration)**.

Refitting

3 Thoroughly check the rocker shaft, rocker arms and camshaft bearing cap seating surface for any signs of excessive wear or damage.

4 Smear some grease (VAG No G000 100) onto the contact face of each rocker arm adjustment screw, and refit the rocker shaft assembly, tightening the new retaining bolts as follows. Starting from the inside out, hand-tighten the bolts. Again, from the inside out, tighten the bolts to the Stage one torque setting. Finally, from the inside out, tighten the bolts to the Stage two angle tightening setting.

5 Attach a DTI (Dial Test Indicator) gauge to the cylinder head upper surface, and position the DTI probe against the top of the adjustment screw. Turn the crankshaft until the rocker arm roller is on the highest point of its corresponding camshaft lobe, and the adjustment screw is at its lowest. Once this position has been established, remove the DTI gauge, screw the adjustment screw in until firm resistance is felt, and the injector spring cannot be compressed further. Turn the adjustment screw anti-clockwise 180°, and tighten the locknut to the specified torque. Repeat this procedure for any other injectors that have been refitted.

6 Refit the camshaft cover and upper timing belt cover, as described in Section 4.

7 Start the engine and check that it runs correctly.

10 Camshaft and hydraulic tappets – removal, inspection and refitting

Note: *A new camshaft oil seal will be required on refitting.*

Removal

1 Turn the crankshaft to position No 1 piston at TDC on the firing stroke, and lock the camshaft and the fuel injection sprocket in position, as described in Section 3.

2 Remove the timing belt as described in Section 7.

3 Remove the camshaft sprocket and hub as described in Section 8.

4 Remove the tandem fuel/brake vacuum pump as described in Chapter 4B, Section 9.

5 Remove the pump injector rocker arms and shaft as described in Section 9.

6 Check the camshaft bearing caps for identification markings **(see illustration)**. The bearing caps are normally stamped with their respective cylinder numbers. If no marks are present, make suitable marks using a scriber or punch. The caps should be numbered from 1 to 5, with No 1 at the timing belt end of the engine. Note on which side of the bearing caps the marks are made to ensure that they are refitted the correct way round.

7 The camshaft rotates in shell bearings. As the camshaft bearing caps are removed, recover the shell bearing halves from the camshaft. Number the back of the bearings with a felt pen to ensure that, if re-used, the bearings are fitted to their original locations.

9.2 Starting with the outer bolts first, carefully and evenly slacken the rocker shaft retaining bolts

10.6 Check the camshaft bearing caps (arrowed) for markings

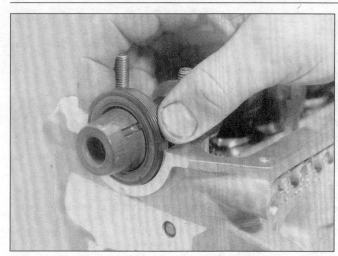

10.11 Remove the camshaft oil seal

10.17 Checking camshaft endfloat using a DTI gauge

Note: *Fitted into the cylinder head, under each camshaft bearing cap, is a washer for each cylinder head bolt.*

8 Unscrew the securing nuts, and remove Nos 1, 3 and 5 bearing caps.

9 Working progressively, in a diagonal sequence, slacken the nuts securing Nos 2 and 4 bearing caps. Note that as the nuts are slackened, the valve springs will push the camshaft up.

10 Once the nuts securing Nos 2 and 4 bearing caps have been fully slackened, lift off the bearing caps.

11 Carefully lift the camshaft from the cylinder head, keeping it level and supported at both ends as it is removed so that the journals and lobes are not damaged. Remove the oil seal from the end of the camshaft and discard it – a new one will be required for refitting **(see illustration)**.

12 Lift the hydraulic tappets from the bores in the cylinder head, and store them with the valve contact surfaces facing downwards, to prevent the oil from draining out. It is recommended that the tappets are kept immersed in oil for the period they are removed from the cylinder head. Make a note of the position of each tappet, as they must be refitted in their original locations on reassembly – accelerated wear leading to early failure will result if the tappets are interchanged.

13 Recover the lower shell bearing halves from the cylinder head; number the back of the shells with a felt pen to ensure that, if re-used, the bearings are fitted to their original locations.

Inspection

14 With the camshaft removed, examine the bearing caps and the bearing locations in the cylinder head for signs of obvious wear or pitting. If evident, a new cylinder head will probably be required. Also check that the oil supply holes in the cylinder head are free from obstructions.

15 Visually inspect the camshaft for evidence of wear on the surfaces of the lobes and journals. Normally their surfaces should be smooth and have a dull shine; look for scoring, erosion or pitting and areas that appear highly polished, indicating excessive wear. Accelerated wear will occur once the hardened exterior of the camshaft has been damaged, so always renew worn items.

Note: *If these symptoms are visible on the tips of the camshaft lobes, check the corresponding tappet, as it will probably be worn as well.*

16 If the machined surfaces of the camshaft appear discoloured or blued, it is likely that it has been overheated at some point, probably due to inadequate lubrication. This may have distorted the shaft, so check the run-out as follows: place the camshaft between two V-blocks and using a DTI gauge, measure the run-out at the centre journal. If it exceeds the figure quoted in the Specifications at the start of this Chapter, renew the camshaft.

17 To measure the camshaft endfloat, temporarily refit the camshaft to the cylinder head, then fit Nos 1 and 5 bearing caps and tighten the retaining nuts to the specified torque setting. Anchor a DTI gauge to the timing belt end of the cylinder head **(see illustration)**. Push the camshaft to one end of the cylinder head as far as it will travel, then rest the DTI gauge probe on the end face of the camshaft, and zero the gauge. Push the camshaft as far as it will go to the other end of the cylinder head, and record the gauge reading. Verify the reading by pushing the camshaft back to its original position and checking that the gauge indicates zero again.

Note: *The hydraulic tappets must not be fitted whilst this measurement is being taken.*

18 Check that the camshaft endfloat measurement is within the limit listed in the Specifications. If the measurement is outside

the specified limit, wear is unlikely to be confined to any one component, so renewal of the camshaft, cylinder head and bearing caps must be considered.

19 The camshaft bearing running clearance should now be measured. This will be difficult to achieve without a range of micrometers or internal/external expanding calipers, measure the outside diameters of the camshaft bearing surfaces and the internal diameters formed by the bearing caps and shell bearings and the bearing locations in the cylinder head. The difference between these two measurements is the running clearance.

20 Compare the camshaft running clearance measurements with the figure given in the Specifications. If any are outside the specified tolerance, the camshaft, cylinder head and bearing caps and shell bearings where applicable should be renewed.

21 Inspect the hydraulic tappets for obvious signs of wear or damage, and renew if necessary. Check that the oil holes in the tappets are free from obstructions.

Refitting

22 Smear some clean engine oil onto the sides of the hydraulic tappets, and offer them into position in their original bores in the cylinder head. Push them down until they contact the valves, and then lubricate the camshaft lobe contact surfaces.

23 Lubricate the camshaft and cylinder head bearing journals and shell bearings with clean engine oil.

24 Carefully lower the camshaft into position in the cylinder head making sure that the cam lobes for No 1 cylinder are pointing upwards.

25 Refit a new camshaft oil seal on the end of the camshaft. Make sure that the closed end of the seal faces the camshaft sprocket end of the camshaft, and take care not to damage the seal lip. Locate the seal against the seat in the cylinder head.

26 Oil the upper surfaces of the camshaft bearing journals and shell bearings, then fit Nos 2 and 4 bearing caps. Ensure that they are fitted the right way round and in the correct locations, and then progressively tighten the retaining nuts in a diagonal sequence to the specified torque. Note that as the nuts are tightened, the camshaft will be forced down against the pressure of the valve springs.

27 Fit bearing caps 1, 3 and 5 over the camshaft and progressively tighten the nuts to the specified torque. Note that it may be necessary to locate No 5 bearing cap by tapping lightly on the end of the camshaft.

28 Refit the injector rocker arms as described in Section 9.

29 Refit the tandem fuel/brake vacuum pump as described in Chapter 4B.

30 Refit the camshaft sprocket and hub as described in Section 8.

31 Refit the timing belt as described in Section 7.

---

11 Hydraulic tappets – testing

⚠️ *Warning: After fitting hydraulic tappets, wait a minimum of 30 minutes (or preferably, leave overnight) before starting the engine; to allow the tappets time to settle, otherwise the valve heads will strike the pistons.*

1 The hydraulic tappets are self-adjusting, and require no attention whilst in service.

2 If the hydraulic tappets become excessively noisy, their operation can be checked as described below.

3 Start the engine, and run it until it reaches normal operating temperature, increase the engine speed to approximately 2500 rpm for 2 minutes.

4 If any hydraulic tappets are heard to be noisy, carry out the following checks.

5 Remove the camshaft cover as described in Section 4.

6 Using a socket or spanner on the crankshaft sprocket bolt, turn the crankshaft until the tip of the camshaft lobe above the tappet to be checked is pointing vertically upwards.

7 Using feeler blades, check the clearance between the top of the tappet, and the cam lobe. If the play is in excess of 0.1 mm, renew the relevant tappet. If the play is less than 0.1 mm, or there is no play, proceed as follows.

8 Press down on the tappet using a wooden or plastic instrument **(see illustration)**. If free play in excess of 1.0 mm is present before the tappet contacts the valve stem, renew the relevant tappet.

9 On completion, refit the camshaft cover as described in Section 4.

---

12 Camshaft oil seals – renewal

Right-hand oil seal

1 Remove the timing belt as described in Section 7.

2 Remove the camshaft sprocket and hub, as described in Section 8.

3 Drill two small holes into the existing oil seal, diagonally opposite each other. Take great care to avoid drilling through into the seal housing or camshaft sealing surface. Thread two self-tapping screws into the holes, and using a pair of pliers, pull on the heads of the screws to extract the oil seal.

4 Clean out the seal housing and the sealing surface of the camshaft by wiping it with a lint-free cloth. Remove any swarf or burrs that may cause the seal to leak.

5 Do not lubricate the lip and outer edge of the new oil seal, push it over the camshaft

until it is positioned in place above its housing. To prevent damage to the sealing lips, wrap some adhesive tape around the end of the camshaft.

6 Using a hammer and a socket of suitable diameter, drive the seal squarely into its housing.

Note: *Select a socket that bears only on the hard outer surface of the seal, not the inner lip that can easily be damaged.*

7 Refit the camshaft sprocket and its hub, as described in Section 8.

8 Refit and tension the timing belt as described in Section 7.

Left-hand oil seal

9 The left-hand camshaft oil seal is formed by the brake vacuum pump seal. Refer to Chapter 9 for details of brake vacuum pump removal and refitting.

---

13 Cylinder head – removal, inspection and refitting

Note: *The cylinder head must be removed with the engine cold. New cylinder head bolts and a new cylinder head gasket will be required on refitting, and suitable studs will be required to guide the cylinder head into position – see text.*

Removal

1 Switch off the ignition and all electrical consumers, and remove the ignition key.

2 Drain the cooling system and engine oil as described in Chapter 1.

3 Remove the cover from the plenum chamber located just in front of the windscreen. Also, unbolt and remove the panel from the rear of the engine compartment **(see illustration)**.

4 Remove the air cleaner assembly complete with the air mass meter and air ducts.

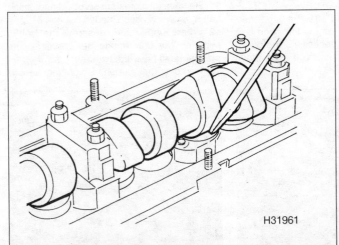

H31961

11.8 Press down on the tappet using a wooden or plastic instrument

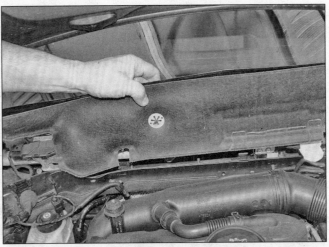

13.3 Removing the panel from the rear of the engine compartment (where fitted)

13.4a Disconnect the wiring...

13.4b...and vacuum hose...

13.4c...then release the clip...

13.4d...undo the screw...

13.4e...remove the upper...

13.4f...and lower covers...

13.4g...and remove the air cleaner...

13.4h...and the ducting from the turbocharger

6 Remove the fuel filter from its mounting bracket and position to one side.
7 Remove the front exhaust pipe as described in Chapter 4C.
8 Remove the turbocharger support and oil return line from the turbocharger. Also, remove the oil supply pipe and place to one side.
9 Remove the camshaft cover as described in Section 4.
10 Remove the timing belt as described in Section 7. Where the right-hand engine mounting has been removed, ensure the engine is supported adequately on a trolley jack and block of wood.
11 Remove the camshaft sprocket and timing belt tensioner as described in Section 8.
12 Where applicable, unscrew the bolt(s) securing the rear timing belt cover to the cylinder head (see illustrations).
13 Remove the camshaft position sensor

Also unbolt and remove the duct from the turbocharger (see illustrations).
5 Disconnect the fuel supply and return lines, and also the coolant hoses from the cylinder head. In the interests of safety, it is

recommended that the fuel be siphoned from the tandem pump on the left-hand end of the cylinder head. If necessary, the pump may be unbolted and removed (see illustration).

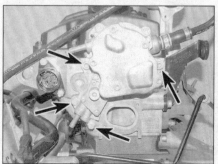

13.5 Undo the four tandem pump retaining bolts (arrowed)

13.12a Where applicable, undo the bolt (arrowed) from the inner cover...

13.12b...and the one (arrowed) on the side of the cover

13.13 Unscrew the bolt and remove the camshaft position sensor

13.14 EGR connecting pipe at the flap housing

13.15 Disconnect the central connector for the injectors

from the right-hand end of the cylinder head **(see illustration)**.

14 Remove the exhaust gas recirculation connecting pipe **(see illustration)**.

15 Note the locations of all the electrical wiring, then disconnect them methodically **(see illustration)**.

16 Disconnect all vacuum and coolant hoses **(see illustrations)**.

17 Using a multi-splined tool, undo the cylinder head bolts, working from the outside-in, evenly and gradually **(see illustration)**. Check that nothing remains connected, and lift the cylinder head from the engine block. Seek assistance if possible, as it is a heavy assembly.

18 Remove the gasket from the top of the block, noting the locating dowels. If the dowels are a loose fit, remove them and store them with the head for safekeeping. Do not discard the gasket yet – it will be needed for identification purposes. If desired, the manifolds can be removed from the cylinder head with reference to Chapter 4B, Section 5 (inlet manifold) or Chapter 4C, Section 7 (exhaust manifold).

Inspection

19 Dismantling and inspection of the cylinder head is covered in Chapter 2D.

Cylinder head gasket selection

Note: *A dial test indicator (DTI) will be required for this operation.*

20 Examine the old cylinder head gasket for manufacturer's identification markings **(see**

13.16a Disconnect the coolant hose from the end of the cylinder head

illustration)**. These will be in the form of holes or notches, and a part number on the edge of the gasket. Unless new pistons have been fitted, the new cylinder head gasket must be of the same type as the old one.

21 If new piston assemblies have been fitted as part of an engine overhaul, or if a new short engine is to be fitted, the projection of the piston crowns above the cylinder head mating face of the cylinder block at TDC must be measured. This measurement is used to determine the thickness of the new cylinder head gasket required.

22 Anchor a dial test indicator (DTI) to the top face (cylinder head gasket mating face) of the cylinder block, and zero the gauge on the gasket mating face.

23 Rest the gauge probe on No 1 piston crown, and turn the crankshaft slowly by hand until the piston reaches TDC. Measure and

13.16b Disconnect the vacuum pipes (arrowed)

record the maximum piston projection at TDC **(see illustration)**.

24 Repeat the measurement for the remaining pistons, and record the results.

25 If the measurements differ from piston-to-piston, take the highest figure, and use this to determine the thickness of the head gasket required as follows.

Piston projection	Gasket identification (number of holes/notches)
0.91 to 1.00 mm	1
0.01 to 1.10 mm	2
1.11 to 1.20 mm	3

26 Purchase a new gasket according to the results of the measurements.

Refitting

Note: *If an Audi exchange cylinder head,*

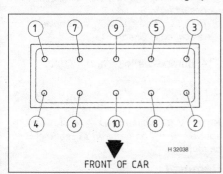

13.17 Cylinder head bolt slackening sequence

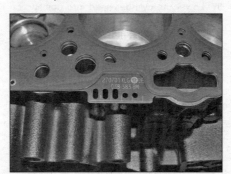

13.20 The thickness of the cylinder head gasket can be identified by notches or holes

13.23 Measuring the piston projection at TDC using a dial gauge

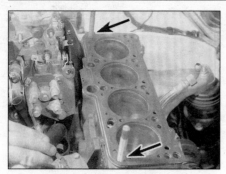
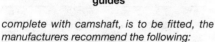

13.35 Two of the old head bolts (arrowed) can be used as cylinder head alignment guides

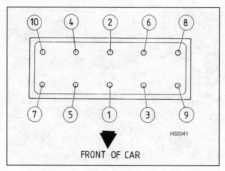

13.40a Cylinder head bolt tightening sequence

13.40b Using a torque wrench to tighten the cylinder head bolts

complete with camshaft, is to be fitted, the manufacturers recommend the following:

a) *Lubricate the contact surfaces between the tappets and the cam lobes before fitting the camshaft cover.*

b) *Do not remove the plastic protectors from the open valves until immediately before fitting the cylinder head.*

c) *Additionally, if a new cylinder head is fitted, Audi recommend that the coolant be renewed.*

27 The mating faces of the cylinder head and block must be perfectly clean before refitting the head. Use a scraper to remove all traces of gasket and carbon, also clean the tops of the pistons. Take particular care with the aluminium surfaces, as the soft metal is easily damaged.

28 Make sure that debris is not allowed to enter the oil and water passages – this is particularly important for the oil circuit, as carbon could block the oil supply to the camshaft and crankshaft bearings. Using adhesive tape and paper, seal the water, oil and bolt holes in the cylinder block.

29 To prevent carbon entering the gap between the pistons and bores, smear a little grease in the gap. After cleaning a piston, rotate the crankshaft to that the piston moves down the bore, and then wipe out the grease and carbon with a cloth rag. Clean the other piston crowns in the same way.

30 Check the head and block for nicks, deep scratches and other damage. If slight, they may be removed carefully with a file.

13.42 Angle-tighten the cylinder head bolts

More serious damage may be repaired by machining, but this is a specialist job.

31 If warpage of the cylinder head is suspected, use a straight-edge to check it for distortion, as described in Chapter 2D.

32 Ensure that the cylinder head bolt holes in the crankcase are clean and free of oil. Syringe or soak up any oil left in the bolt holes. This is most important in order that the correct bolt tightening torque can be applied, and to prevent the possibility of the block being cracked by hydraulic pressure when the bolts are tightened.

33 Turn the crankshaft anti-clockwise all the pistons at an equal height, approximately half-way down their bores from the TDC position (see Section 3). This will eliminate any risk of piston-to-valve contact as the cylinder head is refitted.

34 Where applicable, refit the manifolds with reference to Chapter 4B and/or Chapter 4C

35 To guide the cylinder head into position, screw two long studs (or old cylinder head bolts with the heads cut off, and slots cut in the ends to enable the bolts to be unscrewed) into the cylinder block **(see illustration)**.

36 Ensure that the cylinder head locating dowels are in place in the cylinder block, and then fit the new cylinder head gasket over the dowels, ensuring that the part number is uppermost. Where applicable, the OBEN/TOP marking should also be uppermost. Note that Audi recommend that the gasket is only removed from its packaging immediately prior to fitting.

37 Lower the cylinder head into position on the gasket, ensuring that it engages correctly over the guide studs and dowels.

38 Fit the new cylinder head bolts to the eight remaining bolt locations, and screw them in as far as possible by hand.

39 Unscrew the two guide studs from the exhaust side of the cylinder block, then screw in the two remaining new cylinder head bolts as far as possible by hand.

40 Working progressively, in sequence, tighten all the cylinder head bolts to the specified Stage 1 torque **(see illustrations)**.

41 Again working progressively, in sequence, tighten all the cylinder head bolts to the specified Stage 2 torque.

42 Tighten all the cylinder head bolts, in sequence, through the specified Stage 3 angle **(see illustration)**.

43 Finally, tighten all the cylinder head bolts, in sequence, through the specified Stage 4 angle.

44 After finally tightening the cylinder head bolts, turn the camshaft so that the cam lobes for No 1 cylinder are pointing upwards.

45 Where applicable, reconnect the lifting tackle to the engine lifting brackets on the cylinder head, and then adjust the lifting tackle to support the engine. Once the engine is adequately supported using the cylinder head brackets, disconnect the lifting tackle from the bracket bolted to the cylinder block, and unbolt the improvised engine lifting bracket from the cylinder block. Alternatively, remove the trolley jack and block of wood from under the sump.

46 The remainder of the refitting procedure is a reversal of the removal procedure, bearing in mind the following points.

a) *Refit the injector rocker shaft with reference to Chapter 4B.*

b) *Refit the camshaft cover with reference to Section 4.*

c) *Use new sealing rings when reconnecting the turbocharger oil return pipe to the cylinder block.*

d) *Reconnect the exhaust front section to the turbocharger, with reference to Chapter 4C.*

e) *Refit the timing belt tensioner with reference to Section 8.*

f) *Refit the camshaft sprocket as described in Section 8, and refit the timing belt as described in Section 7.*

g) *Refill the cooling system and engine oil as described in Chapter 1.*

14 Sump – removal and refitting

Note: *VAG sealant (D 176 404 A2 or equivalent) will be required to seal the sump on refitting.*

Removal

1 Apply the handbrake, then jack up the front of the vehicle and support securely on axle

14.4 Disconnect the wiring connector from the oil level/temperature sender

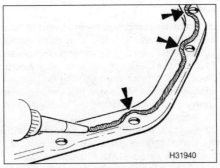

14.9 Apply the sealant around the inside of the bolt holes

stands (see 'Jacking and vehicle support' in Reference Chapter).

2 Remove the securing screws and withdraw the engine undertray.

3 Drain the engine oil as described in Chapter 1, Section 3.

4 Where fitted, disconnect the wiring connector from the oil level/temperature sender in the sump **(see illustration)**.

5 Unscrew and remove the bolts securing the sump to the cylinder block, and the bolts securing the sump to the transmission casing, then withdraw the sump. If necessary, release the sump by tapping with a soft-faced hammer.

6 If desired, unbolt the oil baffle plate from the cylinder block.

Refitting

7 Begin refitting by thoroughly cleaning the mating faces of the sump and cylinder block. Ensure that all traces of old sealant are removed.

8 Where applicable, refit the oil baffle plate, and tighten the securing bolts.

9 Ensure that the cylinder block mating face of the sump is free from all traces of old sealant, oil and grease, and then apply a 2.0 to 3.0 mm thick bead of silicone sealant (VAG D 176 404 A2 or equivalent) to the sump **(see illustration)**. Note that the sealant should be run around the inside of the bolt holes in the sump. The sump must be fitted within 5 minutes of applying the sealant.

10 Offer the sump up to the cylinder block, then refit the sump-to-cylinder block bolts, and lightly tighten them by hand, working progressively in a diagonal sequence.

Note: If the sump is being refitted with the engine and transmission separated, make sure that the sump is flush with the flywheel end of the cylinder block.

11 Refit the sump-to-transmission casing bolts, and tighten them lightly, using a socket.

12 Again working in a diagonal sequence, lightly tighten the sump-to-cylinder block bolts, using a socket.

13 Tighten the sump-to-transmission casing bolts to the specified torque.

14 Working in a diagonal sequence, progressively tighten the sump-to-cylinder block bolts to the specified torque.

15 Refit the wiring connector to the oil level/

temperature sender (where fitted), then refit the engine undertray(s), and lower the vehicle to the ground.

16 Allow at least 30 minutes from the time of refitting the sump for the sealant to cure, then refill the engine with oil, with reference to Chapter 1, Section 3.

15 Oil pump, drive chain and sprockets – removal, inspection and refitting

Oil pump

Removal

1 Remove the sump as described in Section 14.

2 Unscrew the securing bolts, and remove the oil baffle from the cylinder block.

3 Unscrew and remove the three mounting bolts, and release the oil pump from the dowels in the crankcase **(see illustration)**.

Unhook the oil pump drive sprocket from the chain and withdraw the oil pump and oil pick-up pipe from the engine. Note that the tensioner will attempt to tighten the chain, and it may be necessary to use a screwdriver to hold it in its released position before releasing the oil pump sprocket from the chain.

4 If desired, unscrew the flange bolts and remove the suction pipe from the oil pump. Recover the O-ring seal. Unscrew the bolts and remove the cover from the oil pump.

Note: If the oil pick-up pipe is removed from the oil pump, a new O-ring will be required on refitting.

Inspection

5 Clean the pump thoroughly, and inspect the gear teeth/rotors for signs of damage or wear. If evident, renew the oil pump.

6 To remove the sprocket from the oil pump, unscrew the retaining bolt and slide off the sprocket (note that the sprocket can only be fitted in one position).

Refitting

7 Prime the pump with oil by pouring oil into the pick-up pipe aperture while turning the driveshaft.

8 Refit the cover to the oil pump and tighten the bolts securely. Where applicable, refit the pick-up pipe to the oil pump, using a new O-ring seal, and tighten the securing bolts.

9 If the drive chain, crankshaft sprocket and tensioner have been removed, delay refitting them until after the oil pump has been mounted on the cylinder block. If they have not been removed, use a screwdriver to press the tensioner against its spring to provide sufficient slack in the chain to refit the oil pump.

1 Oil pump
2 Oil pump sprocket
3 Bolt
4 Oil pump drive chain
5 Crankshaft oil seal housing
6 Bolt
7 Drive chain tensioner
8 Sump
9 Seal
10 Sump drain plug
11 Dowels
12 O-ring
13 Oil pick-up pipe
14 Oil baffle
15 Seal
16 Oil level/ temperature sender
17 Bolt
18 Oil spray jet
19 bolt

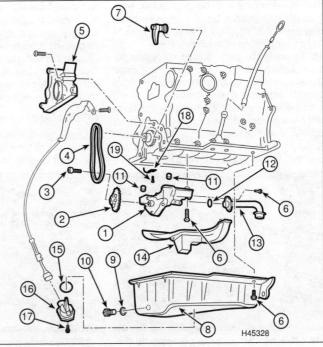

15.3 Sump and oil pump components

10 Engage the oil pump sprocket with the drive chain, and then locate the oil pump on the dowels. Refit and tighten the three mounting bolts to the specified torque.

11 Where applicable, refit the drive chain, tensioner and crankshaft sprocket using a reversal of the removal procedure.

12 Refit the oil baffle, and tighten the securing bolts.

13 Refit the sump as described in Section 14.

Drive chain and sprockets

Note: *VAG sealant (D 176 404 A2 or equivalent) will be required to seal the crankshaft oil seal housing on refitting, and it is advisable to fit a new crankshaft oil seal.*

Removal

14 Proceed as described in paragraphs 1 and 2.

15 To remove the oil pump sprocket, unscrew the securing bolt, then pull the sprocket from the pump shaft, and unhook it from the drive chain.

16 To remove the chain, remove the timing belt as described in Section 7, then unbolt the crankshaft oil seal housing from the cylinder block. Unbolt the chain tensioner from the cylinder block, and then unhook the chain from the sprocket on the end of the crankshaft.

17 The oil pump drive sprocket is a press-fit on the crankshaft, and cannot easily be removed. Consult a Audi dealer for advice if the sprocket is worn or damaged.

Inspection

18 Examine the chain for wear and damage. Wear is usually indicated by excessive lateral play between the links, and excessive noise in operation. It is wise to renew the chain in any case if the engine is to be overhauled. Note that the rollers on a very badly worn chain may be slightly grooved. If there is any doubt as to the condition of the chain, renew it.

19 Examine the teeth on the sprockets for wear. Each tooth forms an inverted V. If worn, the side of each tooth under tension will be slightly concave in shape when compared with the other side of the tooth (ie, the teeth will have a hooked appearance). If the teeth appear worn, the sprocket should be renewed (consult an Audi dealer for advice if the crankshaft sprocket is worn or damaged).

Refitting

20 If the oil pump has been removed, refit the oil pump as described previously in this Section before refitting the chain and sprocket.

21 Refit the chain tensioner to the cylinder block, and tighten the securing bolt to the specified torque. Make sure that the tensioner spring is correctly positioned to pretension the tensioner arm.

22 Engage the oil pump sprocket with the chain, then engage the chain with the crankshaft sprocket. Use a screwdriver to press the tensioner against its spring to provide sufficient slack in the chain to engage the sprocket with the oil pump. Note that the sprocket will only fit in one position.

23 Refit the oil pump sprocket bolt, and tighten to the specified torque.

24 Fit a new crankshaft oil seal to the housing, and refit the housing as described in Section 17.

25 Where applicable, refit the oil baffle, and tighten the securing bolts.

26 Refit the sump as described in Section 14.

16 Flywheel – removal, inspection and refitting

Removal

1 Remove the transmission (see Chapter 7A, Section 3) and clutch (see Chapter 6, Section 6).

2 The flywheel can only be fitted in one position due to the offset of the flywheel mounting holes in the end of the crankshaft.

3 Rotate the outside of the dual-mass flywheel so that the bolts align with the holes (if necessary).

4 Unscrew the bolts and remove the flywheel. Using a locking tool, counter-hold the flywheel to prevent it from turning **(see illustration)**. Discard the bolts, as new ones must be fitted.

Note: *In order not to damage the flywheel, do not allow the bolt heads to make contact with the flywheel during the unscrewing procedure.*

Inspection

5 Check the dual-mass flywheel for wear and damage. Examine the starter ring gear for excessive wear to the teeth. If the driveplate

or its ring gear are damaged, the complete driveplate must be renewed. The flywheel ring gear, however, may be renewed separately from the flywheel, but the work should be entrusted to an Audi dealer. If the clutch friction face is discoloured or scored excessively, it may be possible to regrind it, but this work should also be entrusted to an Audi dealer.

6 The following are guidelines only, but should indicate whether professional inspection is necessary. The dual-mass flywheel should be checked as follows:

Warpage

7 Place a straight edge across the face of the drive surface, and check by trying to insert a feeler gauge between the straight edge and the drive surface **(see illustration)**. The flywheel will normally warp like a bowl – ie. Higher on the outer edge. If the warpage is more than 0.40 mm, the flywheel may need replacing.

Free rotational movement

8 This is the distance the drive surface of the flywheel can be turned independently of the flywheel primary element, using finger effort alone. Move the drive surface in one direction and make a mark where the locating pin aligns with the flywheel edge. Move the drive surface in the other direction (finger pressure only) and make another mark **(see illustration)**. The total of free movement should not exceed 20.0 mm. If it's more, the flywheel may need replacing.

Total rotational movement

9 This is the total distance the drive surface can be turned independently of the flywheel primary element. Insert two bolts into the clutch pressure plate/damper unit mounting holes, and with the crankshaft/flywheel held stationary, use a lever/pry bar between the bolts and use some effort to move the drive surface fully in one direction – make a mark where the locating pin aligns with the flywheel edge. Now force the drive surface fully in the opposite direction, and make another mark. The total rotational movement should not exceed 44.00 mm. If it does, have the flywheel professionally inspected.

Lateral movement

10 The lateral movement (up and down) of the drive surface in relation to the primary element of the flywheel, should not exceed 2.0 mm. If it does, the flywheel may need replacing. This

16.4 Use a locking tool to counterhold the flywheel

16.7 Flywheel warpage check – see text

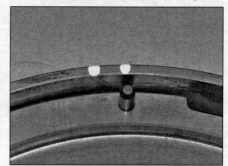

16.8 Flywheel free rotational movement check alignment marks – see text

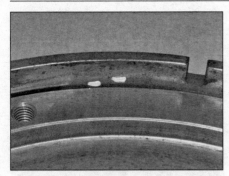

16.10 Flywheel lateral movement check marks – see text

16.12 Use new bolts when refitting

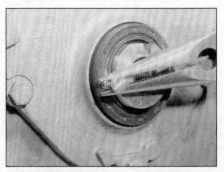

17.2 Removing the crankshaft oil seal using self-tapping screws

can be checked by pressing the drive surface down on one side into the flywheel (flywheel horizontal) and making an alignment mark between the drive surface and the inner edge of the primary element. Now press down on the opposite side of the drive surface, and make another mark above the original one. The difference between the two marks is the lateral movement **(see illustration)**.

11 There should be no cracks in the drive surface of the flywheel. If cracks are evident, the flywheel may need replacing.

Refitting

12 Refitting is a reversal of removal. Use new bolts when refitting the flywheel or driveplate **(see illustration)**, and coat the threads of the bolts (if not already coated with locking compound) with locking fluid before inserting them. Tighten them to the specified torque.

17 Crankshaft oil seals – renewal

Note: The oil seals are a PTFE (Teflon) type and are fitted dry, without using any grease or oil. These have a wider sealing lip and have been introduced instead of the coil spring type oil seal.
Note: If the oil seal housing is removed, suitable sealant (VAG D 176 404 A2, or equivalent) will be required to seal the housing on refitting.

Timing belt end oil seal

1 Remove the timing belt as described in

Section 7, and the crankshaft sprocket with reference to Section 8.

2 To remove the seal without removing the housing, drill two small holes diagonally opposite each other, insert self-tapping screws, and pull on the heads of the screws with pliers **(see illustration)**.

3 Alternatively, to remove the oil seal complete with its housing, proceed as follows.

a) *Remove the sump as described in Section 14. This is necessary to ensure a satisfactory seal between the sump and oil seal housing on refitting.*

b) *Unbolt and remove the oil seal housing.*

c) *Working on the bench, lever the oil seal from the housing using a suitable screwdriver. Take care not to damage the seal seating in the housing **(see illustration)**.*

4 Thoroughly clean the oil seal seating in the housing.

5 Wind a length of tape around the end of the crankshaft to protect the oil seal lips as the seal (and housing, where applicable) is fitted.

6 Fit a new oil seal to the housing, pressing or driving it into position using a socket or tube of suitable diameter. Ensure that the socket or tube bears only on the hard outer ring of the seal, and take care not to damage the seal lips. Press or drive the seal into position until it is seated on the shoulder in the housing. Make sure that the closed end of the seal is facing outwards.

7 If the oil seal housing has been removed, proceed as follows; otherwise proceed to paragraph 11.

8 Clean all traces of old sealant from the

crankshaft oil seal housing and the cylinder block, then coat the cylinder block mating faces of the oil seal housing with a 2.0 to 3.0 mm thick bead of sealant (VAG D 176 404 A2, or equivalent). Note that the seal housing must be refitted within 5 minutes of applying the sealant.

Caution: DO NOT put excessive amounts of sealant onto the housing as it may get into the sump and block the oil pick-up pipe.

9 Refit the oil seal housing, and tighten the bolts progressively to the specified torque **(see illustration)**.

10 Refit the sump as described in Section 14.

11 Refit the crankshaft sprocket with reference to Section 8, and the timing belt as described in Section 7.

Flywheel end oil seal

12 Remove the flywheel as described in Section 16.

13 Remove the sump as described in Section 14. This is necessary to ensure a satisfactory seal between the sump and oil seal housing on refitting.

14 Unbolt and remove the oil seal housing, complete with the oil seal.

15 The new oil seal will be supplied ready-fitted to a new oil seal housing.

16 Thoroughly clean the oil seal housing mating face on the cylinder block.

17 New oil seal/housing assemblies are supplied with a fitting tool to prevent damage to the oil seal as it is being fitted. Locate the tool over the end of the crankshaft **(see illustration)**.

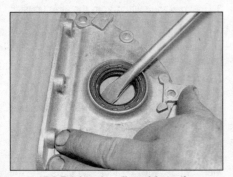

17.3 Prising the oil seal from the crankshaft oil seal housing

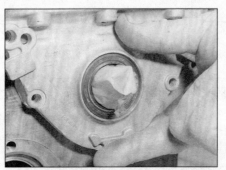

17.9 Slide the oil seal housing over the end of the crankshaft

17.17 Locate the crankshaft oil seal fitting tool over the end of the crankshaft

17.19a Fit the oil seal/housing assembly over the end of the crankshaft

17.19b then tighten the securing bolts to the specified torque

18 If the original oil seal housing was fitted using sealant, apply a thin bead of suitable sealant (VAG D 176 404 A2, or equivalent) to the cylinder block mating face of the oil seal housing. Note that the seal housing must be refitted within 5 minutes of applying the sealant.

Caution: DO NOT put excessive amounts of sealant onto the housing as it may get into the sump and block the oil pick-up pipe.

19 Carefully fit the oil seal/housing assembly over the end of the crankshaft, then refit the securing bolts and tighten the bolts progressively, in a diagonal sequence, to the specified torque **(see illustrations)**.

20 Remove the oil seal protector tool from the end of the crankshaft.

21 Refit the sump as described in Section 14.

22 Refit the flywheel as described in Section 16.

18 Engine/transmission mountings – inspection and renewal

1 Refer to Chapter 2A, Section 16 for the basic procedure, however, note that the right-hand engine mounting is slightly different.

19 Engine oil cooler – removal and refitting

Note: *New sealing rings will be required on refitting.*

Removal

1 The oil cooler is mounted under the oil filter housing on the front of the cylinder block **(see illustration)**.

2 Position a container beneath the oil filter to catch escaping oil and coolant.

3 Clamp the oil cooler coolant hoses to minimise coolant spillage, then remove the clips, and disconnect the hoses from the oil cooler. Be prepared for coolant spillage.

4 Unscrew the oil cooler securing plate from the bottom of the oil filter housing, then slide off the oil cooler. Recover the O-rings from the top and bottom of the oil cooler.

Refitting

5 Refitting is a reversal of removal, bearing in mind the following points:

a) Use new oil cooler O-rings.

b) Tighten the oil cooler securing plate securely.

c) On completion, check and if necessary top-up the oil and coolant levels.

20 Oil pressure warning light switch – removal and refitting

Removal

1 The oil pressure warning light switch is fitted to the oil filter housing. Remove the engine top cover to gain access to the switch.

2 Disconnect the wiring connector and wipe clean the area around the switch.

3 Unscrew the switch from the filter housing and remove it, along with its sealing washer. If the switch is to be left removed from the engine for any length of time, plug the oil filter housing aperture.

Refitting

4 Examine the sealing washer for signs of damage or deterioration and if necessary renew.

5 Refit the switch, complete with washer, and tighten it to the specified torque.

6 Securely reconnect the wiring connector then check and, if necessary, top-up the engine oil as described in *Weekly checks*. On completion, refit the engine top cover.

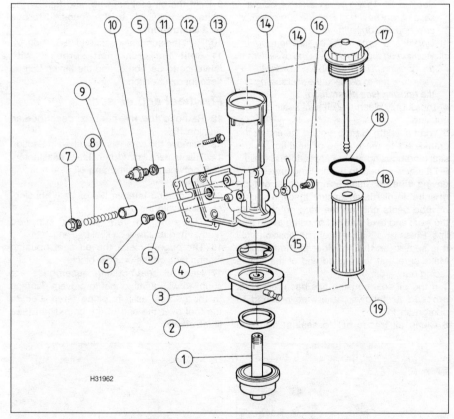

19.1 Oil filter and oil cooler mounting details

1 Oil cooler securing plate	8 Oil pressure relief valve spring (not fitted to all models)	10 Oil pressure warning light switch	14 Seal
2 O-ring		11 Gasket	15 Oil supply pipe to turbo
3 Oil cooler	9 Oil pressure relief valve piston (not fitted to all models)	12 Mounting bolt	16 Banjo bolt – turbo
4 O-ring		13 Oil filter housing	17 Oil filter cover
5 Washer			18 O-ring
6 Sealing plug			19 Oil filter
7 Sealing plug			

Chapter 2 Part C
2.0 litre engine in-car repair procedures

Contents

Degrees of difficulty

| **Easy,** suitable for novice with little experience | | **Fairly easy,** suitable for beginner with some experience | | **Fairly difficult,** suitable for competent DIY mechanic | | **Difficult,** suitable for experienced DIY mechanic | | **Very difficult,** suitable for expert DIY or professional | |

Specifications

General

Manufacturer's engine codes:
    1968 cc (2.0 litre), 16-valve, DOHC . . . .   CBAA, CBAB, CBBB, CFFA, CFFB and CFGB

Maximum outputs:

	Power	Torque
Engine code CBAA & CFFA	100 kW @ 4200 rpm	320 Nm @ 1750 to 2500 rpm
Engine code CBAB & CFFB.	103 kW @ 4200 rpm	320 Nm @ 1750 to 2500 rpm
Engine code CBBB & CFGB.	125 kW @ 4200 rpm	350 Nm @ 1750 to 2500 rpm

Bore . . . .   81.0 mm
Stroke. . . . .   95.5 mm
Compression ratio . . . .   16.5 : 1
Compression pressures:
    Minimum compression pressure . . . .   Approximately 19.0 bar
    Maximum difference between cylinders. . . . .   Approximately 5.0 bar
Firing order. . . . .   1 – 3 – 4 – 2
No 1 cylinder location. . . . .   Timing belt end

Note: *See 'Vehicle identification' in Reference Chapter for the location of engine code markings.*

Lubrication system

Oil pump type..	Gear type, belt-driven from crankshaft, or driven by front balance shaft
Oil pressure switch (green cap)........................	0.5 bar
Oil pressure switch (brown cap).......................	0.7 bar
Oil pressure (oil temperature 80°C):	
Minimum @ idling..................................	0.6 bar
Minimum @ 2000 rpm:	
CBAA, CBAB & CBBB........................	2.0 bar
CFFA, CFFB & CFGB........................	1.0 bar
Maximum @ high rpm:	
CBAA, CBAB & CBBB........................	7.0 bar
CFFA, CFFB & CFGB........................	5.0 bar

Torque wrench settings

	Nm	lbf ft
Ancillary (alternator, etc) bracket mounting bolts: *		
Stage 1..	40	30
Stage 2..	Angle-tighten a further 45°	
Auxiliary drivebelt tensioner securing bolt:		
Stage 1..	20	15
Stage 2..	Angle-tighten a further 180°	
Balance shaft drivegear bolts: *		
Stage 1..	20	15
Stage 2..	Angle-tighten a further 90°	
Balance shaft housing to cylinder block: *		
M7:		
Stage 1......................................	13	10
Stage 2......................................	Angle-tighten a further 90°	
M8:		
Stage 1......................................	20	15
Stage 2......................................	Angle-tighten a further 90°	
Balance shaft idler gear: *		
Stage 1..	90	66
Stage 2..	Angle-tighten a further 90°	
Big-end bearing caps bolts: *		
Stage 1..	30	22
Stage 2..	Angle-tighten a further 90°	
Camshaft bearing frame bolts/nut........................	10	7
Camshaft cover bolts.................................	10	7
Camshaft sprocket hub centre bolt.....................	100	74
Camshaft sprocket-to-hub bolts: *		
Stage 1..	20	15
Stage 2..	Angle-tighten a further 45°	
Common rail bolts...................................	22	16
Coolant pump bolts..................................	15	11
Crankshaft oil seal housing bolts......................	15	11
Crankshaft pulley-to-sprocket bolts: *		
Stage 1..	10	7
Stage 2..	Angle-tighten a further 90°	
Crankshaft sprocket bolt: *		
Stage 1..	180	133
Stage 2..	Angle-tighten a further 90°	
Stage 3..	Angle-tighten a further 45°	
Cylinder head bolts: *		
Stage 1..	30	22
Stage 2..	50	37
Stage 3..	Angle-tighten a further 90°	
Stage 4..	Angle-tighten a further 90°	
Engine mountings: *		
RH engine mounting:		
Mounting bracket to engine:		
Stage 1....................................	40	30
Stage 2....................................	Angle-tighten a further 180°	
Mounting to body:		
Stage 1....................................	40	30
Stage 2....................................	Angle-tighten a further 90°	
Mounting to bracket:		
Stage 1....................................	60	44
Stage 2....................................	Angle-tighten a further 90°	

Torque wrench settings (continued)

	Nm	lbf ft
Engine mountings: * (continued)		
LH engine/transmission mounting:		
Mounting to body:		
Stage 1	40	30
Stage 2	Angle-tighten a further 90°	
Mounting to bracket on transmission:		
Stage 1	60	44
Stage 2	Angle-tighten a further 90°	
Rear mounting link:		
M10 strength class 8.8:		
Stage 1	40	30
Stage 2	Angle-tighten a further 90°	
M10 strength class 10.9:		
Stage 1	50	37
Stage 2	Angle-tighten a further 90°	
M12:		
Stage 1	60	44
Stage 2	Angle-tighten a further 90°	
Flywheel: *		
Stage 1	60	44
Stage 2	Angle-tighten a further 90°	
Fuel injector:		
Retaining nuts	22	16
Cover bolts	5	4
Fuel pump hub nut	95	70
Fuel pump sprocket bolts: *		
Stage 1	20	15
Stage 2	Angle-tighten a further 90°	
Intermediate gear bolt: *		
Stage 1	90	66
Stage 2	Angle-tighten a further 90°	
Main bearing cap bolts: *		
Stage 1	65	48
Stage 2	Angle-tighten a further 90°	
Oil cooler screws (CFFA, CFFB & CFGB)	11	7
Oil cooler centre bolt (CBAA, CBAB & CBBB)	25	18
Oil drain plug*	30	22
Oil filter housing-to-cylinder block bolts: *		
Stage 1	15	11
Stage 2	Angle-tighten a further 90°	
Oil filter cover	25	18
Oil level/temperature sensor-to-sump bolts	10	7
Oil pick-up pipe securing bolts	10	7
Oil pressure warning light switch	20	15
Oil pump to cylinder block securing bolts	16	12
Oil pump to balance shaft securing bolts	9	6
Piston oil spray jet bolt	25	18
Sump:		
Sump-to-cylinder block bolts	15	11
Sump-to-transmission bolts	45	33
Thermostat housing	15	11
Timing belt outer cover bolts	10	7
Timing belt tensioner roller securing nut:		
Stage 1	20	15
Stage 2	Angle-tighten a further 45°	
Timing belt idler pulleys:		
Lower idler roller nut	20	15
Upper idler roller (small) bolt	20	15
Upper idler roller (large) bolt: *		
Stage 1	50	37
Stage 2	Angle-tighten a further 90°	

*Do not re-use fasteners

1 General Information

How to use this Chapter

1 This Part of Chapter 2 describes those repair procedures that can reasonably be carried out on the engine while it remains in the vehicle. If the engine has been removed from the vehicle and is being dismantled as described in Part D, any preliminary dismantling procedures can be ignored.

2 Note that while it may be possible physically to overhaul certain items while the engine is in the vehicle, such tasks are not usually carried out as separate operations, and usually require the execution of several additional procedures (not to mention the cleaning of components and of oilways); for this reason, all such tasks are classed as major overhaul procedures, and are described in Part D of this Chapter.

Engine description

3 Throughout this Chapter, engines are referred to by type, and are identified and referred to by the manufacturer's code letters. A listing of all engines covered, together with their code letters, is given in the Specifications at the start of this Chapter.

4 The engines are water-cooled, double overhead camshafts (DOHC), in-line four-cylinder units, with cast-iron cylinder blocks and aluminium-silicon alloy cylinder heads. All are mounted transversely at the front of the vehicle, with the transmission bolted to the left-hand end of the engine.

5 The crankshaft is of five-bearing type, and thrustwashers are fitted to the centre main bearing to control crankshaft endfloat.

6 Drive for the exhaust camshaft is by a toothed timing belt from the crankshaft, with the intake camshaft driven by interlocking gears at the left-hand end of both camshafts. The gears incorporate a toothed backlash compensator element. Each camshaft is mounted at the top of the cylinder head, and is secured by a bearing frame/ladder.

7 The valves are closed by coil springs, and run in guides pressed into the cylinder head. The valves are operated by roller rocker arms incorporating hydraulic tappets.

8 On certain engines, a twin, counter-rotating balance shaft assembly is fitted to the base of the cylinder block. The rearmost balance shaft is driven by a gear on the crankshaft, via an intermediate gear bolted to the balance shaft housing. The two balance shafts are geared together.

9 On engines without a balance shaft, the gear-type oil pump is driven via a toothed belt from a sprocket on the crankshaft. On engines with a balance shaft the oil pump is driven by the front balance shaft. On all engines, oil is drawn from the sump through a strainer, and then forced through an externally-mounted, renewable filter. From there, it is distributed to the cylinder head, where it lubricates the camshaft journals and hydraulic tappets, and also to the crankcase, where it lubricates the main bearings, connecting rod big-ends, gudgeon pins and cylinder bores. A coolant-fed oil cooler is fitted to the oil filter housing on all engines. Oil jets are fitted to the base of each cylinder – these spray oil onto the underside of the pistons, to improve cooling.

10 All engines are fitted with a brake servo vacuum pump driven by the camshaft on the transmission end of the cylinder head.

11 On all engines, engine coolant is circulated by a pump, driven by the timing belt. For details of the cooling system, refer to Chapter 3.

Operations with engine in car

12 The following operations can be performed without removing the engine:
a) Compression pressure – testing.
b) Camshaft cover – removal and refitting.
c) Crankshaft pulley – removal and refitting.
d) Timing belt covers – removal and refitting.
e) Timing belt – removal, refitting and adjustment.
f) Timing belt tensioner and sprockets – removal and refitting.
g) Camshaft oil seals – renewal.
h) Camshafts and hydraulic tappets – removal, inspection and refitting.
i) Cylinder head – removal and refitting.
j) Cylinder head and pistons – decarbonising.
k) Sump – removal and refitting.
l) Oil pump – removal, overhaul and refitting.
m) Crankshaft oil seals – renewal.
n) Engine/transmission mountings – inspection and renewal.
o) Flywheel – removal, inspection and refitting.

Note: It is possible to remove the pistons and connecting rods (after removing the cylinder head and sump) without removing the engine. However, this is not recommended. Work of this nature is more easily and thoroughly completed with the engine on the bench, as described in Chapter 2D.

2 Compression and leakdown tests – description and interpretation

Compression test

Note: A compression tester suitable for use with diesel engines will be required for this test.

1 When engine performance is down, or if misfiring occurs which cannot be attributed to the ignition or fuel systems, a compression test can provide diagnostic clues as to the engine's condition. If the test is performed regularly, it can give warning of trouble before any other symptoms become apparent.

2 The engine must be fully warmed-up to normal operating temperature, the battery must be fully charged, and you will require the aid of an assistant.

3 Remove the glow plugs as described in Chapter 5, Section 11, and then fit a compression tester to the No 1 cylinder glow plug hole. The type of tester that bolts into the plug thread is preferred.

Note: Part of the glow plug removal procedure is to disconnect the fuel injector wiring plugs. As a result of the plugs being disconnected and the engine cranked, faults will be stored in the ECU memory. These must be erased after the compression test.

4 Have your assistant crank the engine for several seconds on the starter motor. After one or two revolutions, the compression pressure should build-up to a maximum figure and then stabilise. Record the highest reading obtained.

5 Repeat the test on the remaining cylinders, recording the pressure in each.

6 The cause of poor compression is less easy to establish on a diesel engine than on a petrol engine. The effect of introducing oil into the cylinders (wet testing) is not conclusive, because there is a risk that the oil will sit in the recess on the piston crown, instead of passing to the rings. However, the following can be used as a rough guide to diagnosis.

7 All cylinders should produce very similar pressures. Any difference greater than that specified indicates the existence of a fault. Note that the compression should build-up quickly in a healthy engine. Low compression on the first stroke, followed by gradually increasing pressure on successive strokes, indicates worn piston rings. A low compression reading on the first stroke, which does not build-up during successive strokes, indicates leaking valves or a blown head gasket (a cracked head could also be the cause).

8 A low reading from two adjacent cylinders is almost certainly due to the head gasket having blown between them and the presence of coolant in the engine oil will confirm this.

9 On completion, remove the compression tester, and refit the glow plugs, with reference to Chapter 5, Section 11.

10 Reconnect the wiring to the injector solenoids. Finally, have an Audi dealer or suitably equipped specialist erase the fault codes from the ECU memory.

Leakdown test

11 A leakdown test measures the rate at which compressed air fed into the cylinder is lost. It is an alternative to a compression test, and in many ways it is better, since the escaping air provides easy identification of where pressure loss is occurring (piston rings, valves or head gasket).

12 The equipment required for leakdown testing is unlikely to be available to the home mechanic. If poor compression is suspected, have the test performed by a suitably equipped garage.

3 Engine assembly and valve timing marks – general information and usage

General information

1 TDC is the highest point in the cylinder that each piston reaches as it travels up-and-down when the crankshaft turns. Each piston reaches TDC at the end of the compression stroke and again at the end of the exhaust stroke, but TDC generally refers to piston position on the compression stroke. No 1 piston is at the timing belt end of the engine.

2 Positioning No 1 piston at TDC is an essential part of many procedures, such as timing belt removal and camshaft removal.

3 The design of the engines covered in this Chapter is such that piston-to-valve contact may occur if the camshaft or crankshaft is turned with the timing belt removed. For this reason, it is important to ensure that the camshaft and crankshaft do not move in relation to each other once the timing belt has been removed from the engine.

Setting TDC on No 1 cylinder

Note: *VAG special tool T10050 is required to lock the crankshaft sprocket in the TDC position. Alternatively obtain a tool from automotive tool specialists.*

4 Remove the auxiliary drivebelt as described in Chapter 1, Section 27.

5 Remove the crankshaft pulley as described in Section 5.

6 Remove the timing belt outer covers as described in Section 6.

7 Using a spanner or socket on the crankshaft sprocket bolt, turn the crankshaft in the normal direction of rotation (clockwise) until the alignment mark on the face of the sprocket is almost vertical, and the hole in the camshaft sprocket hub aligns with the hole in the cylinder head **(see illustration)**.

8 While in this position it should be possible to insert the VAG tool T10050 to lock the crankshaft, and a 6 mm diameter rod/drill bit to lock the camshafts **(see illustrations)**.

Note: *The mark on the crankshaft sprocket and the mark on the VAG tool must align,*

3.7 The alignment mark (arrowed) on the crankshaft sprocket should be almost vertical

3.8b ...so the marks on the tool and sprocket align (arrowed)

whilst at the same time the shaft of tool must engage in the drilling in the crankshaft oil seal housing.

9 The engine is now set to TDC on No 1 cylinder.

4 Camshaft cover – removal and refitting

Removal

1 Remove the fuel injectors as described in (Chapter 4A, Section 4) and the fuel rail as described in (Chapter 4A, Section 11).

2 Remove the timing belt upper cover as described in Section 6.

3.8a Fit the tool to the hole in the oil seal housing (arrowed)...

3.8c Insert a 6 mm drill bit/rod to lock the camshaft hub

3 Note their fitted positions, then disconnect the vacuum hoses from the camshaft cover, and release them and the wiring loom from the retaining clips at the left-hand end of the cover **(see illustration)**.

4 Squeeze together the sides of the collar, and disconnect the breather hose from the camshaft cover **(see illustration)**.

5 Release the wiring from the clips at the rear of the cover, then unscrew the camshaft cover retaining bolts and lift the cover away. If the cover sticks, do not attempt to lever it off – instead free it by working around the cover and tapping it lightly with a soft-faced mallet **(see illustration)**.

6 Recover the camshaft cover gasket. Inspect the gasket carefully, and renew it if damage or deterioration is evident – note that

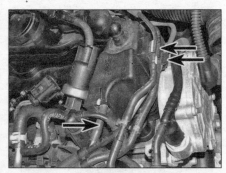

4.3 Disconnect the vacuum hoses from the camshaft cover (arrowed)

4.4 Squeeze together the sides of the collar (arrowed) and disconnect the breather hose

4.5 Undo the bolts and lift away the camshaft cover

4.6a Renew the cover seal if necessary

4.6b Bolts and seals must be pushed fully through the cover before fitting the gasket

5.4 Undo the pulley bolts, counterholding it with a socket on the centre sprocket bolt

the retaining bolts and seals must be pushed fully through the cover **(see illustrations)**.

7 Clean the mating surfaces of the cylinder head and camshaft cover thoroughly, removing all traces of oil – take care to avoid damaging the surfaces as you do this.

Refitting

8 Refit the camshaft cover by following the removal procedure in reverse, tightening the cover retaining bolts to the specified torque starting with the centre bolts and working outwards.

5 Crankshaft pulley – removal and refitting

Removal

1 Switch off the ignition and all electrical consumers and remove the ignition key.
2 Raise the front right-hand side of the vehicle, and support securely on axle stands (see *Jacking and vehicle support* in Reference Chapter). Remove the roadwheel.
3 Remove the securing fasteners and withdraw the lower section of the front wheel arch liner.
4 Slacken the bolts securing the crankshaft pulley to the sprocket **(see illustration)**. If necessary, the pulley can be prevented from turning by counterholding with a spanner or socket on the crankshaft sprocket bolt.
5 Remove the auxiliary drivebelt, as described in Chapter 1, Section 27.
6 Unscrew the bolts securing the pulley to the sprocket, and remove the pulley. Discard the bolts – new ones must be fitted.

Refitting

7 Refit the pulley over the locating peg on the crankshaft sprocket, then fit the new pulley securing bolts.
8 Refit the auxiliary drivebelt as described in Chapter 1, Section 27.
9 Prevent the crankshaft from turning as

during removal, then fit the pulley securing bolts, and tighten to the specified torque.
10 Refit the wheel arch liner.
11 Refit the roadwheel and lower the vehicle to the ground.

6 Timing belt covers – removal and refitting

Upper outer cover

1 Pull the engine top cover upwards to release the mountings.
2 Release the hoses from the retaining clips on the right-hand side of the cylinder head

6.2 Unclip the hoses from their retaining clips

6.5 Supplementary fuel pump retaining bolts (arrowed)

and move them to one side **(see illustration)**.
3 Disconnect the wiring plug, undo the retaining bolt, and remove the pressure differential sender (for particulate filter) including bracket from the top of the engine mounting and move it to one side.
4 Undo the retaining bolt, then twist the washer reservoir filler neck to remove it from engine compartment **(see illustration)**.
5 Slide up the hose retaining clips, then undo the two retaining bolts and remove the supplementary fuel pump **(see illustration)**.
6 Disconnect the radiator outlet temperature sensor wiring plug from the sensor in the right-hand coolant pipe **(see illustration)**. Undo the retaining nut and bolt and move the coolant pipe clear of the timing belt cover.

6.4 Remove the washer reservoir filler neck

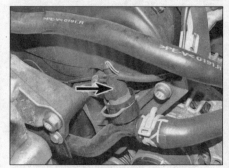

6.6 Disconnect the temperature sensor wiring plug (arrowed)

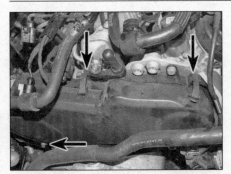

6.7a Release the clips (arrowed)...

6.7b...and manoeuvre the timing belt upper cover from place

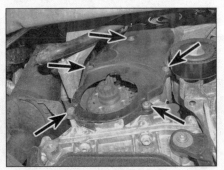

6.11a Undo the lower cover retaining bolts (arrowed)...

6.11b ...and manoeuvre the lower cover from place

6.15a Remove the retaining bolts...

6.15b ...and remove the rear cover

7 Release the three clips and remove the timing belt upper cover **(see illustrations)**.

8 Refitting is a reversal of removal, noting that the lower edge of the upper cover engages with the centre cover.

Lower outer cover

9 Remove the upper cover as described previously.

10 If not already done, remove the crankshaft pulley as described in Chapter 2A, Section 5.

11 Unscrew the five bolts securing the lower cover, and remove it **(see illustrations)**.

12 Refitting is a reversal of removal; noting that the upper edge of the lower cover engages with the upper cover.

Rear cover

13 Remove the timing belt, tensioner and sprockets as described in Chapter 2A, Sections 7 and 8.

14 Undo the retaining bolt and remove the rear hub cover from the end of the camshaft.

15 Slacken and withdraw the retaining bolts and lift the timing belt inner cover from the studs on the end of the engine, and remove it from the engine compartment**(see illustrations)**. It may be required to remove the coolant pump (Chapter 3), before the rear cover can be removed.

16 Refitting is a reversal of removal.

7   Timing belt – removal, inspection and refitting

Note: *There are two types of tensioner fitted to this engine and they are not interchangeable (see illustration). Check to see which type is fitted before removing the timing belt. Type A tensioner requires a locking pin for installation and it tensions the belt by rotating clockwise. Type B tensioner does not require a locking pin for installation and it tensions the belt by rotating anti-clockwise. See text.*

Removal

1 The primary function of the toothed timing belt is to drive the camshaft, but it also drives the coolant pump and high-pressure fuel pump. Should the belt slip or break in service, the valve timing will be disturbed and piston-to-valve contact may occur, resulting in serious engine damage. For this reason, it is important that the timing belt is tensioned correctly, and inspected regularly for signs of wear or deterioration.

2 Switch off the ignition and all electrical consumers and remove the ignition key.

3 Set the engine to TDC on No. 1 cylinder as described in Section 3.

4 Slacken the three bolts securing the

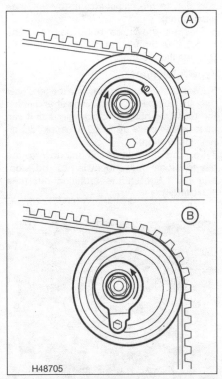

7.0 Two types of tensioner type (A) and (B)

A Roller tensions clockwise
B Roller tensions anti-clockwise

7.4 Slacken the sprocket-to-hub bolts (arrowed)

7.5 Slacken the high-pressure fuel pump sprocket bolts (arrowed)

7.6 Insert an Allen key, slacken the nut, and rotate the hub anti-clockwise until a 2 mm rod/drill bit (arrowed) can be inserted to lock the hub to the pulley

7.7 Rotate the tensioner hub clockwise until it hits the stop

sprocket to the camshaft hub by 90° **(see illustration)**.

5 Slacken the three bolts securing the sprocket to the high-pressure fuel pump by 90° **(see illustration)**.

Type A tensioner

6 Insert a suitable Allen key into the tensioner hub, then slacken the retaining nut and rotate the tensioner hub anti-clockwise until it can be locked in place using a 2.0 mm pin/drill bit **(see illustration)**.

7 Leaving the pin in place, now rotate the tensioner hub clockwise to the stop, and hand-tighten the retaining nut **(see illustration)**.

Type B tensioner

8 Insert a suitable Allen key into the tensioner hub, then slacken the retaining nut and rotate the tensioner hub clockwise, until the tensioner hub is loosened. When in position hand-tighten the retaining nut.

All engines

9 If the original timing belt is to be refitted, mark the running direction of the belt, to ensure correct refitting.

Caution: If the belt appears to be in good condition and can be re-used, it is essential that it is refitted the same way around, otherwise accelerated wear will result, leading to premature failure.

10 Slide the belt from the sprockets, taking

care not to twist or kink the belt excessively if it is to be re-used.

Inspection

11 Examine the belt for evidence of contamination by coolant or lubricant. If this is the case, find the source of the contamination before progressing any further. Check the belt for signs of wear or damage, particularly around the leading edges of the belt teeth. Renew the belt if its condition is in doubt; the cost of belt renewal is negligible compared with potential cost of the engine repairs, should the belt fail in service. The belt must be renewed if it has covered the mileage given in Chapter 1, however, if it has covered less, it is prudent to renew it regardless of condition, as a precautionary measure.

12 If the timing belt is not going to be refitted for some time, it is a wise precaution to hang a warning label on the steering wheel, to remind yourself (and others) not to attempt to start the engine. Have the battery disconnected to prevent any engine damage.

13 If the tensioner roller is to be renewed, the engine mounting will also need to be removed, as described in Section 17. Then the tensioner removed as described in Section 8.

Refitting

14 Ensure that the crankshaft and camshaft are still set to TDC on No 1 cylinder, as described in Section 3. The camshaft sprocket bolts should be renewed, and slackened at this point.

15 Renew the high-pressure fuel pump sprocket bolts one at a time. They should also be slackened.

16 Using a screwdriver on the bolts heads, rotate the high-pressure fuel pump clockwise until a 6.0 mm locking pin/drill bit can be inserted into the housing adjacent to the sprocket, locking the pump in place **(see illustration)**.

17 Rotate the camshaft sprocket and high-pressure fuel pump sprocket fully clockwise so that the securing bolts are at the end of the elongated holes **(see illustrations)**.

18 Loop the timing belt loosely under the crankshaft sprocket.

7.16 Rotate the high-pressure fuel pump clockwise until a 6 mm drill bit/rod can be inserted into the housing and hub(arrowed)

7.17a Rotate the sprockets fully clockwise until the fuel pump sprocket…

7.17b …and camshaft sprocket bolts are at the end of the elongated holes

7.20 Timing belt routing

7.21a Rotate the tensioner clockwise...

Note: *Observe any direction of rotation markings on the belt.*

19 Fit the belt around the tensioner pulley, engage the timing belt teeth with the camshaft sprockets, then manoeuvre it into position around the coolant pump sprocket and the fuel pump sprocket. Make sure that the belt teeth seat correctly on the sprockets.

Note: *Slight adjustment to the position of the camshaft sprocket may be necessary to achieve this. Avoid bending the belt back on itself or twisting it excessively as you do this.*

20 Finally, fit the belt around the idler roller **(see illustration)**. Ensure that any slack in the belt is in the section of belt that passes over the tensioner roller.

Type A tensioner

21 Loosen the timing belt tensioner securing nut, and pull out the tensioner locking pin. Turn the tensioner clockwise with an Allen key until the pointer is just past the middle of the gap in the tensioner base plate **(see illustrations)**. With the tensioner held in this position, tighten the securing nut to the specified torque and angle.

Type B tensioner

22 Loosen the timing belt tensioner securing nut, and turn the tensioner anti-clockwise with an Allen key until the pointer is just past the middle of the gap in the tensioner base plate **(see illustration)**. With the tensioner held in this position, tighten the securing nut to the specified torque and angle.

All engines

23 Counterhold the camshaft sprocket and fuel pump sprocket with a home made tool to prevent any rotation, and then tighten the camshaft sprocket and fuel pump sprocket bolts to 20 Nm **(see illustrations)**.

24 Remove the sprockets' locking tools and the crankshaft locking tool **(see illustrations)**.

25 Using a spanner or wrench and socket on the crankshaft pulley centre bolt, rotate the crankshaft clockwise through two complete revolutions. Reset the engine to TDC on No.1

7.21b ...until the pointer (arrowed) is just past the gap in the base plate

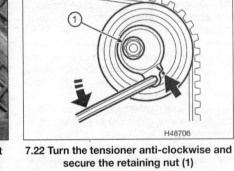

7.22 Turn the tensioner anti-clockwise and secure the retaining nut (1)

7.23a Counterhold the camshaft sprocket...

7.23b ...and the pump sprocket, while the bolts are tightened

7.24a Remove the upper locking pins...

7.24b ...and crankshaft locking tool

7.26 Check the pointer (arrowed) is centred or within 5mm to the right of the gap in the base plate

7.27 Slight misalignment of the pump sprocket timing hole (arrowed) is acceptable

8.4 Coolant pipe upper mounting bolt and lower mounting nut (arrowed)

cylinder, with reference to Section 3 and refit the crankshaft locking tool.

26 Check that the tensioner roller indicator arm is centred, or within a maximum of 5 mm to the right of the notch in the base plate **(see illustration)**. If not, hold the tensioner hub stationary with an Allen key, slacken the retaining nut and position the arm in the centre of the notch. Tighten the retaining nut to the specified torque. Remove the Allen key.

27 Check that the camshaft sprocket locking pin can still be inserted. **Note:** *It's very difficult to align the locking point of the fuel pump hub again* **(see illustration)**. *However, a slight misalignment of holes will not affect engine performance.*

28 If the camshaft sprocket locking pin cannot be inserted, pull the crankshaft locking tool slight away from the engine, and rotate the crankshaft anti-clockwise slightly past TDC. Now slowly rotate the crankshaft clockwise until the camshaft sprocket locking tool can be inserted.

29 If the locating pin of the crankshaft locking tool is to the left of the corresponding hole, slacken the camshaft sprocket bolts, slowly rotate the crankshaft clockwise until the locking tool can be fully inserted. Tighten the camshaft sprocket bolts to 20 Nm.

30 If the locating pin of the crankshaft locking tool is to the right of the corresponding hole, slacken the camshaft sprocket bolts, rotate

the crankshaft anti-clockwise slightly until the pin is to the left of the hole, then slowly rotate it clockwise until the lock tool can be fully inserted. Tighten the camshaft sprocket bolts to 20 Nm.

31 Remove the crankshaft and camshaft locking tools, then rotate the crankshaft 2 complete revolutions clockwise and check the locking tools can be reinserted. If necessary, repeat the adjustment procedure described previously.

32 Tighten the camshaft and fuel pump sprocket bolts to the specified torque.

33 The remainder of refitting is a reversal of removal.

8 Timing belt tensioner and sprockets – removal and refitting

Timing belt tensioner

Removal

1 In order to remove the timing belt tensioner, then engine mounting bracket must first be removed. Either support the engine from above using a crossbeam or an engine hoist, or support if from underneath with a trolley jack and block of wood.

2 Remove the timing belt as described in Section 7.

3 Undo the bolts and remove the right-hand engine mounting.

4 Undo the bolt securing the coolant pipe to the mounting bracket **(see illustration)**.

5 Working in the wheel arch area, undo the nut securing the lower end of the coolant pipe.

6 Undo the 3 retaining bolts and remove the engine mounting bracket **(see illustration)**.

7 Unscrew the timing belt tensioner nut, and remove the tensioner from the engine.

Refitting

8 When refitting the tensioner to the engine, ensure that the lug on the tensioner backplate engages with the corresponding cut-out in the rear timing belt cover, then refit the tensioner nut **(see illustration)**.

9 The remainder of refitting is a reversal of removal.

Idler pulleys

Removal

10 Remove the timing belt as described in Section Section 7.

11 Unscrew the relevant idler pulley/roller securing bolt/nut, and then withdraw the pulley **(see illustration)**.

Refitting

12 Refit the pulley and tighten the securing bolt or nut to the specified torque.

Note: *Renew the large roller/pulley retaining bolt (where applicable).*

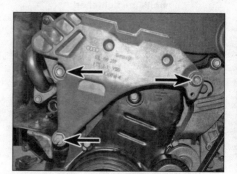

8.6 Engine mounting bracket bolts (arrowed)

8.8 Ensure the lug on the backplate engages with the cut-out in the timing belt cover (arrowed)

8.11 Timing belt idler pulleys (arrowed)

8.27 Fabricate a home-made tool to counterhold the hub. Undo the bolt...

8.28...and slide the hub from the camshaft

8.29 Ensure the integral key aligns with the keyway in the camshaft (arrowed)

13 Refit and tension the timing belt as described in Section 7.

Crankshaft sprocket

Note: *A new crankshaft sprocket securing bolt must be used on refitting.*

Removal

14 Remove the timing belt as described in Section 7.

15 The sprocket securing bolt must now be slackened, and the crankshaft must be prevented from turning as the sprocket bolt is unscrewed. To hold the sprocket, make up a suitable tool, and bolt it to the sprocket using two bolts bolted into two of the crankshaft pulley bolt holes.

16 Hold the sprocket using the tool, then slacken the sprocket securing bolt. Take care, as the bolt is very tight. Do not allow the crankshaft to turn as the bolt is slackened.

17 Unscrew the bolt, and slide the sprocket from the end of the crankshaft, noting which way round the sprocket's raised boss is fitted.

Refitting

18 Commence refitting by positioning the sprocket on the end of the crankshaft.

19 Fit a new sprocket securing bolt, then counter hold the sprocket using the method employed on removal, and tighten the bolt to the specified torque in the two stages given in the Specifications.

20 Refit the timing belt as described in Section 7.

Camshaft sprocket

Removal

21 Remove the timing belt as described in Section 7, then rotate the crankshaft 90° anti-clockwise to prevent any accidental piston-to-valve contact.

22 Unscrew and remove the three retaining bolts and remove the camshaft sprocket from the camshaft hub.

Refitting

23 Refit the sprocket ensuring that it is fitted the correct way round, as noted before removal, then insert the new sprocket bolts, and tighten by hand only at this stage.

24 If the crankshaft has been turned, turn the crankshaft clockwise 90° back to TDC.

25 Refit and tension the timing belt as described in Section 7.

Camshaft hub

Note: *VAG technicians use special tool T10051 to counter hold the hub, however it is possible to fabricate a suitable alternative.*

Removal

26 Remove the camshaft sprocket as described previously in this Section.

27 Engage special tool T10051 with the three locating holes in the face of the hub to prevent the hub from turning. If this tool is not available, fabricate a suitable alternative. Whilst holding the tool, undo the central hub retaining bolt about two turns **(see illustration)**.

28 Slide the hub from the camshaft. If necessary, attach Audi tool T10052 (or a similar three-legged puller) to the hub, and evenly tighten the puller until the hub is free of the camshaft taper **(see illustration)**.

Refitting

29 Ensure that the camshaft taper and the hub centre are clean and dry, locate the hub on the taper, noting that the built-in key in the hub taper must align with the keyway in the camshaft taper **(see illustration)**.

30 Hold the hub in this position with tool T10051 (or similar home-made tool), and tighten the central bolt to the specified torque.

31 Refit the camshaft sprocket as described previously in this Section.

Coolant pump sprocket

32 The coolant pump sprocket is integral with the coolant pump. Refer to Chapter 3 for details of coolant pump removal.

---

9 Camshaft and hydraulic tappets – removal, inspection and refitting

---

Note: *A new camshaft oil seal(s) will be required on refitting. VAG removal tool T40094 (or similar tool) will be required to refit the camshafts – this is necessary to prevent*

damage to the retaining frame and cylinder head as the camshafts are refitted.

Removal

1 Remove the camshaft hub as described in Section 8.

2 Remove the camshaft cover as described in Section 4.

3 Remove the brake vacuum pump as described in Chapter 9, Section 21.

4 Progressively unscrew the camshaft retaining frame bolts in the reverse of the sequence shown in **illustration 9.20**, and carefully remove the retaining frame.

5 Carefully lift the camshafts from the cylinder head, keeping them identified for location. Remove the oil seal from the end of the camshaft and discard it – a new one will be required for refitting.

6 Lift the rocker arms and hydraulic tappets from place. Store the rockers and tappets in a container with numbered compartments to ensure they are refitted to their correct locations. It is recommended that the tappets are kept immersed in oil for the period they are removed from the cylinder head.

Inspection

7 With the camshafts removed, examine the retaining frame and the bearing locations in the cylinder head for signs of obvious wear or pitting. If evident, a new cylinder head will probably be required. Also check that the oil supply holes in the cylinder head are free from obstructions.

8 Visually inspect the camshafts for evidence of wear on the surfaces of the lobes and journals. Normally their surfaces should be smooth and have a dull shine; look for scoring, erosion or pitting and areas that appear highly polished, indicating excessive wear. Accelerated wear will occur once the hardened exterior of the camshaft has been damaged, so always renew worn items.

Note: *If these symptoms are visible on the tips of the camshaft lobes, check the corresponding rocker arm, as it will probably be worn as well.*

9 If the machined surfaces of the camshaft appear discoloured or blued, it is likely that it has been overheated at some point,

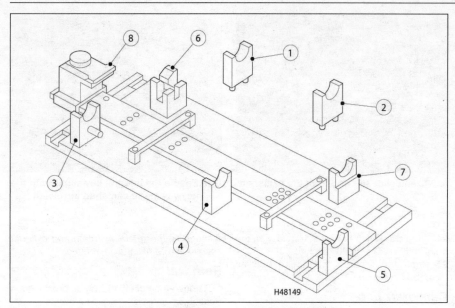

9.12a The different elements of tool No T40094

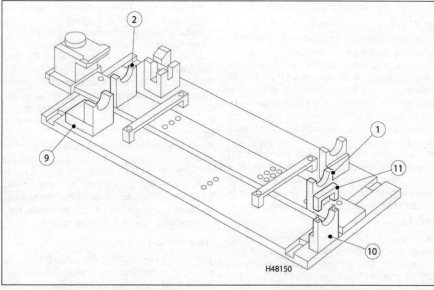

9.12b Position tools No 1, 2, 9 and 10 as shown

probably due to inadequate lubrication. This may have distorted the shaft, so have the camshaft runout and endfloat checked by an automotive engine reconditioning specialist.

10 Inspect the hydraulic tappets for obvious signs of wear or damage, and renew if necessary. Check that the oil holes in the tappets are free from obstructions.

Refitting

11 Oil the rocker arms and hydraulic tappets, and then refit them to their original positions.

⚠ **Warning: After fitting hydraulic tappets, wait a minimum of 30 minutes (or preferably, leave overnight) before starting the engine, to allow the tappets time to settle, otherwise the valve heads will strike the pistons.**

12 To set up the tool, remove the supports number 3, 4 and 5, then install the supports number 1, 2, 9 and 10 as shown (**see illustrations**).

13 Position the inlet camshaft as shown with the cylinder head bolt indent facing outwards, then slide the support number 8 into the slot in the end of the camshaft and remove any free play with a 0.50 mm feeler gauge (**see illustration**).

14 Position the exhaust camshaft on supports numbers 9 and 10, and fit the tool No 11 into the slot in the end of the camshaft (**see illustration**).

15 Fit the clamping tool No T40096 to the gear on the exhaust camshaft, tightening the knurled thumb wheel until the faces of the gear teeth are in alignment. If necessary, use a 13 mm spanner (**see illustration**).

16 Slide the exhaust camshaft towards the inlet camshaft until the gear teeth engage.

17 Ensure the gasket faces of the retaining frame are clean, then apply a smear of clean engine oil to the bearing surfaces and lower the frame into position over the camshafts. Ensure the bearing surfaces locate correctly on the camshafts.

18 Fit the clamping tool No T40095 over the camshafts and frame, and tighten the

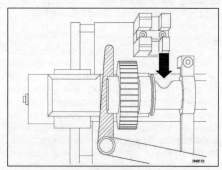

9.13 Position the inlet camshaft on the tool with the bolt indent (arrowed) facing outwards, then slide tool No 8 in to the slot in the end of the camshaft and use a 0.50 mm feeler gauge to remove any free play

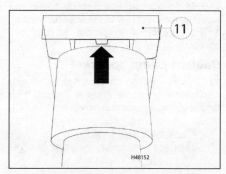

9.14 Fit tool No 11 into the slot (arrowed) in the end of the exhaust camshaft

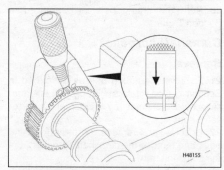

9.15 Tighten the thumbwheel to align the gear teeth. Ensure the clamping jaw with the arrow in seated on the wider gear

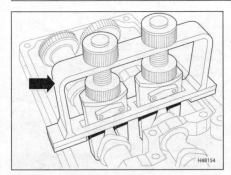

9.18 Secure the camshafts in place in the frame using tool No T40095 (arrowed)

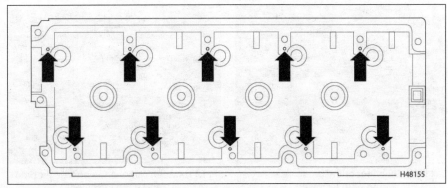

9.19 Apply a 2.0 mm thick bead of sealant to the area shown by the thick, black line. Take care not to block the oil holes (arrowed)

thumbwheels to hold the camshafts in position in the frame **(see illustration)**.

19 Ensure the sealing surfaces of the cylinder head are clean, and then apply a 2.0 mm wide bead of sealant (D 176 501 A1 or equivalent) as shown. Take care not to apply too much sealant, ensuring the oil holes supply holes are not blocked **(see illustration)**.

20 Slide out tool No's 8 and 11, then lift the camshafts, retaining frame and clamping tool from the tool No T40094. Place the camshafts, frame and tool in place on the cylinder head. Progressively and carefully, hand-tighten the frame retaining bolts in the sequence shown, until the retaining frame makes contact with the cylinder head over the complete surface, then tighten the bolts to the specified torque, again in the correct sequence **(see illustration)**.

21 Remove the gear aligning tool (T40096) and the clamping tool (T40095).

22 Renew the camshaft oil seal (Section 10), then drive in a new sealing cap.

23 The remainder of refitting is a reversal of removal.

10 Camshaft oil seals – renewal

Right-hand oil seal

1 Remove the camshaft sprocket and hub, as described in Section 8.

2 Drill two small holes into the existing oil

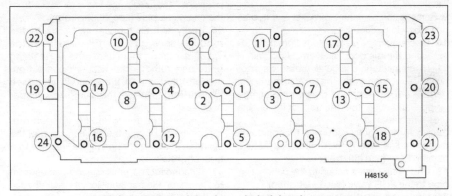

9.20 Camshaft retaining frame bolt tightening sequence

seal, diagonally opposite each other. Take great care to avoid drilling through into the seal housing or camshaft sealing surface. Thread two self-tapping screws into the holes, and using a pair of pliers, pull on the heads of the screws to extract the oil seal **(see illustration)**.

3 Clean out the seal housing and the sealing surface of the camshaft by wiping it with a lint-free cloth. Remove any swarf or burrs that may cause the seal to leak.

4 Do not lubricate the lip and outer edge of the new oil seal, push it over the camshaft until it is positioned in place above its housing. To prevent damage to the sealing lips, wrap some adhesive tape around the end of the camshaft.

5 Using a hammer and a socket of suitable diameter, drive the seal squarely into its housing.

Note: *Select a socket that bears only on the hard outer surface of the seal, not the inner lip that can easily be damaged.*

6 Refit the camshaft sprocket and its hub, as described in Section 8.

Left-hand oil seal

7 The left-hand camshaft oil seal is formed, by the brake vacuum pump seal, which is fitted to the cylinder head. Refer to Chapter 9, Section 21 for details of brake vacuum pump removal and refitting.

11 Cylinder head – removal, inspection and refitting

Note: *The cylinder head must be removed with the engine cold. New cylinder head bolts and a new cylinder head gasket will be required on refitting, and suitable studs will be required to guide the cylinder head into position – see text.*

Removal

1 Remove the battery as described in Chapter 5, Section 3.

2 Drain the cooling system (Chapter 1, Section 31) and engine oil (Chapter 1, Section 3).

3 Pull the plastic cover on the top of the engine upwards from its mountings.

4 Remove the air cleaner assembly as described in Chapter 4A, Section 2.

5 Undo the 3 bolts and remove the battery tray.

6 Remove the radiator cooling fan(s) and shroud as described in Chapter 3, Section 5.

7 Undo the bolts and remove the air hose/duct from the intercooler to the turbocharger. Release the wiring looms from the clips as necessary to enable the duct to be manoeuvred from place.

10.2 Bolt in a self-tapping screw, then pull the bolt and seal from place

11.11a Disconnect the pressure sensor wiring plug (arrowed)...

11.11b...then remove the charge air pipe and hose (arrowed)

11.12 Oil level dipstick guide tube bolt (arrowed)

8 Remove the camshaft cover as described in Section 4.

9 Remove the camshaft sprocket and hub as described in Section 8.

10 Disconnect the wiring plugs from the EGR valve and throttle body/intake manifold flap.

11 Disconnect the charge air pressure sensor wiring plug, then undo the 2 retaining bolts, release the clamps, and remove the charge air pipe and hose from the front of the engine **(see illustrations)**.

12 Undo the bolt securing the oil level dipstick guide tube to the throttle body/intake manifold flap **(see illustration)**.

13 Undo the 2 bolts securing the connecting pipe to the EGR valve **(see illustration)**.

14 Undo the front retaining bolt, twist the charge air pipe clockwise and disconnect

it from the turbocharger. Note their fitted positions, and unclip the vacuum hoses from the charge air pipe **(see illustration)**.

15 Apply a little lubrication spray to the rubber sleeve, pull up the pipe from the vacuum pump, then undo the 4 retaining bolts and remove the vacuum pump from the left-hand end of the cylinder head **(see illustration)**. Renew the pump-to-cylinder head seal.

16 Disconnect the coolant temperature sensor wiring plug at the left-hand end of the cylinder head, and release the wiring loom from any retaining clips.

17 Disconnect the gear change cables from the levers on the transmission, as described in Chapter 7A, Section 2 (manual transmission), or Chapter 7B, Section 4 (DSG transmission).

18 Undo the bolts/nut, securing the gear-change bracket to the top of the transmission. Move the bracket and cables to one side.

19 Undo the bolts securing the EGR pipe to the cooler at the left-hand end of the engine, and the nut securing the bracket to the cylinder head, then remove the pipe **(see illustration)**. Recover the gasket at each end.

20 Working underneath the vehicle, slacken the Allen bolt and release the clamp securing the diesel particulate filter/catalytic converter to the turbocharger, then undo the bolts/nuts securing the brackets to the cylinder block/head and lay the filter/converter to one side.

21 Undo the nuts and multi-spline bolts securing the EGR pipe to the right-hand end of the exhaust manifold and EGR cooler **(see illustration)**. Remove the pipe and recover the gaskets.

22 Trace the exhaust manifold gas temperature sensor wiring back, releasing it from any retaining clips, disconnect its wiring plug at the bulkhead, and slide it from the retaining bracket. Unclip the wiring loom from the top of the turbocharger heat shield.

23 Undo the bolt securing the support bracket/oil return pipe to the underside of the turbocharger, and then undo the bolt securing the top of the support bracket to the underside of the turbocharger. Now pull and twist the support bracket to disconnect it from the oil return pipe at the top. Remove

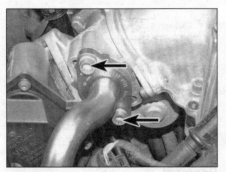

11.13 EGR pipe-to-valve bolts (arrowed)

11.14 Charge air pipe retaining bolt (arrowed). Note the position of the vacuum hoses

11.15 With some lubrication, the hose connection pulls up from the vacuum pump

11.19 EGR pipe-to-cooler bolts (arrowed)

11.21 Remove the EGR pipe between the manifold and cooler

11.23a Undo the banjo bolt at the base of the turbocharger support bracket/oil return pipe and the bolt at the top

11.23b Note the 2 O-ring seals (arrowed) at the base of the oil return pipe

11.26 Undo the bolt (arrowed) securing the timing belt guard

the pipe/bracket **(see illustrations)**. Note the O-ring and copper sealing washer on the lower banjo bolt, and the two O-rings fitted to the base of the oil return pipe still fitted to the turbocharger.

24 Note their fitted locations, then release the clamps and disconnect the various coolant hoses from the cylinder head.

25 Undo the bolt securing the turbocharger oil supply pipe bracket at the left-hand end of the cylinder head, the nut securing the bracket on the rear of the head, then undo the union bolts and remove the pipe. Renew any seals.

26 Undo the bolt securing the timing belt guard adjacent to the timing belt tensioner, and the bolt securing the camshaft position sensor, then remove the tensioner retaining nut **(see illustration)**.

27 Disconnect the turbocharger wastegate position sensor wiring plug, and the intake manifold changeover valve wiring plug. Note their fitted positions and disconnect the vacuum hoses from the EGR cooler (where the plastic pipe joins the metal pipe at the back of the cylinder head) and the turbocharger wastegate actuator. Undo the nuts securing the boost pressure solenoid valve to the

bulkhead. Release the loom wiring plug, lay the wiring loom and vacuum hoses over the front of the engine, clear of the cylinder head **(see illustration)**. Make a final check to ensure all relevant wiring and vacuum hoses have been disconnected. Note the loom/hose routing to aid refitting.

28 Using an M12 multi-splined tool (12-pointed star), undo the cylinder head bolts, working from the outside-in, evenly and gradually **(see illustration)**. Remove the bolts and recover the washers. Check that nothing remains connected, and starting at the gearbox side, lift the cylinder head from the engine block, sliding the belt tensioner from the mounting stud as the cylinder head is removed. Seek assistance if possible, as it is a heavy assembly.

29 Remove the gasket from the top of the block, noting the locating dowels. If the dowels are a loose fit, remove them and store them with the head for safekeeping. Do not discard the gasket yet – it will be needed for identification purposes. If desired, the manifolds can be removed from the cylinder head with reference to Chapter 4A, Section 5 (inlet manifold) or Chapter 4C Section 7 (turbocharger/exhaust manifold).

11.27 Undo the boost pressure solenoid valve nuts (arrowed)

Inspection

30 Dismantling and inspection of the cylinder head is covered in Chapter 2D.

Cylinder head gasket selection

Note: *A dial test indicator (DTI) will be required for this operation.*

31 Examine the old cylinder head gasket for manufacturer's identification markings **(see illustration)**. These will be in the form of holes, and a part number on the edge of the gasket. Unless new pistons have been fitted,

11.28 Undo the cylinder head bolts using a M12 multi-splined (12-pointed star) tool

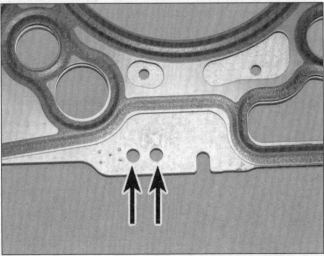

11.31 The holes (arrowed) identify the thickness of the cylinder head gasket

the new cylinder head gasket must be of the same type as the old one.

32 If new piston assemblies have been fitted as part of an engine overhaul, or if a new short engine is to be fitted, the projection of the piston crowns above the cylinder head mating face of the cylinder block at TDC must be measured. This measurement is used to determine the thickness of the new cylinder head gasket required.

33 Anchor a dial test indicator (DTI) to the top face (cylinder head gasket mating face) of the cylinder block, and zero the gauge on the gasket mating face.

34 Rest the gauge probe on No 1 piston crown, and turn the crankshaft slowly by hand until the piston reaches TDC. Measure and record the maximum piston projection at TDC **(see illustration)**.

35 Repeat the measurement for the remaining pistons, and record the results.

36 If the measurements differ from piston-to-piston, take the highest figure, and use this to determine the thickness of the head gasket required as follows.

Piston projection	Gasket identification (number of holes)
0.91 to 1.00 mm	1
1.01 to 1.10 mm	2
1.11 to 1.20 mm	3

37 Purchase a new gasket according to the results of the measurements.

Refitting

38 The mating faces of the cylinder head and block must be perfectly clean before refitting the head. Use a scraper to remove all traces of gasket and carbon, also clean the tops of the pistons. Take particular care with the aluminium surfaces, as the soft metal is easily damaged.

39 Make sure that debris is not allowed to enter the oil and water passages – this is particularly important for the oil circuit, as carbon could block the oil supply to the camshaft and crankshaft bearings. Using adhesive tape and paper, seal the water, oil and bolt holes in the cylinder block.

40 To prevent carbon entering the gap

11.34 Measure the piston protrusion using a DTI guage

between the pistons and bores, smear a little grease in the gap. After cleaning a piston, rotate the crankshaft to that the piston moves down the bore, and then wipe out the grease and carbon with a cloth rag. Clean the other piston crowns in the same way.

41 Check the head and block for nicks, deep scratches and other damage. If slight, they may be removed carefully with a file. More serious damage may be repaired by machining, but this is a specialist job.

42 If warpage of the cylinder head is suspected, use a straight-edge to check it for distortion, as described in Chapter 2D.

43 Ensure that the cylinder head bolt holes in the crankcase are clean and free of oil. Syringe or soak up any oil left in the bolt holes. This is most important in order that the correct bolt tightening torque can be applied, and to prevent the possibility of the block being cracked by hydraulic pressure when the bolts are tightened.

44 Turn the crankshaft anti-clockwise all the pistons at an equal height, approximately halfway down their bores from the TDC position (see Section 3). This will eliminate any risk of piston-to-valve contact as the cylinder head is refitted.

45 Where applicable, refit the manifolds with reference to Chapter 4A, Section 5 (inlet manifold) or Chapter 4C, Section 7 (turbocharger/exhaust manifold).

46 Ensure that the cylinder head locating dowels are in place in the cylinder block, and then fit the new cylinder head gasket over

11.46 Ensure the dowels are in place, then fit the new gasket with the part number uppermost (arrowed)

the dowels, ensuring that the part number is uppermost **(see illustration)**. Note that Audi recommend that the gasket is only removed from its packaging immediately prior to fitting.

47 Lower the cylinder head into position on the gasket, ensuring that it engages correctly over the dowels. Refit the timing belt tensioner as the cylinder head is refitted.

48 Fit the washers in place then fit the new cylinder head bolts to the locations, and bolt them in as far as possible by hand. Do not oil the bolt threads.

49 Working progressively, in sequence, tighten all the cylinder head bolts to the specified Stage 1 torque **(see illustrations)**.

50 Again working progressively, in sequence, tighten all the cylinder head bolts to the specified Stage 2 torque.

51 Tighten all the cylinder head bolts, in sequence, through the specified Stage 3 angle **(see illustration)**.

52 Finally, tighten all the cylinder head bolts, in sequence, through the specified Stage 4 angle.

53 The remainder of the refitting procedure is a reversal of the removal procedure, noting the following points:

a) *Tighten all fasteners to their specified torque where given.*

b) *Renew all seals and gaskets.*

c) *Refill the cooling system, as described in Chapter 1, Section 31.*

d) *Refill the engine oil, as described in Chapter 1, Section 3.*

e) *Ensure all wiring is correctly routed.*

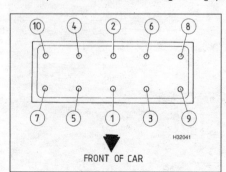
11.49a Cylinder head bolt tightening sequence

11.49b Tighten the cylinder head bolts to the Stage 1 torque

11.51 Use an angle-tightening gauge

12 Sump – removal and refitting

Removal

1 Apply the handbrake, then jack up the front of the vehicle and support securely on axle stands (see *Jacking and vehicle support* in the Reference chapter).
2 Remove the securing bolts and withdraw the engine undershield.
3 Drain the engine oil as described in Chapter 1, Section 3.
4 Release the clamp, raise the retaining clip and remove the air duct from the intercooler outlet **(see illustration)**.
5 Undo the retaining bolts, release the clamp and remove the charge air pipe from the front of the cylinder block **(see illustration 11.11a and 11.11b)**. Disconnect the charge air pressure sensor wiring plug as the pipe is withdrawn.
6 Undo the retaining bolt and move the electric coolant circulation pump to one side **(see illustration)**.
7 Undo the bolt securing the turbo-to-intercooler air pipe to the sump.
8 Disconnect the wiring connector from the oil level/temperature sender in the sump.
9 Pull the sump insulation cover downwards at the rear to release the retaining clips, then prise down the centre clip and pull the clip on the front side of the cover downwards (where fitted) **(see illustrations)**.
10 Unscrew and remove the bolts securing the sump to the cylinder block, and the bolts securing the sump to the transmission casing, then withdraw the sump. If necessary, release the sump by tapping with a soft-faced hammer.

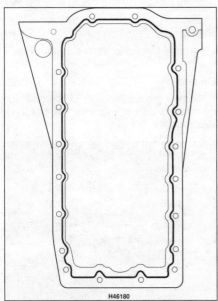

12.12 Apply a bead of sealant around the inside of the bolt holes

12.4 Raise the clip (arrowed) and disconnect the air duct from the intercooler

12.9a Pull the insulation down at the rear to release the clips (arrowed)

Refitting

11 Begin refitting by thoroughly cleaning the mating faces of the sump and cylinder block. Ensure that all traces of old sealant are removed.
12 Ensure that the cylinder block mating face of the sump is free from all traces of old sealant, oil and grease, and then apply a 2.0 to 3.0 mm thick bead of silicone sealant (VW D 176 404 A2 or equivalent) to the sump **(see illustration)**. Note that the sealant should be run around the inside of the bolt holes in the sump. The sump must be fitted within 5 minutes of applying the sealant.
13 Offer the sump up to the cylinder block, then refit the sump-to-cylinder block bolts, and lightly tighten them by hand, working progressively in a diagonal sequence.

13.2 Remove the oil pick-up pipe/filter

12.6 Electric coolant circulation pump retaining bolt (arrowed)

12.9b At the front, prise down the centre pin and pull the clip downwards (arrowed)

Note: *If the sump is being refitted with the engine and transmission separated, make sure that the sump is flush with the flywheel end of the cylinder block.*
14 Refit the sump-to-transmission casing bolts, and tighten them lightly, using a socket.
15 Again working in a diagonal sequence, lightly tighten the sump-to-cylinder block bolts, using a socket.
16 Tighten the sump-to-transmission casing bolts to the specified torque.
17 Working in a diagonal sequence, progressively tighten the sump-to-cylinder block bolts to the specified torque.
18 The remainder of refitting is a reversal of removal, noting to allow at least 30 minutes from the time of refitting the sump for the sealant to dry, then refill the engine with oil, with reference to Chapter 1, Section 7.

13 Oil pump and drive belt (engines without a balance shaft) – removal, inspection and refitting

Oil pump removal

1 Remove the sump as described in Section 12.
2 Unscrew the flange bolts and remove the oil pick-up pipe/filter from the oil pump **(see illustration)**. Recover the O-ring seal and discard, as a new one will be required for refitting.

13.3 Remove the oil baffle plate bolt (which is also one of the oil pump mounting bolts)

13.4 Oil pump mounting bolts (arrowed)

3 Unscrew the securing bolt, and remove the oil baffle from the cylinder block **(see illustration)**.

4 Unscrew and remove the mounting bolts, and release the oil pump from the dowels in the crankcase **(see illustration)**. Unhook the oil pump drive sprocket from the belt and withdraw the oil pump and oil pick-up pipe from the engine. Note, the bolt holding the baffle plate is also one of the pump mounting bolts.

Oil pump inspection

5 Clean the pump thoroughly, and inspect for signs of damage or wear. If evident, renew the oil pump.

Oil pump refitting

6 Prime the pump with oil by pouring oil into the pick-up pipe aperture while turning the driveshaft.

7 If the drive belt and crankshaft sprocket have been removed, delay refitting them until after the oil pump has been mounted on the cylinder block.

8 Engage the oil pump sprocket with the drive belt, and then locate the oil pump on the dowels. Refit and tighten the mounting bolts to the specified torque.

9 Where applicable, refit the drive belt and

crankshaft sprocket using a reversal of the removal procedure.

10 Refit the oil baffle plate, and tighten the securing bolt.

11 Refit the pick-up pipe to the oil pump, using a new O-ring seal, and tighten the securing bolts **(see illustration)**.

12 Refit the sump as described in Section 12.

Oil pump drive belt and sprockets

Note: Audi sealant (D 176 404 A2 or equivalent) will be required to seal the crankshaft oil seal housing on refitting, and it is advisable to fit a new crankshaft oil seal.

Removal

13 Proceed as described in paragraphs 1 and 2.

14 To remove the belt, remove the timing belt as described in Section 7, then unbolt the crankshaft oil seal housing from the cylinder block, as described in Chapter 2A, Section 15. Unhook the belt from the sprocket on the end of the crankshaft.

15 The oil pump drive sprocket is a press-fit on the crankshaft, and cannot easily be removed. Consult an Audi dealer for advice if the sprocket is worn or damaged.

Inspection

16 It is wise to renew the belt in any case if

the engine is to be overhauled, If there is any doubt as to the condition of the belt, renew it.

Refitting

17 If the oil pump has been removed, refit the oil pump as described previously in this Section before refitting the belt and sprocket.

18 Engage the oil pump sprocket with the belt, then engage the belt with the crankshaft sprocket.

19 Fit a new crankshaft oil seal to the housing, and refit the housing as described in Section 16.

20 Where applicable, refit the oil baffle and pick-up pipe, and tighten the securing bolts.

21 Refit the sump as described in Section 12.

14 Oil pump and balance shaft assembly – removal, inspection and refitting

Removal

1 Remove the sump as described in Section 12.

Oil pump

2 Remove the retaining circlip, then pull the oil pump shaft out using an M3 bolt **(see illustrations)**.

13.11 Fit a new seal to the end of the oil pick-up pipe

14.2a Remove the circlip...

14.2b ...and pull out the oil pump shaft using an M3 bolt

14.3 Oil pump pick-up pipe bolts (arrowed)

14.4 Oil pump mounting bolts (arrowed)

14.9 Renew the pick-up pipe O-ring seal

3 Undo the retaining bolts, and then detach the pick-up pipe from the pump **(see illustration)**.

4 Undo the bolts and detach the oil pump from the balance shaft assembly **(see illustration)**.

Balance shaft assembly

5 Lock the camshafts and crankshaft at TDC on No 1 cylinder as described in Section 3.

6 Working gradually and evenly, undo the retaining bolts and detach the balance shaft assembly from the base of the cylinder block.

Inspection

7 At the time of writing, it would appear that no parts are available for the oil pump or balance shaft assembly. If defective, the oil pump or balance shaft assembly must be renewed. Consult an Audi dealer or parts specialist.

Refitting

Oil pump

8 Refit the pump to the balance shaft assembly and tighten the retaining bolts to the specified torque.

9 Refit the oil pick-up pipe using a new O-ring, then tighten the retaining bolts to the specified torque **(see illustration)**.

10 Push the driveshaft into place, and secure it with the circlip.

11 The remainder of refitting is a reversal of removal.

Balance shaft assembly

Note: *If the original balance shaft assembly is being refitted, it's essential that neither the drivegear on the crankshaft or the crankshaft itself has been renewed, or the idler gear bolt has been slackened. If they have, proceed under the heading for the installation of a new balance shaft assembly.*

Refitting the original assembly

12 Rotate the balance shaft until VAG tool No T10255 can be fitted into the groove on the left-hand end of the rear shaft **(see illustrations)**.

13 Ensure the engine is still locked at TDC for No 1 cylinder, and then position the balance shaft assembly over the locating dowels on the base of the cylinder block. The idler gear must engage with the drivegear of the crankshaft, and there must be noticeable backlash.

14 Fit the new balance shaft assembly retaining bolts, and working from the centre outwards, tighten them to the specified torque. Remove the special tool.

15 The remainder of refitting is a reversal of removal.

Fitting a new balance shaft assembly

16 New balance shaft assemblies are supplied with an idler gear with a special coating. Once fitted, the coating wears down to give the correct backlash between the gears.

17 Ensure the engine is still locked at TDC for No 1 cylinder as described in Section 3.

18 Slacken the idler gear retaining bolt 90°.

19 Position the balance shaft assembly over the locating dowels on the base of the cylinder block, ensuring the white mark on the idler gear is centrally aligned with the crankshaft drivegear. Idler gears not marked with a white mark can be installed in any position.

20 Fit the new balance shaft assembly retaining bolts, and working from the centre outwards, tighten them to the specified torque.

21 Rotate the balance shaft until VAG tool No T10255 can be fitted into the groove on the left-hand end of the rear shaft **(see illustration 14.12a, 14.12b and 14.12c)**.

22 Fit the balance shaft drivegear onto the shaft so the holes in the gear align with the holes in the shaft. Tighten the retaining bolts to the specified torque.

23 Have an assistant push the idler gear between the two gears to remove any backlash. At the same time, rotate the balance shaft anti-clockwise slightly, and tighten the idler gear retaining bolt to the specified torque. Remove the balance shaft locking tool.

24 The remainder of refitting is a reversal of removal.

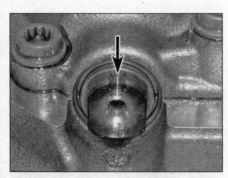

14.12a Rotate the balance shaft until the groove (arrowed) on the end of the rear shaft is vertical...

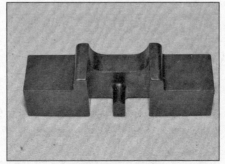

14.12b...and tool No T10255...

14.12c...can be fitted

15.5a Use a locking tool to counterhold the flywheel

15.9 Flywheel warpage check – see text

15 Flywheel – removal, inspection and refitting

Removal

1 On manual transmission models, remove the transmission (Chapter 7A, Section 3) and clutch (Chapter 6, Section 6).

2 On automatic transmission models, remove the semi-automatic (DSG) transmission as described in Chapter 7B, Section 2.

3 Manual models are fitted with a dual-mass flywheel, which can only be fitted in one position due to the offset of the mounting bolt holes in the end of the crankshaft.

4 Rotate the outside of the dual-mass flywheel so that the bolts align with the holes (if necessary).

5 Unscrew the bolts and remove the flywheel. Use a locking tool to counterhold the flywheel **(see illustration)**. Discard the bolts, as new ones must be fitted.

Note: *In order not to damage the flywheel, do not allow the bolt heads to make contact with the flywheel during the unscrewing procedure.*

Inspection

6 Check the flywheel for wear and damage. Examine the starter ring gear for excessive wear to the teeth. If the driveplate or its ring gear is damaged, the complete driveplate must be renewed. The flywheel ring gear, however, may be renewed separately from the flywheel, but the work should be entrusted to an Audi dealer. If the clutch friction face is discoloured or scored excessively, it may be possible to regrind it, but this work should also be entrusted to an Audi dealer.

7 The following are guidelines only, but should indicate whether professional inspection is necessary. The dual-mass flywheel should be checked as follows:

8 There should be no cracks in the drive surface of the flywheel. If cracks are evident, the flywheel may need renewing.

Warpage

9 Place a straightedge across the face of the drive surface, and check by trying to insert a feeler gauge between the straightedge and the drive surface **(see illustration)**. The flywheel will normally warp like a bowl – i.e. higher on the outer edge. If the warpage is more than 0.40 mm, the flywheel may need renewing.

Free rotational movement

10 This is the distance the drive surface of the flywheel can be turned independently of the flywheel primary element, using finger effort alone. Move the drive surface in one direction and make a mark where the locating pin aligns with the flywheel edge. Move the drive surface in the other direction (finger pressure only) and make another mark **(see illustration)**. The total of free movement should not exceed 20.0 mm. If it's more, the flywheel may need renewing.

Total rotational movement

11 This is the total distance the drive surface can be turned independently of the flywheel primary element. Insert two bolts into the clutch pressure plate/damper unit mounting holes, and with the crankshaft/flywheel held stationary, use a lever/pry bar between the bolts and use some effort to move the drive surface fully in one direction – make a mark where the locating pin aligns with the flywheel edge. Now force the drive surface fully in the opposite direction, and make another mark. The total rotational movement should not exceed 44.0 mm. If it does, have the flywheel professionally inspected.

Lateral movement

12 The lateral movement (up and down) of the drive surface in relation to the primary element of the flywheel should not exceed 2.0 mm. If it does, the flywheel may need renewing. This can be checked by pressing the drive surface down on one side into the flywheel (flywheel horizontal) and making an alignment mark between the drive surface and the inner edge of the primary element. Now press down on the opposite side of the drive surface, and make another mark above the original one. The difference between the two marks is the lateral movement **(see illustration)**.

Refitting

13 Refitting is a reversal of removal. Use new bolts when refitting the flywheel or driveplate, and coat the threads of the bolts with locking fluid before inserting them. Tighten them to the specified torque.

16 Crankshaft oil seals – renewal

Note: *The oil seals are a PTFE (Teflon) type and are fitted dry, without using any grease or oil. These have a wider sealing lip and have been introduced instead of the coil spring type oil seal.*

Timing belt end oil seal

1 Remove the timing belt as described in Section 7, and the crankshaft sprocket with reference to Section 8.

2 To remove the seal without removing the housing, drill two small holes diagonally opposite each other, insert self-tapping screws, and pull on the heads of the screws with pliers **(see illustration)**.

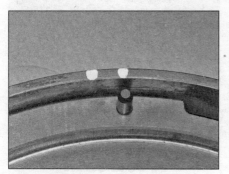

15.10 Flywheel free rotational movement check alignment marks – see text

15.12 Flywheel lateral movement check marks – see text

16.2 Pull the screw and seal from place using pliers

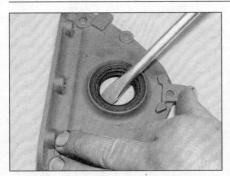
16.3 Prise the oil seal from the crankshaft oil seal housing

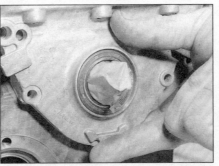
16.9 Slide the oil seal housing over the end of the crankshaft

16.13 Sealing flange bolts (arrowed)

3 Alternatively, to remove the oil seal complete with its housing, proceed as follows.
a) *Remove the sump as described in Section 12. This is necessary to ensure a satisfactory seal between the sump and oil seal housing on refitting.*
b) *Unscrew and remove the oil seal housing.*
c) *Working on the bench, lever the oil seal from the housing using a suitable screwdriver. Take care not to damage the seal seating in the housing (see illustration).*

4 Thoroughly clean the oil seal seating in the housing.

5 Wind a length of tape around the end of the crankshaft to protect the oil seal lips as the seal (and housing, where applicable) is fitted.

6 Fit a new oil seal to the housing, pressing or driving it into position using a socket or tube of suitable diameter. Ensure that the socket or tube bears only on the hard outer ring of the seal, and take care not to damage the seal lips. Press or drive the seal into position until it is seated on the shoulder in the housing. Make sure that the closed end of the seal is facing outwards.

7 If the oil seal housing has been removed, proceed as follows, otherwise proceed to paragraph 11.

8 Clean all traces of old sealant from the crankshaft oil seal housing and the cylinder block, then coat the cylinder block mating faces of the oil seal housing with a 2.0 to 3.0 mm thick bead of silicone sealant (VW D 176 404 A2, or equivalent). Note that the seal housing must be refitted within 5 minutes of applying the sealant.

Caution: DO NOT put excessive amounts of sealant onto the housing as it may get into the sump and block the oil pick-up pipe.

9 Refit the oil seal housing, and tighten the bolts progressively to the specified torque **(see illustration)**.

10 Refit the sump as described in Section 12.

11 Refit the crankshaft sprocket with reference to Section 8, and the timing belt as described in Section 7.

Flywheel end oil seal

Note: *In these engines, the seal, sealing flange and sender wheel are a complete unit. Special tools are required to refit the sealing flange,*

and press the sender wheel onto the end of the crankshaft. It is not possible to accurately fit these parts without the tools, which may be available from Audi (part No T10134) and are available from aftermarket automotive tool specialists.

12 Remove the flywheel as described in Section 15, then prise the intermediate plate from the locating dowels on the cylinder block.

13 Undo the bolts securing the sealing flange to the cylinder block **(see illustration)**.

14 Insert three 6 x 35 mm bolts into the threaded holes in the sealing flange. Tighten the bolts gradually and evenly, and press the sealing flange and sender wheel from the crankshaft/cylinder block **(see illustration)**. The seal, sender wheel and sealing flange are supplied as a complete unit.

16.14 Bolt in three 6 x 35 mm bolts (arrowed) and draw the sealing flange and sender wheel from place

16.16b...then clamp it in a vice

15 Ensure the mating face of the cylinder block is clean and free from debris. The new sealing flange/seal/sender wheel assembly is supplied with a sealing lip support ring, which serves as a fitting sleeve, and must not be removed prior to installation. Equally, the sender wheel must not be separated from the assembly.

16 If using the Audi tool, proceed as follows. If using an aftermarket tool specialist's product, follow the instructions supplied with the tool. Rotate the large spindle nut until it's level with the end of the clamping surface of the spindle, then clamp the spindle in a vice **(see illustrations)**.

17 Press the tool housing downwards until it rests on the nut and washer. Rotate the nut until the inner part of the tool is at the same height as the housing **(see illustration)**.

16.16a Rotate the nut until it is level with the end of the clamping surface (arrowed)...

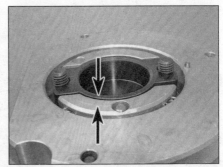
16.17 Rotate the nut until the inner part of the tool is flush with the housing (arrowed)

16.18a Remove the securing clip...

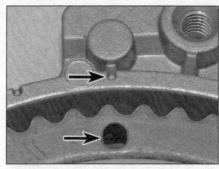

16.18b...the hole in the sender wheel should align with the marking on the flange (arrowed)

16.19a Press the assembly downwards on a clean, flat surface...

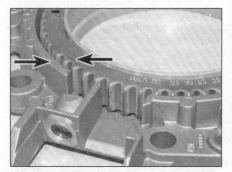

16.19b...so the upper edge of the sender wheel is level with the edge of the flange (arrowed)

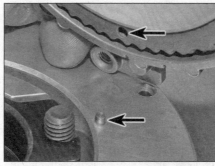

16.20 Fit the flange to the tool, ensuring the pin locates in the hole (arrowed)

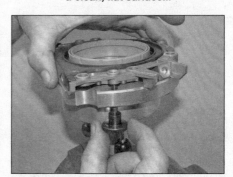

16.21 With the pin engaged in the hole, tighten the 3 knurled bolts to secure the flange to the tool

18 Remove the seal securing clip. The hole on the sender wheel must align with the marking on the sealing flange (see illustrations).

16.23 Unscrew the nut to the end of the thread, and push the spindle in as far as possible

19 Place the flange outer side down on a clean, flat surface, then press the seal guide fitting sleeve (supplied ready fitted), housing, and sender wheel downwards until all the components are flat on the surface. In this position the upper edge of the sender wheel should be level with the edge of the sealing flange (see illustrations).

20 Place the sealing flange on the assembly tool, so the pin locates in the hole in the sender wheel (see illustration).

21 Push the sealing flange and guide fitting sleeve against the tool whilst tightening the 3 knurled bolts. Ensure the pin is still located in the sender wheel (see illustration).

22 Ensure the end of the crankshaft is clean, and is locked at TDC on No 1 cylinder as described in Section 3.

23 Unscrew the large nut to the end of

the spindle threads, then press the spindle inwards as far as possible (see illustration).

24 Align the flat side of the assembly with the sump flange, then secure the tool to the crankshaft using the integral Allen bolts (see illustration). Only hand-tighten the bolts.

25 Insert two M7 x 35 mm bolts to guide the sealing flange to the cylinder block (see illustration).

26 Using hand-pressure alone, push the tool assembly onto the crankshaft until the seal guide fitting sleeve contacts the crankshaft flange, then push the guide pin (black knob) into the hole in the crankshaft. This is to ensure the sender wheel reaches its correct installation position (see illustration).

27 Rotate the large nut until it makes contact with the tool housing, then tighten it to 35 Nm (26 lbf ft). After tightening this nut, a small air

16.24 Hand-tighten the Allen bolts to secure the tool to the crankshaft (arrowed)

16.25 Use 2 M7 x 35 mm bolts (arrowed) to guide the sealing flange

16.26 Push the black knob (arrowed) into the hole in the crankshaft

16.27 After tightening the spindle nut there should be an air gap between the sealing flange and the cylinder block(arrowed)

16.29 Measure the fitted depth of the sender wheel in relation to the end of the crankshaft

17.7 Unbolt the supplementary fuel pump from the top of the mounting

gap must still be present between the sealing flange and cylinder block **(see illustration)**.

28 Unscrew the large nut; the two M7 x 35 mm bolts, the three knurled bolts and the Allen bolts securing the tool to the crankshaft. Remove the tool, and pull the seal guide fitting sleeve from place (if it didn't come out with the tool).

29 Use a vernier caliper or feeler gauge to measure the fitted depth of the sender wheel in relation to the crankshaft flange **(see illustration)**. The correct depth is 0.5 mm.

30 If the gap is correct, fit the sealing flange bolts and tighten them to the specified torque.

31 If the gap is too small, re-attach the tool to the sealing flange and crankshaft, then refit the two M7 x 35 mm guide bolts to the flange. Tighten the large spindle nut to 40 Nm (30 lbf ft), remove the tool and measure the air gap. If the gap is still too small, re-attach the tool and tighten the spindle nut to 45 Nm (33 lbf ft). Measure the gap again. When the gap is correct, refit the flange retaining bolts, and tighten them to the specified torque.

32 The remainder of refitting is a reversal of removal.

17 Engine/transmission mountings – inspection and renewal

Inspection

1 If improved access is required, jack up the front of the vehicle, and support it securely on

axle stands (see *Jacking and vehicle support* in the Reference chapter). Remove the engine top cover, which also incorporates the air filter, and then remove the engine undershield(s).

2 Check the mounting rubbers to see if they are cracked, hardened or separated from the metal at any point; renew the mounting if any such damage or deterioration is evident.

3 Check that all the mountings are securely tightened; use a torque wrench to check if possible.

4 Using a large screwdriver or a crowbar, check for wear in the mounting by carefully levering against it to check for free play. Where this is not possible, enlist the aid of an assistant to move the engine/transmission back-and-forth, or from side-to-side, whilst you observe the mounting. While some free play is to be expected, even from new components, excessive wear should be obvious. If excessive free play is found, check first that the fasteners are correctly secured, and then renew any worn components as described in the following paragraphs.

Renewal

Note: *New mounting securing bolts will be required on refitting.*

Right-hand mounting

5 Attach a hoist and lifting tackle to the engine lifting brackets on the cylinder head, and raise the hoist to just take the weight of the engine. Alternatively the engine can be supported on a trolley jack under the engine.

Use a block of wood between the sump and the head of the jack, to prevent any damage to the sump.

6 For improved access, unscrew the coolant reservoir and move it to one side, leaving the coolant hoses connected.

7 Where fitted, undo the retaining bolts and move the supplementary fuel pump to one side **(see illustration)**.

8 Undo the retaining bolts and move the fuel filter to one side **(see illustration)**. Where applicable, move any wiring harnesses, pipes or hoses to one side to enable removal of the engine mounting.

9 Unscrew the bolts securing the mounting to the engine bracket, and then unscrew the bolts securing it to the body. Also, unscrew the movement limiter. Withdraw the mounting from the engine compartment **(see illustration)**.

10 Refitting is a reversal of removal, bearing in mind the following points.

a) *Use new securing bolts.*

b) *There must be at least 13.5 mm between the engine mounting bracket and the right-hand side chassis member (see illustration).*

c) *The side of the mounting support arm must be parallel to the side of the engine mounting bracket.*

d) *Tighten all fixings to the specified torque.*

Left-hand mounting

11 Remove the engine top cover.

12 Attach a hoist and lifting tackle to the

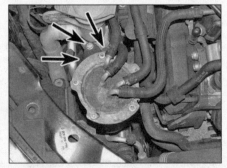

17.8 Undo the filter retaining bolts/nut (arrowed)

17.9 Right-hand engine mounting

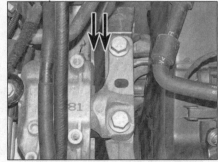

17.10 There must be at least 13.5 mm between the bracket and the chassis member (arrowed)

17.19 Rear lower mounting arm-to-transmission bolts (arrowed)

engine lifting brackets on the cylinder head, and raise the hoist to just take the weight of the engine and transmission. Alternatively the engine can be supported on a trolley jack under the transmission. Use a block of wood between the transmission and the head of the jack, to prevent any damage to the transmission.

13 Remove the battery and battery tray, as described in Chapter 5, Section 3.

14 Unscrew the bolts securing the mounting to the transmission, and the remaining bolts securing the mounting to the body, then lift the mounting from the engine compartment.

15 Refitting is a reversal of removal, bearing in mind the following points:

a) *Use new mounting bolts.*
b) *The edges of the mounting support arm must be parallel to the edge of the mounting.*
c) *Tighten all fixings to the specified torque.*

Rear mounting (torque arm)

16 Apply the handbrake, then jack up the front of the vehicle and support securely on axle stands (see *Jacking and vehicle support* in the Reference chapter). Remove the engine undershield(s) for access to the rear mounting (torque arm).

17 Support the rear of the transmission beneath the final drive housing. To do this, use a trolley jack and block of wood, or alternatively wedge a block of wood between the transmission and the subframe.

18 Working under the vehicle, unscrew and remove the bolt securing the mounting to the subframe.

19 Unscrew the two bolts securing the mounting to the transmission, then withdraw the mounting from under the vehicle (**see illustration**).

20 Refitting is a reversal of removal, but use new mounting securing bolts, and tighten all fixings to the specified torque.

---

18 Engine oil cooler/filter housing – removal and refitting

Removal

Engine codes CFFA, CFFB & CFGB

1 The oil cooler is mounted on the lower part of the oil filter housing on the front of the cylinder block, which is the same as the 1.6 litre engine. Refer to Chapter 2A, Section 17, for the removal refitting procedure

Engine codes CBAA, CBAB & CBBB

2 The oil cooler is mounted on the lower part of the oil filter housing on the front of the cylinder block.

3 Position a container beneath the oil filter housing to catch escaping oil and coolant.

4 Clamp the oil cooler coolant hoses to minimise coolant spillage, and disconnect them from the top of the cooler. If required, drain the cooling system as described in Chapter 1, Section 31.

5 Unscrew the oil cooler centre bolt and lower the oil cooler from oil filter housing (**see illustration**). Recover the O-rings from between the cooler and the oil filter housing, new ones will be required for refitting.

6 If required, undo the retaining bolts and remove the oil filter housing from the cylinder block.

Refitting

7 Refitting is a reversal of removal, bearing in mind the following points:

a) *Use new oil cooler and housing O-rings.*
b) *Tighten the oil cooler and filter housing bolts to the correct torque.*
c) *On completion, check and if necessary top-up the oil and coolant levels.*

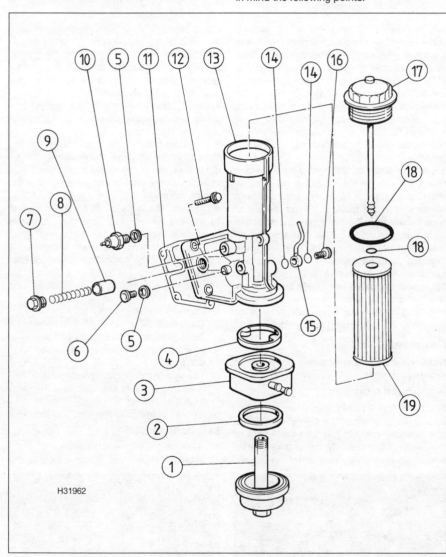

H31962

18.5 Oil filter/cooler mounting details

1 *Oil cooler securing plate*	8 *Oil pressure relief valve spring (not on all models)*	12 *Mounting bolt*
2 *O-ring*	9 *Oil pressure relief valve piston (not on all models)*	13 *Oil filter housing*
3 *Oil cooler*		14 *Seal*
4 *O-ring*	10 *Oil pressure warning light switch*	15 *Oil supply pipe to turbo*
5 *Washer*		16 *Banjo bolt*
6 *Sealing plug*	11 *Gasket*	17 *Oil filter cover*
7 *Sealing plug*		18 *O-ring*
		19 *Oil filter*

19 Oil pressure warning light switch – removal and refitting

Removal

Engine codes CBAA, CBAB & CBBB

1 The oil pressure warning light switch is fitted to the oil filter housing **(see illustration)**. Remove the engine top cover to gain access to the switch (see Section 4).

2 Disconnect the wiring connector and wipe clean the area around the switch.

3 Unscrew the switch from the filter housing and remove it, along with its sealing washer. If the switch is to be left removed from the engine for any length of time, plug the oil filter housing aperture.

19.1 Oil pressure warning light switch on filter housing

Engine codes CFFA, CFFB & CFGB

4 The oil pressure warning light switch is fitted to the left-hand rear of the cylinder head, which is the same as the 1.6 litre engine. Refer to Chapter 2A, Section 18, for the removal and refitting procedure.

Refitting

5 Examine the sealing washer for signs of damage or deterioration and if necessary renew.

6 Refit the switch, complete with washer, and tighten it to the specified torque.

7 Securely reconnect the wiring connector then check and, if necessary, top-up the engine oil as described in 'Weekly checks'. On completion, refit the engine top cover(s).

20 Oil level/temperature sender – removal and refitting

1 The oil level/temperature sender is fitted to bottom of the sump, which is the same as the 1.6 litre engine. Refer to Chapter 2A, Section 19, for the removal refitting procedure

Notes

Chapter 2 Part D
Engine removal and overhaul procedures

Contents

Degrees of difficulty

Easy, suitable for novice with little experience	Fairly easy, suitable for beginner with some experience	Fairly difficult, suitable for competent DIY mechanic	Difficult, suitable for experienced DIY mechanic	Very difficult, suitable for expert DIY or professional

Specifications

Engine codes*

1.6 litre engines . . . . CAYB and CAYC
1.9 litre engines . . . . BLS and BXE
2.0 litre engines . . . . CBAA, CBAB, CBBB, CFFA, CFFB and CFGB

Note: *See 'Vehicle identification' in Reference Chapter for the location of engine code markings.*

Piston rings

	New	Wear limit
End gaps:		
1.6 litre engines:		
Compression rings	0.20 to 0.40 mm	1.0 mm
Oil scraper ring	0.25 to 0.50 mm	1.0 mm
1.9 litre engines:		
Compression rings	0.20 to 0.40 mm	1.0 mm
Oil scraper ring	0.25 to 0.50 mm	1.0 mm
2.0 litre engines:		
Compression rings	0.25 to 0.50 mm	1.0 mm
Oil scraper ring	0.25 to 0.50 mm	1.0 mm
Ring-to-groove clearance:		
1st compression ring	0.06 to 0.09 mm	0.25 mm
2nd compression ring	0.05 to 0.08 mm	0.25 mm
Oil scraper ring	0.03 to 0.06 mm	0.15 mm

Crankshaft

Endfloat	New	Wear limit
1.6 litre engines	0.07 to 0.17 mm	0.37 mm
1.9 litre engines	0.07 to 0.23 mm	0.30 mm
2.0 litre engines	0.07 to 0.23 mm	0.30 mm

Spigot bearing

Fitted depth in end of crankshaft:

1.6 litre engines	1.5 to 1.8 mm
1.9 litre engines	1.5 mm
2.0 litre engines	2.0 mm

Cylinder head

Minimum permissible dimension between top of valve stem and top surface of cylinder head	No reworking permitted
Minimum cylinder head height	No reworking permitted
Maximum cylinder head gasket face distortion	0.1 mm

Valves

Valve stem diameter:	Inlet valves	Exhaust valves
1.6 litre engines	5.968 to 5.982 mm	5.958 to 5.972 mm
1.9 litre engines	6.980 mm	6.956 mm
2.0 litre engines	5.968 to 5.982 mm	5.958 to 5.972 mm
Valve seat angle (all engines)	45°	45°

Torque wrench settings

Refer to, Chapters 2B, 2B or 2C, as applicable.

1 General Information

How to use this Chapter

1 Included in this Part of Chapter 2 are details of removing the engine from the car and general overhaul procedures for the cylinder head, cylinder block and all other engine internal components.

2 The information given ranges from advice concerning preparation for an overhaul and the purchase of new parts, to detailed step-by-step procedures covering removal, inspection, renovation and refitting of engine internal components.

3 After Section 8, all instructions are based on the assumption that the engine has been removed from the car. For information concerning in-car engine repair, as well as the removal and refitting of those external components necessary for full overhaul, refer to the relevant in-car repair procedure section (Chapters 2A, 2B or 2C) and to Section 2 of this Chapter. Ignore any preliminary dismantling operations described in the relevant in-car repair sections that are no longer relevant once the engine has been removed from the car.

4 Apart from torque wrench settings, which are given at the beginning of the relevant in-car repair procedure in Chapters 2A, 2B or 2C, all specifications relating to engine overhaul are given at the beginning of this Part of Chapter 2.

2 Engine overhaul – general information

1 It is not always easy to determine when, or if, an engine should be completely overhauled, as a number of factors must be considered.

2 High mileage is not necessarily an indication that an overhaul is needed, while low mileage does not preclude the need for an overhaul. Frequency of servicing is probably the most important consideration. An engine, which has had regular and frequent oil and filter changes, as well as other required maintenance, should give many thousands of miles of reliable service. Conversely, a neglected engine may require an overhaul very early in its life.

3 Excessive oil consumption is an indication that piston rings, valve seals and/or valve guides are in need of attention. Make sure that oil leaks are not responsible before deciding that the rings and/or guides are worn. Perform a compression (or leakdown) test to determine the likely cause of the problem.

4 Check the oil pressure with a gauge fitted in place of the oil pressure switch, and then compare it with that specified (see Specifications in Part A, B or C of this Chapter). If it is extremely low, the main and big-end bearings, and/or the oil pump, are probably worn.

5 Loss of power, rough running, knocking or metallic engine noises, excessive valve gear noise, and high fuel consumption may also point to the need for an overhaul, especially if they are all present at the same time. If a complete service does not remedy the situation, major mechanical work is the only solution.

6 An engine overhaul involves restoring all internal parts to the specification of a new engine. During an overhaul, the pistons and the piston rings are renewed. New main and big-end bearings are generally fitted (where possible); if necessary, the crankshaft may be renewed to restore the journals. The valves are also serviced as well, since they are usually in less-than-perfect condition at this point. While the engine is being overhauled, other components, such as the starter and alternator, can be overhauled as well. The end result should be an as-new engine that will give many trouble-free miles.

Note: *Critical cooling system components such as the hoses, thermostat and coolant pump should be renewed when an engine is overhauled. The radiator should be checked carefully, to ensure that it is not clogged or leaking. Also, it is a good idea to renew the oil pump whenever the engine is overhauled.*

7 Before beginning the engine overhaul, read through the entire procedure, to familiarise yourself with the scope and requirements of the job. Overhauling an engine is not difficult if you follow carefully all of the instructions, have the necessary tools and equipment, and pay close attention to all specifications. It can, however, be time-consuming. Plan on the car being off the road for a minimum of two weeks, especially if parts must be taken to an engineering works for repair or reconditioning. Check on the availability of parts and make sure that any necessary special tools and equipment are obtained in advance. Most work can be done with typical hand tools, although a number of precision measuring tools are required for inspecting parts to determine if they must be renewed. Often the engineering works will handle the inspection of parts and offer advice concerning reconditioning and renewal.

Note: *Always wait until the engine has been completely dismantled, and until all components (especially the cylinder block and the crankshaft) have been inspected, before deciding what service and repair operations must be performed by an engineering works. The condition of these components will be the major factor to consider when determining whether to overhaul the original engine, or to buy a reconditioned unit. Do not, therefore, purchase parts or have overhaul work done on other components until they have been thoroughly inspected. As a general rule, time is the primary cost of an overhaul, so it does not pay to fit worn or sub-standard parts.*

8 As a final note, to ensure maximum life and minimum trouble from a reconditioned engine, everything must be assembled with care, in a spotlessly clean environment.

3 Engine/transmission removal – preparation and precautions

1 If you have decided that the engine must be removed for overhaul or major repair work, several preliminary steps should be taken.

2 Locating a suitable place to work is extremely important. Adequate workspace, along with storage space for the vehicle, will be needed. If a workshop or garage is not available, at the very least a solid, level, clean work surface is required.

3 If possible, clear some shelving close to the work area and use it to store the engine components and ancillaries as they are removed and dismantled. In this manner, the components stand a better chance of staying clean and undamaged during the overhaul. Laying out components in groups together with their fixings bolts, screws, etc, will save time and avoid confusion when the engine is refitted.

4 Clean the engine compartment and engine before beginning the removal procedure; this will help visibility and help to keep tools clean.

5 The help of an assistant is essential; there are certain instances when one person cannot safely perform all of the operations required to remove the engine from the vehicle. Safety is of primary importance, considering the potential hazards involved in this kind of operation. A second person should always be in attendance to offer help in an emergency. If this is the first time you have removed an engine, advice and aid from someone more experienced would also be beneficial.

6 Plan the operation ahead of time. Before starting work, obtain (or arrange for the hire of) all of the tools and equipment you will need. Access to the following items will allow the task of removing and refitting the engine to be completed safely and with relative ease: a hoist and lifting tackle – rated in excess of the weight of the engine, complete sets of spanners and sockets as described at the rear of this manual, wooden blocks, and plenty of rags and cleaning solvent for mopping-up spilled oil, coolant and fuel. A selection of different-sized plastic storage bins will also prove useful for keeping dismantled components grouped together. If any of the equipment must be hired, make sure that you arrange for it in advance, and perform all of the operations possible without it beforehand; this may save you time and money.

7 Plan on the vehicle being out of use for quite a while, especially if you intend to carry out an engine overhaul. Read through the whole of this Section and work out a strategy based on your own experience, and the tools, time and workspace available to you. Some of the overhaul processes may have to be carried out by an Audi dealer or an engineering works – these establishments often have busy schedules, so it would be prudent to consult them before removing or dismantling the engine, to get an idea of the amount of time required to carry out the work.

8 When removing the engine from the vehicle, be methodical about the disconnection of external components. Labelling cables and hoses as they are removed will greatly assist the refitting process.

9 Always be extremely careful when lifting the engine from the engine compartment. Serious injury can result from careless actions. If help is required, it is better to wait until it is available rather than risk personal injury and/or damage components by continuing alone. By planning ahead and taking your time, a job of this nature, although major, can be accomplished successfully and without incident.

4 Engine and transmission – removal and refitting

Removal

1 The engine and transmission assembly is lowered from the engine compartment and withdrawn from under the car. Access to the front of the engine is gained by moving the lock carrier assembly to its Service position, or alternatively removing it completely after evacuating the air conditioning system (by an air conditioning specialist).

2 Switch off the ignition and all electrical consumers, and remove the ignition key.

3 Remove the engine top cover and air cleaner assembly (Chapter 4A, Section 2 or Chapter 4B, Section 2).

4 Remove the battery as described in Chapter 5, Section 3 then remove the battery tray **(see illustrations)**.

5 Apply the handbrake, then jack up the front of the vehicle and support it on axle stands (see *'Jacking and vehicle support'*

4.4a Remove the battery box...

4.4b...and tray

4.6a Disconnect the bonnet release cable…

4.6b…unscrew the crossmember mounting bolts/screws (arrowed)…

4.6c…remove the front bumper crossmember…

4.6d …and fit the threaded rods (arrowed) into the upper mounting holes

4.6e Undo the outer retaining bolts each side (arrowed)…

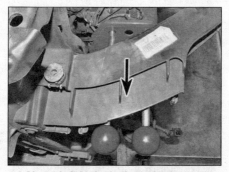

4.6f…and slide the lock carrier forwards along the threaded rods

in Reference Chapter). Remove both front roadwheels.

6 Move the lock carrier, located at the front of the engine compartment, to its Service position as follows.

a) *Remove the front bumper (Chapter 11, Section 6).*
b) *Disconnect the bonnet release cable over the right-hand headlight* **(see illustration)**.
c) *Remove the turbocharger charge air ducts.*
d) *Undo the four mounting bolts and three retaining screws from each side of the front bumper crossmember and remove it* **(see illustrations)**.
e) *Support the lock carrier, then unscrew the mounting bolts and substitute them with*

threaded rods on each side of the car **(see illustration)**.
f) *Undo the outer retaining bolts on the inner wing panel* **(see illustrations)**.
g) *Carefully pull the lock carrier forwards approximately 10 cm to provide access to the front of the engine.*

7 Alternatively, the air conditioning system may be evacuated by a specialist, and the lock carrier removed completely from the front of the car to provide additional working space.

⚠ **Warning: Have the air conditioning system discharged by a suitably qualified specialist before attempting to remove any of the air conditioning system components.**

8 Drain the cooling system as described in Chapter 1, Section 31. On some models the electric cooling fan temperature sensor may be removed from the bottom hose to drain the system, otherwise remove the bottom hose from the radiator **(see illustration)**.

9 Noting their locations, disconnect all wiring, coolant hoses, vacuum hoses and fuel lines from the engine/transmission, with reference to the relevant chapters of this Manual. Alternatively, the engine wiring loom may remain on the engine by disconnecting it from the left-hand side of the engine compartment, and removing the engine management ECU located on the bulkhead **(see illustrations)**. Tape over or plug fuel lines to prevent entry of dust and dirt.

4.8 Removing the bottom hose to drain the cooling system

4.9a Remove the wiring from the supports on the front of the engine

4.9b Engine wiring loom support on exhaust manifold

4.11 Remove the rear engine support/ torque arm

4.12 Disconnect the gearchange cables

4.15 Suspend the driveshafts clear of the transmission

10 Remove the front exhaust pipe with reference to Chapter 4C, Section 11.

11 Unbolt the rear engine support/torque arm from the transmission **(see illustration)**.

12 Disconnect the gearchange mechanism with reference to Chapter 7A, Section 2 (manual transmission) or Chapter 7B, Section 4 (DSG transmission) **(see illustration)**.

13 On manual transmission models, remove the clutch slave cylinder.

Note: *Do not depress the clutch pedal once the slave cylinder has been removed.*

14 Refer to Chapter 3, Section 11, and unbolt the air conditioning compressor from the front of the engine, without disconnecting the refrigerant lines. Suspend the compressor to one side of the engine compartment.

15 Refer to Chapter 8, Section 2, and disconnect the driveshafts from the transmission drive flanges. Suspend them from the underbody **(see illustration)**.

16 Unbolt the washer fluid reservoir for access to the right-engine mounting. Also unbolt the coolant expansion tank and place to one side.

17 Connect a hoist and lifting tackle to the engine lifting brackets on the cylinder head, and raise the hoist to just take the weight of the engine/transmission.

18 Unbolt the right- and left-hand engine mountings with reference to Chapter 2A, Section 16, Chapter 2B, Section 18 or Chapter 2C Section 17.

19 Make a final check to ensure that all relevant wiring, hoses and pipes have been disconnected, then carefully swivel the engine/transmission assembly away from the sides of the engine compartment, lower it, and withdraw forwards from the front of the car.

Separation

Engine and manual transmission

20 Remove the starter motor (Chapter 5, Section 8).

21 Where applicable, unscrew the bolt securing the small engine-to-transmission plate to the transmission.

22 Ensure that both engine and transmission are adequately supported, and then unscrew the remaining engine-to-transmission bolts, noting the location of each bolt, and the locations of any brackets secured by the bolts.

23 Carefully withdraw the transmission from the engine, ensuring that the weight of the transmission is not allowed to hang on the input shaft while it is engaged with the clutch friction disc. Recover the engine-to-transmission plate.

Engine and DSG (dual clutch) transmission

24 Remove the starter motor (Chapter 5, Section 8).

25 Disconnect the coolant hoses from the gearbox oil cooler. Plug the openings to prevent contamination.

26 Disconnect the wiring harness between the engine and gearbox, and move to one side.

27 Ensure that both engine and transmission are adequately supported, and then unscrew the engine-to-transmission bolts, noting the location of each bolt, and the locations of any brackets secured by the bolts.

28 Carefully withdraw the transmission from the engine (take care – the transmission is heavy).

Reconnection and refitting

29 Reconnection and refitting are a reversal of removal, bearing in mind the following points:

a) *Smear the splines of the transmission input shaft with a little high melting-point grease.*

b) *Ensure that any brackets noted before removal are in place on the engine-to-transmission bolts.*

c) *Tighten all fixings to the specified torque, where given.*

d) *Where applicable, have the air conditioning system recharged with refrigerant by a suitably qualified professional.*

e) *Ensure that all wiring, hoses and pipes are correctly reconnected and routed as noted before removal.*

f) *Ensure that the fuel lines are correctly reconnected.*

g) *On completion, refill the cooling system as described in Chapter 1, Section 31.*

5 Engine overhaul – preliminary information

1 It is much easier to dismantle and work on the engine if it is mounted on a portable engine stand. These stands can often be hired from a tool hire shop. Before the engine is mounted on a stand, the flywheel should be removed, so that the stand bolts can be tightened into the end of the cylinder block/ crankcase.

Note: *Do not measure cylinder bore dimensions with the engine mounted on this type of stand.*

2 If a stand is not available, it is possible to dismantle the engine with it blocked up on a sturdy workbench, or on the floor. Be very careful not to tip or drop the engine when working without a stand.

3 If you intend to obtain a reconditioned engine, all ancillaries must be removed first, to be transferred to the new engine (just as they will if you are doing a complete engine overhaul yourself). These components include the following (it may be necessary to transfer additional components, such as the oil level dipstick/tube assembly, oil filter housing, etc, depending on which components are supplied with the reconditioned engine:

a) *Alternator (including mounting brackets) and starter motor (Chapter 5).*

b) *The glow plug/preheating system components (Chapter 5).*

c) *All fuel system components, including fuel injectors, all sensors and actuators (Chapter 4A or 4B).*

d) *The brake vacuum pump (Chapter 9).*

e) *All electrical switches, actuators and sensors, and the engine wiring harness (Chapter 4A or 4B).*

f) *Inlet and exhaust manifolds/turbocharger (Chapters 4A, 4B and 4C).*

g) *Engine mountings (see Chapter 2A, 2B or 2C).*

h) *Clutch components (Chapter 6).*

Note: *When removing the external components from the engine, pay close attention to details that may be helpful or important during refitting. Note the fitted* *position of gaskets, seals, spacers, pins, washers, bolts, and other small components.*

4 If you are obtaining a short engine (the engine cylinder block/crankcase, crankshaft, pistons and connecting rods, all fully assembled), then the cylinder head, sump, oil pump, timing belt, (together with tensioner, idler pulleys and timing belt covers), auxiliary drivebelt (together with its tensioner), coolant pump, thermostat housing, coolant outlet elbows, oil filter housing and oil cooler will also have to be removed.

5 If you are planning a full overhaul, the engine can be dismantled in the order given below:

a) *Inlet and exhaust manifolds (see the relevant part of Chapter 4).*
b) *Timing belt, sprockets and tensioner (see the relevant part of Chapter 2).*
c) *Cylinder head (see the relevant part of Chapter 2).*

d) *Flywheel/driveplate (see the relevant part of Chapter 2).*
e) *Sump (see the relevant part of Chapter 2).*
f) *Oil pump (see the relevant part of Chapter 2).*
g) *Piston/connecting rod assemblies (see Section 9).*
h) *Crankshaft (see Section 10).*

6 Cylinder head – dismantling

Note: *A valve spring compressor tool will be required for this operation.*

1 With the cylinder head removed, proceed as follows.

2 Remove the inlet and exhaust manifolds and turbocharger as described in Chapters 4A and 4B.

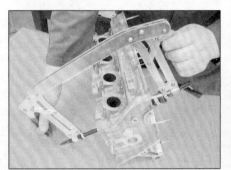

6.9a Compress a valve spring with a compressor tool

6.9c...and valve spring

6.10b...to remove the valve stem oil seals

6.9b Remove the spring cap...

6.10a Use a removal tool...

6.11 Removing a valve

3 Remove the camshaft and hydraulic tappets, as described in Chapter 2A, Section 9, Chapter 2B, Section 10 or Chapter 2C, Section 9.

4 Remove the glow plugs, with reference to Chapter 5, Section 11.

5 Remove the fuel injectors, with reference to Chapter 4A, Section 4 or Chapter 4B, Section 4.

6 Unscrew the nut and remove the timing belt tensioner pulley from the stud on the timing belt end of the cylinder head.

7 Unbolt any remaining auxiliary brackets and/or engine lifting brackets from the cylinder head as necessary, noting their locations to aid refitting.

8 Turn the cylinder head over, and rest it on one side.

9 Using a valve spring compressor, compress each valve spring in turn until the split collets can be removed. Release the compressor, and lift off the spring cap and spring. If, when the valve spring compressor is screwed down, the spring cap refuses to free and expose the split collets, gently tap the top of the tool, directly over the spring cap, with a light hammer. This will free the retainer **(see illustrations)**.

10 Using a pair of pliers, or a removal tool, carefully extract the valve stem oil seal from the top of the valve guide **(see illustrations)**.

11 Withdraw the valve from the gasket side of the cylinder head **(see illustration)**.

12 It is essential that each valve is stored together with its collets, cap, spring and spring seat. The valves should be kept in their correct sequences, unless they are so badly worn that they are to be renewed.

7 Cylinder head and valves – cleaning and inspection

1 Thorough cleaning of the cylinder head and valve components, followed by a detailed inspection, will enable you to decide how much valve service work must be carried out during engine overhaul.

Note: *If the engine has been severely overheated, it is best to assume that the cylinder head is warped. Check carefully for signs of this.*

Cleaning

2 Using a suitable degreasing agent, remove all traces of oil deposits from the cylinder head, paying particular attention to the camshaft bearing surfaces, hydraulic tappet bores, valve guides and oil ways. Scrape off any traces of old gasket from the mating surfaces, taking care not to score or gouge them. If using emery paper, do not use a grade of less than 100. Turn the head over and, using a blunt blade, scrape any carbon deposits from the combustion chambers and ports. Finally, wash the entire head casting with a suitable solvent to remove the remaining debris.

7.7 Measure the distortion of the cylinder head gasket surface

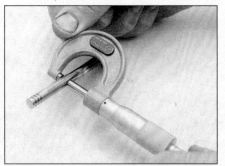

7.10 Measure the diameter of the valve stems using a micrometer

7.13 Measure the free length of each valve spring

3 Clean the valve heads and stems using a fine wire brush (or a power-operated wire brush). If the valve is covered with heavy carbon deposits, scrape off the majority of the deposits with a blunt blade first, then use the wire brush.

4 Thoroughly clean the remainder of the components using solvent and allow them to dry completely. Discard the oil seals, as new ones must be fitted when the cylinder head is reassembled.

Inspection

Cylinder head

5 Examine the head casting closely to identify any damage or cracks that may have developed. Cracks can often be identified from evidence of coolant or oil leakage. Pay particular attention to the areas around the valve seats and fuel injector holes. If cracking is discovered in this area, Audi state that the cylinder head may be re-used, provided the cracks are no larger than 0.5 mm wide. More serious damage will mean the renewal of the cylinder head casting.

6 Moderately pitted and scorched valve seats can be repaired by lapping the valves in during reassembly, as described later in this Chapter. The valve seats must not be recut.

7 Measure any distortion of the gasket surfaces using a straight-edge and a set of feeler blades. Take one measurement longitudinally on the manifold mating surface(s). Take several measurements across the head gasket surface, to assess the level

of distortion in all planes **(see illustration)**. Compare the measurements with the figures in the Specifications.

8 If the head is distorted beyond the specified limit, the head must be renewed.

Camshaft

9 Inspection of the camshaft is covered in Chapters 2A, 2B or 2C as applicable.

Valves and associated components

10 Examine each valve closely for signs of wear. Inspect the valve stems for wear ridges, scoring or variations in diameter; measure their diameters at several points along their lengths with a micrometer, and compare with the figures given in the Specifications **(see illustration)**.

11 The valve heads should not be cracked, badly pitted or charred. Note that light pitting of the valve head can be rectified by lapping-in the valves during reassembly, as described in Section 8.

12 Check that the valve stem end face is free from excessive pitting or indentation; this could be caused by defective hydraulic tappets.

13 Using vernier calipers, measure the free length of each of the valve springs. As a manufacturer's figure is not quoted, the only way to check the length of the springs is by comparison with a new component. Note that valve springs are usually renewed during a major engine overhaul **(see illustration)**.

14 Stand each spring on its end on a flat surface, against an engineer's square **(see**

illustration). Check the squareness of the spring visually, and renew it if it appears distorted.

15 Renew the valve stem oil seals regardless of their apparent condition.

8 Cylinder head – reassembly

Note: *A valve spring compressor tool will be required for this operation.*

1 To achieve a gas-tight seal between the valves and their seats, it will be necessary to lap-in (or grind-in) the valves. To complete this process you will need a quantity of fine/ coarse grinding paste and a grinding tool – this can either be of the rubber sucker type, or the automatic type which is driven by a rotary power tool.

2 Smear a small quantity of fine grinding paste on the sealing face of the valve head. Turn the cylinder head over so that the combustion chambers are facing upwards and insert the valve into the correct guide. Attach the grinding tool to the valve head and using a backward/forward rotary action, grind the valve head into its seat. Periodically lift the valve and rotate it to redistribute the grinding paste **(see illustration)**.

3 Continue this process until the contact between valve and seat produces an unbroken, matt grey ring of uniform width, on both faces. Repeat the operation on the remaining valves.

4 If the valves and seats are so badly pitted that coarse grinding paste must be used, bear in that there is a maximum protrusion of the end of the valve stem from the valve guide. Refer to an Audi dealer or engine reconditioning specialist. If this minimum dimension is outside the limit due to excessive grinding-in, the hydraulic tappets may not operate correctly, and the cylinder head must be renewed.

5 Assuming the repair is feasible, work as described previously, but use coarse grinding paste initially, to achieve a dull finish on the valve face and seat. Wash off the coarse paste with solvent and repeat the process using fine grinding paste to obtain the correct finish.

7.14 Check the squareness of a valve spring

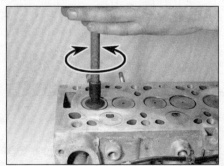

8.2 Grinding-in a valve

8.8a Lubricate the valve stem with clean engine oil

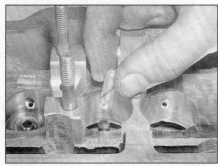

8.8b Fit a protective sleeve over the valve stem before fitting the stem seal

8.9 Use a long-reach socket to fit a valve stem oil seal

6 When all the valves have been ground in, remove all traces of grinding paste from the cylinder head and valves using solvent, and allow the head and valves to dry completely.

7 Turn the cylinder head on its side.

8 Working on one valve at a time, lubricate the valve stem with clean engine oil, and insert the valve into its guide. Fit one of the protective plastic sleeves (where supplied) to fit over the end of the valve stem – this will protect the oil seal as it is being fitted **(see illustrations)**.

9 Dip a new valve stem seal in clean engine oil, and carefully push it over the valve stem and onto the top of the valve guide – take care not to damage the stem seal as it is fitted. Use a suitable long-reach socket or a valve stem seal fitting tool to press the seal firmly into position **(see illustration)**. Remove the protective sleeve from the valve stem.

10 Locate the valve spring over the valve stem, ensuring that the lower end of the spring seats correctly on the cylinder head **(see illustration)**.

11 Fit the upper spring seat over the top of the spring, then using a valve spring compressor, compress the spring until the upper seat is pushed beyond the collet grooves in the valve stem. Refit the split collets. Gradually release the spring compressor, checking that the collets remain correctly seated as the spring extends. When correctly seated, the upper spring seat should force the collets securely into the grooves in the end of the valve stem **(see illustrations)**.

12 Repeat this process for the remaining sets of valve components, ensuring that all components are refitted to their original locations. To settle the components after installation, strike the end of each valve

stem with a mallet, using a block of wood to protect the stem from damage. Check before progressing any further that the split collets remain firmly seated in the grooves in the end of the valve stem.

13 Refit any auxiliary brackets and/or engine lifting brackets to their original locations, as noted before removal.

14 Refit the timing belt tensioner pulley to the stud on the cylinder head, and refit the securing nut.

15 Refit the components removed in paragraphs 2 to 5.

9 Piston/connecting rod assemblies – removal

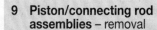

1 Remove the cylinder head, sump and oil baffle plate, oil pump and pick-up pipe and, where applicable, the balance shaft assembly as described in as applicable.

2 Inspect the tops of the cylinder bores for ridges at the point where the pistons reach top dead centre. These must be removed otherwise the pistons may be damaged when they are pushed out of their bores. Use a scraper or ridge reamer to remove the ridges. Such a ridge indicates excessive wear of the cylinder bore.

3 Check the connecting rods and big-end caps for identification markings. Both connecting rods and caps should be marked with the cylinder number on one side of each assembly. Note that No 1 cylinder is at the timing belt end of the engine. If no marks are present, using a hammer and centre-punch, paint or similar, mark each connecting rod and big-end bearing cap with its respective cylinder number – note on which side of the connecting rods and caps the marks are made **(see illustration)**.

4 Similarly, check the piston crowns for direction markings. An arrow on each piston crown should point towards the timing belt end of the engine. On some engines, this mark may be obscured by carbon build-up, in which case the piston crown should be cleaned to check for a mark. In some cases, the direction arrow may have worn off, in

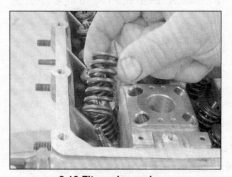

8.10 Fit a valve spring...

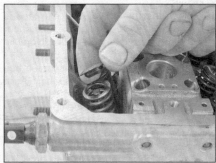

8.11a ...and upper spring seat...

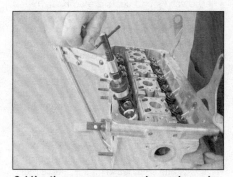

8.11b ...then compress a valve spring using a compressor tool

8.11c Use grease to hold the split collets in the groove

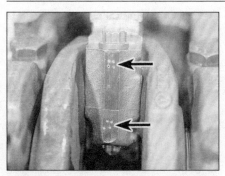

9.3 Mark the big-end caps and connecting rods with their cylinder numbers (arrowed)

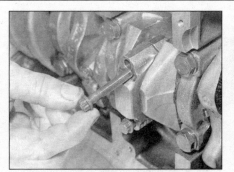

9.6a Unscrew the big-end bearing cap bolts...

9.6b...and remove the cap

which case a suitable mark should be made on the piston crown using a scriber – do not deeply score the piston crown, but ensure that the mark is easily visible.

5 Turn the crankshaft to bring No's 1 and 4 pistons to bottom dead centre.

6 Unscrew the bolts or nuts, as applicable, from No 1 piston big-end bearing cap. Lift off the cap, and recover the bottom half bearing shell. If the bearing shells are to be re-used, tape the cap and bearing shell together. Note that if the bearing shells are to be re-used, they must be fitted to the original connecting rod and cap **(see illustrations)**.

7 Where the bearing caps are secured with nuts, wrap the threaded ends of the bolts with insulating tape to prevent them scratching the crankpins and bores when the pistons are removed **(see illustration)**.

8 Using a hammer handle, push the piston

up through the bore, and remove it from the top of the cylinder block. Where applicable, take care not to damage the piston cooling oil spray jets in the cylinder block as the piston/connecting rod assembly is removed. Recover the upper bearing shell, and tape it to the connecting rod for safe-keeping.

9 Loosely refit the big-end cap to the connecting rod, and secure with the bolts or nuts, as applicable – this will help to keep the components in their correct order.

10 Remove No.4 piston assembly in the same way.

11 Turn the crankshaft as necessary to bring No's 2 and 3 pistons to bottom dead centre, and remove them in the same way.

12 Where applicable, remove the securing bolts, and withdraw the piston cooling oil spray jets from the bottom of the cylinder block **(see illustrations)**.

10 Crankshaft – removal

Note: If no work is to be done on the pistons and connecting rods, there is no need to push the pistons out of the cylinder bores. The pistons should just be pushed far enough up the bores so that they are positioned clear of the crankshaft journals.

1 Remove the timing belt and crankshaft sprocket, sump and oil baffle plate, oil pump and pick-up pipe, flywheel, and the crankshaft oil seal housings.

2 Remove the pistons and connecting rods, or disconnect them from the crankshaft, as described in Section 9 (see Note at the beginning of this Section).

3 Check the crankshaft endfloat as described in Section 13, then proceed as follows.

4 The main bearing caps should be numbered 1 to 5 from the timing belt end of the engine. If the bearing caps are not marked, mark them accordingly using a centre-punch. Note the orientation of the markings to ensure correct refitting.

5 Slacken and remove the main bearing cap bolts, and lift off each cap. If the caps appear to be stuck, tap them with a soft-faced mallet to free them from the cylinder block **(see illustration)**. Recover the lower bearing shells, and tape them to their caps for safekeeping.

6 Recover the lower crankshaft endfloat control thrustwasher halves from either side

9.7 Wrap the threaded ends of the bolts with tape

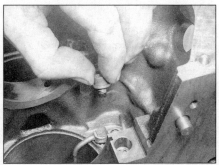

9.12a Remove the securing bolts...

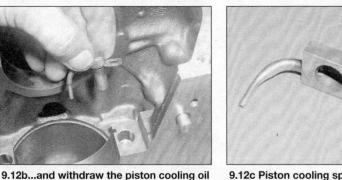

9.12b...and withdraw the piston cooling oil spray jets

9.12c Piston cooling spray jet and retainer

10.5 Slacken and remove the main bearing cap bolts

of the No 3 main bearing cap, noting their orientation.

7 Lift the crankshaft from the cylinder block. Take care, as the crankshaft is heavy. On engines with a crankshaft speed/position sensor fitted, lay the crankshaft on wooden blocks – do not rest the crankshaft on the sensor wheel.

8 Recover the upper bearing shells from the cylinder block, and tape them to their respective caps for safekeeping. Similarly, recover the upper crankshaft endfloat control thrustwasher halves, noting their orientation.

9 On engines with a crankshaft speed/position sensor wheel, unscrew the securing bolts, and remove the sensor wheel, noting which way round it is fitted.

11 Cylinder block/crankcase – cleaning and inspection

Cleaning

1 Remove all external components and electrical switches/sensors from the block, including mounting brackets, coolant pump, oil filter housing, oil cooler and EGR cooler **(see illustration)**, etc. For complete cleaning, the core plugs should ideally be removed. Drill a small hole in the plugs, and then insert a self-tapping screw into the hole. Extract the plugs by pulling on the screw with a pair of grips, or by using a slide hammer.

2 Scrape all traces of gasket and sealant from the cylinder block/crankcase, taking care not to damage the sealing surfaces.

3 Remove all oil gallery plugs (where fitted). The plugs are usually very tight – they may have to be drilled out, and the holes re-tapped. Use new plugs when the engine is reassembled.

4 If the casting is extremely dirty, it should be steam-cleaned. After this, clean all oil holes and galleries one more time. Flush all internal passages with warm water until the water runs clear. Dry thoroughly, and apply a light film of oil to all mating surfaces and cylinder bores, to prevent rusting. If you have access to compressed air, use it to speed up the drying

process, and to blow out all the oil holes and galleries.

 Warning: Wear eye protection when using compressed air.

5 If the castings are not very dirty, you can do an adequate cleaning job with hot, soapy water and a stiff brush. Take plenty of time, and do a thorough job. Regardless of the cleaning method used, be sure to clean all oil holes and galleries very thoroughly, and to dry all components well. Protect the cylinder bores as described above, to prevent rusting.

6 Where applicable, check the piston cooling oil spray jets for damage, and renew if necessary. Check the oil spray hole and the oil passages for blockage.

7 All threaded holes must be clean, to ensure accurate torque readings during reassembly. To clean the threads, run the correct-size tap into each of the holes to remove rust, corrosion, thread sealant or sludge, and to restore damaged threads **(see illustration)**. If possible, use compressed air to clear the holes free of debris produced by this operation.

Note: *Take extra care to exclude all cleaning liquid from blind tapped holes, as the casting may be cracked by hydraulic action if a bolt is threaded into a hole containing liquid.*

8 After coating the mating surfaces of the new core plugs with suitable sealant, fit them to the cylinder block. Make sure that they are driven in straight and seated correctly, or leakage could result.

9 Apply suitable sealant to the new oil gallery plugs, and insert them into the holes in the block. Tighten them securely.

10 If the engine is not going to be reassembled immediately, cover it with a large plastic bag to keep it clean; protect all mating surfaces and the cylinder bores, to prevent rusting.

Inspection

11 Visually check the castings for cracks and corrosion. Look for stripped threads in the threaded holes. If there has been any history of internal coolant leakage, it may be worthwhile having an engine overhaul specialist check the cylinder block/crankcase

for cracks with special equipment. If defects are found, have them repaired, if possible, or renew the assembly.

12 Check each cylinder bore for scuffing and scoring.

13 If in any doubt as the condition of the cylinder block have the block/bores inspected and measured by an engine reconditioning specialist. They will be able to advise on whether the block is serviceable, whether a re-bore is necessary, and supply the appropriate pistons and rings.

14 If the bores are in reasonably good condition and not excessively worn, then it may only be necessary to renew the piston rings.

15 If this is the case, the bores should be honed, to allow the new rings to bed-in correctly and provide the best possible seal. Consult an engine reconditioning specialist

16 The cylinder block/crankcase should now be completely clean and dry, with all components checked for wear or damage, and repaired or overhauled as necessary.

17 Apply a light coating of engine oil to the mating surfaces and cylinder bores to prevent rust forming.

18 Refit as many ancillary components as possible, for safekeeping. If reassembly is not to start immediately, cover the block with a large plastic bag to keep it clean, and protect the machined surfaces as described above to prevent rusting.

12 Piston/connecting rod assemblies – cleaning and inspection

Cleaning

1 Before the inspection process can begin, the piston/connecting rod assemblies must be cleaned, and the original piston rings removed from the pistons.

2 The rings should have smooth, polished working surfaces, with no dull or carbon-coated sections (showing that the ring is not sealing correctly against the bore wall, so allowing combustion gases to blow by) and no traces of wear on their top and bottom surfaces. The end gaps should be clear of carbon, but not polished (indicating a too-small end gap), and all the rings (including the elements of the oil control ring) should be free to rotate in their grooves, but without excessive up-and-down movement. If the rings appear to be in good condition, they are probably fit for further use; check the end gaps (in an unworn part of the bore) as described in Section 16.

3 If any of the rings appears to be worn or damaged, or has an end gap significantly different from the specified value, the usual course of action is to renew all of them as a set.

Note: *While it is usual to renew piston rings when an engine is overhauled, they may be*

11.1 EGR cooler located on the rear of the engine

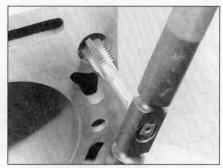

11.7 To clean the cylinder block threads, run a correct-size tap into the holes

re-used if in acceptable condition. If re-using the rings, make sure that each ring is marked during removal to ensure that it is refitted correctly.

4 Carefully expand the old rings over the top of the pistons. The use of two or three old feeler blades will be helpful in preventing the rings dropping into empty grooves **(see illustration)**. Be careful not to scratch the piston with the ends of the ring. The rings are brittle, and will snap if they are spread too far. They are also very sharp – protect your hands and fingers. Note that the third ring incorporates an expander. Keep each set of rings with its piston if the old rings are to be re-used. Note which way up each ring is fitted to ensure correct refitting.

5 Scrape away all traces of carbon from the top of the piston. A hand-held wire brush (or a piece of fine emery cloth) can be used, once the majority of the deposits have been scraped away.

6 Remove the carbon from the ring grooves in the piston, using an old ring. Break the ring in half to do this (be careful not to cut your fingers – piston rings are sharp). Be careful to remove only the carbon deposits – do not remove any metal, and do not nick or scratch the sides of the ring grooves.

7 Once the deposits have been removed, clean the piston/connecting rod assembly with paraffin or a suitable solvent, and dry thoroughly. Make sure that the oil return holes in the ring grooves are clear.

Inspection

8 If the pistons and cylinder bores are not damaged or worn excessively, and if the cylinder block does not need to be re-bored, the original pistons can be refitted.

9 Have the pistons and cylinder bore measure by an engine reconditioning specialist. They will be able to advise on possible repairs, and supply the correct replacement parts.

10 Normal piston wear shows up as even vertical wear on the piston thrust surfaces, and slight looseness of the top ring in its groove. New piston rings should always be used when the engine is reassembled.

11 Carefully inspect each piston for cracks around the skirt, around the gudgeon pin holes, and at the piston ring 'lands' (between the ring grooves).

12 Look for scoring and scuffing on the piston skirt, holes in the piston crown, and burned areas at the edge of the crown. If the skirt is scored or scuffed, the engine may have been suffering from overheating, and/or abnormal combustion, which caused excessively high operating temperatures. The cooling and lubrication systems should be checked thoroughly.

13 Scorch marks on the sides of the pistons show that blow-by has occurred.

14 A hole in the piston crown, or burned areas at the edge of the piston crown, indicates that abnormal combustion (pre-ignition, knocking, or detonation) has been occurring.

12.4 Old feeler blades can be used to prevent piston rings from dropping into empty grooves

15 If any of the above problems exist, the causes must be investigated and corrected, or the damage will occur again. The causes may include incorrect injection pump timing, inlet air leaks or a faulty fuel injector.

16 Corrosion of the piston, in the form of pitting, indicates that coolant has been leaking into the combustion chamber and/or the crankcase. Again, the cause must be corrected, or the problem may persist in the rebuilt engine.

17 Locate a new piston ring in the appropriate groove and measure the ring-to-groove clearance using a feeler blade **(see illustration)**. Note that the rings are of different widths, so use the correct ring for the groove. Compare the measurements with those listed; if the clearances are outside of the tolerance band, then the piston must be renewed. Confirm this by checking the width of the piston ring with a micrometer.

18 Examine each connecting rod carefully for signs of damage, such as cracks around the big-end and small-end bearings. Check that the rod is not bent or distorted. Damage is highly unlikely, unless the engine has been seized or badly overheated. Detailed checking of the connecting rod assembly can only be carried out by an Audi dealer or engine repair specialist with the necessary equipment.

19 The gudgeon pins are of the floating type, secured in position by two circlips. The pistons and connecting rods can be separated as follows.

20 Using a small flat-bladed screwdriver,

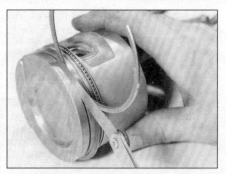

12.17 Measure the piston ring-to-groove clearance using a feeler blade

prise out the circlips, and push out the gudgeon pin **(see illustrations)**. Hand pressure should be sufficient to remove the pin. Identify the piston and rod to ensure correct reassembly. Discard the circlips – new ones must be used on refitting. If the gudgeon pin proves difficult to remove, heat the piston to 60°C with hot water – the resulting expansion will then allow the two components to be separated.

21 Examine the gudgeon pin and connecting rod small-end bearing for signs of wear or damage. It should be possible to push the gudgeon pin through the connecting rod bush by hand, without noticeable play. Wear can be cured by renewing both the pin and bush. Bush renewal, however, is a specialist job – press facilities are required, and the new bush must be reamed accurately.

22 Examine all components, and obtain any new parts from your Audi dealer or engine reconditioning specialist. If new pistons are purchased, they will be supplied complete with gudgeon pins and circlips. Circlips can also be purchased individually.

23 The orientation of the piston with respect to the connecting rod must be correct when the two are reassembled. The piston crown is marked with an arrow (which may be obscured by carbon deposits); this must point towards the timing belt end of the engine when the piston is installed. The connecting rod and its bearing cap both have recesses machined into them on one side, close to their mating surfaces – these recesses must both face the

12.20a Use a small flat-bladed screwdriver to prise out the circlip...

12.20b...then push out the gudgeon pin and separate the piston and connecting rod

same way as the arrow on the piston crown (ie, towards the timing belt end of the engine) when correctly installed. Reassemble the two components to satisfy this requirement **(see illustrations)**.

24 Apply a smear of clean engine oil to the gudgeon pin. Slide it into the piston and through the connecting rod small-end. Check that the piston pivots freely on the rod, then secure the gudgeon pin in position with two new circlips. Ensure that each circlip is correctly located in its groove in the piston.

25 Repeat the cleaning and inspection process for the remaining pistons and connecting rods.

13 Crankshaft – checking endfloat, spigot bearing, and inspection

Checking endfloat

1 If the crankshaft endfloat is to be checked, this must be done when the crankshaft is still installed in the cylinder block/crankcase, but is free to move (see Section 10).

2 Check the endfloat using a dial gauge in contact with the end of the crankshaft. Push the crankshaft fully one way, and then zero the gauge. Push the crankshaft fully the other way, and check the endfloat. The result can be compared with the specified amount, and will give an indication as to whether new thrustwasher halves are required **(see illustration)**. Note that all thrustwashers must be of the same thickness.

3 If a dial gauge is not available, feeler blades can be used. First push the crankshaft fully

12.23a The piston crown is marked with an arrow which must point towards the timing belt end of the engine

towards the flywheel end of the engine, and then use feeler blades to measure the gap between the web of No 3 crankpin and the thrustwasher halves **(see illustration)**.

Spigot bearing

Note: *On 7-speed DSG semi-automatic transmissions, the spigot needle roller bearing needs to be renewed; every time the transmission is removed from the engine.*

4 On some models, there is a bearing positioned in the end of the crankshaft, which supports the transmission shaft.

5 Remove the transmission as described in Chapter 7A (manual transmission) or Chapter 7B (DSG transmissions)

6 Remove the clutch assembly as described in Chapter 6.

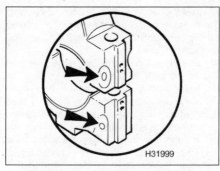

12.23b The recesses (arrowed) in the connecting rod and bearing cap must face the timing belt end of the engine

7 Before removing the bearing, check the fitted depth of the bearing inside the end of the crankshaft **(see illustration)**. See specifications at the beginning of this Chapter to find the relevant depth for each engine.

8 Using an internal puller, slide the bearing out from the centre of the crankshaft **(see illustrations)**.

9 Using a drift, drive the bearing into the end of the crankshaft **(see illustration)**, taking care not to drive it in to far, as noted on removal. Also see specifications at the beginning of Chapter for depth of bearing.

⚠️ **Warning: If the new bearing is driven into the end of the crankshaft to far, then it will need to be completely removed and another new one fitted.**

13.2 Measure crankshaft endfloat using a dial gauge

13.3 Measure crankshaft endfloat using feeler blades

13.7 Check the depth of the bearing using a vernier gauge

13.8a Using an internal bearing puller...

13.8b...to withdraw the bearing

13.9 Using a drift to carefully tap the bearing back into position

Inspection

10 Clean the crankshaft using paraffin or a suitable solvent, and dry it, preferably with compressed air if available. Be sure to clean the oil holes with a pipe cleaner or similar probe, to ensure that they are not obstructed.

 Warning: Wear eye protection when using compressed air.

11 Check the main and big-end bearing journals for uneven wear, scoring, pitting and cracking.

12 Big-end bearing wear is accompanied by distinct metallic knocking when the engine is running (particularly noticeable when the engine is pulling from low speed) and some loss of oil pressure.

13 Main bearing wear is accompanied by severe engine vibration and rumble – getting progressively worse as engine speed increases – and again by loss of oil pressure.

14 Check the bearing journal for roughness by running a finger lightly over the bearing surface. Any roughness (which will be accompanied by obvious bearing wear) indicates that the crankshaft requires regrinding (where possible) or renewal.

15 If the crankshaft has been reground, check for burrs around the crankshaft oil holes (the holes are usually chamfered, so burrs should not be a problem unless regrinding has been carried out carelessly). Remove any burrs with a fine file or scraper, and thoroughly clean the oil holes as described previously.

16 Have the crankshaft measured and inspected by an engine reconditioning specialist. They will be able to advise any possible repairs and supply the correct parts.

17 Check the oil seal contact surfaces at each end of the crankshaft for wear and damage. If the seal has worn a deep groove in the surface of the crankshaft, consult an engine overhaul specialist; repair may be possible, but otherwise a new crankshaft will be required.

18 If the crankshaft journals have not already been reground, it may be possible to have the crankshaft reconditioned, and to fit undersize shells (see Section 17). If no undersize shells are available and the crankshaft has worn beyond the specified limits, it will have to be renewed. Consult your Audi dealer or engine specialist for further information on parts availability.

14 Main and big-end bearings – inspection and selection

Inspection

1 Even though the main and big-end bearings should be renewed during the engine overhaul, the old bearings should be retained for close examination, as they may reveal valuable information about the condition of the engine **(see illustration)**.

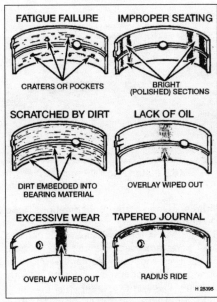

14.1 Typical bearing failures

2 Bearing failure can occur due to lack of lubrication, the presence of dirt or other foreign particles, overloading the engine, or corrosion. Regardless of the cause of bearing failure, the cause must be corrected before the engine is reassembled, to prevent it from happening again.

3 When examining the bearing shells, remove them from the cylinder block/crankcase, the main bearing caps, the connecting rods and the connecting rod big-end bearing caps. Lay them out on a clean surface in the same general position as their location in the engine. This will enable you to match any bearing problems with the corresponding crankshaft journal. Do not touch any shell's internal bearing surface with your fingers while checking it, or the delicate surface may be scratched.

4 Dirt and other foreign matter get into the engine in a variety of ways. It may be left in the engine during assembly, or it may pass through filters or the crankcase ventilation system. It may get into the oil, and from there into the bearings. Metal chips from machining operations and normal engine wear are often present. Abrasives are sometimes left in engine components after reconditioning, especially when parts are not thoroughly cleaned using the proper cleaning methods. Whatever the source, these foreign objects often end up embedded in the soft bearing material, and are easily recognised. Large particles will not embed in the bearing, but will score or gouge the bearing and journal. The best prevention for this cause of bearing failure is to clean all parts thoroughly, and keep everything spotlessly clean during engine assembly. Frequent and regular engine oil and filter changes are also recommended.

5 Lack of lubrication (or lubrication

breakdown) has a number of interrelated causes. Excessive heat (which thins the oil), overloading (which squeezes the oil from the bearing face) and oil leakage (from excessive bearing clearances, worn oil pump or high engine speeds) all contribute to lubrication breakdown. Blocked oil passages, which usually are the result of misaligned oil holes in a bearing shell, will also oil-starve a bearing, and destroy it. When lack of lubrication is the cause of bearing failure, the bearing material is wiped or extruded from the steel backing of the bearing. Temperatures may increase to the point where the steel backing turns blue from overheating.

6 Driving habits can have a definite effect on bearing life. Full-throttle, low-speed operation (labouring the engine) puts very high loads on bearings, tending to squeeze out the oil film. These loads cause the bearings to flex, which produces fine cracks in the bearing face (fatigue failure). Eventually, the bearing material will loosen in pieces, and tear away from the steel backing.

7 Short-distance driving leads to corrosion of bearings, because insufficient engine heat is produced to drive off the condensed water and corrosive gases. These products collect in the engine oil, forming acid and sludge. As the oil is carried to the engine bearings, the acid attacks and corrodes the bearing material.

8 Incorrect bearing installation during engine assembly will lead to bearing failure as well. Tight-fitting bearings leave insufficient bearing running clearance, and will result in oil starvation. Dirt or foreign particles trapped behind a bearing shell result in high spots on the bearing, which lead to failure.

9 Do not touch any shell's internal bearing surface with your fingers during re-assembly, as there is a risk of scratching the delicate surface, or of depositing particles of dirt on it.

10 As mentioned at the beginning of this Section, the bearing shells should be renewed as a matter of course during engine overhaul. To do otherwise is false economy.

Selection

11 Main and big-end bearings for the engines described in this Chapter are available in standard sizes and a range of undersizes to suit reground crankshafts.

12 Have the crankshaft measured by an engine reconditioning specialist. They will be able to supply the correctly sized bearings.

15 Engine overhaul – reassembly sequence

1 Before reassembly begins, ensure that all new parts have been obtained, and that all necessary tools are available. Read through the entire procedure to familiarise yourself with the work involved, and to ensure that all items necessary for reassembly of the engine are at hand. In addition to all normal tools and

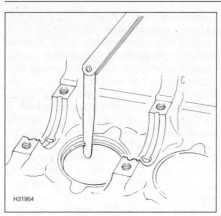

16.4 Check a piston ring end gap using a feeler blade

materials, thread-locking compound will be needed. A suitable tube of liquid sealant will also be required for the joint faces that are fitted without gaskets.

2 In order to save time and avoid problems, engine reassembly can be carried out in the following order, referring to Part A, B or C of this Chapter unless otherwise stated. Where applicable, use new gaskets and seals when refitting the various components.

a) *Crankshaft (Section 17).*
b) *Piston/connecting rod assemblies (Section 18).*
c) *Oil pump.*
d) *Sump.*
e) *Flywheel.*
f) *Cylinder head.*
g) *Timing belt, tensioner and sprockets.*
h) *Engine external components.*

3 At this stage, all engine components should be absolutely clean and dry, with all faults repaired. The components should be laid out (or in individual containers) on a completely clean work surface.

16 Piston rings – refitting

1 Before fitting new piston rings, the ring end gaps must be checked as follows.
2 Lay out the piston/connecting rod assemblies and the new piston ring sets, so that the ring sets will be matched with the same piston and cylinder during the end gap measurement and subsequent engine reassembly.
3 Insert the top ring into the first cylinder, and push it down the bore using the top of the piston. This will ensure that the ring remains square with the cylinder walls. Position the ring approximately 15.0 mm the bottom of the cylinder bore, at the lower limit of ring travel. Note that the top and second compression rings are different.
4 Measure the end gap using feeler blades, and compare the measurements with the

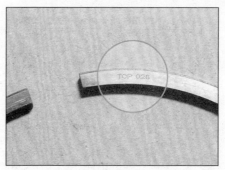

16.9 Piston ring TOP marking

figures given in the Specifications **(see illustration)**.
5 If the gap is too small (unlikely if genuine Audi parts are used), it must be enlarged, or the ring ends may contact each other during engine operation, causing serious damage. Ideally, new piston rings providing the correct end gap should be fitted. As a last resort, the end gap can be increased by filing the ring ends very carefully with a fine file. Mount the file in a vice equipped with soft jaws, slip the ring over the file with the ends contacting the file face, and slowly move the ring to remove material from the ends. Take care, as piston rings are sharp, and are easily broken.
6 With new piston rings, it is unlikely that the end gap will be too large. If the gaps are too large, check that you have the correct rings for your engine and for the particular cylinder bore size.
7 Repeat the checking procedure for each ring in the first cylinder, and then for the rings in the remaining cylinders. Remember to keep rings, pistons and cylinders matched up.
8 Once the ring end gaps have been checked and if necessary corrected, the rings can be fitted to the pistons.
9 Fit the piston rings using the same technique as for removal. Fit the bottom (oil control) ring first, and work up. Note that a two- or three-section oil control ring may be fitted; where a two-section ring is

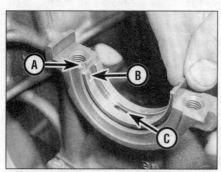

17.2 Bearing shell correctly refitted

A *Recess in cylinder block*
B *Lug on bearing shell*
C *Oil hole*

fitted, first insert the wire expander, then fit the ring. Ensure that the rings are fitted the correct way up – the top surface of the rings is normally marked TOP **(see illustration)**. Offset the piston ring gaps by 120° from each other.

Note: *Always follow any instructions supplied with the new piston ring sets – different manufacturers may specify different procedures. Do not mix up the top and second compression rings, as they have different cross-sections.*

17 Crankshaft – refitting

1 Wipe off the surfaces of the bearing shells in the crankcase and bearing caps.
2 Press the bearing shells into their locations, ensuring that the tab on each shell engages in the notch in the cylinder block or bearing cap, and that the oil holes In the cylinder block and bearing shell are aligned **(see illustration)**. Take care not to touch any shells bearing surface with your fingers.
3 Where applicable, refit the crankshaft speed/position sensor wheel, and tighten the securing bolts to the specified torque. Make sure that the sensor wheel is correctly orientated as noted before removal.
4 Liberally coat the bearing shells in the crankcase with clean engine oil of the appropriate grade **(see illustration)**. Make sure that the bearing shells are still correctly seated in their locations.
5 Lower the crankshaft into position so that No 1 cylinder crankpin is at BDC, ready for fitting No 1 piston. Ensure that the crankshaft endfloat control thrustwasher halves, either side of the No 3 main bearing location, remain in position. Where applicable, take care not to damage the crankshaft speed/position sensor wheel as the crankshaft is lowered into position.
6 Lubricate the lower bearing shells in the main bearing caps with clean engine oil. Make sure that the crankshaft endfloat control thrustwasher halves are still correctly

17.4 Lubricate the upper bearing shells

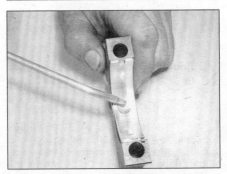

17.6a Lubricate the lower bearing shells...

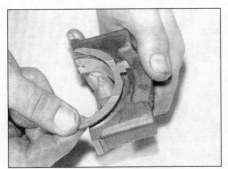

17.6b...and make sure that the thrustwashers are correctly seated

17.7 Fitting No 1 main bearing cap

seated either side of No 3 bearing cap **(see illustrations)**.

7 Fit the main bearing caps in the correct order and orientation – No 1 bearing cap must be at the timing belt end of the engine and the bearing shell tab locating recesses in the crankcase and bearing caps must be adjacent to each other **(see illustration)**. Insert the bearing cap bolts (using new bolts where necessary), and hand-tighten them only.

8 Working from the centre bearing cap outwards, tighten the bearing cap bolts to their specified torque. On engines where two Stages are given for the torque, tighten all bolts to the Stage 1 torque, then go round again, and tighten all bolts through the Stage 2 angle **(see illustrations)**.

9 Check that the crankshaft rotates freely by turning it by hand. If resistance is felt, recheck the bearing running clearances, as described previously.

10 Check the crankshaft endfloat as described at the beginning of Section 13. If the thrust surfaces of the crankshaft have been checked and new thrustwashers have been fitted, then the endfloat should be within specification.

11 Refit the pistons and connecting rods or reconnect them to the crankshaft as described in Section.

12 Refit the crankshaft oil seal housings, flywheel, oil pump and pick-up pipe, sump and oil baffle plate, and the crankshaft sprocket and timing belt.

17.8a Tighten the main bearing cap bolts to the specified torque...

17.8b...then through the specified angle

connecting rods. Tap the old bolts out of the connecting rods using a soft-faced mallet, and tap the new bolts into position.

4 Ensure that the bearing shells are correctly fitted, as described at the beginning of this Section. If new shells are being fitted, ensure that all traces of the protective grease are cleaned off using paraffin. Wipe dry the shells and connecting rods with a lint-free cloth.

5 Lubricate the cylinder bores, the pistons, piston rings and upper bearing shells with clean engine oil **(see illustrations)**. Lay out each piston/connecting rod assembly in order on a clean work surface. Where the bearing caps are secured with nuts, pad the threaded ends of the bolts with insulating tape to prevent them scratching the crankpins and bores when the pistons are refitted.

6 Start with piston/connecting rod assembly No 1. Make sure that the piston rings are still spaced as described in Section 16, then clamp them in position with a piston ring compressor tool.

7 Insert the piston/connecting rod assembly into the top of cylinder No 1. Lower the big-end in first, guiding it to protect the cylinder bores. Where oil jets are located at the bottoms of the bores, take particular care not to damage them when guiding the connecting rods onto the crankpins.

8 Ensure that the orientation of the piston in its cylinder is correct – the piston crown, connecting rod and big-end bearing cap have markings, which must point towards the timing belt end of the engine when the piston

18 Piston/connecting rod assemblies – refitting

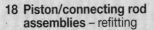

Note: *A piston ring compressor tool will be required for this operation.*

1 Note that the following procedure assumes that the crankshaft main bearing caps are in place.

2 Where applicable, refit the piston cooling oil spray jets to the bottom of the cylinder block, and tighten the securing bolts to the specified torque.

3 On engines where the big-end bearing caps are secured by nuts, fit new bolts to the

18.5a Lubricate the pistons...

18.5b...and big-end upper bearing shells with clean engine oil

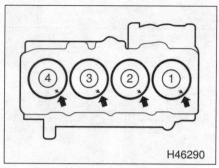

18.8 Piston orientation and coding

18.9 Using a hammer handle to tap the piston into its bore

18.13a Tighten the big-end bearing cap bolts/nuts to the specified torque...

18.13b...then through the specified angle

is installed in the bore **(see illustration)** – refer to Section 12 for details.

9 Using a block of wood or hammer handle against the piston crown, tap the assembly into the cylinder until the piston crown is flush with the top of the cylinder **(see illustration)**.

10 Ensure that the bearing shell is still correctly installed in the connecting rod, and then liberally lubricate the crankpin and both bearing shells with clean engine oil.

11 Taking care not to mark the cylinder bores; tap the piston/connecting rod assembly down the bore and onto the crankpin. On engines where the big-end caps are secured by nuts, remove the insulating tape from the threaded ends of the connecting rod bolts. Oil the bolt threads, and on engines where the big-end caps are secured by bolts, oil the undersides of the bolt heads.

12 Fit the big-end bearing cap, tightening its retaining nuts or bolts (as applicable) finger-tight at first. The connecting rod and its bearing cap both have recesses machined into them on one side, close to their mating

surfaces – these recesses must both face the same way as the arrow on the piston crown (i.e. towards the timing end of the engine) when correctly installed. Reassemble the two components to satisfy this requirement.

13 Tighten the retaining bolts or nuts (as applicable) to the specified torque and angle, in the two stages given in the Specifications **(see illustrations)**.

14 Refit the other three remaining piston/connecting rod assemblies in the same way.

15 Rotate the crankshaft by hand. Check that it turns freely; some stiffness is to be expected if new parts have been fitted, but there should be no binding or tight spots.

16 If new pistons have been fitted, or if a new short engine has been fitted, the projection of the piston crowns above the cylinder head mating face of the cylinder block at TDC must be measured. This measurement is used to determine the thickness of the new cylinder head gasket required. This procedure is described as part of the Cylinder head – removal, inspection and refitting procedure.

17 Refit the balance shaft assembly (where applicable), oil pump and pick-up pipe, sump and oil baffle plate and cylinder head.

19 Engine – initial start-up after overhaul and reassembly

1 Refit the remainder of the engine components in the order listed in Section 5 of this Chapter. Refit the engine to the vehicle as described in Section. Double-check the engine oil and coolant levels, and make a final check that everything has been reconnected. Make sure that there are no tools or rags left in the engine compartment.

2 Where necessary, reconnect the battery leads with reference to 'Disconnecting the battery' in Reference Chapter.

3 Disconnect the injector harness wiring plug at the end of the cylinder head.

4 Turn the engine using the starter motor until the oil pressure warning lamp goes out.

5 If the lamp fails to extinguish after several seconds of cranking, check the engine oil level and oil filter security. Assuming these are correct, check the security of the oil pressure switch cabling – do not progress any further until you are satisfied that oil is being pumped around the engine at sufficient pressure.

6 Reconnect the injector harness wiring plug.

7 Start the engine, but be aware that as fuel system components have been disturbed, the cranking time may be a little longer than usual.

8 While the engine is idling, check for fuel, water and oil leaks. Don't be alarmed if there are some odd smells and the occasional plume of smoke as components heat up and burn off oil deposits.

9 Assuming all is well; keep the engine idling until hot water is felt circulating through the top hose.

10 After a few minutes, recheck the oil and coolant levels, and top-up as necessary.

11 There is no need to retighten the cylinder head bolts once the engine has been run following reassembly.

12 If new pistons, rings or crankshaft bearings have been fitted, the engine must be treated as new, and run-in for the first 600 miles. Do not operate the engine at full-throttle, or allow it to labour at low engine speeds in any gear. It is recommended that the engine oil and filter be changed at the end of this period.

Chapter 3
Cooling, heating and air conditioning systems

Contents

Degrees of difficulty

Easy, suitable for novice with little experience 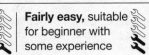	Fairly easy, suitable for beginner with some experience	Fairly difficult, suitable for competent DIY mechanic	Difficult, suitable for experienced DIY mechanic	Very difficult, suitable for expert DIY or professional

Specifications

Cooling system pressure cap

Opening pressure	1.4 to 1.6 bar

Thermostat

	Begins to open	Fully open
1.6 litre engines	92°C	107°C
1.9 litre engines	85°C	105°C
2.0 litre engines	85°C	105°C

Torque wrench settings

	Nm	lbf ft
Coolant pump bolts	15	11
Radiator	5	4
Radiator cooling fan shroud bolts	5	4
Thermostat cover bolts	15	11

1 General information and precautions

1 A pressurised cooling system is used, with a pump, an aluminium crossflow radiator, two electric cooling fans, a thermostat and a heater matrix, electric coolant circulation pump, engine oil cooler as well as the interconnecting hoses. On semi-automatic (DSG) transmission models, there is also a separate transmission oil cooler. The thermostat is located in the front, right-hand side of the cylinder block, in the coolant return from the radiator.

2 The system functions as follows. Coolant is circulated through the cylinder block and head passages by the coolant pump which is driven by the timing belt. The coolant cools the cylinder bores, combustion surfaces and valve seats of the engine.

3 When the engine is cold, the thermostat is closed and the coolant only circulates around the engine and the heater matrix in the passenger compartment, however, when the engine reaches a predetermined temperature, the thermostat opens and the coolant passes through the radiator for additional cooling. The coolant enters the top of the radiator and is cooled, as it circulates down through the cooling tubes, by the inrush of air when the car is in forward motion. Airflow is supplemented by the action of the electric cooling fans when necessary. Upon leaving the bottom of the radiator, the coolant returns to the engine and the cycle is repeated.

4 Refer to Section 11 for information on the air conditioning system.

Precautions

⚠️ *Warning: Do not attempt to remove the expansion tank filler cap or disturb any part of the cooling system while the engine is hot, as there is a high risk of scalding. If the expansion tank filler cap must be removed before the engine and radiator have fully cooled (even though this is not recommended) the pressure in the cooling system must first be relieved. Cover the cap with a thick layer of cloth, to avoid scalding, and slowly unscrew the filler cap until a*

hissing sound can be heard. When the hissing has stopped, indicating that the pressure has reduced, slowly unscrew the filler cap until it can be removed; if more hissing sounds are heard, wait until they have stopped before unscrewing the cap completely. At all times keep well away from the filler cap opening.

• Do not allow antifreeze to come into contact with skin or painted surfaces of the vehicle. Rinse off spills immediately with plenty of water. Never leave antifreeze lying around in an open container or in a puddle in the driveway or on the garage floor. Children and pets are attracted by its sweet smell. Antifreeze can be fatal if ingested.

• If the engine is hot, the electric cooling fan may start rotating even if the engine is not running, so be careful to keep hands, hair and loose clothing well clear when working in the engine compartment.

• Refer to Section 11 for additional precautions to be observed when working on models with air conditioning.

2 Cooling system hoses – disconnection and renewal

Note: *Refer to the warnings given in Section 1 of this Chapter before proceeding.*

1 If the checks described in the relevant part of Chapter reveal a faulty hose, it must be renewed as follows.

2 First drain the cooling system as described in Chapter 1 Section 31. If the coolant is not due for renewal, it may be re-used if it is collected in a clean container.

3 To disconnect a hose, release its retaining clips, then move them along the hose, clear of the relevant inlet/outlet union. Carefully work the hose free.

4 In order to disconnect the radiator inlet and outlet hoses, apply pressure to hold the hose on to the relevant union, pull out the spring clip and pull the hose from the union **(see illustration)**. Note that the radiator inlet and outlet unions are fragile; do not use excessive force when attempting to remove the hoses. If a hose proves to be difficult to remove, try to release it by rotating the hose ends before attempting to free it.

5 When fitting a hose, first slide the clips onto the hose, and then work the hose into position. If clamp type clips were originally fitted, it is a good idea to use screw type clips when refitting the hose. If the hose is stiff, use a little soapy water as a lubricant, or soften the hose by soaking it in hot water.

6 Work the hose into position, checking that it is correctly routed, and then slide each clip along the hose until it passes over the flared end of the relevant union, before securing it in position with the retaining clip.

7 Prior to refitting a radiator inlet or outlet hose, renew the connection O-ring regardless of condition. The connections are a push-fit over the radiator unions.

8 Refill the cooling system as described in Chapter 1 Section 31.

9 Check thoroughly for leaks as soon as possible after disturbing any part of the cooling system.

3 Radiator – removal, inspection and refitting

Removal

1 Switch off the ignition and all electrical consumers.

2 Undo the retaining screws and securing clips from the air cleaner housing and ducting and remove it from in front of the battery tray.

3 Move the lock/radiator carrier, located at the front of the engine compartment, to its Service position as described in Chapter 2D, Section 4.

Warning: If the refrigerant lines have not been disconnected, take care not to damage them when moving the front panel forward. Disconnect any securing clips to allow the pipes to move slightly.

4 Drain the cooling system as described in Chapter 1 Section 31. On some models, the electric cooling fan temperature sensor may be removed from the bottom hose to drain the system, otherwise disconnect the bottom hose from the radiator **(see illustration)**.

5 Disconnect the coolant hoses from the radiator by pulling out the clips and easing off the hoses **(see illustration)**.

2.4 Pull out the spring clip and pull the hose from the union

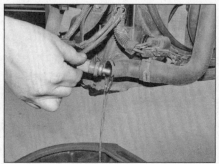

3.4 Removing the cooling fan temperature sensor to drain the cooling system

3.5 Pull out the clip (arrowed) with a screwdriver and disconnect the hoses from the radiator

3.7a Release the retaining clip arrowed...

3.7b...and undo the two retaining screws

3.12a Radiator lower mounting rubber grommets on the lock carrier...

6 Disconnect the wiring from the cooling fan connector at the bottom left-hand side of the radiator and remove the fan assembly as described in Section 5 of this Chapter.

7 Release the securing clip and disconnect the hose from the left-hand side of the intercooler. Then working at the rear of the radiator undo the two retaining screws at each side of the radiator **(see illustrations)**. Move the top of the radiator slightly to the rear, and withdraw it upwards from the lower mounting rubber grommets in the lock carrier.

Inspection

8 If the radiator has been removed due to suspected blockage, reverse flush it as described in Chapter 1, Section 31.

9 Clean dirt and debris from the radiator fins, using an airline (in which case, wear eye protection) or a soft brush. Be careful, as the fins are sharp and easily damaged.

10 If necessary, a radiator specialist can perform a 'flow test' on the radiator, to establish whether an internal blockage exists.

11 A leaking radiator must be referred to a specialist for permanent repair. Do not attempt to weld or solder a leaking radiator, as damage may result.

12 Check the radiator mounting rubbers, and renew if necessary **(see illustrations)**.

Refitting

13 Refitting is a reversal of removal. On

3.12b...and upper mounting rubbers on the radiator

completion, refill the cooling system using the correct type of antifreeze as described in Chapter 1, Section 31.

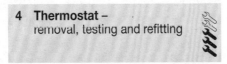

4   Thermostat –
removal, testing and refitting

1.6 and 2.0 litre engines engines
Removal

1 The thermostat is located behind the alternator at the front right-hand side of the engine cylinder block **(see illustration)**. There are two types of thermostat fitted:

a) *Single hose to the thermostat cover, and the thermostat can be renewed separately.*

4.1 Location of thermostat (arrowed)

b) *Three hoses to the thermostat housing, the thermostat is part of the housing and can only be renewed as a complete assembly.*

2 Drain the cooling system as described in Chapter 1 Section 31. If the coolant is not due for renewal, it may be re-used if it is collected in a clean container.

3 Slacken the retaining clips and remove the rubber hose from the intercooler and charge air ducting to the throttle housing/inlet manifold **(see illustration)**.

4 Undo the bolt on the right-hand end of the sump, and disconnect the wiring connector from the charge pressure/temperature sensor on the charge air ducting **(see illustrations)**.

5 Slacken the clip securing the charge air ducting to the throttle housing/inlet manifold, then undo the bolt at the rear of the air-conditioning compressor and withdraw the

4.3 Remove the intercooler lower hose

4.4a Undo the charge air pipe retaining bolt (arrowed)

4.4b Disconnect the charge air pressure sensor wiring connector

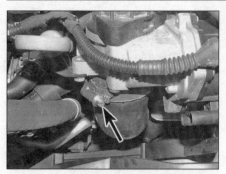

4.5a Slacken the hose retaining clip (arrowed)...

4.5b...undo the retaining bolt arrowed...

4.5c and remove the charge air pipe

4.7 Release the retaining clip (arrowed)

4.8a Remove the thermostat housing...

4.8b...and renew the seal

ducting out from the front of the engine **(see illustrations)**.

6 To make access easier, remove the alternator as described in Chapter 5, Section 5.

7 Release the securing clip(s) and disconnect the coolant hose(s) from the thermostat cover/housing **(see illustration)**.

8 Unscrew the two securing bolts, and remove the thermostat cover/housing complete with the thermostat. Note the locations of any brackets secured by the bolts. Recover the O-ring if it is loose **(see illustrations)**.

9 On models with one hose connections to the thermostat cover, remove the thermostat by twisting the thermostat 90° anti-clockwise, and then pull it from the cover.

10 On models with three hose connections to the thermostat housing, the thermostat cannot be removed, renew the complete unit.

Testing

Note: *If there is any question about the operation of the thermostat, it's best to renew it – they are not usually expensive items. Testing involves heating in, or over, an open pan of boiling water, which carries with it the risk of scalding. A thermostat that has seen more than five years' service may well be past its best already.*

11 A rough test of the thermostat, may be made by suspending it with a piece of string in a container full of water, but not touching the container. Heat the water to bring it to the boil – the thermostat must open by the time the water boils. If not, renew it.

12 If a thermometer is available, the precise opening temperature of the thermostat may be determined, and compared with the figures

given in the Specifications. The opening temperature is also marked on the thermostat.

13 A thermostat which fails to close as the water cools must also be renewed.

Refitting

14 Refitting is a reversal of removal, bearing in mind the following points.

a) *Refit the thermostat using a new O-ring.*

b) *Insert the thermostat into the cover and twist 90° clockwise (where applicable). The thermostat should be fitted with the brace almost vertical.*

c) *Ensure that any brackets are in place on the thermostat cover bolts as noted before removal.*

d) *Refit the alternator (where applicable) with reference to Chapter 5, Section 5.*

e) *Refill the cooling system with the correct type and quantity of coolant as described in Chapter 1 Section 31.*

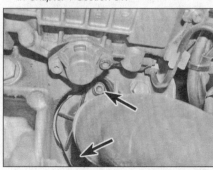

4.18a Thermostat cover bolts (arrowed)

1.9 litre engines

Removal

15 The thermostat is located behind a connection flange in the front side of the engine block, at the timing belt end.

16 Drain the cooling system as described in Chapter 1 Section 31. Prise out the sealing caps, undo the retaining nuts and remove the engine covers.

17 Release the securing clip and disconnect the coolant hose from the thermostat cover/connection flange.

18 Unscrew the two securing bolts, and remove the thermostat cover/connection flange complete with the thermostat. Note the locations of any brackets secured by the bolts. Recover the O-ring if it is loose **(see illustrations)**.

19 To remove the thermostat from the cover, twist the thermostat 90° anti-clockwise, and pull it from the cover.

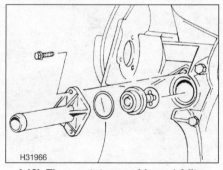

4.18b Thermostat assembly on 1.9 litre engines

Testing

20 Proceed as described in paragraphs 11 to 13.

Refitting

21 Refitting is a reversal of removal, bearing in mind the following points.

a) *Refit the thermostat using a new O-ring*
b) *Insert the thermostat into the cover and twist 90° clockwise.*
c) *The thermostat should be fitted with the brace almost vertical.*
d) *Ensure that any brackets are in place on the thermostat cover bolts as noted before removal.*
e) *Refill the cooling system with the correct type and quantity of coolant as described in Chapter 1 Section 31.*

5 Electric cooling fans – testing, removal and refitting

Testing

1 Two electric cooling fans are fitted to all models. The cooling fans are supplied with current through the ignition switch, cooling fan control unit (located on the motor), temperature sensor, the relays and fuses/fusible link (see Chapter 12). The circuit is activated by the temperature sensor mounted in the outlet elbow at the bottom, left-hand side of the radiator, or by the engine management ECU which activates it according to the engine coolant temperature sensor. Testing of the cooling fan circuit is as follows.

2 If a fan does not appear to work, first check the fuses and fusible links. If they are good, run the engine until normal operating temperature is reached, then allow it to idle. If the fan does not cut-in within a few minutes, the cause may be the temperature sender (where applicable), which can be checked by an Audi dealer using specialist diagnostic equipment.

3 Check the motors by disconnecting the motor wiring connector, and then connecting a 12 volt supply directly to the motor terminals. If the motor is faulty, it must be renewed, as no spares are available.

4 If the fan still fails to operate, check the cooling fan circuit wiring (Chapter 12). Check each wire for continuity and ensure that all connections are clean and free of corrosion.

5 On models with a cooling fan control unit, if no fault can be found, then it is likely that the cooling fan control unit is faulty. Testing of the unit should be entrusted to an Audi dealer or specialist; if the unit is faulty it must be renewed.

Removal

6 Switch off the ignition and all electrical consumers. Remove the plastic cover from the top of the engine.

7 Undo the retaining screws and securing clips from the air filter housing and ducting and remove it from in front of the battery tray.

8 On some models it will be necessary to

5.10 Disconnect the wiring...

move the lock/radiator carrier to its Service position as follows to allow for more room (See Chapter 2D Section 4).

9 Release the securing clip and disconnect the hose from the left-hand side lower part of the intercooler.

10 Disconnect the wiring plug for the cooling fan motors **(see illustration)**.

11 Unscrew the bolts securing the cooling fan shroud to the radiator, and withdraw either upwards or downwards according to model **(see illustrations)**.

12 To remove the fans and motors from the shroud, first disconnect and release the wiring plugs, then unscrew the nuts and remove the units **(see illustrations)**.

Refitting

13 Refitting is a reversal of removal.

5.11a...undo the retaining screws...

5.11b...and remove the cooling fan assembly upwards...

5.11c...or out through the bottom – depending on model

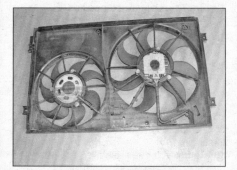

5.11d Cooling fan shroud and motors removed from the radiator

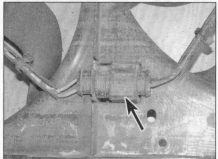

5.12a Disconnect and release the wiring plugs (arrowed)...

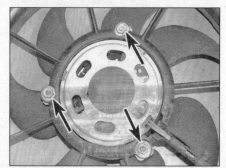

5.12b...and unscrew the motor retaining nuts (arrowed)

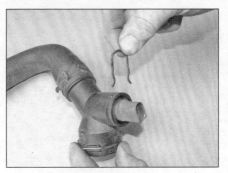

6.6a Pull out the clip...

6.6b...remove the sensor...

6.6c...and recover the O-ring seals from the elbow and sensor

6 Cooling system electrical sensors – testing, removal and refitting

Testing

1 The sensors contains a thermistor, which consists of an electronic component whose electrical resistance decreases at a predetermined rate as its temperature rises. When the coolant is cold, the sensor resistance is high, current flow through the gauge is reduced, and the gauge needle points towards the 'cold' end of the scale. No resistance-to-temperature values are available. Therefore the only method of accurately checking the sensor is with dedicated diagnostic equipment, and should be entrusted to an Audi dealer or specialist. If the sensor is faulty, it must be renewed.

Removal and refitting

Cooling fan temperature sensor

2 Where fitted, the sensor is located in the outlet elbow at the bottom left-hand side of the radiator.

3 The engine and radiator should be cold before removing the sensor. Switch off the ignition and all electrical consumers.

4 Either drain the cooling system (as described in Chapter 1 Section 31), or have ready a suitable plug which can be used to plug the sensor aperture whilst it is removed.

5 Disconnect the wiring plug from the sensor.

6 Pull out the clip and remove the sensor from the elbow. Recover the O-ring seals from the elbow and sensor (see illustrations).

7 Refitting is a reversal of removal. On completion, refill the cooling system with the correct type and quantity of coolant as described in Chapter 1 Section 31, or top-up as described in *Weekly checks*.

8 Start the engine and run it until it reaches normal operating temperature, then continue to run the engine and check that the cooling fan cuts in and functions correctly.

Coolant temperature sensor – 1.9 litre engines

9 The sensor is located on the thermostat housing at the left-hand end of the cylinder head (see illustration).

10 Remove the engine top cover.

11 Disconnect the wiring from the sensor (see illustration). Partially drain the cooling system to below the level of the sensor (as described in Chapter 1 Section 31).

12 Pull out the retaining clip and withdraw the sensor from the housing. Recover the O-ring (see illustrations).

13 Refitting is a reversal of removal. Bearing in mind the following points.

a) Refit the sensor with a new O-ring.
b) Refill the cooling system as described in Chapter 1 Section 31, or top-up as described in 'Weekly checks'.

Coolant temperature sensor – 1.6 and 2.0 litre engines

14 Two sensors are fitted to these engines, one located in the upper hose at the right-hand side of the engine and one in the coolant housing on the left-hand side of the cylinder head.

Sensor fitted to coolant housing

15 Remove the plastic cover from the top of the engine.

16 Remove the air cleaner assembly as described in Chapter 4A, Section 2.

17 Slacken the retaining clip, undo the two retaining bolts and move the charge air

6.9 Engine coolant temperature sensor (arrowed) on 1.9 litre engines

6.11 Disconnect the wiring...

6.12a...then pull out the retaining clip...

6.12b...and withdraw the coolant temperature sensor and O-ring seal from the thermostat housing

6.17a Slacken the retaining clip (arrowed)...

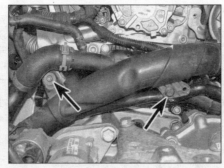

6.17b...and undo the two retaining bolts (arrowed)

6.18 Disconnect the wiring connector (arrowed)

6.19a Pull out the clip and remove the sensor...

6.19b...recover the O-ring from the housing

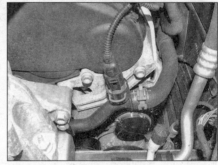

6.21 Coolant hose temperature sensor

ducting away from the coolant housing **(see illustrations)**.

18 Disconnect the wiring from the sensor **(see illustration)**. Partially drain the cooling system to below the level of the sensor (as described in Chapter 1, Section 31).

19 Pull out the retaining clip and withdraw the sensor from the housing. Recover the O-ring **(see illustrations)**.

20 Refitting is a reversal of removal. Bearing in mind the following points.

a) *Refit the sensor with a new O-ring.*

b) *Refill the cooling system as described in Chapter 1, Section 31, otherwise top-up as described in 'Weekly checks'.*

Sensor fitted to coolant hose

21 The sensor is located in the hose positioned on the right-hand side of the engine **(see illustration)**. Remove the sensor from the hose as described in paragraphs 15 to 20.

22 Refitting is a reversal of removal.

7 Coolant pump – removal and refitting

Belt driven coolant pump

1 Drain the cooling system as described in Chapter 1 Section 31.

2 Remove the timing belt as described in Chapter 2A Section 7,

3 Unscrew the coolant pump retaining bolts, and remove the pump from the engine block. Recover the O-ring seal from the groove in the pump. If the pump is faulty, it must be renewed **(see illustrations)**.

4 Refitting is a reversal of removal, bearing in mind the following points.

a) *Fit the coolant pump with a new O-ring.*

b) *Lubricate the O-ring with coolant.*

c) *Refill the cooling system as described in Chapter 1 Section 31.*

Electric circulation pump

5 Raise the front of the vehicle and support is securely on axle stands (see *'Jacking and vehicle support'* in Reference Chapter).

6 Undo the fasteners and remove the engine undertray.

7.3a Undo the coolant pump bolts...

7.3b...remove it from the cylinder block...

7.3c...and renew the O-ring seal

7.7 Disconnect the wiring connector (arrowed)

7.8 Disconnect the coolant hoses (arrowed)

7 Disconnect the wiring plug connector to the pump **(see illustration)**.

8 Fit hose clamps to the coolant hoses connected to the pump, and release the clips and disconnect the hoses from the pump **(see illustration)**. Be prepared for some loss of coolant.

9 Undo the retaining bolt and remove the pump **(see illustration)**.

10 Refitting is a reversal of removal. Top up the coolant, as described in 'Weekly checks'.

8 Heating and ventilation system – general information

1 The heating/ventilation system consists of a four-speed blower motor (housed in the passenger compartment), face-level vents in the centre and at each end of the facia, and air ducts to the front and rear footwells.

2 The control unit is located in the facia, and the controls operate flap valves to deflect and mix the air flowing through the various parts of the heating/ventilation system. The flap valves are contained in the air distribution housing, which acts as a central distribution unit, passing air to the various ducts and vents.

3 Cold air enters the system through the grille at the rear of the engine compartment. A pollen filter is fitted to filter out dust, soot,

7.9 Undo the pump bracket retaining bolt (arrowed)

pollen and spores from the air entering the vehicle.

4 The airflow, which can be boosted by the blower, flows through the various ducts, according to the settings of the controls. Stale air is expelled through ducts beneath the rear bumper. If warm air is required, the cold air is passed through the heater matrix, which is heated by the engine coolant.

5 If necessary, the outside air supply can be closed off, allowing the air inside the vehicle to be recirculated. This can be useful to prevent unpleasant odours entering from outside the vehicle, but should only be used briefly, as the recirculated air quality inside the vehicle will soon deteriorate.

9 Heating/ventilation system components – removal and refitting

Models without air conditioning

Heater/ventilation control unit

1 Switch off the ignition and all electrical consumers, then note the position of the outer control knobs, as they will need to be in this position for refitting.

2 Remove the radio as described in Chapter 12 Section 21.

9.14 Slacken the bolt arrowed

3 Unclip the facia from the heater control panel and then undo the eight retaining screws and remove the control unit from the facia.

4 Disconnect the wiring by releasing the securing clip as the panel is withdrawn.

5 Refitting is a reversal of removal, but ensure the control knobs are positioned as previously-noted as these will only fit on the shafts in one position. Check the operation of the controls.

Temperature flap control cable

6 Remove the heater/ventilation control unit from the facia as described previously.

7 Reach into the facia and disconnect the inner cable and release the cable outer.

8 Remove the centre console as described in Chapter 11 Section 26.

9 Disconnect the inner and outer cable(s) from the temperature flap(s) at each side of the heater unit. Note the routing and position of the cable(s) before removing.

10 Refitting is a reversal of removal, but check that the temperature control knob can be turned easily.

Heater matrix

11 At the rear of the engine compartment, depending on model, remove the bulkhead trim from the plenum chamber.

12 Using hose clamps, clamp the heater matrix inlet and return hoses located on the bulkhead at the rear of the engine compartment. Place a container beneath the hoses, then loosen the clips and disconnect them. Note the location of the hoses for correct refitting.

13 With the hoses disconnected, remove the coolant from the matrix by blowing air into the upper tube, preferably using an airline. This will then push any coolant through the matrix and out of the lower tube.

14 Loosen (but do not remove) the bolt located between the matrix upper and lower tubes **(see illustration)**. This will make removal of the matrix easier.

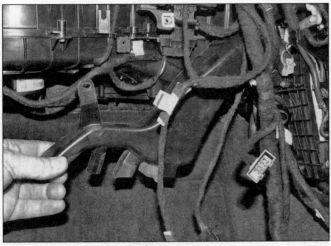

9.16 Remove the air vent

9.17 Remove the air vent flap motor

15 Remove the glovebox as described in Chapter 11 Section 25.

16 Undo the retaining screws and remove the air vent to the passenger side footwell **(see illustration)**.

17 Undo the retaining bolts and remove the air vent flap motor from the side of the heater unit **(see illustration)**.

18 Unclip the wiring loom from the plastic cover, then undo the retaining bolts and remove heater matrix cover **(see illustrations)**.

19 Place cloth rags or similar on the floor beneath the heater matrix, then release the pipe clamps and pull the coolant pipes from the matrix **(see illustration)**. Discard the seals,

as new ones will be required for refitting. Audi supply a new sealing kit, which includes new clamps also.

20 Pull the heater matrix and slide it out from the heater unit **(see illustration)**.

21 Refitting is a reversal of removal, noting the following.

a) *Make sure the seal is fitted correctly around the perimeter of the matrix.*

b) *When reconnecting the coolant pipes, apply a small amount of rubber grease to the new seals and fit them to the matrix. Make sure the conical ends of the pipes locate in the matrix correctly* **(see illustrations)**. *After reconnecting the*

pipes, the clamps must turn easily before tightening them securely.

c) *Check that the rubber grommet in the bulkhead is correctly located in its hole.*

d) *Top-up the coolant level with reference to 'Weekly checks'.*

Heater unit

22 Remove the facia panel as described in Chapter 11 Section 27.

23 Remove the front seats as described in Chapter 11 Section 22.

24 Remove the right- and left-hand rear footwell ducts from the heater unit. It is recommended that the complete floor carpet

9.18a Unclip the wiring loom...

9.18b...and remove the matrix cover

9.19 Remove the two pipe retaining clamps (arrowed)

9.20 Withdraw the matrix from the heater housing

9.21a Fit new seals to the heater matrix...

9.21b...and make sure the pipes seal correctly

9.24a Remove the carpet...

9.24b...then remove the right- and left-hand rear footwell ducts from the heater unit

be removed first, as the ducts are located below the carpets **(see illustrations)**. Also remove the centre console air duct.

25 Remove the wiper arms and windscreen lower trim panel with reference to Chapter 12 Section 17. Undo the crossmember front mounting bolt from inside the scuttle panel **(see illustration)**.

26 At the rear of the engine compartment, depending on model, remove the bulkhead trim from the plenum chamber.

27 Using hose clamps, clamp the heater matrix inlet and return hoses located on the bulkhead at the rear of the engine compartment. Place a container beneath the hoses, then pull out the clips and disconnect them **(see illustrations)**. Note the location of the hoses for correct refitting.

28 With the hoses disconnected, remove the coolant from the matrix by blowing air into the upper tube, preferably using an airline. This will then push any coolant through the matrix and out of the lower tube.

29 Inside the car, place cloth rags or similar on the floor beneath the heater unit, to catch any spillage.

30 Note the location and routing of all wiring, then disconnect it from the heater unit and crossmember. Also note the location of plastic cable ties to ensure correct refitting.

31 Undo the retaining screws and remove the air vents to the front passenger and driver's side footwells **(see illustration)**.

32 Unbolt and remove the two central support legs located over the rear of the heater unit **(see illustration)**.

33 Unbolt the retaining bracket from the driver's side of the crossmember **(see illustration)**.

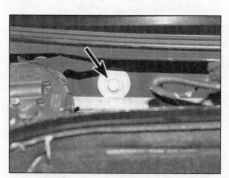

9.25 Facia crossmember securing bolt (arrowed)

9.27a Pull out the clips...

9.27b...and disconnect the hoses from the heater matrix

9.31 Remove the front footwell air vents

9.32 Remove the central support legs (one side arrowed)

9.33 Remove the upper mounting plate

9.34a Remove the front...

9.34b...and rear air inlet ducts...

9.35a Remove the upper support brackets...

9.35b...and remove the centre support brackets

34 Release the retaining clips and remove the air inlet ducts from the top of the heater (**see illustrations**).

35 Undo the bolts and remove the remaining support bracket from the centre of the heater unit (**see illustrations**).

36 Undo the retaining bolts/screws and remove the fusebox and relay panel from the brackets on the crossmember (**see illustrations**).

9.36a Unbolt the fusebox...

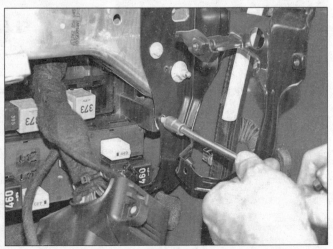

9.36b...and relay panel from the right-hand side of the crossmember

9.37a Undo the right-hand mounting bolts...

9.37b the left-hand mounting bolts...

9.37c...and withdraw the facia crossmember from the vehicle

37 Undo the bolts/nuts from the brackets at each end of the crossmember, make sure there are no other brackets or wiring attached and remove the crossmember from the vehicle **(see illustrations)**.
38 Check for any remaining screws or bolts around the heater unit.
39 Carefully pull the heater unit from the bulkhead, taking care not to damage or bend the matrix tubes on the bulkhead **(see illustration)**. The help of an assistant may be required. Be prepared for coolant spillage as the assembly is removed from inside the car.
40 If necessary, the heater may be further dismantled on the bench.
41 Refitting is a reversal of removal, but

top-up the coolant with reference to Weekly checks.

Heater blower motor

42 Switch off the ignition and all electrical consumers.
43 Remove the passenger side glovebox as described in Chapter 11 Section 25.
44 Where fitted, remove the cover from under the heater blower motor. Disconnect the wiring from the blower motor **(see illustration)**.
45 Lift the locking tab and turn the blower motor anti-clockwise to remove it from the heater housing **(see illustrations)**.
Note: *On some models there may be a screw fitted, if so remove screw before removal.*
46 Refitting is a reversal of removal.

Heater blower motor series resistor

47 Remove the blower motor as described previously, see paragraphs 42 to 46.
48 Undo the screws and remove the cover from under the heater blower motor.
49 Disconnect the wiring from the blower series resistor, undo the retaining bolts and remove the resistor from the blower motor housing **(see illustration)**.
Caution: The resistor may be very hot if the heater has recently been in use.
50 Refitting is the reverse of removal.

Air flap positioning motors

51 Remove the passenger side glovebox as described in Chapter 11 Section 25.
52 Disconnect the wiring connector, then

9.39 Removing the complete heater housing assembly

9.44 Disconnect the wiring connector

9.45a Release the locking tab and turn...

9.45b...to remove the blower motor

9.45c Some motors may have a retaining screw fitted (arrowed)

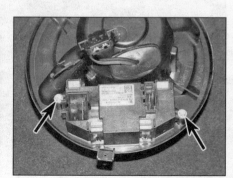

9.49 Resistor retaining screws (arrowed)

9.52a Flap motor retaining bolts (arrowed)

9.52b Removing the flap motor from the left-hand side of the heater unit

9.54 Withdraw the plastic trim

9.55 Carefully unclip the trim panel from the switches

9.56 Release the clips (arrowed) and push downwards

9.57 Disconnect the wiring connectors

undo the retaining bolts and remove the flap motor from the heater housing **(see illustrations)**.

53 Refitting is a reversal of removal.

Models with air conditioning

Heater/ventilation control unit

54 Unclip the trim from under the heater control panel **(see illustration)**.

55 Using a lever, carefully unclip the trim from the switch panel above the control panel **(see illustration)**.

56 Using a lever, carefully unclip the top edge of the heater control panel from the facia and remove it downwards from the facia panel **(see illustration)**.

57 Disconnect the wiring connectors as it is removed **(see illustration)**.

Heater matrix

58 The procedure is as described previously in this section for models without air conditioning.

Heater/air conditioning unit

Warning: Refer to the precautions given in Section 11.

59 It is not possible to remove the unit without opening the refrigerant circuit to the evaporator; therefore this task must be entrusted to an Audi dealer or an air conditioning specialist. With the refrigerant evacuated, the procedure is as described for models without air conditioning, except for the following.

a) Unscrew the bolts securing the refrigerant

lines to the evaporator on the bulkhead at the rear of the engine compartment, and detach them. Recover the seals and plug the lines and evaporator openings to prevent entry of foreign matter and water

9.59a Unscrew the bolts and remove the refrigerant lines from the evaporator

9.59c Remove the footrest...

vapour. Discard the seals; new ones must be used on refitting **(see illustrations)**.

b) Remove the footrest and condensation water drainage hose from the driver's side of the heater unit **(see illustrations)**.

9.59b Plug the lines and evaporator while they are disconnected

9.59d...and condensation water drainage hose from the heater unit

9.63 Unscrew the bolts securing the two sections of the heater housing

9.68 Unscrew the bolts (arrowed) and separate the refrigerant lines

9.69 Condenser retaining screw – one shown

Caution: The air conditioning compressor is driven permanently by the auxiliary drivebelt, and is not fitted with a magnetic clutch. It is not recommended that the engine is started without refrigerant being present in the system, as the compressor may overheat causing internal damage. Note also that if the refrigerant circuit is not opened within 10 minutes of evacuation, slight pressure may develop due to re-evaporation.

Air conditioning evaporator

 Warning: Refer to the precautions given in Section 11.

60 Have the refrigerant evacuated from the air conditioning system by an Audi dealer or refrigeration specialist.

Caution: The air conditioning compressor is driven permanently by the auxiliary drivebelt, and is not fitted with a magnetic clutch. It is not recommended that the engine is started without refrigerant being present in the system, as the compressor may overheat causing internal damage. Note also that if the refrigerant circuit is not opened within 10 minutes of evacuation, slight pressure may develop due to re-evaporation.

61 Remove the heater/air conditioning unit as described earlier in this Section.

62 Remove the heater matrix as described earlier in this Section.

63 Undo the retaining screws from around the heater unit and split it into two parts to access the evaporator **(see illustration)**.

64 Remove the evaporator from the housing together with the refrigerant lines and rubber grommet.

65 Refitting is a reversal of removal; renew the seals and have the system recharged by an Audi dealer or refrigeration specialist.

Air conditioning condenser

Warning: Refer to the precautions given in Section 11.

66 The condenser is attached to the front of the radiator. Have the refrigerant evacuated from the air conditioning system by an Audi dealer or refrigeration specialist.

Caution: The air conditioning compressor is driven permanently by the auxiliary drivebelt, and is not fitted with a magnetic clutch. It is not recommended that the engine be started without refrigerant being present in the system, as the compressor may overheat causing internal damage. Note also that if the refrigerant circuit is not opened within 10 minutes of evacuation, slight pressure may develop due to re-evaporation.

67 Remove the radiator as described in Section 3 of this Chapter.

68 Undo the screws and disconnect the refrigerant lines from the condenser **(see illustration)**. Recover the seals and plug the

lines and condenser openings to prevent entry of foreign matter and water vapour.

69 Undo the retaining screws from each side of the condenser and carefully remove it from the lock/radiator carrier, taking care not to damage its fins **(see illustration)**.

70 Refitting is a reversal of removal; renew the seals and have the system recharged by an Audi dealer or refrigeration specialist.

Heater blower motor

71 The procedure is as described previously in this section for models without air conditioning.

Heater blower motor series resistor

72 The procedure is as described previously in this section for models without air conditioning.

Air flap positioning motors

73 The procedure is as described previously in this section for models without air conditioning.

Auxiliary heater

74 Remove the glovebox assembly as described in Chapter 11 Section 25.

75 Disconnect the wiring connector from the auxiliary heater unit **(see illustration)**.

76 Undo the retaining bolts and slide the auxiliary heater out from the heater assembly **(see illustration)**.

77 Refitting is a reversal of removal.

9.75 Disconnect the wiring connectors

9.76 Removing the auxiliary heater

10 Heating/ventilation system vents – removal and refitting

1 Remove the air vents by carefully levering them out from the facia panel **(see illustrations)**.
2 To refit, carefully push the vent into position until the locating clips engage.

11 Air conditioning system – general information and precautions

1 Air conditioning is fitted as standard to most models, and is available as manually-operated (Climatic) or automatically-operated (Climatronic). The Climatronic system works in conjunction with the heating and air conditioning systems to maintain a selected vehicle interior temperature fully automatically.
2 The air conditioning system enables the temperature of incoming air to be lowered, and dehumidifies the air, which makes for rapid demisting and increased comfort. The cooling side of the system works in the same way as a domestic refrigerator. Refrigerant gas is drawn into a belt-driven compressor and passes into a condenser mounted in front of the radiator, where it loses heat and becomes liquid. The liquid passes through an expansion valve to an evaporator, where it changes from liquid under high pressure to gas under low pressure. This change is accompanied by a drop in temperature, which cools the evaporator. The refrigerant returns to the compressor and the cycle begins again.
3 Air blown through the evaporator passes to the air distribution unit, where it is mixed with hot air blown through the heater matrix to achieve the desired temperature in the passenger compartment.
4 The heating side of the system works in the same way as on models without air conditioning.
5 The operation of the system is controlled electronically by coolant temperature switches, and pressure switches which are screwed into the compressor high-pressure line. Any problems with the system should be referred to an Audi dealer or an air conditioning specialist.
6 The only operation, which can be carried out easily without discharging the refrigerant, is the renewal of the compressor drivebelt, which is covered in Chapter 1. Removal of the evaporator and condenser requires the evacuation of the refrigerant. If necessary the compressor can be unbolted and moved aside, without disconnecting its flexible hoses, after removing the drivebelt **(see illustration)**.

Precautions

7 When an air conditioning system is fitted, it

is necessary to observe special precautions whenever dealing with any part of the system, its associated components and any items which require disconnection of the system. If for any reason the system must be disconnected, entrust this task to your Audi dealer or an air conditioning specialist.
8 Do not operate the air conditioning system if it is known to be short of refrigerant, as this may damage the compressor.

⚠ *Warning: The refrigeration circuit contains a refrigerant and it is therefore dangerous to disconnect any part of the system without specialised knowledge and equipment. The refrigerant is potentially dangerous and should only be handled by qualified persons. If it is splashed onto the skin it can cause frostbite. It is not itself poisonous, but in the presence of a naked flame (including a cigarette) it forms a poisonous gas. Uncontrolled discharging of the refrigerant is dangerous and potentially damaging to the environment.*

12 Climatronic system components – removal and refitting

Sunlight penetration sensor

1 Switch off the ignition and all electrical consumers.
2 Using a small lever, carefully prise the cover from the top, centre of the facia panel **(see illustration)**.

10.1a Carefully prise out the vent...

10.1b...and withdraw it from the facia

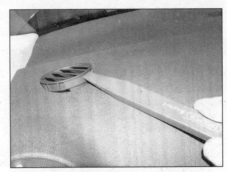
10.1c...and prising the upper vent...

10.1d...from the top of the facia

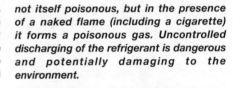

11.6 Air conditioning compressor bolted to the front of the cylinder block

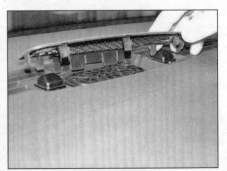
12.2 Unclip the trim cover...

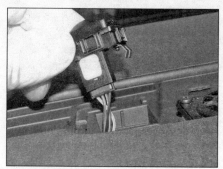

12.3 ...and remove the sensor

12.6 Air vent temperature sensor (arrowed)

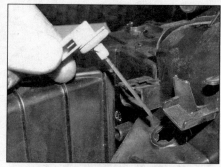

12.8 Turn the sensor 90° and withdraw from air vent

12.11 Ambient temperature sender location at the front of the radiator/condenser

3 Unclip the sensor and disconnect the wiring plug as it is removed **(see illustration)**.
4 Refitting is a reversal of removal.

Air vent temperature sender

Note: *There are a four air vent temperature sender units fitted in the air ducting, one in each piece of air ducting going to each air vent on the facia.*
5 Switch off the ignition and all electrical consumers.
6 Depending on temperature sender to be removed, either unclip the trim panel from the relevant end of the facia, or remove the glovebox or lower facia trim panels as described in Chapter 11 **(see illustration)**.
7 Disconnect the wiring plug from the sender.
8 Turn the sender through 90°, and withdraw it from the housing **(see illustration)**.
9 Refitting is a reversal of removal.

Ambient temperature sender

10 Remove the front bumper as described in Chapter 11 Section 6.
11 Unclip the sender from its retainer and disconnect the wiring **(see illustration)**.
12 Refitting is a reversal of removal. Make sure the wiring is fully connected to prevent entry of water.

Chapter 4 Part A
Fuel systems – 1.6 and 2.0 litre engines

Contents

Degrees of difficulty

| **Easy,** suitable for novice with little experience | | **Fairly easy,** suitable for beginner with some experience | | **Fairly difficult,** suitable for competent DIY mechanic | | **Difficult,** suitable for experienced DIY mechanic | | **Very difficult,** suitable for expert DIY or professional | |

Specifications

Engine codes

1.6 litre engines . . . .   CAYB and CAYC
2.0 litre engines . . . .   CBAA, CBAB, CBBB, CFFA, CFFB and CFGB
Note: *See 'Vehicle identification' in Reference Chapter for the location of engine code markings.*

General

Fuel injection system . . . .   Electronic, direct, common rail injection
Firing order   1-3-4-2
Maximum engine speed . . . .   N/A (ECU controlled)
Engine fast idle speed . . . .   N/A (ECU controlled)
Turbocharger type . . . .   Garrett or KKK

Torque wrench settings

	Nm	lbf ft
Camshaft position sensor (Hall sender)	10	7
EGR pipe flange-to-inlet manifold bolts	8	6
Engine speed/TDC sender	5	4
Flap motor housing	10	7
Fuel pressure regulating valve (left-hand end of fuel rail)	80	59
Fuel pressure sender (right-hand end of fuel rail)	100	74
Fuel pump bolts*:		
Two lower bolts (long):		
Stage 1	20	15
Stage 2	Angle-tighten a further 180°	
One upper bolt (short):		
Stage 1	20	15
Stage 2	Angle-tighten a further 45°	
Fuel rail	22	16
High-pressure fuel pipe unions	28	20
Injector clamp/cover mounting:		
1.6 litre engines		
Clamp bolt*:		
Stage 1	8	6
Stage 2	Angle-tighten a further 180°	
2.0 litre engines (CFFA, CFFB and CFGB):		
Clamp bolt*:		
Stage 1	8	6
Stage 2	Angle-tighten a further 180°	
2.0 litre engines (CBAA, CBAB and CBBB):		
Clamp nut	10	7
Cover bolt	5	4
Inlet manifold to cylinder head	8	6
Oxygen (Lambda probe) sensor	50	37
Toothed belt pulley on high-pressure pump bolts*	20	15

Do not re-use fasteners

1 General information and precautions

General information

1 All engines covered in this Chapter are fitted with a direct-injection fuelling system, incorporating a fuel tank, an engine-bay mounted fuel filter with an integral water separator, fuel supply and return lines and four fuel injectors.

2 The fuel system is the familiar Common Rail system, where fuel is supplied from a timing belt-driven high-pressure pump to a common fuel rail (or reservoir). The four injectors are fitted into the cylinder head and are connected to the fuel rail by rigid metal pipes. The precise timing of the pre-, main, and post-injections are controlled by the engine management ECU and an electrically operated Piezo crystal incorporated into the injector design. All engines are fitted with a turbocharger.

3 The direct-injection fuelling system is controlled electronically by a diesel engine management system, comprising an Electronic Control Unit (ECU) and its associated sensors, actuators and wiring. In addition, the ECU manages the operation of the Exhaust Gas Recirculation (EGR) emission control system (Chapter 4C), the turbocharger boost pressure control system and the glow plug control system (Chapter 5).

4 A flap valve/throttle valve module fitted to the intake manifold is closed by the ECU for 3 seconds as the engine is switched off, to minimise the air intake as the engine shuts down. This minimises the vibration felt as the pistons come up against the volume of highly compressed air present in the combustion chambers.

5 It should be noted that fault diagnosis of the diesel engine management system is only possible with dedicated electronic test equipment. Problems with the system's operation should therefore be referred to an Audi dealer or suitably equipped specialist for assessment. Once the fault has been identified, the removal/refitting sequences detailed in the following Sections will then allow the appropriate component(s) to be renewed as required.

6 The Electronic On-Board Diagnostic (EOBD) connector is located under the driver's side of the facia.

Precautions

7 Many of the operations described in this Chapter involve the disconnection of fuel lines, which may cause an amount of fuel spillage. Before commencing work, refer to the warnings below and the information in *Safety first!*.

⚠ *Warning: When working on any part of the fuel system, avoid direct contact skin contact with diesel fuel – wear protective clothing and gloves when handling fuel system components. Ensure that the work area is* well ventilated to prevent the build-up of diesel fuel vapour.

⚠ *Warning: Fuel injectors operate at extremely high pressures and the jet of fuel produced at the nozzle is capable of piercing skin, with potentially fatal results. When working with pressurised injectors, take care to avoid exposing any part of the body to the fuel spray. It is recommended that a diesel fuel systems specialist should carry out any pressure testing of the fuel system components.*

⚠ *Warning: Under no circumstances should diesel fuel be allowed to come into contact with coolant hoses – wipe off accidental spillage immediately. Hoses that have been contaminated with fuel for an extended period should be renewed.*

⚠ *Warning: Diesel fuel systems are particularly sensitive to contamination from dirt, air and water. Pay particular attention to cleanliness when working on any part of the fuel system, to prevent the ingress of dirt. Thoroughly clean the area around fuel unions before disconnecting them. Only use lint-free cloths and clean fuel for component cleansing.*

 Warning: Store dismantled components in sealed containers to prevent contamination and the formation of condensation.

2.1a Unclip the cover from the air intake

2.1b Release the securing clips...

2.1c...and remove the air ducting

2 Air cleaner assembly – removal and refitting

Removal

1 Unclip the plastic cover from the air intake ducting, then release the two securing clips (one at each side) and remove the ducting from the front crossmember **(see illustrations)**.
Note: *On some models there may be a retaining screw securing the inner part of the lower ducting to the crossmember.*
2 Disconnect the wiring plug from the air mass meter **(see illustration)**.
3 Disconnect the vacuum pipe from the air intake hose **(see illustration)**.
4 Loosen the clip and disconnect the air duct from the air mass meter **(see illustration)**.
5 Undo the retaining bolt and lift the air cleaner assembly upwards to release it from the locating pegs **(see illustrations)**. As the air cleaner is removed, withdraw the water drain hose, under the air cleaner assembly out from the inner wing panel.

Refitting

6 Refit the air cleaner by following the removal procedure in reverse. Make sure the assembly is located correctly on the lower mounting pegs **(see illustration)**.

2.2 Disconnect the air mass meter wiring plug

2.3 Disconnect the vacuum pipe

2.4 Disconnect the air intake hose

2.5a Undo the retaining screw...

2.5b...and remove the air cleaner assembly out of the engine compartment

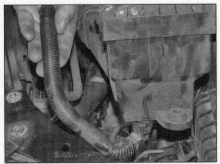

2.5c Release the drain tube as it is removed

2.6 Make sure the assembly is located correctly on the mounting pegs (arrowed)

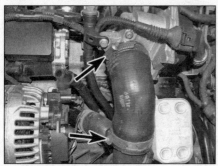

3.2 Slacken the retaining clips and remove the intake hose

3.3 Disconnect the wiring connector

3.4 Undo the dipstick tube retaining bolt

3 Diesel engine management system – component removal and refitting

Throttle valve housing/module

1 Remove the engine upper trim cover.
2 Slacken the retaining clips and remove the air intake rubber hose from the throttle housing **(see illustration)**. If required, undo the bolts securing the air intake plastic hose from the intercooler to the throttle housing, this will allow easier removal of the intake rubber hose.
3 Disconnect the wiring plug connector, from the throttle housing/module **(see illustration)**.
4 Undo the retaining bolt and disconnect the dipstick guide tube from the throttle housing **(see illustration)**.

5 Unscrew and remove the retaining bolts, then lift the throttle housing/module away from the inlet manifold **(see illustrations)**. Recover the O-ring seal; a new one will be required for refitting.
6 Refitting is a reversal of removal, noting the following:
a) *Use a new throttle housing-to-inlet manifold seal* **(see illustration)**.
b) *Tighten the throttle housing bolts evenly to the specified torque.*
c) *Ensure that all hoses and electrical connectors are refitted securely.*

Inlet manifold flap motor

Note: *On some engines there is an electrically operated flap motor located on the inlet manifold, this is not fitted to all models.*
7 Remove the engine upper trim cover

8 Disconnect the flap control motor wiring plug from the lower part of the housing **(see illustration)**.
9 Unscrew the bolts securing the flap motor housing to the manifold **(see illustration)**, remove the flap housing and recover the O-ring seal.
10 Refitting is a reversal of removal. Renew the O-ring seal if it appears damaged.

Air mass meter

11 The air mass meter is located in the outlet from the air cleaner assembly on the left-hand side of the engine compartment.
12 Disconnect the wiring plug connector from the air mass meter **(see illustration)**.
13 Slacken the retaining clip and disconnect

3.5a Undo the three retaining bolts ...

3.5b ... and remove the throttle housing module

3.6 Fit a new seal to the housing on refitting

3.8 Disconnect the wiring connector

3.9 Undo the three retaining bolts (arrowed)

3.12 Disconnect the air mass meter wiring plug

3.13 Disconnect the air intake hose

3.16 Charge air pressure sensor location (arrowed)

3.19 Fuel pressure regulator valve (arrowed)

the air intake ducting from the air mass meter **(see illustration)**.

14 Undo the retaining screws securing the meter to the air cleaner. Withdraw the meter and recover the O-ring seal.

Caution: Handle the air mass meter carefully – its internal components are easily damaged.

15 Refitting is a reversal of removal. Renew the O-ring seal if it appears damaged.

Charge air pressure/ temperature sensor

16 The charge air pressure/temperature sensor is fitted in the air ducting from the intercooler to the throttle housing/inlet manifold, just below the air-conditioning compressor **(see illustration)**. Jack up the front of the vehicle and support it on axle stands (see *Jacking and vehicle support* in Reference chapter), and then remove the engine undertray.

17 Disconnect the wiring then undo the two retaining screws and remove the sensor from the intake ducting.

18 Refit the sensor by reversing the removal procedure, using a new O-ring seal.

Fuel pressure regulating valve

19 The fuel pressure regulating valve is fitted to the left-hand end of the fuel rail **(see illustration)**. If the valve is removed from the fuel rail, then it will need to be renewed, as it has a deformable sealing lip as part of the valve.

20 To check the operation of the regulating valve, first disconnect the fuel return hose from the fuel rail and plug the end **(see illustration)**. Then fit a piece of hose to the fuel rail and the other end into a container. There are three checks that can be made, the first two with the engine running and the third if the vehicle will not start:

a) Start the engine and run at idle for 30 seconds, there should be approx. 75ml of fuel (1.6 litre engines) or 100ml of fuel (2.0 litre engines) in the container.

b) Start engine and increase engine speed to 2000rpm, there should be 0ml of fuel in the container (allow for a few droplets of fuel).

c) On vehicles that will not run, turn the ignition key and crank the engine, there should be 0ml of fuel in the container (allow for a few droplets of fuel).

21 If any of these readings are not attained, renew the regulating valve.

22 To renew the valve, remove the fuel rail as described in Section 11.

23 Clean around the valve, then slacken the valve from the end of the fuel rail **(see illustration)** ; counterhold the fuel rail using the flats on the housing. Plug the end of the rail to prevent dirt from entering.

24 Fit the new valve by reversing the removal procedure, making sure that the threads are all clean before fitting. Check the deformable seal on the new valve, before fitting, to check it is not damaged. Apply a small amount of Molybdenum grease to seal and threads.

3.20 Disconnect the fuel hose (arrowed)

3.26 Disconnect the wiring connector from the fuel pressure sender

Fuel pressure sender

25 The fuel pressure sender is fitted to the right-hand end of the fuel rail. If the engine will not start, disconnect the fuel pressure sender wiring connector and see if the engine will start. If the engine starts, the fuel pressure sender is faulty. With the connector removed a value is taken from the control unit, so that the engine will start, in this mode the maximum engine speed is limited to 3000rpm.

26 To renew the sender, first disconnect the wiring plug connector **(see illustration)**.

27 Clean around the sender, then slacken it from the end of the fuel rail **(see illustration)**; plug the end of the rail to prevent dirt from entering.

28 Refit the pressure sender by reversing the removal procedure, making sure that

3.23 Pressure regulator valve fitted to the left-hand end of the fuel rail

3.27 The fuel pressure sender is fitted to the right-hand end of the fuel rail

3.29 Fuel temperature sensor (arrowed)

3.33 Camshaft position sensor (arrowed)

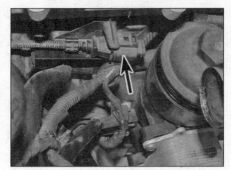

3.35 Disconnect the sensor wiring connector (arrowed)

the threads are all clean before refitting. The sender has a deformable seal, check for damage. Keep the threads free of oil and grease.

Fuel temperature sensor

29 The fuel temperature sensor is located in the fuel supply line at the top of the high-pressure fuel pump **(see illustration)**, on some 2.0 litre engines.

30 First, disconnect the wiring connector, then release the securing clips and disconnect the hoses from the sensor assembly.

31 Refit the fuel temperature sensor by reversing the removal procedure.

Coolant temperature sensors

32 Refer to Chapter 3, Section 6.

Camshaft position sensor

33 The camshaft position sensor (Hall sender) is located behind the timing belt cover, below the camshaft sprocket **(see illustration)**.

34 Remove the timing belt, as described in Chapter 2A, Section 7 (1.6 litre engine) or Chapter 2C, Section 7 (2.0 litre engine).

35 Disconnect the sensor wiring plug connector, located at the rear of the oil filter housing against the cylinder block **(see illustration)**.

36 To make access easier undo the retaining bolt and remove the timing belt idler pulley **(see illustration)**.

37 Using a screwdriver prise out the aperture cover in the rear plastic cover, then withdraw the wiring plug through the cover, unhooking it from the rear cover **(see illustration)**.

38 Undo the retaining bolt and remove the camshaft sensor from the cylinder head.

39 Refitting is a reversal of removal, but tighten the bolt to the specified torque setting and fit rubber plugs to the aperture for the wiring in the rear plastic cover.

Engine speed/TDC sensor

40 The engine speed/TDC sensor is mounted on the front cylinder block, adjacent to the mating surface of the block and transmission bellhousing **(see illustration)**.

41 Access is from beneath the engine compartment. Apply the handbrake, and then jack up the front of the vehicle and support it on axle stands (see *Jacking and vehicle support* Reference chapter). Remove the engine undertray.

42 Remove the retaining screw and withdraw the sensor from the cylinder block **(see illustrations)**.

43 Refit the sensor by reversing the removal procedure.

Oxygen (lambda probe) sensor

⚠️ *Warning: Working on the sensors is only advisable with the engine (and therefore the exhaust system) completely cold. The particulate filter in particular will be very hot for some time after the engine has been switched off.*

3.36 Unbolt the Idler pulley

3.37 Prise up the aperture cover (arrowed)

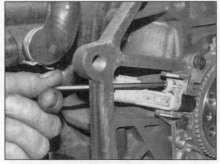

3.40 Crankshaft position speed sensor (arrowed)

3.42a Undo the retaining bolt...

3.42b ...and withdraw the sensor

3.44 Oxygen sensor (arrowed)

3.45 Disconnect the wiring connector on the bulkhead

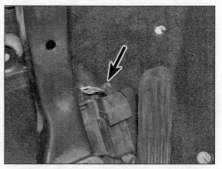

3.50 Release the wiring connector locking clip (arrowed)

44 All models have a sensor threaded into the top of the catalytic converter/particulate filter **(see illustration)**.
Note: *On some models there may be a second sensor in the front pipe after the catalytic converter/particulate filter. Do not confuse exhaust gas sensors fitted to the exhaust system.*
45 Working from the sensor, trace the wiring harness from the oxygen sensor back to the connector, and disconnect it **(see illustration)**. Unclip the sensor wiring from any retaining clips, noting how it is routed.
46 Access to the upstream sensor is possible on some models from above, while the downstream sensor (where fitted) is only accessible from below.
47 Unscrew and remove the sensor, taking care to avoid damaging the sensor probe as it is removed.
Note: *As a flying lead remains connected to the sensor after it has been disconnected, if the correct-size spanner is not available, a slotted socket will be required to remove the sensor.*
48 Apply a little high-temperature anti-seize grease to the sensor threads – avoid contaminating the probe tip.
49 Refit the sensor, tightening it to the correct torque. Reconnect the wiring; making sure that the wiring loom is secured in its retaining clips.

Throttle pedal/position sensor

50 Release the securing clip and disconnect the wiring connector from the top of the accelerator pedal **(see illustration)**.
51 Prise off the cap, and undo the screw securing the throttle pedal to the bulkhead **(see illustration)**.
52 The throttle pedal is clipped to two metal pegs in the floor panel, using a lever and thin screwdriver, release the securing clips **(see illustration)**.
53 The outer clip can be released by pressing the screwdriver inwards to release the securing clip, whilst levering the pedal upwards. Then insert the screwdriver into the inner slot and push it to the left to release the

securing clip **(see illustrations)**. Withdraw the throttle pedal from the floor panel and out from the vehicle.
54 Refitting is a reversal of removal.

Clutch pedal switch

55 The clutch pedal switch is clipped to the clutch master cylinder on the pedal bracket. Remove the master cylinder as described in Chapter 6, Section 4.
56 Unclip the pedal switch from the bottom of the master cylinder.
57 Refitting is a reversal of removal.

Electronic control unit (ECU)

Caution: Always wait at least 30 seconds after switching off the ignition before

3.51 Undo the pedal retaining bolt (arrowed)

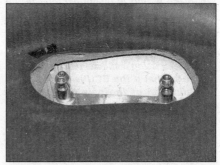

3.52 Throttle pedal securing pegs in the floor panel

3.53a Release the outer clip by pressing the screwdriver forwards

3.53b Release the inner clip by pushing the screwdriver inwards, and then to the left to release the clip

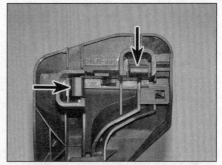

3.53c Direction (arrowed) to release the two securing clips

3.58 Electronic control unit located in scuttle panel

3.59 Unclip the control unit from the mounting bracket

3.60a Cut a slot in the end of the shear bolts (arrowed)...

3.60b...and use a screwdriver to remove them

disconnecting the wiring from the ECU. *When the wiring is disconnected, all the learned values are erased, although any Specifications of the fault memory are retained. After reconnecting the wiring, the basic settings must be reinstated by an Audi dealer using a special test instrument. Note also that if the ECU is renewed, the identification of the new ECU must be transferred to the immobiliser control unit by an Audi dealer.*

58 The ECU is located centrally behind the engine compartment bulkhead **(see illustration)**, under the windscreen cowl panel. Remove the wiper arms and cowl panel as for windscreen wiper motor removal and refitting, described in Chapter 12, Section 18.

59 Release the ECU from the lower tray and withdraw it from inside the bulkhead **(see illustration)**. Disconnect the battery negative lead and position it away from the terminal. Refer to 'Disconnecting the battery' in the Reference Chapter.

60 Place a piece of cardboard under the ECU and either drill out the shear bolts that are holding the wiring connector security cover together, or cut a slot in them and unscrew them with a screwdriver **(see illustrations)**. New shear bolts will be required for refitting.

61 Lever the top part upwards and remove the security cover from around the ECU **(see illustrations)**.

62 Disconnect the wiring plugs from the ECU by sliding the locking levers outwards,

to release them from the top of the ECU **(see illustration)**. Remove the ECU from the vehicle.

63 Refitting is a reversal of removal, using new shear bolts to secure the wiring cover. Bear in mind the comments made in the Caution above – the ECU will not work correctly until it has been electronically coded.

4 Injectors – general information, removal and refitting

> ⚠ *Warning: Exercise extreme caution when working on the fuel injectors. Never expose the hands or any part of the body to injector spray, as the high pressure can cause the fuel to penetrate the skin, with possibly fatal results. You are strongly advised to have any work which involves testing the injectors under pressure carried out by a dealer or fuel injection specialist. Refer to the precautions given in Section 1 of this Chapter before proceeding.*

General information

1 Injectors do deteriorate with prolonged use, and it is reasonable to expect them to need reconditioning or renewal after 60,000 miles (100,000 km) or so. Accurate testing, overhaul and calibration of the injectors must be left to a specialist.

Removal

Note: *Take care not to allow dirt into the injectors or fuel pipes during this procedure. Do not drop the injectors or allow the needles at their tips to become damaged. The injectors are precision-made to fine limits, and must not be handled roughly. Keep the injectors identified for position to ensure correct refitting.*

2 Pull the plastic cover over the engine upwards from its mountings. Where fitted, remove the foam insulation over the injectors.

3 Ensure the area around the injectors and the pipes/return hoses is clean and free from debris. The use of a vacuum cleaner is recommended. Plug all fuel lines when they

3.61a Pull the clamp upwards...

3.61b...and remove it from around the control unit

3.62 Pull out the locking slides at each side to disconnect the wiring

4.3 Fit sealing caps to prevent dirt ingress

4.4 Disconnect the wiring plugs from the injectors

4.5a Remove the retaining clips...

4.5b ...and disconnect the fuel return pipes

4.6a Use two spanners to counterhold the fuel pipe to the injector...

4.6b ...and remove the high pressure fuel pipes

have been disconnected to prevent any dirt ingress **(see illustration)**.

1.6 litre engines

4 Disconnect the injector wiring plug connectors **(see illustration)**.

5 Using a pair of long-nose pliers, withdraw the retaining clip from the side of the injector and remove the fuel return hose **(see illustrations)**. Discard the O-ring seals, as new ones will be required for refitting.

6 Counterhold the injector with an open-ended spanner when releasing the pipe union. Undo the unions and remove the high-pressure pipes from between the fuel rail and the injectors **(see illustrations)**. Plug the openings to prevent contamination.

7 Undo the bolt securing the injector clamp **(see illustration)**, note that one clamp secures two injectors in place.

8 Audi technicians use a slide hammer (tool

T10055) and adapter (T10402) to pull the injector from the cylinder head. If this tool is not available, it may be possible to fabricate an equivalent tool to pull the injector out of the cylinder head.

9 Two injectors will need to be removed together, as the clamping piece is slotted into both injectors. Recover the copper seal and O-rings and discard. New ones must be used for refitting **(see illustration)**.

Note: *The injectors can only be refitted to their original positions. Mark the injectors to avoid confusion if refitting the original injectors.*

2.0 litre engines (CFFA, CFFB and CFGB)

10 Disconnect the injector wiring plug connectors.

11 Push the return hose connector downwards at its outer tabs, then pull up the centre piece and disconnect them from the

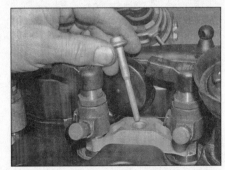

4.7 Remove the injector clamp retaining bolts

top of the injectors **(see illustrations)**. Plug the openings to prevent contamination.

12 Undo the unions and remove the high-pressure pipes from between the fuel

4.9 Remove two injectors at a time with retaining clamp

4.11a Hold down the outer tabs, and prise up the centre piece (arrowed)...

4.11b...then pull the return hose connector upwards from the injector

4.16 Lever up the clip (arrowed) and disconnect the injector wiring plugs

4.18 Undo the unions and remove the high-pressure pipes between the common rail and the injectors

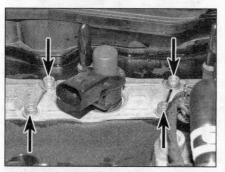

4.19a Undo the injector clamp cover bolts (arrowed)...

4.19b ...then lift and rotate it 90°

and the pipes/return hoses is clean and free from debris. The use of a vacuum cleaner is recommended. Push the return hose connector downwards at its tabs, then pull up the centre piece and disconnect them from the injectors **(see illustrations 4.11a and 4.11b)**.

18 Undo the unions remove the high-pressure pipes between the common fuel rail and the injectors **(see illustration)**. Plug the openings to prevent contamination.

19 Undo the bolts securing the injector clamp cover, the slightly lift the cover and rotate it 90° for access to the injector retaining nuts **(see illustrations)**.

20 Unscrew the injector retaining nuts.

21 Audi technicians use a slide hammer (tool T10055) and adapter (T10055/1) to pull the injector from the cylinder head. This is a slide hammer with an adapter that screws onto the top of the injector. If this tool is not available, it is possible to fabricate an equivalent using slide hammer with the union from an old injector pipe brazed/welded onto the end. Screw the tool onto the top of the injector, and pull the injector out using a few gently taps. Recover the clamping piece, copper seal and O-rings and discard. New ones must be used for refitting **(see illustrations)**.

rail and the injectors. Counterhold the injector with an open-ended spanner when releasing the pipe union **(see illustrations 4.6a and 4.6b)**.

13 Undo the bolt securing the injector clamp between the two injectors, note that one clamp secures two injectors in place.

14 Audi technicians use a slide hammer (tool T10055) and adapter (T10415) to pull the injector from the cylinder head. If this tool is not available, it may be possible to fabricate an equivalent tool to pull the injector out of the cylinder head.

15 Two injectors will need to be removed together, as the clamping piece is slotted into both injectors. Recover the copper seal and O-rings and discard. New ones must be used for refitting.

Note: *The injectors can only be refitted to their original positions. Mark the injectors to avoid confusion if refitting the original injectors.*

2.0 litre engines (CBAA, CBAB and CBBB)

16 Disconnect the injector wiring plugs **(see illustration)**.

17 Ensure the area around the injectors

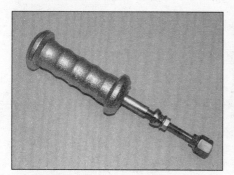

4.21a We attached an old injector pipe union onto the end of the slide hammer...

4.21b ...screwed it onto the top of the injector...

4.21c ...and pulled it from the cylinder head

4.22a Carefully prise out the seal...

4.22b ...making sure the spring does not fall into the cover

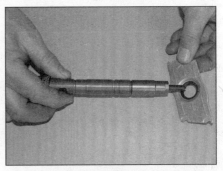

4.24 Slide the new cover plate onto the injector

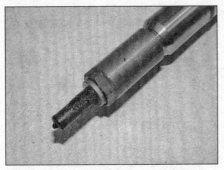

4.25a Clean off the carbon around the end of the injector...

4.25b...and fit a new sealing washer

4.26 Fit new O-ring seals to the fuel return lines

Note: *The injectors can only be refitted to their original positions. Mark the injectors to avoid confusion if refitting the original injectors.*

Refitting

22 If required, renew the injector seals in the top of the camshaft cover. Using a screwdriver, prise the seal out from the cover; the new seal can then be pressed firmly into the cover **(see illustrations)**. There are different size seals depending on engine code, make sure the correct seals are supplied. Also make sure the spring on the inside lip of the seal does not drop into the camshaft cover.

23 Ensure the area around the injector locations in the cylinder head are clean and free from debris. Use a vacuum cleaner if available. Clean any carbon deposits from the injector and sealing surfaces with a cloth soaked in clean engine oil or rust-releasing spray.

24 On 2.0 litre engines (CBAA, CBAB and CBBB), if new cover plates are to be fitted, slide them on now **(see illustration)**.

25 To remove the copper sealing washer, spray rust-releasing spray around the injector nozzle, then clamp the seal in a vice, and use a twisting motion to pull the injector from the seal. Push the new copper seal into place **(see illustrations)**. Do not touch the very end of the injector, or you could block up the nozzle.

26 On 1.6 litre engines, apply a little clean engine oil to the return pipe connection, and fit the new O-ring **(see illustration)**.

27 On 2.0 litre engines, apply a little clean engine oil to the return pipe connection on the injector, and fit the new O-ring **(see illustration)**.

28 To renew the main injector O-ring seal, Audi specify the use of tool no. T10377. This tool allows the O-ring to slide over the end of the injector without twisting. With care, the seals can be fitted without the tool **(see illustrations)**.

29 On 2.0 litre engines (CBAA, CBAB and CBBB), slide the new clamping piece onto injector as shown **(see illustration)**.

4.27 Fit the new return pipe O-ring (arrowed) to the top of the injector

4.28 Fit a new main O-ring seal without twisting it

4.29 Slide the new clamping piece (arrowed) onto the injector

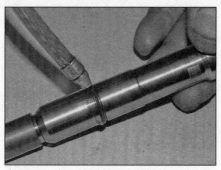

4.30a Lubricate the seal with some clean oil...

4.30b ...then slide the injectors down into the cylinder head

4.33 Fit new clips to secure the fuel return lines

30 Apply a smear of clean engine oil to the main O-ring seal, and insert the injector into place in the cylinder head **(see illustrations)**. Note that if the original injectors are being refitted, they must go into their original positions. Tighten the injector clamping bolt/nut to the specified torque.

31 On 2.0 litre engines (CBAA, CBAB and CBBB), rotate the cover back to position and tighten the retaining bolt to the specified torque.

32 Refit the high-pressure fuel pipes and tighten the unions to the specified torque. Note that the pipes may be re-used providing the tapered seats are undamaged and the pipes are not deformed, constricted or corroded. Counterhold the injector with an open-ended spanner when tightening the pipe union.

33 On 1.6 litre engines, when fitting the return hoses to the sides of the injector, use new securing clips **(see illustration)**.

34 The remainder of refitting is a reversal of removal, noting the following:

a) *If one or more injectors have been renewed, the 'injector delivery calibration values' and 'injector voltage calibration values' must be entered into the ECM using Audi diagnostic equipment. Entrust this task to an Audi dealer or suitably equipped specialist.*

b) *After completion of the work, the fuel system must be bled as described in Section 10.*

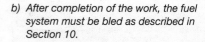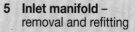

5 Inlet manifold – removal and refitting

Removal

Plastic manifold

1 Remove the throttle housing, as described in Section 3 of this Chapter.

2 Remove the fuel rail from the top of the inlet manifold, as described in Section 11 of this Chapter.

3 Undo the two retaining screws and move the coolant return pipe to one side **(see illustration)**.

4 Undo the two retaining screws and move the fuel return pipe to one side **(see illustration)**.

5 Where fitted, disconnect the wiring plug connector from the manifold flap motor **(see illustration)**.

6 Undo the retaining screw and remove the EGR cooler changeover valve from the manifold **(see illustration)**.

7 Slacken the retaining clamp and disconnect the EGR pipe **(see illustration)**.

8 Undo the manifold retaining bolts, starting

5.3 Undo the coolant pipe retaining screws (arrowed)

5.4 Undo the fuel line retaining screws (arrowed)

5.5 Disconnect the wiring connector (arrowed)

5.6 Undo the solenoid valve mounting bracket securing bolt (arrowed)

5.7 Slacken the EGR pipe retaining clamp (arrowed)

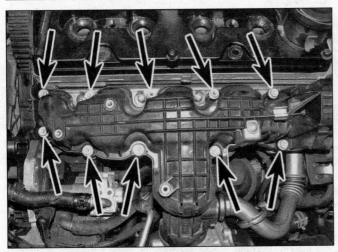

5.8a Undo the retaining bolts (arrowed)...

5.8b ...and remove the inlet manifold

from the outside and working inwards in a diagonal sequence **(see illustrations)**. Lift the manifold from the cylinder head and retrieve the gasket seals; discard, as new ones will be required for refitting.

Aluminium manifold

9 Remove the throttle housing and manifold flap motor (where fitted), as described in Section 3 of this Chapter.
10 Using thin, long-nosed pliers, carefully pull the wiring plugs from the top of the glow plugs **(see illustration)**.
11 With reference to Section 4, disconnect

the fuel return pipes from the injectors, fuel rail, and high-pressure pump.
12 Undo the retaining nut and remove the fuel return pipe **(see illustration)**.
13 Undo the unions and disconnect the high-pressure fuel pipe between the pump and fuel rail.
14 Disconnect the wiring plug from the manifold change-over motor.
15 Where applicable, undo the 2 retaining bolts and pull the engine oil level dipstick guide tube upwards from place.
16 Undo the retaining bolts, starting from the outside and working inwards in a diagonal

sequence, then manoeuvre the manifold from position.

Refitting

17 Refitting is a reversal of removal, using new seals and gaskets **(see illustration)**. Remember to renew any self-locking nuts. Tighten the manifold retaining bolts to the specified torque setting, starting from the inside and working outwards in a diagonal sequence.

6 Fuel filter – renewal

Note: *Observe the precautions in Section 1 before working on any component in the fuel system.*
1 Refer to Chapter 1, Section 8.

5.8c Cover the inlet manifold recess with tape

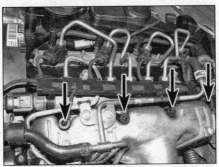

5.10 Pull the wiring plugs from the glow plugs

7 Fuel lift pump and gauge sender unit – removal and refitting

Note: *Observe the precautions in Section 1 before working on any component in the fuel system.*

⚠️ **Warning: Avoid direct skin contact with fuel – wear protective clothing and gloves when handling fuel system components. Ensure that the work area is well-ventilated to prevent the build-up of fuel vapour.**

General information

1 The fuel lift pump and gauge sender unit are combined in one assembly, which is mounted in the top of the fuel tank. Access is beneath the rear seat cushion in the floor panel. The unit protrudes into the fuel tank, and its removal involves exposing the contents of the tank to the atmosphere.

5.12 Fuel return pipe nut (arrowed)

5.17 Renew the inlet manifold seals

7.4a Disconnect the wiring connector block...

7.4b...then prise up the cover and disconnect the wiring from the pump/ gauge unit

7.5 Fuel supply and return hoses

Removal

2 Ensure that the vehicle is parked on a level surface, then disconnect the battery negative lead and position it away from the terminal. Refer to 'Disconnecting the battery' in Reference chapter.

3 Remove the rear seat cushion, and lift the carpet section from the floor panel.

4 Unclip and disconnect the wiring connector block, then prise up the cover and disconnect the wiring from the top of the lift pump/gauge sender unit **(see illustrations)**.

5 Pad the area around the supply and return fuel hoses with rags to absorb any spilt fuel from the fuel lines, and then squeeze the catches to release the hose clips and

disconnect them **(see illustration)**. Observe the supply and return arrow markings on the ports – label the fuel hoses accordingly to ensure correct refitting later. The supply pipe is black, and may have white markings, while the return pipe is blue, or has blue markings.

6 Note the position of the alignment marks, then unscrew and remove the securing ring. Use a pair of water pump pliers (or home-made tool) to grip and rotate the securing ring **(see illustrations)**.

7 Lift out the lift pump/gauge sender unit, holding it above the level of the fuel in the tank until the excess fuel has drained out. Recover the flange and seal **(see illustration)**.

8 With the pump/sender unit removed from

the car, place it on an absorbent card or rag **(see illustration)**. Inspect the float at the end of the sender unit swinging arm for punctures and fuel ingress – renew the unit if it appears damaged.

9 The fuel pick-up incorporated in the assembly is spring-loaded to ensure that it always draws fuel from the lowest part of the tank. Check that the pick-up is free to move under spring tension with respect to the sender unit body.

10 Inspect the rubber seal from the fuel tank aperture for signs of fatigue – renew it if necessary **(see illustration)**.

11 Inspect the sender unit wiper and track; clean off any dirt and debris that may have

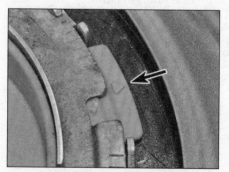

7.6a Note the alignment marks...

7.6b...then use a suitable tool to unscrew...

7.6c...and remove the securing ring

7.7 Removing the lift pump/gauge sender unit from the fuel tank

7.8 Lift pump/gauge sender unit removed from the car

7.10 If not removed with the unit, recover the rubber seal and check its condition

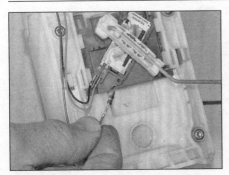

7.12a Disconnect the small wires...

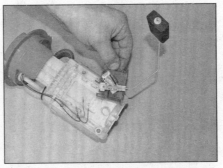

7.12b...then undo the screws and slide out the sender unit

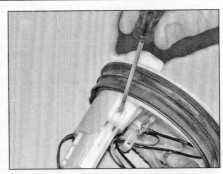

7.13a Prise up the retaining tags...

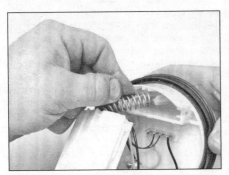

7.13b...and recover the spring fitted under the top plate

7.14a Locate the seal in the tank aperture...

7.14b...then fit the lift pump/sender unit

accumulated, and look for breaks in the track.

12 If required, the sender unit can be separated from the assembly, as follows. Disconnect the two small wires (note their positions), then remove the four screws and slide the unit downwards to remove **(see illustrations)**.

13 The unit top plate can be removed by releasing the plastic tags at either side; recover the large spring, which fits onto a peg on the plate underside **(see illustrations)**.

Refitting

14 Refit the lift pump/sender unit by following the removal procedure in reverse, noting the following points:

a) Take care not to bend the float arm as the unit is refitted.

b) Smear the outside of tank aperture rubber seal with clean fuel or lubricating spray, to ease fitting. Locate the seal in the tank aperture before fitting the lift pump/sender unit **(see illustrations)**.

c) The arrow markings on the sender unit body and the access aperture must be aligned.

d) Reconnect the fuel hoses to the correct ports – observe the direction-of-flow arrow markings, and refer to paragraph 5. Ensure that the fuel hose fittings click fully into place.

e) On completion, check that all associated pipes are securely clipped to the tank, then run the engine and check for fuel leaks.

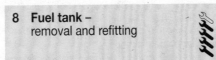

8 Fuel tank – removal and refitting

Note: *Observe the precautions in before working on any component in the fuel system.*

Removal

1 Before the tank can be removed, it must be drained of as much fuel as possible. As no drain plug is provided, it is preferable to carry out this operation with the tank almost empty.

2 Open the fuel filler flap, and unscrew the fuel filler cap – leave the cap loosely in place.

3 Disconnect the battery negative lead and position it away from the terminal. Refer to *'Disconnecting the battery'* in Reference chapter. Using a hand pump or siphon, remove any remaining fuel from the bottom of the tank.

4 Loosen the right-hand rear wheel bolts, then jack up the rear of the car and remove the right-hand rear wheel.

5 Remove the right-hand rear wheel arch liner as described in Chapter 11 Section 21.

6 Gain access to the top of the fuel pump/sender unit as described in Section 7, and disconnect the wiring harness from the top of the pump/sender unit at the multiway connector.

7 Unscrew the fuel filler flap unit retaining screw (on the side opposite the flap hinge), and ease the flap unit out of position. Recover the rubber seal, which fits around the filler neck.

8 Unbolt the filler pipe from the body.

9 Release the mounting rubbers and support the rear of the exhaust system to allow removal of the fuel tank.

10 Disconnect the fuel and charcoal canister breather lines as necessary.

11 Position a trolley jack under the centre of the tank. Insert a block of wood between the jack head and the tank to prevent damage to the tank surface. Raise the jack until it just takes the weight of the tank.

12 Unscrew the mounting bolt and detach the tank strap.

13 Lower the jack and tank away from the underside of the vehicle. If necessary, unscrew the nuts and remove the heat shield from the tank.

14 If the tank is contaminated with sediment or water, remove the fuel pump/sender unit (see Section 7) and swill the tank out with clean fuel. The tank is injection-moulded from a synthetic material, and if damaged, it should be renewed. However, in certain cases it may be possible to have small leaks or minor damage repaired. Seek the advice of a suitable specialist before attempting to repair the fuel tank.

Refitting

15 Refitting is the reverse of the removal procedure, noting the following points:

a) When lifting the tank back into position, make sure the mounting rubbers are correctly positioned, and take care to ensure none of the hoses get trapped between the tank and vehicle body.

b) *Ensure that all pipes and hoses are correctly routed, are not kinked, and are securely held in position with their retaining clips.*
c) *Tighten the tank strap retaining bolt to the specified torque.*
d) *On completion, refill the tank with fuel, and exhaustively check for signs of leakage prior to taking the vehicle out on the road.*

9 Fuel pump – removal and refitting

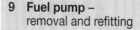

Removal

1.6 litre engines

1 Remove the timing belt and pump sprocket as described in
Chapter 2A, Section 8.
2 Disconnect the wiring connector from the fuel metering valve on top of the fuel pump **(see illustration)**.
3 Undo the two retaining screws and move the coolant return pipe to one side **(see illustration 5.3)**.
4 Undo the two retaining screws and move the fuel return pipe to one side **(see illustration 5.4)**.
5 Undo the pipe retaining bracket screw and the two retaining bolts, then remove the lifting eye from the front of the engine **(see illustration)**.
6 Slacken the fuel pipe unions and remove the high-pressure pipe from the pump to the fuel rail **(see illustration)**.

9.2 Disconnect the pump wiring connector

7 Release the retaining clips and disconnect the two fuel hoses from the top of the fuel pump **(see illustration)**.
8 Counterhold the pump hub using VAG tool No. T10051, and undo the pump hub nut. In the absence of this special tool, counterhold the hub using something to lock the sprocket, whilst the centre nut is slackened **(see illustration)**.
9 Using a suitable two-legged puller (VAG tool No. T40064) and two bolts, remove the hub complete with sprocket from the pump shaft.
10 Undo the 3 retaining bolts and remove the pump **(see illustration)**.

2.0 litre engines

11 Remove the timing belt and pump sprocket as described in Chapter 2C, Section 8.
12 Disconnect the fuel supply hose from the pump **(see illustration)**. Plug all openings to prevent contamination.

9.5 Remove the lifting bracket from above the fuel pump

13 Disconnect the wiring plug from the sensor on the pump.
14 Slacken the unions and disconnect the high-pressure fuel pipe between the pump and common fuel rail. Undo the retaining screws to release the fuel pipe from the support brackets.
15 On some models it may be necessary to disconnect he wiring connectors from the glow plugs. Pulling only under the ridge at the top of the connectors, disconnect the wiring connectors.
Note: *Take care not to damage the connectors or wiring, as the glow plug wiring loom/connectors are only available as a complete assembly.*
16 Undo the bolts securing the coolant pipe to the intake manifold, and position the pipe to one side.
17 Disconnect the fuel return pipes from the pump and the common fuel rail **(see illustration)**.

9.6 Remove the high pressure fuel line from the pump

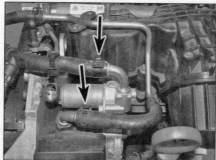

9.7 Disconnect the fuel hoses (arrowed) from the pump

9.8 Remove the fuel pump centre hub nut

9.10 Fuel pump mounting bolts (arrowed)

9.12 Release the clip (arrowed) and disconnect the fuel supply hose

9.17 Fuel pump return hose (arrowed)

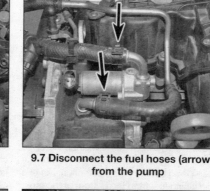

9.18 Counterhold the pump hub with a C-spanner, and undo the nut

9.19a Use a two-legged puller and 8 mm bolts to pull the hub from the pump shaft

9.19b Note the locating peg (arrowed) in the pump shaft

18 Counterhold the pump hub using VAG tool No. T10051, and undo the pump hub nut. In the absence of this special tool, counterhold the hub using a suitable C-spanner **(see illustration)**.

19 Using a suitable two-legged puller and two 8 mm bolts, remove the hub from the pump shaft **(see illustrations)**.

20 Undo the 3 retaining bolts and remove the pump.

Refitting

21 Refitting is a reversal of removal, noting the following points:

a) *Ensure all fuel pipes/hose connections are clean and free from debris.*

b) *The high-pressure fuel pipe from the pump to the common rail maybe re-used providing it's not been damaged.*

c) *Tighten all fasteners to their specified torque where given.*

d) *Fill the pump with clean fuel through the fuel supply pipe aperture prior to starting (see illustration).*

e) *Bleed the fuel system as described in Section 10.*

Supplementary fuel pump

Removal

22 The supplementary fuel pump is not fitted to all models, where fitted, it is located on a bracket bolted to the top of the right-hand engine mounting **(see illustration)**.

23 Disconnect the wiring plug from the exhaust gas pressure sensor, then undo the retaining bolt and move the sensor and

9.23 Undo the retaining screw (arrowed)

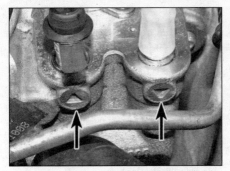

9.21 The triangles adjacent to the pump apertures indicate fuel flow (arrowed)

bracket to one side **(see illustration)**.

24 Undo the retaining bolts and lift the supplementary fuel pump upwards to access the fuel pipes and wiring plug **(see illustration)**.

25 Release the fuel hoses from the retaining clips, and disconnect the fuel pump wiring plug.

26 Release the clamps and disconnect the fuel supply pipe from the fuel filter. Plug/cover the openings to prevent contamination.

27 Disconnect the fuel temperature sensor wiring plug, release the clamp and disconnect the fuel supply pipe from the high-pressure fuel pump. Plug/cover the openings to prevent contamination.

Refitting

28 Refitting is a reversal of removal, noting the following points:

9.24 Undo the bolts and remove the pump bracket

9.22 Supplementary fuel pump location (arrowed)

a) *Ensure the hoses are not kinked.*

b) *Ensure all connections are clean and free from debris.*

c) *Note the hose connections: The return hose is blue (or blue markings), and the supply hose is black.*

d) *Bleed the system as described in Section 10.*

10 Fuel system bleeding

1 Prime the high pressure fuel pump by filling it with clean diesel through the fuel supply aperture **(see illustration 9.21)**, then operate the starter for shorts bursts (no more than 10 seconds at a time) until the engine starts. Operate the engine at a fast idle (approx 2000 rpm) for several minutes before allowing it to return to its normal idle speed.

2 If the engine fails to start, it must be filled/bled using Audi diagnostic equipment (VAS5051 etc.). Using this equipment operates the electric fuel pumps for 3 minutes.

3 Once the engine has been started, test drive the vehicle over a distance of at least 15 miles with at least one period of full acceleration. If there is any air left in the fuel system, the engine management ECU may switch to 'limp home' mode, and store a fault code. Have the fault code cleared and road test the vehicle again.

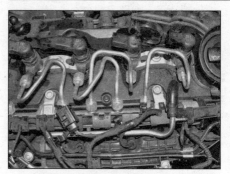

11.3a Remove the high pressure pipes from the rail and injectors...

11.3b ...and fit sealing caps to prevent dirt ingress

11.4a Disconnect the hose from the return pipe...

11 Fuel rail –
removal and refitting

Note: *Observe the precautions in Section 1 before working on any component in the fuel system.*

Removal

1 Pull the plastic cover on the top of the engine upwards from it's mountings and remove the foam insulation (where fitted). Ensure the area around the fuel rail and pipes is clean and free from debris. If available, use a vacuum cleaner.

2 Disconnect the wiring connectors from the fuel injectors.

3 Counterhold the injector with an open-ended spanner when releasing the pipe union. Undo the unions and remove the high-pressure pipes from between the fuel rail and the injectors **(see illustrations)**. Plug the openings to prevent contamination.

4 Release the retaining clips and disconnect the fuel return hose from the fuel rail **(see illustrations)**

5 Undo the retaining bolts, disconnect the coolant return hose from the expansion tank, and move the coolant pipe/hose to one side **(see illustration 5.3)**.

6 Slacken the fuel pipe unions and remove the high-pressure pipe from the pump to the fuel rail **(see illustration 9.6)**.

7 Disconnect the wiring plugs from the glow plugs, fuel pressure regulating valve, and the fuel pressure sensor at each end of the fuel rail. Unclip the wiring loom retaining bracket from the top of the fuel rail and move it to one side **(see illustration)**.

8 Undo the multi-spline retaining bolts and remove the fuel rail **(see illustrations)**.

9 If required, note their fitted positions, then unscrew the fuel pressure sensor and pressure regulating valve from the fuel rail, as described in Section 3.

Note: *Audi insist that once removed, the pressure regulating valve cannot be re-used.*

Refitting

10 Where applicable, refit the fuel pressure sensor and the new regulating valve to the fuel rail, and tighten them to the specified torque. Note that the threads of the sensors must be clean and free from oil and grease.

11.4b ...and the return pipe from the fuel rail

11 The remainder of refitting is a reversal of removal, noting the following points:

a) *Refit the high-pressure fuel pipes and tighten the unions to the specified torque. Note that the high-pressure fuel pipes may be re-used providing the tapered seats are undamaged and the pipes are not deformed, constricted or corroded.*

b) *After completion of the work, the fuel system must be bled as described in Section 10.*

11.7 Lift the wiring loom over and place to one side

11.8a Undo the fuel rail mounting bolts (arrowed) – CAYB & CAYC engines

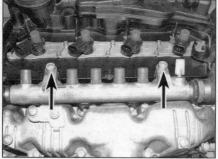

11.8b Undo the fuel rail mounting bolts (arrowed) – CBAA, CBAB & CBBB engines

Chapter 4 Part B
Fuel system – 1.9 litre engines

Contents

Degrees of difficulty

Easy, suitable for novice with little experience	Fairly easy, suitable for beginner with some experience	Fairly difficult, suitable for competent DIY mechanic	Difficult, suitable for experienced DIY mechanic	Very difficult, suitable for expert DIY or professional

Specifications

Engine codes

1.9 litre, 8-valve, turbo, SOHC	BLS and BXE

Note: *See 'Vehicle identification' in Reference chapter for the location of engine code markings.*

General

Fuel injection system	Electronic, direct, unit injectors
Firing order	1-3-4-2
Maximum engine speed.	N/A (ECU controlled)
Engine fast idle speed	N/A (ECU controlled)

Tandem pump

Fuel pressure at 1500 rpm	3.5 bar

Turbocharger

Type	Garrett or KKK

Torque wrench settings

	Nm	lbf ft
EGR pipe flange bolts	25	18
EGR valve mounting bolt	10	7
Engine speed sender	5	4
Flap motor housing	10	7
Injector clamp/mounting bolt: *		
Stage 1.	12	9
Stage 2.	Angle-tighten a further 270°	
Inlet manifold to cylinder head	22	16
Pump injector rocker shaft bolts: *		
Stage 1.	20	15
Stage 2.	Angle-tighten a further 90°	
Tandem pump bolts:		
Upper 20	15	
Lower 10	7	

*Do not re-use fastener

1 General information and precautions

1 The engines covered in this Chapter are fitted with a direct-injection fuelling system, with a fuel tank, an engine-bay mounted fuel filter with an integral water separator, fuel supply and return lines and four fuel injectors. Most models also have a fuel cooler mounted beneath the right-hand side of the car, bolted to the underside of the body.

2 The fuel is delivered by a camshaft driven 'tandem pump' at low pressure to the injectors (known as 'Unit injectors'). A 'roller rocker' assembly, mounted above the camshaft bearing caps, uses an extra set of camshaft lobes to compress the top of each injector once per firing cycle. This arrangement creates far higher injection pressures. The precise timing of the pre-injection and main injection is controlled by the engine management ECU and a solenoid on each injector. The resultant effect of this system is improved engine torque and power output, greater combustion efficiency, and lower exhaust emissions. All are fitted with a turbocharger.

3 The direct-injection fuelling system is controlled electronically by a diesel engine management system, comprising an Electronic Control Unit (ECU) and its associated sensors, actuators and wiring. In addition, the ECU manages the operation of the Exhaust Gas Recirculation (EGR) emission control system (Chapter 4C), the turbocharger boost pressure control system (Chapter 4C) and the glow plug control system (Chapter 5).

4 An electrically-operated flap valve is fitted to the inlet manifold to increase the vacuum when the engine speed is less than 2200 rpm; this is necessary to operate the EGR system efficiently, the flap valve is closed by the ECU for 3 seconds as the engine is switched off, to minimise the air inlet as the engine shuts down. This minimises the vibration felt as the pistons come up against the volume of highly compressed air present in the combustion chambers. On some models, there is a vacuum reservoir mounted on the front of the engine, which provides the vacuum supply to a vacuum capsule, which operates the flap.

5 It should be noted that fault diagnosis of the diesel engine management system is only possible with dedicated electronic test equipment. Problems with the system's operation should therefore be referred to an Audi dealer or suitably-equipped specialist for assessment. Once the fault has been identified, the removal/refitting sequences detailed in the following Sections will then allow the appropriate component(s) to be renewed as required.

Precautions

6 Many of the operations described in this Chapter involve the disconnection of fuel lines, which may cause an amount of fuel spillage. Before commencing work, refer to the warnings below and the information in *Safety first!*

⚠ *Warning: When working on any part of the fuel system, avoid direct contact skin contact with diesel fuel – wear protective clothing and gloves when handling fuel system components. Ensure that the work area is well ventilated to prevent the build-up of diesel fuel vapour.*

⚠ *Warning: Fuel injectors operate at extremely high pressures and the jet of fuel produced at the nozzle is capable of piercing skin, with potentially fatal results. When working with pressurised injectors, take care to avoid exposing any part of the body to the fuel spray. It is recommended that a diesel fuel systems specialist should carry out any pressure testing of the fuel system components.*

⚠ *Warning: Under no circumstances should diesel fuel be allowed to come into contact with coolant hoses – wipe off accidental spillage immediately. Hoses that have been contaminated with fuel for an extended period should be renewed.*

⚠ *Warning: Diesel fuel systems are particularly sensitive to contamination from dirt, air and water. Pay particular attention to cleanliness when working on any part of the fuel system, to prevent the ingress of dirt. Thoroughly clean the area around*

fuel unions before disconnecting them. Only use lint-free cloths and clean fuel for component cleansing.

⚠ *Warning: Store dismantled components in sealed containers to prevent contamination and the formation of condensation.*

2 Air cleaner assembly – removal and refitting

Removal

1 Loosen the clip and disconnect the air duct from the air mass meter.

2 Disconnect the wiring from the air mass meter. Also disconnect the vacuum hose below the air mass meter wiring connector **(see illustrations)**.

3 Undo the screws and lift the air cleaner lid complete with air mass meter from the base.

4 Lift out the air filter element, noting how it is fitted.

5 Disconnect the air duct from the front of the base, then unscrew the mounting nuts and withdraw the base from the engine compartment.

Refitting

6 Refit the air cleaner by following the removal procedure in reverse.

3 Diesel engine management system – component removal and refitting

Throttle pedal/position sensor

1 Refer to the procedures in Chapter 4A, Section 3.

Coolant temperature sensor (left-hand end of cylinder head)
Removal

2 Refer to Chapter 1, Section 31 and drain approximately one quarter of the coolant from the engine. Alternatively, be prepared for coolant spillage as the sensor is removed.

3 Remove the engine top cover.

4 The sensor is located on the left-hand end of the cylinder head, on the rear of the coolant outlet.

5 Remove the securing clip, then extract the sensor from its housing and recover the O-ring seal.

Refitting

6 Refit the coolant temperature sensor by reversing the removal procedure, using a new O-ring seal. Refer to Chapter 1 or Weekly checks and top-up the cooling system.

Coolant temperature sensor (radiator bottom outlet)
Removal

7 Drain the cooling system with reference to Chapter 1, Section 31. Alternatively, be

2.2a Disconnect the air mass meter wiring plug...

2.2b and the vacuum hose below it

3.10 Fuel temperature sensor

3.15 Charge air pressure sensor (arrowed)

3.23 Air mass meter (arrowed)

prepared for coolant spillage as the sensor is removed.

8 Remove the securing clip, then extract the sensor from the outlet elbow and recover the O-ring seal.

Refitting

9 Refit the coolant temperature sensor by reversing the removal procedure, using a new O-ring seal. Refer to Chapter 1 or Weekly checks and top-up the cooling system.

Fuel temperature sensor

Removal

10 The fuel temperature sensor is located in the fuel return line to the fuel filter in the engine compartment (see illustration). First, disconnect the wiring.

11 Remove the securing clip, then extract the sensor from the fuel line housing and recover the O-ring seal.

Refitting

12 Refit the fuel temperature sensor by reversing the removal procedure, using a new O-ring seal.

Inlet air temperature sensor

13 An air temperature sensor is built into the air mass meter – this sensor is an integral part of the air mass meter, and cannot be renewed separately.

Charge air pressure/ temperature sensor

Removal

14 The charge air pressure and temperature sensor is fitted either on the intercooler inlet elbow, or on the air hose from the intercooler to the inlet manifold depending on model. Jack up the front of the vehicle and support it on axle stands (see 'Jacking and vehicle support' in Reference chapter) then remove the engine undertray.

15 Disconnect the wiring then undo the screw and remove the sensor from its location (see illustration).

Refitting

16 Refit the inlet air temperature sensor by reversing the removal procedure, using a new O-ring seal.

Engine speed sensor

Removal

17 The engine speed sensor is mounted on the front cylinder block, adjacent to the mating surface of the block and transmission bellhousing.

18 Access is from beneath the engine compartment. Jack up the front of the vehicle and support it on axle stands (see 'Jacking and vehicle support' in Reference chapter) then remove the engine undertray.

19 Fit hose clamps to the hoses attached to the oil cooler, then disconnect them. Be prepared for some loss of coolant.

20 Unbolt and remove the oil filter bracket.

21 Remove the retaining screw and withdraw the sensor from the cylinder block.

Refitting

22 Refit the sensor by reversing the removal procedure.

Air mass meter

Removal

23 The air mass meter is located in the outlet from the air cleaner assembly on the left-hand side of the engine compartment (see illustration).

24 Loosen the clips and disconnect the air ducting from the air mass meter.

25 Disconnect the wiring and the vacuum hose. Undo the retaining screws securing the meter to the air cleaner. Withdraw the meter and recover the O-ring seal.

3.29 Inlet manifold flap motor

Caution: Handle the air mass meter carefully – its internal components are easily damaged.

Refitting

26 Refitting is a reversal of removal. Renew the O-ring seal if it appears damaged.

Absolute pressure (altitude) sensor

27 The absolute pressure sensor is an integral part of the ECU, and hence cannot be renewed separately.

Inlet manifold flap motor/ housing

Removal

28 Remove the engine top cover.

29 Loosen the clip (or release the spring clip) and disconnect the air trunking from the flap housing (see illustration).

30 Disconnect the flap control motor wiring plug from the housing.

31 Unscrew the bolts securing the flap housing to the EGR valve/housing/manifold, remove the flap housing and recover the O-ring seal.

Refitting

32 Refitting is a reversal of removal. Renew the O-ring seal if it appears damaged.

Clutch pedal switch

Removal

33 The clutch pedal switch is clipped to the clutch master cylinder on the pedal bracket. Remove the master cylinder as described in Chapter 6, Section 4.

34 Unclip the pedal switch from the bottom of the master cylinder.

Refitting

35 Refitting is a reversal of removal.

Electronic control unit (ECU)

Caution: Always wait at least 30 seconds after switching off the ignition before disconnecting the wiring from the ECU. When the wiring is disconnected, all the learned values are erased, however any Specifications of the fault memory are retained. After reconnecting the wiring, the basic settings must be reinstated by an Audi dealer using a special test instrument. Note also that if the ECU is renewed, the identification of the new ECU must be transferred to the immobiliser control unit by an Audi dealer.

36 Refer to the procedures in Chapter 4A, Section 3.

4 Injectors – general information, removal and refitting

⚠️ **Warning: Exercise extreme caution when working on the fuel injectors. Never expose the hands or any part of the body to injector spray, as the high working pressure can cause the fuel to penetrate the skin, with possibly fatal results. You are strongly advised to have any work which involves testing the injectors under pressure carried out by a dealer or fuel injection specialist. Refer to the precautions given in Section 1 of this Chapter before proceeding.**

General information

1 Injectors deteriorate with prolonged use, and it is reasonable to expect them to need reconditioning or renewal after 60 000 miles or so. Accurate testing, overhaul and calibration of the injectors must be left to a specialist.

Removal

Note: *Take care not to allow dirt into the injectors or fuel pipes during this procedure.*

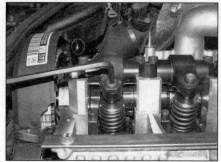

4.4 Undo the adjustment screw until the rocker arm lies against the plunger pin of the injector

Do not drop the injectors or allow the needles at their tips to become damaged. The injectors are precision-made to fine limits, and must not be handled roughly. Keep the injectors identified for position to ensure correct refitting.

2 With reference to Chapter 2B, remove the upper timing belt cover and camshaft cover.

3 Using a spanner or socket, turn the crankshaft pulley until the rocker arm for the injector which is to be removed, is at its highest, ie, the injector plunger spring is under the least amount of tension.

4 Slacken the locknut of the adjustment screw on the end of the rocker arm above the injector, and undo the adjustment screw until the rocker arm lies against the plunger pin of the injector **(see illustration)**.

5 Starting at the outside and working in, gradually and evenly slacken and remove

4.6 Remove the clamping block securing bolt (arrowed)

the rocker shaft retaining bolts. Lift off the rocker shaft. Check the contact face of each adjustment screw, and renew any that show signs of wear.

6 Undo the clamping block securing bolt and remove the block from the side of the injector **(see illustration)**.

7 Using a small screwdriver, carefully prise the wiring connector from the injector.

8 Audi technicians use a slide hammer (tool T10055) to pull the injector from the cylinder head. This is a slide hammer, which engages in the side of the injector. If this tool is not available, it is possible to fabricate an equivalent using a short section of angle iron, a length of threaded rod, a cylindrical weight, and two locknuts. Weld/braze the rod to the angle iron, slide the weight over the rod, and lock the two nuts together at the end of the rod to provide the stop for the weight **(see illustration)**. Seat the slide hammer/tool in the slot on the side on the injector, and pull the injector out using a few gently taps. Recover circlip, the heat shield and O-rings and discard. New ones must be used for refitting **(see illustration)**.

9 If required, the injector wiring loom/rail can be removed from the cylinder head by undoing the two retaining nuts/bolts at the back of the head. To prevent the wiring connectors fouling the cylinder head casting as the assembly is withdrawn, insert the connectors into the storage slots in the plastic wiring rail. Carefully push the assembly to the rear, and out of the casting **(see illustrations)**.

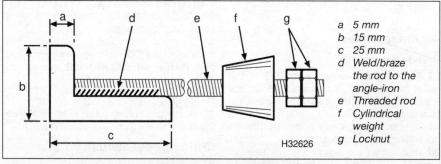

a	5 mm
b	15 mm
c	25 mm
d	Weld/braze the rod to the angle-iron
e	Threaded rod
f	Cylindrical weight
g	Locknut

H32626

4.8a Unit injector removal tool

4.8b Seat the slide hammer/tool in the slot on the side on the injector, and pull the injector out

4.9a Undo the two nuts at the back of the head and slide the injector loom/rail out

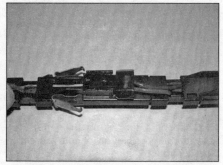

4.9b The injector connectors will slide into the loom/rail to prevent them from being damaged as the assembly is withdrawn/ inserted into the cylinder head

4.10 Care must be used to ensure that the injector O-rings are fitted without being twisted

Refitting

10 Prior to refitting the injectors, the three O-rings, heat insulation washer and clip must be renewed. Due to the high injection pressures, it is essential that the O-rings are fitted without being twisted. Audi recommend the use of three special assembly sleeves to install the O-rings squarely. It may be prudent to entrust O-ring renewal to an Audi dealer or suitably-equipped injection specialist, rather than risk subsequent leaks **(see illustration)**.

11 After renewing the O-rings, fit the heat shield and secure it in place with the circlip **(see illustration)**.

12 Smear clean engine oil onto the O-rings, and push the injector evenly down into the cylinder head onto its stop.

13 Fit the clamping block alongside the injector, but only hand-tighten the new retaining bolt at this stage.

14 It is essential that the injectors are fitted at right-angles to the clamping block. In order to achieve this, measure the distance from the rear face of the cylinder head to the rounded section of the injector **(see illustrations)**. The dimensions (a) are as follows:

Cylinder 1 = 333.0 ± 0.8 mm
Cylinder 2 = 245.0 ± 0.8 mm
Cylinder 3 = 153.6 ± 0.8 mm
Cylinder 4 = 65.6 ± 0.8 mm

15 Once the injector(s) are aligned correctly, tighten the clamping bolt to the specified Stage 1 torque setting, and the Stage 2 angle tightening setting.

Note: *If an injector has been renewed, it is essential that the adjustment screw, locknut of the corresponding rocker and ball-pin are renewed at the same time. The ball-pins simply pull out of the injector spring cap. There is an O-ring in each spring cap to stop the ball-pins from falling out.*

16 Smear some grease (VAG No G000 100) onto the contact face of each rocker arm adjustment screw, and refit the rocker shaft assembly to the camshaft bearing caps, tightening the retaining bolts as follows. Starting from the inside out, hand-tighten the

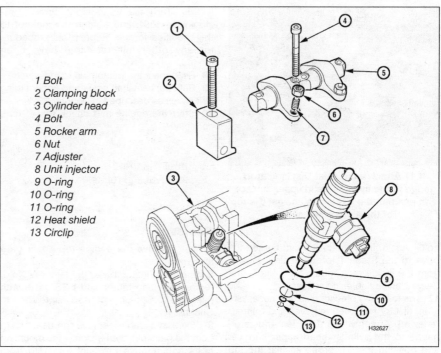

1 Bolt
2 Clamping block
3 Cylinder head
4 Bolt
5 Rocker arm
6 Nut
7 Adjuster
8 Unit injector
9 O-ring
10 O-ring
11 O-ring
12 Heat shield
13 Circlip

4.11 Unit injector details

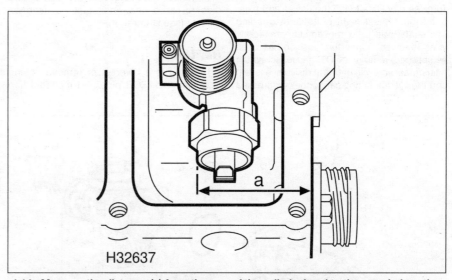

4.14a Measure the distance (a) from the rear of the cylinder head to the rounded section of the injector (see text)

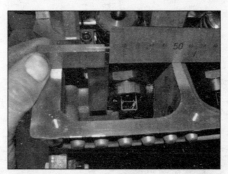

4.14b Use a set square against the edge of the injector...

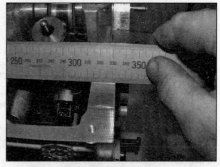

4.14c ...and measure the distance to the rear of the cylinder head

4.17 Attach a DTI (Dial Test Indicator) gauge to the cylinder head upper surface, and position the DTI probe against the top of the adjustment screw

bolts. Again, from the inside out, tighten the bolts to the Stage 1 torque setting. Finally, from the inside out, tighten the bolts to the Stage 2 angle tightening setting.

17 The following procedure is only necessary if an injector has been removed and refitted/ renewed. Attach a DTI (Dial Test Indicator) gauge to the cylinder head upper surface, and position the DTI probe against the top of the adjustment screw **(see illustration)**. Turn the crankshaft until the rocker arm roller is on the highest point of its corresponding camshaft lobe, and the adjustment screw is at its lowest. Once this position has been established, remove the DTI gauge, screw the adjustment screw in until firm resistance is felt, and the injector spring cannot be compressed

further. Turn the adjustment screw anti-clockwise 180°, and tighten the locknut to the specified torque. Repeat this procedure for any other injectors that have been refitted.

18 Reconnect the wiring plug to the injector.

19 Refit the camshaft cover and upper timing belt cover, as described in Chapter 2B.

20 Start the engine and check that it runs correctly.

5 Inlet manifold – removal and refitting

Removal

1 First, remove the engine top cover **(see illustration)**.

2 Where not integral with the inlet manifold, remove the flap motor and EGR valve with reference to Section 3 of this Chapter, and to Chapter 4C.

3 Where applicable, remove the heat shield from the manifold, then unscrew the mounting bolts and remove the inlet manifold from the cylinder head. Recover the gasket and discard, as a new one must be used on refitting **(see illustration)**.

Refitting

4 Refitting is a reversal of removal, using new manifold, EGR pipe and manifold flap

assembly gaskets/O-rings. Tighten the mounting bolts to the specified torque.

6 Fuel filter – renewal

Note: *Observe the precautions in Section 1 before working on any component in the fuel system.*

1 Refer to Chapter 1, Section 8.

7 Fuel gauge sender unit – removal and refitting

Note: *Observe the precautions in Section 1 before working on any component in the fuel system.*

⚠ **Warning: Avoid direct skin contact with fuel – wear protective clothing and gloves when handling fuel system components. Ensure that the work area is well ventilated to prevent the build-up of fuel vapour.**

1 The fuel gauge sender unit is mounted in the top of the fuel tank. Access is beneath the rear seat cushion in the floor panel. The unit protrudes into the fuel tank, and its removal involves exposing the contents of the tank to the atmosphere.

2 Refer to the procedures in Chapter 4A, Section 7, for removal and refitting procedures.

8 Fuel tank – removal and refitting

Note: *Observe the precautions in Section 1 before working on any component in the fuel system.*

1 Refer to the procedures in Chapter 4A, Section 8.

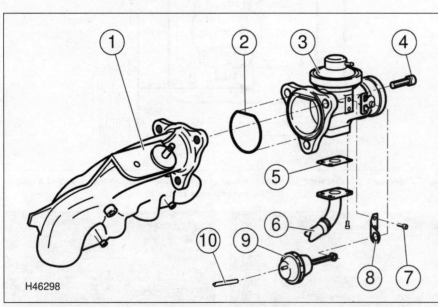

5.1 Inlet manifold details

1 Inlet manifold
2 O-ring seal
3 Combined EGR valve and flap housing
4 Screw
5 Gasket
6 EGR pipe

7 Screw
8 Bracket
9 Vacuum actuator (not on all engines) – electric on others
10 Vacuum hose to solenoid (not on all engines) – electric on others

5.3 Unscrew the inlet manifold mounting bolts

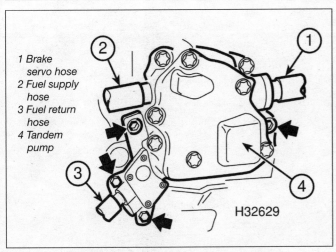

1 Brake
  servo hose
2 Fuel supply
  hose
3 Fuel return
  hose
4 Tandem
  pump

H32629

9.4 Tandem fuel pump securing bolts (arrowed)

9.7 Ensure that the tandem pump pinion engages correctly with the drive slot in the camshaft

9 Tandem fuel pump –
removal and refitting

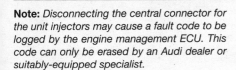

Note: *Disconnecting the central connector for the unit injectors may cause a fault code to be logged by the engine management ECU. This code can only be erased by an Audi dealer or suitably-equipped specialist.*

Removal

1 The tandem fuel pump is located on the left-hand end of the cylinder head. It is effectively a vacuum pump (for the braking system) and a fuel lift pump (for the fuel injection system). First, remove the engine top cover.

2 Disconnect the fuel supply hose (marked white) and the return hose (marked blue) from the fuel filter and drain all fuel from the hoses into a suitable container.

3 Remove the air cleaner assembly together with the air mass meter and air ducting, with reference to Section 2.

4 Release the retaining clip (where fitted) and disconnect the brake servo pipe from the tandem pump **(see illustration)**.

5 Disconnect the fuel supply hose (marked white) and the return hose (marked blue) from the tandem pump.

6 Unscrew the four retaining bolts and remove the tandem pump from the cylinder head. Recover the gasket and discard, as a new one must be used on refitting. There are no serviceable parts within the tandem pump. If the pump is faulty, it must be renewed.

Refitting

7 Refitting is a reversal of removal, but use a new gasket and tighten the mounting bolts to the specified torque. Ensure the pump pinion engages correctly with the drive slot in the camshaft **(see illustration)**. It is recommended that the tandem pump is primed with fuel as follows. Disconnect the fuel filter return hose (marked blue), and connect the hose to a hand vacuum pump. Operate the vacuum pump until fuel comes out of the return hose. Take care not to suck any fuel into the vacuum pump. Reconnect the return hose to the fuel filter.

8 Have the engine management ECU's fault memory interrogated and erased by an Audi dealer or suitably-equipped specialist.

Chapter 4 Part C
Emission control and exhaust systems

Contents

Degrees of difficulty

| **Easy,** suitable for novice with little experience | 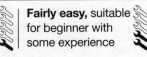 | **Fairly easy,** suitable for beginner with some experience | | **Fairly difficult,** suitable for competent DIY mechanic | | **Difficult,** suitable for experienced DIY mechanic | | **Very difficult,** suitable for expert DIY or professional | |

Specifications

Engine codes

1.6 litre, 16-valve, turbo, DOHC. . . . .   CAYB and CAYC
1.9 litre, 8-valve, turbo, SOHC. . . . .   BLS and BXE
2.0 litre 16-valve, turbo, DOHC . . . .   CBAA, CBAB, CBBB, CFFA, CFFB and CFGB
See 'Vehicle identification' in Reference Chapter for the location of engine code markings.

Emission control applications

1.6 and 2.0 litre engines. . . . .   Particulate filter in downpipe, with catalytic converter and oxygen (lambda probe) sensor, EGR system with exhaust gas temperature sensors and exhaust gas pressure sensor.

1.9 litre engines . . . .   One catalyst in downpipe, EGR system OR Particulate filter/catalyst in downpipe with oxygen sensor, exhaust gas temperature sensor and exhaust gas pressure sensor, EGR system

Torque wrench settings

	Nm	lbf ft
1.6 and 2.0 litre engines:		
Catalytic converter/particulate filter mounting bracket nuts/bolts . . .	25	18
EGR cooler mounting bolts	9	6
EGR recirculation metal pipes (all engines except CBAA, CBAB and CBBB):		
to-cooler bolts	9	6
to-cylinder head bolts.	9	6
to-exhaust manifold nuts	25	18
to-inlet manifold clamp bolt	5	4
EGR recirculation metal pipes (CBAA, CBAB and CBBB engines):		
to-EGR valve bolts	20	15
to-cooler bolts	20	15
to-exhaust manifold nuts	20	15
EGR valve bolts (CBAA, CBAB and CBBB engines)	8	6
Exhaust clamp nuts	25	18
Exhaust gas temperature sensors:		
to-exhaust manifold	45	33
to-top of catalytic converter/particulate filter	60	45
to-front pipe after catalytic converter/particulate filter.	60	45
Exhaust/turbocharger manifold to cylinder head:		
CBAA, CBAB and CBBB engines.	20	15
All engines except CBAA, CBAB, and CBBB.	25	18
Turbocharger pulsation damper bolts	10	7
Turbocharger oil return pipe flange bolts: *		
CBAA, CBAB and CBBB engines.	15	11
All engines except CBAA, CBAB and CBBB	17	13
Turbocharger oil return banjo bolt*.	40	30
Turbocharger oil supply banjo bolt (all engines except		
CBAA, CBAB and CBBB)	30	22
Turbocharger oil supply union nut (CBAA, CBAB and CBBB engines). .	22	16
Turbocharger-to-downpipe/catalytic converter clamp.	7	5
1.9 litre engines:		
EGR pipe nuts/bolts.	22	16
Exhaust clamp nuts	25	18
Exhaust manifold-to-downpipe nuts*.	25	18
Turbocharger/exhaust manifold: *		
BLS engines	25	18
Except BLS engines	20	15
Turbocharger oil return pipe flange bolts	17	13
Turbocharger oil return union nut.	30	22
Turbocharger oil supply union nut	22	16
Turbocharger-to-downpipe clamp	7	5

Do not re-use fasteners

1 General Information

Emission control systems

1 All engines have a crankcase emission control system, and in addition, are fitted with a catalytic converter/particulate filter. All engines are also equipped with an Exhaust Gas Recirculation (EGR) system to reduce exhaust emissions.

Crankcase emission control

2 To reduce the emission of unburned hydrocarbons from the crankcase into the atmosphere, the engine is sealed and the blow-by gases and oil vapour are drawn from inside the crankcase, through a wire mesh oil separator, into the inlet tract to be burned by the engine during normal combustion.

3 Under conditions of high manifold depression, the gases will be sucked positively out of the crankcase. Under conditions of low manifold depression, the gases are forced out of the crankcase by the (relatively) higher crankcase pressure. If the engine is worn, the raised crankcase pressure (due to increased blow-by) will cause some of the flow to return under all manifold conditions.

Exhaust emission control

4 An oxidation catalyst is fitted in the exhaust system of all models. This has the effect of removing a large proportion of the gaseous hydrocarbons, carbon monoxide and particulates present in the exhaust gas. On some models, a particulate filter is also fitted in order to filter out soot particles.

5 An Exhaust Gas Recirculation (EGR) system is fitted to all models. This reduces the level of nitrogen oxides produced during combustion by introducing a proportion of the exhaust gas back into the inlet manifold under certain engine operating conditions. The system is controlled electronically by the engine management ECU.

Exhaust systems

6 On 1.6 and 2.0 litre engines, the exhaust system consists of the exhaust manifold, front pipe with catalytic converter/particulate filter and the tailpipe and silencer. On 1.9 litre engines, the system consists of the exhaust manifold, front pipe with catalytic converter/particulate filter, intermediate pipe and silencer, and tailpipe and silencer. On all engines, the turbocharger is integral with the exhaust manifold, and is driven by the exhaust gases.

7 The system is supported by various metal brackets screwed to the vehicle floor, with rubber vibration dampers fitted to suppress noise.

2 Crankcase emission system
– general information

1 The crankcase emission control system consists of hoses connecting the crankcase to the air cleaner or inlet manifold.

2 The system requires no attention other than to check at regular intervals that the hoses and pressure-regulating valve are free of blockages and in good condition.

3 Exhaust Gas Recirculation (EGR) system (1.6 and 2.0 litre engines) – component removal

1 The EGR system consists of the EGR valve, which directs exhaust gas from the exhaust manifold to the inlet manifold, and a control (changeover) valve that actuates the system according to engine load and speed **(see illustration)**. There is a vacuum-operated changeover unit, which is fitted on the EGR cooler for recirculating the exhaust gas. All this is connected by a series of vacuum hoses, and metal corrugated cooler pipes. There is also a recirculation potentiometer fitted to the EGR valve, this is controlled directly from the engine management ECU, which then activates the control motor.

2 On 2.0 litre (CBAA, CBAB and CBBB engines), the EGR valve is mounted between the throttle valve module and the inlet manifold. On the side of the EGR valve is a metal connecting pipe that goes to the exhaust gas cooler, which is bolted to the rear of the cylinder block. The gas cooler uses coolant from the engine cooling system to cool the exhaust gases before passing them to the inlet manifold. The system is activated by a solenoid valve mounted at the front of the inlet manifold, which is controlled by the ECU.

3 On all other engines the EGR valve is integral with the exhaust gas cooler, which is bolted to the rear of the cylinder block. It is joined to the exhaust manifold and cylinder head, by flanged corrugated metal pipes. The system is activated by a solenoid valve mounted at the front of the inlet manifold, which is controlled by the ECU.

EGR cooler 'change-over' solenoid valve

4 The EGR vacuum-solenoid valve is mounted on the front of the inlet manifold **(see illustration)**. Do not confuse the EGR solenoid with the turbo charge pressure control solenoid, which is mounted on the bulkhead.

5 Disconnect the wiring plug from the solenoid valve **(see illustration)**.

6 Unclip the valve from the mounting

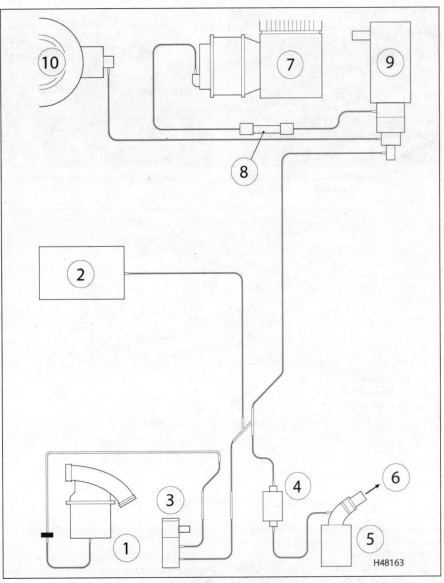

3.1 Vacuum hose layout

1 EGR cooler changeover vacuum unit
2 Cylinder head cover
3 EGR cooler changeover valve
4 Non-return valve
5 Vacuum pump connection
6 To brake servo
7 Air filter
8 Silencer
9 Charge pressure control solenoid valve

3.4 EGR cooler solenoid valve (arrowed)

3.5 Disconnect the wiring connector...

3.6 ...then unclip the valve from the bracket

3.9 EGR pipe-to-valve bolts (arrowed)

12 Refitting is a reversal of removal, using a new EGR valve O-ring seal, and tightening the retaining bolts to the specified torque.

All other engine codes

13 The EGR valve is incorporated into the EGR cooler, remove the cooler as described in paragraphs 20 to 26. At the time of writing, it was not possible to separate the EGR valve from the cooler.

EGR cooler

14 Remove the exhaust front pipe/catalytic converter/particulate filter as described in Section 11.

15 Drain the cooling system as described in Chapter 1, Section 31. If required the coolant hoses can be clamped before removal, to save draining the complete system.

Engine codes CBAA, CBAB and CBBB

16 Release the retaining clips and disconnect the coolant hoses from the EGR cooler. Be prepared for coolant spillage.

17 Undo the retaining bolts and disconnect the EGR metal connecting pipes from each end of the cooler.

18 Undo the upper bolts and lower banjo bolt and remove the turbocharger oil return pipe/support from the rear of the engine.

19 Disconnect the vacuum hose from vacuum unit on the lower part of the cooler, then undo the retaining bolts, and remove the cooler from the rear of the engine **(see illustration)**.

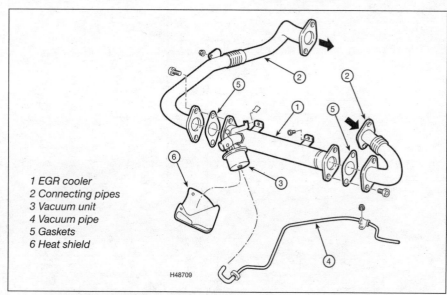

1 EGR cooler
2 Connecting pipes
3 Vacuum unit
4 Vacuum pipe
5 Gaskets
6 Heat shield

H48709

3.19 EGR cooler system – CBAA, CBAB and CBBB engines

All other engine codes

20 Release the retaining clips and disconnect the coolant hoses from each end of the EGR cooler **(see illustrations)**. Be prepared for coolant spillage.

21 Undo the two retaining screws from the cooler, the two retaining nuts from the exhaust manifold and remove the EGR metal connecting pipe **(see illustration)**.

22 Undo the two retaining screws from the cooler, the two retaining screws from the

bracket **(see illustration)**, then identify the vacuum hoses for refitting and disconnect them from the valve.

7 Refitting is a reversal of removal. Ensure that the hoses and wiring plug are reconnected securely and correctly.

EGR valve

Engine codes CBAA, CBAB and CBBB

8 Remove the throttle valve housing from the

inlet manifold, as described in Chapter 4A, Section 3.

9 Undo the bolts securing the pipe to the left-hand side of the EGR valve **(see illustration)**.

10 Disconnect the wiring plug connector from the right-hand side of the EGR valve.

11 Undo the bolts and detach the valve from the inlet manifold. Discard the O-ring seal – a new one must be fitted.

3.20a Disconnect the coolant hose from the cooler

3.20b Release the retaining clips (arrowed) and remove hose

3.21 Remove the EGR pipe from the cooler to the manifold

3.22a Undo the EGR pipe bolts (arrowed) to the cooler

3.22b Undo the EGR pipe bolts (arrowed) to the cylinder head

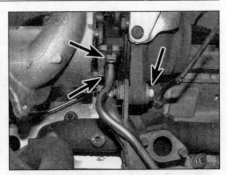

3.23a Undo the upper bolts (arrowed)...

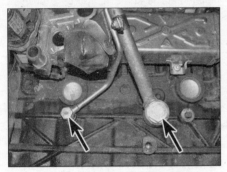

3.23b ...and lower banjo bolts...

3.23c ...then remove the pipes and support bracket

3.24 Disconnect the wiring connector from the EGR valve

cylinder head and remove the EGR metal connecting pipe (see illustrations).

23 Undo the upper bolts and lower banjo bolt and remove the turbocharger oil return pipe/support from the rear of the engine (see illustrations).

24 Disconnect the wiring plug connector from the EGR valve (see illustration).

25 Disconnect the vacuum hose from vacuum unit on the lower part of the cooler (see illustration), then undo the four retaining bolts, and remove the cooler from the rear of the engine.

26 Refitting is a reversal of removal, using new gaskets (see illustration), and tightening the retaining bolts to the specified torque.

4 Exhaust Gas Recirculation (EGR) system (1.9 litre engines) – component removal

1 The EGR system consists of the EGR valve, which directs exhaust gas from the exhaust manifold to the inlet manifold, and a control valve, which actuates the system according to engine load and speed. On engines with a vacuum-operated EGR system, the control valve is a solenoid valve that opens vacuum from the inlet manifold to the EGR valve actuator when the solenoid is energised by the engine management ECU.

2 Where a recirculation potentiometer is

fitted, control of the system is directly from the engine management ECU that activates the control motor.

3 The EGR valve is located as follows:

a) *Engine code BXE – the EGR valve is located between the flap housing and inlet manifold, and is joined to the exhaust manifold by a flanged pipe (see illustration). A vacuum solenoid control valve is mounted on the engine compartment bulkhead.*

b) *Engine code BLS – the EGR valve is integral with a gas recirculation potentiometer located on a housing located between the flap housing and inlet manifold. A flanged pipe connects*

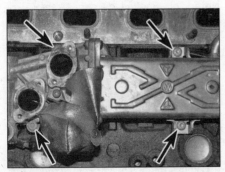

3.25 EGR cooler securing bolts (arrowed)

3.26 Fit new gaskets to the EGR pipes

4.3 EGR valve location on engine (arrowed)

4.4 EGR solenoid valve location

4.10 EGR connecting pipe retaining bolts (arrowed)

4.11 Disconnect the wiring connector (arrowed)

the housing to the exhaust manifold. A vacuum solenoid control valve is mounted on the engine compartment bulkhead.

EGR vacuum-solenoid valve

4 The EGR vacuum-solenoid valve is mounted on the bulkhead at the rear of the engine compartment **(see illustration)**. Do not confuse the EGR solenoid with the turbo boost pressure solenoid, which is mounted further to the left (left as seen from the driver's seat).

5 Disconnect the wiring plug from the solenoid valve. On some models access can be improved by removing the cover from the engine compartment fusebox.

6 Identify and disconnect the vacuum hoses.

7 Unscrew the solenoid valve mounting bolt, and remove the valve from the bulkhead.

8 Refitting is a reversal of removal. Ensure that the hoses and wiring plug are reconnected securely and correctly.

EGR valve

Engine code BXE

9 Remove the inlet manifold flap motor/housing as described in Chapter 4B, Section 3.

10 Unscrew the bolts and separate the connecting pipe from the EGR valve **(see illustration)**. Recover the gasket and discard it, as a new one must be used on refitting.

11 Disconnect the wiring connector from the EGR valve **(see illustration)**.

12 Remove the EGR valve from the inlet manifold and recover the O-ring seal.

13 Refitting is a reversal of removal, but renew the gasket and O-ring seal.

Enginecode BLS

14 Remove the engine top cover.

15 Disconnect the wiring from the combined EGR valve and re-circulation potentiometer.

16 Unscrew the mounting bolts and remove the EGR valve/potentiometer from the inlet housing. Recover the O-ring seal and discard, as a new one must be used on refitting.

17 To remove the inlet housing, first remove the inlet manifold flap motor/housing as described in Chapter 4B, Section 3, then remove the EGR valve as described earlier in this sub-Section. Unbolt the connecting

pipe and recover the gasket, then unbolt the housing from the inlet manifold. Recover the O-ring seal. Discard the O-ring seal and gasket, as new ones must be used on refitting.

18 Refitting is a reversal of removal, but fit a new gasket and O-ring seals. Note that if the combined EGR valve and potentiometer unit is renewed, after initially switching on the ignition, the ignition must be switched off then on again. Wait one complete minute to allow the control unit to learn the position of the valve, and check that an audible click is heard from the main relay, and then switch the ignition off.

5 Turbocharger – general information and precautions

1 A turbocharger is fitted to all engines, and is integral with the exhaust manifold.

2 The turbocharger increases engine efficiency by raising the pressure in the inlet manifold above atmospheric pressure. Instead of the air simply being sucked into the cylinders, it is forced in.

3 Energy for the operation of the turbocharger comes from the exhaust gas. The gas flows through a specially-shaped housing (the turbine housing) and in so doing, spins the turbine wheel. The turbine wheel is attached to a shaft, at the end of which is another vaned wheel, known as the compressor wheel. The compressor wheel spins in its own housing, and compresses the inducted air on the way to the inlet manifold.

4 Between the turbocharger and the inlet manifold, the compressed air passes through an intercooler (see Section 11 for details). The purpose of the intercooler is to remove from the inducted air some of the heat gained in being compressed. Because cooler air is denser, removal of this heat further increases engine efficiency.

5 Boost pressure (the pressure in the inlet manifold) is limited by a wastegate, which diverts the exhaust gas away from the turbine wheel in response to a pressure-sensitive actuator.

6 The turbo shaft is pressure-lubricated by an oil feed pipe from the engine oil filter

mounting. The shaft 'floats' on a cushion of oil. Oil is returned to the sump through a return pipe that connects to the sump.

Precautions

7 The turbocharger operates at extremely high speeds and temperatures. Certain precautions must be observed to avoid premature failure of the turbo, or injury to the operator.

• *Do not operate the turbo with any parts exposed – foreign objects falling onto the rotating vanes could cause excessive damage and (if ejected) personal injury.*

• *Cover the turbocharger air inlet ducts to prevent debris entering, and clean using lint-free cloths only.*

• *Do not race the engine immediately after start-up, especially if it is cold. Give the oil a few seconds to circulate.*

• *Observe the recommended intervals for oil and filter changing, and use a reputable oil of the specified quality. Neglect of oil changing, or use of inferior oil, can cause carbon formation on the turbo shaft and subsequent failure.*

• *Thoroughly clean the area around all oil pipe unions before disconnecting them, to prevent the ingress of dirt.*

• *Store dismantled components in a sealed container to prevent contamination.*

6 Turbocharger and exhaust manifold (1.6 and 2.0 litre engines) – removal and refitting

Note: *This Section describes removal of the turbocharger together with the exhaust manifold. On all engines covered in this manual, the turbocharger cannot be removed from the exhaust manifold.*

Removal

1 Apply the handbrake, then jack up the front of the vehicle and support it on axle stands (see 'Jacking and vehicle support' in Reference chapter). Remove the engine compartment undertray and the engine top cover.

2 Remove the bulkhead panel from the rear of the engine compartment, as described in Chapter 12, Section 18.

6.5a Disconnecting the breather hose...

6.5b ...undo the retaining screw...

6.5c ...and disconnect the air intake hose

3 Remove the air cleaner assembly and ducting as described in Chapter 4A, Section 2.

4 Remove the exhaust front pipe/catalytic converter/particulate filter as described in Section 11.

5 Undo the retaining bolt, unclip the breather pipe and disconnect the air intake hose from the turbocharger (**see illustrations**).

6 Disconnect the wiring connector and vacuum pipe from the vacuum unit on top of the turbocharger (**see illustrations**).

7 Located at the engine compartment bulkhead, disconnect the exhaust gas temperature sensor wiring plugs, and detach the connector from the bulkhead bracket (**see illustrations**). Note that there is one wiring connector behind the mounting plate on the bulkhead, trace the wiring back from the relevant sensor, noting its routing and releasing it from any retaining clips.

8 Slacken the retaining clips, undo the two retaining bolts and withdraw the pulsation damper from the charge air ducting to the turbo (**see illustration**).

9 Undo the retaining screws and remove the EGR metal connecting pipes, with reference to Section 3.

10 Undo the two upper securing bolts and the lower banjo bolts for the oil supply and return for the turbocharger. Then remove the oil return pipe/support from the rear of the engine (**see illustrations 3.23a, 3.23b and 3.23c**).

11 Undo the two retaining screws and remove the heat shield from the manifold (**see illustration**).

6.6a Disconnect the wiring connector...

6.6b ...and the vacuum hose from the vacuum pump

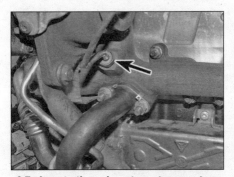

6.7a Locate the exhaust gas temperature sensor (arrowed)...

6.7b ...and disconnect the wiring connector on the bulkhead

12 Check around the turbocharger/exhaust manifold and unclip any wiring or hoses still connected, noting their fitted position and the routing of all cables.

13 Undo the retaining nuts and manoeuvre the exhaust manifold/turbocharger assembly out from the engine compartment (**see illustration**).

6.8 Disconnect the charge air pipe/pulsation damper from the turbocharger

6.11 Undo the two retaining screws from the heat shield

6.13 Remove the turbocharger/manifold from the engine compartment

6.14a Fit a new exhaust manifold gasket...

6.14b ...oil return/supply pipe gasket...

6.14c ...oil return banjo bolt...

6.14d ...and oil supply sealing washers

7.6 Disconnect the oil return pipe and support bracket (arrowed)

7.9 Oxygen (lambda) sensor (arrowed)

Refitting

14 Refit the turbocharger by following the removal procedure in reverse, noting the following points:

a) *Renew exhaust maniflold gaskets, sealing washers and O-rings* **(see illustration)**.

b) *Fit a new gasket to the oil return pipe upper flange* **(see illustration)**.

c) *Fit a new banjo bolt to the oil return pipe* **(see illustration)**.

d) *Fit new sealing washers to the oil supply pipe* **(see illustration)**.

e) *Before reconnecting the oil supply pipe, fill the turbocharger with fresh oil using an oil can.*

f) *Tighten all nuts and bolts to the specified torque, where given.*

g) *Ensure that the air hose clips are securely tightened, to prevent air leaks.*

h) *When the engine is started after refitting, allow it to idle for approximately one minute to give the oil time to circulate around the turbine shaft bearings. Check for signs of oil or coolant leakage from the relevant unions.*

7 Turbocharger and exhaust manifold (1.9 litre engines) – removal and refitting

Note: *This Section describes removal of the turbocharger together with the exhaust manifold. On all engines covered in this Manual, the turbocharger cannot be detached from the exhaust manifold.*

Removal

1 Apply the handbrake, then jack up the front of the vehicle and support it on axle stands (see '*Jacking and vehicle support*' in Reference chapter). Remove the engine compartment undertray and the engine top cover.

2 Remove the right-hand driveshaft as described in Chapter 8, Section 2.

3 Remove the front suspension subframe as follows:

a) *Unbolt the exhaust system mounting from the subframe.*

b) *Unbolt the heat shield from the subframe.*

c) *Remove the engine rear-mounting link from the subframe and transmission with reference to Chapter 2B, Section 18.*

d) *Support the subframe on a trolley jack, then unscrew the bolts securing the steering gear and anti-roll bar to the subframe.*

e) *Unscrew the mounting bolts and lower the subframe to the ground.*

4 On engine code BLS detach the particulate filter from the turbocharger as follows:

a) *Disconnect the wiring from the exhaust gas pressure sensor, then unbolt the sensor.*

b) *Disconnect the wiring from the particulate filter then loosen the clamp and detach the filter from the turbocharger.*

5 Where fitted, unscrew the bolts from the auxiliary heater coolant pipes.

6 Unbolt the turbocharger support bracket then undo bolts from the turbocharger oil return pipe **(see illustration)**.

7 Remove the EGR cooler connecting pipe, and disconnect the charge pressure duct from the turbocharger.

8 Disconnect the vacuum hose, and then unscrew the oil supply line union nut.

9 Trace the wiring from the oxygen sensor(s) and disconnect the wiring connector **(see illustration)**. The sensor can remain fitted to the exhaust manifold while it is removed, taking care not to damage it on removal.

10 Unscrew the exhaust manifold mounting bolts.

11 Push the engine forwards as far as possible, then slide the exhaust manifold off its studs and lower it together with the turbocharger from the engine. Recover the gasket from the cylinder head and discard it as a new one must be used on refitting.

Refitting

12 Refit the turbocharger by following the removal procedure in reverse, noting the following points:

a) *Renew all gaskets, sealing washers and O-rings.*

b) *Before reconnecting the oil supply pipe, fill the turbocharger with fresh oil using an oil can.*

c) *Tighten all nuts and bolts to the specified torque, where given.*

d) *Ensure that the air hose clips are securely tightened, to prevent air leaks.*

e) *When the engine is started after refitting, allow it to idle for approximately one minute to give the oil time to circulate around the turbine shaft bearings. Check for signs of oil or coolant leakage from the relevant unions.*

8.2 Boost pressure solenoid location

8 Turbocharger boost control system components – description, removal and refitting

Description

1 The turbocharger wastgate valve is operated by vacuum supplied by the brake vacuum pump mounted on the left-hand end of the cylinder head. The vacuum supply is controlled by an electrically-operated solenoid valve activated by the engine management ECU. The solenoid valve is mounted on the bulkhead at the rear of the engine compartment. On engines fitted with a particulate filter, the valve has three hoses connecting it to the air cleaner, turbocharger and inlet manifold. On all other engines, the valve has six hoses connecting it to the non-return valve, EGR valve, bypass/intake manifold flap, air filter, vacuum reservoir and turbocharger. It is important that the hoses are connected correctly to the solenoid valve.

Boost pressure solenoid valve

2 The boost pressure solenoid valve is mounted at the rear of the engine compartment, on the left-hand side of the bulkhead (see illustration).
3 Disconnect the wiring from the boost pressure valve.
4 Remove the vacuum hoses from the ports on the boost control valve, noting their order of connection carefully to aid correct refitting.

5 Remove the retaining nuts and withdraw the valve.
6 Refitting is a reversal of removal.

Boost pressure valve (wastegate)

7 The boost pressure valve is an integral part of the turbocharger, and cannot be renewed separately.

9 Intercooler – general information, removal and refitting

1 The intercooler is effectively an 'air radiator', used to cool the pressurised inlet air before it enters the engine.
2 When the turbocharger compresses the inlet air, one side effect is that the air is heated, causing the air to expand. If the inlet air can be cooled, a greater effective volume of air will be inducted, and the engine will produce more power.
3 The compressed air from the turbocharger, which would normally be fed straight into the inlet manifold, is instead ducted around the engine to the base of the intercooler. The intercooler is mounted at the front of the car, in the airflow. The heated air entering the base of the unit rises upwards, and is cooled by the airflow over the intercooler fins, much as with the radiator. When it reaches the top of the intercooler, the cooled air is then ducted into the throttle housing.

Removal

4 The intercooler is located in front of the radiator on the lock carrier (the crossmember incorporating the headlights and radiator grille). Remove the radiator as described in Chapter 3, Section 3 for access to the intercooler. This procedure includes moving the lock carrier to its Service position.
5 Release the air ducts from the inlet and outlet elbows at the bottom of the intercooler (see illustrations).
6 Undo the screws securing the air conditioning condenser to the intercooler, secure the intercooler in place so as to remove the intercooler.
7 Undo the screws from the mounting

rubbers to the lock carrier (see illustration), and lift the intercooler upwards from the lower mountings, taking care not to damage the cooling fins.
8 Examine the mounting rubbers and renew them if necessary. Also, examine the intercooler for any damage, and check the air hoses for splits.

Refitting

9 Refitting is a reversal of removal, referring to Chapter 3, Section 3 when refitting the radiator. Ensure that the air hose clips are securely refitted, to prevent air leaks.

10 Exhaust manifold and catalytic converter/particulate filter – removal and refitting

1 The exhaust manifold and turbocharger are integral, and removal and refitting procedures are described in Section 6 for 1.6 and 2.0 litre engines, and in Section 7 for 1.9 litre engines.

11 Exhaust system – component renewal

⚠️ **Warning: Allow ample time for the exhaust system to cool before starting work. In particular, note that the catalytic converter runs at very high temperatures. If there is any chance that the system may still be hot, wear suitable gloves.**

Removal

Note: *The following procedures describe the general work required for component renewal. Some differences will be experienced according to model, but the procedures are essentially the same*

1 The original Audi system fitted in the factory is in multiple sections, depending on engine type. On all models. the front section includes the catalytic converter/particulate filter, and can be removed complete. On 1.9 litre models, the original rear section cannot be removed in one piece, as it passes over the rear axle – the pipe must be cut through

9.5a Release the retaining clips (arrowed)...

9.5b...and remove the air hoses

9.7 Intercooler mounting bolts – one side arrowed

between the centre and rear silencers, at a point marked on the pipe.

2 To remove part of the system, first jack up the front or rear of the car and support it on axle stands (see *'Jacking and vehicle support'* in Reference chapter). Alternatively, position the car over an inspection pit or on car ramps. Before removing the front part of the exhaust system, trace the wiring from the oxygen sensor(s) and disconnect the wiring connector. The sensor can remain fitted to the exhaust while it is removed, taking care not to damage it on removal.

Front pipe and catalytic converter or particulate filter

Caution: Handle the flexible, braided section of the front pipe carefully, and do not bend it excessively.

3 Unscrew the clamp bolt securing the front exhaust pipe to the turbocharger or exhaust manifold.

4 Unscrew the clamp bolt securing the front pipe to the centre/rear exhaust sections, and free the clamp so that both sections can be moved independently.

5 Release the front pipe from the mounting rubbers, then lower the front pipe, and twist it from the centre section. Lower it to the ground and withdraw from under the car.

Rear pipe and silencers

6 If the factory-fitted Audi centre/rear section is being worked on, examine the pipe between the two silencers for three pairs of punch marks, or three line markings. The centre marking indicates the point at which to cut the pipe, while the outer marks indicate the position for the ends of the new clamp

required when refitting. Cut through the pipe using the centre mark as a guide, making the cut as square to the pipe as possible if either resulting section is to be re-used.

7 If the factory-fitted rear section has already been renewed, unscrew the clamp bolts between the two sections.

Centre silencer

8 To remove the centre silencer, first loosen the bolts on the clamps at the front and rear of the centre silencer. Release the centre silencer from the rubber mountings, then twist from the front and rear sections, and withdraw from under the car.

Rear silencer

9 The rear silencer is supported by a rubber mounting, which is bolted to the underside of the car. Unscrew the clamp bolt securing the rear silencer to the centre silencer.

10 Release the silencer from the rubber mountings, then twist it from the centre section and withdraw from under the car.

Refitting

11 Each section is refitted by a reversal of the removal sequence, noting the following points:

a) *Ensure that all traces of corrosion have been removed from the flanges or pipe ends, and renew all necessary gaskets.*

b) *The design of the clamps used between the exhaust sections means that they play a greater role in ensuring a gas-tight seal – fit new clamps if they are in less than perfect condition.*

c) *When fitting the clamps, use the markings on the pipes as a guide to the clamp's correct fitted position.*

d) *Inspect the mountings for signs of damage or deterioration, and renew as necessary.*

e) *If using exhaust assembly paste, make sure this is only applied to joints downstream of the catalyst.*

f) *Prior to tightening the exhaust system mountings and clamps, ensure that all rubber mountings are correctly located and that there is adequate clearance between the exhaust system and vehicle underbody*

12 Catalytic converter – general information and precautions

1 The catalytic converter/particulate filter needs to be treated with respect to avoid problems. The unit is a reliable and simple device which needs no maintenance in itself, but there are some facts of which an owner should be aware if the converter/particulate filter is to function properly for its full service life:

a) *DO NOT use fuel or engine oil additives – these may contain substances harmful to the catalytic converter.*

b) *DO NOT continue to use the car if the engine burns (engine) oil to the extent of leaving a visible trail of blue smoke.*

c) *Remember that the catalytic converter is FRAGILE – do not strike it with tools during servicing work, and take care handling it when removing it from the car for any reason.*

d) *The catalytic converter, used on a well-maintained and well-driven car, should last for between 50,000 and 100,000 miles – if the converter is no longer effective, it must be renewed.*

Chapter 5
Starting and charging systems

Contents

Degrees of difficulty

Easy, suitable for novice with little experience 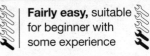	**Fairly easy,** suitable for beginner with some experience	**Fairly difficult,** suitable for competent DIY mechanic	**Difficult,** suitable for experienced DIY mechanic	**Very difficult,** suitable for expert DIY or professional

Specifications

General
System type . . . . 12 volt, negative earth

Starter motor
Rating . . . . 12V, 2.0 kW

Battery
Ratings . . . . 36 to 72 Ah (depending on model and market)

Alternator
Rating . . . . 55, 60, 70 or 90 amp
Minimum brush length . . . . 5.0 mm

Torque wrench settings	Nm	lbf ft
Alternator mounting bolts:		
1.6 litre engines	20	15
1.9 litre engines	25	18
2.0 litre engines:		
All engines except CBBB and CFGB	20	15
CBBB and CFGB engines	25	18
Glow plugs	15	11
Starter mounting bolts:		
M10	40	30
M12	75	55

1 General information and precautions

1 The engine electrical system consists mainly of the charging and starting systems, and the engine pre/post-heating system. Because of their engine-related functions, these are covered separately from the body electrical devices such as the lights, instruments, etc (which are covered in Chapter 12).

2 The electrical system is of the 12 volt negative earth type.

3 The battery is of the low maintenance or maintenance-free (sealed for life) type and is charged by the alternator, which is belt-driven from the crankshaft pulley.

4 The starter motor is of the pre-engaged type, with an integral solenoid. On starting, the solenoid moves the drive pinion into engagement with the flywheel ring gear before the starter motor is energised. Once the engine has started, a one-way clutch prevents the motor armature being driven by the engine until the pinion disengages from the flywheel.

5 Further details of the various systems are given in the relevant Sections of this Chapter. While some repair procedures are given, the usual course of action is to renew the component concerned.

Precautions

Warning: It is necessary to take extra care when working on the electrical system to avoid damage to semi-conductor devices (diodes and transistors), and to avoid the risk of personal injury. In addition to the precautions given in 'Safety first!' observe the following when working on the system:

• *Always remove rings, watches, etc, before working on the electrical system.* Even with the battery disconnected, capacitive discharge could occur if a component's live terminal is earthed through a metal object. This could cause a shock or nasty burn.

• *Do not reverse the battery connections.* Components such as the alternator, electronic control units, or any other components having semi-conductor circuitry could be irreparably damaged.

• *Never disconnect the battery terminals, the alternator, any electrical wiring or any test instruments when the engine is running.*

• *Do not allow the engine to turn the alternator when the alternator is not connected.*

• *Never test for alternator output by flashing the output lead to earth.*

• *Always ensure that the battery negative lead is disconnected when working on the electrical system.*

• Before using electric-arc welding equipment on the car, *disconnect the battery, alternator and components such as the*

electronic control units (where applicable) to protect them from the risk of damage.

Caution: Certain audio units fitted as standard equipment by Audi have a built-in security code to deter thieves. If the power source to the unit is cut, the anti-theft system will activate. Even if the power source is immediately reconnected, the unit will not function until the correct security code has been entered. Therefore, if you do not know the correct security code for the unit, do not disconnect the battery negative terminal or remove the audio unit from the vehicle. Refer to your Audi dealer for further information on whether the unit fitted to your car has a security code. Refer to 'Disconnecting the battery' in Reference chapter.

2 Battery – testing and charging

Testing

Standard and low-maintenance battery

1 If the vehicle covers a small annual mileage, it is worthwhile checking the specific gravity of the electrolyte every three months to determine the state of charge of the battery. Remove the battery (see Section 3) then remove the cell caps/cover (as applicable) and use a hydrometer to make the check, comparing the results with the following table. Note that the specific gravity readings assume an electrolyte temperature of 15°C; for every 10°C below 15°C subtract 0.007. For every 10°C above 15°C add 0.007. If the electrolyte level of any cell is low, top it up to the MAX level mark with distilled water.

	Above 25°C	Below 25°C
Fully-charged	1.210 to 1.230	1.270 to 1.290
70% charged	1.170 to 1.190	1.230 to 1.250
Discharged	1.050 to 1.070	1.110 to 1.130

2 If the battery condition is suspect, first check the specific gravity of electrolyte in each cell. A variation of 0.040 or more between any cells indicates loss of electrolyte or deterioration of the internal plates.

3 If the specific gravity variation is 0.040 or more, the battery should be renewed. If the cell variation is satisfactory but the battery is discharged, it should be recharged as described later in this Section.

Maintenance-free battery

4 In cases where a sealed for life maintenance-free battery is fitted, topping-up and testing of the electrolyte in each cell is not possible. The condition of the battery can therefore only be tested using a battery condition indicator or a voltmeter.

5 Certain models may be fitted with a maintenance-free battery with a built-in charge condition indicator. The indicator is

located in the top of the battery casing, and indicates the condition of the battery from its colour. If the indicator shows green, then the battery is in a good state of charge. If the indicator turns darker, eventually to black, then the battery requires charging, as described later in this Section. If the indicator shows clear/yellow, then the electrolyte level in the battery is too low to allow further use, and the battery should be renewed. Do not attempt to charge, load or jump-start a battery when the indicator shows clear/yellow.

All battery types

6 If testing the battery using a voltmeter, connect the voltmeter across the battery and note the voltage. The test is only accurate if the battery has not been subjected to any kind of charge for the previous six hours. If this is not the case, switch on the headlights for 30 seconds, then wait four to five minutes before testing the battery after switching off the headlights. All other electrical circuits must be switched off, so check that the doors and tailgate are fully shut when making the test.

7 If the voltage reading is less than 12.2 volts, then the battery is discharged, whilst a reading of 12.2 to 12.4 volts indicates a partially discharged condition. The battery should be recharged as described later in this Section.

Charging

Note: *The following is intended as a guide only. Always refer to the manufacturer's recommendations (often printed on a label attached to the battery) before charging a battery.*

8 If the battery is to be recharged, we recommend that you use a low current battery charger. Note that it is not necessary to disconnect the battery leads when using a low current battery charger. If the battery is disconnected (eg, if it is to be removed and recharged on the bench), note that certain 'learned' values will be lost from the engine management ECU memory, requiring the car to be driven over a short distance after refitting the battery. Also, when the battery is reconnected, the warning lights for the ESP and electro-mechanical steering will light up and stay on. They will extinguish if you drive briefly in a straight line at a speed of 9 to 13 mph.

Standard and low maintenance battery

9 Charge the battery at a rate equivalent to 10% of the battery capacity (eg, for a 45 Ah battery charge at 4.5 A) and continue to charge the battery at this rate until no further rise in specific gravity is noted over a four-hour period.

10 Alternatively, a trickle charger charging at the rate of 1.5 amps can safely be used overnight.

11 Specially rapid boost charges, which are

claimed to restore the power of the battery in 1 to 2 hours, are not recommended, as they can cause serious damage to the battery plates through overheating.

12 While charging the battery, note that the temperature of the electrolyte should never exceed 38°C.

Maintenance-free battery

13 This battery type takes considerably longer to fully recharge than the standard type, the time taken being dependent on the extent of discharge, but it can take anything up to three days.

14 The battery should be removed from the car, and a constant voltage type charger is required, to be set, when connected, to 13.9 to 14.9 volts with a charger current below 25 amps. Using this method, the battery should be useable within three hours, giving a voltage reading of 12.5 volts, but this is for a partially discharged battery and, as mentioned, full charging can take far longer.

15 If the battery is to be charged from a fully discharged state (condition reading less than 12.2 volts), have it recharged by your local automotive electrician, as the charge rate is higher and constant supervision during charging is necessary.

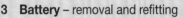

3.1 Lift the cover from the insulation box to gain access to the battery terminals.

3 Unscrew the retaining clamp bolt **(see illustration)**, then lift the battery from the plastic insulator box.
4 Unclip and remove the plastic insulation box **(see illustration)**.
5 If necessary, unbolt and remove the battery tray **(see illustration)**.

Refitting

6 Refit the battery by following the removal procedure in reverse. Tighten the clamp bolt securely.

---

3 Battery – removal and refitting

Note: *If the vehicle has a security-coded radio, make sure that you have the code number before disconnecting the battery. If necessary, a 'code-saver' or 'memory-saver' can be used to preserve the radio code and any other relevant memory values whilst the battery is disconnected (see 'Disconnecting the battery' in Reference chapter.*

Removal

1 The battery is located on the left-hand side of the engine compartment. Lift the insulation box cover to gain access to the battery **(see illustration)**.
2 Loosen the clamp nut and disconnect the battery negative (-) then positive (+) leads from the terminals **(see illustration)**.

---

4 Alternator/charging system – testing in vehicle

Note: *Refer to Section 1 of this Chapter before starting work.*

1 If the charge warning light fails to illuminate when the ignition is switched on, first check the alternator wiring connections for security. If the light still fails to illuminate, check the continuity of the warning light feed wire from the alternator to the bulbholder. If all is satisfactory, the alternator is at fault and should be renewed or taken to an auto-electrician for testing and repair.
2 Similarly, if the charge warning light comes on with the ignition, but is then slow to go out when the engine is started, this may indicate an impending alternator problem. Check all the items listed in the preceding paragraph,

3.2 Disconnecting the battery positive terminal

and refer to an auto-electrical specialist if no obvious faults are found.
3 If the charge warning light illuminates when the engine is running, stop the engine and check that the auxiliary drivebelt is not broken (see Chapter 1, Section 9) and that the alternator connections are secure. If all is so far satisfactory, check the alternator brushes and slip-rings as described in Section 6. If the fault persists, the alternator should be renewed, or taken to an auto-electrician for testing and repair.
4 If the alternator output is suspect even though the warning light functions correctly, the regulated voltage may be checked as follows.
5 Connect a voltmeter across the battery terminals, and start the engine.
6 Increase the engine speed until the voltmeter reading remains steady; the reading should be approximately 12 to 13 volts, and no more than 14 volts.
7 Switch on as many electrical accessories (eg, the headlights, heated rear window and heater blower) as possible, and check that the alternator maintains the regulated voltage at around 13 to 14 volts.
8 If the regulated voltage is not as stated, this may be due to worn brushes, weak brush springs, a faulty voltage regulator, a faulty diode, a severed phase winding or worn or damaged slip-rings. The brushes and slip-rings may be checked (see Section 6), but if the fault persists, the alternator should be renewed or taken to an auto-electrician.

3.3 Battery retaining clamp bolt (arrowed)

3.4 Unclip and remove the plastic insulation box

3.5 Battery tray and retaining bolts (arrowed)

5.4 Remove the air intake hose (arrowed)

5.5 Move the fuel filter to one side

5.8 Disconnecting the alternator wiring plug connector

5.9 Pull the plastic cover off and undo the retaining nut

5 Alternator – removal and refitting

Removal

1 Disconnect the battery negative lead and position it away from the terminal, refer to 'Disconnecting the battery' in Reference chapter.
2 Pull the engine trim cover upward to release it from the top of the engine.
3 Remove the radiator cooling fans from the rear of the radiator as described in Chapter 3, Section 5.
4 Slacken the retaining clips and remove the air intake hose from the throttle housing **(see illustration)**. To give more access to the alternator, also undo the retaining bolts and lower the plastic air ducting away from the rear of the alternator.
5 Undo the retaining bolts, and then move the fuel filter to one side **(see illustration)**. The fuel pipes do not need to be disconnected from the filter.
6 Remove the auxiliary drivebelt as described in Chapter 1, Section 27. Mark the drivebelt

for direction to ensure it is refitted in the same position.
7 Remove the air conditioning compressor from below the alternator, as described in Chapter 3, Section 11. The air-conditioning pipes do not need to be disconnected from the compressor, move the compressor to one side and secure it in place under the vehicle with cable-tie or similar.
8 Release the retaining clip and disconnect the wiring connector from the alternator **(see illustration)**.
9 Remove the protective plastic cap, unscrew and remove the nut (washer), then disconnect the battery positive cable from the alternator terminal. Where applicable, unscrew the nut and remove the cable guide **(see illustration)**.
10 Unscrew and remove the lower, then upper bolts, then lift the alternator away from its bracket **(see illustrations)**.

Refitting

11 Refitting is a reversal of removal. Refer to Chapter 1, Section 27, for details of refitting and tensioning the auxiliary drivebelt. Tighten the alternator mounting bolts to the specified torque. Before fitting the alternator, it may be necessary to tap the sliding sleeve in the alternator housing back a couple of millimeters **(see illustration)**, so that it can be refitted to the mounting bracket eassier.

6 Alternator brush holder/ regulator module – renewal

Removal

1 Remove the alternator, as described in Section 5.
2 Place the alternator on a clean work surface, with the pulley facing down.

Bosch

3 Undo the screw and the two retaining nuts,

5.10 Alternator mounting bolts (arrowed)

5.11 Tap the spacer (arrowed) down slightly to aid refitting

6.3 On the Bosch type, remove the outer cover...

6.4a...undo the screws (arrowed)...

6.4b...and remove the brush holder/ regulator

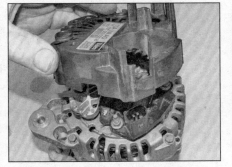

6.5 On the Valeo type, remove the outer plastic cover...

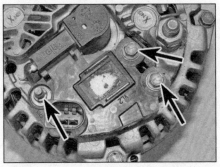

6.6a...undo the two bolts and single nut (arrowed)...

6.6b...and remove the voltage regulator

and lift away the outer plastic cover **(see illustration)**.
4 Unscrew the three securing screws, and remove the voltage regulator **(see illustrations)**.

Valeo

5 Prise off the spring clips, and remove the outer plastic cover **(see illustration)**.
6 Undo the two screws and single nut, and remove the voltage regulator **(see illustrations)**.
7 Slide off the brush cover by depressing the lugs on each side.

Inspection

8 Measure the free length of the brush contacts **(see illustration)**. Check the measurement with the Specifications; renew the module if the brushes are worn below the minimum limit.

6.8 Measure the brush length

9 Clean and inspect the surfaces of the slip-rings **(see illustration)**, at the end of the alternator shaft. If they are excessively worn, or damaged, the alternator must be renewed.

Refitting

Bosch

10 Refit the voltage regulator using a reversal of the removal procedure, tightening the screws securely. On completion, refer to Section 5 and refit the alternator.

Valeo

11 Depress the carbon brushes into the housing, then refit the voltage regulator and tighten the screws and nut securely. Slide on the brush cover until it is heard to engage. On completion, refer to Section 5 and refit the alternator.

6.9 Clean and inspect the surfaces of the slip-rings

7 Starting system – testing

Note: *Refer to Section 1 of this Chapter before starting work.*
1 If the starter motor fails to operate when the ignition key is turned to the appropriate position, the following possible causes may be to blame:
a) *The battery is faulty.*
b) *The electrical connections between the switch, solenoid, battery and starter motor are somewhere failing to pass the necessary current from the battery through the starter to earth.*
c) *The solenoid is faulty.*
d) *The starter motor is mechanically or electrically defective.*
2 To check the battery, switch on the headlights. If they dim after a few seconds, this indicates that the battery is discharged – recharge (see Section 2) or renew the battery. If the headlights glow brightly, operate the ignition switch and observe the lights. If they dim, then this indicates that current is reaching the starter motor, therefore the fault must lie in the starter motor. If the lights continue to glow brightly (and no clicking sound can be heard from the starter motor solenoid), this indicates that there is a fault in the circuit or solenoid – see following paragraphs. If the starter motor turns slowly when operated, but the battery is in good condition, then this indicates that either the starter motor is faulty, or there is

considerable resistance somewhere in the circuit.

3 If a fault in the circuit is suspected, disconnect the battery leads (including the earth connection to the body), the starter/solenoid wiring and the engine/transmission earth strap. Refer to *'Disconnecting the battery'* in Reference chapter. Thoroughly clean the connections, and reconnect the leads and wiring, then use a voltmeter or test light to check that full battery voltage is available at the battery positive lead connection to the solenoid, and that the earth is sound.

4 If the battery and all connections are in good condition, check the circuit by disconnecting the wire from the solenoid blade terminal. Connect a voltmeter or test light between the wire end and a good earth (such as the battery negative terminal), and check that the wire is live when the ignition switch is turned to the start position. If it is, then the circuit is sound – if not the circuit wiring can be checked as described in Chapter 12.

5 The solenoid contacts can be checked by connecting a voltmeter or test light between the battery positive feed connection on the starter side of the solenoid, and earth. When the ignition switch is turned to the start position, there should be a reading or lighted bulb, as applicable. If there is no reading or lighted bulb, the solenoid is faulty and should be renewed.

6 If the circuit and solenoid are proved sound,

the fault must lie in the starter motor. It may be possible to have the starter motor overhauled by a specialist, but check on the availability and cost of spares before proceeding, as it may prove more economical to obtain a new or exchange motor.

8 Starter motor –
   removal and refitting

Removal

1 Disconnect the battery negative lead. Refer to *'Disconnecting the battery'* in Reference chapter.

2 Apply the handbrake, then jack up the front of the vehicle and support it on axle stands (see *'Jacking and vehicle support'* in Reference chapter). Remove the engine undertray.

3 Pull the engine trim cover upward to release it from the top of the engine.

4 Remove the air cleaner air cleaner as described in Chapter 4A, Section 2 or Chapter 4B Section 2.

5 Release the securing clip and disconnect the wiring connector from the solenoid **(see illustration)**.

6 Unclip the plastic cover from the wiring connector and unscrew the nut to disconnect the battery positive lead from the starter motor **(see illustrations)**.

8.5 Disconnecting the starter wiring plug connector

7 Where applicable, unscrew the nut from the upper starter bolt and disconnect the earth cable **(see illustration)**.

8 Unscrew the nut from the lower starter mounting bolt, and then remove the wiring loom support bracket **(see illustration)**.

9 Unscrew the mounting bolts noting their fitted position, then guide the starter motor out of the bellhousing aperture and out of the engine compartment **(see illustrations)**.

Note: *On vehicle with DSG transmissions, the starter motor upper bolt is also one of the transmission securing bolts.*

Refitting

10 Refit the starter motor by following the removal procedure in reverse. Tighten the mounting bolts to the specified torque.

8.6a Remove the plastic cap, undo the nut...

8.6b ...and disconnect the wiring from the starter motor

8.7 Disconnect the earth cable – where fitted

8.8 Removing the wiring loom support bracket

8.9a Starter motor mounting bolts (arrowed)

8.9b The upper bolt also secures the transmission – DSG transmissions

9 Starter motor – testing and overhaul

1 If the starter motor is thought to be defective, it should be removed from the vehicle and taken to an auto-electrician for assessment. In the majority of cases, new starter motor brushes can be fitted at a reasonable cost. However, check the cost of repairs first as it may prove more economical to purchase a new or exchange motor.

10 Preheating system – general Information

1 To assist cold starting, diesel engine models are fitted with a preheating system, which consists of four glow plugs, a glow plug control unit, a facia-mounted warning light and the associated electrical wiring. The glow plug control unit on some models, is incorporated in the ECU, other models have a control unit/relay located under the fusebox in the engine compartment (see Section 12).
2 The glow plugs are miniature electric heating elements, encapsulated in a metal case with a probe at one end and electrical connection at the other. Each inlet tract has a glow plug threaded into it, which is positioned directly in line with the incoming spray of fuel. When the glow plug is energised, the fuel passing over it is heated, allowing its optimum combustion temperature to be achieved more readily in the combustion chamber.
3 The duration of the preheating period is governed by the ECU, which monitors the temperature of the engine through the coolant temperature sensor and alters the preheating time to suit the conditions. Preheating only takes place at coolant temperature below 9°C.
4 A facia-mounted warning light informs the driver that preheating is taking place. The light extinguishes when sufficient preheating has taken place to allow the engine to be started, but power will still be supplied to the glow plugs for a further period until the engine is started. If no attempt is made to start the engine, the power supply to the glow plugs is switched off to prevent battery drain and glow plug burn-out. If the warning light flashes, or comes on during normal driving, this indicates a fault with the diesel engine management system, which should be investigated by an Audi dealer as soon as possible.
5 After the engine has been started, the glow plugs continue to operate for a further period of time. This helps to improve fuel combustion whilst the engine is warming-up, resulting in quieter, smoother running and reduced exhaust emissions.

11 Glow plugs – testing, removal and refitting

⚠ *Warning: A correctly functioning glow plug will become red-hot in a very short time. This should be in mind when removing the glow plugs, if they have recently been in use. If a glow plug is dropped, it may be damaged internally, which could result in ceramic fragments entering the engine causing extensive damage. Do not fit a glow plug that has been dropped.*

Testing

1 If the system malfunctions, testing is ultimately by substitution of known good units, but some preliminary checks may be made as described in the following paragraphs.
2 Before testing the system, use a multi-meter to check that the battery voltage is at least 11.5. Switch off the ignition.
3 Pull the engine upper trim cover upwards to remove it from the top of the engine.
4 Disconnect the wiring plug from the coolant temperature sender at the left-hand end of the engine (left as seen from the driver's seat) – refer to Chapter 3. Disconnecting the sender in this way simulates a cold engine, which is a requirement for the glow plug system to activate.
5 Disconnect the wiring connector from the most convenient glow plug, and connect a suitable multimeter between the wiring connector and a good earth.
6 Have an assistant switch on the ignition for approximately 20 seconds.

7 Battery voltage should be displayed – note that the voltage will drop to zero when the preheating period ends.
8 If no supply voltage can be detected at the glow plug, then either the glow plug relay (where applicable) or the supply wiring must be faulty. Also check that the glow plug fuse or fusible link has not blown – if it has, this may indicate a serious wiring fault; consult an Audi dealer for advice.
9 To locate a faulty glow plug, first disconnect the battery negative cable and position it away from the terminal. Refer to *'Disconnecting the battery'* in Reference chapter.
10 Disconnect the wiring plug from the glow plug terminal. Measure the electrical resistance between the glow plug terminal and the engine earth **(see illustration)**. At the time of writing, this information is not available – as a guide, a resistance of more than a few ohms indicates that the plug is defective.
11 If a suitable ammeter is available, connect it between the glow plug and its wiring connector, and measure the steady-state current consumption (ignore the initial current surge, which will be about 50% higher). As a guide, high current consumption (or no current draw at all) indicates a faulty glow plug.
12 As a final check, remove the glow plugs and inspect them visually, as described in the next sub-Section. A badly burned or charred stem may be an indication of a faulty fuel injector.

Removal

Note: *Refer to the Warning at the start of this Section before proceeding.*
13 Pull the plastic cover on the top of the engine upwards from its mountings.
14 Where fitted, remove the noise insulation from above the injectors.
15 To make access easier, disconnect the wiring plugs from the injectors, exhaust gas pressure sensor, and fuel rail pressure sensor **(see illustration)**.
16 Undo the retaining bolts and detach the coolant pipe from the inlet manifold. Move the pipe to the front of the manifold.
17 Release the retaining clip and disconnect the fuel return hose from the fuel rail **(see illustration)**. Be prepared for fuel spillage.
18 Release the retaining clips and disconnect

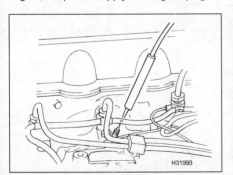

11.10 Testing the glow plugs using a multimeter

11.15 Disconnect the wiring plugs from the injectors

11.17 Disconnect the return hose from the fuel rail

11.19a Using long nose pliers...

11.19b...pull the connectors from the top of the glow plugs

the fuel return pipe connectors from the top of the fuel rail. Plug the openings to prevent contamination. Move the entire fuel return pipe assembly to the one side.

19 Pull the connectors from the top of the glow plugs and move the wiring loom to one side. Be sure to only pull on the underside of the ridge at the top of the connectors **(see illustrations)**.

20 Clean the area around the glow plugs; use a vacuum cleaner if possible. Spray brake cleaner (or similar) around the glow plug opening, letting it penetrate briefly, and then blow out with compressed air.

12.1 Glow plug control unit location (arrowed)

12.3 Slide the control unit out and disconnect the wiring connector

Caution: Always wear protective goggles to protect your eyes, when using compressed air.

21 Using a universal joint, extension and a deep 10 mm socket, unscrew and remove the glow plug(s) from the cylinder head. Note that the plug must be kept 'straight' when being removed, as it can be easily damaged.

Refitting

22 Refitting is a reversal of removal, but tighten the glow plugs to the specified torque.

12 Glow plug control unit – removal and refitting

Note: *The glow plug control unit may be incorporated inside the engine management ECU. Follow the procedure below for models with separate glow plug control unit.*

Removal

1 The glow plug control unit (where applicable) is located under the fuse box in the engine compartment **(see illustration)**.

2 To gain access to the control unit, remove the battery and battery tray, as described in Section 3.

3 Release the retaining clip and slide the control unit mounting bracket from the underside of the fusebox housing **(see illustration)**.

4 Disconnect the wiring connector and remove the control unit

Refitting

5 Refitting is a reversal of removal.

Chapter 6
Clutch

Contents

Degrees of difficulty

Easy, suitable for novice with little experience 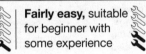	**Fairly easy,** suitable for beginner with some experience	**Fairly difficult,** suitable for competent DIY mechanic	**Difficult,** suitable for experienced DIY mechanic	**Very difficult,** suitable for expert DIY or professional

Specifications

General

Type:
Luk clutch .... Single dry friction disc, diaphragm spring with spring-loaded hub, self-adjusting pressure plate (SAC)
Sachs clutch .... Single dry friction disc, diaphragm spring with spring-loaded hub
Clutch operation .... Hydraulic with master and slave cylinders
Transmissions:
1.6 litre engines .... 5-speed, type 0A4
1.9 litre engines .... 5-speed, type 0AF
2.0 litre engines .... 6-speed, type 02Q

Torque wrench settings	Nm	lbf ft
Clutch pedal mounting bracket nuts*	25	18
Clutch pedal pivot nut*	25	18
Clutch pressure plate-to-flywheel bolts*:		
M7 bolt	20	15
M6 bolt	13	10
Clutch release bearing guide sleeve bolts:		
0AF transmissions*:		
Stage 1	5	4
Stage 2	Angle-tighten a further 90º	
0A4 transmissions	20	15
Clutch release bearing/slave cylinder bolts (02Q transmissions)	12	9
Clutch slave cylinder bolts	20	15

*Do not re-use fasteners

2.3a Clutch slave cylinder bleed screw (arrowed) – 0AF and 0A4 transmissions

2.3b Clutch bleed screw (arrowed) – 02Q transmissions

1 General Information

1 The clutch is of single dry plate type, incorporating a diaphragm spring pressure plate, and is hydraulically operated.

2 The pressure plate is bolted to the rear face of the flywheel, and the friction disc is located between the pressure plate and the flywheel friction surface. The friction disc hub is splined to the transmission input shaft and is free to slide along the splines. Friction lining material is riveted to each side of the disc, and the disc hub incorporates cushioning springs to absorb transmission shocks and ensure a smooth take-up of drive.

3 On all transmissions except 02Q, when the clutch pedal is depressed, the slave cylinder pushrod moves the release lever forwards. On 02Q transmissions, the slave cylinder is fitted concentrically around the transmission input shaft within the bellhousing. The release bearing is forced onto the pressure plate diaphragm spring fingers. As the centre of the diaphragm spring is pushed in, the outer part of the spring moves out and releases the pressure plate from the friction disc. Drive then ceases to be transmitted to the transmission.

4 When the clutch pedal is released, the diaphragm spring forces the pressure plate into contact with the linings on the friction disc, and at the same time pushes the disc slightly forward along the input shaft splines into engagement with the flywheel. The friction disc is now firmly sandwiched between the pressure plate and flywheel. This causes drive to be taken up.

5 As the linings wear on the friction disc, the pressure plate rest position moves closer to the flywheel resulting in the 'rest' position of the diaphragm spring fingers being raised. The hydraulic system requires no adjustment since the quantity of hydraulic fluid in the circuit automatically compensates for wear every time the clutch pedal is operated.

2 Hydraulic system – bleeding

Warning: Hydraulic fluid is poisonous, thoroughly wash off spills from bare skin without delay. Seek immediate medical advice if any fluid is swallowed or gets into the eyes. Certain types of hydraulic fluid are inflammable and may ignite when brought into contact with hot components. Hydraulic fluid is also an effective paint stripper. If spillage occurs onto painted bodywork or fittings, it should be washed off immediately, using copious quantities of cold water. It is also hygroscopic (i.e. it can absorb moisture from the air) which then renders it useless. Old fluid may have suffered contamination, and should never be re-used.

Note: *Suitable pressure-bleeding equipment will be required for this operation.*

1 If any part of the hydraulic system is dismantled, or if air has accidentally entered the system, the system will need to be bled. The presence of air is characterised by the pedal having a spongy feel and it results in difficulty in changing gear.

2 The design of the clutch hydraulic system does not allow bleeding to be carried out using the conventional method of pumping the clutch pedal. In order to remove all air present in the system, it is necessary to use pressure bleeding equipment. This is available from auto accessory shops at relatively low cost.

3 The pressure bleeding equipment should be connected to the brake/clutch hydraulic fluid reservoir in accordance with the manufacturer's instructions. The system is bled through the bleed screw of the clutch slave cylinder (all transmissions except 02Q), which is located on the top of the transmission housing. On 02Q transmissions, the slave cylinder bleed screw is located at the front of the transmission, above the starter motor **(see illustrations)**.

4 Bleed the system until the fluid being ejected is free from air bubbles. Close the bleed screw, then disconnect and remove the bleeding equipment.

5 Check the operation of the clutch to see that it is satisfactory. If air still remains in the system, repeat the bleeding operation.

6 Discard any fluid that is bled from the system, even if it looks clean. Hydraulic fluid absorbs water and its re-use can cause internal corrosion of the master and slave cylinders, leading to excessive wear and failure of the seals.

3 Clutch pedal – removal and refitting

Removal

1 Move the driver's seat fully to the rear, and adjust the steering column to its highest position.

2 Remove the steering column trim panels and lower facia trim panel, with reference to Chapter 11 Section 27

3 Unbolt the crash bar from in front of the clutch pedal **(see illustration)**.

4 Undo the pivot nut and bolt from the top of the clutch pedal, withdraw the bolt and

3.3 Undo the crash bar retaining bolt (arrowed)

3.4a Undo the retaining nut (arrowed)...

3.4b...remove the pivot bolt...

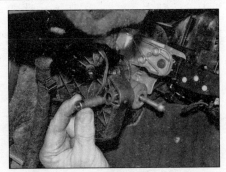

3.4c...and withdraw the pivot bush

3.5 Remove the spring assembly

3.6a Release the securing clips...

3.6b...and disengage the pushrod securing clip (arrowed)

remove the pivot bush from the top of the pedal **(see illustrations)**.

5 With the pedal lowered, the clutch pedal spring assembly can be removed from inside the clutch pedal mounting bracket **(see illustration)**.

6 Using a couple of screwdrivers, squeeze together the tabs at each side of the pushrod securing clip, and separate the pedal from the pushrod **(see illustrations)**.

Refitting

7 Refitting is a reversal of removal, bearing in mind the following points:

a) *Press the pushrod securing clip firmly into the pedal until it is heard to engage.*

b) *Make sure the clutch spring assembly is located correctly in the clutch pedal mounting bracket.*

c) *On completion, check the brake/clutch fluid level, and top-up if necessary.*

4 Master cylinder – removal, overhaul and refitting

Note: *Refer to the warning at the beginning of Section regarding the hazards of working with hydraulic fluid.*

Removal

1 The clutch master cylinder is located inside the car on the clutch pedal mounting bracket. Hydraulic fluid for the unit is supplied from the brake master cylinder reservoir **(see illustration)**.

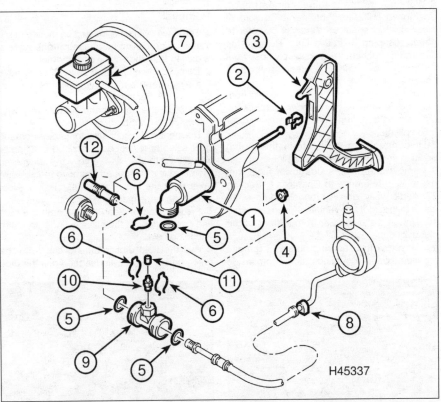

4.1 Clutch hydraulic system layout – 02Q transmission

1 Clutch master cylinder
2 Push rod retaining clip
3 Clutch pedal
4 Self-locking nut

5 O-ring seals
6 Securing clips
7 Brake fluid reservoir
8 Fluid pipe retaining clip

9 T-piece connector
10 Clutch bleed valve
11 Dust cap
12 Slave cylinder connection

H45337

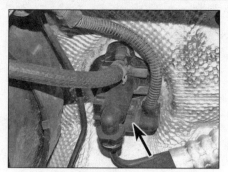

4.3 Clutch master cylinder viewed from the engine compartment

2 Before proceeding, place cloth rags on the carpet inside the car to prevent damage from spilt hydraulic fluid.

3 Working in the engine compartment, clamp the hydraulic fluid hose leading from the brake fluid reservoir to the clutch master cylinder using a brake hose clamp **(see illustration)**.

4 Similarly, clamp the rubber section of the hydraulic hose leading from the master cylinder to the slave cylinder using a brake hose clamp, to prevent loss of hydraulic fluid.

5 Remove the engine top cover. Additionally, on LHD models, remove the battery and battery tray with reference to Chapter 5, Section 3.

6 Working in the engine compartment, position a suitable container, or a wad of clean cloth, beneath the master cylinder to catch escaping hydraulic fluid. Release the clip and disconnect the fluid supply hose from the master cylinder – be prepared for fluid spillage.

7 Pull the fluid outlet hose retaining clip from the union on the master cylinder, then pull the pipe from the union. Again, be prepared for fluid spillage.

8 Disconnect the wiring from the clutch position sender on the master cylinder.

9 Remove the driver's side lower facia trim panel, with reference to Chapter 11, Section 27. Additionally, on LHD models, remove the cable guide, footwell vent and fuse/relay box.

10 Unbolt the crash bar from in front of the clutch pedal.

11 Unscrew the securing nuts and remove the clutch pedal mounting bracket from inside

the car. Note that the upper nut is difficult to locate.

12 Squeeze together the tabs of the pushrod retaining clip, and separate the pedal from the pushrod. Hold the pedal away from the bracket using a 40 mm wood block or similar.

13 Release the clip and withdraw the master cylinder from the mounting bracket by twisting it anti-clockwise.

Overhaul

14 No spare parts are available from Audi for the master cylinder. If the master cylinder is faulty or worn, the complete assembly must be renewed.

Refitting

15 Refitting is a reversal of removal, but bleed the clutch hydraulic system as described in Section 2.

---

5 Slave cylinder – removal, overhaul and refitting

Note: *Refer to the warning at the beginning of Section regarding the hazards of working with hydraulic fluid.*

0A4 and 0AF (5-speed) transmissions

Removal

1 The slave cylinder is located on the top of the transmission casing **(see illustration)**. Access is gained from the engine compartment.

2 Remove the engine top cover, then remove the air cleaner assembly, with reference to Chapter 4A, Section 2.

3 Remove the battery and battery tray with reference to Chapter 5, Section 3.

4 Disconnect the gear selector cables from the gear selector levers, as described in Chapter 7A. Extract the clip and remove the relay lever, then unscrew the nut and remove the selector lever from the top of the transmission. Also, unbolt the cable mounting bracket.

5 Place a wad of clean rag beneath the fluid line connection on the slave cylinder to catch escaping fluid.

6 Pull the fluid pipe retaining clip from the union on the slave cylinder, then pull the pipe

from the union. Release the fluid line from the bracket **(see illustration)**, and position it clear of the slave cylinder. Be prepared for fluid spillage.

7 Unscrew the two bolts securing the slave cylinder to the transmission casing, and withdraw the slave cylinder from the transmission **(see illustration)**.

Overhaul

8 No spare parts are available from Audi for the slave cylinder. If the slave cylinder is faulty or worn, the complete assembly must be renewed.

Refitting

9 Refitting is a reversal of removal, bearing in mind the following points:
a) *Tighten all fixings to the specified torque where given.*
b) *On completion, bleed the clutch hydraulic system as described in Section 2.*

02Q (6-speed) transmission

10 The slave cylinder is part of the release bearing unit and is located inside the transmission bellhousing. For the removal and refitting procedure of the clutch release bearing/slave cylinder, see Section 7 in this Chapter.

---

6 Clutch friction disc and pressure plate – removal, inspection and refitting

⚠️ *Warning: Dust created by clutch wear and deposited on the clutch components may contain asbestos, which is a health hazard. DO NOT blow it out with compressed air or inhale any of it. DO NOT use petrol or petroleum-based solvents to clean off the dust. Brake system cleaner or methylated spirit should be used to flush the dust into a suitable receptacle. After the clutch components are wiped clean with clean rags, dispose of the contaminated rags and cleaner in a sealed container.*

Note: *New clutch pressure plate securing bolts will be required on refitting. It is recommended that a friction disc centralising tool be used when refitting the clutch.*

5.1 Clutch slave cylinder (arrowed) – 0A4 and 0AF transmissions

5.6 Clutch hydraulic fluid line and support bracket

5.7 Removing the clutch slave cylinder

6.3a Undo the pressure plate retaining bolts (arrowed)

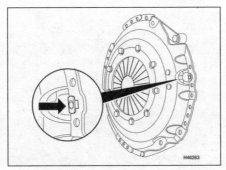

6.3b Ensure the stop pin is free to move

6.11 The friction disc should be marked 'Getriebeseite' or 'Gearbox side'

Removal

1 Access to the clutch is obtained by removing the transmission as described in, Section.

2 Mark the clutch pressure plate and flywheel in relation to each other.

3 Hold the flywheel stationary, and then unscrew the clutch pressure plate bolts ¼ of a turn at a time **(see illustration)**. With the bolts unscrewed two or three turns, check that the pressure plate is not binding on the dowel pins. If necessary, use a screwdriver to release the pressure plate. On models with the Sachs clutch, as the bolts are removed the stop pin must slacken. If it doesn't, press the pin towards the flywheel **(see illustration)**.

4 Remove all the bolts, then lift the clutch pressure plate and friction disc from the flywheel.

Inspection

Note: *Due to the amount of work necessary to remove and refit clutch components, it is usually considered good practice to renew the clutch friction disc, pressure plate assembly and release bearing as a matched set, even if only one of these is actually worn enough to require renewal. It is also worth considering the renewal of the clutch components on*

a preventative basis if the engine and/or transmission have been removed for some other reason.

5 Clean the pressure plate friction surface, clutch friction disc and flywheel. Do not inhale the dust, as it may contain asbestos which is dangerous to health.

6 Examine the fingers of the diaphragm spring for wear or scoring. If the depth of wear exceeds half the thickness of the fingers, a new pressure plate assembly must be fitted.

7 Examine the pressure plate for scoring, cracking, distortion and discoloration. Light scoring is acceptable, but if excessive, a new pressure plate assembly must be fitted. If the distortion of the friction surface exceeds 1.0 mm, renew it.

8 Examine the friction disc linings for wear and cracking, and for contamination with oil or grease. The linings are worn excessively if they are worn down to, or near, the rivets. Check the disc hub and splines for wear by temporarily fitting it on the transmission input shaft. Renew the friction disc as necessary.

9 Examine the flywheel friction surface for scoring, cracking and discoloration (caused by overheating). If excessive, it may be possible to have the flywheel machined by an engineering works, otherwise it should be renewed.

10 Ensure that all parts are clean, and free of oil or grease, before reassembling. Apply just a small amount of lithium-based grease (VW No. G000100) to the splines of the friction disc hub. Do not use copper-based grease. Note that new pressure plates and clutch covers

may be coated with protective grease. It is only permissible to clean the grease away from the friction disc lining contact area. Removal of the grease from other areas will shorten the service life of the clutch.

Refitting

11 Commence reassembly by locating the friction disc on the flywheel, with the raised side of the hub facing outwards (normally marked 'Getriebeseite' or 'Gearbox side'). If possible, the centralising tool (see paragraph 20) should be used to hold the disc on the flywheel at this stage **(see illustration)**.

Models with self-adjusting clutch (SAC)

12 On models with a Self-adjusting clutch (SAC), where a new friction disc is fitted, but the pressure plate is to be re-used, it is necessary to reset the pressure plate adjusting ring prior to assembly as follows.

13 Insert three 8 mm bolts into the pressure plate mounting holes at intervals of 120°. The bolts should be inserted from the flywheel side, and retained by nuts **(see illustration)**.

14 Place the pressure plate face down on the bed of an hydraulic press so that only the heads of the bolts make contact with the press bed, then place a circular spacer over the ends of the diaphragm springs fingers.

15 Use 2 screwdrivers to attempt to rotate the adjuster ring anti-clockwise. Apply just enough pressure with the hydraulic press until it's just possible to move the adjuster ring **(see illustration)**.

6.13 Insert three 8 mm bolts from the flywheel side, and secure with nuts

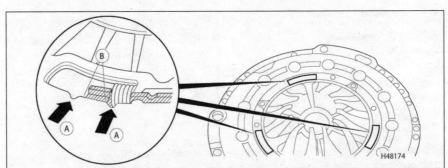

6.15 The edges of the adjuster ring (B) must be between the notches (A)

16 Once the adjuster ring edges are between the notches, relieve the pressure. The ring is now reset.

Note: *New pressure plates are supplied in this reset position.*

All models

17 Locate the clutch pressure plate on the disc, and fit it onto the location dowels **(see illustration)**. If refitting the original pressure plate, make sure that the previously-made marks are aligned.

18 Insert the bolts finger-tight to hold the pressure plate in position.

19 The friction disc must now be centralised, to ensure correct alignment of the transmission input shaft with the disc centre. To do this, a proprietary tool may be used, or alternatively, use a wooden mandrel made to fit inside the friction disc and the hole in the centre of the crankshaft. Insert the tool through the friction disc into the crankshaft, and make sure that it is central.

20 Tighten the pressure plate bolts progressively and in diagonal sequence, until the specified torque setting is achieved, then remove the centralising tool **(see illustration)**.

21 Check the release bearing in the transmission bellhousing for smooth operation, and if necessary renew it with reference to Section 7.

22 Refit the transmission with reference to, Section.

6.17 Fit the pressure plate over the locating dowel pins (arrowed)

6.20 With the pressure plate screws tightened, remove the centralising tool

7 Release bearing and lever – removal, inspection and refitting

0A4 and 0AF (5-speed) transmissions

Removal

1 Remove the transmission as described in, Section.

2 Using a screwdriver, prise the release lever from the ball-stud on the transmission housing. If this proves difficult, push the retaining spring from the release lever first **(see illustration)**. Where applicable, remove

the plastic pad from the stud.

3 Slide the release bearing, together with the lever, from the guide sleeve, and withdraw it over the transmission input shaft **(see illustration)**.

4 Separate the release bearing from the lever **(see illustrations)**.

5 If the guide sleeve is worn excessively, unbolt it and remove the O-ring seal **(see illustration)**.

Inspection

6 Spin the release bearing by hand, and check it for smooth running. Any tendency to seize or run rough will necessitate renewal of the bearing. If the bearing is to be re-used, wipe it clean with a dry cloth; the bearing

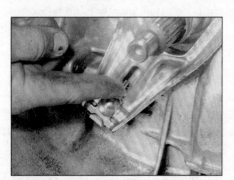

7.2 Push the spring clip to release the arm from the ball-stud

7.3 Release lever and bearing removed from the transmission

7.4a Use a screwdriver to depress the retaining tags...

7.4b...then remove the release bearing from the arm

7.4c Release arm and separated bearing removed from the transmission

7.5 Guide sleeve on the transmission (arrowed)

7.8 Fitting the guide sleeve with assembled release bearing and lever

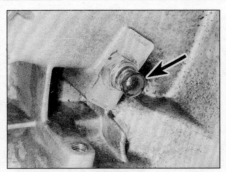

7.9 Lubricate the ball-stud with a little grease

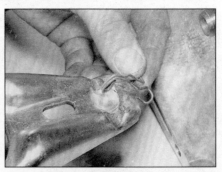

7.11a Locate the spring over the end of the release lever...

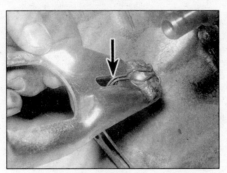

7.11b...and press the spring into the hole...

7.11c...then press the release lever onto the ball-stud until the spring clip holds it in position

should not be washed in a liquid solvent, as this will remove the internal grease.

7 Clean the release lever, ball-stud and guide sleeve.

Refitting

8 If the guide sleeve was removed, locate a new O-ring seal over the input shaft, then fit the guide sleeve and tighten the bolts to the specified torque. If preferred, the guide sleeve may be assembled to the release bearing and lever, and the components fitted over the input shaft as one unit **(see illustration)**.

9 Lubricate the ball-stud in the transmission bellhousing with molybdenum sulphide-based grease **(see illustration)**. Also smear a little grease on the release-bearing surface, which contacts the diaphragm spring fingers in the clutch cover.

10 Push the release bearing into position on the release lever.

11 Fit the retaining spring onto the release lever, then press the release lever onto the ball-stud until the retaining spring holds it in position **(see illustrations)**.

12 Refit the transmission as described in, Section.

02Q (6-speed) transmission

Note: *The release bearing and slave cylinder are one unit which cannot be renewed separately*

Removal

13 Remove the transmission as described in, Section.

14 Undo the three retaining bolts from the release bearing/slave cylinder unit.

15 Withdraw the release bearing/slave cylinder unit from the transmission housing, and remove it over the input shaft **(see illustration)**.

16 Remove the O-ring and input shaft seal and discard; new ones will be required for refitting.

Inspection

17 Spin the release bearing by hand, and check it for smooth running. Any tendency to

seize or run rough will necessitate renewal of the bearing. If the bearing is to be re-used, wipe it clean with a dry cloth; the bearing should not be washed in a liquid solvent, as this will remove the internal grease.

18 Check for fluid leaks around the slave cylinder and hose connection.

Refitting

19 Lubricate slave cylinder hose connection

O-ring with some clean brake fluid for refitting.

20 Press the new input shaft seal into position, making sure it sits squarely in the housing.

21 Refit the release bearing/slave cylinder and tighten the retaining bolts to the specified torque setting.

22 Refit the transmission as described in, Section.

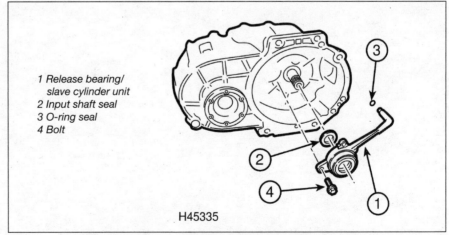

1 Release bearing/
  slave cylinder unit
2 Input shaft seal
3 O-ring seal
4 Bolt

H45335

7.15 Release bearing/slave cylinder unit – 02Q transmission

Chapter 7 Part A
Manual transmission

Contents

Degrees of difficulty

Easy, suitable for novice with little experience	**Fairly easy,** suitable for beginner with some experience	**Fairly difficult,** suitable for competent DIY mechanic	**Difficult,** suitable for experienced DIY mechanic	**Very difficult,** suitable for expert DIY or professional

Specifications

General

Type .... Transversely mounted, front-wheel-drive layout with integral transaxle differential/final drive, 5 or 6 forward speeds and 1 reverse

Transmissions:
  5-speed:
    1.6 litre engines............................... Type 0A4
    1.9 litre engines............................... Type 0AF
  6-speed:
    2.0 litre engines............................... Type 02Q

Torque wrench settings	**Nm**	**lbf ft**
Gearchange bracket....................................	20	15
Reversing light switch	20	15
Selector lever	23	17
Transmission to engine:		
M12 bolts	80	59
M10 bolt	40	30

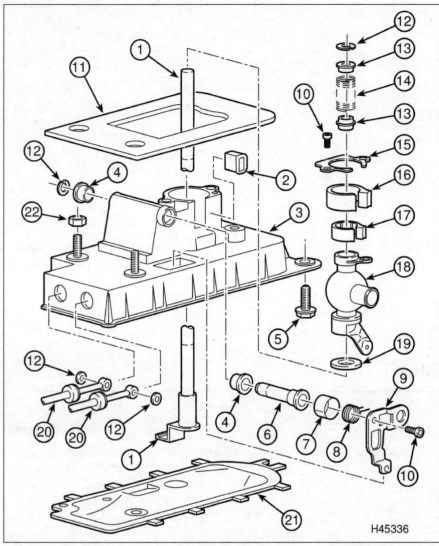

1.3a Gear linkage layout

1 Selector lever	9 Selector lever gate	17 Bearing
2 Damper	10 Retaining screw	18 Selector lever ball/
3 Selector lever housing	11 Housing seal	guide
4 Bush – bearing	12 Securing clip	19 Damping washer
5 Bolt	13 Bush	20 Gear selector cable
6 Fulcrum pin	14 Spring	21 Baseplate
7 Bush – guide	15 Cover plate	22 Securing nut
8 Spring	16 Damper collar	

1.3b Transmission end of the gearchange cables

2.3 Push the collar down and lock in position

1 General Information

1 The manual transmission is bolted directly to the left-hand end of the engine. This layout has the advantage of providing the shortest possible drive path to the front wheels, as well as locating the transmission in the airflow through engine bay, optimising cooling. The unit is cased in aluminium alloy.

2 Drive from the crankshaft is transmitted through the clutch to the gearbox input shaft, which is splined to accept the clutch friction disc.

3 All forward gears are fitted with synchromesh. The floor-mounted gear lever is connected to the gearbox by shift cables **(see illustrations)**. Levers on the transmission actuate internal selector forks, which are connected to the synchromesh sleeves. The sleeves are locked to the gearbox shafts but can slide axially by means of splined hubs, and they press baulk rings into contact with the respective gear/pinion. The coned surfaces between the baulk rings and the pinion/gear act as a friction clutch, which progressively matches the speed of the synchromesh sleeve (and hence the gearbox shaft) with that of the gear/pinion. This allows gearchanges to be carried out smoothly.

4 Drive is transmitted to the differential crownwheel, which rotates the differential case and planetary gears, thus driving the sun gears and driveshafts. The rotation of the differential planetary gears on their shaft allows the inner roadwheel to rotate at a slower speed than the outer roadwheel during cornering.

2 Gearchange linkage – adjustment

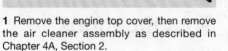

1 Remove the engine top cover, then remove the air cleaner assembly as described in Chapter 4A, Section 2.

2 Remove the battery and battery tray as described in Chapter 5, Section 3

3 With the gearchange set in the neutral position, push the two locking collars (one on each cable) forwards to compress the springs, turn them clockwise (looking from the driver's seat) to lock into position **(see illustration)**.

4 Press down on the selector shaft on the top of the transmission, and push the locking pin into the transmission while turning it clockwise until it engages, and the selector shaft cannot move **(see illustration)**.

5 Working inside the vehicle, unclip the gear lever gaiter from the centre console. Still in the neutral position, move the gear lever as far to the left as possible and insert the locking

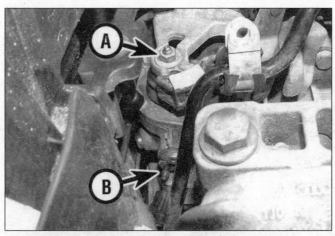

2.4 Press down on (A), then push in locking pin (B)

2.5 Locking the gear lever in position using a drill bit

pin (or drill bit) through the hole in the base of the gear lever and into the hole in the housing **(see illustration)**.

6 Working back in the engine bay, turn the two locking collars on the cables anti-clockwise so that the springs will release them back into position and lock the cables **(see illustration)**.

7 With the cable adjustment set, the locking pin can now be turned anti-clockwise to its original position pointing upwards.

8 Inside the vehicle, remove the locking pin from the gear lever, and then check the operation of the selector mechanism. When the gear lever is at rest in neutral, it should be central, ready to select 3rd or 4th. The gear lever gaiter can now be refitted to the centre console.

9 Refit the battery tray, battery and air cleaner assembly.

3 Manual transmission – removal and refitting

Removal

1 Select a solid, level surface to park the vehicle upon. Give yourself enough space to move around it easily. Apply the handbrake and chock the rear wheels.

3.5b Gearchange bracket

2 Raise the front of the vehicle and support it securely on axle stands (see *'Jacking and vehicle support'* in Reference chapter). Where fitted, remove the engine/transmission undertray. Position a suitable container beneath the transmission, then unscrew the drain plug and drain the transmission oil.

3 Remove the engine top cover, then remove the air cleaner assembly as described in Chapter 4A, Section 2.

4 Remove the battery and battery tray with reference to Chapter 5, Section 3.

5 Disconnect the gear selector cables from the gear selector levers. Extract the clip and remove the relay lever, then unscrew the nut and remove the selector lever from the top of

2.6 Release the two locking collars (arrowed) back into position

3.6 Remove the support bracket (arrowed) – 0A4 transmissions

the transmission. Also, unbolt and remove the gearchange bracket **(see illustrations)**.

6 Undo the retaining bolts, and then remove the support bracket **(see illustration)**, from the top of the transmission (04A transmissions).

7 On models with the clutch slave cylinder on the top of the transmission (all except 02Q transmissions), undo the retaining bolts and place the cylinder to one side, with reference to Chapter 6, Section 5.

8 On 02Q transmissions, seal the slave cylinder flexible hose using a hose clamp, then prise out the clip and pull the fluid pipe from the bleeder connection on the slave cylinder supply pipe **(see illustration)**. Refer to Chapter 6, Section 5.

3.5a Disconnecting the gearchange cables

3.8 Prise up the clip a little and pull the hose from the connection – 02Q transmissions

3.13a Reversing light switch (arrowed)...

3.13b...neutral switch (arrowed) – depending on transmission

9 Unbolt the earth cable from the engine/ transmission or subframe.

10 Unscrew and remove the upper bolts securing the transmission to the engine.

11 With reference to Chapter 5, Section 8, remove the starter motor.

12 Remove the lower left-hand wheel arch liner.

13 Disconnect the wiring from the reversing light switch **(see illustrations)**, and where fitted, the neutral position switch on vehicles with a start/stop system.

14 Where fitted unbolt the metal shield from around the right-hand driveshaft.

15 Slacken the clamp securing the exhaust intermediate pipe to the rear section and undo the front mounting bracket bolts **(see illustrations)**. This will allow the engine to be moved forwards and backwards during the transmission removal and alignment procedures. Consequently, there is no need to completely separate the exhaust pipe sections.

16 With reference to Chapter 8, Section 2, unscrew and remove the bolts securing the driveshafts to the transmission output flanges. Tie the right-hand driveshaft to one side, and then tie the left-hand driveshaft to the suspension strut, so that the shaft is as high as possible **(see illustration)**. Alternatively, completely remove the driveshaft as described in Chapter 8, Section 2.

17 Remove the radiator cooling fans, as described in Chapter 3, Section 5. Cover the rear of the radiator to prevent it from getting damaged as the engine/transmission is moved forward.

18 Unbolt the engine rear mounting torque arm from the bottom of the transmission **(see illustration)**.

19 Where applicable, unbolt the flywheel cover plate from the transmission bellhousing.

20 Using a suitable hoist, support the weight of the engine.

21 Unscrew the bolts securing the transmission mounting to the body. Also, unbolt the mounting bracket from the transmission.

22 Lower the engine/transmission assembly slightly and, using a trolley jack, support the transmission. Position the jack so that it can be withdrawn from the left-hand side of the car. As the engine/transmission is moved, make sure any wiring or hoses are not damaged.

23 Unscrew and remove the remaining lower transmission-to-engine mounting bolts, including the bolt located on the left-hand rear of the engine **(see illustration)**.

24 Carefully pull the transmission directly

3.15a Slacken the exhaust clamp...

3.15b ...and undo the exhaust mounting bracket bolts (arrowed)

3.16 Support the driveshafts

3.18 Unbolt the engine rear mounting torque arm

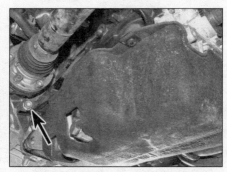

3.23 Undo the rear mounting bolt (arrowed)

3.25a Hold the drive flange in position...

3.25b ...whilst removing the centre bolt...

3.25c ...then slide the drive flange from the transmission

away from the engine, taking care not to allow its weight to rest on the clutch friction disc hub. A second person is helpful to pull the engine as far forwards as possible.

25 On models with driveshafts that have a bolted flange, it will be necessary to manouvre the right-hand driveshaft flange, from around the flywheel on removal. If required, hold the drive flange in position and undo the centre securing bolt, then the drive flange can be removed **(see illustrations)**, make removal of the transmission easier.

Warning: Support the transmission to ensure that it remains steady on the jack head. Keep the transmission level until the input shaft is fully withdrawn from the clutch friction disc.

26 When the transmission is clear of the locating dowels and clutch components, lower the transmission to the ground and withdraw from under the car.

Refitting

27 Refitting the transmission is essentially a reversal of the removal procedure, but note the following points:

a) *Apply a smear of high melting-point grease to the clutch friction disc hub splines; take care to avoid contaminating the friction surfaces.*

b) *In order to align the transmission with the flywheel, gently pull the engine forward as the transmission is manoeuvred into place.*

c) *Tighten the transmission-to-engine bolts to the specified torque.*

d) *Refer to the relevant part of Chapter 2 and tighten the engine mounting bolts to the correct torque.*

e) *Refer to Chapter 8, and tighten the driveshaft bolts to the specified torque.*

f) *On completion, refer to Section 2 and check the gearchange linkage/cable adjustment.*

g) *Refill the transmission with the correct grade and quantity of oil. Refer to 'Lubricants and fluids' and to Chapter 1, as appropriate.*

4 Manual transmission overhaul – general information

1 The overhaul of a manual transmission is a complex (and often expensive) task for the DIY home mechanic to undertake, which requires access to specialist equipment. It involves dismantling and reassembly of many small components, measuring clearances precisely and if necessary, adjusting them by selecting shims and spacers. Internal transmission components are also often difficult to obtain and in many instances, extremely expensive. Because of this, if the transmission develops a fault or becomes noisy, the best course of action is to have the unit overhauled by a specialist repairer or to obtain an exchange reconditioned unit.

2 Nevertheless, it is not impossible for the more experienced mechanic to overhaul the transmission if the special tools are available and the job is carried out in a deliberate step-by-step manner, to ensure nothing is overlooked.

3 The tools necessary for an overhaul include internal and external circlip pliers, bearing pullers, a slide hammer, a set of pin punches, a dial test indicator and possibly a hydraulic press. In addition, a large, sturdy workbench and a vice will be required.

4 During dismantling of the transmission,

5.7 Reversing light switch on the transmission

make careful notes of how each component is fitted to make reassembly easier and accurate.

5 Before dismantling the transmission, it will help if you have some idea of where the problem lies. Certain problems can be closely related to specific areas in the transmission, which can make component examination and renewal easier. Refer to *Fault finding* in Reference chapter for more information.

5 Reversing light switch – testing, removal and refitting

Testing

1 Ensure that the ignition switch is turned to the OFF position.

2 Unplug the wiring harness from the reversing light switch at the connector. The switch is located on the top or front of the transmission casing.

3 Connect the probes of a continuity tester, or multimeter set to the resistance measurement function, across the terminals of the reversing light switch.

4 The switch contacts are normally open, so with any gear other than reverse selected; the tester/meter should indicate an open circuit or infinite resistance. When reverse gear is selected, the switch contacts should close, causing the tester/meter to indicate continuity or zero resistance.

5 If the switch does not operate correctly, it should be renewed.

Removal

6 Ensure that the ignition switch is turned to the OFF position.

7 Unplug the wiring harness from the reversing light switch at the connector **(see illustration)**.

8 Unscrew the switch from the transmission casing, and recover the sealing ring.

Refitting

9 Refitting is a reversal of removal.

Chapter 7 Part B
DSG semi-automatic transmission

Contents

Degrees of difficulty

Easy, suitable for novice with little experience	**Fairly easy,** suitable for beginner with some experience	**Fairly difficult,** suitable for competent DIY mechanic	**Difficult,** suitable for experienced DIY mechanic	**Very difficult,** suitable for expert DIY or professional

Specifications

General

Description	DSG (Direct Shift Gearbox) semi-automatic 6- or 7-forward speeds and 1 reverse. Integral transaxle differential/final drive transmission with multi-plate clutch or dual-clutch.
Transmission type number:	
1.6 litre engine:	
7-speed.	0AM
2.0 litre engine:	
6-speed.	02E
Transmission capacity:	
Type 0AM – 7-speed transmission	1.7 litres
Type 02E – 6-speed transmission	5.2 litres
Clutch type:	
6-speed (02E) transmission	Multi-plate (wet clutch), 4 outer plates, 4 inner plates and 1 drive plate.
7-speed (0AM) transmission.	Two (Dual-clutch) dry friction discs, with spring loaded centre hub.
Clutch operation.	Mechatronic unit (mechanical and electronic).

Torque wrench settings

	Nm	lbf ft
Driveshaft flange bolt	30	22
Transmission-to-engine bolts:		
M10 bolts	40	30
M12 bolts	80	59
Transmission mounting bracket-to-casing bolts*:		
Stage 1	40	30
Stage 2	Angle-tighten a further 90°	
Transmission mounting-to-bracket bolts*:		
Stage 1	60	44
Stage 2	Angle-tighten a further 90°	
Drain plug (0AM transmission)	30	22
Drain/level plug (02E transmission)	45	31
Oil level tube (02E transmission)	3	2

*Do not re-use fasteners

1 General Information

1 The Audi semi-automatic Direct Shift Gearbox (DSG) has six- or seven-forward speeds (and one reverse). In contrast to traditional automatic transmissions where a fluid flywheel (torque converter) transmits the power from the engine to the gearbox, the DSG has a multi-plate clutch in the six-speed transmission and a twin-clutch in the seven-speed transmission. The main advantages of the DSG transmission, is near-instant gear changes, with seamless, highly efficient drive, resulting in less exhaust emissions and improved fuel consumption.

2 On the front of the transmission housing is a mechatronic unit, this is made up of mechanical and electronic components. The electronic part of the unit uses information from sensors (e.g. engine speed, road speed, driving mode etc.) to determine the optimum gear and shift commands, the mechanical part then selects the correct gear required. On 6-speed (02E) transmissions, the unit is inside the transmission housing with a pressed steel cover, bolted to the front of the transmission casing. On 7-speed (0AM) transmissions, it is a sealed unit, and is bolted to the front of the transmission **(see illustration)**

3 On 6-speed (02E) transmissions, the clutch is of a multi-plate type, which runs in the transmission oil. It is made up of four outer plates, which have teeth on the outer edge to locate in the clutch housing, four inner plates with teeth on the inner edge that locate on the clutch inner hub, and one drive plate that is located on the outside of the clutch plate assembly. The four larger outer plates (C1) operate 1st, 3rd, 5th and reverse gears, and then the four smaller inner plates (C2) operate 2nd, 4th and 6th gears. With this system whilst 'C1' has a gear engaged, then 'C2' will

pre-select the next gear ready to change gear. The assembly requires special care, as all the components in the assembly are balanced together, during manufacture. The clutch assembly is sealed inside the bell housing by a clutch end cover, which also forms a seal, to prevent loss of oil. If the end cover is removed for any reason, it will need to be renewed.

4 On 7-speed (0AM) transmissions, the clutch is of a dual-clutch dry plate type, which has two friction discs and a spring loaded centre hub **(see illustration)**. The clutch friction disc nearest the engine is operated by the larger outer release lever (K1) and operates 1st, 3rd, 5th & 7th gears. The clutch friction disc nearest the transmission is operated by the smaller inner release lever (K2) and operates 2nd, 4th, 6th & Reverse gears. With this system whilst 'K1' has a gear engaged, then 'K2' will pre-select the next gear ready to change gear. The clutch assembly can only be purchased as a complete unit, and if renewed, new release levers will also need to be renewed.

5 A fault diagnosis system is integrated into the control unit, but analysis can only be undertaken with specialised equipment. It is important that any transmission fault be identified and rectified at the earliest possible opportunity. An Audi dealer or suitable equipped specialist can 'interrogate' the ECU fault memory for stored fault codes, enabling him to pinpoint the fault quickly. Once the fault has been corrected and any fault codes have been cleared, normal transmission operation is restored.

6 Because of the need for special test equipment, the complexity of some of the parts, and the need for scrupulous cleanliness when these transmissions, the work which the owner can do is limited. Most major repairs and overhaul operations should be left to an Audi dealer or specialist, who will be equipped with the necessary equipment for fault diagnosis and repair. The information in this Chapter is therefore limited to a description of the removal

and refitting of the transmission as a complete unit. The removal, refitting and adjustment of the selector cable is also described.

7 In the event of a transmission problem occurring, consult an Audi dealer or transmission specialist before removing the transmission from the vehicle, since the majority of fault diagnosis is best carried out with the transmission still in the vehicle.

2 Transmission – removal and refitting

Removal

1 The transmission is removed downwards from the engine compartment. First, select a solid, level surface to park the vehicle upon. Give yourself enough space to move around it easily. Select P, apply the handbrake, and chock the rear wheels.

2 Loosen the front wheel bolts, and the driveshaft hub bolts. Do not undo the hub bolt more than 90° at this point; otherwise the wheel bearing could be damaged, whilst the weight is still on the wheels.

3 Raise the front of the vehicle and rest it securely on axle stands (see 'Jacking and vehicle support' in Reference chapter). Remove the front wheels. Allow a suitable working clearance underneath for the eventual withdrawal of the transmission. Undo the fasteners and remove the engine/transmission undershield.

4 Drain the transmission oil, as described in Section 6.

⚠️ *Warning: The mechatronic unit on the front of the 7-speed (0AM) transmission is a sealed unit. If any oil is lost from this unit, it will need to be renewed, as it cannot be refilled. Remove the breather cap (see illustration) from the top of the unit and cover with a blanking plug, to prevent any loss of oil.*

1.2 Mechatronic unit – 0AM transmissions

1.4 Clutch assembly – 0AM transmissions

2.4 Breather cap on the mechatronic unit – 0AM transmissions

2.10 Clamp the transmission cooler hoses (arrowed) – 02E transmissions

2.11a Wiring plug and earth cable (arrowed) – 02E transmissions

2.11b Wiring plug connections...

2.11c...on the front of the transmission – 0AM transmissions

2.12 Undo the earth cable securing nut

5 Remove the air cleaner assembly as described in Chapter 4A, Section 2.

6 Undo the retaining clips and remove the turbocharger intake hose and charge air pipe to the intercooler.

7 Remove the front subframe, as described in Chapter 10, Section 23.

8 Remove the starter motor as described in Chapter 5, Section 8.

9 Disconnect the selector cable from the selector shaft lever on the top of the transmission, as described in Section 4. Position the cable to one side, noting that the retaining clip/circlip must be renewed.

10 On 6-speed (02E) transmissions there is a fluid cooler located on top of the transmission. Clamp off the cooler hoses with brake hose type clamps. Release the retaining clips and detach the hoses from the cooler **(see illustration)**. Take great care not to spill any

coolant into the transmission unit, as this will cause damage.

11 Disconnect the wiring plug connectors from the front of the transmission **(see illustrations)**. If required, undo the nuts and detach the wiring loom retainer from the gearbox cover.

a) *6-speed 02E transmissions – rotate the collar anti-clockwise to disconnect.*

b) *7-speed 0AM transmissions – slide the locking lever upwards to disconnect.*

12 Disconnect the earth cable from either the transmission or the vehicle body **(see illustration)**.

13 Remove the upper engine-to-transmission mounting bolts.

14 Remove the radiator cooling fan assembly as described in Chapter 3, Section 5.

15 Undo the bolts and slide rearwards the exhaust pipe connecting piece between the

front and rear sections of the exhaust system. Also undo the retaining bolts and remove the exhaust front mounting bracket **(see illustration)**.

16 Disconnect the wiring plug from the engine oil level/temperature sensor on the sump **(see illustration)** ; this is to prevent it getting damaged when the engine moves forward.

17 With reference to Chapter 8, Section 2, unscrew and remove the bolts securing the driveshafts to the transmission output flanges. Tie the right-hand driveshaft to one side, and then tie the left-hand driveshaft to the suspension strut, so that the shaft is as high as possible **(see illustration)**. Alternatively, completely remove the driveshaft as described in Chapter 8, Section 2.

18 Support the engine with a hoist or support bar located on the front wing inner channels.

2.15 Undo the exhaust mounting retaining bolts

2.16 Disconnect the oil level/temperature sensor wiring connector

2.17 Fasten the driveshaft to one side

2.24a Hold the drive flange in position...

2.24b ...whilst removing the centre bolt...

2.24c ...then slide the drive flange from the transmission

Depending on the engine, temporarily remove components as necessary to attach the hoist.
19 Position a trolley jack underneath the transmission, and raise it to just take the weight of the unit.
20 Undo and remove the bolts securing the left-hand gearbox mounting. By controlling both the engine hoist/support bar and the trolley jack, lower the transmission slightly. To make removal easier undo the retaining bolts and remove the mounting bracket from the top of the transmission casing.
21 On 6-speed (02E) transmissions, undo the retaining bolt and remove the small cover plate located above the right-hand driveshaft flange.
22 Lower the engine/transmission until there is sufficient clearance between the upper edge of the transmission and the left-hand chassis member.
23 Unscrew and remove the lower bolts securing the transmission to the engine, noting the bolt locations, as they are of different sizes and lengths.
24 On models with driveshafts that have a bolted flange, hold the flange in position and undo the flange securing bolt, then the flange can be removed (see illustrations).
25 Check that all the fixings and attachments are clear of the transmission. Enlist the aid of an assistant to help in guiding and supporting the transmission during its removal.
26 The transmission is located on engine alignment dowels, and if stuck on them, it may be necessary to carefully tap and prise the transmission free of the dowels to allow separation. Once the transmission is disconnected from the location dowels, swivel the unit out and lower it out of the vehicle.

 Warning: Support the transmission to ensure that it remains steady on the jack head.

27 When the transmission is clear of the locating dowels and clutch components, lower the transmission to the ground and withdraw from under the car. Make sure that the transmission does not fall and lose any transmission oil. Also make sure that the clutch assembly comes away with the transmission, and stays inside the bell-housing.

Refitting

28 Refitting the transmission is essentially a reversal of the removal procedure, but note the following points:
a) On 7-speed (0AM) transmissions, renew the needle bearing in the end of the crankshaft (see Chapter 2D, Section 13).
b) When reconnecting the transmission to the engine, ensure that the location dowels are in position, and that the transmission is correctly aligned with them before pushing it fully into engagement with the engine.
c) Tighten all retaining bolts to their specified torque wrench settings.
d) Be sure to guide the selector cable into the support bracket as the transmission is refitted – renew the retaining clips.
e) Adjust the selector cable, as described in Section 4.
f) Refer to Chapter 8, Section 2, and then tighten the driveshaft bolts to the specified torque.
g) On completion, check the coolant level.
h) If a new transmission unit has been fitted, it may be necessary to have the transmission ECM 'matched' to the engine management ECM electronically, to ensure correct operation – seek the advice of your Audi dealer or suitably equipped specialist.
i) Refill the transmission with the correct grade and quantity of oil, as described in Section 6.

3 Transmission overhaul – general information

1 In the event of a fault occurring, it will be necessary to establish whether the fault is electrical, mechanical or hydraulic in nature, before repair work can be contemplated. Diagnosis requires detailed knowledge of the transmission's operation and construction, as well as access to specialised test equipment, and so is deemed to be beyond the scope of this manual. It is therefore essential that problems with the automatic transmission be referred to an Audi dealer or specialist for assessment.
2 Although it is possible to remove the clutch assembly from out of the bell housing, it is not possible to fit a new assembly without the use of special tools. When a new clutch is purchased, there are a number of shims and retaining clips of different thickness in the kit, therefore without the correct tools, it is not possible to correctly install the assembly back in place.
3 Note that a faulty transmission should not be removed before the vehicle has been assessed by a dealer or specialist, as fault diagnosis is best carried out with the transmission still in the vehicle.

4 Selector lever housing and cable – removal, refitting and adjustment

Note: The selector lever housing and cable should not be separated, therefore remove the housing and cable as a complete unit.

Removal

1 Move the selector lever to the P position, and remove the battery and battery tray as described in Chapter 5, Section 3.
2 Remove the air cleaner housing as described in Chapter 4A, Section 2.
3 Working inside the vehicle, remove the centre console and gear selector knob, as described in Chapter 11, Section 26.
4 Disconnect the wiring connector from the front of the gear selector housing (see illustration).

4.4 Disconnect the wiring connector

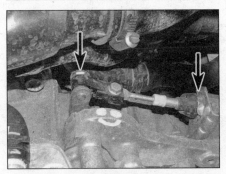

4.6 Selector cable clip and outer cable circlip (arrowed)

4.7 Prise the inner cable from the ball joint

4.8 Release the outer cable securing clip

6-speed (02E) transmission

5 Working inside the engine compartment, slacken the adjustment screw on the cable end fitting at the transmission end **(see illustration 4.16b)**.

6 Prise out the clips securing the cable to the lever on the transmission, and the outer cable to the support bracket **(see illustration)**. Withdraw the cable from the support bracket and discard the clips – new ones must be fitted.

7-speed (0AM) transmission

7 Working inside the engine compartment, use a pair of long-nose pliers to release the cable end fitting from the ball head on the selector lever **(see illustration)**.

8 Prise out the clip securing the outer cable and withdraw the cable from the support bracket on the transmission **(see illustration)**. Discard the retaining clip as a new one must be fitted.

All transmissions

9 Raise the front of the vehicle and support it securely on axle stands (see *'Jacking and vehicle support'* in Reference chapter).

10 Remove the centre tunnel front heat shield from the underside of the vehicle to gain access to the base of the selector lever housing and cable. It may be necessary to separate the exhaust downpipe from the intermediate pipe with reference to Chapter 4A.

11 Working inside the vehicle, undo the retaining nuts **(see illustration)**, then remove the bracket and lower the gear selector housing downwards. Withdraw it complete with selector cable out from under the vehicle. It may be useful having the aid of an assistant at this point, to be under the vehicle when lowering the selector housing.

Refitting

12 Refitting is the reversal of the removal procedure, noting the following points:

a) *Do not grease the cable end fittings. This is stated by Audi.*

b) *Ensure that the cable is correctly routed and secured, as noted on removal.*

c) *Take care not to bend or kink the cable.*

d) *Carry out the cable adjustment procedure described below before reconnecting the cable at the transmission end.*

e) *When refitting the outer cable to the support bracket, use new clips.*

Adjustment

13 Inside the car, move the selector lever to the 'P' position.

14 If not already done, disconnect the cable from the selector lever on the transmission.

15 Move the selector lever inside the vehicle from 'P' to 'S' and back, repeatedly, to check that everything moves easily. Audi recommend that you do not grease the cable.

16 Reconnect the cable to the lever at the transmission, and then slacken the cable adjusting bolt **(see illustrations)**.

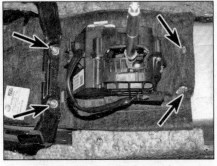

4.11 Gearchange housing mounting nuts (arrowed)

17 Check that both the selector lever inside the car and the lever on the transmission are in their 'P' positions. Gently rock the levers backwards and forwards to make sure the cable is settled. Do not move either lever out of the 'P' position.

18 The transmission lever is in the 'P' position when:

a) *6-speed 02E transmissions – it's pushed all the way back towards the bulkhead*

b) *7-speed 0AM transmissions – it's pushed back towards the selector cable mounting bracket (see illustration)*

19 When in position, tighten the cable adjusting bolt.

20 Verify the operation of the selector lever by shifting through all gear positions and checking that every gear can be selected smoothly and without delay.

4.16a Secure the outer cable in the bracket...

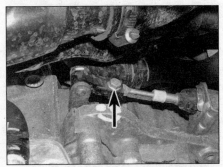

4.16b ...and slacken the cable adjustment bolt (arrowed)

4.18 Push the lever in the direction of the arrow

5 Emergency release of selector lever

1 If the vehicles battery is disconnected or discharged, it is possible to release the selector lever from its locked position. First, ensure the handbrake is fully applied.

2 Carefully prise up the selector lever gaiter surround trim from the console and move it to one side **(see illustration)**.

3 Press the yellow plastic wedge downwards **(see illustration)**. It should now be possible to move the selector lever to the desired position.

6 Transmission oil renewal

7-speed dual clutch 0AM transmission

Note: *This transmission is fitted to 1.6-litre engines. The transmission is filled for life, and does not have an oil level checking procedure. If there has been an oil leak from the transmission, after the leak has been rectified, renew the transmission oil as described in the following paragraphs.*

1 Take the vehicle on a short journey to warm the transmission oil, and then park the car on a level surface. For improved access to the drain plug, apply the handbrake, then jack up the front of the vehicle and support it on axle stands (see *'Jacking and vehicle support'* in Reference chapter), but note that the rear of the vehicle should also be raised to ensure all oil is drained.

2 Undo the retaining screws and remove the engine undertray. Wipe clean the area around the transmission drain plug, which is situated on the lower rear of the transmission **(see illustration)**.

3 Place a container under the transmission casing, then unscrew the drain plug from the base of the differential housing, and allow the oil to drain.

4 Remove the battery and battery tray as described in Chapter 5 Section 3.

5.2 Prise up the selector lever gaiter surround trim

5 Remove the air cleaner assembly as described in Chapter 4A Section 2.

6 When the oil has finished draining, clean the surrounding area, refit the drain plug and tighten it to the specified torque.

7 Unclip the breather cap from the selector cover plate on the top of the transmission casing **(see illustration)**.

8 Using a length of hose, and funnel, add 1.7 litres of new oil to the transmission. Only use VAG recommended oil, for 7-speed dual clutch 0AM transmission.

9 Refit the breather cap, making sure that it is secure. Renew if damaged.

10 The remainder of refitting is a reversal of removal.

6-speed dual clutch 02E transmission

Note: *An accurate fluid level check can only be made with the transmission fluid at a temperature of between 35°C and 45°C, and if it is not possible to ascertain this temperature, it is strongly recommended that the check be made by an Audi dealer who will have the instrumentation to check the temperature and to check the transmission electronics for fault codes. Over-filling or under-filling adversely affects the function of the transmission.*

11 Take the vehicle on a short journey to warm the transmission oil. And then park the vehicle on level ground and engage P with the selector lever. Raise the front and rear of the vehicle and support it on axle stands (see *'Jacking and vehicle support'* in Reference chapter), ensuring the vehicle is kept level.

5.3 Press down the yellow plastic peg

Undo the retaining screws and remove the engine undertray to gain access to the base of the transmission unit.

12 Start the engine and run it at idle speed until the transmission fluid temperature reaches 35°C.

13 Unscrew the fluid level plug from the bottom of the transmission sump **(see illustration)**.

14 If fluid continually drips from the level tube as the fluid temperature increases, the fluid level is correct and does not need to be topped-up. Note that there will be some fluid already present in the level tube, and it will be necessary to observe when this amount has drained before making the level check. Make sure that the check is made before the fluid temperature reaches 45°C.

15 If no fluid drips from the level tube, even when the fluid temperature has reached 45°C, it will be necessary to add fluid. Audi technicians use an adapter which screws into the bottom of the transmission sump, however, a tube inserted up through the drain plug (into the space above the fluid); will allow fluid to be added. Ideally, the fluid should be allowed to cool before adding the fluid.

16 Check the condition of the seal on the level plug and renew it if necessary by cutting off the old seal and fitting a new one. Refit the plug and tighten to the specified torque.

17 Refit the engine undertray, tighten the retaining screws securely, and lower the vehicle to the ground.

18 Frequent need for topping-up indicates that there is a leak, which should be corrected as soon as possible.

6.2 Transmission oil drain plug – 0AM transmissions

6.7 Breather cap on selector cover – 0AM transmissions

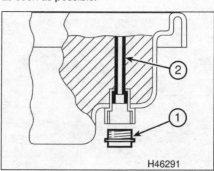

6.13 Transmission fluid level check – 02E transmissions

1 Level plug   2 Level tube

Chapter 8
Driveshafts

Contents

Degrees of difficulty

Easy, suitable for novice with little experience	**Fairly easy,** suitable for beginner with some experience	**Fairly difficult,** suitable for competent DIY mechanic	**Difficult,** suitable for experienced DIY mechanic	**Very difficult,** suitable for expert DIY or professional

Specifications

General

Driveshaft type . . . . Steel shafts with outer constant velocity joints and inner tripod or constant velocity joints (according to type). Some models have an intermediate shaft from the right-hand side of the transmission to the driveshaft

Type code differences:
  VL 90 or VL 100 . . . . CV joints each end, inner joint diameter 90 mm or 100 mm bolted to transmission drive flanges on each side

  VL 107 . . . . CV joints each end, inner joint diameter 107 mm bolted to drive flange on transmission (LH side) or flange on end of intermediate shaft (RH side)

  AAR 2600i . . . . CV outer joint, tripod inner joint located in housing splined to sun gear
  AAR 3300i . . . . CV outer joint, tripod inner joint housing bolted to transmission drive flange (LH side) or joint located in housing formed on end of intermediate shaft (RH side)

Lubrication

Overhaul and repair . . . . Use only special grease supplied in sachets with gaiter/overhaul kits; joints are otherwise pre-packed with grease and sealed

Joint grease type
  All joints except (inner triple roller joint) . . . . VAG G 000 603 grease
  Inner triple roller joint . . . . VAG G 000 605 grease
Joint grease quantity
  Outer joint . . . . 120 g
  Inner joint . . . . 140 g

Torque wrench settings

	Nm	lbf ft
Driveshaft-to-transmission flange bolts:		
Stage 1	10	7
Stage 2:		
M8	40	30
M10	70	52
Hub bolt*:		
Hexagon (6-sided bolt) and bi-hexagonal		
(12-sided bolt) without ribbing on the face:		
Stage 1	200	148
Stage 2	Angle-tighten a further 180°	
Bi-hexagonal (12-sided bolt) with ribbing on the face:		
Stage 1	70	52
Stage 2	Angle-tighten a further 90°	
Intermediate shaft bearing to bracket	20	15
Intermediate shaft bracket to block:		
Stage 1	5	4
Stage 2	35	26
Lower arm-to-balljoint nuts*	60	44
Wheel bolts	120	89

Do not re-use fasteners

1 General Information

1 Drive is transmitted from the differential to the front wheels by means of two steel driveshafts of either solid or hollow construction (depending on model). Both driveshafts are splined at their outer ends, to accept the wheel hubs, and are secured to the hub by a large bolt. The inner end of each driveshaft is either bolted to a transmission drive flange or splined directly into the differential sun gear. Some models are fitted with an intermediate driveshaft, with its own support bearing, between the transmission and right-hand driveshaft.

2 Ball-bearing type constant velocity (CV) joints are fitted to the outer ends of each driveshaft, to ensure the smooth and efficient transmission of drive at all the angles possible as the roadwheels move up-and-down with the suspension, and as they turn from side-to-side under steering.

3 The inner ends of each driveshaft (except for the AAR type driveshafts) are fitted with

ball and cage type constant velocity (CV) joint. The AAR driveshafts have a triple roller type (tripod) joint fitted to the inner end of the driveshaft.

4 Plastic gaiters are fitted over both CV joints with steel clips. The gaiters contain the grease, which lubricates the joints, and also protect the joints from the entry of dirt and debris.

2 Driveshafts – removal and refitting

Note: *A new hub bolt will be required on refitting. There are two different types of bolts fitted, one is ribbed (see illustration) under the face of the bolt head and one is smooth. The torque setting is different for each type of bolt (see Specifications), so it is important to make sure you check which is fitted.*

Removal

1 Remove the wheel trim/hub cap (as applicable) then apply the handbrake, and partially unscrew, by a maximum of 90°, the relevant hub bolt with the vehicle resting on

its wheels – note that the bolt is very tight, and a suitable extension bar will probably be required to aid unscrewing. Also unscrew the roadwheel securing bolts.

Caution: Do not loosen the bolt more than 90° with the vehicle standing on the ground, as the wheel bearings may be damaged.

2 Apply the handbrake, then jack up the front of the vehicle and support it on axle stands (see '*Jacking and vehicle support*' in Reference chapter). Remove the appropriate front roadwheel.

3 Remove the retaining screws and/or clips, and remove the undershields from beneath the engine/transmission unit to gain access to the driveshafts. Where necessary, also unbolt the heat shield from the transmission housing to improve access to the driveshaft inner joint **(see illustration)**.

4 Unscrew and remove the hub bolt **(see illustration)**.

Note: *Discard the bolt and obtain a new one of the same type.*

5 Unscrew the three nuts securing the front suspension lower arm balljoint to the lower arm. Discard the nuts as new ones must be used on refitting.

2.0 Flange of bolt (arrowed) is ribbed

2.3 Remove the heat shield

2.4 Driveshaft/hub bolt hexagon type (arrowed)

2.8 Driveshaft inner joint and flange bolts

2.15 Locate a new gasket on the inner joint

6 Lever the lower arm downwards to release it from the balljoint studs, then pull the hub carrier outwards, and at the same time withdraw the driveshaft outer constant velocity joint from the hub. If the joint splines are a tight fit in the hub, tap the joint out of the hub using a soft-faced mallet and drift. If this fails to free the driveshaft from the hub, the joint will have to be pressed out using a suitable tool bolted to the hub.

7 Proceed as follows according to type.

Caution: Support the driveshaft by suspending it with wire or string – do not allow it to hang under its own weight, or the joint may be damaged.

Inner joint with drive flange

8 Using a multi-splined tool, unscrew and remove the bolts securing the inner driveshaft joint to the transmission flange and, where applicable, recover the retaining plates from underneath the bolts **(see illustration)**.

Inner joint splined to differential sun gear

9 Position a container beneath the transmission to catch spilt oil, then pull out the driveshaft. The internal driveshaft circlip may be tight in the transmission side gear, in which case careful use of a lever against the transmission casing will be required. Lever against a block of wood to prevent damage to the casing, and take care not to damage the oil seal as the driveshaft is being removed.

Note: *Pull only on the inner joint housing, not the driveshaft itself, otherwise the gaiter may be damaged.*

Inner joint tripod located in housing on end of intermediate shaft

10 Mark the inner joint housing and driveshaft in relation to each other, then loosen the clip, ease off the rubber gaiter, and pull the tripod out of the housing.

All types

11 Manoeuvre the driveshaft out from

underneath the vehicle and (where fitted) recover the gasket from the end of the inner constant velocity joint.

Note: *Discard the gasket and obtain a new one.*

Caution: Do not allow the vehicle to rest on its wheels with one or both driveshaft(s) removed, as damage to the wheel bearings may result.

12 If moving the vehicle is unavoidable, temporarily insert the outer end of the driveshaft(s) in the hub(s), and tighten the driveshaft retaining bolt(s); in this case, the inner end(s) of the driveshaft(s) must be supported, for example by suspending with string from the vehicle underbody.

Refitting

13 Where applicable, check the condition of the circlip on the inner end of the driveshaft, and if necessary, renew it.

14 As applicable, clean the splines on each end of the driveshaft and in the hub and apply a little oil, and where applicable wipe clean the oil seal in the transmission casing. Check the oil seal and if necessary renew it as described in Chapter 7A or 7B. Smear a little oil on the lips of the oil seal before fitting the driveshaft.

Inner joint with drive flange

15 Ensure that the transmission flange and inner joint mating surfaces are clean and dry. Where necessary, fit a new gasket to the joint by peeling off its backing foil and sticking it in position **(see illustration)**.

16 Manoeuvre the driveshaft into position, and align the inner joint holes with those on the transmission flange. Refit the retaining bolts and where necessary, the plates. Tighten the retaining bolts to the specified torque.

Inner joint splined to differential sun gear

17 Locate the inner end of the driveshaft into the transmission – turn the driveshaft as necessary to engage the splines. Press in the

driveshaft until the internal circlip engages the groove. Check that the circlip is engaged by attempting to pull out the driveshaft with only moderate force.

Inner joint tripod located in housing on end of intermediate shaft

18 Fill the inner joint with the specified quantity of grease, and then locate the driveshaft tripod into the housing, aligning the previously-made marks. Ease the gaiter onto the housing, and refit the clip.

All types

19 With the lower arm levered downwards, engage the outer joint with the hub. Fit the new hub bolt and use it to draw the joint fully into position.

20 Align the balljoint studs with the holes in the lower arm, then release the arm and fit the three new nuts. Tighten the nuts to the specified torque.

21 Where applicable, fit new rear engine/transmission mounting-to-subframe bolts, and tighten the bolts to the specified torque.

22 Tighten the driveshaft bolt to the Stage 1 torque.

Note: *The bolt must be tightened with the wheel clear of the ground.*

23 Refit the roadwheel and lower the vehicle to the ground, then angle-tighten the driveshaft bolt through the Stage 2 angle.

24 Once the driveshaft bolt is correctly tightened, tighten the wheel bolts to the specified torque and refit the wheel trim/hub cap.

3 Driveshaft rubber gaiters – renewal

1 Remove the driveshaft from the car, as described in Section 2. Continue as described under the relevant sub-heading. Driveshafts with a tripod type inner joint

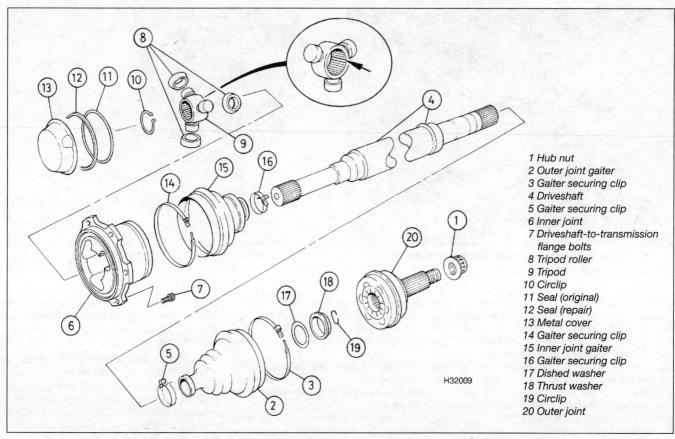

1 Hub nut
2 Outer joint gaiter
3 Gaiter securing clip
4 Driveshaft
5 Gaiter securing clip
6 Inner joint
7 Driveshaft-to-transmission flange bolts
8 Tripod roller
9 Tripod
10 Circlip
11 Seal (original)
12 Seal (repair)
13 Metal cover
14 Gaiter securing clip
15 Inner joint gaiter
16 Gaiter securing clip
17 Dished washer
18 Thrust washer
19 Circlip
20 Outer joint

H32009

3.1a Driveshaft components – models with press-fit metal cover on inner end of inner CV joint

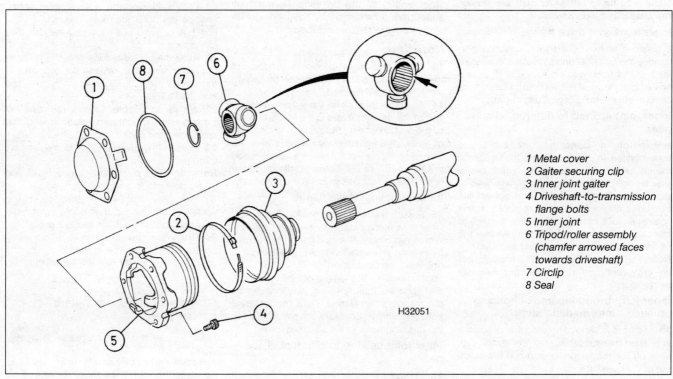

1 Metal cover
2 Gaiter securing clip
3 Inner joint gaiter
4 Driveshaft-to-transmission flange bolts
5 Inner joint
6 Tripod/roller assembly (chamfer arrowed faces towards driveshaft)
7 Circlip
8 Seal

H32051

3.1b Inner driveshaft joint components – models with cover on inner end of inner CV joint secured by tabs

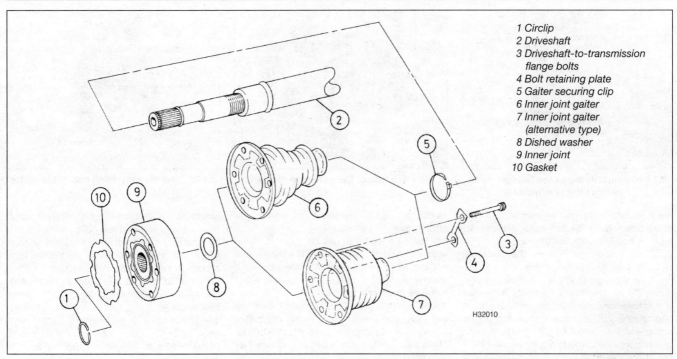

1 Circlip
2 Driveshaft
3 Driveshaft-to-transmission flange bolts
4 Bolt retaining plate
5 Gaiter securing clip
6 Inner joint gaiter
7 Inner joint gaiter (alternative type)
8 Dished washer
9 Inner joint
10 Gasket

H32010

3.1c Inner driveshaft components – certain manual transmission models

can be identified by the shape of the inner CV joint; the driveshaft retaining bolt holes are in extensions from the joint, giving it a six-pointed star-shaped exterior, in contrast to the smooth, circular shape of the ball-and-cage joint **(see illustrations)**.

Outer CV joint gaiter

2 Secure the driveshaft in a vice equipped with soft jaws, and release the two outer joint gaiter retaining clips **(see illustration)**. If necessary, the retaining clips can be cut to release them.
3 Slide the rubber gaiter down the shaft to expose the constant velocity joint, and scoop out excess grease **(see illustration)**.
4 Using a soft-faced mallet, tap the joint off the end of the driveshaft **(see illustration)**.
5 Remove the circlip from the driveshaft groove, and slide off the thrustwasher and dished washer, noting which way around it is fitted **(see illustration)**.

6 Slide the rubber gaiter off the driveshaft and discard it **(see illustration)**.
7 Thoroughly clean the constant velocity joint(s) using paraffin, or a suitable solvent, and dry thoroughly. Carry out a visual inspection as follows.

8 Move the inner splined driving member from side-to-side to expose each ball in turn at the top of its track. Examine the balls for cracks, flat spots or signs of surface pitting.
9 Inspect the ball tracks on the inner and outer members. If the tracks have widened,

3.2 Release the outer joint gaiter clips...

3.3...and slide the gaiter away from the joint

3.4 Use a mallet to drive the outer joint from the driveshaft

3.5 Removing the circlip, thrustwasher and dished washer

3.6 Removing the outer gaiter

3.11 Temporarily tape over the splines to protect the new gaiter

3.14a Pack half of the grease in the joint...

3.14b...and the remaining half in the gaiter

the balls will no longer be a tight fit. At the same time, check the ball cage windows for wear or cracking between the windows.

10 If on inspection any of the constant velocity joint components are found to be worn or damaged, it will be necessary to renew the complete joint assembly. If the joint is in satisfactory condition, obtain a new gaiter and retaining clips, a constant velocity joint circlip and the correct type of grease. Grease is often supplied with the joint repair kit – if not, use good-quality molybdenum disulphide grease.

11 Tape over the splines on the end of the driveshaft, to protect the new gaiter as it is slid into place (see illustration).

12 Slide the new gaiter onto the end of the driveshaft, then remove the protective tape from the driveshaft splines.

13 Slide on the dished washer, making sure

its convex side is innermost, followed by the thrustwasher.

14 Pack the joint with half the quantity of the specified type of grease. Work the grease well into the bearing tracks whilst twisting the joint, and fill the rubber gaiter with the remaining half (see illustrations).

15 Fit a new circlip to the driveshaft, then tap the joint onto the driveshaft until the circlip engages in its groove (see illustrations). Make sure that the joint is securely retained by the circlip.

16 Ease the gaiter over the joint, and ensure that the gaiter lips are correctly located on both the driveshaft and constant velocity joint. Lift the outer sealing lip of the gaiter to equalise air pressure within the gaiter (see illustration).

17 Fit the large metal retaining clip to the gaiter. Pull the clip as tight as possible, and

locate the hooks on the clip in their slots. Remove any slack in the gaiter retaining clip by carefully compressing the raised section of the clip. In the absence of the special tool, a pair of side-cutters may be used, taking care not to cut the clip (see illustrations). Secure the small retaining clip using the same procedure.

18 Check the constant velocity joint moves freely in all directions, then refit the driveshaft to the vehicle, as described in Section 2.

Tripod inner CV joint gaiter

Press-fit metal cover

19 This type of joint can be recognised from the press-fit metal cover fitted to the end of the CV joint outer member. The cover is round. On models where the inner CV joint gaiter has been renewed previously, a metal cover will not be fitted, in which case this type of joint can be recognised during dismantling by the fact that the tripod rollers are a loose fit on the tripod, and will slide off easily (if the rollers are secured to the tripod, proceed as described in paragraphs 45 to 61).

20 Release the two outer joint gaiter retaining clips. If necessary, the retaining clips can be cut to release them. Slide the rubber gaiter down the shaft, away from the joint outer member.

21 Carefully secure the joint outer member in a vice equipped with soft jaws.

22 Drive a screwdriver through the side of the metal cap over the end of the joint outer member, and use the screwdriver to lever the

3.15a Fit a new circlip...

3.15b...then refit the outer joint

3.16 Seat the gaiter on the outer joint and driveshaft, then lift its inner lip to equalise the air pressure

3.17a Fit the large metal retaining clip...

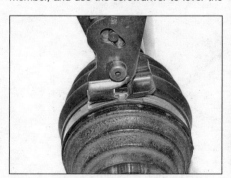

3.17b...and use a suitable tool to tighten it

3.32 Check the tripod rollers and outer member for signs of wear

3.34a Tape over the driveshaft splines to protect the new gaiter...

3.34b...then lever the gaiter carefully over the ridge on the driveshaft

cap off the outer member. If the cap cannot be levered off, drive a second screwdriver through the opposite side of the cap, and use the two screwdrivers to lever off the cap.

23 Scoop out excess grease from the joint, then remove the O-ring from the groove in the end of the joint outer member.

24 Using a suitable marker pen or a scriber, make alignment marks between the end of the driveshaft, the tripod roller assembly, and the outer member.

25 Support the driveshaft and the joint, and withdraw the outer member from the vice. As the assembly is removed from the vice, make sure that the rollers do not fall off the tripod.

26 Slowly slide the joint outer member down the driveshaft, away from the joint, making sure that the rollers stay on the tripod.

27 Mark the rollers and the arms of the tripod, so that the rollers can be refitted in their original positions, then lift off the rollers and place them to one side on a dry, clean surface.

28 Remove the circlip from the end of the driveshaft.

29 Press or drive the driveshaft from the tripod, taking great care not to damage the surfaces of the roller locating arms.

30 Slide the outer member and the rubber gaiter from the end of the driveshaft.

31 Thoroughly clean the joint components using paraffin, or a suitable solvent, and dry thoroughly. Carry out a visual inspection as follows.

32 Inspect the tripod rollers and the joint outer member for signs of wear, pitting or

scuffing on their mating surfaces. Check that the joint rollers rotate smoothly, with no traces of roughness **(see illustration)**.

33 If the rollers or outer member shown signs of wear or damage, it will be necessary to renew the complete driveshaft, since the joint is not available separately. If the joint is in satisfactory condition, obtain a repair kit, consisting of a new gaiter, retaining clips, circlip, and the correct type and quantity of grease.

34 Tape over the splines on the end of the driveshaft to protect the new gaiter as it is slid into place, and then slide the new gaiter and securing clips, and the joint outer member over the end of the driveshaft **(see illustrations)**. Remove the protective tape from the driveshaft splines.

35 Press or drive the tripod onto the end of the driveshaft until it contacts the stop, ensuring that the marks made on the end of the driveshaft and the tripod before dismantling are aligned. Note that the chamfered edge of the internal splines on the tripod should face towards the driveshaft.

36 Fit the new circlip to retain the tripod on the end of the driveshaft.

37 Refit the rollers to the tripod, ensuring that they are refitted in their original locations, as noted before removal.

38 Work half of the grease supplied with the repair kit into the inner end of the joint outer member, then slide the outer member over the tripod, ensuring that the marks made during dismantling are aligned, and clamp the outer member in the vice.

39 Work the rest of the grease supplied with the repair kit into the rear of the joint outer member **(see illustration)**.

40 Slide the rubber gaiter up the driveshaft onto the joint outer member, and secure with the large clip, as described in paragraph 17.

41 Lift the gaiter outer end to equalise the air pressure in the gaiter, then secure the outer gaiter securing clip in position using the same method used previously **(see illustration)**.

42 Check that the grease in the joint outer member is evenly distributed around the tripod rollers.

43 Wipe any excess grease from the inner face of the joint outer member, then fit the rectangular profile O-ring provided in the repair kit into the groove in the inner face of the joint outer member. The rectangular profile of the seal acts as a grease seal, and takes the place of the metal cover prised off during dismantling.

44 Check the driveshaft joint moves freely in all directions, then refit the driveshaft to the vehicle, as described in Section 2. To prevent the tripod joint from being pushed back down the driveshaft during refitting, temporarily stick adhesive tape over the open end of the joint outer member **(see illustration)**. Remove the tape just before reconnecting the inner end of the driveshaft to the transmission.

Metal cover secured by tabs

45 This type of joint can be recognised from the metal cover fitted to the end of the CV joint outer member. The cover fits over the end of the outer member flange, and the driveshaft-

3.39 Work the grease into the joint outer member

3.41 Lift the gaiter outer end to equalise the air pressure

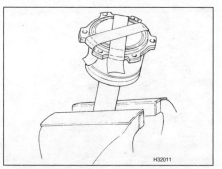

3.44 Tape over the end of the driveshaft joint

3.62 Release the gaiter small securing clip...

3.63...drive the metal ring from the joint outer member

to-transmission flange bolts pass through the cover. The cover is secured to the outer member flange by three tabs. If the cover is a press-fit, or if no cover is fitted, proceed as described in paragraphs 19 to 44.

46 Proceed as described in paragraphs 20 and 21.

47 Using a screwdriver, prise up the tabs of the metal cap over the end of the joint outer member. Lever the cover from the joint outer member.

48 Proceed as described in paragraphs 23 and 24.

49 Support the driveshaft and the joint, and withdraw the outer member from the vice. Slide the joint outer member down the driveshaft, away from the joint.

50 Remove the circlip from the end of the driveshaft.

51 Press or drive the driveshaft from the tripod, taking great care not to damage the rollers.

52 Proceed as described in paragraphs 30 to 36, taking care not to damage the rollers as the tripod is refitted.

53 Work half of the grease supplied with the repair kit into the inner end of the joint outer member, then slide the outer member over the tripod, ensuring that the marks made during dismantling are aligned, and clamp the outer member in the vice.

54 Work the rest of the grease supplied with the repair kit into the rear of the joint outer member.

55 Slide the rubber gaiter up the driveshaft onto the joint outer member, ensuring that the end of the gaiter seats in the groove in the joint outer member, and secure with the large clip as described in paragraph 17.

56 Lift the gaiter outer end to equalise the air pressure in the gaiter, then secure the outer gaiter securing clip in position using the same method used previously.

57 Check that the grease in the joint outer member is evenly distributed around the tripod rollers.

58 Wipe any excess grease from the inner face of the joint outer member, then fit the O-ring provided in the repair kit into the groove in the inner face of the joint outer member.

59 Fit the new cover supplied in the repair kit to the inner end of the joint outer member, ensuring that the bolt holes in the outer member and cover are aligned.

60 Secure the cover by bending the securing tabs around the edge of the outer member flange.

61 Check the driveshaft joint moves freely in all directions, then refit the driveshaft to the vehicle, as described in Section 2.

Ball-and-cage type inner CV joint

62 Secure the driveshaft in a vice equipped with soft jaws, then release the gaiter small securing clip, securing the gaiter to the driveshaft (see illustration).

63 Using a hammer and a small drift, carefully drive the gaiter metal ring from the joint outer member (see illustration).

64 Slide the gaiter down the driveshaft to expose the constant velocity joint, and scoop out excess grease.

65 Remove the circlip from the end of the driveshaft using circlip pliers (see illustration).

66 Press or drive the driveshaft from the joint, taking great care not to damage the joint. Recover the dished washer fitted between the constant velocity joint and the gaiter (see illustrations).

67 Slide the gaiter from the end of the driveshaft (see illustration).

3.65 Remove the circlip...

3.66a...followed by the joint...

3.66b...dished washer...

3.67...and gaiter

3.68a Tilt the splined hub and cage to remove the ball-bearings...

3.68b...then separate the hub from the cage

3.68c Inner CV joint gaiter repair kit

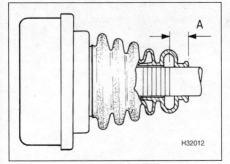

3.72 Installation position of inner joint gaiter on left-hand driveshaft

A = 17.0 mm

3.73a Pack the inner joint with half of the grease...

3.73b...then pack the gaiter with the remaining half

68 Proceed as described previously in paragraphs 7 to 12 **(see illustrations)**.

69 Slide the dished washer onto the driveshaft, making sure its convex side is innermost.

70 Fit the joint to the end of the driveshaft, noting that the chamfered edge of the internal splines on the joint should face towards the driveshaft. Drive or press the joint into position until it contacts the shoulder on the driveshaft.

71 Fit a new circlip to retain the joint on the end of the driveshaft.

72 It the left-hand driveshaft is being worked on, mark the final installation position of the gaiter outboard end on the driveshaft using tape or paint – do not scratch the surface of the driveshaft **(see illustration)**.

73 Pack the joint with the half the recommended quantity of grease (see Specifications0), and then pack the gaiter with the remaining half **(see illustrations)**.

74 Slide the gaiter up the driveshaft, and press or drive the gaiter metal ring onto the joint outer member. To ensure the bolt holes are correctly positioned, temporarily fit one of the flange bolts **(see illustrations)**.

75 If the left-hand driveshaft is being worked on, slide the outboard end of the gaiter into position using the mark made previously (see paragraph 72), then secure the outer gaiter securing clip in position as described in paragraph 17.

76 If the right-hand driveshaft is being worked on, slide the outboard end of the

gaiter into position on the driveshaft, then secure the outer gaiter securing clip in position as described in paragraph 17 **(see illustration)**.

77 Check the driveshaft joint moves freely in all directions, then refit the driveshaft to the vehicle, as described in Section 2.

4 Driveshaft overhaul –
general information

1 If any of the checks described in Chapter 1 reveal wear in any driveshaft joint, first remove the roadwheel trim or centre cap (as applicable) and check that the hub bolt is tight. If the bolt is loose, obtain a new one,

3.74a Temporarily fit one of the flange bolts to ensure the bolt holes are correctly aligned...

3.74b...then drive the metal ring onto the joint outer member

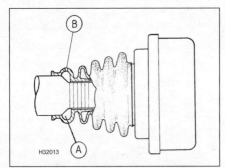

3.76 Installation position of inner joint gaiter on right-hand driveshaft

A Vent chamber in gaiter   B Vent hole

and tighten it to the specified torque (see Section 2). If the bolt is tight, refit the centre cap/trim, and repeat the check on the other hub bolt.

2 Road test the vehicle, and listen for a metallic clicking from the front of the vehicle as the vehicle is driven slowly in a circle on full-lock. If a clicking noise is heard, this indicates wear in the outer constant velocity joint; this means that the joint must be renewed.

3 If vibration consistent with roadspeed is felt through the car when accelerating, there is a possibility of wear in the inner constant velocity joints.

4 To check the joints for wear, remove the driveshafts, then dismantle them as described in Section 3. If any wear or free play is found, the affected joint must be renewed. Refer to an Audi dealer for information on the availability of driveshaft components.

5 Intermediate driveshaft and support bearing assembly – removal, overhaul and refitting

Removal

1 Remove the right-hand driveshaft as described in Section 2.

2 Unscrew the three bolts securing the intermediate driveshaft to the bearing bracket on the rear of the cylinder block.

3 Position a container beneath the transmission to catch spilled oil/fluid when the intermediate shaft is removed.

4 Pull the driveshaft from the transmission splined sun gear/input shaft, and withdraw through the bearing bracket.

5 Remove the O-ring seal from the input shaft and discard, as a new one must be used on refitting.

Overhaul

6 Inspect the intermediate driveshaft and bearing for excessive wear and damage, and renew as necessary.

7 Ideally, a hydraulic press will be required to press the driveshaft from the bearing, although it may be possible to drive it out with a soft-faced mallet, while supporting the bearing in a vice.

8 Using a suitable metal tube, press or drive the new bearing fully into position on the driveshaft. Press only on the bearing inner race.

Refitting

9 Refitting is a reversal of removal, but note the following additional points:

a) *Fit a new O-ring seal to the input shaft.*

b) *Tighten all mounting nuts/bolts to the specified torque, where given.*

c) *Top-up the transmission oil/fluid.*

Chapter 9
Braking system

Contents

Degrees of difficulty

Easy, suitable for novice with little experience	**Fairly easy,** suitable for beginner with some experience	**Fairly difficult,** suitable for competent DIY mechanic	**Difficult,** suitable for experienced DIY mechanic	**Very difficult,** suitable for expert DIY or professional

Specifications

Front brakes
Caliper type . . . . FSIII or FN3 (according to model)
Disc diameter:
  FSIII . . . . 280 mm
  FN3 . . . . 288 or 312 mm
Disc thickness.
  New:
    FSIII . . . . 22.0 mm
    FN3 . . . . 25.0 mm
  Minimum permissible thickness:
    FSIII . . . . 19.0 mm
    FN3 . . . . 22.0 mm
Maximum disc run-out . . . . 0.1 mm
Brake pad lining thickness (all models):
  New . . . . 14.0 mm
  Minimum. . . . . 2.0 mm

Rear disc brakes
Caliper type . . . . C38 or CII38 (according to model)
Disc diameter:
  Type C38. . . . . 255 mm
  Type CII38. . . . . 286 mm
Disc thickness:
  New:
    Type C38. . . . . 10.0 mm
    Type CII38. . . . . 12.0 mm
  Minimum thickness:
    Type C38. . . . . 8.0 mm
    Type CII38. . . . . 10.0 mm
Maximum disc run-out . . . . 0.1 mm
Brake pad lining thickness (all models):
  New . . . . 11.0 mm
  Minimum. . . . . 2.0 mm

Torque wrench settings

	Nm	lbf ft
ABS control unit retaining bolts	8	6
ABS wheel sensor retaining bolts	8	6
Brake pedal pivot shaft nut	25	18
Front brake caliper:		
Guide pins	30	22
Mounting bracket bolts (FN3)	125	92
Front brake disc shield	10	7
Hydraulic brake line union nuts	14	10
Master cylinder mounting nuts	25	18
Rear brake caliper:		
Guide pin bolts*	35	26
Mounting bracket bolts	65	48
Roadwheel bolts	120	89
Servo unit electric vacuum pump bracket to transmission	25	18
Servo unit electric vacuum pump to bracket	8	6
Servo unit mechanical vacuum pump:		
1.9 litre engines:		
Upper bolts	20	15
Lower bolts	10	7
1.6 and 2.0 litre engines	10	7
Servo unit mounting nuts	25	18

*Do not re-use fasteners

1 General information and precautions

1 The braking system is of servo-assisted, diagonal dual-circuit hydraulic type. The arrangement of the hydraulic system is such that each circuit operates one front and one rear brake from a tandem master cylinder. Under normal circumstances, both circuits operate in unison, but, if there is hydraulic failure in one circuit, full braking force will still be available at two wheels. Vacuum for the servo unit is supplied from a combined fuel lift pump and vacuum pump, driven off the end of the camshaft.

2 All models covered by this manual are equipped with disc brakes at the front and rear. ABS is fitted as standard to all models (refer to Section 19 for further information on ABS operation).

3 The front disc brakes are actuated by single-piston sliding type calipers, which ensure that equal pressure is applied to each disc pad.

4 The rear brakes are also actuated by single-piston sliding calipers, which incorporate independent mechanical handbrake mechanisms as well.

Precautions

5 When servicing any part of the system, work carefully and methodically; also observe scrupulous cleanliness when overhauling any part of the hydraulic system. Always renew components in axle sets (where applicable) if in doubt about their condition, and use only genuine Audi parts, or at least those of known good quality. Note the warnings given in *Safety first!* and at relevant points in this Chapter concerning the dangers of asbestos dust and hydraulic fluid.

2 Hydraulic system – bleeding

Warning: Hydraulic fluid is poisonous; wash off immediately and thoroughly in the case of skin contact, and seek immediate medical advice if any fluid is swallowed or gets into the eyes. Certain types of hydraulic fluid are flammable, and may ignite when allowed into contact with hot components; when servicing any hydraulic system, it is safest to assume that the fluid is flammable, and to take precautions against the risk of fire as though it is petrol that is being handled. Hydraulic fluid is also an effective paint stripper, and will attack plastics; if any is spilt, it should be washed off immediately, using copious quantities of fresh water. Finally, it is hygroscopic (it absorbs moisture from the air) – old fluid may be contaminated and unfit for further use. When topping-up or renewing the fluid, always use the recommended type, and ensure that it comes from a freshly-opened sealed container.

Note: *Audi specify that at least 0.25 litre of brake fluid should be expelled from each caliper.*

General

1 The correct operation of any hydraulic system is only possible after removing all air from the components and circuit; this is achieved by bleeding the system. Since the clutch hydraulic system also uses fluid from the brake system reservoir, it should also be bled at the same time by referring to Chapter 6, Section 2.

2 During the bleeding procedure, add only clean, unused hydraulic fluid of the recommended type; never re-use fluid that has already been bled from the system. Ensure that sufficient fluid is available before starting work.

3 If there is any possibility of incorrect fluid being already in the system, the brake components and circuit must be flushed completely with uncontaminated, correct fluid, and new seals should be fitted to the various components.

4 If hydraulic fluid has been lost from the system, or air has entered because of a leak, ensure that the fault is cured before continuing further.

5 Park the vehicle on level ground, then chock the wheels and release the handbrake.

6 Check that all pipes and hoses are secure, unions tight and bleed screws closed. Clean any dirt from around the bleed screws.

7 Unscrew the master cylinder reservoir cap, and top the reservoir up to the MAX level line; refit the cap loosely, and remember to maintain the fluid level at least above the MIN level line throughout the procedure, or there is a risk of further air entering the system.

8 There are a number of one-man, do-it-yourself brake bleeding kits currently available from motor accessory shops. It is recommended that one of these kits is used whenever possible, as they greatly simplify the bleeding operation, and reduce the risk of expelled air and fluid being drawn back into the system. If such a kit is not available, the basic (two-man) method must be used, which is described in detail below.

9 If a kit is to be used, prepare the vehicle as described previously, and follow the kit manufacturer's instructions, as the procedure may vary slightly according to the type being used; generally, they are as outlined below in the relevant sub-section.

10 Whichever method is used, the same sequence must be followed (paragraph 12) to ensure the removal of all air from the system.

Bleeding sequence

11 If the system has been only partially disconnected, and suitable precautions were taken to minimise fluid loss, it should be necessary only to bleed that part of the system.

12 If the complete system is to be bled, then it should be done working in the following sequence:

RHD models

a) Right-hand front brake.
b) Left-hand front brake.
c) Right-hand rear brake.
d) Left-hand rear brake.

LHD models

a) Left-hand front brake.
b) Right-hand front brake.
c) Left-hand rear brake.
d) Right-hand rear brake.

13 If the hydraulic fluid has run dry in either chamber of the reservoir, the system must be pre-bled as follows, before carrying out the bleeding sequence described above:

a) Bleed the front left and right brakes simultaneously.
b) Bleed the rear left and right brakes simultaneously.

Bleeding

Basic (two-man) method

14 Collect together a clean glass jar of reasonable size, a suitable length of plastic or rubber tubing which is a tight fit over the bleed screw, and a ring spanner to fit the screw. The help of an assistant will also be required.

15 Remove the dust cap from the first screw in the sequence **(see illustration)**. Fit the spanner and tube to the screw, place the other end of the tube in the jar, and pour in sufficient fluid to cover the end of the tube.

16 Ensure that the master cylinder reservoir fluid level is maintained at least above the MIN level line throughout the procedure.

17 Have the assistant fully depress the brake pedal several times to build-up pressure, and then maintain it on the final downstroke.

18 While pedal pressure is maintained, unscrew the bleed screw (approximately one turn) and allow the compressed fluid and air to flow into the jar. The assistant should maintain pedal pressure, following it down to the floor if necessary, and should not release it until instructed to do so. When the flow stops, tighten the bleed screw again, have the assistant release the pedal slowly, and recheck the reservoir fluid level.

19 Repeat the steps given in paragraphs 16 and 17 until the fluid emerging from the bleed screw is free from air bubbles. If the master cylinder has been drained and refilled, and air is being bled from the first screw in the sequence, allow approximately five seconds between cycles for the master cylinder passages to refill.

20 When no more air bubbles appear, tighten the bleed screw securely, remove the tube and spanner, and refit the dust cap. Do not over tighten the bleed screw.

21 Repeat the procedure on the remaining screws in the sequence, until all air is removed from the system and the brake pedal feels firm again.

Using a one-way valve kit

22 As their name implies, these kits consist of a length of tubing with a one-way valve fitted, to prevent expelled air and fluid being drawn back into the system; some kits include a translucent container, which can be positioned so that the air bubbles can be more easily seen flowing from the end of the tube.

23 The kit is connected to the bleed screw, which is then opened. The user returns to the driver's seat, depresses the brake pedal with a smooth, steady stroke, and slowly releases it; this is repeated until the expelled fluid is clear of air bubbles **(see illustration)**.

24 Note that these kits simplify work so much that it is easy to forget the master cylinder reservoir fluid level; ensure that this is maintained at least above the MIN level line at all times.

Using a pressure-bleeding kit

25 These kits are usually operated by the reservoir of pressurised air contained in the spare tyre. However, note that it will be probably necessary to reduce the pressure to less than 1.0 bar (14.5 psi); refer to the instructions supplied with the kit.

26 By connecting a pressurised, fluid-filled container to the master cylinder reservoir, bleeding can be carried out simply by opening each screw in turn (in the specified sequence), and allowing the fluid to flow out until no more air bubbles can be seen in the expelled fluid.

27 This method has the advantage that the large reservoir of fluid provides an additional safeguard against air being drawn into the system during bleeding.

28 Pressure-bleeding is particularly effective when bleeding 'difficult' systems, or when bleeding the complete system at the time of routine fluid renewal.

All methods

29 When bleeding is complete, and firm pedal feel is restored, wash off any spilt fluid, tighten the bleed screws securely, and refit their dust caps.

30 Check the hydraulic fluid level in the master cylinder reservoir, and top-up if necessary (see Weekly checks).

31 Discard any hydraulic fluid that has been bled from the system; it will not be fit for re-use.

32 Check the feel of the brake pedal. If it feels at all spongy, air must still be present in the system, and further bleeding is required. Failure to bleed satisfactorily after a reasonable repetition of the bleeding procedure may be due to worn master cylinder seals.

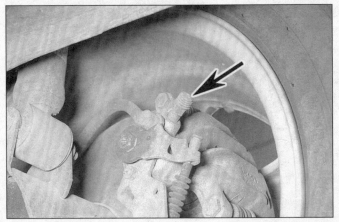

2.15 Remove the dust cap (arrowed) from the first screw in the sequence

2.23 Bleeding a brake using a one-way valve kit

3 Hydraulic pipes and hoses – renewal

Note: *Refer to the warning in Section 2 concerning the dangers of hydraulic fluid.*

1 If any pipe or hose is to be renewed, minimise fluid loss by first removing the master cylinder reservoir cap, then tightening it down onto a piece of polythene to obtain an airtight seal. Alternatively, flexible hoses can be sealed, if required, using a proprietary brake hose clamp; metal brake pipe unions can be plugged (if care is taken not to allow dirt into the system) or capped immediately they are disconnected. Place a wad of rag under any union that is to be disconnected, to catch any spilt fluid.

2 If a flexible hose is to be disconnected, where applicable unscrew the brake pipe union nut before removing the spring clip which secures the hose to its mounting bracket.

3 To unscrew the union nuts, it is preferable to obtain a brake pipe spanner of the correct size; these are available from most large motor accessory shops. Failing this, a close-fitting open-ended spanner will be required, though if the nuts are tight or corroded, their flats may be rounded-off if the spanner slips. In such a case, a self-locking wrench is often the only way to unscrew a stubborn union, but it follows that the pipe and the damaged nuts must be renewed on reassembly. Always clean a union and surrounding area before disconnecting it. If disconnecting a component with more than one union, make a careful note of the connections before disturbing any of them.

4 If a brake pipe is to be renewed, it can be obtained, cut to length and with the union nuts and end flares in place, from Audi dealers. All that is then necessary is to bend it to shape, following the line of the original, before fitting it to the car. Alternatively, most motor accessory shops can make up brake pipes from kits, but this requires very careful measurement of the original, to ensure that the new pipe is of the correct length. The safest answer is usually to take the original to the shop as a pattern.

5 On refitting, do not overtighten the union nuts. It is not necessary to exercise brute force to obtain a sound joint.

6 Ensure that the pipes and hoses are correctly routed, with no kinks, and that they are secured in the clips or brackets provided. After fitting, remove the polythene from the reservoir, and bleed the hydraulic system as described in Section 2. Check carefully for fluid leaks, around the complete brake system and wash off any spilt brake fluid.

4 Front brake pads – removal, inspection and refitting

⚠️ **Warning: Renew both sets of brake pads at the same time – never renew the pads on only one wheel, as uneven braking may result. Note that the dust created by wear of the pads may contain asbestos, which** is a health hazard. Never blow it out with compressed air, and do not inhale any of it. An approved filtering mask should be worn when working on the brakes. DO NOT use petrol or petroleum-based solvents to clean brake parts; use brake cleaner or methylated spirit only.

FSIII calipers

Removal

1 Apply the handbrake, then jack up the front of the vehicle and support it on axle stands (see *'Jacking and vehicle support'* in Reference chapter) Remove the front roadwheels.

2 Trace the brake pad wear sensor wiring (where fitted) back from the pads, and disconnect it from the wiring connector **(see illustration)**. Note the routing of the wiring, and free it from any relevant retaining clips.

3 Where applicable, to improve access, undo the retaining bolts and remove the air deflector shield from the caliper.

4 Remove the two protective rubber caps and, using a suitable hexagon key, slacken and remove the two caliper guide pins from the caliper **(see illustrations)**. Then lift the caliper, together with pads, away from the hub carrier, and tie it to the suspension strut using a suitable piece of wire. Do not allow the caliper to hang unsupported on the flexible brake hose.

5 Remove the two brake pads from the caliper, noting that the inner pad is retained in the piston by a spring clip **(see illustrations)**. If the

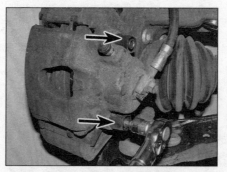

4.2 Disconnect the brake pad wear sensor wiring connector

4.4a Unscrew the caliper guide pins...

4.4b...and remove them

4.5a Removing the outer pad...

4.5b...and inner pad from the caliper

4.5c Front brake pads

4.9 Open the bleed nipple as the piston is pushed back into the caliper

4.10 The inboard pad is labelled 'Piston side'

outer pad remains on the carrier, remove it. If the original pads are to be refitted, mark them so that they can be refitted in their original positions.

Inspection

6 First measure the thickness of each brake pad. If either pad is worn at any point to the specified minimum thickness or less, all four pads must be renewed. Also, the pads should be renewed if any are fouled with oil or grease; there is no satisfactory way of degreasing friction material, once contaminated. If any of the brake pads are worn unevenly, or are fouled with oil or grease, trace and rectify the cause before reassembly. New brake pad kits are available from Audi dealers.

7 If the brake pads are still serviceable, carefully clean them using a clean, fine wire brush or similar, paying particular attention to the sides and back of the metal backing. Clean out the grooves in the friction material (where applicable), and pick out any large embedded particles of dirt or debris. Carefully clean the pad locations in the caliper body/ mounting bracket.

8 Prior to fitting the pads, check that the guide pins are free to slide easily in the caliper body bushes, and are a reasonably tight fit. Brush the dust and dirt from the caliper and piston, but do not inhale it, as it is injurious to health. Inspect the dust seal around the piston for damage, and the piston for evidence of fluid leaks, corrosion or damage. If attention to any of these components is necessary, refer to Section 5.

Refitting

9 If new brake pads are to be fitted, the caliper piston must be pushed back into the cylinder to make room for them. Either use a G-clamp or similar tool, or use suitable pieces of wood as levers. To avoid any dirt entering the ABS solenoid valves, connect a pipe to the bleed nipple and, as the piston is pushed

back, open the nipple and allow the displaced fluid to flow through the pipe into a suitable container (see illustration).

Caution: Pushing back the piston causes a reverse-flow of brake fluid, which has been known to 'flip' the master cylinder rubber seals, resulting in a total loss of braking. To avoid this, clamp the caliper flexible hose and open the bleed screw – as the piston is pushed back, the fluid can be directed into a suitable container using a hose attached to the bleed screw. Close the screw just before the piston is pushed fully back, to ensure no air enters the system.

10 Fit the new pads into the caliper. The inboard pad (piston side) is marked 'Piston side' (see illustration).

11 Position the caliper and pads over the brake disc ensuring that the lug on the caliper engages correctly with the hub carrier (see illustration). Pass the pad warning sensor wiring (where fitted) through the caliper aperture.

12 Position the caliper until it is possible to install the caliper guide pins. Apply a little copper grease to the pins before refitting them, and tighten them to the specified torque (see illustration).

Note: *Do not exert excess pressure on the caliper, as this will deform the pad springs, resulting in noisy operation of the brakes.*

13 Where applicable, reconnect the brake pad wear sensor wiring connectors, ensuring that the wiring is correctly routed. Where applicable, refit the air deflector shield to the caliper.

14 Depress the brake pedal repeatedly, until the pads are pressed into firm contact with the brake disc, and normal (non-assisted) pedal pressure is restored.

15 Repeat the above procedure on the remaining front brake caliper.

16 Refit the roadwheels, then lower the vehicle to the ground and tighten the roadwheel bolts to the specified torque.

17 New pads will not give full braking efficiency until they have bedded-in. Be prepared for this, and avoid hard braking as far as possible for the first hundred miles or so after pad renewal.

FN3 calipers
Removal

18 Proceed as described in paragraphs 1 and 2.

19 Using a screwdriver, lever the brake pad

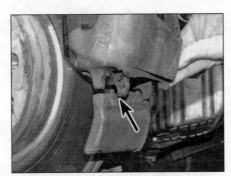

4.11 Ensure the pads and caliper are correctly located on the carrier

4.12 Apply copper grease to the guide pins before inserting them

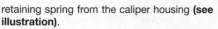

4.19 Unclip the spring from the caliper housing

4.20a Remove the plastic covers...

4.20b...and undo the caliper guide pins

retaining spring from the caliper housing **(see illustration)**.

20 Remove the two protective rubber caps and using a suitable hexagon key, slacken and remove the two caliper guide pins from the caliper **(see illustrations)**. Then lift the caliper away from the brake pads and hub, and tie it to the suspension strut using a suitable piece of wire. Do not allow the caliper to hang unsupported on the flexible brake hose.

21 Withdraw the two brake pads from the caliper mounting bracket. If the original pads are to be refitted, identify them so that they can be refitted in their original locations. Where applicable, disconnect the pad wear sensor wiring connector.

Inspection

22 Examine the pads and caliper as described previously in paragraphs 6 to 8. If new pads are to be refitted, refer to paragraph

9 before attempting to push the piston back into the caliper.

Refitting

23 Where applicable, remove the protective foil from the outer pad backplate. Install the outer pad in the caliper mounting bracket, ensuring that the friction material of the pad is against the brake disc. Install the inner (piston side) pad into the caliper. If the original pads are being refitted, ensure that they are refitted to their original locations as noted before removal. The inner pad is fitted with a retaining clip, which engages with the recess in the piston. Where applicable, note that the pad with the wear sensor wiring should be installed as the inner pad. New pads are marked with an arrow on the backing plate, which identifies the direction of rotation. Consequently, the pads should be fitted with the arrows pointing to the ground **(see illustrations)**.

24 Press the caliper into position. Install and tighten the guide pins to the specified torque **(see illustration)**.

25 Refit the brake pad retaining spring to the caliper housing **(see illustration)**.

26 Where applicable, reconnect the brake pad wear sensor wiring connectors, ensuring that the wiring is correctly routed.

27 Depress the brake pedal repeatedly until the pads are pressed into firm contact with the brake disc, and normal (non-assisted) pedal pressure is restored.

28 Repeat the above procedure on the remaining front brake caliper.

29 Refit the roadwheels, then lower the vehicle to the ground and tighten the roadwheel bolts to the specified torque.

30 Check the hydraulic fluid level as described in *Weekly checks*.

31 New pads will not give full braking efficiency until they have bedded-in. Be prepared for this and avoid hard braking (where possible) in the first hundred miles or so after pad renewal.

4.23a Fit the outer pad to the caliper mounting bracket...

4.23b...and refit the inner pad to the caliper piston

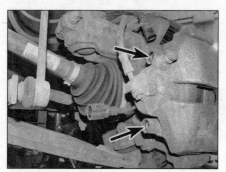

4.24 Install the caliper guide pins (arrowed)

4.25 Refit the retaining spring (arrowed)

5 Front brake caliper – removal, overhaul and refitting

Note: *Before starting work, refer to the warning at the beginning of Section 2 concerning the dangers of hydraulic fluid, and to the warning at the beginning of Section 4 concerning the dangers of asbestos dust.*

Removal

1 Apply the handbrake, then jack up the front of the vehicle and support it on axle stands (see 'Jacking and vehicle support' in Reference chapter). Remove the appropriate roadwheel.

2 Minimise fluid loss by first removing the master cylinder reservoir cap, and then tightening it down onto a piece of polythene, to obtain an airtight seal. Alternatively, use a brake hose clamp, a G-clamp or a similar tool to clamp the flexible hose.

3 Clean the area around the union, then loosen the brake hose union nut.

4 Remove the brake pads as described in Section 4.

5 Unscrew the caliper from the end of the brake hose and remove it from the vehicle.

Overhaul

6 With the caliper on the bench, wipe away all traces of dust and dirt, but avoid inhaling the dust, as it is injurious to health.

7 Withdraw the partially-ejected piston from the caliper body, and remove the dust seal.

8 Using a small screwdriver, extract the piston hydraulic seal, taking great care not to damage the caliper bore **(see illustration)**.

9 Thoroughly clean all components, using only methylated spirit, isopropyl alcohol or clean hydraulic fluid as a cleaning medium. Never use mineral-based solvents such as petrol or paraffin, as they will attack the hydraulic system rubber components. Dry the components immediately, using compressed air or a clean, lint-free cloth. Use compressed air to blow clear the fluid passages.

10 Check all components, and renew any that are worn or damaged. Check particularly the cylinder bore and piston; these should be renewed if they are scratched, worn or corroded in any way (note that this means the renewal of the complete caliper body assembly). Similarly check the condition of the spacers/guide pins and their bushes/bores (as applicable); both spacers/pins should be undamaged and (when cleaned) a reasonably tight sliding fit in their bores. If there is any doubt about the condition of any component, renew it.

11 If the assembly is fit for further use, obtain the appropriate repair kit; the components are available from Audi dealers in various combinations.

12 Renew all rubber seals, dust covers and caps disturbed on dismantling as a matter of course; these should never be re-used.

13 On reassembly, ensure that all components are clean and dry.

14 Thinly coat the piston and piston seal with brake fitting paste (VAG part no G 052 150 A2). This should be included in the Audi caliper overhaul/repair kit.

15 Fit the new piston (fluid) seal, using only your fingers (no tools) to manipulate it into the cylinder bore groove. Fit the new dust seal to the piston, and refit the piston to the cylinder bore using a twisting motion; ensure that the piston enters squarely into the bore. Press the

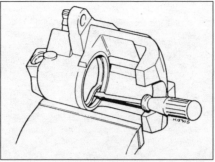

5.8 Use a small screwdriver to extract the caliper piston hydraulic seal

piston fully into the bore, then press the dust seal into the caliper body.

Refitting

16 Screw the caliper fully onto the flexible hose union.

17 Refit the brake pads as described in Section 4.

18 Securely tighten the brake pipe union nut.

19 Remove the brake hose clamp or polythene, as applicable, and bleed the hydraulic system as described in Section 2. Note that, providing the precautions described were taken to minimise brake fluid loss, it should only be necessary to bleed the relevant front brake.

20 Refit the roadwheel, then lower the vehicle to the ground and tighten the roadwheel bolts to the specified torque.

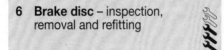

6 Brake disc – inspection, removal and refitting

Note: *Before starting work, refer to the warning at the beginning of Section 4 concerning the dangers of asbestos dust.*
Note: *If either disc requires renewal, BOTH should be renewed at the same time, to ensure even and consistent braking. New brake pads should also be fitted.*

Front brake disc

Inspection

1 Apply the handbrake, then jack up the front of the vehicle and support it on axle

stands (see *'Jacking and vehicle support'* in Reference chapter). Remove the appropriate roadwheel.

2 Slowly rotate the brake disc so that the full area of both sides can be checked; remove the brake pads if better access is required to the inboard surface. Light scoring is normal in the area swept by the brake pads, but if heavy scoring or cracks are found, the disc must be renewed.

3 It is normal to find a lip of rust and brake dust around the perimeter of the disc; this can be scraped off if required. If, however, a lip has formed due to excessive wear of the brake pad swept area, then the disc thickness must be measured using a micrometer. Take measurements at several places around the disc, at the inside and outside of the pad swept area; if the disc has worn at any point to the specified minimum thickness or less, the disc must be renewed.

4 If the disc is thought to be warped, it can be checked for run-out. Either use a dial gauge mounted on any convenient fixed point, while the disc is slowly rotated, or use feeler blades to measure (at several points all around the disc) the clearance between the disc and a fixed point, such as the caliper mounting bracket. If the measurements obtained are at the specified maximum or beyond, the disc is excessively warped, and must be renewed; however, it is worth checking first that the hub bearing is in good condition (see Chapter 1, Section 17). If the run-out is excessive, the disc must be renewed **(see illustration)**.

5 Check the disc for cracks, especially around the wheel bolt holes, and any other wear or damage, and renew if necessary.

Removal

6 Remove the brake pads as described in Section 4.

7 On models with FN3 front brake calipers, unscrew the two bolts securing the brake caliper mounting bracket to the hub carrier, then slide the caliper assembly off the disc. Using a piece of wire or string, tie the caliper to the front suspension coil spring, to avoid placing any strain on the brake hose.

8 Use chalk or paint to mark the relationship of the disc to the hub, then remove the screw securing the brake disc to the hub, and remove the disc **(see illustrations)**. If it is tight, apply

6.4 Using a DTI gauge to measure disc run-out

6.8a Undo the screw...

6.8b ...and remove the front brake disc

6.13 Lift away the disc

8.3 Counterhold the guide pin bolts

8.4 Remove the caliper

penetrating fluid, and tap its rear face gently with a hide or plastic mallet. The use of excessive force could cause the disc to be damaged.

Refitting

9 Refitting is the reverse of the removal procedure, noting the following points:
a) *Ensure that the mating surfaces of the disc and hub are clean and flat.*
b) *Align (if applicable) the marks made on removal, and securely tighten the disc retaining screw.*
c) *If a new disc has been fitted, use a suitable solvent to wipe any preservative coating from the disc, before refitting the caliper.*
d) *On models with FN3 brake calipers, slide the caliper into position over the disc, making sure the pads pass either side of the disc. Tighten the caliper bracket mounting bolts to the specified torque.*
e) *Fit the brake pads as described in Section 4.*
f) *Refit the roadwheel, then lower the vehicle to the ground and tighten the roadwheel bolts to the specified torque. On completion, repeatedly depress the brake pedal until normal (non-assisted) pedal pressure returns.*

Rear brake disc

Inspection

10 Firmly chock the front wheels, then jack up the rear of the car and support it on axle stands (see 'Jacking and vehicle support' in Reference chapter. Remove the appropriate rear roadwheel.
11 Inspect the disc as described in paragraphs 2 to 5.

Removal

12 Unscrew the two bolts securing the brake caliper mounting bracket in position, then slide the caliper assembly off the disc. Using a piece of wire or string, tie the caliper to the rear suspension coil spring, to avoid placing any strain on the hydraulic brake hose.
13 Use chalk or paint to mark the relationship of the disc to the hub, then remove the screw securing the brake disc to the hub, and remove the disc **(see illustration)**. If it is tight, apply penetrating fluid, and tap its rear face gently with a hide or plastic mallet. The use of excessive force could cause the disc to be damaged.

Refitting

14 Refitting is a reversal of the removal procedure, noting the following points:
a) *Ensure that the mating surfaces of the disc and hub are clean and flat.*
b) *Align (if applicable) the marks made on removal, and securely tighten the disc retaining screw.*
c) *If a new disc has been fitted, use a suitable solvent to wipe any preservative coating from the disc, before refitting the caliper.*
d) *Slide the caliper into position over the disc, making sure the pads pass either side of the disc. Tighten the caliper bracket mounting bolts to the specified torque. If new discs have been fitted and there is insufficient clearance between the pads to accommodate the new, thicker disc, it may be necessary to push the piston back into the caliper body as described in Section 8.*
e) *Refit the roadwheel, then lower the vehicle to the ground and tighten the roadwheel*

bolts to the specified torque. On completion, repeatedly depress the brake pedal until normal (non-assisted) pedal pressure returns.

7 Front brake disc shield – removal and refitting

Removal

1 Remove the brake disc as described in Section 6.
2 Unscrew the securing bolts, and remove the brake disc shield.

Refitting

3 Refitting is a reversal of removal. Tighten the shield retaining bolts to the specified torque. Refit the brake disc with reference to Section 6.

8 Rear brake pads – removal, inspection and refitting

Note: *Before starting work, refer to the warning at the beginning of Section 4 concerning the dangers of asbestos dust. New guide pin bolts will be required on refitting.*

Removal

1 Chock the front wheels, then jack up the rear of the vehicle and support it on axle stands (see 'Jacking and vehicle support' in Reference chapter). Remove the rear wheels.
2 If required, slacken the handbrake cable and detach it from the caliper as described in Section 16.
3 Slacken and remove the guide pin bolts, using a slim open-ended spanner to prevent the guide pins from rotating **(see illustration)**. Discard the bolts – new ones must be used on refitting.
4 Lift the caliper away from the brake pads, and tie it to the suspension strut using a suitable piece of wire **(see illustration)**. Do not allow the caliper to hang unsupported on the flexible brake hose.
5 Withdraw the two brake pads from the caliper mounting bracket **(see illustrations)**,

8.5a Remove the outer rear brake pad...

8.5b ...and inner rear brake pad

8.10a Refit the anti-rattle shims (arrowed)

8.10b Some brake pads have anti-rattle springs attached (arrowed)

and on the CII38 type, recover the pad anti-rattle shims from the mounting bracket, noting their correct fitted locations.

Inspection

6 First measure the thickness of each brake pad. If either pad is worn at any point to the specified minimum thickness or less, all four pads must be renewed. Also, the pads should be renewed if any are fouled with oil or grease; there is no satisfactory way of degreasing friction material, once contaminated. If any of the brake pads are worn unevenly, or fouled with oil or grease, trace and rectify the cause before reassembly.

7 If the brake pads are still serviceable, carefully clean them using a clean, fine wire brush or similar, paying particular attention to the sides and back of the metal backing. Clean out the grooves in the friction material (where applicable), and pick out any large embedded particles of dirt or debris. Carefully clean the pad locations in the caliper body/ mounting bracket.

8 Prior to fitting the pads, check that the guide pins are free to slide easily in the caliper bracket, and check that the rubber guide pin gaiters are undamaged. Brush the dust and dirt from the caliper and piston, but do not inhale it, as it is injurious to health. Inspect the dust seal around the piston for damage, and the piston for evidence of fluid leaks, corrosion or damage. If attention to any of these components is necessary, refer to Section 9.

Refitting

9 If new brake pads are to be fitted, it will be necessary to retract the piston fully; by rotating it in a clockwise direction as it is pushed into the caliper bore (see **Haynes Hint**). To avoid any dirt entering the ABS solenoid valves, connect a pipe to the bleed nipple, and as the piston is pushed back open the nipple and allow the displaced fluid to flow through the pipe into a suitable container.

 HAYNES HINT *In the absence of the special tool, the piston can be screwed back into the caliper using a pair of circlip pliers.*

Caution: Pushing back the piston causes a reverse-flow of brake fluid, which has been known to 'flip' the master cylinder rubber seals, resulting in a total loss of braking. To avoid this, clamp the caliper flexible hose and open the bleed screw – as the piston is pushed back, the fluid can be directed into a suitable container using a hose attached to the bleed screw. Close the screw just before the piston is pushed fully back, to ensure no air enters the system.

10 On the CII38 type, fit the pad anti-rattle shims to the caliper mounting bracket, ensuring that they are correctly located **Note:** *On the C38 type, the anti-rattle springs are attached to the pads themselves. Install the pads in the mounting bracket, ensuring that each pad's friction material is against the brake disc.* Remove the protective foil from the outer pad backing plate **(see illustrations)**.

11 Slide the caliper back into position over the pads.

12 Press the caliper into position, then install the new guide pin bolts, tightening them to the specified torque setting while retaining the guide pin with an open-ended spanner **(see illustration)**.

13 Depress the brake pedal repeatedly, until the pads are pressed into firm contact with the brake disc, and normal (non-assisted) pedal pressure is restored.

14 Repeat the above procedure on the remaining rear brake caliper.

15 Reconnect the handbrake cables to the calipers, and adjust the handbrake as described in Section 14.

8.12 Hold the guide pin whilst tightening the guide pin bolt

16 Refit the roadwheels, then lower the vehicle to the ground and tighten the roadwheel bolts to the specified torque setting.

17 Check the hydraulic fluid level as described in *Weekly checks*.

18 New pads will not give full braking efficiency until they have bedded-in. Be prepared for this, and avoid hard braking as far as possible for the first hundred miles or so after pad renewal.

---

9   Rear brake caliper – removal, overhaul and refitting

Note: *Before starting work, refer to the warning at the beginning of Section 2 concerning the dangers of hydraulic fluid, and to the warning at the beginning of Section 4 concerning the dangers of asbestos dust.*

Removal

1 Chock the front wheels, then jack up the rear of the vehicle and support on axle stands (see *'Jacking and vehicle support'* in Reference chapter). Remove the relevant rear wheel.

2 Minimise fluid loss by first removing the master cylinder reservoir cap, and then tightening it down onto a piece of polythene, to obtain an airtight seal. Alternatively, use a brake hose clamp, a G-clamp or a similar tool to clamp the flexible hose.

3 Clean the area around the union on the caliper, and then loosen the brake hose union nut.

4 Lift the caliper from the brake pads as described in Section 8.

5 Unscrew the caliper from the end of the flexible hose and remove it from the vehicle.

Overhaul

Note: *It is not possible to overhaul the brake caliper handbrake mechanism. If the mechanism is faulty, or fluid is leaking from the handbrake lever seal the caliper assembly must be renewed.*

6 With the caliper on the bench, wipe away all traces of dust and dirt, but avoid inhaling the dust, as it is injurious to health.

7 Using a small screwdriver, carefully prise out the dust seal from the caliper, taking care not to damage the piston.

8 Remove the piston from the caliper bore by rotating it in an anti-clockwise direction. This can be achieved using a suitable pair of circlip pliers engaged in the caliper piston slots. Once the piston turns freely but does not come out any further, the piston can be withdrawn by hand.

9 Using a small screwdriver, extract the piston hydraulic seal(s), taking care not to damage the caliper bore.

10 Withdraw the guide pins from the caliper, and remove the guide sleeve gaiters.

11 Thoroughly clean all components, using

only methylated spirit, isopropyl alcohol or clean hydraulic fluid as a cleaning medium. Never use mineral-based solvents such as petrol or paraffin, as they will attack the hydraulic system rubber components. Dry the components immediately, using compressed air or a clean, lint-free cloth. Use compressed air to blow clear the fluid passages.

12 Check all components, and renew any that are worn or damaged. Check particularly the cylinder bore and piston; these should be renewed (note that this means the renewal of the complete caliper body assembly) if they are scratched, worn or corroded in any way. Similarly check the condition of the spacers/guide pins and their bushes/bores (as applicable); both spacers/pins should be undamaged and (when cleaned) a reasonably tight sliding fit in their bores. If there is any doubt about the condition of any component, renew it.

13 If the assembly is fit for further use, obtain the appropriate repair kit; the components are available from Audi dealers in various combinations.

14 Renew all rubber seals, dust covers and caps disturbed on dismantling as a matter of course; these should never be re-used.

15 On reassembly, ensure that all components are clean and dry.

16 Smear a thin coat of brake fitting paste (VAG part no G 052 150 A2) on the piston,

seal and caliper bore. This should be included in the overhaul/repair kit. Fit the new piston (fluid) seal, using only the fingers (no tools) to manipulate into the cylinder bore groove.

17 Fit the new dust seal to the piston groove, then refit the piston assembly. Turn the piston in a clockwise direction, using the method employed on dismantling, until it is fully retracted into the caliper bore.

18 Press the dust seal into position in the caliper housing.

19 Apply the grease supplied in the repair kit, or a copper-based brake grease or anti-seize compound, to the guide pins. Fit the new gaiters to the guide pins and fit the pins to the caliper ensuring that the gaiters are correctly located in the grooves on both the pins and caliper.

20 Prior to refitting, fill the caliper with fresh hydraulic fluid by slackening the bleed screw and pumping the fluid through the caliper until bubble-free fluid is expelled from the union hole.

Refitting

21 Screw the caliper fully onto the flexible hose union.

22 Refit the caliper over the brake pads as described in paragraphs 10 to 12 of Section 8.

23 Securely tighten the brake pipe union nut.

24 Remove the brake hose clamp or remove the polythene from the fluid reservoir, as

applicable, and bleed the hydraulic system as described in Section 2. Note that, providing the precautions described were taken to minimise brake fluid loss, it should only be necessary to bleed the relevant rear brake.

25 Connect the handbrake cable to the caliper, and adjust the handbrake as described in Section 14.

26 Refit the roadwheel, then lower the vehicle to the ground and tighten the roadwheel bolts to the specified torque. On completion, check the hydraulic fluid level as described in *Weekly checks*.

10 Brake pedal – removal and refitting

Removal

1 Disconnect the battery negative lead. Refer to *'Disconnecting the battery'* in Reference chapter.

2 With reference to Chapter 11, remove the driver's side lower facia trim panels, and the trim panel below the facia.

3 Where fitted, unscrew the two retaining screws and remove the connecting plate between the clutch and brake pedals.

4 Where fitted to the pedal bracket, remove the brake light switch as described in Section 18.

Note: *On later models, the switch is located on the brake master cylinder.*

5 It is now necessary to release the brake pedal from the ball on the vacuum servo pushrod. To do this, an Audi special tool is available, but a suitable alternative can be improvised. Note that the plastic lugs in the pedal are very stiff, and it will not be possible to release them by hand. Depress and hold down the pedal, then, using the tool, release the securing lugs, and pull the pedal from the servo pushrod **(see illustrations)**.

6 Undo the upper retaining nut and bolt and remove the pedal from the mounting bracket **(see illustration)**.

10.5a Improvised special tool constructed from a modified exhaust clamp, used to release the brake pedal from the servo pushrod

10.5b Using the tool to release the brake pedal...

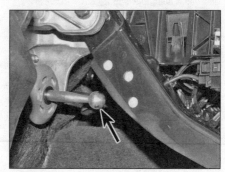

10.5c ...from the servo pushrod (arrowed)

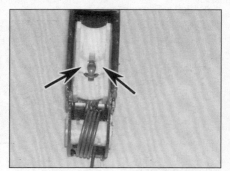

10.5d Rear view of the brake pedal (removed) showing plastic lugs (arrowed) securing pedal to pushrod

10.6 Undo the pedal upper pivot bolt (arrowed)

7 If required, unscrew the nuts/bolts securing the pedal support bracket to the bulkhead/servo and remove mounting bracket.

8 Carefully clean all components, and renew any that are worn or damaged.

Refitting

9 Prior to refitting, apply a smear of multi-purpose grease to the pivot shaft and pedal bearing surfaces.

10 Pull the servo unit pushrod down, and at the same time manoeuvre the pedal into position, ensuring that the pivot bush is correctly located.

11 If removed, tighten the pedal bracket retaining nuts/bolts securely.

12 Hold the servo unit pushrod, and push the pedal back onto the pushrod ball. Make sure the pedal is securely fastened to the pushrod.

13 Insert the pedal pivot bolt and tighten the retaining nut to the to the specified torque.

14 Refit the brake light switch, as described in Section 18.

15 Where fitted, refit the connecting plate between the clutch and brake pedals, and tighten the two retaining bolts securely.

16 Refit the facia trim panels as described in Chapter 11.

11 Servo unit – testing, removal and refitting

Testing

1 To test the operation of the servo unit, depress the footbrake several times to exhaust the vacuum, then start the engine whilst keeping the pedal firmly depressed. As the engine starts, there should be a noticeable 'give' in the brake pedal as the vacuum builds-up. Allow the engine to run for at least two minutes, and then switch it off. If the brake pedal is now depressed, it should feel normal, but further applications should result in the pedal feeling firmer, with the pedal stroke decreasing with each application.

2 If the servo does not operate as described, first inspect the servo unit non-return valve as described in Section 12. Also check the operation of the vacuum pump as described in, Section 21.

3 If the servo unit still fails to operate satisfactorily, the fault lies within the unit itself. Repairs to the unit are not possible – if faulty, the servo unit must be renewed.

Removal

4 Remove the master cylinder as described in Section 13.

5 Where applicable remove the heat shield from the servo, then carefully ease the vacuum hose out from the sealing grommet in the front of the servo. Where applicable, also disconnect the wiring from the servo vacuum sensor, then extract the retaining circlip with a screwdriver, and withdraw the sensor from the servo.

6 On LHD models with manual transmission, refer to Chapter 7A and disconnect the gearchange cables from the levers on the transmission, then unbolt the gearchange support bracket and tie it to one side.

7 With reference to Chapter 11, remove the driver's side lower facia trim panels, and the trim panel below the facia.

8 Where fitted, unscrew the two retaining screws and remove the connecting plate between the clutch and brake pedals (manual transmission models only). Also, where fitted, remove the air duct and cover for access to the servo mounting nuts.

9 It is now necessary to release the brake pedal from the ball on the vacuum servo pushrod. To do this, an Audi special tool is available, but a suitable alternative can be improvised. Note that the plastic lugs in the pedal are very stiff, and it will not be possible to release them by hand. Using the tool, release the securing lugs, and pull the pedal from the servo pushrod (see illustration 10.5a).

10 Again working in the footwell, undo the nuts securing the servo unit to the bulkhead, then return to the engine compartment and manoeuvre the servo unit out of position, and recover the gasket where fitted.

Refitting

11 Check the servo unit vacuum hose sealing grommet for signs of damage or deterioration, and renew if necessary.

12 Where applicable, fit a new gasket to the rear of the servo unit, and then reposition the unit in the engine compartment.

13 From inside the vehicle, ensure that the servo unit pushrod is correctly engaged with the brake pedal, and push the pedal onto the pushrod ball. Check the pushrod ball is securely engaged, then refit the servo unit mounting nuts and tighten them to the specified torque.

14 As applicable, refit the connecting plate, air duct and cover.

15 Refit the facia trim panels.

16 On LHD models with manual transmission, refit the gearchange cables and support bracket.

17 Carefully ease the vacuum hose back into position in the servo, taking great care not to displace the sealing grommet. Refit the heat shield to the servo and, where applicable, refit the vacuum sensor and wiring.

18 Refit the master cylinder as described in Section 13 of this Chapter.

19 On completion, start the engine and check for air leaks at the vacuum hose-to-servo unit connection; check the operation of the braking system.

12 Servo non-return valve – testing, removal and refitting

1 The non-return valve is located in the vacuum hose leading from the inlet manifold or vacuum pump to the brake servo.

Removal

2 Ease the vacuum hose out of the servo unit, taking care not to displace the grommet.

3 Note the routing of the hose, then slacken the retaining clip(s) and disconnect the opposite end of the hose assembly from the manifold/pump/hose, and remove it from the car.

Testing

4 Examine the check valve and vacuum hose for signs of damage, and renew if necessary.

5 The valve may be tested, by blowing through it in both directions; air should flow through the valve in one direction only; when blown through from the servo unit end of the valve. Renew the valve if this is not the case.

6 Examine the servo unit rubber sealing grommet for signs of damage or deterioration, and renew as necessary.

Refitting

7 Ensure that the sealing grommet is correctly fitted to the servo unit.

8 Ease the hose union into position in the servo, taking great care not to displace or damage the grommet.

9 Ensure that the hose is correctly routed, and connect it to the inlet manifold/pump/hose, ensuring the hose is secured in the retaining clips.

10 On completion, start the engine and check the valve-to-servo unit connection for signs of air leaks.

13 Master cylinder – removal, overhaul and refitting

Note: *Before starting work, refer to the warning at the beginning of Section 2 concerning the dangers of hydraulic fluid. A new master cylinder O-ring will be required on refitting.*

Removal

1 Disconnect the battery negative lead. Refer to 'Disconnecting the battery' in Reference chapter. Remove the engine top cover and air inlet ducting.

2 On LHD models, remove the battery and tray with reference to Chapter 5, Section 3.

3 Remove the master cylinder reservoir cap (disconnect the wiring plug from the brake fluid level warning switch), and siphon

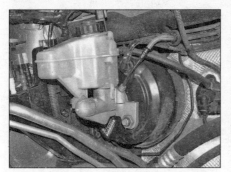

13.3a Brake master cylinder and fluid reservoir

13.3b Filler cap incorporating brake fluid level warning switch

13.5 Clutch fluid supply hose and union

the hydraulic fluid from the reservoir **(see illustrations).**

Note: *Do not siphon the fluid by mouth, as it is poisonous; use a syringe or an old poultry baster.*

4 Disconnect the wiring from the brake light switch (where applicable).

5 On manual transmission models, disconnect and plug the clutch master cylinder supply hose from the master cylinder reservoir **(see illustration).**

6 Wipe clean the area around the brake pipe unions on the side of the master cylinder, and place absorbent rags beneath the pipe unions to catch any leaking fluid. Make a note of the correct fitted positions of the unions, then unscrew the union nuts and carefully withdraw the pipes. Plug or tape over the pipe ends and master cylinder orifices, to minimise the loss of brake fluid, and to prevent the entry of dirt into the system. Wash off any spilt fluid immediately with cold water.

7 Unscrew and remove the two nuts and washers securing the master cylinder to the vacuum servo unit, remove the heat shield (where fitted), then withdraw the unit from the engine compartment **(see illustration).** Remove the O-ring from the rear of the master cylinder, and discard it.

Overhaul

8 If the master cylinder is faulty, it must be renewed. Repair kits are not available from an Audi dealer, so the cylinder must be treated as a sealed unit.

9 The only items which can be renewed are the mounting seals for the fluid reservoir; if these show signs of deterioration, prise them out with a screwdriver. Lubricate the new seals with clean brake fluid, and press them into the master cylinder ports.

Refitting

10 Remove all traces of dirt from the master cylinder and servo unit mating surfaces, and fit a new O-ring to the groove on the master cylinder body.

11 Fit the master cylinder to the servo unit, ensuring that the servo unit pushrod enters the master cylinder bore centrally. Refit the heat shield (where applicable), and the master cylinder mounting nuts and washers, and tighten them to the specified torque.

12 Wipe clean the brake pipe unions, then refit them to the master cylinder ports and tighten them securely.

13 On manual transmission models, reconnect the clutch master cylinder supply hose to the reservoir.

14 Refill the master cylinder reservoir with new fluid, and bleed the complete hydraulic system as described in Section 2.

15 Reconnect the wiring to the brake level sender unit and brake light switch as applicable.

16 On LHD models, refit the battery tray and battery.

17 Refit the air ducting where necessary, then reconnect the battery negative lead.

14 Handbrake – adjustment

1 To check the handbrake adjustment, first apply the footbrake firmly several times to establish correct pad-to-disc clearance, then apply and release the handbrake several times.

2 Applying normal moderate pressure, pull the handbrake lever to the fully applied position, counting the number of clicks from the handbrake ratchet mechanism. If adjustment is correct, there should be approximately 4 to 7 clicks before the handbrake is fully applied. If this is not the case, adjust as follows.

3 Remove the rear ashtray and unclip the cover from the rear of the centre console **(see illustration),** to gain access to the handbrake lever.

4 Chock the front wheels, then jack up the rear of the vehicle and support it on axle stands (see *'Jacking and vehicle support'* in Reference chapter).

5 With the handbrake fully released, slacken the handbrake adjuster nut until both the rear caliper handbrake levers are back against their stops **(see illustration).**

6 From this point, tighten the adjuster nut until both handbrake levers just move off the caliper stops. Ensure that the gap between each caliper handbrake lever and its stop is between 1.0 and 1.5 mm, and ensure both the right- and left-hand gaps are equal **(see**

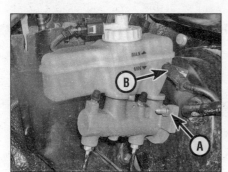

13.7 Master cylinder retaining nuts (A), and clutch master cylinder supply hose (B)

14.3 Remove the rear storage compartment

14.5 Slacken the adjuster nut (arrowed)

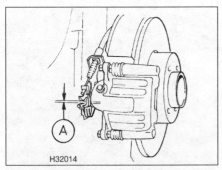

14.6 Turn the adjuster nut until a gap (A) of between 1.0 and 1.5 mm can be seen

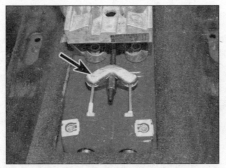

15.4a Handbrake cables and equaliser plate

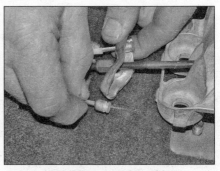

15.4b Disengage the cables

illustration). Check that both wheels/discs rotate freely, and then check the adjustment by applying the handbrake fully and counting the clicks from the handbrake ratchet (see paragraph 2). If necessary, re-adjust.

7 Once adjustment is correct, refit the handbrake cover and ashtray to the centre console.

15 Handbrake lever – removal and refitting

Removal

1 Remove the centre console as described in Chapter 11, Section 26.

2 If desired, remove the handbrake lever cover sleeve by depressing the locating tag with a screwdriver, then sliding the sleeve from the lever.

3 Unclip the handbrake 'on' warning light switch from the handbrake lever mounting bracket **(see illustration 17.3)**.

4 Slacken the handbrake cable adjuster nut sufficiently to allow the ends of the cables to be disengaged from the equaliser plate **(see illustrations)**.

5 Unscrew the retaining nuts, and withdraw the lever and bracket assembly from the floor **(see illustration)**.

Refitting

6 Refitting is a reversal of removal, bearing in mind the following points.

a) *Prior to refitting the handbrake cover, adjust the handbrake as described in Section 14.*

b) *Check the operation of the handbrake 'on' warning switch prior to refitting the centre console.*

16 Handbrake cables – removal and refitting

Removal

1 Remove the centre console as described in Chapter 11, Section 26, to gain access to the handbrake lever. The handbrake cable consists of two sections, a right- and a left-hand section, which are linked to the lever by an equaliser plate. Each section can be removed individually.

2 Chock the front wheels, then jack up the rear of the car and support it on axle stands (see *'Jacking and vehicle support'* in Reference chapter).

3 Slacken the handbrake cable adjuster nut sufficiently to allow the ends of the cables to be disengaged from the equaliser plate.

4 Working back along the length of the cable, note its correct routing, and free it from all the relevant guides and retaining clips.

5 Disengage the inner cable from the caliper handbrake lever, then remove the outer cable retaining clip and detach the cable from the caliper **(see illustration)**. Withdraw the cable from underneath the vehicle.

Refitting

6 Refitting is a reversal of removal, bearing in mind the following points.

a) *When locating the handbrake cable sheath in the guide on the rear trailing arm, the cable clamping ring must lie in the middle of the clip.*

b) *Before refitting the centre console, adjust the handbrake as described in Section 14.*

17 Handbrake 'on' warning light switch – removal and refitting

Removal

1 Remove the centre console as described in Chapter 11, Section 26.

2 Disconnect the wiring plug from the switch.

3 Squeeze the securing lugs, and withdraw the switch from the handbrake lever assembly **(see illustration)**.

Refitting

4 Refitting is a reversal of removal.

18 Brake light switch – removal and refitting

Pedal bracket switch

Removal

1 The brake light switch is located on the brake pedal bracket beneath the facia.

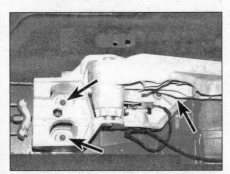

15.5 Handbrake assembly mounting nuts (arrowed)

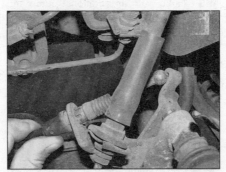

16.5 Release the cable inner from its lever and withdraw the cable from the caliper

17.3 Removing the handbrake 'on' warning light switch

18.3 Disconnect the brake switch

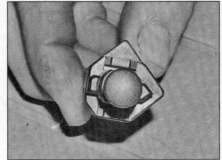

18.6 Align the shaped lug with the corresponding cut-out in the bracket

20.1 ABS hydraulic unit

2 Working in the driver's footwell, remove the lower facia panel; see Chapter 11, Section 27.
3 Reach up behind the facia and disconnect the wiring connector from the switch **(see illustration)**.
4 Twist the switch through 90° and release it from the mounting bracket.

Refitting

5 Prior to installation, fully extend the brake light switch plunger.
6 Fully depress and hold the brake pedal, then manoeuvre the switch into position. Align the shaped lug of the switch with the corresponding cut-out in the bracket **(see illustration)**. Secure the switch in position it by pushing it into the bracket and twisting it through 90°, then release the brake pedal.
7 Reconnect the wiring connector, and check the operation of the brake lights. The brake lights should illuminate after the brake pedal has travelled approximately 5 mm. If the switch is not functioning correctly, it is faulty and must be renewed; no adjustment is possible.
8 On completion, refit the lower facia panel.

Master cylinder switch

9 On certain models, the brake light switch is located on the master cylinder. Remove the engine top cover, and where applicable, remove the air inlet ducting to improve access.
10 Disconnect the wiring from the switch.
11 Unscrew the mounting bolt, then pull the switch from the bottom of the master cylinder, and remove it from the locking lug at the top.

Refitting

12 Refitting is a reversal of removal, but tighten the mounting bolt securely.

19 Anti-lock braking system (ABS) – general information and precautions

1 The anti-lock braking system (ABS) fitted as standard to all models prevents wheel lock-up under heavy braking, and not only optimises stopping distances, but also improves steering control. By electronically monitoring the speed of each roadwheel in relation to the other wheels, the system can detect when a wheel is about to lock-up, before control is actually lost. The brake fluid pressure applied to that wheel's brake caliper is then decreased and restored ('modulated') several times a second until control is regained. The system components are: four wheel speed sensors, a hydraulic unit with integral Electronic Control Unit (ECU), brake lines and a dashboard-mounted warning light. The four wheel sensors are mounted on the wheel hub carriers. Each wheel has a rotating toothed hub mounted on the driveshaft (front) or on the hub (rear). The wheel speed sensors are mounted in close proximity to these hubs. The teeth produce a voltage waveform whose frequency varies with the speed of the hubs. These waveforms are transmitted to the ECU, and used to calculate the rotational speed of each wheel. The ECU has a self-diagnostic facility, to inhibit the operation of the ABS if a fault is detected, lighting the dashboard-mounted warning light. The braking system will then revert to conventional, non-ABS operation. If the nature of the fault is not immediately obvious upon inspection, the vehicle must be taken to an Audi dealer, who will have the diagnostic equipment required to interrogate the ABS ECU electronically and pinpoint the problem.
2 There are two ABS systems fitted to the models covered in this Manual.
• The Mark 70 version includes a traction control system (TCS), which uses the basic ABS system, with an additional pump and valves fitted to the hydraulic actuator. If wheelspin is detected at a speed below 30 mph, one of the valves opens, to allow the pump to pressurise the relevant brake, until the spinning wheel slows to a rotational speed corresponding to the speed of the vehicle. This has the effect of transferring torque to the wheel with most traction. At the same time, the throttle plate is closed slightly, to reduce the torque from the engine.
• The Mark 60 version includes electronic differential locking (EDL) and an electronic stability programme (ESP). The EDL system applies the brake of the spinning wheel in order to transfer torque to the wheel with the better grip. On models with ESP, the system recognises critical driving conditions and stabilises the vehicle by individual wheel braking and by intervention in the engine control, which occurs independently of the position of the brake and accelerator pedals.
3 The operation of the ABS system is entirely dependent on electrical signals. To prevent the system responding to any inaccurate signals, a built-in safety circuit monitors all signals received by the ECU. If an inaccurate signal or low battery voltage is detected, the ABS system is automatically shut down, and the warning light on the instrument panel is illuminated, to inform the driver that the ABS system is not operational. Normal braking will still be available, however.
4 If a fault does develop in the ABS system, the car must be taken to an Audi dealer for fault diagnosis and repair.

20 Anti-lock braking system (ABS) components – removal and refitting

Hydraulic unit

1 Removal and refitting of the hydraulic unit is best entrusted to an Audi dealer, as a fault diagnosis check must be performed on completion using specialist equipment **(see illustration)**.

Electronic control unit (ECU)

2 The ECU is mounted underneath the hydraulic unit. Although it can be separated from the hydraulic unit, due to the delicacy of the components and the need for absolute cleanliness, it is recommended that the work be entrusted to an Audi dealer.

Front wheel sensor

Removal

3 Chock the rear wheels, then firmly apply the handbrake, jack up the front of the car and support on axle stands (see *Jacking and vehicle support* in Reference chapter). Remove the appropriate front roadwheel.
4 Disconnect the electrical connector from the sensor by carefully lifting up the retaining

20.4 Disconnect the wiring...

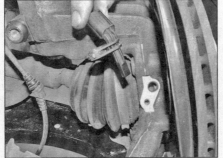

20.5...and unbolt the front wheel sensor

20.11 Rear wheel sensor securing bolt (arrowed)

tag, and pulling the connector from the sensor **(see illustration)**.

5 Slacken and remove the hexagon socket-head bolt securing the sensor to the hub carrier, and remove the sensor from the car **(see illustration)**.

Refitting

6 Ensure that the sensor and hub carrier sealing faces are clean.

7 Apply a thin coat of multi-purpose grease to the mounting hole inner surface, then fit the sensor to the hub carrier. Refit the retaining bolt and tighten it to the specified torque.

8 Ensure that the sensor wiring is correctly routed and retained by all the necessary clips, and reconnect the wiring connector.

9 Refit the roadwheel, then lower the car to the ground and tighten the roadwheel bolts to the specified torque.

Rear wheel sensor

Removal

10 Chock the front wheels, then jack up the rear of the car and support it on axle stands (see *'Jacking and vehicle support'* in Reference chapter). Remove the appropriate roadwheel.

11 Remove the rear wheel speed sensor as described in paragraphs 4 and 5 **(see illustration)**.

Refitting

12 Refit the sensor as described above in paragraphs 6 to 9.

Front reluctor rings

13 The front reluctor rings are integral with

the wheel bearings, and can only be inspected after removal of the driveshafts. If faulty, the bearings must be renewed.

Rear reluctor rings

14 The rear reluctor rings are integral with the rear wheel bearings, and can only be inspected after removal of the rear hubs. If faulty, the rear hub complete with bearing must be renewed as described in Chapter 10.

---

21 Servo unit mechanical vacuum pump – testing, removal and refitting

---

Testing

1 The operation of the braking system vacuum pump can be checked using a vacuum gauge. First, remove the engine top cover and the air cleaner assembly.

Note: *On 1.9 litre engines vacuum pump is combined with the fuel lift pump to form what is known as a 'Tandem pump'.*

2 Disconnect the vacuum hose from the pump, and connect the gauge to the pump union using a suitable length of hose.

3 Start the engine and allow it to idle, and then measure the vacuum created by the pump. As a guide, after one minute, a minimum of approximately 500 mm Hg should be recorded. If the vacuum registered is significantly less than this, it is likely that the pump is faulty. However, seek the advice of an Audi dealer before condemning the pump.

4 Reconnect the vacuum hose. Overhaul of

the vacuum pump is not possible, since no major components are available separately for it. If faulty, the complete pump assembly must be renewed.

Removal

1.9 litre engines

Note: *A new pump O-ring will be required on refitting.*

5 Release the retaining clip (where fitted), and disconnect the vacuum hose from the top of pump.

6 Note the locations of the fuel supply (white) and return (blue) hoses, then disconnect them.

7 Unscrew the two main upper mounting bolts and the two small lower mounting bolts.

8 Withdraw the vacuum pump from the cylinder head, and recover the O-ring seals. Discard them and obtain new ones for using on refitting.

1.6 and 2.0 litre engines

Note: *A new pump O-ring will be required on refitting.*

9 Disconnect the small vacuum pipe from the vacuum hose connector on the top of the vacuum pump **(see illustration)**.

10 Release the securing clips and remove the air intake hose from across the end of the cylinder head, to access the vacuum pump.

11 Pull the vacuum hose from the top of the pump, noting the rubber seal may stay on the vacuum pump outlet pipe **(see illustration)**.

12 Unscrew the four mounting bolts and withdraw the vacuum pump from the cylinder head **(see illustration)**. Recover the O-ring

21.9 Disconnect the small vacuum pipe

21.11 Remove the vacuum hose and rubber seal

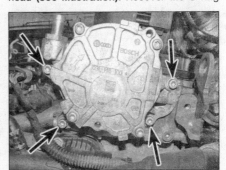

21.12 Vacuum pump securing bolts (arrowed)

seal and discard, as a new one will be required for refitting.

Refitting

1.9 litre engines

13 Fit the new O-ring seals to the vacuum pump, and apply a smear of oil to aid installation.

14 Manoeuvre the vacuum pump into position, making sure that the slot in the pump drive gear aligns with the slot on the pump driveshaft.

15 Refit the pump retaining bolts, and tighten to the specified torque.

16 Reconnect the fuel hoses.

17 Reconnect the vacuum hose and secure with the retaining clip (where fitted).

18 Refit the air filter housing and engine top cover.

1.6 and 2.0 litre engines

19 Fit the new O-ring seal to the vacuum pump, and apply a smear of oil to aid installation.

20 Manoeuvre the vacuum pump into position, making sure the slot in the pump drive gear engages with the slot on the pump driveshaft.

21 Refit the pump retaining bolts and tighten them to the specified torque.

22 Reconnect the vacuum hoses and secure with the retaining clip (where fitted). If the vacuum hose seal is still fitted to the outlet pipe on the vacuum pump, remove it and fit it inside the end of the vacuum hose before refitting.

23 Refit the air intake hose and engine top cover.

22 Servo unit electric vacuum pump – testing, removal and refitting

Note: *The electric vacuum pump is only fitted to certain models with the DSG semi-automatic transmission.*

Testing

1 With the engine stopped, depress the brake pedal several times to exhaust the vacuum in the servo unit. The pedal will become firm.

2 Start the engine, and then slowly depress the brake pedal. An audible 'click' must be heard as the electric vacuum pump is activated, and the pedal will be easier to depress. Confirmation that the pump is running can be made by an assistant touching the pump as the pedal is depressed.

3 Overhaul of the electric vacuum pump is not possible, therefore, if faulty, the pump must be renewed.

Removal

4 The electric brake vacuum pump is located on a bracket on the front of the transmission. Apply the handbrake, and then jack up the front of the vehicle and support it on axle stands (refer to 'Jacking and vehicle support' in Reference chapter). Remove the left-hand front roadwheel.

5 Disconnect the vacuum hose from the pump.

6 Disconnect the wiring from the vacuum pump and release it from the clip.

7 Unscrew the bolts securing the bracket to the transmission and withdraw the assembly from the transmission.

8 Unbolt the bracket from the vacuum pump.

Refitting

9 Refitting is a reversal of removal, but tighten the mounting bolts to the specified torque.

Chapter 10
Suspension and steering systems

Contents

Degrees of difficulty

Easy, suitable for novice with little experience	Fairly easy, suitable for beginner with some experience	Fairly difficult, suitable for competent DIY mechanic	Difficult, suitable for experienced DIY mechanic	Very difficult, suitable for expert DIY or professional

Specifications

Front suspension
Type . . . .   Independent, with MacPherson struts incorporating coil springs, telescopic shock absorbers and anti-roll bar

Rear suspension
Type . . . .   Trailing arm with Multi-link transverse arms, separate gas-filled telescopic shock absorbers, coil springs and anti-roll bar

Steering
Type . . . .   Rack-and-pinion. Electro-mechanical power assistance standard

Wheel alignment and steering angles
Front wheel:
  Camber angle:
    Standard suspension . . . .   -30' ± 30'
    Sports suspension . . . .   -41' ± 30'
    Heavy duty suspension . . . .   -14' ± 30'
    Maximum difference between sides (all models) . . . .   30'
  Castor angle:
    Standard suspension . . . .   7° 34' ± 30'
    Sports suspension . . . .   7° 47' ± 30'
    Heavy duty suspension . . . .   7° 17' ± 30'
    Maximum difference between sides (all models) . . . .   30'
  Toe setting . . . .   10' ± 10'
  Toe-out on turns (20° left or right):
    Standard suspension . . . .   1° 38' ± 20'
    Sports suspension . . . .   1° 40' ± 20'
    Heavy duty suspension . . . .   1° 38' ± 20'
Rear wheel:
  Camber angle . . . .   -1°20' ± 30'
  Maximum difference between sides . . . .   30'
  Toe setting . . . .   +10' ± 12.5'

Roadwheels

Type . . . . Aluminium alloy

Tyres

Size . . . . 205/55R16, 205/50R17, 225/45R17 and 225/40R18
Pressures . . . . Refer to the tyre pressure data sticker on the edge of the driver's side front door

Torque wrench settings	Nm	lbf ft
Steering		
Steering column:		
To mounting bracket.	20	15
Mounting bracket to body	20	15
Strut to mounting bracket/body.	20	15
Universal joint to steering gear:		
Stage 1	20	15
Stage 2	Angle-tighten a further 90°	
Steering gear:		
To subframe:		
Stage 1	50	37
Stage 2	Angle-tighten a further 90°	
Shield	6	4
Steering wheel to column.	50	37
Track rod end to track rod	55	41
Track rod end to wheel bearing housing:		
Stage 1	20	15
Stage 2	Angle-tighten a further 90°	
Track rod to steering gear rack	100	74
Front suspension		
Anti-roll bar link	65	48
Anti-roll bar to subframe:		
Stage 1	20	15
Stage 2	Angle-tighten a further 90°	
Driveshaft bolt	See Chapter 8	
Hub to wheel bearing housing:		
Stage 1	70	52
Stage 2	Angle-tighten a further 90°	
Lower arm:		
To bracket: *		
Stage 1	70	52
Stage 2	Angle-tighten a further 180°	
To front wheel bearing housing (lower balljoint)*	60	44
Mounting bracket to body:		
Stage 1	70	52
Stage 2	Angle-tighten a further 90°	
Mounting bracket to bracket:		
Stage 1	50	37
Stage 2	Angle-tighten a further 90°	
Rear engine mounting:		
To subframe:		
Stage 1	100	74
Stage 2	Angle-tighten a further 90°	
To transmission:		
Stage 1	40	30
Stage 2	Angle-tighten a further 90°	
Subframe-to-underbody/bracket bolts: *		
Stage 1	70	52
Stage 2	Angle-tighten a further 90°	
Splash plate to wheel bearing housing	10	7
Suspension strut:		
Bottom clamp: *		
Stage 1	70	52
Stage 2	Angle-tighten a further 90°	
Upper mounting: *		
Stage 1	15	11
Stage 2	Angle-tighten a further 90°	
Upper piston rod	60	44
Vehicle level sender to subframe and lower arm	9	7

Torque wrench settings (continued)

	Nm	lbf ft
Rear suspension		
ABS speed sensor	8	6
Anti-roll bar:		
To subframe:		
Stage 1	25	18
Stage 2	Angle-tighten a further 45°	
Anti-roll bar link	40	30
Hub to wheel bearing housing: *		
Stage 1	180	133
Stage 2	Angle-tighten a further 180°	
Lower transverse link to wheel bearing housing:		
Stage 1	90	66
Stage 2	Angle-tighten a further 90°	
Radius rods:		
To body:		
Stage 1	40	30
Stage 2	Angle-tighten a further 90°	
To subframe:		
Stage 1	90	66
Stage 2	Angle-tighten a further 45°	
Shock absorber:		
To wheel bearing housing	180	133
To shock absorber mounting bracket	25	18
To body:		
Stage 1	50	37
Stage 2	Angle-tighten a further 45°	
Splash plate to wheel bearing housing	12	9
Stone deflector to transverse link	8	6
Subframe to body:		
Stage 1	90	66
Stage 2	Angle-tighten a further 90°	
Track control rod to subframe:		
Stage 1	90	66
Stage 2	Angle-tighten a further 90°	
Track control rod to wheel bearing housing:		
Stage 1	130	96
Stage 2	Angle-tighten a further 90°	
Trailing arm:		
To wheel bearing housing		
Stage 1	90	66
Stage 2	Angle-tighten a further 90°	
To mounting bracket:		
Stage 1	90	66
Stage 2	Angle-tighten a further 90°	
Mounting bracket to underbody:		
Stage 1	50	37
Stage 2	Angle-tighten a further 45°	
Transverse links to subframe	95	70
Upper transverse link to wheel bearing housing:		
Stage 1	130	96
Stage 2	Angle-tighten a further 90°	
Vehicle level sender	5	4

Roadwheels

	Nm	lbf ft
Roadwheel bolts	120	89

Do not re-use fastenings

1 General Information

1 The independent front suspension is of the MacPherson strut type, incorporating coil springs and integral telescopic shock absorbers. The struts are located by transverse lower suspension arms, which use rubber inner mounting bushes, and incorporate a balljoint at the outer ends. The front wheel bearing housings, which carry the wheel bearings, brake calipers and the hub/disc assemblies, are attached to the MacPherson struts by clamp bolts, and connected to the lower arms through the balljoints. A front anti-roll bar is fitted to all models. The anti-roll bar is rubber-mounted, and is connected to both lower suspension arms by short links.

2 The rear suspension consists of a trailing arm, rubber-mounted at its front end to the underbody, a wheel bearing housing, lower main transverse link and coil spring, track control rod, upper transverse link, and separate shock absorber. A rear anti-roll bar

is fitted to all models. The anti-roll bar is rubber-mounted on the rear subframe, and is connected to the wheel bearing housings on each side by a short connecting link.

3 The safety steering column incorporates an intermediate shaft at its lower end. The intermediate shaft is connected to both the steering column and steering gear by universal joints, although the shaft is supplied as part of the column assembly and cannot be separated. Both the inner steering column and intermediate shaft have splined sections, which collapse during a major frontal impact. The outer column is also telescopic with two sections, to facilitate reach adjustment.

4 The steering gear is mounted onto the front subframe, and is connected by two track rods, with balljoints at their inner and outer ends, to the steering arms projecting rearwards from the wheel bearing housings. The track rod ends are threaded to the track rods in order to allow adjustment of the front wheel toe setting. The steering gear has electro-mechanical assistance, and incorporates an integral control unit. It is only functional when the engine is running. There are no hydraulic components, and steering assistance is automatically matched to the vehicle speed, steering wheel torque and steering wheel angle.

2 Front wheel bearing housing – removal and refitting

Note: *Renewal of the hub bearings does not require removal of the wheel bearing housing (see Section 3). This Section describes removal of the wheel bearing housing leaving the suspension strut in position, however, if necessary, it can be removed together with the suspension strut, and then separated on the bench. All self-locking nuts and bolts disturbed on removal must be renewed as a matter of course.*

Removal

Note: *A new hub bolt will be required on refitting. There are two different types of bolts fitted, one is ribbed under the face of the bolt head and one is smooth. The torque*

2.4 Removing the brake hose/wiring bracket

setting is different for each type of bolt, so it is important to make sure you check which is fitted Refer to the information contained in Chapter 8 Section 2.

1 Remove the wheel trim/hub cap (as applicable) and loosen the driveshaft retaining bolt (hub bolt) by 90° with the vehicle resting on its wheels. Also loosen the wheel bolts.

Note: *Do not loosen the hub bolt more than 90° at this stage, or the wheel bearing may be damaged.*

2 Apply the handbrake, then jack up the front of the vehicle and support it on axle stands (see *'Jacking and vehicle support'* in Reference chapter). Remove the front roadwheel.

3 Unscrew and remove the driveshaft retaining bolt.

4 Remove the ABS wheel sensor as described in Chapter 9, Section 20. Also, unbolt the brake hose/wiring bracket from the strut **(see illustrations)**.

5 Remove the brake disc as described in Chapter 9, Section 6.

6 Unbolt the splash plate from the wheel bearing housing.

7 Loosen the nut securing the steering track rod balljoint to the wheel bearing housing. To do this, fit a ring spanner to the nut, and then hold the balljoint pin stationary using an Allen key. With the nut removed, it may be possible to release the balljoint from the wheel bearing housing by turning the balljoint pin with an Allen key. If not, leave the nut on by a few turns to protect the threads, then use a universal balljoint separator to release the

2.8 Lower balljoint-to-arm retaining nuts

balljoint. Remove the nut completely once the taper has been released.

8 Unscrew the front suspension lower balljoint-to-lower arm retaining nuts **(see illustration)**, then lever the lower arm down to release the balljoint studs from the arm. Now use a soft-faced mallet to tap the driveshaft from the hub splines while pulling out the bottom end of the wheel bearing housing. If the driveshaft is tight on the splines, it may be necessary to use a puller bolted to the hub to remove it. Tie the driveshaft to one side.

9 Note which way round it is fitted, then unscrew the nut and remove the clamp bolt securing the wheel bearing housing to the bottom of the strut.

10 The wheel bearing housing must now be released from the strut. To do this, Audi technicians insert a special tool into the split wheel bearing housing, and turn it through 90° to open up the clamp. A similar tool can be made out of an old screwdriver, or alternatively a suitable cold chisel can be driven into the split as a wedge. Slightly press inwards the top of the wheel bearing housing, and then push it downwards from the bottom of the strut **(see illustrations)**.

Refitting

11 Ensure that the driveshaft outer joint and hub splines are clean and dry, and then lubricate the splines with fresh engine oil. Also lubricate the threads and contact surface of the hub nut/bolt with oil.

12 Lift the wheel bearing assembly into

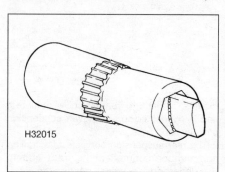
2.10a Tool used by Audi technicians to open up the split wheel bearing housing

2.10b Using a cold chisel to open up the wheel bearing housing and release the suspension strut

2.10c Withdrawing the wheel bearing housing from the bottom of the suspension strut

3.6 Splash plate mounting bolts (wheel bearing housing removed)

3.8a Removing the front hub/wheel bearing from the wheel bearing housing

3.8b Front hub/wheel bearing

position, and engage the hub with the splines on the outer end of the driveshaft. Fit the new hub bolt, tightening it by hand only at this stage.

13 Engage the wheel bearing housing with the bottom of the suspension strut; making sure that the hole in the side plate aligns with the holes in the split housing. Remove the tool used to open the split.

14 Insert the strut-to-wheel bearing housing clamp bolt from the front, and fit the new retaining nut. Tighten the nut to the specified torque.

15 Refit the lower arm balljoint to the lower arm, and tighten the nuts to the specified torque.

16 Refit the track rod balljoint to the wheel bearing housing, then fit a new retaining nut and tighten it to the specified torque. If necessary, hold the balljoint pin with an Allen key while tightening the nut.

17 Refit the splash plate and tighten the bolts.

18 Refit the brake disc and caliper with reference to Chapter 9, Section 6.

19 Refit the ABS wheel sensor as described in Chapter 9.

20 Have an assistant depress the brake pedal, and then tighten the driveshaft retaining bolt to the Stage 1 torque given in the Specifications.

21 Refit the roadwheel and lower the vehicle to the ground, then angle-tighten the driveshaft bolt through the Stage 2 angle. Refit the wheel trim/hub cap.

3 Front hub bearings – renewal

Note: *The bearing is a sealed, pre-adjusted and pre-lubricated, double-row roller type, and requires no maintenance. It is bolted to the wheel bearing housing.*

Note: *A new hub bolt will be required on refitting. There are two different types of bolts fitted, one is ribbed under the face of the bolt head and one is smooth. The torque setting is different for each type of bolt, so it is important to make sure you check which is fitted. Refer to the information contained in Chapter 8, Section 2.*

1 Remove the wheel trim/hub cap (as applicable) and loosen the driveshaft retaining

bolt (hub bolt) with the vehicle resting on its wheels.

Note: *Do not loosen the hub bolt more than 90° at this stage, or the wheel bearing may be damaged.*

2 Apply the handbrake, then jack up the front of the vehicle and support it on axle stands (see 'Jacking and vehicle support' in Reference chapter). Remove the front roadwheel.

3 Unscrew and remove the driveshaft retaining bolt.

4 Remove the ABS wheel sensor as described in Chapter 9, Section 20.

5 Remove the brake disc as described in Chapter 9, Section 6. This procedure includes removing the brake caliper; however do not disconnect the hydraulic brake hose from the caliper. Using a piece of wire or string, tie the caliper to the front suspension coil spring, to avoid placing any strain on the hydraulic brake hose.

6 Unbolt the splash plate from the wheel bearing housing **(see illustration)**.

7 Press the driveshaft outer stub towards the transmission as far as possible, then unscrew and remove the wheel bearing retaining bolts from the rear of the housing.

8 Remove the hub/wheel bearing complete with hub from the outside of the housing while sliding it from the driveshaft splines **(see illustrations)**.

9 Fit the new wheel bearing to the housing and engage the hub splines with the driveshaft outer stub.

10 Refit the splash plate and tighten the bolts.

11 Refit the brake disc and caliper with reference to Chapter 9, Section 6.

12 Refit the ABS wheel sensor as described in Chapter 9, Section 20.

13 Pull the driveshaft outer stub fully into the hub and fit a new hub bolt, hand-tight at this stage.

14 Have an assistant depress the brake pedal, and then tighten the driveshaft retaining bolt to the Stage 1 torque given in the Specifications.

15 Refit the roadwheel and lower the vehicle to the ground, then angle-tighten the driveshaft bolt through the Stage 2 angle. Refit the wheel trim/hub cap.

4 Front suspension strut – removal, overhaul and refitting

Note: *This section describes removal of the suspension strut leaving the wheel bearing housing in position, however, if necessary, it can be removed together with the wheel bearing housing, then separated on the bench. All self-locking nuts and bolts disturbed on removal must be renewed as a matter of course.*

Removal

Note: *A new hub bolt will be required on refitting. There are two different types of bolts fitted, one is ribbed under the face of the bolt head and one is smooth. The torque setting is different for each type of bolt, so it is important to make sure you check which is fitted. Refer to the information contained in Chapter 8, Section 2.*

1 Remove the wheel trim/hub cap (as applicable) and loosen the driveshaft retaining bolt (hub bolt) with the vehicle resting on its wheels.

Note: *Do not loosen the hub bolt more than 90° at this stage, or the wheel bearing may be damaged.*

2 Apply the handbrake, then jack up the front of the vehicle and support it on axle stands (see 'Jacking and vehicle support' in Reference chapter). Remove the appropriate roadwheel.

3 Unscrew the nut and disconnect the anti-roll bar link from the strut **(see illustration)**.

4.3 Disconnect the anti-roll bar link from the strut

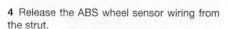

4.5 Unscrew and remove the driveshaft retaining bolt

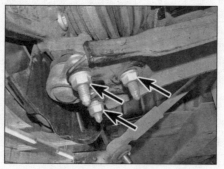

4.6a Unscrew the nuts...

4.6b...and detach the lower arm from the balljoint studs...

4 Release the ABS wheel sensor wiring from the strut.

5 Unscrew and remove the driveshaft retaining bolt **(see illustration)**.

6 Unscrew the front suspension lower balljoint-to-lower arm retaining nuts, then lever the lower arm down to release the balljoint studs. Now use a soft-faced mallet to tap the driveshaft from the hub splines while pulling out the bottom end of the wheel bearing housing **(see illustrations)**. If the driveshaft is tight on the splines, it may be necessary to use a puller bolted to the hub to remove it. Tie the driveshaft to one side, then refit the lower balljoint to the lower arm and secure with the nuts, hand-tightened.

7 Note which way round it is fitted, then unscrew the nut and remove the clamp bolt securing the wheel bearing housing to the bottom of the strut **(see illustration)**.

8 The wheel bearing housing must now

be released from the strut. To do this, Audi technicians insert a special tool into the split wheel bearing housing, and turn it through 90° to open up the clamp. A similar tool such as an Allen key can be used, or alternatively a suitable cold chisel can be driven into the split as a wedge. Slightly press inwards the top of the wheel bearing housing, and then push it downwards from the bottom of the strut **(see illustration)**. Support the wheel bearing housing to one side without straining the hydraulic brake hose.

9 Remove the wiper arms (Chapter 12, Section 17) and the plenum chamber cover (Chapter 12, Section 18).

10 To ensure correct refitting, mark the strut upper mounting in relation to the body. If the reason for removing the strut is overhaul, loosen the upper mounting centre nut one turn, while holding the piston rod with an Allen key.

11 Support the strut, then unscrew the upper

mounting bolts and lower the strut from under the wheel arch **(see illustrations)**.

Overhaul

⚠️ *Warning: Before attempting to dismantle the suspension strut, a suitable tool to hold the coil spring in compression must be obtained. Adjustable coil spring compressors are readily available, and are recommended for this operation. Any attempt to dismantle the strut without such a tool is likely to result in damage or personal injury.*

12 With the strut removed from the car, clean away all external dirt. If necessary, mount it upright in a vice during the dismantling procedure.

13 Fit the spring compressor, and compress the coil spring until all tension is relieved from the upper spring seat **(see illustration)**.

14 Unscrew and remove the upper centre

4.6c...now remove the driveshaft from the hub splines

4.7 Remove the clamp bolt...

4.8 then use a suitable tool to expand the split, so that the strut can be pulled from the wheel bearing housing

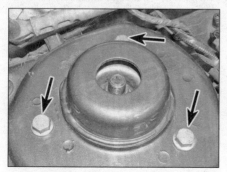

4.11a Unscrew the upper mounting bolts...

4.11b...and lower the strut from under the wheel arch

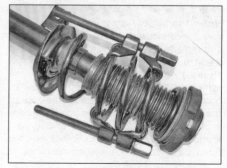

4.13 Compress the coil spring with the compressor tool

retaining nut, whilst retaining the strut piston with a suitable Allen key, then remove the mounting, thrust bearing, and coil spring **(see illustrations)**.

15 Remove the protective sleeve and upper bearing race, and then remove the bump stop from the upper mounting **(see illustrations)**.

16 With the strut assembly now completely dismantled, examine all the components for wear, damage or deformation, and check the bearing for smoothness of operation. Renew any of the components as necessary.

17 Examine the strut for signs of fluid leakage. Check the strut piston for signs of pitting along its entire length, and check the strut body for signs of damage. While holding it in an upright position, test the operation of the strut by moving the piston through a full stroke, and then through short strokes of 50 to 100 mm. In both cases, the resistance felt should be smooth and continuous. If the resistance is jerky, or uneven, or if there is any visible sign of wear or damage to the strut, renewal is necessary.

18 If any doubt exists about the condition of the coil spring, carefully remove the spring compressors, and check the spring for distortion and signs of cracking. Renew the spring if it is damaged or distorted, or if there is any doubt as to its condition.

19 Inspect all other components for signs of damage or deterioration, and renew as necessary.

20 Assemble the bump stop to the upper mounting, then refit the upper bearing race and protective sleeve to the mounting. The larger diameter of the bump stop must be against the upper mounting.

21 Fit the coil spring (together with the compressor tool) onto the strut, making sure its lower (larger diameter) end is correctly located against the spring seat stop.

22 Refit the thrust bearing and upper mounting, then screw on a new retaining nut. Tighten the nut to the specified torque while holding the piston rod with an Allen key.

Refitting

23 Manoeuvre the strut into position under the wheel arch, and locate in the suspension strut turret in the previously-noted position. If a new strut is being fitted, locate it so that

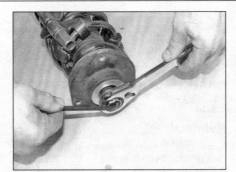

4.14a Unscrew the upper centre nut...

one of the two arrows marked on the upper mounting points forwards, and the bolt holes are aligned. Insert the bolts and tighten to the specified torque.

24 Refit the plenum chamber cover and wiper arms.

25 Engage the wheel bearing housing with the bottom of the suspension strut; making sure that the hole in the side plate aligns with the holes in the split housing. Raise the housing, while pressing it inwards to assist entry. Use a trolley jack if necessary. When fully entered, remove the tool used to open the split.

26 Insert the new strut-to-wheel bearing housing bolt from the front, and fit the new retaining nut. Tighten the nut to the specified torque.

27 Unscrew the nuts from the lower balljoint and lever down the lower arm to release it from the wheel bearing housing. Insert the outer end of the driveshaft through the hub and engage it with the splines. Fit the new hub bolt, tightening it by hand only at this stage.

28 Refit the lower arm balljoint to the lower arm, and tighten the nuts to the specified torque. Where applicable, refit the headlight range control sensor arm to the lower arm and tighten the nut.

29 Attach the ABS wheel sensor wiring to the strut.

30 Have an assistant depress the brake pedal, and then tighten the driveshaft retaining bolt to the Stage 1 torque given in the Specifications.

31 Refit the roadwheel and lower the vehicle to the ground, then angle-tighten the

4.14b...then remove the mounting, thrust bearing and coil spring

driveshaft bolt through the Stage 2 angle. Refit the wheel trim/hub cap.

5 Front suspension lower arm – removal, overhaul and refitting

Note: *The lower arm is available in either cast steel or sheet steel – when renewing the arm, make sure the correct type is fitted according to model. Audi subframe locating pins (T10096) or similar are required for the work in this Section, to ensure correct front wheel alignment. All self-locking nuts and bolts disturbed on removal must be renewed as a matter of course.*

Removal

1 Apply the handbrake, then jack up the front of the vehicle and support it on axle stands (see 'Jacking and vehicle support' in Reference chapter). Remove the appropriate front roadwheel and the engine compartment undertray.

2 Unscrew the front suspension lower balljoint-to-lower arm retaining nuts, then lever down the lower arm to release the arm from the balljoint studs.

3 At this stage, Audi technicians use locating pins T10096 in place of the rear outer subframe mounting bolts to ensure correct front wheel alignment. If these pins are not available, only remove and refit one lower arm at a time, and mark the position of the subframe accurately with dabs of paint.

4.15a Remove the protective sleeve...

4.15b...and upper bearing race...

4.15c...then remove the bump stop from the upper mounting

4 Unscrew and remove the rear outer mounting bolt and, where available, substitute it with a locating pin tightened to 20 Nm (15 lbf ft).

5 Unscrew and remove the front mounting bolt, then support the lower arm and unscrew the two rear inner mounting bolts. Remove the lower arm from beneath the car.

Overhaul

6 Thoroughly clean the lower arm, then check carefully for cracks or any other signs of wear or damage, paying particular attention to the rubber mounting bushes. If either bush requires renewal, take the lower arm to an Audi dealer or suitably-equipped garage. Alternatively, a hydraulic press and suitable spacers may be used to press the bushes out of the arm and rear bracket, and to install the new ones. Dip the bushes in a mild solution of washing-up liquid and water. Note the following:

a) *When fitting a new front mounting bush, it must be initially tilted with one lip in the bore. As the bush is inserted, it will straighten up. Make sure the bush is centred in its bore.*

b) *After pressing a new rear mounting bush into the rear mounting bracket, press the bracket and bush fully onto the lower arm rear pivot.*

Refitting

7 Locate the lower arm on the subframe and insert the front mounting bolt loosely.

8 Insert the two rear outer mounting bolts loosely, then position the inner bolt hole in the exact position noted during removal. If an Audi location pin was used on removal, the bracket will be correctly positioned on the pin. Tighten the two outer bolts to the specified torque, then remove the pin and refit the inner bolt, and tighten to the specified torque.

9 Tighten the front mounting bolt to the specified torque.

10 Lever down the lower arm and locate the balljoint studs in their holes. Fit the new nuts and tighten to the specified torque.

11 Refit the roadwheel and undertray, and lower the car to the ground.

6.2 Front suspension lower arm balljoint retaining nut

6 Front suspension lower arm balljoint – removal, inspection and refitting

Note: *All self-locking nuts and bolts disturbed on removal must be renewed as a matter of course.*

Removal

1 Remove the wheel bearing housing as described in Section 2.

2 Unscrew and remove the balljoint retaining nut **(see illustration)**, then release the balljoint from the wheel bearing housing using a universal balljoint separator. Withdraw the balljoint.

Inspection

3 With the balljoint removed, check that it moves freely, without any sign of roughness. Check also that the balljoint rubber gaiter shows no sign of deterioration, and is free from cracks and splits. Renew as necessary.

Refitting

4 Fit the balljoint to the wheel bearing housing and fit the new retaining nut. Tighten the nut to the specified torque setting, noting that the balljoint shank can be retained with an Allen key if necessary to prevent it from rotating.

5 Refit the wheel bearing housing with reference to Section 2.

7 Front anti-roll bar – removal and refitting

Note: *As the subframe must be lowered during this procedure, Audi subframe locating pins (T10096) or similar are required ensuring correct front wheel alignment. All self-locking nuts and bolts disturbed on removal must be renewed as a matter of course.*

Removal

1 Apply the handbrake, then jack up the front of the vehicle and support it on axle stands (see '*Jacking and vehicle support*' in Reference chapter). Remove both front

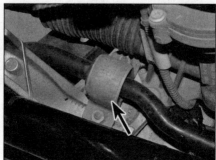

7.5 Front anti-roll bar clamp (arrowed) on the subframe

roadwheels and the engine compartment undertray.

2 Inside the car, undo the nuts and remove the trim beneath the foot pedals for access to the steering column universal joint. Unscrew the clamp bolt and pull the universal joint from the steering gear pinion.

3 The anti-roll bar may be removed with or without the side links. Unscrew the nuts securing the links to the struts or anti-roll bar as required.

4 Working on each side in turn, unscrew the front suspension lower balljoint-to-lower arm retaining nuts, then disconnect the track rod ends with reference to Section 25.

5 Unscrew the bolts securing the anti-roll bar clamps to the subframe **(see illustration)**. Mark the anti-roll bar to indicate which way round it is fitted, and the position of the rubber mounting bushes; this will aid refitting.

6 Unscrew and remove the engine/ transmission rear mounting bolts from the transmission.

7 Support the subframe with a trolley jack and block of wood. If not using the special Audi locating pins T10096, accurately mark the position of the subframe to ensure correct wheel alignment.

8 Unscrew the mounting bolts and slightly lower the subframe, taking care not to damage the electrical wiring. Where available, fit the Audi locating pins to facilitate refitting.

9 Lift the anti-roll bar forwards over the bracket, and lower it to the floor.

10 Carefully examine the anti-roll bar components for signs of wear, damage or deterioration, paying particular attention to the rubber mounting bushes. Renew worn components as necessary.

Refitting

11 Refitting is a reversal of removal but tighten all nuts and bolts to the specified torque where given. When refitting the subframe, align it with the marks made on removal, or use the special Audi location pins before tightening the mounting bolts. To assist entry of the steering gear gaiter through the bulkhead, apply a soapy solution to it. Have the front wheel alignment checked at the earliest opportunity.

8 Front anti-roll bar connecting link – removal and refitting

Note: *All self-locking nuts and bolts disturbed on removal must be renewed as a matter of course.*

Removal

1 Apply the handbrake, then jack up the front of the vehicle and support it on axle stands (see '*Jacking and vehicle support*' in Reference chapter). Remove the relevant front roadwheel.

2 Unscrew and remove the nuts securing the link to the strut and anti-roll bar.

3 Inspect the link rubbers for signs of damage or deterioration. If evident, renew the link complete.

Refitting

4 Refitting is a reversal of removal, but tighten the nuts to the specified torque.

9 Rear wheel bearing housing – removal and refitting

Removal

1 Chock the front wheels, then jack up the rear of the vehicle and support it on axle stands (see *'Jacking and vehicle support'* in Reference chapter).

2 Remove the rear coil spring as described in Section 15.

3 Remove the rear hub as described in Section 10.

4 Unbolt the splash plate from the rear wheel bearing housing.

5 Disconnect the wiring, then unscrew the mounting bolt and remove the ABS sensor from the rear wheel bearing housing.

6 Unscrew the bolt securing the rear shock absorber to the rear wheel bearing housing.

7 Unscrew the bolts securing the upper transverse link and lower transverse links to the rear wheel bearing housing.

8 Unscrew the bolt securing the rear track control rod to the rear wheel bearing housing.

9 Support the rear wheel bearing housing, and then unscrew the mounting bolts from the trailing arm. Also, undo the nut and disconnect the anti-roll bar link from the trailing arm.

10 Withdraw the rear wheel bearing housing from the car.

Refitting

Note: *Do not fully tighten the rear wheel bearing housing mounting bolts until the coil spring and shock absorber have been fitted, and the suspension is fully extended.*

11 Attach the rear wheel bearing housing to the rear track control rod, and the upper and lower transverse links, and hand-tighten the bolts.

12 Fit the wheel bearing housing to the trailing arm and insert the rear, upper bolt loosely.

13 Insert the two remaining bolts securing the trailing arm to the rear wheel bearing housing, and tighten them to the specified torque.

14 Refit the splash plate and tighten the bolts to the specified torque.

15 Refit the rear hub with reference to Section 10.

16 Position the centre of the rear hub the following ride-height distance from the centre of the wheel arch, according to model. Use the trolley jack to adjust the position:

a) *Standard running gear = 380 ± 10 mm*

b) *Heavy duty running gear = 400 ± 10 mm*

c) *Sports running gear = 365 ± 10 mm*

17 Tighten the following bolts to their specified torque, in the order given:

a) *Track control rod.*

b) *Lower transverse link.*

c) *Upper transverse link. Position the washer so that it clears the splash plate.*

18 Refit the shock absorber lower mounting bolt and tighten to the specified torque.

19 Remove the trolley jack, then refit the rear coil spring with reference to Section 15.

20 Refit the ABS sensor and tighten the mounting bolt. Reconnect the wiring.

21 Refit the roadwheel, then lower the vehicle to the ground, tighten the roadwheel bolts, and refit the wheel trim/hub cap. Have the rear wheel alignment checked and if necessary adjusted by an Audi dealer.

10 Rear hub/wheel bearings – checking and renewal

Note: *The rear wheel bearings cannot be renewed independently of the rear hub, because the outer races are formed in the hub itself. If excessive wear is evident, the rear hub must be renewed complete. The rear hub nut must always be renewed after removal.*

Removal

1 Chock the front roadwheels, then jack up the rear of the vehicle and support on axle stands (see *'Jacking and vehicle support'* in Reference chapter). Release the handbrake and remove the relevant rear roadwheel.

2 Remove the rear brake caliper and mounting bracket with reference to Chapter 9, Section 9. Do not disconnect the hydraulic brake pipe. Move the caliper just clear of the brake disc, without bending the hydraulic pipe excessively, and support it with welding rod or on an axle stand.

3 Undo the crosshead screw then withdraw the brake disc from the hub.

4 Remove the dust cap from the centre of the hub using a screwdriver or cold chisel **(see illustration)**.

5 Unscrew and remove the hub bolt, using a multi-spline key. Note that it is tightened to a high torque and a socket extension bar may be required to loosen it. The bolt must be renewed whenever removed.

6 Using a suitable puller, pull the hub and bearings from the stub axle. The bearing inner race will remain on the stub axle, and a puller will be required to remove it; use a sharp cold chisel to move the race away from the stub axle base so that the puller legs can fully engage the race.

7 Examine the hub and bearings for wear, pitting and damage. If any damage is evident, renew the hub complete.

Refitting

8 Wipe clean the stub axle, then check that

10.4 Removing the dust cap

the bearing races are adequately lubricated with suitable grease. Check that the inner bearing race is located correctly in the hub. Also make sure that the ABS rotor is pressed firmly onto the inner end of the hub.

9 Locate the hub as far as possible on the stub axle.

10 Screw on the new bolt and tighten it to the specified torque.

11 Check the dust cap for damage and renew it if necessary. Use a hammer to carefully tap the cap into the hub.

Note: *A badly fitting dust cap will allow moisture to enter the bearing, reducing its service life.*

12 Refit the brake disc and tighten the crosshead screw.

13 Refit the rear brake mounting bracket and caliper with reference to Chapter 9, Section 9.

14 Refit the roadwheel and lower the vehicle to the ground.

11 Rear radius rods – removal and refitting

Removal

1 The rear radius rods (where fitted) extend from the front of the rear subframe to the underbody, just in front of the trailing arms. The bolts on the subframe must only be loosened or tightened with the vehicle resting on its wheels. First, mark the position of the radius rods on the underbody and subframe, using marking pens or dabs of paint, and then loosen the bolts securing the radius rod to the subframe.

2 Chock the front roadwheels, then jack up the rear of the vehicle and support on axle stands (see *'Jacking and vehicle support'* in Reference chapter).

3 Unscrew the mounting bolts and remove the radius rod from under the vehicle.

Refitting

4 Locate the radius rod on the underbody and subframe and insert the mounting bolts loosely.

5 Align the radius rod with the marks made on removal, then tighten the two underbody bolts to the specified torque.

6 Lower the vehicle to the ground, and then tighten the bolts securing the radius rod to the subframe to the specified torque. Have the rear wheel alignment checked and if necessary adjusted by an Audi dealer.

12 Rear track control rod – removal and refitting

Removal

1 Chock the front roadwheels, then jack up the rear of the vehicle and support on axle stands (see *'Jacking and vehicle support'* Reference chapter). Remove the relevant rear roadwheel.
2 Note the fitted position of the rear track control rod, with the 'closed' side facing forwards. Also, note which way round the mounting bolts are fitted.
3 Unscrew and remove the mounting bolts and nuts, and withdraw the track control rod from under the vehicle. Note the location of the special 'star' washer beneath the head of the bolt securing the outer end of the rod to the wheel bearing housing.

Refitting

4 Refitting is a reversal of removal, but tighten the bolts to the specified torque and position the rod and bolts as previously-noted. Check that a clearance exists between the special 'star' washer and the track control rod. Have the rear wheel alignment checked and if necessary adjusted by an Audi dealer.

13 Rear transverse links – removal and refitting

Upper link

Removal

1 Chock the front roadwheels, then jack up the rear of the vehicle and support on axle stands (see *'Jacking and vehicle support'* in Reference chapter). Remove the roadwheel.

2 Remove the rear coil spring as described in Section 15.
3 Release the ABS speed sensor wiring from the upper link, then unscrew the bolt securing the link to the wheel bearing housing.
4 At the inner end of the upper link, mark the position of the eccentric bolt and subframe in relation to each other. This alignment determines the camber setting of the rear wheels.
5 Note which way round the eccentric bolt is fitted, then unscrew and remove it and withdraw the upper link.

Refitting

6 Refitting is a reversal of removal, but delay fully-tightening the mounting bolts until the rear suspension is set to the correct ride-height given in Section 9. Make sure the eccentric bolt is correctly aligned as previously noted, and also position the 'star' washer to provide a clearance between one of its points and the splash plate. Have the rear wheel alignment checked and if necessary adjusted by an Audi dealer.

Lower transverse link

Removal

7 Chock the front roadwheels, then jack up the rear of the vehicle and support on axle stands (see *'Jacking and vehicle support'* in Reference chapter). Remove the roadwheel.
8 Remove the rear coil spring as described in Section 15.
9 Unscrew the bolt securing the lower transverse link to the wheel bearing housing.
10 On models with headlight range control, unscrew the nut and disconnect the sensor arm from the link.
11 At the inner end of the upper link, mark the position of the eccentric bolt and subframe in relation to each other. This alignment determines the camber setting of the rear wheels.
12 Refer to Chapter 4C and lower the rear section of the exhaust system for improved access. Support the exhaust on an axle stand.
13 Unscrew and remove the inner bolt and withdraw the lower transverse link from under the car.

Refitting

14 Refitting is a reversal of removal, but delay fully-tightening the mounting bolts until the rear suspension is set to the correct ride-height given in Section 9. Make sure the eccentric bolt is correctly aligned as previously-noted, and also position the 'star' washer to provide a clearance between one of its points and the splash plate. Have the rear wheel alignment checked and if necessary adjusted by an Audi dealer.

14 Rear trailing arm and bracket – removal, overhaul and refitting

Removal

1 Chock the front roadwheels, then jack up the rear of the vehicle and support on axle stands (see *'Jacking and vehicle support'* in Reference chapter). Remove the roadwheel.
2 Remove the rear coil spring as described in Section 15.
3 Unscrew the bolt securing the handbrake cable support to the trailing arm.
4 Unscrew the nut and detach the anti-roll bar link.
5 Unscrew the bolts securing the trailing arm to the rear wheel bearing housing.
6 Mark the position of the trailing arm front mounting bracket in relation to the underbody.
7 Support the front mounting bracket on a trolley jack, then unscrew the bolts, lower the assembly and withdraw the rear trailing arm and bracket from under the vehicle.

Overhaul

8 Thoroughly clean the trailing arm and bracket, then unscrew the front pivot bolt and separate the arm from the bracket. Check carefully for cracks or any other signs of wear or damage, paying particular attention to the rubber mounting bush.
9 If the bush requires renewal, take the arm to an Audi dealer or suitably-equipped garage. Alternatively, a hydraulic press and suitable spacers may be used to press the bush out of the arm, and to install the new one. Dip the bush in a mild solution of washing-up liquid

14.9a Make a vertical line on the arm as shown...

A = 114.0 mm

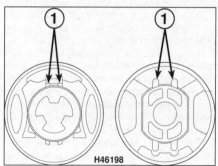

14.9b ...then press in the new bush so that the line is between the two projections (1)

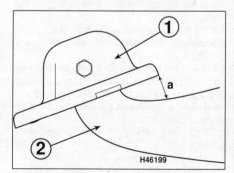

14.10 Mounting bracket assembly to trailing arm

1 Mounting bracket 2 Trailing arm a = 34.0 mm

15.2a Rear coil spring

15.2b Compress the rear coil spring with the special tool...

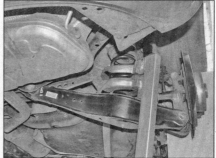

15.2c...then remove it from the trailing arm and underbody

and water. When fitting the new bush to the front of the trailing arm, it is important to position it correctly. Make a vertical line on the arm, and then press in the new bush so that the line is between the two projections **(see illustrations)**.

10 With the new bush in position, locate the front of the arm in the bracket, and insert the bolt. Position the arm in relation to the bracket as shown **(see illustration)** then tighten the bolt/nut to the specified torque. There are two types of bush.

Refitting

11 Fit the trailing arm to the wheel bearing housing and insert the bolts loosely.
12 Fit the anti-roll bar link and screw on the nut loosely.
13 Raise the front mounting bracket and locate it on the underbody in its previously-noted position. Insert the new bolts and tighten to the specified torque.
14 Lower the jack then tighten the arm-to-housing bolts to the specified torque.
15 Tighten the anti-roll bar link nut.
16 Refit the handbrake cable support and tighten the bolt.
17 Refit the rear coil spring with reference to Section 15.
18 Refit the roadwheel and lower the vehicle to the ground. Have the rear wheel alignment checked and if necessary adjusted by an Audi dealer.

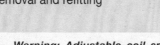

15 Rear coil spring – removal and refitting

⚠ *Warning: Adjustable coil spring compressors are readily available, and are recommended for this operation. Any attempt to remove the coil spring without such a tool is likely to result in damage or personal injury.*

Removal

1 Chock the front roadwheels, then jack up the rear of the vehicle and support on axle stands (see *'Jacking and vehicle support'* in Reference chapter). Remove the relevant rear roadwheel.
2 Fit the tool to the coil spring and compress it until it can be removed from the trailing arm and underbody **(see illustrations)**. With the coil spring on the bench, carefully release the tension of the tool and remove it.
3 With the coil spring removed, recover the upper and lower spring seats and check them for damage. Obtain new ones if necessary, but note that they are different, the lower one having a location pin, which enters a hole in the lower transverse link. Also clean thoroughly the spring locations on the underbody and trailing arm.

Refitting

4 Refitting is a reversal of removal, but make

sure that the lower spring seat engages the hole in the lower transverse link, the lower end of the coil spring abuts the stop on the seat, and the upper seat is correctly engaged with the lug on the underbody **(see illustrations)**.

16 Rear shock absorber – removal and refitting

Note: *All self-locking nuts and bolts disturbed on removal must be renewed as a matter of course.*

Removal

1 Before removing the shock absorber, an idea of how effective it is can be gained by depressing the rear corner of the car. If the shock absorber is in good condition, the body should rise then settle in its normal position. If the body oscillates more than this, the shock absorber is defective.
Note: *To ensure even rear suspension, both rear shock absorbers should be renewed at the same time.*
2 Chock the front roadwheels, then jack up the rear of the vehicle and support on axle stands (see *'Jacking and vehicle support'* in Reference chapter). Remove the relevant rear roadwheel.
3 Remove the wheel arch liner **(see illustration)**.
4 Position a trolley jack and block of wood

15.4a Rear coil spring located in the lower transverse link...

15.4b...and underbody

16.3 Removing the rear wheel arch liner

16.5a Unscrew the rear shock absorber lower mounting bolt...

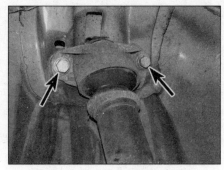

16.5b.....and upper mounting bolts (arrowed)

16.6a Remove the cap...

16.6b...unscrew the nut while holding the piston...

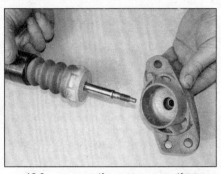

16.6c...remove the upper mounting bracket...

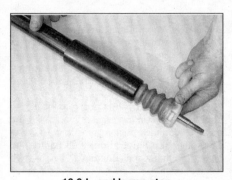

16.6d...and bump stop

beneath the coil spring position on the trailing arm, and raise the arm so that the shock absorber is slightly compressed. Note on some models, it may be necessary to remove the stone protection guard first. If preferred, the rear coil spring may be removed completely at this stage.

5 Unscrew the lower mounting bolt, then unscrew the upper mounting bolts and withdraw the shock absorber **(see illustrations)**.

6 With the shock absorber on the bench, remove the cap, then unscrew the nut from the top of the piston rod and remove the upper mounting bracket, followed by the bump stop, and where fitted the support ring, protective tube, and protective cap **(see illustrations)**.

Note: *Two types of bump stop are supplied; a short version with a support ring, and a long version without a support ring.*

7 If necessary, the action of the shock

17.4 Rear anti-roll bar mounting clamp (arrowed)

absorber can be checked by mounting it upright in a vice. Fully depress the rod, and then pull it up fully. The piston rod must move smoothly over its complete length.

Refitting

8 Locate the components removed from the top of the shock absorber in their correct order, and screw on a new nut. Tighten the nut and fit the cap.

9 Locate the shock absorber in the rear wheel arch, then insert the upper mounting bolts and tighten to the specified torque.

10 Extend the shock absorber if necessary, and insert the lower mounting bolt loosely.

11 Raise the trailing arm until the rear suspension is set to the correct ride-height given in Section 9, then fully tighten the shock absorber lower mounting bolt.

12 Refit the rear coil spring with reference to Section 15.

13 Refit the wheel arch liner.

14 Refit the roadwheel and lower the vehicle to the ground.

17 Rear anti-roll bar – removal and refitting

Removal

1 Chock the front roadwheels, then jack up the rear of the vehicle and support on axle stands (see *'Jacking and vehicle support'* in Reference chapter). Remove both rear roadwheels.

2 Working on each side in turn, unscrew the nut and detach the side links from the anti-roll bar. Note that on early models with two balljoints, a metal shield is fitted between the link and the anti-roll bar. No shield is fitted to later models with a rubber bush connection to the bar (see Section 18).

3 Mark the anti-roll bar to indicate which way round it is fitted, and the position of the rubber mounting bushes; this will aid refitting.

4 Unscrew the bolts securing the anti-roll bar clamps to the rear subframe, and recover the clamps **(see illustration)**.

Refitting

5 Refitting is a reversal of removal but tighten all nuts and bolts to the specified torque.

18 Rear anti-roll bar connecting link – removal and refitting

Removal

1 Chock the front roadwheels, then jack up the rear of the vehicle and support on axle stands (see *'Jacking and vehicle support'* in Reference chapter). Remove the relevant rear roadwheel.

2 Note that on early models with two balljoints, a metal shield is fitted between the link and the anti-roll bar. No shield is fitted to later models with a rubber bush connection to the bar – on this type, the link connection to the trailing arm is a balljoint type.

3 Unscrew the nuts securing the link to the

20.5 Unscrew and remove the retaining bolt

20.6a The steering wheel should be marked for its central position

anti-roll bar and trailing arm, and withdraw it from under the vehicle. On the early type, recover the metal shield.

4 Inspect the link rubbers/balljoints for signs of damage or deterioration. If evident, renew the link complete.

Refitting

5 Refitting is a reversal of removal, but tighten the nuts to the specified torque.

19 Vehicle level sender – removal and refitting

Removal

1 The front sender for the headlight range control system is located on the left-hand side of the front subframe, and incorporates an arm and link attached to the left-hand front lower suspension arm. The rear sender is bolted to the rear subframe, and an arm and link is attached to a bracket on the lower transverse link. The system is controlled by an ECU located behind a cover on the passenger's side of the instrument panel.

2 To remove the front sender, apply the handbrake then jack up the front of the vehicle and support it on axle stands (see 'Jacking and vehicle support' in Reference chapter). Remove the front roadwheel, and then note the position of the sender on the lower arm. Unscrew the nut and disconnect the link and bracket from the lower arm. Disconnect the wiring then unscrew the bolt and remove the sender from the front subframe.

3 To remove the rear sender, chock the front roadwheels then jack up the rear of the vehicle and support on axle stands (see 'Jacking and vehicle support' in Reference chapter). Disconnect the wiring from the sender. Unscrew the bolts securing the link and bracket to the lower transverse link, then

unscrew the bolts and remove the sender from the rear subframe.

Refitting

4 Refitting is a reversal of removal, but tighten the mounting bolts to the specified torque. If necessary, have the sender outputs checked by an Audi dealer. This work requires the use of special equipment, which may not be available to the home mechanic.

20 Steering wheel – removal and refitting

20.6b Removing the steering wheel

⚠ **Warning: During the airbag removal and refitting procedures, avoid sitting in the front seats.**

Removal

1 Set the front wheels in the straight-ahead position, and release the steering lock by inserting the ignition key.

2 Disconnect the battery negative (earth) lead and position it away from the terminal (see 'Disconnecting the battery' in Reference chapter).

3 Adjust the steering column to its highest position, then extend it into the passenger compartment as far as possible, and lock it in this position.

4 Remove the driver's airbag as described in Chapter 12, Section 26.

Warning: Position the airbag in a safe and secure place, away from the work area.

5 Using a multi-spline socket, unscrew and remove the retaining bolt, while holding the steering wheel stationary **(see illustration).**

Note: *The steering wheel retaining bolt can be re-used up to 5 times, after which it must be renewed. It is recommended that the nut is marked with a centre punch to indicate the number of times it has been unscrewed.*

6 Check if the steering wheel is marked in relation to the column. If not, use a dab of

paint to mark them, then ease the steering wheel from the column splines by firmly rocking it side-to-side **(see illustrations).**

Refitting

7 Locate the steering wheel on the column splines making sure that the previously made marks are correctly aligned.

8 Refit the retaining bolt and tighten to the specified torque while holding the steering wheel stationary.

9 Refit the driver's airbag with reference to Chapter 12, Section 26.

10 Reconnect the battery negative (earth) lead.

21 Steering column – removal, inspection and refitting

Removal

1 Disconnect the battery negative lead, and position it away from the terminal (see 'Disconnecting the battery' in Reference chapter).

2 Adjust the steering column to its lowest position and extend it into the passenger compartment as far as possible, then lock it

21.2 Remove the height adjuster handle

21.3a Release the gap cover...

21.3b...then unclip and remove the upper shroud

21.5a Undo the upper screws...

21.5b...and the lower screw...

21.5c...and remove the lower shroud from the steering column

in this position. Undo the screws and remove the column height and reach adjustment handle **(see illustration)**.

3 Release the gap cover, then unclip and remove the upper shroud from the steering column **(see illustrations)**.

4 Remove the steering wheel as described in Section 20, and return the steering to the straight-ahead position.

5 Undo the two upper screws and single lower screw and remove the lower shroud from the steering column **(see illustrations)**.

6 Remove the fusebox cover and light switch (see Chapter 12), then undo the screws and remove the lower facia panel located next to the steering column. On models with a storage

compartment, remove the compartment first for access to the lower screws.

7 Remove the switch carrier from the top of the steering column as described in Section 22.

Note: *This work requires fitting new shear-head bolts. If it is not imperative to remove the carrier, leave it in position on the steering column.*

8 Undo the retaining screw and remove the footwell vent from under the steering column **(see illustration)**.

9 Disconnect the wiring from the ignition switch.

10 Remove the cable guide from below the steering column. To do this, carefully prise up the lugs from the retaining clips.

11 Undo the nuts and remove the trim beneath the foot pedals for access to the steering column universal joint. Unscrew the clamp bolt and pull the universal joint from the steering gear pinion. Note that the pinion shaft has a cut-out to enable fitting of the clamp bolt, and the splined pinion shaft incorporates a flat making it impossible to assemble the joint to the shaft in the wrong position. Discard the clamp bolt; a new one should be used on refitting.

12 Unscrew the nut and disconnect the earth cable, then remove the wiring harness from the steering column **(see illustration)**.

13 Note that the inner and outer columns, and the intermediate shaft, are telescopic to

21.8 Remove the footwell air vent

21.12 Undo the earth wire retaining nut (arrowed)

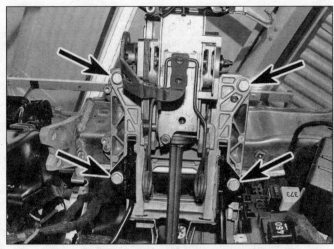

21.14a Steering column mounting bolts (arrowed)

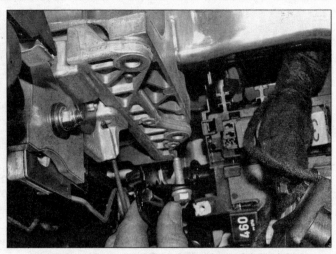

21.14b Note the lower bolts support the pedal crash bars

facilitate the reach adjustment. It is important to keep the splined sections of the inner steering column engaged with each other while the steering column is removed. If they become detached due to the outer column sections being separated, especially on a vehicle which has completed a high mileage, it is possible that rattling noises may occur.

14 Unscrew and remove two diagonally-opposite mounting bolts, then support the steering column and unscrew the two remaining bolts **(see illustrations)**.

Note: *The two lower mounting bolts have safety bars fitted to them. They are fitted above the clutch and brake pedals, to prevent them being forced up in case of an accident.*

15 Lower the steering column and withdraw it from inside the car **(see illustration)**. Discard the bolts, as new ones must be used on refitting. Note that the mounting bracket on the bulkhead has location pins, which align the steering column.

Caution: Do not carry the steering column by suspending it from the universal joint or intermediate shaft, as this will damage the universal joint and steering column bushes. Also, do not bend the joints by more than 90º.

16 If necessary, remove the ignition switch/steering column lock with reference to Section 22.

Inspection

17 The steering column is designed to collapse in the event of a front-end crash, to prevent the steering wheel injuring the driver. Before refitting the steering column, examine the column and mountings for signs of damage and deformation.

18 Check the inner column sections for signs of free play in the column bushes. If any damage or wear is found on the steering column bushes, the column must be renewed as an assembly.

19 The intermediate shaft is permanently attached to the inner column and cannot be renewed separately. Inspect the universal joints for excessive wear. If evident, the complete steering column must be renewed.

Refitting

20 Where removed, refit the ignition switch/steering column lock/switch carrier with reference to Section 22.

21 Refit the steering column to the bulkhead bracket, insert the new mounting bolts, and tighten to the specified torque.

22 Reconnect the earth cable and tighten the bolt. Refit the wiring harness.

23 Attach the universal joint on the steering gear pinion splines, insert the new clamp bolt, and tighten to the specified torque.

24 Refit the foot pedal trim and tighten the nuts.

25 Refit the cable guide, making sure that the retaining lugs engage on both sides.

26 Reconnect the wiring to the ignition switch.

27 Refit the footwell vent under the steering column.

28 Refit the light switch with reference to Chapter 12.

29 Refit the facia lower trim panel and tighten the screws, then refit the light switch and fusebox cover.

30 Refit the lower and upper shrouds and tighten the screws. Refit the gap cover.

31 Refit the column height and reach adjustment handle and tighten the screws.

32 Refit the steering wheel with reference to Section 20.

33 Reconnect the battery negative lead.

34 On models with ESP, the steering angle sensor basic settings must be set by an Audi dealer using specialist diagnostic equipment.

22 Ignition switch and steering column lock/switch carrier – removal and refitting

Ignition switch

Removal

1 Disconnect the battery negative lead, and position it away from the terminal (see *'Disconnecting the battery'* in Reference chapter).

2 Remove the steering wheel as described in Section 20.

3 Undo the screws and remove the column height and reach adjustment handle.

4 Release the gap cover, then unclip and remove the upper shroud from the steering column.

5 Undo the two upper screws and single lower screw and remove the lower shroud from the steering column.

6 Carefully disconnect the plug from the ignition switch **(see illustration)**.

7 Insert the ignition key and turn to the Drive

21.15 Lower the steering column and remove

22.6 Disconnect the wiring connector from the switch

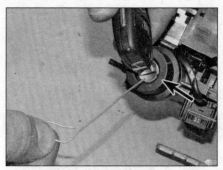

22.7a Align the hole with the mark on the cover (arrowed)...

22.7b...and insert 1.2 mm wire through the lock cylinder...

22.7c...to release the locking lever (arrowed)

position (90º), where a hole will align with the dot on the plastic cover. Insert a piece of wire 1.2 mm in diameter in the drilling next to the ignition key, depress it, then withdraw the lock cylinder from the housing **(see illustrations)**.

Refitting

8 Refit the switch to the steering lock housing, withdraw piece of wire and press in until the retaining clip engages.

9 Withdraw the ignition key and check ignition switch is secure.

10 Reconnect the wiring plug to the ignition switch.

11 Refit the upper and lower shrouds, and tighten the screws. Also, refit the gap cover.

12 Refit the column height and reach adjustment handle, and tighten the screws.

13 Refit the steering wheel with reference to Section 20.

14 Reconnect the battery negative lead.

Steering lock/switch carrier

Removal

15 The steering column lock is integral with the wiper and indicator switch carrier, which is secured to the steering column with shear-head bolts.

16 Disconnect the battery negative lead, and position it away from the terminal (see *'Disconnecting the battery'* in Reference chapter).

17 Check that the front wheels are pointing straight-ahead and the steering wheel is in its centre position, then remove the steering wheel as described in Section 20.

18 Undo the screws and remove the column height and reach adjustment handle.

19 Release the gap cover, then unclip and remove the upper shroud from the steering column.

20 Undo the two upper screws and single lower screw and remove the lower shroud from the steering column. As the shroud is being removed, release it from the height and reach adjustment handle.

21 Remove the steering column electronics control unit. To do this, undo the single retaining screw, then insert a 2.5 mm diameter rod or similar through the hole provided, and release the centre clip. Now use a screwdriver to release the rear clip. Pull down the control unit from the column switch carrier and disconnect the wiring **(see illustrations)**.

22.21a Undo the retaining screw...

22.21b...and insert 2.5 mm rod to release the upper clip...

22.21c... and use a screwdriver to release the lower clip..

22.21d...then lower the control unit from the column

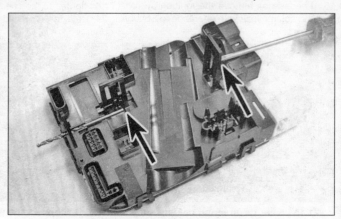

22.21e Showing the position of the retaining clips

22.22a Release the retaining clips...

22.22b...and withdraw the airbag clock spring from the column

22 The airbag clock spring/slip-ring must be held in its central position while it is removed, to ensure correct refitting. Unclip the airbag clock spring/slip-ring from the combination switch carrier by lifting the retaining hooks **(see illustrations)**.

23 On models with ESP, pull the steering angle sensor directly away from the combination switch carrier **(see illustration)**.

24 Remove the indicator and windscreen wiper switches by inserting a 1.0 mm feeler gauge through the slot provided to release the switch from the carrier **(see illustrations)**.

25 Disconnect the wiring from the immobiliser coil on the ignition lock housing.

26 The steering column lock/switch carrier is secured by shear-head bolts, and the heads are broken off in the tightening procedure. To remove the old bolts, either drill them out, or use a sharp cold chisel to cut off their heads or turn them anti-clockwise. Withdraw the carrier from the steering column.

Refitting

27 If removed, refit the lock cylinder with the ignition key in the Drive position, then remove the wire. Make sure that the immobiliser coil connection is located correctly in the guide when inserting the lock cylinder.

28 Locate the lock/switch carrier on the outer column as far as possible, and insert the new shear-head bolts. Tighten the bolts until their heads break off.

29 The remaining procedure is a reversal of removal, but refer to Chapter 12 when refitting the airbag clock spring/slip-ring to check that it is in its central position.

22.23 Removing the steering angle sensor

22.24a Release the retaining clip and insert a feeler gauge as shown...

22.24b...and withdraw the light switch...

22.24c...and the same to remove the wiper switch

23 Steering gear assembly – removal, overhaul and refitting

Note: *As the subframe must be lowered during this procedure, Audi subframe locating pins (T10096) or similar are required to ensure correct front wheel alignment. New subframe mounting bolts, track rod balljoint nuts, steering gear retaining bolts, and an intermediate shaft universal joint clamp bolt will be required on refitting.*

Removal

1 Disconnect the battery negative lead (refer to *'Disconnecting the battery'* in Reference chapter).

2 Apply the handbrake, then jack up the front of the vehicle and support it on axle stands positioned on the underbody, leaving the subframe free (see *Jacking and vehicle support* in Reference chapter). Position the steering straight-ahead, and then remove both front roadwheels. Also remove the engine compartment undertray.

3 Inside the vehicle, undo the screws and remove the plastic cover for access to the universal joint connecting the steering inner column to the steering gear pinion. Unscrew and remove the clamp bolt, and pull the universal joint from the pinion splines. **Note:** *The steering gear pinion incorporates a cut-out for the clamp bolt, and therefore the joint can only be fitted in one position. Discard the clamp bolt; a new one should be used on refitting.*

4 Working on each side in turn, unscrew the nuts from the track rod ends, then use a balljoint separator tool to release the ends from the steering arms on the front wheel bearing housings.

5 Working on each side in turn, unscrew the nuts securing the anti-roll bar links to the struts.

6 Working on each side in turn, unscrew the front suspension lower balljoint-to-lower arm retaining nuts, then lever the lower arms down to release the balljoint studs.

7 Unscrew and remove the engine/transmission rear mounting bolts from the transmission.

8 Unbolt the exhaust system mounting from the subframe.

9 Unbolt the exhaust system heat shield from the subframe.

10 Support the subframe with a trolley jack and block of wood. If not using the special Audi locating pins T10096, accurately mark the position of the subframe to ensure correct wheel alignment.

11 Unscrew the mounting bolts and slightly lower the subframe, taking care not to damage the electrical wiring. Where available, fit the Audi locating pins to facilitate refitting.

12 Unbolt the heat shield from over the steering gear.

13 Remove the cable guide and disconnect all wiring from the steering gear. Release the wiring from all clips.

Caution: Do not touch the wiring terminals on the electronic control unit, as a static electricity discharge may damage the internal components.

14 Lower the subframe together with the steering gear to the floor.

15 Unbolt the steering gear from the subframe, and carefully place it on the floor taking care not to damage the electronic control unit.

Overhaul

16 Examine the steering gear assembly for signs of wear or damage, and check that the rack moves freely throughout the full length of its travel, with no signs of roughness or excessive free play between the steering gear pinion and rack.

17 It is not possible to overhaul the steering gear assembly housing components, and if it is faulty, the assembly must be renewed. The only components which can be renewed individually are the steering gear gaiters, the track rod end balljoints and the track rods, as described later in this Chapter.

Refitting

18 Locate the steering gear on the subframe, and insert and tighten the bolts for the gear and anti-roll bar before inserting the subframe bolts.

19 Raise the subframe sufficiently to refit the cable guide and reconnect all the wiring to the steering gear. Secure the wiring in the clips.

20 Refit the heat shield, then raise the subframe onto the underbody and align it with the marks made on removal, or use the special Audi location pins before tightening the mounting bolts. To assist entry of steering gear gaiter through the bulkhead, apply a soapy solution to it.

21 Refit the exhaust heat shield and mounting, then refit the engine/transmission rear mounting bolts to the transmission and tighten to the specified torque.

22 Locate the front suspension lower balljoints in the lower arms, screw on the new nuts and tighten to the specified torque.

23 Refit the track rod ends with new nuts, and tighten them to the specified torque.

24 Inside the car, attach the universal joint on the steering gear pinion splines, insert the new clamp bolt, and tighten to the specified torque.

25 Refit the engine compartment undertray, then refit the wheels and lower the car to the ground.

26 Reconnect the battery negative lead. Have the front wheel alignment checked at the earliest opportunity.

27 On models with ESP, the steering angle sensor basic settings have to be reset, this must be done by an Audi dealer using specialist diagnostic equipment. If a new steering gear has been fitted, it must also be adapted to the vehicle by an Audi dealer.

24 Steering gear rubber gaiters and track rods – renewal

Steering gear rubber gaiters

1 Remove the track rod end balljoint as described in Section 25. Also, unscrew the locking nut after noting its position.

2 Wipe clean the rubber gaiter to prevent entry of dirt or moisture. Note the fitted position of the gaiter on the track rod, then release the retaining clips and slide the gaiter off the steering gear housing and track rod.

3 Wipe clean the track rod and the steering gear housing, and then apply a film of suitable grease to the surface of the rack. To do this, turn the steering wheel as necessary to fully extend the rack from the housing, then reposition it in its central position.

4 Carefully slide the new gaiter onto the track rod, and locate it on the steering gear housing. Position the gaiter as previously-noted on removal, making sure that it is not twisted, then lift the outer sealing lip of the gaiter to equalise air pressure within the gaiter.

5 Secure the gaiter in position with new retaining clips. Where crimped-type clips are used, pull the clip as tight as possible, and locate the hooks in their slots. Remove any slack in the clip by carefully compressing the raised section. In the absence of the special crimping tool, a pair of side-cutters may be used, taking care not to cut the clip.

6 Screw on the locking nut, then refit the track rod end balljoint as described in Section 25.

Track rods

7 Remove the relevant steering gear rubber gaiter as described earlier. If there is insufficient working room with the steering gear mounted in the car, remove it as described in Section 23 and hold it in a vice while renewing the track rod.

8 Hold the steering rack stationary with one spanner on the flats provided, then loosen the balljoint nut with another spanner. Fully unscrew the nut and remove the track rod from the rack.

9 Locate the new track rod on the end of the steering rack and screw on the nut. Hold the rack stationary with one spanner and tighten the balljoint nut to the specified torque. A crow's foot adapter may be required since the track rod prevents access with a socket, and care must be taken to apply the correct torque in this situation.

10 Refit the steering gear or rubber gaiter with reference to the earlier paragraphs or Section 23. On completion check and, if necessary, adjust the front wheel alignment as described in Section 26.

25.4a Using an Allen key to hold the balljoint shank while loosening the nut

25.4b Using a balljoint separator to release the track rod balljoint from the steering arm on the wheel bearinghousing

25.5 Unscrewing the track rod end from the track rod

25 Track rod end – removal and refitting

Note: *A new balljoint retaining nut will be required on refitting.*

Removal

1 Apply the handbrake, then jack up the front of the vehicle and support it on axle stands (see *'Jacking and vehicle support'* in Reference chapter). Remove the relevant roadwheel.

2 If the track rod end is to be re-used, mark its position in relation to the track rod to facilitate refitting.

3 Unscrew the track rod end locknut by a quarter of a turn. Do not move the locknut from this position, as it will serve as a handy reference mark on refitting.

4 Loosen and remove the nut securing the track rod end balljoint to the wheel bearing housing, and release the balljoint tapered shank using a universal balljoint separator. Note that the balljoint shank has a hexagon hole – hold the shank with an Allen key while loosening the nut **(see illustrations)**.

5 Counting the exact number of turns necessary to do so, unscrew the track rod end from the track rod **(see illustration)**.

6 Carefully clean the balljoint and the threads. Renew the balljoint if its movement is sloppy or too stiff, if excessively worn, or if damaged in any way; carefully check the stud taper and threads. If the balljoint gaiter is damaged, the complete balljoint assembly must be renewed; it is not possible to obtain the gaiter separately.

Refitting

7 Screw the track rod end onto the track rod by the number of turns noted on removal. This should bring the track rod end to within a quarter of a turn of the locknut, with the alignment marks that were made on removal (if applicable) lined up. Tighten the locknut.

8 Refit the balljoint shank to the steering arm on the wheel bearing housing, then fit a new retaining nut and tighten it to the specified torque. Hold the shank with an Allen key if necessary.

9 Refit the roadwheel, then lower the car to the ground and tighten the roadwheel bolts to the specified torque.

10 Check and, if necessary, adjust the front wheel toe setting as described in Section 26.

26 Wheel alignment and steering angles – general information

Definitions

1 A car's steering and suspension geometry is defined in three basic settings – all angles are expressed in degrees; the steering axis is defined as an imaginary line drawn through the axis of the suspension strut, extended where necessary to contact the ground.

2 Camber is the angle between each roadwheel and a vertical line drawn through its centre and tyre contact patch, when viewed from the front or rear of the car. Positive camber is when the roadwheels are tilted outwards from the vertical at the top; negative camber is when they are tilted inwards.

3 Camber angle is only adjustable by loosening the front suspension subframe mounting bolts and moving it slightly to one side. This also alters the Castor angle. The camber angle can be checked using a camber checking gauge.

4 Castor is the angle between the steering axis and a vertical line drawn through each roadwheel's centre and tyre contact patch, when viewed from the side of the car. Positive castor is when the steering axis is tilted so that it contacts the ground ahead of the vertical; negative castor is when it contacts the ground behind the vertical. Slight castor angle adjustment is possible by loosening the front suspension subframe bolts and moving it slightly to one side. This also alters the Camber angle.

5 Castor is not easily adjustable, and is given for reference only; while it can be checked using a castor checking gauge, if the figure obtained is significantly different from that specified, the car must be taken for careful checking by a professional, as the fault can only be caused by wear or damage to the body or suspension components.

6 Toe is the difference, viewed from above, between lines drawn through the roadwheel centres and the car's centre-line. Toe-in is when the roadwheels point inwards, towards each other at the front, while toe-out is when they splay outwards from each other at the front.

7 The front wheel toe setting is adjusted by screwing the track rod(s) in/out of the outer balljoint(s) to alter the effective length of the track rod assembly.

8 Rear wheel toe setting is not adjustable, and is given for reference only. While it can be checked, if the figure obtained is significantly different from that specified, the car must be taken for careful checking by a professional, as the fault can only be caused by wear or damage to the body or suspension components.

Checking and adjustment

9 Due to the special measuring equipment necessary to check the wheel alignment, and the skill required to use it properly, the checking and adjustment of these settings is best left to an Audi dealer or similar expert. Note that most tyre-fitting centres now possess sophisticated checking equipment.

Chapter 11
Bodywork and fittings

Contents

Degrees of difficulty

Easy, suitable for novice with little experience	**Fairly easy,** suitable for beginner with some experience	**Fairly difficult,** suitable for competent DIY mechanic	**Difficult,** suitable for experienced DIY mechanic	**Very difficult,** suitable for expert DIY or professional

Specifications

Torque wrench settings	Nm	lbf ft
Bonnet	22	16
Door hinge bolts.	32	24
Door lock	18	13
Window frame bolts	32	24
Front seat mounting retaining bolts	40	30
Seat belt inertia reel mounting bolt: *		
Front	50	37
Rear	55	41
Seat belt upper mounting bolt*	50	37
Seat belt upper height adjuster mounting bolt*	21	16
Seat belt stalk to front seat*	22	16
Tailgate	10	7
Tailgate hinge retaining bolts	24	18

* Renew the bolts if work carried out following an accident

1 General Information

1 The body shell is made of pressed-steel sections, and is available in both three- and five-door Hatchback versions. Most components are welded together, and some use is made of structural adhesives; the front wings are bolted on.

2 The bonnet, door, and some other vulnerable panels are made of zinc-coated metal, and are further protected by being coated with an anti-chip primer before being sprayed.

3 Extensive use is made of plastic materials, mainly in the interior, but also in exterior components. The front and rear bumpers, and front grille, are injection-moulded from a synthetic material that is very strong and yet light. Plastic components such as wheel arch liners are fitted to the underside of the vehicle, to improve the body's resistance to corrosion.

2 Maintenance – bodywork and underframe

1 The general condition of a vehicle's bodywork is the one thing that significantly affects its value. Maintenance is easy, but needs to be regular. Neglect, particularly after minor damage, can lead quickly to further deterioration and costly repair bills. It is important also to keep watch on those parts of the vehicle not immediately visible, for instance the underside, inside all the wheel arches, and the lower part of the engine compartment.

2 The basic maintenance routine for the bodywork is washing – preferably with a lot of water, from a hose. This will remove all the loose solids, which may have stuck to the vehicle. It is important to flush these off in such a way as to prevent grit from scratching the finish. The wheel arches and underframe need washing in the same way, to remove any accumulated mud, which will retain moisture and tend to encourage rust. Paradoxically enough, the best time to clean the underframe and wheel arches is in wet weather, when the mud is thoroughly wet and soft. In very wet weather, the underframe is usually cleaned of large accumulations automatically, and this is a good time for inspection.

3 Periodically, except on vehicles with a wax-based underbody protective coating, it is a good idea to have the whole of the underframe of the vehicle steam-cleaned, engine compartment included, so that a thorough inspection can be carried out to see what minor repairs and renovations are necessary. Steam cleaning is available at many garages, and is necessary for the removal of the accumulation of oily grime, which sometimes is allowed to become thick in certain areas. If steam-cleaning facilities are not available, there are some excellent grease solvents available which can be brush-applied; the dirt can then be simply hosed off. Note that these methods should not be used on vehicles with wax-based underbody protective coating, or the coating will be removed. Such vehicles should be inspected annually, preferably just prior to winter, when the underbody should be washed down, and any damage to the wax coating repaired. Ideally, a completely fresh coat should be applied. It would also be worth considering the use of such wax-based protection for injection into door panels, sills, box sections, etc, as an additional safeguard against rust damage, where such protection is not provided by the vehicle manufacturer.

4 After washing paintwork, wipe off with a chamois leather to give an unspotted clear finish. A coat of clear protective wax polish will give added protection against chemical pollutants in the air. If the paintwork sheen has dulled or oxidised, use a cleaner/polisher combination to restore the brilliance of the shine. This requires a little effort, but such dulling is usually caused because regular washing has been neglected. Care needs to be taken with metallic paintwork, as special non-abrasive cleaner/polisher is required to avoid damage to the finish. Always check that the door and ventilator opening drain holes and pipes are completely clear, so that water can be drained out. Brightwork should be treated in the same way as paintwork. Windscreens and windows can be kept clear of the smeary film, which often appears, by the use of proprietary glass cleaner. Never use any form of wax or other body or chromium polish on glass.

3 Maintenance – upholstery and carpets

1 Mats and carpets should be brushed or vacuum-cleaned regularly, to keep them free of grit. If they are badly stained, remove them from the vehicle for scrubbing or sponging, and make quite sure they are dry before refitting. Seats and interior trim panels can be kept clean by wiping with a damp cloth. If they do become stained (which can be more apparent on light-coloured upholstery), use a little liquid detergent and a soft nail brush to scour the grime out of the grain of the material. Do not forget to keep the headlining clean in the same way as the upholstery. When using liquid cleaners inside the vehicle, do not over-wet the surfaces being cleaned. Excessive damp could get into the seams and padded interior, causing stains, offensive odours or even rot.

2 If the inside of the vehicle gets wet accidentally, it is worthwhile taking some trouble to dry it out properly, particularly where carpets are involved. Do not leave oil or electric heaters inside the vehicle for this purpose.

4 Minor body damage – repair

Scratches

1 If the scratch is very superficial, and does not penetrate to the metal of the bodywork, repair is very simple. Lightly rub the area of the scratch with a paintwork renovator, or a very fine cutting paste, to remove loose paint from the scratch, and to clear the surrounding bodywork of wax polish. Rinse the area with clean water.

2 Apply touch-up paint to the scratch using a fine paint brush; continue to apply fine layers of paint until the surface of the paint in the scratch is level with the surrounding paintwork. Allow the new paint at least two weeks to harden, and then blend it into the surrounding paintwork by rubbing the scratch area with a paintwork renovator or a very fine cutting paste. Finally, apply wax polish.

3 Where the scratch has penetrated right through to the metal of the bodywork, causing the metal to rust, a different repair technique is required. Remove any loose rust from the bottom of the scratch with a penknife, then apply rust-inhibiting paint to prevent the formation of rust in the future. Using a rubber or nylon applicator, fill the scratch with bodystopper paste. If required, this paste can be mixed with cellulose thinners to provide a very thin paste, which is ideal for filling narrow scratches. Before the stopper-paste in the scratch hardens, wrap a piece of smooth cotton rag around the top of a finger. Dip the finger in cellulose thinners, and quickly sweep it across the surface of the stopper-paste in the scratch; this will ensure that the surface of the stopper-paste is slightly hollowed. The scratch can now be painted over as described earlier in this Section.

Dents

4 When deep denting of the vehicle's bodywork has taken place, the first task is to pull the dent out, until the affected bodywork almost attains its original shape. There is little point in trying to restore the original shape completely, as the metal in the damaged area will have stretched on impact, and cannot be reshaped fully to its original contour. It is better to bring the level of the dent up to a point, which is about 3 mm below the level of the surrounding bodywork. In cases where the dent is very shallow anyway, it is not worth trying to pull it out at all. If the underside of the dent is accessible, it can be hammered out gently from behind, using a mallet with a wooden or plastic head. Whilst doing this, hold a suitable block of wood firmly against the outside of the panel, to absorb the impact from the hammer blows and thus prevent a large area of the bodywork from being 'belled-out'.

5 Should the dent be in a section of the bodywork, which has a double skin, or some other factor making it inaccessible from behind, a different technique is called for. Drill several small holes through the metal inside the area – particularly in the deeper section. Then screw long self-tapping screws into the holes, just sufficiently for them to gain a good purchase in the metal. Now the dent can be pulled out by pulling on the protruding heads of the screws with a pair of pliers.

6 The next stage of the repair is the removal of the paint from the damaged area, and from an inch or so of the surrounding 'sound' bodywork. This is accomplished most easily by using a wire brush or abrasive pad on a power drill, although it can be done just as effectively by hand, using sheets of abrasive paper. To complete the preparation for filling, score the surface of the bare metal with a screwdriver or the tang of a file, or alternatively, drill small holes in the affected area. This will provide a really good 'key' for the filler paste.

7 To complete the repair, see the Section on filling and respraying.

Rust holes or gashes

8 Remove all paint from the affected area, and from an inch or so of the surrounding 'sound' bodywork, using an abrasive pad or a wire brush on a power drill. If these are not available, a few sheets of abrasive paper will do the job most effectively. With the paint removed, you will be able to judge the severity of the corrosion, and therefore decide whether to renew the whole panel (if this is possible) or to repair the affected area. New body panels are not as expensive as most people think, and it is often quicker and more satisfactory to fit a new panel than to attempt to repair large areas of corrosion.

9 Remove all fittings from the affected area, except those, which will act as a guide to the original shape of the damaged bodywork (e.g. headlight shells etc). Then, using tin snips or a hacksaw blade, remove all loose metal and any other metal badly affected by corrosion. Hammer the edges of the hole inwards, in order to create a slight depression for the filler paste.

10 Wire-brush the affected area to remove the powdery rust from the surface of the remaining metal. Paint the affected area with rust-inhibiting paint, if the back of the rusted area is accessible, treat this also.

11 Before filling can take place, it will be necessary to block the hole in some way. This can be achieved by the use of aluminium or plastic mesh, or aluminium tape.

12 Aluminium or plastic mesh, or glass-fibre matting, is probably the best material to use

for a large hole. Cut a piece to the approximate size and shape of the hole to be filled, then position it in the hole so that its edges are below the level of the surrounding bodywork. It can be retained in position by several blobs of filler paste around its periphery.

13 Aluminium tape should be used for small or very narrow holes. Pull a piece off the roll, trim it to the approximate size and shape required, then pull off the backing paper (if used) and stick the tape over the hole; it can be overlapped if the thickness of one piece is insufficient. Burnish down the edges of the tape with the handle of a screwdriver or similar, to ensure that the tape is securely attached to the metal underneath.

Filling and respraying

14 Before using this Section, see the Sections on dent, deep scratch, rust holes and gash repairs.

15 Many types of bodyfiller are available, but generally speaking, those proprietary kits, which contain a tin of filler paste and a tube of resin hardener, are best for this type of repair. A wide, flexible plastic or nylon applicator will be found invaluable for imparting a smooth and well-contoured finish to the surface of the filler.

16 Mix up a little filler on a clean piece of card or board – measure the hardener carefully (follow the maker's instructions on the pack), otherwise the filler will set too rapidly or too slowly. Using the applicator, apply the filler paste to the prepared area; draw the applicator across the surface of the filler to achieve the correct contour and to level the surface. As soon as a contour that approximates to the correct one is achieved, stop working the paste – if you carry on too long, the paste will become sticky and begin to 'pick-up' on the applicator. Continue to add thin layers of filler paste at 20-minute intervals, until the level of the filler is just proud of the surrounding bodywork.

17 Once the filler has hardened, the excess can be removed using a metal plane or file. From then on, progressively finer grades of abrasive paper should be used, starting with a 40-grade production paper, and finishing with a 400-grade wet-and-dry paper. Always wrap the abrasive paper around a flat rubber, cork, or wooden block – otherwise the surface of the filler will not be completely flat. During the smoothing of the filler surface, the wet-and-dry paper should be periodically rinsed in water. This will ensure that a very smooth finish is imparted to the filler at the final stage.

18 At this stage, the dent should be surrounded by a ring of bare metal, which in turn should be encircled by the finely 'feathered' edge of the good paintwork. Rinse the repair area with clean water, until all of the dust produced by the rubbing-down operation has gone.

19 Spray the whole area with a light coat of primer – this will show up any imperfections

in the surface of the filler. Repair these imperfections with fresh filler paste or bodystopper, and once more smooth the surface with abrasive paper. Repeat this spray-and-repair procedure until you are satisfied that the surface of the filler, and the feathered edge of the paintwork, are perfect. Clean the repair area with clean water, and allow to dry fully.

20 The repair area is now ready for final spraying. Paint spraying must be carried out in a warm, dry, windless and dust-free atmosphere. This condition can be created artificially if you have access to a large indoor working area, but if you are forced to work in the open, you will have to pick your day very carefully. If you are working indoors, dousing the floor in the work area with water will help to settle the dust, which would otherwise be in the atmosphere. If the repair area is confined to one body panel, mask off the surrounding panels; this will help to minimise the effects of a slight variance in paint colours. Bodywork fittings (e.g. chrome strips, door handles etc) will also need to be masked off. Use genuine masking tape, and several thickness of newspaper, for the masking operations.

21 Before commencing to spray, agitate the aerosol can thoroughly, and then spray a test area (an old tin, or similar) until the technique is mastered. Cover the repair area with a thick coat of primer; the thickness should be built up using several thin layers of paint, rather than one thick one. Using 400-grade wet-and-dry paper, rub down the surface of the primer until it is really smooth. While doing this, the work area should be thoroughly doused with water, and the wet-and-dry paper periodically rinsed in water. Allow to dry before spraying on more paint.

22 Spray on the top coat, again building up the thickness by using several thin layers of paint. Start spraying at one edge of the repair area, and then, using a side-to-side motion, work until the whole repair area and about 2 inches of the surrounding original paintwork is covered. Remove all masking material 10 to 15 minutes after spraying on the final coat of paint.

23 Allow the new paint at least two weeks to harden, then, using a paintwork renovator, or a very fine cutting paste, blend the edges of the paint into the existing paintwork. Finally, apply wax polish.

Plastic components

24 With the use of more and more plastic body components by the vehicle manufacturers (e.g. bumpers. spoilers, and in some cases major body panels), rectification of more serious damage to such items has become a matter of either entrusting repair work to a specialist in this field, or renewing complete components. Repair of such damage by the DIY owner is not really feasible, owing to the cost of the equipment and materials required for effecting such repairs. The basic technique involves making a groove along the line of the crack in the plastic, using a rotary burr in a power drill. The damaged part is then welded back together, using a hot-air gun to heat up and fuse a plastic filler rod into the groove. Any excess plastic is then removed, and the area rubbed down to a smooth finish. It is important that a filler rod of the correct plastic is used, as body components can be made of a variety of different types (e.g. polycarbonate, ABS, polypropylene).

25 Damage of a less serious nature (abrasions, minor cracks etc) can be repaired by the DIY owner using a two-part epoxy filler repair material. Once mixed in equal proportions, this is used in similar fashion to the bodywork filler used on metal panels. The filler is usually cured in twenty to thirty minutes, ready for sanding and painting.

26 If the owner is renewing a complete component himself, or if he has repaired it with epoxy filler, he will be left with the problem of finding a suitable paint for finishing which is compatible with the type of plastic used. At one time, the use of a universal paint was not possible, owing to the complex range of plastics encountered in body component applications. Standard paints, generally speaking, will not bond to plastic or rubber satisfactorily. However, it is now possible to obtain a plastic body parts finishing kit, which consists of a pre-primer

treatment, a primer and coloured top coat. Full instructions are normally supplied with a kit, but basically, the method of use is to first apply the pre-primer to the component concerned, and allow it to dry for up to 30 minutes. Then the primer is applied, and left to dry for about an hour before finally applying the special-coloured top coat. The result is a correctly coloured component, where the paint will flex with the plastic or rubber, a property that standard paint does not normally possess.

5 Major body damage – repair

1 Where serious damage has occurred, or large areas need renewal due to neglect, it means that complete new panels will need welding-in, and this is best left to professionals. If the damage is due to impact, it will also be necessary to check completely the alignment of the body shell, and this can only be carried out accurately by an Audi dealer using special jigs. If the body is left misaligned, it is primarily dangerous, as the car will not handle properly, and secondly, uneven stresses will be imposed on the steering, suspension and possibly transmission, causing abnormal wear, or complete failure, particularly to such items as the tyres.

6 Front bumper – removal and refitting

Removal

1 Apply the handbrake, then jack up the front of the vehicle and support it on axle stands (see *'Jacking and vehicle support'* in Reference chapter).

2 Open the bonnet, and undo the screws securing the upper part of the radiator grille/bumper cover to the engine compartment crossbar (see illustration).

3 Working on each side in turn, undo the screws securing the wheel arch liners to the bumper ends and remove the lower part of the liner (see illustrations).

4 Undo the bumper upper mounting screws/bolts from each side of the bumper (see illustrations).

5 Undo the three securing screws from the lower front edge of the bumper (see illustration).

6 With the help of an assistant, release the bumper ends, and withdraw the front bumper cover from the vehicle until it is possible to disconnect the wiring from the foglights. Also, where applicable, release the headlamp washer hoses.

7 On models with headlamp washers, remove the washer jets as described in Chapter 12, Section 20.

6.2 Undo the bumper/grille upper screws

6.3a Undo the lower retaining screws...

6.3b...and remove the inner liner

6.4a Undo the bumper retaining screws...

6.4b...and retaining bolt

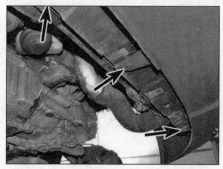

6.5 Unscrew the lower bumper securing screws

6.8a Undo the bolts and screws...

6.8b...and remove the bumper crossmember

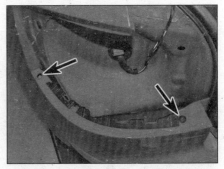

7.2a Remove the bumper upper retaining screws

8 Undo the retaining bolts and screws and remove the front bumper from across the front of the vehicle **(see illustrations)**.

Refitting

9 Refitting is a reverse of the removal procedure, ensuring that the bumper ends engage correctly with the locating guides as the bumper is refitted.

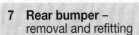

7 Rear bumper – removal and refitting

Removal

1 To improve access, chock the front wheels, and then jack up the rear of the vehicle and support it on axle stands (see *'Jacking and vehicle support'* in Reference chapter).
2 Remove the rear light clusters (as described in Chapter 12, Section 7), and then undo the upper mounting screws **(see illustrations)**.
3 Remove the six screws (three each side) securing the wheel arch liners to the bumper ends **(see illustration)**.
4 Undo the screws from the lower edge of the bumper **(see illustration)**.
5 Working inside the luggage compartment, unclip the plastic trim covers and unscrew the securing nuts from the rear mounting bolts **(see illustrations)**.
Note: *You will need to use a deep 10mm socket to remove the nut from the long*

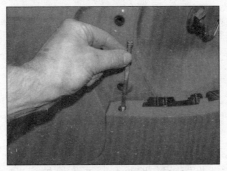

7.2b The front one is a long bolt...

7.3 Remove the rear bumper-to-wheel arch liner screws

mounting bolt, taking care not to drop the securing nut into the chassis.
6 With the help of an assistant, release the bumper cover from the guides at the left-

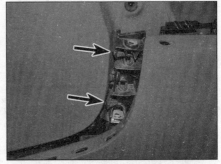

7.2c...that pushes the locking tabs (arrowed) to the secure the bumper

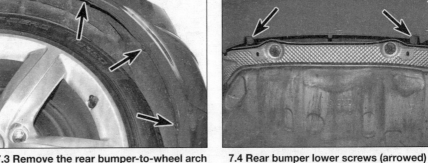

7.4 Rear bumper lower screws (arrowed)

and right-hand ends, and then withdraw the bumper cover from the rear of the vehicle **(see illustration)**.
7 Undo the retaining bolts and remove

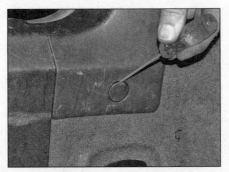

7.5a Unclip the plastic cover and...

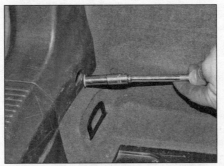

7.5b...and undo the securing nut, using a deep socket

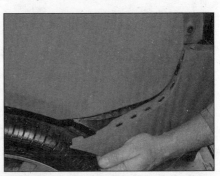

7.6 Unclip the rear bumper at each side of the vehicle

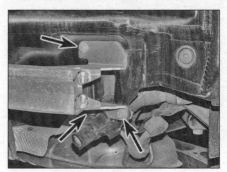

7.7 Rear bumper crossmember mounting bolts

7.8 Rear bumper mounting bolts, secured to bumper

8.2 Release the strut retaining clip

the rear bumper from across the rear of the vehicle **(see illustration)**.

Refitting

8 Refitting is a reverse of the removal procedure, ensuring that the bumper ends engage correctly with the slides as the bumper is refitted. Make sure the mounting bolts in the rear of the bumper cover are secure, before refitting **(see illustration)**.

8 Bonnet – removal, refitting and adjustment

Removal

1 Open the bonnet and using a pencil or felt tip pen, mark the outline of each bonnet hinge relative to the bonnet, to use as a guide on refitting.
2 With the help of an assistant to support the bonnet, release the locking clip and disconnect the gas support strut from the balljoint on the bonnet **(see illustration)**.
3 Undo the bonnet securing nuts **(see illustration)**, and carefully lift the bonnet clear. Store the bonnet out of the way in a safe place.
4 Inspect the bonnet hinges for signs of wear and free play at the pivots, and if necessary renew. Each hinge is secured to the body by two bolts, mark the position of the hinge on the body then undo the retaining bolts and remove it from the vehicle. On refitting, align

the new hinge with the marks and tighten the retaining bolts.

Refitting and adjustment

5 With the aid of an assistant, offer up the bonnet and loosely fit the retaining bolts. Align the hinges with the marks made on removal, and then tighten the retaining nuts securely.
6 Refit the gas strut in the reverse order of removal.
7 Close the bonnet, and check for alignment with the adjacent panels. If necessary, unscrew the hinge nuts and re-align the bonnet. Once the bonnet is correctly aligned, tighten the hinge nuts. Check that the bonnet fastens and releases satisfactorily.

9 Bonnet release cable – removal and refitting

Removal

1 The bonnet release cable is in two sections, with a coupling located to the rear of the right-hand side headlight. To remove either section of cable it will be necessary to first release the coupling by unhooking the pivoting cover, and then unhook the inner cable end from the coupling **(see illustrations 10.3a and 10.3b)**.
2 To release the cable at the bonnet lock, remove the lock as described in Section 10, then depress the end fitting and pull it out.

3 To remove the rear section, first release the coupling as described in paragraph 1.
4 Working inside the vehicle, unclip the driver's side sill trim panel from inside the footwell **(see illustration)**.
5 Undo the retaining screws, and remove the lower facia panel from above the pedal assembly.
6 Undo the two securing screws and remove the bonnet release lever **(see illustration)**.
7 Release the outer cable by unclipping from the lever bracket and detach the inner cable from the lever.
8 Release the cable sealing grommet from the bulkhead.
9 Work along the length of the cable, noting its correct routing, and free it from the retaining clips and ties.
10 Disconnect the outer cable from under the crossmember on the lock housing.
11 Tie a length of string to the end of the cable inside the vehicle, and then withdraw the cable through into the engine compartment.
12 Once the cable is free, untie the string and leave it in position in the vehicle; the string can then be used to draw the new cable back into position.

Refitting

13 Tie the inner end of the string to the end of the cable, then use the string to draw the bonnet release cable back from the engine compartment. Once the cable is through, untie the string.
14 Refitting is a reversal of the removal.

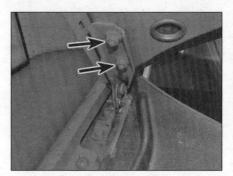

8.3 Bonnet hinge securing nuts

9.4 Unclip the driver's side trim panel

9.6 Bonnet release lever (arrowed) – facia removed for clarity

10.2 Disconnecting the bonnet lock microswitch located over the headlight

10.3a Lift the cable cover...

10.3b...and release the bonnet lock cable at the join adapter

10.4 Unscrew the mounting bolts...

10.5a...prise the lock from the crossmember...

10.5b...and disconnect the cable

15 Ensure the rubber grommet in the bulkhead is fitted correctly, and the cable is correctly routed and secured to all the relevant retaining clips.

16 Before closing the bonnet, check the operation of the release lever and cable.

10 Bonnet lock – removal and refitting

Removal

1 Open the bonnet then remove the radiator grille, as described in Section 6.

2 Disconnect the wiring for the contact microswitch at the connector located at the left-hand side of the radiator above the top hose **(see illustration)**.

3 Disconnect the bonnet cable at the join adapter located over the headlight, by lifting

the cover and releasing the cable end fitting **(see illustrations)**. This will allow the cable to be disconnected from the bonnet lock.

4 Note the location of the three mounting bolts in their slots to ensure correct adjustment on refitting, then unscrew and remove them **(see illustration)**.

5 Prise the lock from the crossmember, then disconnect the cable by lifting the cover and unhooking the cable end fitting from the lock lever **(see illustrations)**.

6 Pull off the wiring support clips beneath the crossmember, then withdraw the lock while at the same time guiding the wiring through the hole in the crossmember.

Refitting

7 Refitting is a reversal of removal. Check that the bonnet fastens and releases satisfactorily before refitting the radiator grille. If adjustment is necessary, loosen the bonnet lock retaining

bolts, and adjust the position of the lock to suit. Finally, tighten the bolts.

11 Door – removal, refitting and adjustment

Removal

1 Open the door then disconnect the wiring at the A- or B-pillar as applicable. To do this, first release the rubber bellows **(see illustration)**, pull out the locking lever and disconnect the wiring plug.

2 Unscrew and remove the upper and lower bolts from the lower hinge, then support the door and unscrew the upper bolt from the upper hinge **(see illustrations)**. Withdraw the door from the A- or B-pillar.

3 Examine the hinges for signs of wear or damage. If renewal is necessary, the hinge

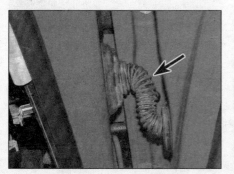

11.1 Rubber bellows for wiring protection

11.2a Front door upper hinge...

11.2b...and lower hinge

11.8 Door lock striker mounted on the B-pillar

retaining bolts are fitted from inside the vehicle A- or B-pillar, making it necessary to remove the relevant trim panel for access to them. Before removing them, accurately mark their position to ensure correct refitting.

Refitting

4 Where renewed, fit the hinges and tighten the bolts to the specified torque. Refit the trim.

5 With the aid of an assistant, offer up the door to the vehicle and locate it on the guide bolts. Fit the new hinge bolts and tighten to the specified torque.

6 Reconnect the wiring plug and secure with the locking lever.

7 Refit the rubber bellows.

Adjustment

8 Close the door and check the door alignment with the surrounding body panels. There must be an even gap all around, and the door must be level with the surrounding body panels. Slight adjustment can be made with the eccentric pin of the upper hinge; loosen the lock bolt then turn the pin as necessary and retighten the lock-bolt. Check that the striker enters the door lock centrally as the door is closed, and if necessary adjust the position of the striker by loosening its mounting bolts **(see illustration)**.

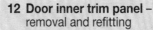

12 Door inner trim panel – removal and refitting

Removal

1 Switch off the ignition.

Front (3-door)

2 Carefully unclip the armrest trim panel by carefully inserting a lever or similar tool under the lower edge, and levering upwards **(see illustrations)**.

3 Undo the two retaining screws securing the grip handle to the door panel **(see illustration)**.

4 Undo the screws from the lower edge of the trim panel **(see illustration)**.

5 Release the door trim panel studs each side, carefully levering between the panel and door with a flat-bladed lever. Work around the outside of the panel, and when all the studs are released, lift the door trim panel upwards and off the window slot. Support the panel away from the door **(see illustration)**.

6 Disconnect any wiring connections from the rear of the panel, and then unhook the cable from the inner door handle, and remove the trim panel from the vehicle **(see illustration)**.

Front (5-door)

7 Using a lever, carefully unclip the speaker trim cover from the top of the door grab handle.

8 Using a lever, carefully unclip the window switch trim cover from bottom of the door grab handle.

9 Undo the two trim retaining screws located at the top and bottom of the grab handle.

10 Release the door trim panel studs, carefully levering between the panel and door with a flat-bladed lever. Work around the outside of the panel, and when all the studs are released, lift the door trim panel upwards and off the window slot. Support the panel away from the door.

11 Where applicable, disconnect the wiring from the trim panel.

12 Unhook the cable from the inner door handle, and remove the trim panel from the vehicle.

12.2a Carefully prise up the trim panel...

12.2b ...and remove it from the door inner trim panel

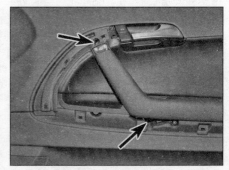

12.3 Undo the door handle securing screws

12.4 Door inner trim panel lower retaining screw

12.5 Release the door panel from the studs...

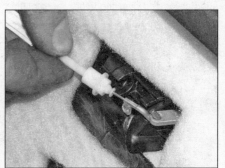

12.6 ...and disconnect the cable from the door release handle

12.13 Unclip the handle upper trim cover

12.14 Unclip the switch trim cover

12.15a Undo the upper...

12.15b...and lower handle retaining screws

12.16a Carefully lever the trim panel...

12.16b...and remove it from the door

Rear doors

13 Using a lever, carefully unclip the speaker trim cover from the top of the door grab handle **(see illustration)**.

14 Using a lever, carefully unclip the window switch trim cover from bottom of the door grab handle **(see illustration)**.

15 Undo the two trim retaining screws located at the top and bottom of the grab handle **(see illustrations)**.

16 Release the door trim panel studs, carefully levering between the panel and door with a flat-bladed lever. Work around the outside of the panel, and when all the studs are released, lift the door trim panel upwards and off the window slot. Support the panel away from the door **(see illustrations)**.

17 Where applicable, disconnect the wiring from the trim panel.

18 Unhook the cable from the inner door handle, and remove the trim panel from the vehicle **(see illustration)**.

Refitting

19 Before refitting, check whether any of the trim panel retaining studs where broken on removal, and renew them as necessary. Refitting of the trim panel is then a reversal of removal. Check the operation of the door electrical equipment.

13 Door handle and lock components – removal and refitting

Removal

Interior door handle

1 Remove the door inner trim panel as described in Section 12.

2 Undo the screws on the inside of the door trim panel, then disconnect the wiring and unclip the door handle to remove it **(see illustrations)**.

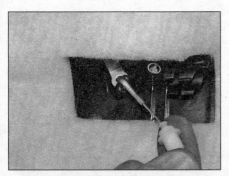

12.18...then unhook the cable from the inner door handle

13.2a Disconnect the wiring connector...

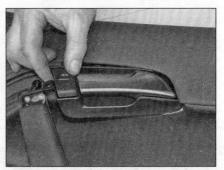

13.2b...then undo the screws and remove the interior door handle

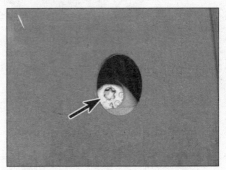

13.3 Lock cylinder retaining screw

13.4 Undo the screw until it comes to the stop

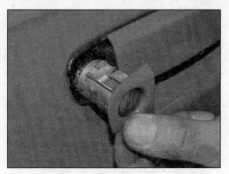

13.5 Removing the door lock cylinder housing

13.6 Unclipping the trim cover from the lock cylinder

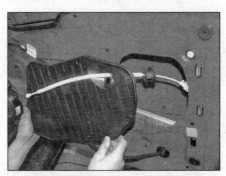

13.10 Unclip the plastic cover from the door panel

13.11 Disconnect the operating rod from the door handle

Front door lock cylinder housing or end cap

3 Open the door, and then unclip the rubber

13.12 Remove the security cover from the door lock assembly

grommet in the rear edge of the door to locate the retaining screw **(see illustration)**.

4 Pull out the door handle, and hold it in this position whilst undoing the Torx retaining screw until it comes to its stop. Do not remove the screw too far or the locking ring may fall into the door **(see illustration)**.

5 Pull the lock cylinder housing out of the door handle, and release the handle to the original position **(see illustration)**. On older vehicles, the housing may be corroded into the door aperture making it difficult to remove.

6 If required, unclip the plastic trim cover from the end of the lock cylinder **(see illustration)**.

Door lock assembly

7 Remove the door inner trim panel as described in Section 12.

8 Remove the door lock cylinder housing as described in paragraphs 3 to 5.

9 Remove the window glass/frame as described in Section 14.

10 Remove the plastic cover from the door panel, unclipping the lock operating cable as it is removed **(see illustration)**.

11 Working through the top of the door aperture, disconnect the top of the operating rod from the door handle unit **(see illustration)**.

12 Working through the door aperture, unclip the security plastic cover from the door lock assembly **(see illustration)**.

13 Release the securing clip and disconnect the bottom of the operating rod from the lock assembly, noting its fitted position **(see illustrations)**.

14 Unclip the rubber grommet and insert a screwdriver to release the locking clip from the rear of the door handle unit **(see illustrations)**.

13.13a Release the locking clip...

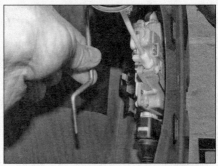

13.13b...and disengage the operating rod

13.14a Remove the rubber grommet...

13.14b...and slide the locking clip to release...

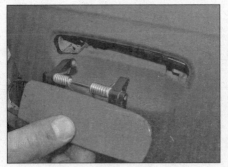

13.15...the outer door handle

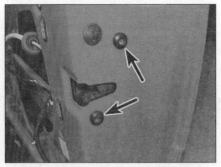

13.16a Undo the door lock retaining screws...

15 With the locking clip released, remove the outer door handle from the mounting bracket **(see illustration)**.

16 Unscrew the two lock mounting bolts and withdraw the lock assembly complete with door handle mounting bracket out from inside the door aperture. Disconnect the wiring connector as it is removed **(see illustrations)**.

17 If required, release the securing clip and unclip the plastic trim cover from the door handle **(see illustrations)**.

Refitting

Interior door handle

18 Clip the handle back into position and secure with the retaining screws on the inside of the door trim. Reconnect the wiring connector and refit the door trim panel as described in Section 12.

Front door lock cylinder housing or end cap

19 Insert the lock cylinder housing in the door. As it is fitted, it should make an audible click as it locates in the mounting plate.

20 Allow the exterior handle to rest lightly against the door panel, and then tighten the Torx retaining screw.

21 Refit the grommet to cover the screw in the end of the door frame.

22 Check the operation of the lock before closing the door, by sliding a screwdriver into

13.16b...remove the lock assembly from inside the door panel...

13.16c...and disconnect the wiring connector

the lock to operate the mechanism. If it does not function correctly, remove the housing and check that the operating rod is located correctly in the exterior handle.

Door lock assembly

23 Refitting is a reversal of removal, making sure the operating rod and flexible cable drive are located correctly in the position noted on removal. Reconnect wiring connector and tighten all bolts securely.

24 Refit the window glass/frame as described in Section 14.

25 Refit the lock cylinder housing or end cap, as described above and check that it functions correctly.

26 Refit the door trim panel as described in Section 12.

14 Door window glass/frame and regulator – removal and refitting

Removal

Window motor and control unit

1 Remove the door inner trim panel as described in Section 12.

2 Disconnect the wiring connectors from the window regulator motor **(see illustration)**.

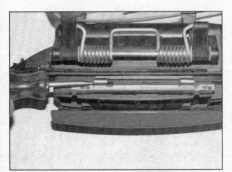

13.17a Slide the locking clip to one side...

13.17b...to release the door handle trim cover

14.2 Disconnect the wiring connector

14.3a Undo the three retaining screws...

14.3b...and remove the motor from the door panel

14.4 Release the securing clips to remove the control unit from the motor

14.6 Rear upper mounting bolt

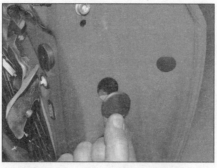

14.7a Remove the rubber grommet...

14.7b...to access the lower mounting bolt

3 Unscrew the mounting bolts and withdraw the regulator motor from the door panel **(see illustrations)**.

4 If required, release the securing clips and withdraw the control unit from the regulator motor **(see illustration)**.

Front door window frame

5 Remove the window motor as described in paragraphs 1 to 3.

6 Pull back the rubber trim cover at the rear of the window frame and undo the upper mounting bolt **(see illustration)**.

7 Unclip the rubber grommet in the rear edge of the door to locate the lower mounting bolt **(see illustrations)**.

8 Pull back the rubber trim cover at the front of the window frame and undo the upper mounting bolt **(see illustrations)**.

9 Undo the lower frame mounting bolt at the front of the door panel, just above the speaker **(see illustration)**.

10 Undo the window regulator assembly securing screws from the door panel **(see illustration)**.

Note: *There are three screws along the top of the door panel on 3-door vehicles and two screws at the top on 5-door vehicles.*

11 Using a pair of grips or similar, release the locating clips for the window regulator from the door panel **(see illustration)**.

12 With all screws and clips released, withdraw the window frame/glass and

14.8a Pull back the rubber trim...

14.8b...and remove the front upper mounting bolt

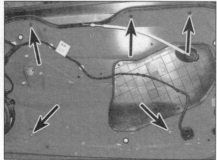

14.9 Undo the front lower mounting bolt

14.10 Window regulator securing screws

14.11 Releasing the motor securing clips from the door panel

14.12 Withdraw the window frame/ regulator assembly from the door panel

14.13 Note the position of the adjusters – rear adjuster shown

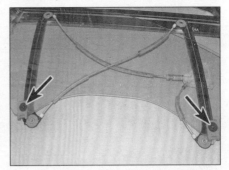

14.15 Window glass securing screws

regulator assembly out through the top of the door panel **(see illustration)**.

13 Note the position of the adjusters (9 mm Allen key) on the lower part of the window frame, where the mounting bolts are fitted **(see illustration)**. Do not turn these as they are set in position for refitting.

Front door window glass

14 Remove the door window frame as described in paragraphs 6 to 13.
15 To remove the glass, undo the two retaining screws from the lower part of the glass and slide the glass out from the guides **(see illustration)**.

Front door window regulator

16 Remove the window glass as described in paragraphs 14 and 15.
17 To remove the window regulator, undo the two retaining screws from the window frame **(see illustration)**.

Rear door window frame

18 Remove the window motor as described in paragraphs 1 to 3.
19 Pull back the rubber trim cover at the rear of the window frame and undo the upper mounting bolt.
20 Unclip the rubber grommet in the rear edge of the door to locate the mounting bolt **(see illustration)**.
21 Undo the lower frame mounting bolt at the rear edge of the door panel **(see illustration)**.
22 Pull back the rubber trim cover at the front of the window frame and undo the upper mounting bolt **(see illustration)**.
23 Unclip the rubber grommet in the front edge of the door to locate the mounting bolt.
24 Undo the window regulator assembly securing screws from the door panel **(see illustrations)**.

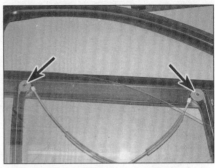

14.17 Window regulator securing screws

25 Using a pair of pliers or similar, release the locating clips for the window regulator from the door panel **(see illustration)**.
26 With all screws and clips released,

14.20 Undo the rear upper mounting bolts

14.21 Undo the lower mounting bolt

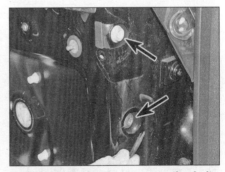

14.22 Undo the front upper mounting bolts

14.24a Window regulator upper securing screws...

14.24b ...and lower securing screws (arrowed)

14.25 Releasing the motor securing clips from the door panel

14.26 Withdraw the window frame/regulator assembly from the door panel

14.27 Note the position of the adjusters – rear adjuster shown

14.29 Window glass securing screws

14.31 Window regulator securing screw

14.33a Position of the window frame...

14.33b...can be adjusted with a 9 mm Allen key

withdraw the window frame/glass and regulator assembly out through the top of the door panel **(see illustration)**.

27 Note the position of the adjusters (9 mm Allen key) on the lower part of the window frame, where the mounting bolts are fitted **(see illustration)**. Do not turn these as they are set in position for refitting.

Rear door window glass

28 Remove the door window frame as described in paragraphs 18 to 27.

29 To remove the glass, undo the two retaining screws from the lower part of the glass and slide the glass out from the guides **(see illustration)**.

Rear door window regulator

30 Remove the window glass as described in paragraphs 28 and 29.

31 To remove the window regulator, undo the retaining screw from the window frame **(see illustration)**.

Refitting

32 Refitting is a reversal of removal, noting the fitted position of the adjusters on the lower part of the window frame (see paragraphs 13 front doors and 27 rear doors).

33 If a new window frame is fitted, a 9mm Allen key will need to be used to adjust the position of the window frame in the door panel **(see illustrations)**. The frame will need to be held in position as the adjusters are wound outwards to contact the inside of the door panel. Close the door to check the position of the frame against the vehicle body. Turn adjusters to get the correct position.

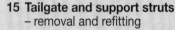

15 Tailgate and support struts – removal and refitting

Removal

Tailgate

1 With the tailgate open, undo the trim panel retaining screws inside the grab handles **(see illustrations)**. Release the trim panel clips, carefully levering between the panel and tailgate with a flat-bladed screwdriver. Work around the outside of the panel, and when all the clips are released, unclip from the upper trim and remove the panel.

2 Unclip the two upper side trims from

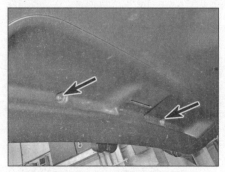

15.1a Remove the retaining screws...

15.1b...unclip the tailgate trim panel...

15.1c...and remove lock trim cover if required

15.2 Unclip the tailgate side trim panels

15.3a Undo the retaining screw (arrowed)...

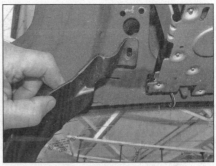

15.3b...and unclip the hinge trim

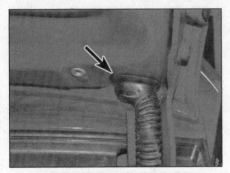

15.5 Wiring harness rubber sleeve

15.11a Lift locking clips and remove upper balljoint...

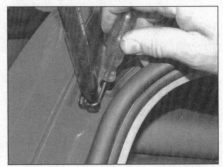

15.11b...and then the lower balljoint

tailgate **(see illustration)**, and then the upper trim from along the top of the tailgate starting from the outer ends and working towards the middle.

3 Undo the retaining screw and carefully unclip the plastic trim covers from the hinge brackets **(see illustrations)**.

Note: *These trim covers are only thin plastic and can crack easily.*

4 Working your way around the tailgate, disconnect the wiring connectors situated behind the trim panel and free the washer hose from the tailgate wiper motor.

5 Tie a piece of string to each end of the wiring then, noting the correct routing of the wiring harness, release the harness rubber sleeve **(see illustration)** from the tailgate and withdraw the wiring. When the end of the wiring appears, untie the string and leave it in position in the tailgate; it can then be used on refitting to draw the wiring into position.

6 Using a suitable marker pen, draw around the outline of each hinge marking its correct position on the tailgate.

7 With the help of an assistant to support the tailgate, remove the support struts as described below.

8 Unscrew and remove the bolts securing the hinges to the tailgate. Where necessary, recover the gaskets, which are fitted between the hinge and vehicle body.

9 Inspect the hinges for signs of wear or damage and renew if necessary. The hinges are secured to the vehicle by nuts or bolts (depending on model), which can be accessed once the headlining rear cover strip has been removed.

Support struts

⚠️ *Warning: The support struts are filled with a gas and must be disposed of safely.*

10 With the help of an assistant, support the tailgate in the open position.

11 Using a small flat-bladed screwdriver lift the locking clip, and pull the gas support strut off its balljoint mounting on the tailgate **(see illustrations)**. Repeat the procedure on the lower strut mounting and remove the strut from the vehicle body.

Note: *If the gas strut is to be re-used, the locking clip must not be taken all the way out, or the clip will be damaged.*

Refitting

Tailgate

12 Refitting is the reverse of removal, aligning the hinges with the marks made before removal. Tighten retaining bolts to the specified torque.

13 On completion, close the tailgate and check its alignment with the surrounding panels. If necessary slight adjustment can be made by unscrewing the retaining bolts and repositioning the tailgate on its hinges. If the tailgate buffers are in need of adjustment, continue as follows.

14 Locate the adjustment buffers on the tailgate. Through the hole in the rubber cap, insert an Allen key and undo the screw until the centre notched slide will move freely in or out of the housing. When the adjustment

buffer has been set to the correct position tighten the centre screw.

Support struts

15 Refitting is a reverse of the removal procedure, ensuring that the strut is securely retained by its retaining clips.

16 Tailgate lock components – removal and refitting

Removal

1 Open up the tailgate and remove the trim panel as described in Section 15.

Note: *If the lock is inoperative, the tailgate can be opened manually by sliding a flat object (key) through the slot in the tailgate trim cover from inside the car **(see illustration)**.*

16.1 Tailgate can be opened through the slot in the tailgate trim panel

16.2 Release the operating rod from the securing clip (arrowed)

16.3 Disconnect the wiring from the tailgate lock

Tailgate lock

2 Release the securing clip and disconnect the operating rod from the tailgate lock **(see illustration)**.

3 Disconnect the wiring from the lock **(see illustration)**.

4 Undo the retaining nuts and remove the lock from the tailgate **(see illustration)**.

Tailgate actuator

5 Release the securing clip and disconnect

the operating rod from the tailgate lock **(see illustration 16.2)**.

6 Slacken the retaining screws holding the actuator to the tailgate, and then withdraw it from inside the tailgate to remove **(see illustrations)**.

Note: *The retaining screws do not have to be completely removed, slacken and then slide the actuator out from the tailgate.*

7 Disconnect the wiring from the actuator as it is removed from the tailgate **(see illustration)**.

16.4 Tailgate lock retaining nuts

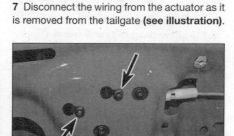

16.6a Slacken the tailgate actuator screws...

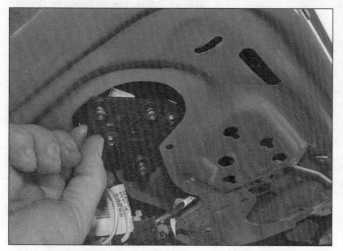

16.6b...and slide the actuator out from the tailgate

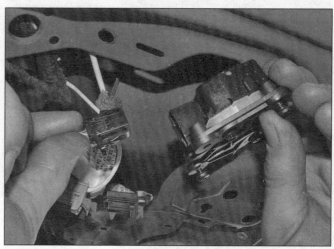

16.7 Disconnect the wiring connector as it is removed

Refitting

8 Refitting is a reversal of removal, however, before refitting the trim panel, check the operation of the lock components.

17 Central locking components – description, removal and refitting

Note: *Before disconnecting the battery, refer to 'Disconnecting the battery' in Reference chapter.*

Description

1 The central locking system consists of the following main components. Note that the central locking and anti-theft alarm systems share some components (see Chapter 12):

a) *Convenience system central control unit located behind the luggage compartment trim.*

b) *Door control units integrated in the window regulator motors.*

c) *Electric door lock actuators integrated in the door locks.*

d) *Fuel tank filler cap flap actuator located behind the luggage compartment trim.*

e) *Tailgate lock actuator located in the tailgate, together with the release button.*

f) *Anti-theft alarm horn located beneath the right-hand front wheel arch.*

g) *Bonnet contact switch located on the bonnet lock.*

h) *Remote control transmitter on the ignition key fob.*

Removal

Convenience system control unit

2 Remove the right-hand trim from the luggage compartment with reference to Section 25.

3 Undo the retaining nuts and remove the plastic mounting bracket. Disconnect the

17.3a Undo the retaining nuts...

17.3b...remove the mounting bracket...

17.3c...and slide the control unit out from the mounting

17.7 Disconnect the wiring connector

17.8a Slacken the fuel flap actuator screws...

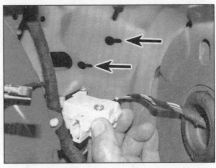

17.8b...and slide the actuator out from the inner body panel

wiring from the control unit and slide it out from its mounting bracket **(see illustrations)**.

Door control unit

4 Remove the window regulator motor as described in Section 14.

Electric door lock actuator

5 Remove the door lock as described in Section 13.

Fuel tank filler cap flap actuator

6 Remove the right-hand trim from the luggage compartment with reference to Section 25.
7 Disconnect the wiring from the actuator **(see illustration)**.
8 Slacken the retaining screws by two turns and then slide the actuator forwards to release it from the inner body panel **(see illustrations)**.

Tailgate lock activator

9 Remove the tailgate lock actuator as described in Section 16.

Anti-theft alarm horn

10 Switch off the ignition.
11 Apply the handbrake, then jack up the front of the vehicle and support it on axle stands (see *'Jacking and vehicle support'* in Reference chapter). Remove the right-hand front roadwheel.
12 Remove the wheel arch liner with reference to Section 21.
13 Use a drill to remove the pop rivets securing the horn to the inner body panel.

14 Withdraw the horn and disconnect the wiring.

Bonnet contact switch

15 Remove the bonnet lock as described in Section 10. If necessary, the operating cable may remain attached to the lock.
16 On the lock, release the tab and push the switch from the slotted holes.

Remote control transmitter battery

17 Using a screwdriver inserted in the slot, separate the transmitter unit from the key.
18 Prise apart the covers, then lever out the battery, noting which way round it is fitted.

Refitting

19 Refitting is a reversal of removal. Use new pop rivets when refitting the anti-theft alarm horn. On completion check the operation of the central locking system.

18 Exterior mirrors and associated components – removal and refitting

Removal

Exterior mirror

1 Remove the door inner trim panel as described in Section 12.
2 Disconnect the wiring for the exterior mirror at the window regulator motor/control unit **(see illustration)**.
3 Undo the retaining screws and remove the speaker from the door panel. Reach up inside the speaker aperture to release the wiring loom from the window frame **(see illustration)**. Also, release the wiring from any support clips.

18.2 Disconnect the wiring connector

18.3 Release the wiring loom from the window frame (removed for clarity)

18.4 Mirror retaining screw (arrowed)

18.5 Removing the exterior door mirror

18.6 Remove the exterior mirror glass...

18.7...and disconnect the wiring

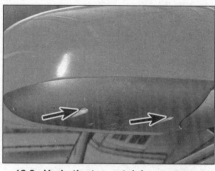

18.9a Undo the two retaining screws...

18.9b...and unclip the lower trim panel

4 Pull back the small trim panel **(see illustration)**, and then unscrew the mounting screw while supporting the exterior mirror.
5 Withdraw the exterior mirror from the door while guiding the wiring through the hole **(see**

18.10 Unclipping the mirror housing

illustration). Where fitted, remove the gasket from the window frame.

Mirror glass

Note: *The mirror glass is clipped into place. Removal of the glass without the Audi special forked tool is likely to result in breakage of the glass. Wear protective gloves and glasses to prevent personal injury.*
6 Press in the top of the mirror glass so that the bottom edge is furthest from the housing. Protect the edge of the housing with masking tape (or a cloth), then insert the special tool and lever the mirror glass from its mounting clips. Take great care when removing the glass; do not use excessive force, as the glass is easily broken. If the Audi special tool is not available, use a flat-bladed lever with tape around to prevent any damage to the mirror housing **(see illustration)**.

7 Disconnect the wiring connectors from the mirror heating element **(see illustration)**.

Mirror housing

8 Remove the mirror glass as described in paragraphs 6 and 7.
9 Undo the two retaining screws and unclip the trim panel from the bottom of the mirror housing **(see illustrations)**.
10 Carefully pull the housing upwards to release the securing clips and withdraw it from its mounting **(see illustration)**.

Mirror motor

11 Remove the mirror glass as described in paragraphs 6 and 7.
12 Undo the three retaining screws and unclip the motor from the mirror mounting bracket **(see illustrations)**.
13 Disconnect the wiring connector from the motor as it is removed **(see illustration)**.

18.12a Undo the retaining screws
(arrowed)...

18.12b...remove the motor...

18.13...and disconnect the wiring
connector

Mirror switch

14 Refer to Chapter 12, Section 4.

Refitting

15 Refitting is the reverse of the relevant removal procedure. When refitting the mirror glass, press firmly at the centre taking care not to use excessive force, as the glass is easily broken.

19 Windscreen and rear window glass – general information

1 These areas of glass are bonded in position with a special adhesive. Renewal of such fixed glass is a difficult, messy and time-consuming task, which is beyond the scope of the home mechanic. It is difficult, unless one has plenty of practice, to obtain a secure, waterproof fit. Furthermore, the task carries a high risk of breakage; this applies especially to the laminated glass windscreen. In view of this, owners are strongly advised to have this sort of work carried out by one of the many specialist windscreen fitters.

20 Sunroof – general information

1 Due to the complexity of the sunroof mechanism, considerable expertise is needed to repair, renew or adjust the sunroof components successfully. Removal of the roof first requires the headlining to be removed, which is a complex and tedious operation, and not a task to be undertaken lightly. Therefore, any problems with the sunroof should be referred to an Audi dealer.

2 On models with an electric sunroof, if the sunroof motor fails to operate, first check the relevant fuse. If the fault cannot be traced and rectified, the sunroof can be opened and closed manually using an Allen key to turn the motor spindle (a suitable key is supplied with the vehicle, and should be clipped onto the inside of the sunroof motor trim).

3 To gain access to the motor, unclip the rear of the trim cover to open. Unclip the Allen key,

21.1a Removing the front lower inner wheel arch liner...

and then insert it fully into the motor opening (against spring pressure). Rotate the key to move the sunroof to the required position.

21 Body exterior fittings – removal and refitting

Wheel arch liners and body under-panels

1 The various plastic covers fitted to the underside of the vehicle are secured in position by a mixture of screws, nuts and retaining clips and removal will be fairly obvious on inspection. Work methodically around the panel removing its retaining screws and releasing its retaining clips until the panel is free and can be removed from the underside of the vehicle (see illustrations). Most clips used on the vehicle are simply prised out of position. Remove the wheels to ease the removal of the wheel arch liners.

2 On refitting, renew any retaining clips that may have been broken on removal, and ensure that the panel is securely retained by all the relevant clips and screws.

Body trim strips and badges

3 The various body trim strips and badges are held in position with a special adhesive tape and locating lugs. Removal requires the trim/badge to be heated, to soften the adhesive, and then carefully lifted away from the surface. Due to the high risk of damage to

21.1b...and the rear inner wheel arch liner

the vehicle's paintwork during this operation, it is recommended that this task should be entrusted to an Audi dealer.

22 Seats – removal and refitting

Note: Refer to the warnings in Chapter 12, Section 25 on side airbags.

Removal

Front seats

Note: The amount of wiring connectors under the seat may vary depending on the vehicle specification.

1 Disconnect the battery negative lead (refer to 'Disconnecting the battery' in Reference chapter).

2 Where fitted, remove the drawer from below the seat.

3 Slide the seat forwards as far as possible and unscrew the rear mounting bolts (see illustration).

4 Slide the seat rearwards as far as possible then remove the wiring connector cover (see illustration).

5 Disconnect the seat wiring (see illustration). Audi technicians fit an adapter to the airbag wiring connector as a safety precaution; wrap the connector with insulation tape instead.

⚠ **Warning: As a precaution against unintentional electrostatic discharge into the airbag, briefly**

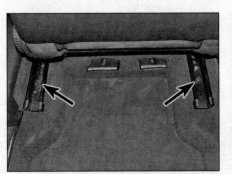

22.3 Seat rear mounting bolts

22.4 Unclip the front seat wiring cover

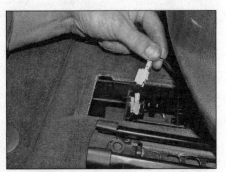

22.5 Disconnect the front seat wiring

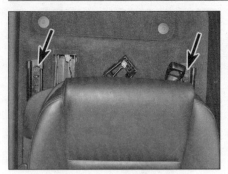

22.6 Seat front mounting bolts

22.7 If required, unclip the plastic housing from the floor

22.8 Unclip the plastic guides from the rear of the seat cushion

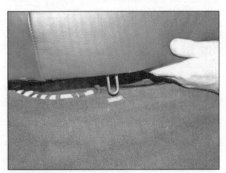

22.9a Lift the front of the cushion...

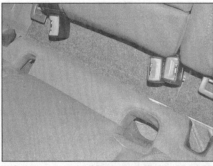

22.9b...then release its rear edge from the seat belt stalks

touch part of the vehicle body before disconnecting the wiring.

6 Unscrew the seat front mounting bolts **(see illustration)**.

7 Check that the wiring harness is released from any clips in the floor **(see illustration)**, and then remove the seat from the vehicle. Do not lift the seat by the seat belt stalk or by the seat adjustment levers. If necessary, have an assistant help to remove the seat, as it is heavy, and surrounding trim panels may be otherwise damaged.

Rear seat cushion

8 At the rear of the seat cushion, unclip the four guides from the child seat mountings **(see illustration)**.

9 Lift the front edge of the cushion from the location sockets, then push the cushion to the rear and pull upwards **(see illustrations)**.

10 Withdraw the rear seat cushion from inside the vehicle.

Rear seat backrest

11 Remove the cushion as described in paragraphs 8 to 10.

12 Fold the backrest forwards, then pull back the carpet and remove the trim from the centre mounting **(see illustration)**.

13 Unbolt the clamp, then remove the right backrest by lifting it from the centre mounting and sliding it off the outer mounting pin **(see illustrations)**.

22.12 Remove the trim from the centre mounting

22.13a Undo the retaining screw...

22.13b...remove the clamp...

22.13c...lift the rear seat backrest from the centre mounting...

22.13d...and slide it off the outer mounting pin

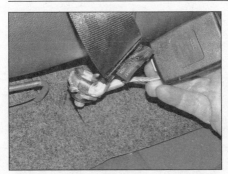

22.14 Remove the rear centre belt securing bolt

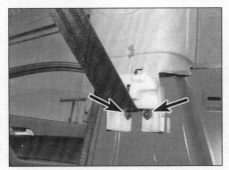

24.11a Upper trim securing screws

24.11b Release the seat belt from the trim panel

14 Unscrew and remove the bolt securing the centre belt and/or buckle assembly to the floor, and remove it from the vehicle **(see illustration)**.

15 Remove the left backrest by lifting it from the centre mounting and sliding it off the outer mounting pin.

Refitting

16 Refitting is a reversal of removal, but tighten the mounting bolts to the specified torque where given.

---

23 Front seat belt tensioning mechanism – general information

1 All models covered in this manual are fitted with a front seat belt tensioner system incorporated in each of the inertia reels. Rear seat belt inertia reels with the tensioner system are only fitted to some models, other models having standard inertia reels.

2 The system is designed to instantaneously take up any slack in the seat belt in the case of a sudden frontal impact, therefore reducing the possibility of injury to the front seat occupants. The seat belt tensioner is triggered by a frontal impact above a predetermined force. Lesser impacts, including impacts from behind, will not trigger the system.

3 When the system is triggered, the explosive gas in the tensioner mechanism retracts and locks the seat belt. This prevents the seat belt moving and keeps the occupant firmly in position in the seat. Once the tensioner has been triggered, the seat belt will be permanently locked and the assembly must be renewed.

4 There is a risk of personal injury if the system is triggered inadvertently when working on the vehicle, and it is therefore strongly recommended that any work involving the seat belt inertia reels be entrusted to an Audi dealer. Note the following warnings before contemplating any work on the front seat belts.

⚠ *Warning: Do not expose the tensioner mechanism to temperatures in excess of 100°C.*

● If the tensioner mechanism is dropped, it must be renewed, even it has suffered no apparent damage.
● Do not allow any solvents to come into contact with the tensioner mechanism.
● Do not attempt to open the tensioner mechanism as it contains explosive gas.
● Tensioners must be discharged before they are disposed of, but this task should be entrusted to an Audi dealer.

---

24 Seat belt components – removal and refitting

⚠ *Warning: Refer to Section 23 before proceeding.*

Front seat belt removal

1 Disconnect the battery negative lead (refer to *'Disconnecting the battery'* in Reference chapter).

5-door models

2 Remove the upper and lower trim panels from the B-pillar with reference to Section 25.

3 Unscrew and remove the seat belt lower anchor mounting bolt and remove the belt from the floor.

4 Unscrew the mounting bolt and remove the inertia reel from the bottom of the B-pillar. Disconnect the wiring from the reel.

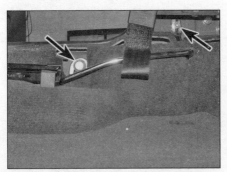

24.12 Front seat belt anchor rail bolts

⚠ *Warning: As a precaution against unintentional electrostatic discharge, briefly touch part of the vehicle body before disconnecting the wiring.*

5 Undo the screws and remove the belt guide from the B-pillar.

6 Unscrew and remove the bolt securing the seat belt upper anchor to the height adjuster on the B-pillar.

7 Remove the seat belt assembly from the vehicle.

8 To remove the belt height adjustment, remove the securing bolt and lift upwards from the pillar.

3-door models

9 Remove the relevant rear seat and backrest as described in Section 22.

10 Remove the sill panel moulding and the side panel trims, with reference to Section 25.

11 Remove the upper trim panel from the B-pillar **(see illustrations)**, with reference to Section 25.

12 Unscrew the bolts securing the anchor rail to the sill, and slide the rail from the end of the seat belt **(see illustration)**.

13 Where applicable, release the locking clip and disconnect the wiring connector from the inertia reel. Unscrew the mounting bolt, and withdraw the reel from the pillar **(see illustrations)**.

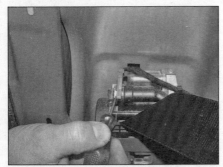

24.13a Release the locking clip...

24.13b...disconnect the wiring connector...

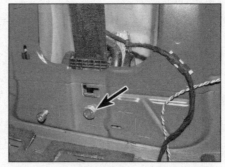

24.13c...and remove the seat belt inertia reel bolt

24.14 Front seat belt upper anchor bolt

⚠️ **Warning: As a precaution against unintentional electrostatic discharge, briefly touch part of the vehicle body before disconnecting the wiring.**

14 Unscrew and remove the bolt securing the seat belt upper anchor to the height adjuster on the B-pillar **(see illustration)**.

15 Remove the seat belt assembly from the vehicle.

16 To remove the belt height adjustment, remove the securing bolt and lift upwards from the pillar **(see illustration)**.

Front seat belt stalk removal

17 Remove the front seat assembly as described in Section 22.

18 Unscrew and remove the bolt securing the stalk to the seat, and remove the stalk.

Rear seat side belt removal

5-door models

19 Remove the rear seat cushion as described in Section 22.

20 Remove the side panel trim.

Note: *Refer to Chapter 12, Section 25 on models with rear side airbags.*

21 Remove the luggage compartment cover side support.

22 Remove the roof frame trim.

23 Remove the trim from the C-pillar.

24 Unbolt the belt from the floor anchorage.

25 Where applicable, release the locking clip and disconnect the wiring connector from the inertia reel. Unscrew the mounting bolt, and withdraw the reel from the pillar.

⚠️ **Warning: As a precaution against unintentional electrostatic discharge, briefly touch part of**

the vehicle body before disconnecting the wiring.

3-door models

26 Remove the rear seat cushion and backrest as described in Section 22.

27 Unclip the sill inner trim panel and slide it forward to release it from the rear side trim panel **(see illustration)**.

28 Unclip the plastic cover and undo the retaining screw at the front of the rear trim panel **(see illustration)**.

29 Undo the retaining screw at the rear of the side trim panel **(see illustration)**.

30 Remove the luggage compartment side trim, unclipping it from bottom of the C-pillar trim panel **(see illustration)**. On left-hand trim, disconnect the wiring connector for the luggage compartment light.

31 Unscrew the bolt and remove the belt anchor from the floor **(see illustration)**.

24.16 Front seat belt height adjuster mounting bolt

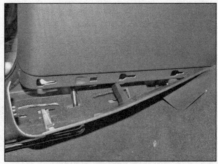

24.27 Unclip the sill trim

24.28 Undo the front retaining screw

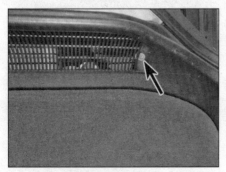

24.29 Undo the rear retaining screw

24.30 Unclip the luggage compartment side trim

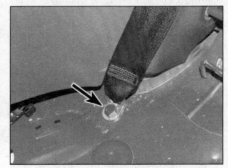

24.31 Rear side seat belt lower mounting bolt

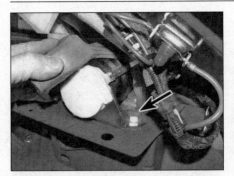
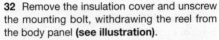

24.32 Rear side inertia seat belt mounting bolt

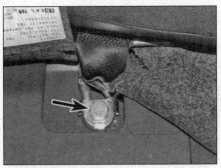
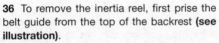

24.35 Rear centre belt lower securing bolt

24.36 Prise out and remove the belt guide trim cover

32 Remove the insulation cover and unscrew the mounting bolt, withdrawing the reel from the body panel **(see illustration)**.

33 Where applicable, release the locking clip and disconnect the wiring connector from the inertia reel.

 Warning: As a precaution against unintentional electrostatic discharge, briefly touch part of the vehicle body before disconnecting the wiring.

Rear centre seat belt & buckle removal

34 Remove the rear seat cushion and backrest as described in Section 22.

35 If not already done, unscrew and remove the bolt securing the centre belt and/or buckle assembly to the floor, and remove it from the vehicle **(see illustration)**.

36 To remove the inertia reel, first prise the belt guide from the top of the backrest **(see illustration)**.

37 Carefully prise the seat catch trim from the top of the backrest **(see illustration)**.

38 Working your way around the seat frame, carefully prise the moulding out from the edge of the backrest **(see illustrations)**.

39 Fold the seat cover and padding upwards to access the mounting bolt. Unbolt and remove the inertia reel **(see illustration)**.

40 While the padding is removed, if required, press the legs at each side of the headrest guides, and then push them out through the top of the seat back **(see illustrations)**.

41 While the padding is removed, if required, undo the securing screws and remove the seat catch from the backrest **(see illustration)**.

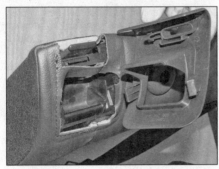

24.37 Unclip the seat catch trim cover

Refitting

42 Refitting is a reversal of the removal procedure, ensuring that all the seat belt units are located correctly and mounting bolts are

24.38a Prise out the moulding from around the edge...

24.38b ...and unclip cover from around the seat pivot

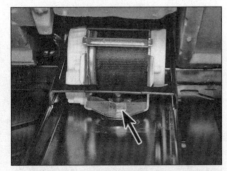

24.39 Inertia reel mounting nut

24.40a Squeeze the two legs in...

24.40b ...and withdraw the headrest guides

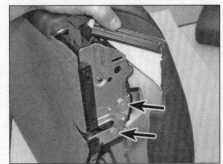

24.41 Seat catch securing bolts

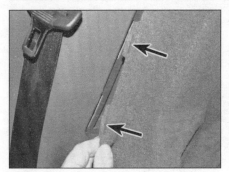

25.1 Rear side trim carpet clipped in position

25.2a Unclip upper rear trim panel...

25.2b...undo the retaining screw...

securely tightened to their specified torque. Check all the trim panels are securely retained by all the relevant retaining clips. When refitting the upper trim panels, ensure that the height adjustment levers engage correctly with the seat belt upper mounting bolt head.

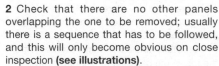

25 Interior trim – removed and refitting

 Warning: Refer to Section 23 before proceeding.

Interior trim panels

1 The interior trim panels are secured using either screws or various types of trim fasteners, usually studs or clips **(see illustration)**.

2 Check that there are no other panels overlapping the one to be removed; usually there is a sequence that has to be followed, and this will only become obvious on close inspection **(see illustrations)**.

3 Remove all obvious fasteners, such as screws. If the panel will not come free, it is held by hidden clips or fasteners. These are usually situated around the edge of the panel and can be prised up to release them; note, however, that they can break quite easily so new ones should be available. The best way of releasing such clips, without the correct type of tool, is to use a large flat-bladed screwdriver. Note in many cases that the adjacent sealing strip must be prised back to release a panel.

4 When removing a panel, never use excessive force or the panel may be damaged; always check carefully that all fasteners or other relevant components have

been removed or released before attempting to withdraw a panel.

5 Refitting is the reverse of the removal procedure; secure the fasteners by pressing them firmly into place and ensure that all disturbed components are correctly secured to prevent rattles.

Glovebox

6 Switch off the ignition.

7 Using a lever, carefully prise out the facia end panel on the passenger side and remove the retaining bolt **(see illustrations)**.

8 Unclip the trim panel from the lower rear part of the glovebox assembly.

9 Undo the two retaining screws at the lower part of the glovebox assembly **(see illustration)**.

10 Open up the glovebox lid, and then undo the retaining screw at the rear of the compartment **(see illustration)**.

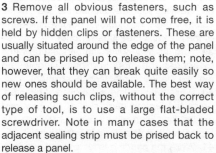

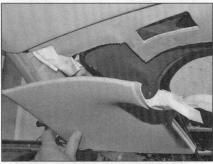

25.2c...and unclip the rear pillar trim

25.7a Using a lever...

25.7b...unclip the facia side trim panel...

25.7c... and undo the retaining bolt

25.9 Glovebox lower securing screws

25.10 Undo the retaining bolt inside glovebox

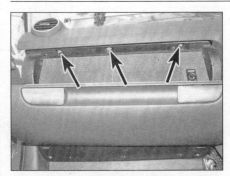

25.11a Undo the glovebox upper securing screws...

25.11b ...and disconnect the wiring connectors

25.13 Unclip the sill trim panel

11 Remove the three retaining screws from inside the front upper edge of the assembly. Slide the glovebox out of position, disconnecting the wiring connector from the glovebox illumination light as it becomes accessible. Where fitted, also disconnect the wiring from the passenger airbag isolation switch **(see illustrations)**.

12 Refitting is the reverse of removal.

Carpets

13 The passenger compartment floor carpet is in one piece and is secured at its edges by trim panels, which have screws or clips to secure them **(see illustration)** ; usually the same type of fasteners used to secure the various trim panels on the vehicle.

14 Carpet removal and refitting is reasonably straightforward but very time-consuming because all adjoining trim panels must be removed first, as must components such as the seats, the centre console and seat belt lower anchorages.

Headlining

15 The headlining is clipped to the roof and can be withdrawn only once all fittings such as the grab handles, sun visors, sunroof (if fitted), and related upper trim panels **(see**

25.15a Unclip the A-pillar trim panel...

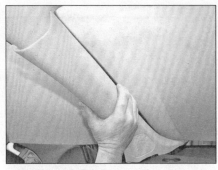

25.15b ...and slide it upwards to remove

illustrations) have been removed and the door, tailgate and sunroof aperture sealing strips have been prised clear.

16 To remove the sun visors and grab handles the plastic covers have to be unclipped first **(see illustration)**, to gain access to the securing screws.

Note: *Headlining removal requires considerable skill and experience if it is to be carried out without damage and is therefore best entrusted to an expert. The headlining also covers the airbag side curtains* **(see illustration)**; *see Section 23 before proceeding with any work.*

Interior mirror

17 To remove the interior mirror, turn the mirror arm anti-clockwise by 90° to release it from the baseplate. When refitting, place the mirror at 90° to the mounted position, then turn until the locking clip locks into place to secure the mirror. On models fitted with rain sensor, unclip the trim around the stem of the mirror and disconnect the wiring connector, then slide the mirror first along and then downwards from the mounting. Note that the base is attached to the windscreen with glass-metal adhesive.

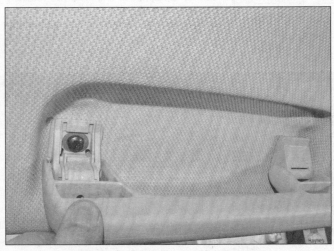

25.16a Grab handle securing screws

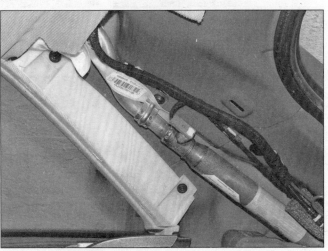

25.16b Rear trim held on by screws – 3-door

26.2a Remove the rear ashtray...

26.2b...and unclip the storage compartment

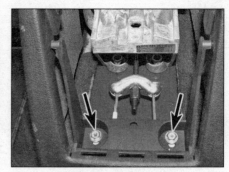

26.4 Rear mounting bolts

26.5a Unclip the gear lever gaiter...

26.5b...and remove the outer trim panel

26 Centre console – removal and refitting

Removal

1 Switch off the ignition.

2 Unclip the ashtray from the rear of the console, and then unclip the rear compartment/switch panel from below the ashtray **(see illustrations)**.

3 On models with centre armrest, undo the mounting bolts from inside the rear of the console and remove the armrest.

4 Undo the two retaining bolts from inside the rear of the console **(see illustration)**.

5 Release the gear/selector lever gaiter from the console and unclip the trim panel from around the gaiter **(see illustrations)**.

6 Using a lever, carefully unclip and remove the trim panel from in front of the ashtray **(see illustrations)**.

7 Undo the two retaining screws from the front ashtray **(see illustration)**.

8 Withdraw the ashtray from the front of the console; disconnect the wiring connector as it is removed **(see illustrations)**.

9 To remove the two grab handles from each side of the console, undo the two retaining bolts at the rear of the grab handles, the two bolts up through to the centre facia panel and

26.6a Using a lever unclip the trim panel...

26.6b...from in front of the ashtray

26.7 Undo the two screws...

26.8a...disconnect the wiring connector...

26.8b...and remove the ashtray

26.9a Undo the rear mounting bolts...

26.9b...the upper mounting bolts...

26.9c...and the front mounting bolts

the two bolts at the front of the grab handles (see illustrations).

10 Using a lever, carefully unclip the trim panel from below the handbrake (see illustrations).

11 Remove the lining mat from the small

oddments recess, and then unclip the cigarette lighter (12 volt socket), including the trim from the console (see illustrations). Disconnect the wiring connector as it is removed.

12 Unclip the plastic covers and undo the retaining screws from each side of the

console at the front edges (see illustrations).

13 Undo the two screws from inside the gear lever recess and lift the rear of the console upwards, withdrawing it over the handbrake lever and out from the vehicle (see illustrations). Disconnect the wiring as applicable.

26.10a Unclip the trim panel...

26.10b...and remove it from the handbrake

26.11a Remove the lining mat...

26.11b...unclip the cigarette lighter trim...

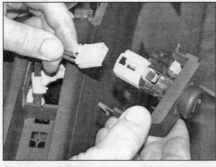

26.11c...and disconnect the wiring connector

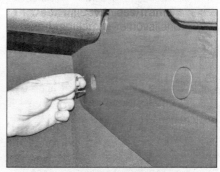

26.12a Unclip the plastic covers...

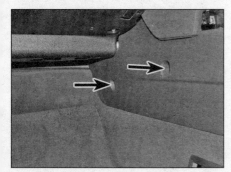

26.12b...and remove the retaining screws

26.13a Undo the front mounting screws...

26.13b...and withdraw the console over the handbrake lever

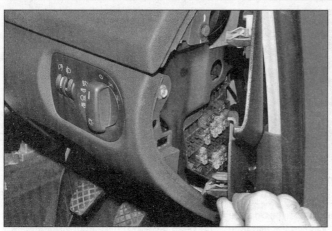

27.2 Unclip the driver's side trim cover from the facia

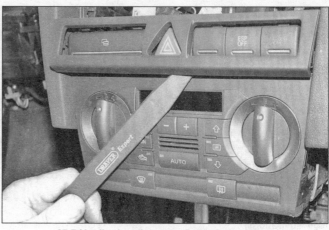

27.7 Unclip the trim cover from the switches

Refitting

14 Refitting is a reversal of removal, making sure all screws and clips are secure to prevent any rattles. Tighten the screws securing the centre console to the facia first, and then work back to the rear of the console.

27 Facia panel assembly – removal and refitting

Note: *Refer to the warnings in Chapter 12 for airbags.*

Removal

1 Disconnect the battery negative lead (refer to *'Disconnecting the battery'* in Reference chapter).
2 Prise out the trim panels from each end of the facia **(see illustration)**.
3 Prise out the covers, then undo the screws and remove the A-pillar upper trim **(see illustrations 25.15a and 25.15b)**. Disconnect the wiring from the speaker, where applicable.
4 Remove the glovebox as described in Section 25.
5 Remove the centre console as described in Section 26.
6 Remove the radio or navigation unit as described in Chapter 12.
7 Using a lever, carefully unclip the trim from

the switch panel **(see illustration)**. Remove the switches from the facia, noting their fitted position.
8 Using a lever, carefully unclip the top edge of the heater control panel from the facia and remove it downwards from the facia panel **(see illustrations)**. Disconnect the wiring connectors as it is removed.
9 Remove the steering column shrouds as follows (refer to Chapter 10 for more information):
a) *Undo the screws and remove the column height and reach adjustment handle.*
b) *Release the gap cover, and then unclip and remove the upper shroud from the steering column.*
c) *Undo the two upper screws and single*

lower screw and remove the lower shroud from the steering column. As the shroud is being removed, release it from the height and reach adjustment handle.
10 Remove the steering column as described in Chapter 10, Section 21.
11 Remove the air vents, by carefully levering them out from the facia panel **(see illustrations)**.
12 Undo the two lower retaining screws and carefully withdraw the instrument panel from the facia. Disconnect the wiring connectors as the panel is being removed.
13 Unclip the trim cover from the centre top of the facia panel. Remove the speaker and sensors, disconnecting the wiring connectors as they are removed **(see illustration)**.

27.8a Unclip the upper part of the heater control panel...

27.8b...and remove it from the facia panel

27.11a Carefully lever the air vent...

27.11b...and withdraw from the facia panel

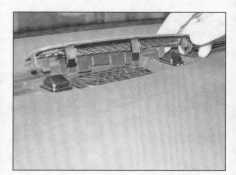

27.13 Unclip the trim from the top centre of the facia

27.14a Turn the switch to release the locking peg (arrowed)

27.14b Disconnect the wiring connector

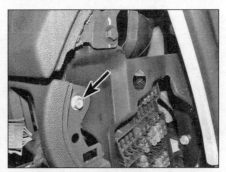

27.15a Undo the retaining bolt...

14 Depress the light switch and turn it clockwise until vertical, to release the locking peg. Then remove the switch from the facia and disconnect the wiring connectors **(see illustrations)**.

15 Undo the retaining bolt and remove the light switch panel **(see illustrations)**.

16 Undo the retaining bolts from the lower edge of the facia, at each side of the centre facia panel **(see illustration)**

17 Undo the retaining screws from inside the radio aperture in the centre facia panel **(see illustration)**

18 Unscrew the bolts securing the front passenger airbag bracket to the facia and remove. Also, disconnect the airbag wiring **(see illustrations)**.

19 Working your way along the facia, unclip any wiring connectors and wiring loom retaining clips, noting their fitted position.

20 Unscrew the retaining bolts from each end of the facia assembly, then, with the help of an assistant, pull out from the bulkhead clips and remove from the vehicle **(see illustrations)**. As the facia is being removed, check for any remaining wiring, and note its routing to aid refitting.

Refitting

21 Refitting is a reversal of the removal procedure, noting the following points:
a) *Ensure the facia guides engage correctly with the clips on the bulkhead. As the facia is being fitted, check that all wiring is routed as noted during removal.*
b) *Insert all of the retaining screws*

27.15b...and remove the light switch trim panel

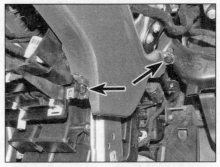

27.16 Facia centre retaining screws (one side shown)

27.17 Undo the retaining screws from the centre of the facia

27.18a Undo the airbag mounting nuts...

hand-tight, then with the facia positioned centrally, fully-tighten the securing screws
c) *Refer to the relevant Chapter for the refitting of any individual components.*

d) *On completion, reconnect the battery and check that all the electrical components and switches function correctly.*

27.18b...and carefully remove it from under the facia panel

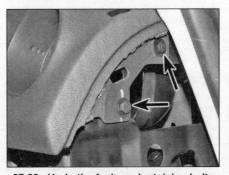

27.20a Undo the facia end retaining bolts (one side shown)...

27.20b...and remove the facia from inside the vehicle

Chapter 12
Body electrical system

Contents

Degrees of difficulty

Easy, suitable for novice with little experience	**Fairly easy,** suitable for beginner with some experience	**Fairly difficult,** suitable for competent DIY mechanic	**Difficult,** suitable for experienced DIY mechanic	**Very difficult,** suitable for expert DIY or professional

Specifications

System type.................................... 12 volt negative earth

Fuses .... Refer to the sticker on the inside of the fusebox cover

Bulbs	Wattage	Type
Brake lights.....................................	21	Bayonet
Daytime running lights	19	PS19W
Direction indicators:		
Front	24	PSY24W
Rear	21	Bayonet
Foglights:		
Front	55	H11
Rear	21	H21W
Glovebox light	5	Wedge
Headlight:		
Halogen:		
Main beam	55	H7
Dipped beam	55	H7
Gas discharge (Xenon):		
Main beam	55	H1
Dipped beam	35	DS2 (80-117 volt)
Interior light	10	Festoon
Reversing lights	21	Bayonet
Sidelight	5	Wedge

Torque wrench setting	Nm	lbf ft
Passenger airbag and brackets	9	7

1 General information and precautions

Warning: *Before carrying out any work on the electrical system, read through the precautions given in 'Safety first!' at the beginning of this manual, and in Chapter 5.*

1 The electrical system is of 12 volt negative earth type. Power for the lights and all electrical accessories is supplied by a lead-acid type battery, which is charged by the alternator.

2 This Chapter covers repair and service procedures for the various electrical components not associated with the engine. Information on the battery, alternator and starter motor can be found in Chapter 5.

3 It should be noted that prior to working on any component in the electrical system, the ignition and all electrical consumers must be switched off. Additionally, where stated, the battery negative lead must be disconnected, however, note the information given in *'Disconnecting the battery'* in Reference chapter as special procedures have to be carried out when reconnecting the battery.

4 Some models are fitted with gas discharge headlight systems (Xenon headlights), which include automatic range control to reduce the possibility of dazzling oncoming drivers. Note the special precautions which apply to these systems as given in Section 5.

2 Electrical fault finding – general information

Note: *Refer to the precautions given in 'Safety first!' and in Chapter 5 before starting work. The following tests relate to testing of the main electrical circuits, and should not be used to test delicate electronic circuits (such as anti-lock braking systems), particularly where an electronic control module is used.*

General

1 A typical electrical circuit consists of an electrical component; any switches, relays, motors, fuses, fusible links or circuit breakers related to that component, and the wiring and connectors which link the component to both the battery and the chassis. To help to pinpoint a problem in an electrical circuit, wiring diagrams are included at the end of this Chapter.

Note: *Many of the circuits are controlled by computerised systems (for instance, the windscreen wipers will only operate with the bonnet closed), so before assuming there are faults, it is worthwhile checking if specific conditions apply.*

2 Before attempting to diagnose an electrical fault, first study the appropriate wiring diagram to obtain a complete understanding of the components included in the particular circuit concerned. The possible sources of a fault can be narrowed down by noting if other components related to the circuit are operating properly. If several components or circuits fail at one time, the problem is likely to be related to a shared fuse or earth connection.

3 Electrical problems usually stem from simple causes, such as loose or corroded connections, a faulty earth connection, a blown fuse, a melted fusible link, or a faulty relay (refer to Section 3 for details of testing relays). Visually inspect the condition of all fuses, wires and connections in a problem circuit before testing the components. Use the wiring diagrams to determine which terminal connections will need to be checked in order to pinpoint the trouble spot.

4 The basic tools required for electrical fault finding include a circuit tester or voltmeter (a 12 volt bulb with a set of test leads can also be used for certain tests); a self-powered test light (sometimes known as a continuity tester); an ohmmeter (to measure resistance); a battery and set of test leads; and a jumper wire, preferably with a circuit breaker or fuse incorporated, which can be used to bypass suspect wires or electrical components. Before attempting to locate a problem with test instruments, use the wiring diagram to determine where to make the connections.

5 To find the source of an intermittent wiring fault (usually due to a poor or dirty connection, or damaged wiring insulation), a wiggle test can be performed on the wiring. This involves wiggling the wiring by hand to see if the fault occurs as the wiring is moved. It should be possible to narrow down the source of the fault to a particular section of wiring. This method of testing can be used in conjunction with any of the tests described in the following sub-Sections.

6 Apart from problems due to poor connections, two basic types of fault can occur in an electrical circuit – open-circuit, or short-circuit.

7 Open-circuit faults are caused by a break somewhere in the circuit, which prevents current from flowing. An open-circuit fault will prevent a component from working, but will not cause the relevant circuit fuse to blow.

8 Short-circuit faults are caused by a short somewhere in the circuit, which allows the current flowing in the circuit to escape along an alternative route, usually to earth. Short-circuit faults are normally caused by a breakdown in wiring insulation, which allows a feed wire to touch either another wire, or an earthed component such as the bodyshell. A short-circuit fault will normally cause the relevant circuit fuse to blow.

Finding an open-circuit

9 To check for an open-circuit, connect one lead of a circuit tester or voltmeter to either the negative battery terminal or a known good earth.

10 Connect the other lead to a connector in the circuit being tested, preferably nearest to the battery or fuse.

11 Switch on the circuit, bearing in mind that some circuits are live only when the ignition switch is moved to a particular position.

12 If voltage is present (indicated either by the tester bulb lighting or a voltmeter reading, as applicable), this means that the section of the circuit between the relevant connector and the battery is problem-free.

13 Continue to check the remainder of the circuit in the same fashion.

14 When a point is reached at which no voltage is present, the problem must lie between that point and the previous test point with voltage. Most problems can be traced to a broken, corroded or loose connection.

Finding a short-circuit

15 To check for a short-circuit; first disconnect the load(s) from the circuit (loads are the components which draw current from a circuit, such as bulbs, motors, heating elements, etc).

16 Remove the relevant fuse from the circuit, and connect a circuit tester or voltmeter to the fuse connections.

17 Switch on the circuit, bearing in mind that some circuits are live only when the ignition switch is moved to a particular position.

18 If voltage is present (indicated either by the tester bulb lighting or a voltmeter reading, as applicable), this means that there is a short circuit.

19 If no voltage is present, but the fuse still blows with the load(s) connected, this indicates an internal fault in the load(s).

Finding an earth fault

20 The battery negative terminal is connected to earth – the metal of the engine/transmission and the car body – and most systems are wired so that they only receive a positive feed, the current returning through the metal of the car body. This means that the component mounting and the body form part of that circuit. Loose or corroded mountings can therefore cause a range of electrical faults, ranging from total failure of a circuit, to a puzzling partial fault. In particular, lights may shine dimly (especially when another circuit sharing the same earth point is in operation), motors (eg, wiper motors or the radiator cooling fan motor) may run slowly, and the operation of one circuit may have an apparently unrelated effect on another. Note that on many vehicles, earth straps are used between certain components, such as the engine/transmission and the body, usually where there is no metal-to-metal contact between components due to flexible rubber mountings, etc.

21 To check whether a component is properly earthed, disconnect the battery (refer to the warnings given in the Reference section at the rear of the manual) and connect one lead of an ohmmeter to a known good earth point. Connect the other lead to the wire or

3.2 Unclip the fusebox trim cover

3.3 Removing a fuse from the facia fusebox

3.8 Fuse and relay box on the left-hand side of the engine compartment

earth connection being tested. The resistance reading should be zero; if not, check the connection as follows.

22 If an earth connection is thought to be faulty, dismantle the connection and clean back to bare metal both the bodyshell and the wire terminal or the component earth connection mating surface. Be careful to remove all traces of dirt and corrosion, and then use a knife to trim away any paint, so that a clean metal-to-metal joint is made. On reassembly, tighten the joint fasteners securely; if a wire terminal is being refitted, use serrated washers between the terminal and the bodyshell to ensure a clean and secure connection. When the connection is remade, prevent the onset of corrosion in the future by applying a coat of petroleum jelly or silicone-based grease or by spraying on (at regular intervals) a proprietary ignition sealer or a water dispersant lubricant.

3 Fuses and relays – general information

Fuses and fusible links

1 Fuses are designed to break a circuit when a predetermined current is reached, in order to protect the components and wiring, which could be damaged by excessive current flow. Any excessive current flow will be due to a fault in the circuit, usually a short-circuit (see Section 2).

2 The main fuses are located in the fusebox on the driver's side of the facia; open the driver's door and unclip the fusebox cover from the end of the facia to gain access to the fuses **(see illustration)**. The fuse locations are marked onto the rear of the fusebox cover.

3 To remove a fuse, first switch off the circuit concerned (or the ignition), and then pull the fuse out of its terminals **(see illustration)**.

4 The wire within the fuse should be visible; if the fuse has blown it will be broken or melted.

5 Always renew a fuse with one of the correct rating; never use a fuse with a different rating from that specified.

6 Refer to the wiring diagrams for details of the fuse ratings and the circuits protected.

The fuse rating is stamped on the top of the fuse; the fuses are also colour-coded as follows.

Colour	Rating
Light brown	5A
Brown	7.5A
Red	10A
Blue	15A
Yellow	20A
White or clear	25A
Green	30A
Orange	40A

7 Never renew a fuse more than once without tracing the source of the trouble. If the new fuse blows immediately, find the cause before renewing it again; a short to earth as a result of faulty insulation is most likely. Where a fuse protects more than one circuit, try to isolate the fault by switching on each circuit in turn (where possible) until the fuse blows again. Always carry a supply of spare fuses of each relevant rating on the vehicle.

8 Additional fuses and relays are located in the fusebox located on the left-hand side of the engine compartment. Unclip and open the fuse holder cover to gain access **(see illustration)**.

9 To renew a fusible link, first disconnect the battery negative terminal (see *'Disconnecting the battery'* in Reference chapter. Unscrew the retaining nuts then remove the blown link from the holder. Fit the new link to its terminals and

reconnect the lead **(see illustration)**. Ensure the link and lead are correctly seated then refit the retaining nuts and tighten securely. Clip the cover back into position then reconnect the battery.

Relays

10 A relay is an electrically-operated switch, which is used for the following reasons:

a) *A relay can switch a heavy current remotely from the circuit in which the current is flowing, allowing the use of lighter-gauge wiring and switch contacts.*

b) *A relay can receive more than one control input, unlike a mechanical switch.*

c) *A relay can have a timer function – for example, the intermittent wiper relay.*

11 Most of the relays are located on the relay plate behind the driver's side facia **(see illustration)** ; however, additional relays are located in the engine compartment fusebox.

12 Access to the relays can be obtained after removing the driver's side lower facia panel as described in Chapter 11, Section 27. Refer to the wiring diagrams, for further identification details of the relays.

13 If a circuit or system controlled by a relay develops a fault, and the relay is suspect, operate the system. If the relay is functioning, it should be possible to hear it click as it is energised. If this is the case, the fault lies with the components or wiring of the system. If the relay is not being energised, then either the relay is not receiving a main supply or a switching voltage, or the relay itself is faulty. Testing is by the substitution of a known

3.9 Fusible links on the front of the engine compartment fusebox

3.11 Relays located behind the facia (driver's side)

4.4 Turn the switch to release the locking peg (arrowed)...

4.5...then withdraw it, and disconnect the wiring connector

4.17 Unclip the trim cover

good unit, but be careful – while some relays are identical in appearance and in operation, others look similar but perform different functions.

14 To remove a relay, first ensure that the relevant circuit is switched off. The relay can then simply be pulled out from the socket, and pushed back into position.

15 The direction indicator/hazard flasher relay is integral with the hazard-warning switch. Refer to Section 4 for the switch removal procedure.

4 Switches –
removal and refitting

Ignition switch

1 Refer to Chapter 10, Section 22.

Wiper and indicator switches

2 Refer to Chapter 10, Section 22.

Lighting switch

3 Switch off the ignition and all electrical consumers and remove the ignition key.
4 With the light switch in position O, press the switch centre inwards and turn it slightly to the right. Hold this position to release the locking peg and then pull the switch from the facia (see illustration).
5 As the switch is withdrawn, disconnect the wiring plug (see illustration).
6 To refit the switch, first reconnect the wiring plug.
7 Hold the switch and press the rotary part inwards and slightly to the right.
8 Insert the switch into the facia, turn the rotary part to position O and release. Check the switch for correct operation.

Headlamp range control and instrument illumination switch

9 Remove the lighting switch as described in paragraphs 3 to 5.
10 Release the clips, and carefully unclip the headlamp control switch from the rear of the trim panel.
11 Refitting is a reversal of removal.

Heated seat/air conditioning/ heated rear window switches

Note: *Depending on model, the switches may be part of the heating control panel, check for availability of parts before removal.*
12 Switch off the ignition and all electrical consumers and remove the ignition key.
13 Carefully prise the switch from its location in the facia panel, using a small flat-bladed screwdriver. Take care not to damage the surrounding trim.
14 Disconnect the wiring plug(s) and withdraw the switch.
15 Reconnect the switch wiring plug, and push the switch firmly into position.

Hazard warning/ESP/ heated rear window switches

Note: *Depending on model, the switches may be part of the heating control panel, check for availability of parts before removal.*
16 Switch off the ignition and all electrical consumers and remove the ignition key.
17 Carefully prise the trim cover from over the switches (see illustration).
18 Unclip the switch from its location in the facia panel and disconnect the wiring connector (see illustrations).
19 Refitting is a reversal of removal, making sure the switch is fitted firmly into position.

Electric window switch/module

20 Switch off the ignition and all electrical consumers, and remove the ignition key.
21 Remove the door trim panel as described in Chapter 11, Section 12.
22 Working on the inside of the door trim panel undo the retaining screws securing the armrest/grab handle to the door trim and disconnect the wiring connectors from the rear of the switches (see illustration).
23 Working on the outside of the door trim panel, undo the two retaining screws from the top of the grab handle (see illustration).

4.18a Withdraw the switch...

4.18b...and disconnect the wiring connector

4.22 Disconnect the wiring connector

4.23 Undo the retaining screws...

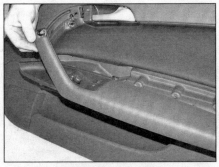

4.24...and remove the armrest/grab handle

4.25a Release the retaining clips...

4.25b...and remove the switch from the armrest

24 Withdraw the armrest/grab handle from the door trim panel **(see illustration)**.
25 Release the locking clips and withdraw the switch module from the plastic housing **(see illustrations)**.
26 Refitting is a reversal of removal.

Electric mirror switch

27 Remove the armrest/grab handle as described in paragraphs 20 to 24.
28 Undo the retaining screw and remove the mirror switch trim from the armrest **(see illustrations)**.
29 Release the locking clips and withdraw the switch module from the plastic housing **(see illustrations)**.
30 Refitting is a reversal of removal.

Heater blower motor switch

31 The switch is integral with the heater control panel, and cannot be removed separately. Refer to Chapter 3, Section 9 for details of heater control panel removal and refitting.

Handbrake 'on' warning switch

32 Refer to Chapter 9, Section 17.

Brake light switch

33 Refer to Chapter 9, Section 18.

Reversing light switch

34 Refer to Chapter 7A, Section 5.

Courtesy light switches

35 The courtesy light switch is integrated into the door lock mechanism, and cannot be renewed independently. If the courtesy light switch is faulty, renew the door lock mechanism as described in Chapter 11, Section 13.

Luggage area light switch

36 The luggage compartment light switch is

integrated into the tailgate lock mechanism, and cannot be renewed independently. If the luggage compartment light switch is faulty, renew the tailgate lock mechanism as described in Chapter 11, Section 16.

Glovebox light switch

37 Switch off the ignition and all electrical consumers and remove the ignition key.
38 Remove the glovebox as described in Chapter 11, Section 25.
39 Release the lug and push out the switch from the glovebox.
40 Refitting is a reversal of removal.

4.28a Undo the retaining screw...

4.28b...and remove the switch panel from the armrest

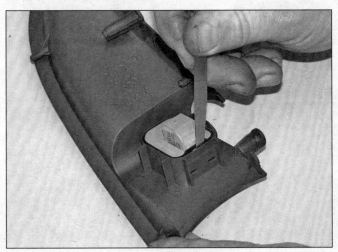

4.29a Release the retaining clips...

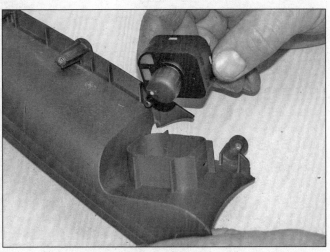

4.29b...and remove the switch from the trim panel

4.43a Disconnect the wiring connector...

4.43b...and unclip the switch from the door trim panel

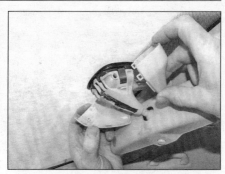

4.46a Remove the mirror base covers...

Interior monitoring deactivation switch

41 Switch off the ignition and all electrical consumers and remove the ignition key.
42 Remove the door inner trim panel as described in Chapter 11, Section 12.
43 Disconnect the wiring plug, and carefully prise the switch from the edge of the door trim panel **(see illustrations)**.
44 Refitting is a reversal of removal.

Rain sensor

45 Switch off the ignition and all electrical consumers and remove the ignition key.
46 The windscreen wipers are automatically activated when droplets of water are detected by the rain sensor, located in the front of the interior mirror base. Separate the left and right mirror base covers, and disconnect the wiring plug **(see illustrations)**.
47 Pull the mirror downwards from the mirror base, remove the stay, and if necessary disconnect the wiring from the sensor **(see illustrations)**.
48 The mirror base is bonded to the windscreen. Whilst it is possible to remove the base by means of a scraper, great care must be exercised to avoid scratching the windscreen.
49 Due to the hazardous chemicals involved, it is recommended that the bonding of the mirror base to the windscreen be entrusted to an Audi dealer or suitably-equipped specialist.
50 With the base in place, refit the mirror to the base.
51 Reconnect the sensor wiring plugs.
52 Refit the two halves of the mirror base covers.

Driver's door locking switch

53 Remove the door inner trim panel as described in Chapter 11, Section 12.
54 Working on the inside of the door trim panel undo the retaining screws securing the door release handle to the door trim and disconnect the wiring connector from the rear of the switch **(see illustrations)**.
55 Release the locking clips and withdraw

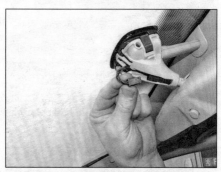

4.46b and disconnect the wiring plug...

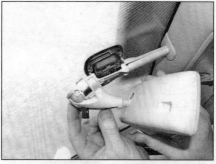

4.47a...then pull the mirror downwards...

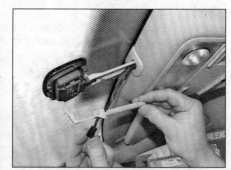

4.47b...remove the stay...

4.47c...and if necessary, disconnect the sensor wiring

4.54a Disconnect the wiring connector, undo the screws...

4.54b...and remove the door handle from the trim panel

4.55a Release the retaining clips...

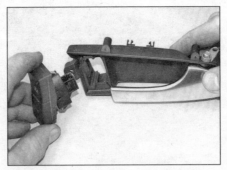

4.55b...and remove the switch from door handle

4 Turn the bulbholder anti-clockwise and withdraw it from the light unit **(see illustration)**.
5 Lift the retaining tabs and disconnect the wiring plug from the rear of the bulb **(see illustration)**.
6 When handling the new bulb, use a tissue or clean cloth to avoid touching the glass with the fingers; moisture and grease from the skin can cause blackening and rapid failure of this type of bulb. If the glass is accidentally touched, wipe it clean using methylated spirit.
7 Connect the wiring plug to the new bulb, then locate the bulbholder in the light unit. Turn the bulbholder clockwise to secure, then refit the plastic cover.

Headlight dip beam

Halogen headlights

Note: *Do not touch the glass envelope of the bulb if it is to be re-used.*
8 Switch off the ignition and all electrical consumers and remove the ignition key.
9 Working in the engine compartment, remove the plastic cover from the rear of the headlight by turning it anti-clockwise **(see illustration)**.
10 Turn the bulbholder anti-clockwise and withdraw it from the light unit **(see illustration)**.
11 Lift the retaining tabs and disconnect the wiring plug from the rear of the bulb **(see illustration)**.
12 When handling the new bulb, use a tissue

the switch from the release handle trim panel **(see illustrations)**.
56 Refitting is a reversal of removal.

5 Bulbs (exterior lights) – renewal

General

1 Whenever a bulb is renewed, note the following points:
a) *Switch off the ignition and all electrical consumers before commencing work.*
b) *Remember that if the light has just been in use the bulb may be extremely hot.*
c) *Always check the bulb contacts and*

holder, ensuring that there is clean metal-to-metal contact. Clean off any corrosion or dirt before fitting a new bulb.
d) *Wherever festoon-type bulbs are fitted ensure that the spring-tensioned arms bear firmly against the bulb contacts.*
e) *Always ensure that the new bulb is of the correct rating and that it is thoroughly clean before fitting it.*

Headlight main beam

Note: *Do not touch the glass envelope of the bulb if it is to be re-used.*
2 Switch off the ignition and all electrical consumers, and remove the ignition key.
3 Working in the engine compartment, remove the plastic cover from the rear of the headlight **(see illustration)**.

5.3 Remove the plastic cover from the rear of the headlight

5.4 Withdraw the bulbholder from the light unit

5.5 Disconnect the wiring plug from the bulb

5.9 Remove the plastic cover by turning it anti-clockwise

5.10 Withdraw the bulbholder from the light unit

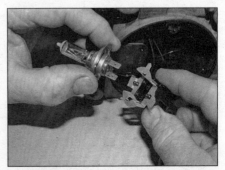

5.11 Disconnect the wiring plug from the bulb

5.18 Remove the plastic cover from the rear of the headlight

5.19 Withdraw the bulbholder from the light unit

5.20 Disconnect the wiring plug from the bulbholder

or clean cloth to avoid touching the glass with the fingers; moisture and grease from the skin can cause blackening and rapid failure of this type of bulb. If the glass is accidentally touched, wipe it clean using methylated spirit.

13 Connect the wiring plug to the new bulb, then locate the bulbholder in the light unit so that the location tab is correctly located in the cut-out.

14 Install the new bulb, ensuring that its location tab is correctly located in the cut-out, and secure it in position with the securing clips.

15 Refit the cover to the headlight unit with the word TOP uppermost.

Gas discharge headlights (Xenon bulbs)

 Warning: The headlight bulb contains gas at very high pressure, and it is recommended

that gloves and eye protection are worn to prevent potential personal injury.

16 Due to the high pressure of gas in this type of bulb, it is recommended that this type of bulb be renewed by an Audi dealer or specialist workshop.

Caution: After refitting a gas discharge headlamp, the basic setting of the Automatic Range Control system should be checked. Because of the requirement for specialised equipment, this can only be carried out by an Audi dealer or suitably-equipped specialist.

Front sidelight/daytime running light

17 Switch off the ignition and all electrical consumers and remove the ignition key.

18 Working in the engine compartment,

remove the plastic cover from the rear of the headlight by turning it anti-clockwise(see illustration).

19 Turn the bulbholder anti-clockwise and withdraw it from the light unit **(see illustration)**.

20 Depress the tab and disconnect the wiring plug from the bulbholder **(see illustration)**. Note that the bulb is integral with the bulbholder.

21 Refitting is a reversal of removal, making sure that the headlight cover is securely refitted.

Front direction indicator

Note: *Do not touch the glass envelope of the bulb if it is to be re-used.*

22 Switch off the ignition and all electrical consumers and remove the ignition key.

23 Working in the engine compartment, remove the plastic cover from the rear of the headlight unit.

24 Turn the bulbholder anti-clockwise and remove it from the headlight complete with bulb **(see illustration)**.

25 Depress the tab and disconnect the wiring plug from the bulbholder **(see illustration)**. Note that the bulb is integral with the bulbholder.

26 Refitting is a reversal of removal, making sure that the headlight cover is securely refitted.

Front foglight

27 Switch off the ignition and all electrical consumers and remove the ignition key.

28 Remove the foglight unit as described in Section 7.

29 Disconnect the wiring connector from the bulb.

30 Turn the bulbholder anticlockwise and remove it from the light unit. Note that the bulb is integral with the bulbholder.

31 Refitting is a reverse of removal.

Rear light cluster

32 Remove the rear light cluster as described in Section 7.

33 Release the retaining clips and remove the bulbholder from the rear of the light cluster **(see illustrations)**.

34 The bulbs are a bayonet-fit in the

5.24 Remove the bulbholder from the headlight

5.25 Disconnect the wiring plug from the bulbholder

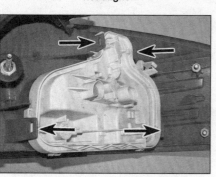

5.33a Release the retaining clips...

5.33b...and remove the bulbholder

5.34 Remove the bulb by depressing and twisting it

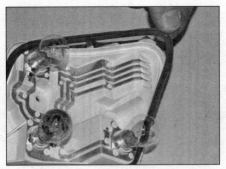

5.35 Make sure the seal is fitted correctly before refitting

5.36 Unclip the cover to access the rear light

bulbholder – depress and twist the relevant bulb to remove it **(see illustration)**.

35 Fit the new bulb using a reversal of the removal procedure. Make sure the sealing ring is fitted correctly to the outside of the bulbholder, to prevent any water ingress **(see illustration)**.

Rear fog/reversing light (5-door model)

Note: *The rear fog/reversing light bulbs are fitted to the rear light cluster on 3-door models, see paragraphs 36 to 39.*

36 The rear fog/reversing light bulbs are located in the tailgate. Open the tailgate and unclip the plastic access cover at the rear of the light unit **(see illustration)**.

37 Disconnect the wiring connector from the rear of the light unit **(see illustration)**.
38 Release the retaining clips and remove the bulbholder from the rear of the light cluster.
39 Rear foglight bulb is a bayonet-fit in the bulbholder – depress and twist the relevant bulb to remove it **(see illustration)**.
40 Reversing light bulb is a wedge-type bulb – pull the relevant bulb to remove it **(see illustration)**.
41 Fit the new bulb using a reversal of the removal procedure.

Number plate light

42 Switch off the ignition and all electrical consumers, and remove the ignition key.
43 Undo the securing screw, and withdraw

the light unit from the tailgate **(see illustrations)**.
44 Unclip the festoon-type bulb from the rear of the light unit **(see illustration)**.
45 Fit the new bulb using a reversal of the removal procedure.

High-level brake light

Note: *The light is of LED design; therefore if faulty the complete unit must be renewed.*

3-door models

46 Switch off the ignition and all electrical consumers and remove the ignition key.
47 Remove the tailgate trim panel as described in Chapter 11, Section 15.
48 Working inside the top of the tailgate,

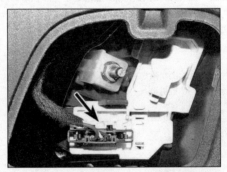

5.37 Disconnect the wiring connector

5.39 Removing a bayonet-type bulb

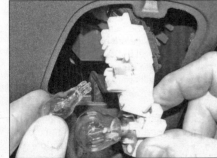

5.40 Removing a wedge-type bulb

5.43a Undo the retaining screw...

5.43b...withdraw the light unit...

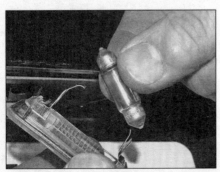

5.44...and remove the festoon-type bulb

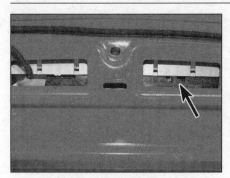

5.48a Slide the lower part (arrowed) to remove

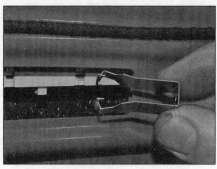

5.48b Retrieve the securing clips from inside the tailgate

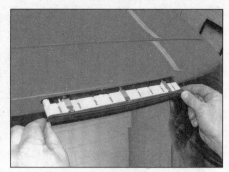

5.49 Withdraw the light unit from the tailgate

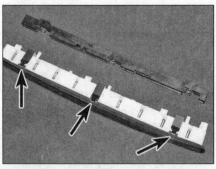

5.50 Make sure the three securing clips are in place

5.51 Reconnect the wiring connector

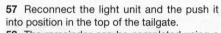

5.55 Release the securing clips

carefully slide the (black), lower part of the light unit to the side to disengage it from the upper (white) part of the light unit. **Note:** *You may need to retrieve the retaining clips from inside the top of the tailgate* **(see illustrations).**

49 The high-level brake light is then removed from the outside of the tailgate, followed by the lower (black) part of the light unit **(see illustration).** Disconnect the light unit as it is removed.

50 Before refitting the light unit, assemble the lower and upper parts of the light, including the three retaining clips **(see illustration).**

51 Reconnect the light unit and then push it into position in the top of the tailgate **(see illustration).**

52 The remainder can be completed using a reversal of the removal procedure.

5-door models

53 Switch off the ignition and all electrical consumers and remove the ignition key.

54 Remove the tailgate trim panel as described in Chapter 11, Section 15.

55 Working inside the top of the tailgate, carefully release the four retaining clips **(see illustration).**

56 The high-level brake light is then removed from the outside of the tailgate **(see illustrations).** Disconnect the light unit as it is removed.

57 Reconnect the light unit and the push it into position in the top of the tailgate.

58 The remainder can be completed using a reversal of the removal procedure.

6 Bulbs (interior lights) – renewal

General

1 Whenever a bulb is renewed, note the following points:

a) *Switch off the ignition and all electrical consumers before commencing work.*

b) *Remember that if the light has just been in use the bulb may be extremely hot.*

c) *Always check the bulb contacts and holder, ensuring that there is clean metal-to-metal contact between them. Clean off any corrosion or dirt before fitting a new bulb*

d) *Wherever festoon-type bulbs are fitted ensure that the live contact(s) bear firmly against the bulb contact.*

e) *Always ensure that the new bulb is of the correct rating and that it is completely clean before fitting it.*

Front courtesy light

2 Carefully prise the lens from the light unit, using a small flat-bladed screwdriver, and

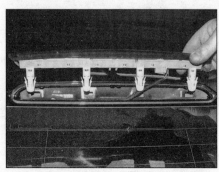

5.56a Withdraw the light unit...

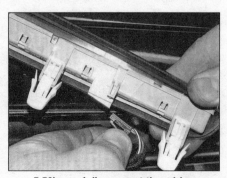

5.56b...and disconnect the wiring connector

6.2a Prise off the lens...

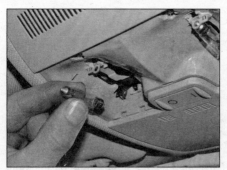

6.2b...then pull the festoon-type bulb from the spring contacts

6.4a Unclip the rear light unit...

then pull the festoon-type bulb from the spring contacts (see illustrations).

3 Fit the new bulb using a reversal of the removal procedure.

Rear courtesy light

4 Using a screwdriver, carefully release the locking clips and withdraw the light unit from the headlining (see illustrations). Disconnect the wiring connector as it is removed.

5 Pull the festoon-type bulb from the rear of the light (see illustration).

6 Fit the new bulb using a reversal of the removal procedure.

Luggage compartment light

7 Carefully prise the light unit from its location in the luggage compartment (see illustrations). Disconnect the wiring connector as it is removed.

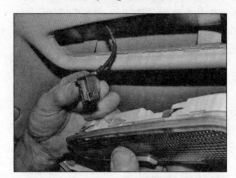

6.4b...and disconnect the wiring connector

8 Unclip the plastic cover from the rear of the light unit (see illustration).

9 The wedge-type bulb is a push-fit in the spring contacts; pull the bulb to remove (see illustration).

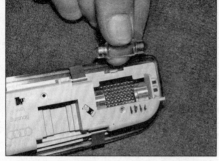

6.5 Pull the festoon-type bulb from the spring contacts

10 Fit the new bulb using a reversal of the removal procedure.

Make-up lights

11 Carefully prise the light unit from its location in the sun visor, and then remove the bulb. The make-up light is activated by lifting the cover of the mirror built into the sun visor.

12 No renewal procedure is recommended for the microswitch in the sun visor. If the switch is faulty, the visor must be renewed.

Glovebox illumination light

13 Open the glovebox, then use a screwdriver to carefully prise the light unit from its location in the glovebox (see illustration). Disconnect the wiring connector as it is removed.

14 Unclip the plastic cover from the rear of the light unit (see illustration 6.8).

15 The wedge-type bulb is a push-fit in the

6.7a Unclip the light unit...

6.7b...and disconnect the wiring connector

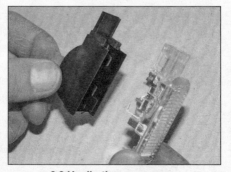

6.8 Unclip the rear cover...

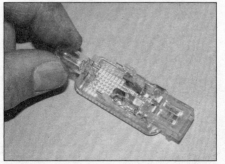

6.9...and pull out the wedge type bulb

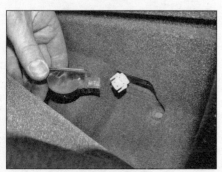

6.13 Unclip the light unit from inside the glovebox

spring contacts; pull the bulb to remove **(see illustration 6.9)**.

16 Fit the new bulb using a reversal of the removal procedure.

Instrument panel illumination/ warning lights

17 The instrument panel illumination/warning lights are non-renewable LEDs.

Cigarette lighter illumination

18 Remove the cigarette lighter as described in Section 14 of this Chapter.
19 Lift the retaining clip, and pull the bulbholder from the rear of the assembly. The bulb is integral with the bulbholder.
20 Fit the new bulb using a reversal of the removal procedure.

Heater/ventilation control panel illumination

21 The control panel is illuminated by LEDs built into the panel. Consequently, if a fault develops, renewal of the panel is necessary.

Switch illumination

22 The switch illumination bulbs are integral with the switches. If a bulb fails, the complete switch must be renewed.

Door warning lights

23 Open the relevant door, and carefully prise out the light unit.
24 Unplug the wiring connector.
25 Unclip the lens from the unit, and release the bulb from the spring contacts.
26 Refitting is a reversal of removal.

7 Exterior light units – removal and refitting

Headlight

1 Remove the front bumper cover, as described in Chapter 11, Section 6.
2 Undo the mounting bolts and pull the headlight unit forward **(see illustrations)**.
3 Pull the headlight slightly forward and disconnect the wiring connector **(see illustration)**.
4 Withdraw the headlamp forwards, while turning it as necessary to clear the front wing.
5 Refitting is a reversal of removal, but on completion, check that the headlight is aligned flush with the surrounding bodywork. If not, slacken the mounting bolts and re-align light unit. Finally, have the headlight alignment checked at the earliest opportunity.
Caution: After refitting a gas discharge headlamp, the basic setting of the Automatic Range Control system should be checked. Because of the requirement for specialised equipment, this can only be carried out by an Audi dealer or suitably-equipped specialist.

Gas discharge light starter unit

⚠️ *Warning: The headlight bulb contains gas at very high pressure, and it is recommended that gloves and eye protection are worn to prevent potential personal injury.*

6 Remove the headlight as described above.
7 Depress the tab and open the dipped beam bulb cover from the rear of the headlight unit.
8 If working on the left-hand light unit, unscrew the two range control motor retaining bolts.
9 Turn the starter unit anti-clockwise (OPEN) as far as possible (this will disconnect the wiring), and remove it from the headlight.
10 Refitting is a reversal of removal.

Gas discharge bulb control unit

11 Remove the headlight as described above.
12 Undo the three retaining screws, and remove the control unit from the headlight. Note that the electrical connections are automatically separated when the unit is removed.
13 Refitting is a reversal of removal.

Direction indicator in exterior mirror

14 There are no conventional bulbs in the exterior mirror, but LED's instead, therefore if the direction indicator is not working, the complete unit must be renewed. Refer to Chapter 11, Section 18.

Rear light cluster

15 Inside the rear luggage compartment, unclip the plastic cover from the securing nut **(see illustration)**.
16 Unscrew the mounting nut and withdraw the rear light cluster from the rear of the vehicle, releasing it from the outer locating pegs **(see illustrations)**.

7.2a Undo the headlight upper outer mounting bolt (arrowed)...

7.2b ...and the two inner mounting bolts (arrowed)...

7.3 Disconnect the wiring connector

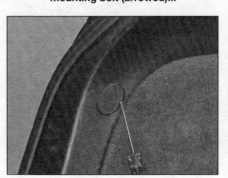

7.15 Unclip the plastic cover...

7.16a ...undo the retaining nut...

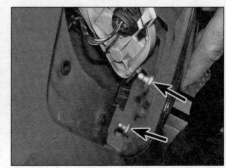

7.16b ...and remove the rear light unit from its locating pegs

7.17 Disconnecting the wiring as it is removed

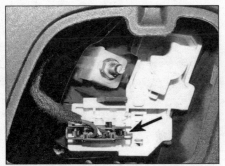

7.22 Disconnect the wiring connector

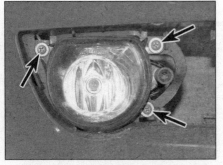

7.27 Front foglight retaining screws

17 Release the locking clip and disconnect the wiring plug from the light unit **(see illustration)**.
18 Refitting is a reversal of removal.

High-level brake light

19 The procedure is described as part of the bulb renewal procedure in Section 5.

Number plate light

20 The procedure is described as part of the rear number plate light bulb renewal procedure in Section 5.

Rear fog/reversing light (5-door)

Note: *The rear fog/reversing light bulbs are fitted to the rear light cluster on 3-door models, see paragraphs 14 to 17.*
21 Open the tailgate and unclip the plastic access cover at the rear of the light unit.
22 Disconnect the wiring connector from the rear of the light unit **(see illustration)**.
23 Undo the mounting nut and withdraw the light unit from the tailgate.
24 Refitting is a reversal of removal.

Front foglight

25 Switch off the ignition and all electrical consumers and remove the ignition key.
26 Reach into the opening at the lower, inner part of the foglight trim, and remove the trim from around the foglight unit.
27 Undo the three retaining screws (two screws on some models) and withdraw

the light unit from the front bumper **(see illustration)**.
28 Release the retaining clip and disconnect the wiring connector as it is removed.
29 Refitting is a reversal of removal.

8 Headlight beam adjustment components – removal and refitting

Headlight adjustment switch

1 The switch is integral with the lighting and instrument illumination switch.
2 Removal and refitting of the switch assembly is covered in Section 4.

Range adjustment motor

3 Remove the headlight (see Section 7).
4 Remove the plastic cover from the rear of the headlight by unclipping it at the top **(see illustration)**.
5 Unscrew the mounting screws **(see illustration)**, then slightly lift the reflector and manoeuvre out the motor. As it is being removed, turn the ball-head to release it.
6 Disconnect the wiring and remove the motor from the headlight.
7 Refitting is a reversal of removal.

Automatic range control ECU

Note: *Although it is possible to remove and refit the ECU, the new unit will need to be*

'coded' before it will function correctly. This task can only be carried out by an Audi dealer or suitably-equipped specialist.
8 The ECU is located behind the glovebox on the passenger end of the facia. Remove the glovebox as described in Chapter 11, Section 25.
9 Release the locking clip and disconnect the wiring connector.
10 Undo the retaining bolts and withdraw the ECU from behind the facia.
11 Refitting is a reversal of removal, but make sure the ECU is correctly located in the bracket before reconnecting the wiring.

Vehicle level sender

12 Refer to Chapter 10, Section 19.

9 Headlight and foglight beam alignment – general information

1 Accurate adjustment of the headlight beam is only possible using optical beam setting equipment and this work should therefore be carried out by an Audi dealer or suitably-equipped workshop.
2 For reference, the headlights can be adjusted using the adjuster assemblies fitted to the top of each light unit **(see illustration)**. The inner adjuster alters the lateral position of the beam whilst the outer adjuster alters the height of the beam.

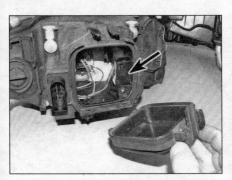

8.4 Headlight range adjuster motor

8.5 Undo the two retaining screws

9.2 Headlight manual adjusters

9.3 Front foglight adjusting screw

10.2a Pull back the gap cover...

10.2b...and unclip the upper column shroud

3 The front foglights can be adjusted by turning the adjuster at the front of the light unit **(see illustration)**.

10 Instrument panel – removal and refitting

Removal

1 Switch off the ignition and all electrical consumers and remove the ignition key. Release the steering wheel adjustment handle, pull the wheel out as far as possible, and set it in the lowest position.

10.3a Undo the two retaining screws...

2 Carefully pull the gap cover out from the instrument panel, and then unclip the upper part of the steering column shroud from the lower part **(see illustrations)**.
3 Undo the two retaining screws from the lower part of the instrument panel and then carefully pull the instrument panel out from the facia **(see illustrations)**.
4 Release the locking lever and disconnect the wiring plug connectors as the panel is withdrawn **(see illustration)**.

Refitting

5 Refitting is a reversal of removal.

11 Instrument panel components – removal and refitting

1 It is not possible to dismantle the instrument panel. If any of the gauges are faulty, the complete instrument panel must be renewed.

12 Service interval indicator – general information and resetting

1 All Audi models are equipped with a service interval indicator. After all necessary

maintenance work has been completed (see Chapter 1), the service interval display code must be reset.
2 Resetting is described in Chapter 1, Section 5.

13 Clock – removal and refitting

1 The clock is integral with the instrument panel, and cannot be removed separately. The instrument panel is a sealed unit, and if the clock, or any other components, are faulty, the complete instrument panel must be renewed. Refer to Section 10 to remove it.

14 Cigarette lighter – removal and refitting

Removal

1 Disconnect the battery negative lead (refer to *'Disconnecting the battery'* in Reference chapter).
2 Remove the lining mat from the small

10.3b...and withdraw the instrument panel

10.4 Disconnect the wiring connector

14.2 Lift out the lining mat...

14.3a...unclip the cigarette lighter trim...

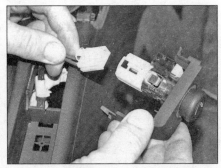

14.3b...and disconnect the wiring connector

oddments recess in the centre console **(see illustration)**.
3 Unclip the cigarette lighter (12 volt socket), including trim from the console **(see illustrations)**. Disconnect the wiring connector as it is removed.
4 Lift the retaining clip, and pull the bulbholder from the rear of the assembly. The bulb is integral with the bulbholder.
5 Push the centre element of the lighter out of the mounting in the trim panel.

Refitting

6 Refitting is a reversal of removal.

15 Horn – removal and refitting

Removal

1 Switch off the ignition and all electrical consumers and remove the ignition key.
2 Remove the front bumper as described in Chapter 11, Section 6.
3 Disconnect the wiring, then unscrew the mounting bolt and withdraw the horn together with the mounting bracket **(see illustration)**.
Note: *On some models there are two*

horns fitted one at each side of the front crossmember.
4 Unscrew the nut and remove the horn from the bracket.

Refitting

5 Refitting is a reversal of removal.

16 Speedometer sensor – general information

1 Unlike earlier models, no electronic speedometer sensor is fitted to the models covered in this Manual. Vehicle speed is determined from the ABS wheel sensor signals, and processed by the engine management ECU.

17 Wiper arm – removal and refitting

Removal

1 Operate the wiper motor, then switch off so that the wiper arms return to the at-rest position.

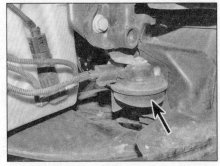

15.3 Horn location (front bumper removed)

2 Stick a piece of masking tape to the glass along the edge of the wiper blade to use as an alignment aid on refitting.
3 On the front wiper arms, prise off the wiper arm spindle nut cover, and then slacken but do not completely remove the spindle nut **(see illustrations)**.
4 On the rear wiper arm, unclip the plastic cover and then unclip the washer jet from the centre of the spindle. Slacken but do not completely remove the spindle nut **(see illustrations 20.12a and 20.12b)**.
5 Lift the blade off the glass and carefully rock the wiper arm from side-to-side, until it

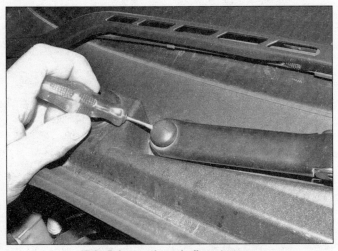

17.3a Prise up the spindle nut cover...

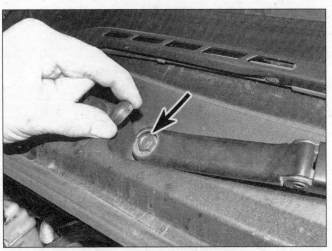

17.3b...and unscrew the spindle nut

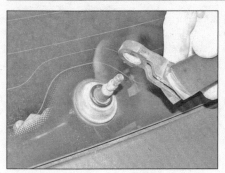

17.5a Remove the tailgate wiper arm...

17.5b...and the front wiper arm

17.5c Using a puller to release the wiper arm from the spindle

releases from the spindle. Remove the spindle nut **(see illustrations)**. The wiper arm can be a tight fit on the splines, if necessary use a puller to release the arm from the spindle.

Note: *If both windscreen wiper arms are to be removed at the same time mark them for identification; the arms are not interchangeable.*

Refitting

6 Ensure that the wiper arm and spindle

18.4 Pull off the rubber sealing strip

splines are clean and dry, and then refit the arm to the spindle, aligning the wiper blade with the tape fitted on removal. Refit the spindle nut, tightening it securely, and clip the nut cover and washer jet (rear wiper) back in position.

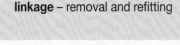

18 Windscreen wiper motor and linkage – removal and refitting

Removal

1 The wiper motor control unit is integrated into the wiper motor. Note that the windscreen wiper system has an APP (alternating park position) function. Every second time the wipers are switched off, the wiper arm is moved up slightly from its lowest position in order to maintain the efficiency of the wiper blades. If the motor crank is disconnected, it must be reset by first deactivating the APP function, however, this requires the use of diagnostic equipment not available to the home mechanic. It is

therefore important to accurately mark the crank in relation to the motor spindle before removing it. Reactivation of the function occurs automatically after 100 cycles of the wiper movement, and this also applies to new motors.

2 Remove the wiper arms as described in Section 17.

3 Disconnect the battery negative lead (refer to *'Disconnecting the battery'* in Reference chapter).

4 Pull off the rubber sealing strip from the top of the bulkhead **(see illustration)**.

5 Unclip the washer jets from the windscreen cowling, disconnect the washer pipe and the wiring connector as it is removed, Refer to Section 20.

6 Starting at each end of the cowling, carefully work your way along the lower edge of the windscreen, pulling the plastic windscreen cowling away from the windscreen seal **(see illustrations)**. Withdraw the cowling out from the bulkhead.

Caution: Do not use a screwdriver lever between the cowling and windscreen, as this is likely to result in the windscreen cracking.

18.6a Remove the plastic windscreen cowling...

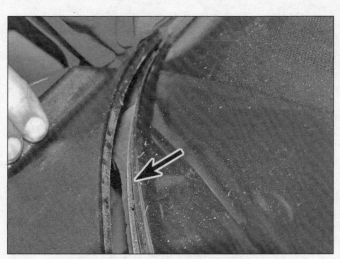

18.6b...unclipping it from the windscreen seal

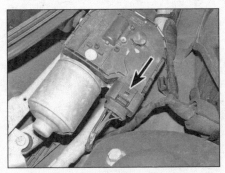

18.7 Disconnecting the wiring plug

18.8a Unscrew the wiper linkage...

18.8b...mounting bolts

7 Disconnect the wiring plug from the wiper motor **(see illustration)**.

8 Unscrew the mounting bolts and manoeuvre the windscreen wiper motor and linkage out from the scuttle **(see illustrations)**.

9 Where applicable, recover the washers and spacers from the motor mounting rubbers, noting their locations, then inspect the rubbers for signs of damage or deterioration, and renew if necessary.

10 To separate the motor from the linkage, proceed as follows.

a) *Make alignment marks between the motor spindle and the linkage to ensure correct alignment on refitting, and note the orientation of the linkage.*

b) *Unscrew the nut securing the linkage crank to the motor spindle.*

c) *Unscrew the three bolts securing the motor to the mounting plate, and then withdraw the motor.*

Refitting

11 Refitting is a reversal of removal, bearing in mind the following points.

a) *If the motor has been separated from the linkage, ensure that the marks made on the motor spindle and linkage before removal are aligned, and ensure that the linkage is orientated as noted before removal.*

b) *Ensure that the washers and spacers are*

fitted to the motor mounting rubbers as noted before removal.

c) *Make sure the locating peg on the wiper motor linkage engages correctly with the rubber grommet in the bulkhead* **(see illustration)**.

d) *Lubricate the windscreen cowling mounting slots with a silicone-based spray lubricant to ease installation. Do not strike the cowling to seat it in position as this could result in the windscreen cracking.*

e) *Refit the wiper arms as described in Section 17.*

19 Rear wiper motor – removal and refitting

Removal

1 Remove the wiper arm as described in Section 17.

2 Recover the wiper motor shaft sealing ring.

3 Open the tailgate, then remove the trim panel as described in Chapter 11, Section 15.

4 Unplug the wiring connector from the motor **(see illustration)**.

5 Disconnect the washer fluid hose from the washer nozzle connector on the motor assembly **(see illustrations)**.

18.11 Wiper linkage locating peg (arrowed)

19.4 Disconnect the wiring connector

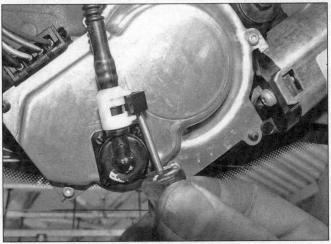

19.5a Release the securing clip...

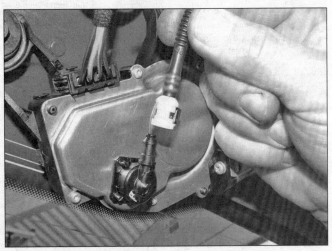

19.5b...and disconnect the washer fluid hose

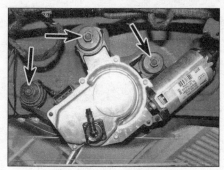

19.6a Undo the retaining nuts...

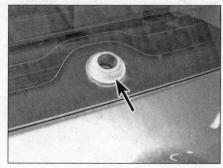

19.6b...and remove the tailgate wiper motor

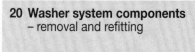

19.6c Tailgate wiper motor rubber grommet

6 Unscrew the three nuts securing the motor, and then withdraw the assembly. If necessary, renew the rubber grommet **(see illustrations)**.

Refitting

7 Refitting is a reversal of removal, but ensure that the motor shaft rubber sealing ring is correctly refitted to prevent water leaks, and refit the wiper arm with reference to Section 17.

20 Washer system components – removal and refitting

Washer fluid reservoir and pumps

Removal

1 Switch off the ignition and all electrical consumers and remove the ignition key.
2 In the engine compartment, unscrew the mounting bolt and remove the extension from the reservoir filler neck **(see illustrations)**.
3 Remove the front bumper as described in Chapter 11, Section 6.
4 Disconnect the wiring from the fluid level sender **(see illustration)**.
5 Note the position of the hose connections to the reservoir for refitting. Release the locking clips and disconnect the hoses from the washer pump motors **(see illustration)**.
Note: *Position a suitable container beneath the reservoir to catch spilt fluid.*
6 Pull the pump motors upwards from the reservoir and disconnect the wiring **(see illustration)**.
7 Unscrew the mounting bolts and remove the reservoir from the vehicle **(see illustrations)**.

Refitting

8 Refitting is a reversal of removal.

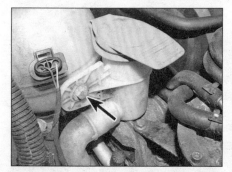

20.2a Undo the retaining bolt...

20.2b...and disconnect the filler neck from the washer bottle

20.4 Disconnect the wiring from the fluid level sender

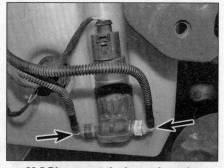

20.5 Disconnect the hoses from the washer pump

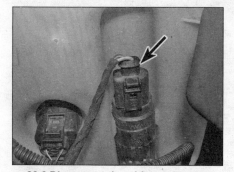

20.6 Disconnect the wiring connector

20.7a Undo the front mounting bolt...

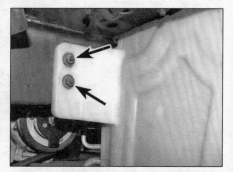

20.7b...and the two rear mounting bolts

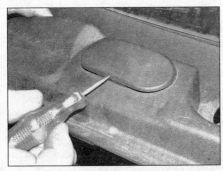

20.9 Unclip the washer jet from the trim panel

20.10a Disconnect the washer pipe...

20.10b...and the wiring connector

20.12a Unclip the plastic cover...

20.12b...and then remove the washer jet

Refitting

22 Refitting is a reversal of removal. Operate the washers several times to bleed any trapped air.

21 Radio/CD player/changer – removal and refitting

Note: *This Section only applies to standard-fit audio equipment.*

Radio/CD player

Removal

1 The radio/CD player is equipped with an electronic anti-theft system linked to the instrument panel. If the voltage supply to the radio is temporarily disconnected, the radio will function again when the supply is reconnected, without entering the safety code number, provided the radio is located in the original vehicle. Should the radio operation be blocked, normal operation can be restored by entering the correct anti-theft code.
2 Remove any CDs, which may be in the unit. Switch off the ignition and all electrical consumers, and remove the ignition key.
3 Insert four radio keys in the slots in the radio/CD player to release the locking clips, and then withdraw the radio/CD player unit from the facia **(see illustrations)**.
4 As the radio/CD player is removed, disconnect

Windscreen washer jets

Removal

9 Open the bonnet, and unclip the washer jets from the windscreen cowling **(see illustration)**.
10 Disconnect the washer pipe and the wiring connector as it is removed from the cowling **(see illustrations)**.

Refitting

11 Refitting is a reversal of removal.

Tailgate washer jet

Removal

12 On the rear wiper arm, unclip the plastic cover from the rear wiper arm and then unclip the washer jet from the centre of the spindle **(see illustrations)**.

Refitting

13 On refitting, ensure that the jet is securely pushed into position. Check the operation of the jet. If necessary, adjust the nozzle, aiming the spray at a point slightly above the area of glass swept by the wiper blade.

Headlight washer jets

Removal

14 Switch off the ignition and all electrical consumers, and remove the ignition key.
15 Carefully pull the washer jet out from the front bumper to its full extent, and hold it. Carefully prise the end cap from the washer jet.

16 Still holding the washer jet, lift the securing clip slightly, and pull the jet from the lift cylinder.

Refitting

17 Refitting is a reversal of removal. Operate the washers several times to bleed any trapped air.

Headlight pop-up washer jet lift cylinder

Removal

18 Remove the washer jet end cap as described in paragraphs 14 and 15.
19 Remove the front bumper as described in Chapter 11, Section 6.
20 Undo the two retaining screws, and withdraw the cylinder.
21 Clamp the hose, squeeze the retaining clip, and disconnect the hose.

21.3a Insert the radio/CD player locking keys...

21.3b...and withdraw the radio/CD player from the facia

21.4a Disconnect the aerial connections...

21.4b...and the wiring block connectors

the wiring connectors and aerial connection from the rear of the unit **(see illustrations)**.

Refitting

5 Refitting is a reversal of removal.

CD changer

Removal

6 The CD changer is located in the glovebox on the passenger side of the facia. It is fitted with special mounting clips, requiring the use of special removal tools (see radio removal), which should be supplied with the vehicle, or may be obtained from an in-car entertainment specialist. Alternatively, two feeler blades can be used.
7 Switch off the ignition and all electrical consumers, and remove the ignition key.
8 Open the glovebox and remove any CDs, which may still be in the unit.
9 Insert the tools into the slots on each side

22.3 Disconnect the wiring connector

of the unit and push them until they snap into place. The CD changer can then be pulled out of the glovebox using the tools, and the wiring connectors disconnected.

Refitting

10 Refitting is a reversal of removal.

22 Loudspeakers – removal and refitting

Front-mounted treble

Removal

1 Switch off the ignition and all electrical consumers, and remove the ignition key.
2 Remove the trim panel from the A-pillar as described in Chapter 11, Section 25.
3 Disconnect the speaker wiring plug **(see illustration)**.

22.13 Door speaker wiring connector

4 Twist the speaker to remove it from the inside of the trim panel.

Refitting

5 Refitting is a reversal of removal.

Rear-mounted treble

Removal

6 The loudspeaker is located behind the inner trim panel at the rear of the passenger compartment. First, switch off the ignition and all electrical consumers, and remove the ignition key.
7 Remove the rear door trim panel as described in Chapter 11, Section 12.
8 Disconnect the speaker wiring plug.
9 Release the retaining clips and withdraw the speaker from the rear of the trim panel.

Refitting

10 Refitting is a reversal of removal.

Door-mounted bass

Removal

11 Switch off the ignition and all electrical consumers, and remove the ignition key.
12 Remove the door trim with reference to Chapter 11, Section 12.
13 Disconnect the wiring plug from the top of the loudspeaker **(see illustration)**.
14 Undo the retaining screws, and then withdraw the speaker from the door **(see illustration)**. Where applicable, recover the rubber sealing ring between the speaker and door trim.
Note: *Some models may be fitted with pop rivets to secure the speakers, and these will need to be drilled out and replaced with new ones.*

Refitting

15 Refitting is a reversal of removal.

Centre mid-range and treble

Removal

16 Switch off the ignition and all electrical consumers, and remove the ignition key.
17 Unclip the trim panel from the centre of the facia **(see illustration)**.
18 Undo the retaining screws and withdraw the speaker from the top of the facia **(see illustration)**.
19 Disconnect the speaker wiring plug

22.17 Unclip the trim panel...

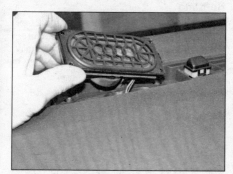

22.18...and remove the speaker from the facia

22.14 Front door loudspeaker retaining screws

Refitting

20 Refitting is a reversal of removal.

Rear bass

Removal

21 The bass loudspeaker is located behind the left-hand inner trim panel in the luggage compartment. First, switch off the ignition and all electrical consumers, and remove the ignition key.

22 Remove the rear luggage compartment trim panel as described in Chapter 11, Section 25.

23 Disconnect the speaker wiring plug.

24 Undo the retaining bolts and nut, and then withdraw the speaker from the rear body panel **(see illustration)**.

Refitting

25 Refitting is a reversal of removal.

---

23 Radio aerials –
removal and refitting

Aerial

Removal

1 The radio aerial is integrated into the rear window, which is bonded in position with a special adhesive. If the aerial is faulty, a new rear window must be fitted.

2 Where fitted the navigation, telephone and

22.24 Rear bass speaker retaining bolts

auxiliary heater telestart aerial is fitted to the rear of the roof panel. First, remove the trim from the C-pillar as described in Chapter 11, Section 25.

3 Undo the screws and remove the two rear grab handles from the headlining.

4 Carefully lower the rear of the headlining and disconnect the wiring. Note the colour-coded wiring as follows:
a) *Violet connector for the telephone.*
b) *Blue connector for the navigation system.*
c) *Remaining connector for the auxiliary heating remote control.*

5 Unscrew the securing nut and withdraw the aerial base from the roof. Hold the aerial base as the nut is being unscrewed to prevent the base from rotating and scratching the roof panel. Recover the rubber spacer.

Refitting

6 Refitting is a reversal of removal, but make

23.7 Aerial amplifier located on the tailgate

sure that the two guide lugs on the rubber spacer are correctly located in the aerial base.

Aerial amplifier

Removal

7 The aerial amplifier is fitted to the top of the tailgate, behind the inner trim panel **(see illustration)**. First, switch off the ignition and all electrical consumers, and remove the ignition key.

8 Remove the inner tailgate trim panels as described in Chapter 11, Section 15.

9 Disconnect the amplifier wiring connectors.

10 Undo the retaining screw and then withdraw the amplifier from the tailgate.

Refitting

11 Refitting is a reversal of removal.

Aerial module

Removal

12 The aerial module is fitted in the tailgate, behind the inner trim panel. First, switch off the ignition and all electrical consumers, and remove the ignition key.

13 Remove the inner tailgate trim panel as described in Chapter 11, Section 15.

14 Release the securing clips and disconnect the module wiring connectors **(see illustrations)**.

15 Remove the two upper mounting bolts and then slacken the lower mounting nuts. Withdraw the module from the lower mounting nut **(see illustrations)**. As the module is removed disconnect the small wiring connector at the rear of the unit, which attaches to the rear screen, taking care not to damage it.

Refitting

16 Refitting is a reversal of removal.

---

24 Anti-theft alarm system and engine immobiliser – general information

Note: *This information is applicable only to the anti-theft alarm system fitted by Audi as standard equipment.*

1 Models in the range are fitted with an anti-theft alarm system as standard

23.14a Disconnect the wiring connectors...

23.14b...and the aerial leads

23.15a Remove the two bolts and slacken the nut...

23.15b...slide the unit out, disconnecting the wiring connector

equipment. The alarm has switches on all the doors (including the tailgate), the bonnet and the ignition switch. If the tailgate, bonnet or any of the doors are opened whilst the alarm is set, the alarm horn will sound and the hazard warning lights will flash. These are also equipped with an internal monitoring system, which will activate the alarm system if any movement in the cabin is detected. The internal monitoring system can be disabled, if required, by a switch on the front door inner trim panel.

2 The alarm is set using the key in the driver's or passenger's front door lock, and tailgate lock, or with the central locking remote control transmitter. The alarm system will then start to monitor its various switches approximately 30 seconds later.

3 With the alarm set, if the tailgate is unlocked, the lock switch sensing will automatically be switched off but the door and bonnet switches will still be active. Once the tailgate is shut and locked again, the switch sensing will be switched back on.

4 All models are fitted with an immobiliser system, which is activated by the ignition switch. A transponder reading coil on the ignition switch reads a code contained within the ignition key. The system sends a signal to the engine management electronic control unit (ECU), which allows the engine to start if the code is correct. If an incorrect ignition key is used, the engine will not start.

5 If a fault is suspected with the alarm or immobiliser systems, the vehicle should be taken to an Audi dealer for examination. They will have access to a special diagnostic tester, which will quickly trace any fault present in the system.

25 Airbag system – general information and precautions

Warning: Before carrying out any operations on the airbag system, disconnect the battery negative lead (see 'Disconnecting the battery' in Reference chapter). When operations are complete, make sure no one is inside the vehicle when the battery is reconnected.

- *Note that the airbags must not be subjected to temperatures in excess of 90°C. When the airbag is removed, ensure that it is stored with the pad upwards to prevent possible inflation.*
- *Do not allow any solvents or cleaning agents to contact the airbag assemblies. They must be cleaned using only a damp cloth.*
- *The airbags and control unit are both sensitive to impact. If either is dropped or damaged they should be renewed.*

1 A driver's airbag, passenger's airbag and side airbags were fitted as standard to the Audi A3 range. Certain models also have curtain airbags located behind the headlining on each side of the car. The airbag system consists of the airbag unit (complete with gas generator), which is fitted to the steering wheel (driver's side), facia (passenger's side), roof (where applicable) and front seats, impact (crash) sensors, the control unit and a warning light in the instrument panel.

2 The airbag system is triggered in the event of a heavy frontal or side impact above a predetermined force; depending on the point of impact. The airbag is inflated within milliseconds and forms a safety cushion between the driver and the steering wheel, the passenger and the facia, and in the case of side impact, between front seat occupants and the sides of the cabin. This prevents contact between the upper body and cabin interior, and therefore greatly reduces the risk of injury. The airbag then deflates almost immediately.

3 Every time the ignition is switched on, the airbag control unit performs a self-test. The self-test takes approximately 3 seconds and during this time the airbag warning light on the facia is illuminated. After the self-test has been completed the warning light should go out. If the warning light fails to come on, remains illuminated after the initial 3 second period or comes on at any time when the vehicle is being driven, there is a fault in the airbag system. The vehicle should then be taken to an Audi dealer for examination at the earliest possible opportunity.

4 After renewing any components on the airbag system, it may be necessary to take the vehicle to your local Audi dealer to have them code the control unit to the specific vehicle.

26 Airbag system components – removal and refitting

Note: *Refer to the warnings in Section 25 before carrying out the following operations.*

1 Disconnect the battery negative lead (refer to 'Disconnecting the battery' in Reference chapter), then continue as described under the relevant heading.

Driver's airbag

Removal

2 Set the front wheels to the straight-ahead position, and release the steering lock by inserting the ignition key.

3 Adjust the steering column to its highest position by releasing the adjustment handle, then extend the steering wheel as far as possible. Lock the column in this position.

4 With the steering wheel in the straight-ahead position, unclip the plastic screw covers from each side of the steering wheel hub **(see illustration)**.

5 Insert a screwdriver into the holes in the rear of the steering wheel hub, and undo the retaining screws **(see illustration)**.

6 Carefully withdraw the airbag module and disconnect the wiring connector **(see illustrations)**.

Caution: To prevent any discharge of static electricity into the airbag circuit, temporarily touch the vehicle bodywork before disconnecting the wiring.

 Warning: Position the airbag in a safe and secure place, away from the work area.

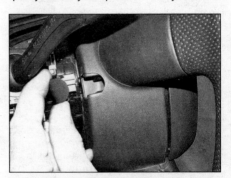

26.4 Unclip the plastic cover...

26.5...and remove the retaining screws

26.6a Withdraw the driver's airbag...

26.6b...then carefully release the wiring connector

26.9 Disconnect the wiring connector...

26.10a...then undo the mounting nuts...

26.10b...and remove the passenger airbag unit

Refitting

7 With the steering wheel in the straight-ahead position, locate the airbag module in position and reconnect the wiring. Carefully press the module into position and tighten the two retaining screws, then fit the plastic screw covers to the steering wheel. Reconnect the battery negative lead, ensuring that nobody is inside the vehicle as the lead is connected.

Passenger's airbag

Removal

8 Remove the passenger side glovebox with reference to Chapter 11, Section 25.
9 Reach up behind the facia panel and disconnect the wiring connector from the passenger's airbag **(see illustration)**.
Caution: To prevent any discharge of static electricity into the airbag circuit, temporarily touch the vehicle bodywork before disconnecting the wiring.
10 Unscrew the mounting bolts and withdraw the airbag unit from under the facia panel **(see illustrations)**. As the airbag unit is removed, check for any other wiring still attached to the unit.

 Warning: Position the airbag in a safe and secure place, away from the work area.

Refitting

11 Refitting is a reversal of removal, but tighten the mounting bolts to the specified torque. Reconnect the battery negative lead, ensuring that nobody is inside the vehicle as the lead is connected.

Front seat side impact airbags

12 The side impact air bags are integral with the seats. As seat upholstery removal requires considerable skill and experience, if it is to be carried out without damage, it is best entrusted to an expert.

Roof curtain airbags

13 This work involves removing the headlining and major dismantling of interior trim panels **(see illustration)**, and is best entrusted to an Audi dealer.

Airbag control unit

Note: *Although it is possible to remove and refit the control unit, the new unit will need to be 'coded' before it will function correctly. This task can only be carried out by an Audi dealer or suitably-equipped specialist.*

Removal

14 The airbag control unit is located beneath the heater unit at the centre of the facia **(see illustration)**.
15 Remove the centre console with reference to Chapter 11, Section 26.
16 Release the locking lever and disconnect the wiring from the control unit **(see illustration)**.
17 Unscrew the nuts and remove the control unit from the vehicle.

Refitting

18 Refitting is the reverse of removal making sure the wiring connector is securely reconnected and the arrow on the top of the unit is facing forward **(see illustration)**.

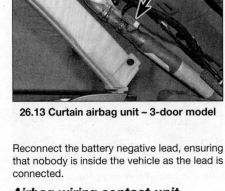

26.13 Curtain airbag unit – 3-door model

Reconnect the battery negative lead, ensuring that nobody is inside the vehicle as the lead is connected.

Airbag wiring contact unit

Removal

19 Check that the front wheels are pointing straight-ahead and the steering wheel is in its centre position, then remove the steering wheel as described in Chapter 10, Section 20.
20 Undo the screws and remove the column height and reach adjustment handle.
21 Carefully prise out the gap cover, and then remove the upper shroud from the steering column.
22 Undo the two upper screws and single lower screw and remove the lower shroud.
23 Remove the steering column electronics control unit. To do this, undo the single retaining screw, then insert a 2.5 mm diameter

26.14 Airbag control unit location – under heater unit

26.16 Release the wiring connector locking lever

26.18 Arrow on unit should always face forward when fitted

26.23a Undo the retaining screw...

26.23b...and insert 2.5 mm rod to release the upper clip...

26.23c...and use a screwdriver to release the lower clip...

rod or similar through the hole provided, and release the centre clip. Now use a screwdriver to release the rear clip. Pull down the control unit from the column switch

26.23d...then lower the control unit from the column

carrier and disconnect the wiring **(see illustrations)**.

24 The airbag clock spring/slip-ring must be held in its central position while it is removed,

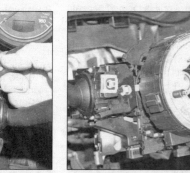

26.23e Showing the position of the retaining clips

to ensure correct refitting. Unclip the airbag clock spring/slip-ring from the combination switch carrier by lifting the retaining hooks **(see illustrations)**.

25 If required, on models with ESP, pull the steering angle sensor directly away from the combination switch carrier **(see illustration)**.

Refitting

26 Refitting is a reversal of removal procedure. Reconnect the battery negative lead, ensuring that no one is inside the vehicle as the lead is connected.

Passenger airbag isolation switch

Removal

27 The switch is located inside the glovebox. To remove it, open the glovebox then use a screwdriver to prise out the switch **(see illustration)**. Disconnect the wiring.

Refitting

28 Refitting is a reversal of removal.

Side crash sensors

Removal

29 Disconnect the battery negative lead (see 'Disconnecting the battery' in Reference chapter).

30 Remove the sill trim panel with reference to Chapter 11, Section 25, and pull back the carpet.

31 Release the securing clip and disconnect the wiring connector from the crash sensor.

26.24a Release the retaining clips...

26.24b...and withdraw the airbag clock spring from the column

26.25 Removing the steering angle sensor

26.27 Unclip the switch from inside the glovebox

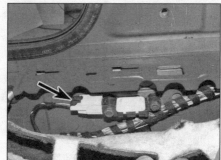

26.31 Side crash sensor at base of B-pillar

26.35a Rear crash sensor on C-pillar –
5-door model

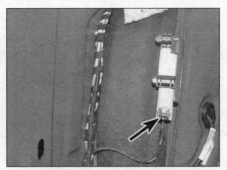

26.35b Rear crash sensor in front of rear
wheel arch – 3-door model

26.38 Front crash sensors – one on each
side of the radiator

Undo the mounting nuts and remove the sensor from the sill panel **(see illustration)**.

Refitting

32 Refitting is a reversal of removal. Make sure that nobody is inside the vehicle when first switching on the ignition.

Rear wheel housing crash sensors

Removal

33 Disconnect the battery negative lead (see *'Disconnecting the battery'* in Reference chapter).

34 Remove the luggage compartment side trim panels with reference to Chapter 11, Section 25. On 3-door models it will be necessary to remove the rear seat side trim panels.

35 Release the securing clip and disconnect the wiring connector from the crash sensor. Undo the mounting nuts and remove the sensor from the rear wheel housing **(see illustrations)**.

Refitting

36 Refitting is a reversal of removal. Make sure that nobody is inside the vehicle when first switching on the ignition.

Front crash sensors

Removal

37 Disconnect the battery negative lead (see *'Disconnecting the battery'* in Reference chapter).

38 Open the bonnet and the sensors are fitted at each side of the radiator on the front panel, at the inside of each headlamp **(see illustration)**.

39 Release the securing clip and disconnect the wiring connector from the crash sensor. Undo the mounting nuts and remove the sensor from the front panel.

Refitting

40 Refitting is a reversal of removal. Make sure that nobody is inside the vehicle when first switching on the ignition.

27 Parking aid components – general information, removal and refitting

General information

1 The parking aid system is available as a standard fitment on highline models, and optional on other models. Four ultrasound sensors located in the rear bumper measure the distance to the closest object behind the car, and inform the driver using acoustic signals from a buzzer located under the rear luggage compartment trim. The nearer the object, the more frequent the acoustic signals.

2 The system includes a control unit and self-diagnosis program, and therefore, in the event of a fault, the vehicle should be taken to an Audi dealer.

Control unit

3 The parking aid control unit is located in the luggage compartment behind the right-hand trim panel. Switch off the ignition and all electrical consumers, and remove the ignition key, then remove the right-hand trim with reference to Chapter 11, Section 25.

4 Depress the locking lugs and disconnect the wiring plugs from the control unit.

5 Unclip the unit from the mounting bracket.

6 Refitting is a reversal of removal.

Range/distance sensor

7 Remove the rear bumper as described in Chapter 11, Section 7.

8 Disconnect the wiring from the sensor.

9 Release the lugs and pull the sensor from the bumper.

10 Refitting is a reversal of removal. Press the sensor firmly into position until the retaining clips engage.

Warning buzzer

11 The warning buzzer is located in the luggage compartment behind the right-hand trim panel. Switch off the ignition and all electrical consumers and remove the ignition key, then remove the right-hand trim with reference to Chapter 11, Section 25.

12 Disconnect the wiring, then release the clips and remove the buzzer from the mounting bracket.

13 Refitting is a reversal of removal.

Fuse box in engine compartment (E-box low) up to 10-2008

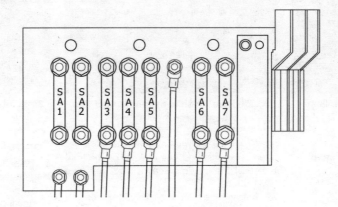

FUSE	VALUE	DESCRIPTION
SA1	200 A	Alternator (150A also used)
SA2	80 A	Power steering control unit
SA3	50 A	Radiator fan control unit, Thermoswitch, radiator Cooling fan
SA4	40 A	Low-output heating relay or not used
SA5	80 A	Positive connections in the main wiring loom, Fuse box in passenger compartment, fuses 12 - 17, 22 - 28, 38, 43
SA6	100 A	Additional air heater control unit Or High-output heating relay (80A also used)
SA7	80 A	Optional equipment (50A also used) Or Electronic damper control unit (30A also used)

Fuse box in engine compartment (E-box low) from 11-2008

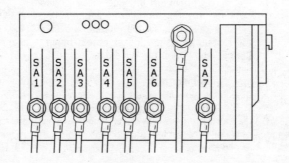

FUSE	VALUE	DESCRIPTION
SA1	200 A	Alternator (150A also used)
SA2	80 A	Power steering control unit
SA3	50 A	Radiator fan control unit, Thermoswitch, radiator Cooling fan
SA4	80 A	High-output heating relay
SA5	80 A	Positive connections in the main wiring loom, Fuse box in passenger compartment, fuses 12 - 17, 22 - 28, 38, 43
SA6	40 A	Low-output heating relay
SA7	80 A	Optional equipment (50A also used) Or Electronic damper control unit (30A also used)

Fuse box in engine compartment (E-box high)

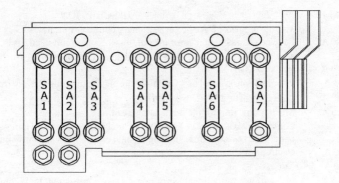

FUSE	VALUE	DESCRIPTION
SA1	200 A	Alternator (150A also used)
SA2	80 A	Power steering control unit
SA3	80 A	Radiator fan control unit
SA4	80 A	Window regulator, Window regulator 2, Fuse box in passenger compartment, fuses 22 - 27
SA5	100 A	Additional air heater control unit
SA6	50 A	Fuse box in passenger compartment, fuses 12 - 17, 19, 44, 45 Or Window regulator, Window regulator 2, Fuse box in passenger compartment, fuses 12 - 17, 19, 22 - 27 (80A also used)
SA7	0 A	Not used

Main fuse and relay box in engine compartment (E-box low)

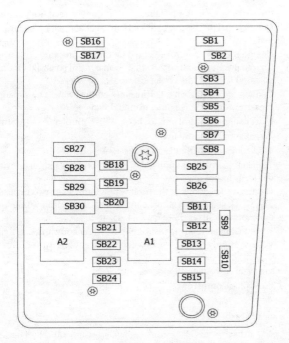

FUSE	VALUE	DESCRIPTION
SB1	40 A	Voltage regulator Fuse box in passenger compartment, fuses 7 - 11 Or Voltage regulator Fuse box in passenger compartment, fuses 7 - 10 or not used
SB2	30 A	Mechatronic unit for the dual-clutch gearbox Or Control unit, steering column electronics (5A also used)
SB3	5 A	Power supply control unit Or Power supply control unit, Battery monitor control unit
SB4	30 A	ABS control unit (20A also used)
SB5	15 A	Mechatronic unit for the dual-clutch gearbox
SB6	5 A	Control unit with display in the dash panel insert Or Control unit with display in the dash panel insert Control unit, steering column electronics Or Control unit, steering column electronics
SB7	0 A	Not used
SB8	15 A	Navigation control unit, Information display control unit, Radio or not used
SB9	5 A	Navigation system with CD drive control unit Navigation system Satellite digital audio receiver control unit Communication control unit Aerial selection control unit Connector T18a or not used
SB10	5 A	Terminal 30 voltage supply relay
SB11	30 A	Additional heater control unit (20A also used)
SB12	5 A	Data bus diagnostic interface
SB13	30 A	Engine control units
SB14	0 A	Not used
SB15	5 A	Fuel pump relay Glow plug control unit, Low-output heating relay, High-output heating relay
SB16	30 A	ABS control unit Or Power supply control unit Right
SB17	15 A	Horns
SB18	30 A	Amplifier Rear audio amplifier Or Voltage regulator, Amplifier, Rear audio amplifier
SB19	30 A	Wiper control unit
SB20	0 A	Not used
SB21	10 A	Oxygen sensor in front of the catalytic converter or not used
SB22	5 A	Clutch pedal position sensor Or Clutch pedal position sensor, Brake light switch, Brake pedal switch
SB23	10 A	Charge pressure control solenoid Or Charge pressure control solenoid EGR valve Or Charge pressure control solenoid Swirl control solenoid Or Charge pressure control solenoid Exhaust gas cooler solenoid
SB24	10 A	Cooling fan control unit, Oil pressure control valve Or Cooling fan control unit, Oil pressure control valve, Inlet manifold flap
SB25	30 A	Power supply control unit Right Or ABS control unit (40A also used)
SB26	30 A	Power supply control unit
SB27	50 A	Glow plug control unit Glow plugs 1 - 4
SB28	40 A	Terminal 15 voltage supply relay Fuse box in passenger compartment, fuses 1 - 6, 29 - 31, 46, 47, 49 or not used
SB29	50 A	Positive connections in the main wiring loom, Fuse box in passenger compartment, fuses 32 - 37, 44, 45, 48 Or Positive connections in the main wiring loom, Fuse box in passenger compartment, fuses 32 - 37, 39, 44, 45, 48
SB30	50 A	X contact relief relay, Fuse box in passenger compartment, fuses 40 - 42 Or Terminal 15 voltage supply relay, Fuse box in passenger compartment, fuses 1 - 6, 19, 20, 29 - 31, 40 - 42, 46, 47, 49
A1		Terminal 30 voltage supply relay
A2		Glow plug control unit

Main fuse and relay box in engine compartment (E-box high)

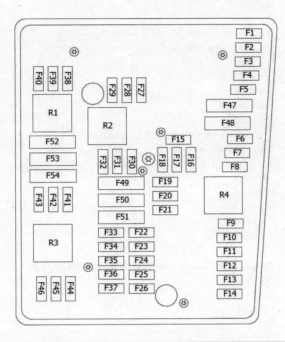

FUSE/RELAY	VALUE	DESCRIPTION
F1	30 A	ABS control unit Or Power supply control unit Right
F2	30 A	ABS control unit (20A also used)
F3	40 A	Voltage regulator Fuse box in passenger compartment, fuses 11 - 17 Or Fuse box in passenger compartment, fuses 7 - 10 or not used
F4	5 A	Power supply control unit
F5	15 A	Horns
F6	0 A	Not used
F7	0 A	Not used
F8	0 A	Not used
F9	0 A	Not used
F10	0 A	Not used
F11	0 A	Not used
F12	0 A	Not used
F13	15 A	Mechatronic unit for the dual-clutch gearbox
F14	0 A	Not used
F15	10 A	Coolant circulation pump
F16	5 A	Control unit, steering column electronics or not used
F17	5 A	Control unit with display in the dash panel insert Or Control unit with display in the dash panel insert Control unit, steering column electronics Or Control unit, steering column electronics
F18	30 A	Amplifier Rear audio amplifier Or Voltage regulator Amplifier Rear audio amplifier
F19	15 A	Navigation control unit Information display control unit Radio or not used
F20	5 A	Navigation system with CD drive control unit Navigation system Communication control unit Aerial selection control unit Connector T18a or not used

F21	0 A	Not used
F22	0 A	Not used
F23	10 A	Engine control units Motronic power supply relay
F24	5 A	Data bus diagnostic interface
F25	0 A	Not used
F26	0 A	Not used
F27	0 A	Not used
F28	0 A	Not used
F29	0 A	Not used
F30	30 A	Additional heater control unit (20A also used)
F31	30 A	Wiper control unit
F32	0 A	Not used
F33	0 A	Not used
F34	0 A	Not used
F35	0 A	Not used
F36	0 A	Not used
F37	0 A	Not used
F38	0 A	Not used
F39	5 A	Clutch pedal position sensor Brake light switch Brake pedal switch or not used
F40	0 A	Not used
F41	0 A	Not used
F42	0 A	Not used
F43	0 A	Not used
F44	0 A	Not used
F45	0 A	Not used
F46	0 A	Not used
F47	30 A	Power supply control unit
F48	40 A	ABS control unit Or Power supply control unit Right (30A also used)
F49	40 A	Terminal 15 voltage supply relay Fuse box in passenger compartment, fuses 1 - 6, 29 - 31, 46, 47, 49 or not used
F50	0 A	Not used
F51	0 A	Not used
F52	50 A	X contact relief relay Fuse box in passenger compartment, fuses 40 - 42 Or Terminal 15 voltage supply relay Fuse box in passenger compartment, fuses 1 - 6, 19, 20, 29 - 31, 40 - 42, 46, 47, 49
F53	50 A	Positive connections in the main wiring loom Fuse box in passenger compartment, fuses 32 - 37, 44, 45, 48 Fuse box in passenger compartment, fuses 32 - 37, 48 Or Positive connections in the main wiring loom Fuse box in passenger compartment, fuses 32 - 37, 39, 44, 45, 48 Fuse box in passenger compartment, fuses 32 - 37, 39, 48
F54	0 A	Not used
R1		Motronic power supply relay or not used
R2		Continued coolant circulation relay or not used
R3		Not used
R4		Fuel pump relay or not used

Fuse box in passenger compartment

FUSE	VALUE	DESCRIPTION
SC1	10 A	Lighting switch, Headlight range control, Trailer detection control unit, Headlight range control unit, Crankcase heater Diagnostic connector (16), Mass airflow meter, Engine Start and Stop system switch
SC2	10 A	Engine control units, ABS control unit, Power steering control unit, Data bus diagnostic interface, Gear selector control unit, Mechatronic unit for the dual-clutch gearbox, Starter relay 1, Starter relay 2, Automatic anti-dazzle rear-view mirror, Brake light switch, Brake pedal switch, Or Engine control units, ABS control unit, Power steering control unit, Data bus diagnostic interface, Gear selector control unit, Mechatronic unit for the dual-clutch gearbox, Starter relay 1, Starter relay 2, Automatic anti-dazzle rear-view mirror
SC3	5 A	Airbag control unit, Passenger's side airbag deactivation light
SC4	5 A	Switch heated rear seats, Tyre pressure monitor switch TCS/ESP button ,Garage door opener, Reversing light switch, Air-conditioning high-pressure sensor, Air quality sensor, Oil level and temperature sensor, Heater control unit, Climatronic control unit, Air-conditioning control unit, Navigation system with CD drive control unit, Parking assistance control unit, Garage door operation control unit, Seat occupied recognition control unit, Control unit, heated front seats, Heated washer jets, Automatic anti-dazzle rear-view mirror, Voltage regulator, Engine Start and Stop system switch
SC5	5 A	Power output control unit for the left headlight
SC6	5 A	Power output control unit for the right headlight
SC7	0 A	Not used
SC8	5 A	Control unit with display in the dash panel insert
SC9	15 A	Navigation control unit, Information display control unit, Radio Connector
SC10	7.5 A	Navigation system Communication control unit, Audio connection Connector T18a
SC11	10 A	Automatic anti-dazzle rear-view mirror
SC12	10 A	Driver's door control unit, Front passenger's door control unit
SC13	10 A	Door control unit, rear left Door control unit, rear right Comfort system control unit Or Door control unit, rear left Door control unit, rear right
SC14	10 A	ABS control unit, Gear selector control unit
SC15	10 A	Front interior light, Rear interior light
SC16	10 A	Rain and light sensor, Heater control unit, Climatronic control unit, Air-conditioning control unit, Tyre pressure monitor control unit,Additional heater remote control receiver, Diagnostic connector (16), Lighting switch
SC17	5 A	Interior monitoring, Vehicle inclination sender, Alarm horn
SC18	5 A	Power supply control unit, Voltage regulator, Engine control unit
SC19	10 A	4WD control unit

SC20	5 A	Electronic damper control unit
SC21	0 A	Not used
SC22	40 A	Fresh-air blower control unit, Blower
SC23	30 A	Driver's side power window
SC24	20 A	Cigarette lighter
SC25	30 A	Heated rear windscreen
SC26	20 A	12V socket
SC27	15 A	Fuel pump relay Relay, fuel pump No. 2 Or Fuel pump relay, Relay fuel pump No. 2, Additional relay fuel pump Additional fuel pump Or Fuel pump relay Additional relay fuel pump, Additional fuel pump
SC28	30 A	Rear left power window, Rear right power window
SC29	0 A	Not used
SC30	20 A	Multifunction switch, Automatic transmission control unit or not used
SC31	0 A	Not used
SC32	30 A	Headlight washer pump
SC33	20 A	Sliding roof control unit
SC34	20 A	Heated rear seat(s) control unit
SC35	0 A	Not used
SC36	10 A	Driver's seat adjustment switch, Front passenger's seat adjustment switch
SC37	20 A	Climatronic control unit, Driver's seat heater control unit, Passenger's seat heater control unit
SC38	30 A	Front passenger's power window
SC39	5 A	GPS system
SC40	40 A	Starter
SC41	15 A	Rear wiper motor
SC42	15 A	Front and rear washer pumps or not used
SC43	20 A	Comfort system control unit Or Power supply control unit
SC44	20 A	Trailer detection control unit
SC45	20 A	Trailer detection control unit
SC46	10 A	Trailer connector socket
SC47	5 A	Connector T18a, Aerial selection control unit
SC48	10 A	12V socket
SC49	5 A	Buzzer Fuse 6 Footwell light(s)

Fuse and relay box in luggage compartment

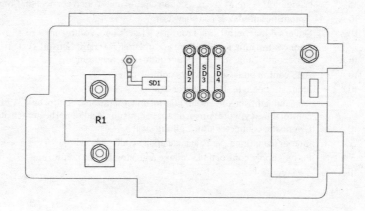

FUSE/RELAY	VALUE	DESCRIPTION
SD1	5 A	Power supply control unit
SD2	125 A	Fuse box in passenger compartment Fuses and relays in engine compartment
SD3	80 A	Fuse box in passenger compartment Fuses and relays in engine compartment
SD4	50 A	Amplifier Optional equipment (30A also used) Or Fuse box in passenger compartment, fuses 12 - 17, 19 Or Fuse box in passenger compartment, fuses 12 - 17, 43
R1		Battery isolation relay Battery cut-out relay

Fuse and relay box in passenger compartment up to 2008

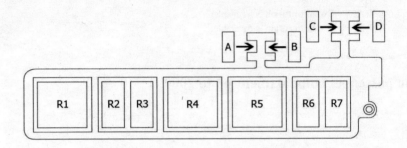

RELAY/FUSE	VALUE	DESCRIPTION
R1		Headlight washer relay
R2		Fuel pump relay Or Low-output heating relay or not used
R3		Fuel pump relay Or Low-output heating relay or not used
R4		Terminal 50 voltage supply relay
R5		Terminal 50 voltage supply relay or not used
R8		Fuel pump relay
R7		Relay, fuel pump No. 2
A	30 A	Window regulator or not used
B	30 A	Window regulator 2 or not used
C	30 A	No information is available
D	30 A	No information is available

Fuse and relay box in passenger compartment from 2009

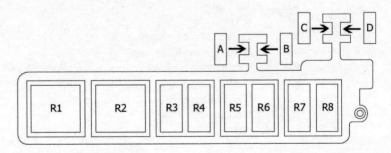

RELAY/FUSE	VALUE	DESCRIPTION
R1		Low-output heating relay
R2		Terminal 50 voltage supply relay or not used
R3		Headlight washer relay Or Starter relay 2
R4		Additional relay, fuel pump Or Starter relay 1
R5		Relay, fuel pump No. 2 or not used
R6		Fuel pump relay or not used
R7		High-output heating relay Or Additional relay, fuel pump or not used
R8		High-output heating relay Or Automatic anti-dazzle rear-view mirror or not used
A	0 A	Not used
B	0 A	Not used
C	30 A	No information is available
D	30 A	No information is available

Relay box in passenger compartment up to 2009

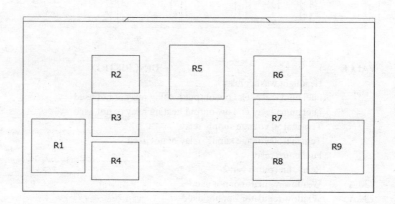

RELAY	DESCRIPTION
R1	Terminal 15 voltage supply relay
R2	Not used
R3	Not used
R4	Terminal 30 voltage supply relay
R5	Heated rear windscreen relay
R6	Horn relay
R7	Washer pump relay 2
R8	Washer pump relay
R9	X contact relief relay

Relay box in passenger compartment from 2010

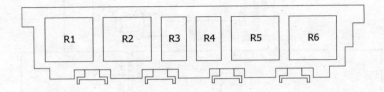

RELAY	DESCRIPTION
R1	Terminal 15 voltage supply relay
R2	Heated rear windscreen relay
R3	Horn relay
R4	Headlight washer relay
R5	X contact relief relay
R6	High-output heating relay

Relay box in engine compartment

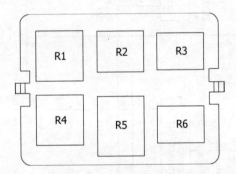

RELAY	DESCRIPTION
R1	Not used
R2	Glow plug control unit or not used
R3	Not used
R4	Continued coolant circulation relay or not used
R5	Secondary air pump relay or not used
R6	Not used

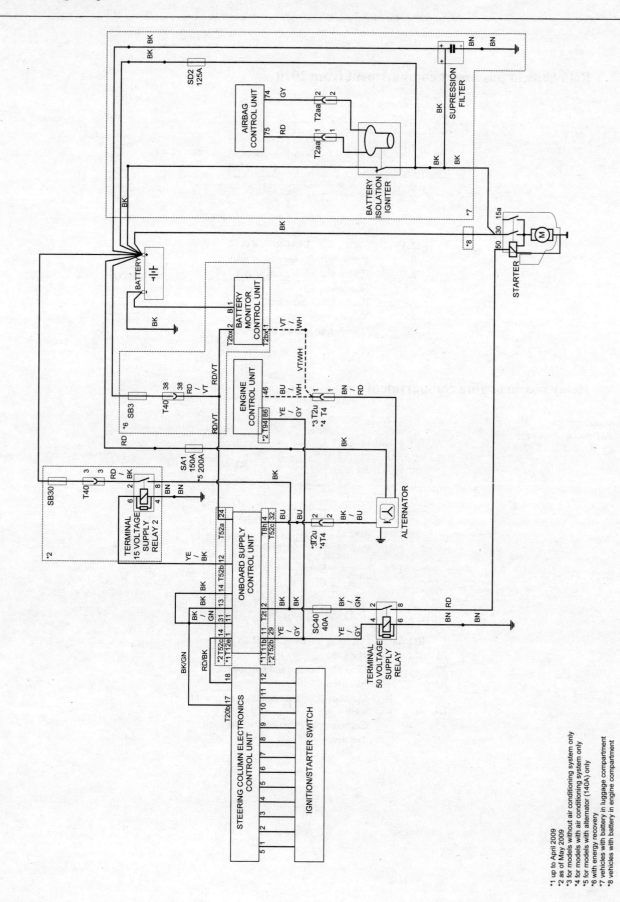

Starting/charging without start-stop system

*1 up to April 2009
*2 as of May 2009
*3 for models without air conditioning system only
*4 for models with air conditioning system only
*5 for models with alternator (140A) only
*6 with energy recovery
*7 vehicles with battery in luggage compartment
*8 vehicles with battery in engine compartment

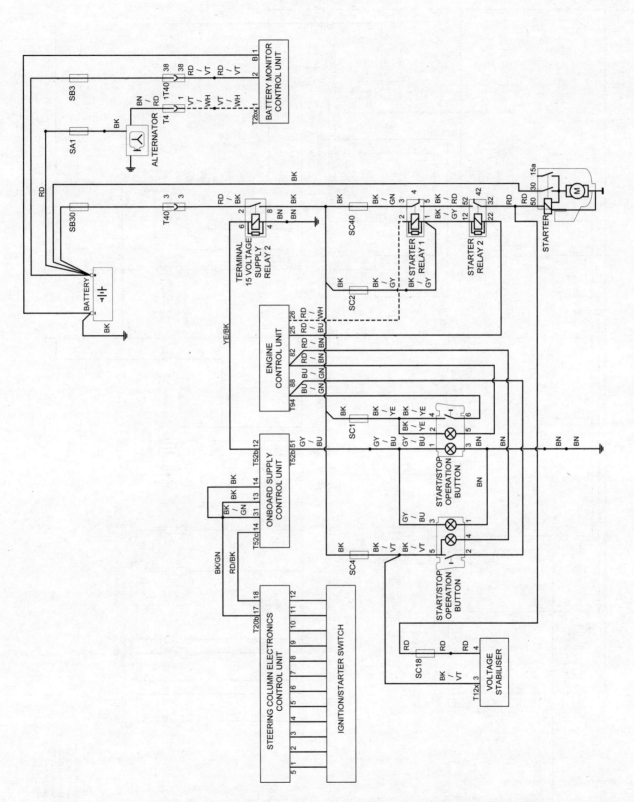

Starting/charging with start-stop system

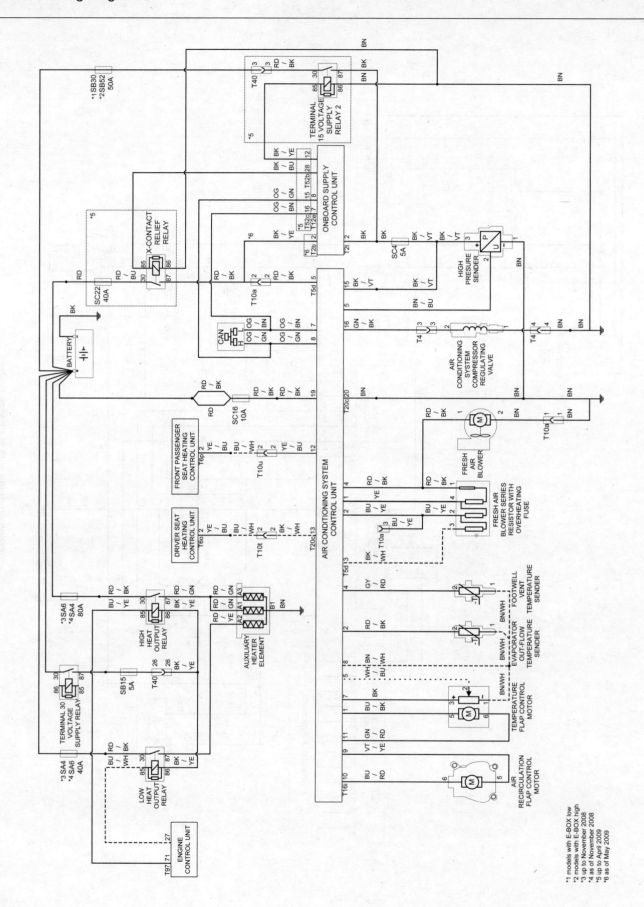

Air conditioning – manual regulation

*1 models with E-BOX low
*2 models with E-BOX high
*3 up to November 2008
*4 as of November 2008
*5 up to April 2009
*6 as of May 2009

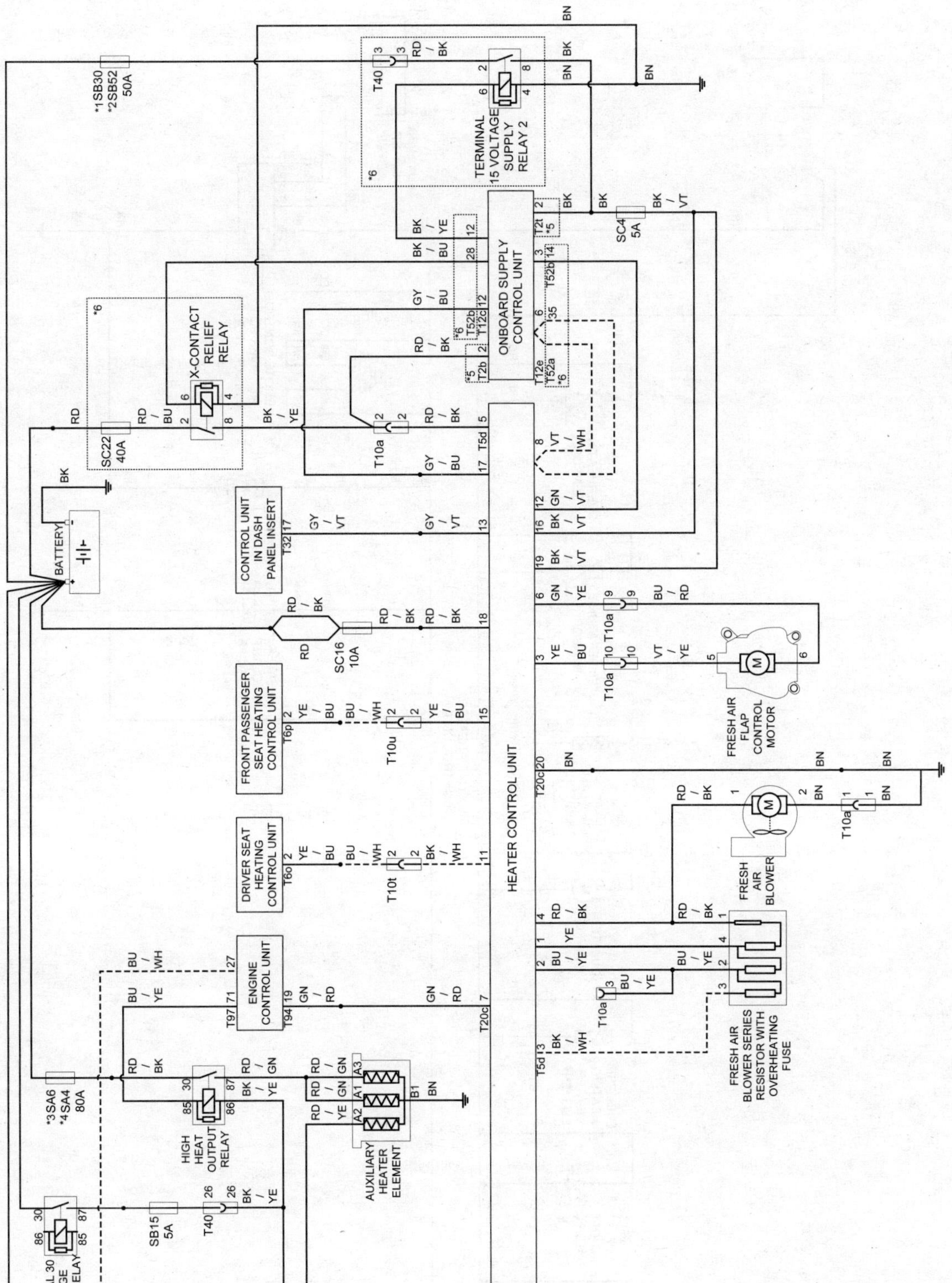

Air conditioning – manual regulation with heater

BN

*1 SB30
*2 SB52
50A

T40 3 3 RD / BK 2 8 BK BN
6 4
TERMINAL 15 VOLTAGE SUPPLY RELAY 2
*6

BN BK

*6

BK BK YE 12 28 T21 *5 BK BK BK VT
BU BU SC4 5A
X-CONTACT RELIEF RELAY
GY BU T52b *6 3 35 T52b 14
RD BK T12c 12 2 T12e T52a 6
ONBOARD SUPPLY CONTROL UNIT
*5 T2b T12e T52a 6
RD RD BU BK YE 2 2 RD BK 5 8 VT
SC22 6 4 T10a 17 T5d WH
40A 2 GY VT
BK
RD RD
BATTERY
BK

CONTROL UNIT IN DASH PANEL INSERT
T32 17 GY / VT GY / VT 13 16 BK VT / YE VT / VT
12 GN VT / VT
19 BK VT / YE

RD BK RD BK 18 6 GN BU 9 BU RD
YE YE 9
RD BK 3 YE 10 T10a VT YE
SC16 BU 10 YE 5 6
10A FRESH AIR FLAP CONTROL MOTOR M 6

FRONT PASSENGER SEAT HEATING CONTROL UNIT
T6p 2 YE BU 2 YE 15
BU WH BU
T10u T20c 20 BN BN BN

DRIVER SEAT HEATING CONTROL UNIT
T6d 2 YE BU 2 BK 11
BU WH WH
T10t RD BK 1 M 2 BN BN
FRESH AIR BLOWER T10a 1 BN

HEATER CONTROL UNIT
4 RD RD BK
BK 1
ENGINE CONTROL UNIT 1 YE YE
T97 71 127 BU BU 2 BU YE 4
T94 19 GN GN BU YE 2
YE RD RD T20c 7 T10a 3
BU / YE GN WH FRESH AIR BLOWER SERIES RESISTOR WITH OVERHEATING FUSE
T5d 13 BK
iWH

*3 SA6
*4 SA4
80A
RD BK
HIGH HEAT OUTPUT RELAY
85 30 RD RD GN GN A3
87 BK RD YE A1
86 YE GN A2 A1
RD RD GN GN B1 BN
AUXILIARY HEATER ELEMENT

TERMINAL 30 VOLTAGE SUPPLY RELAY
86 30 BK 26 BK
85 87 SB15 T40 YE
5A

*3 SA4
*4 SA6
40A
RD BK
LOW HEAT OUTPUT RELAY
85 30 BK YE
86 87 YE

*1 E-BOX low
*2 E-BOX high
*3 up to November 2008
*4 as of November 2008
*5 up to April 2009
*6 as of May 2009

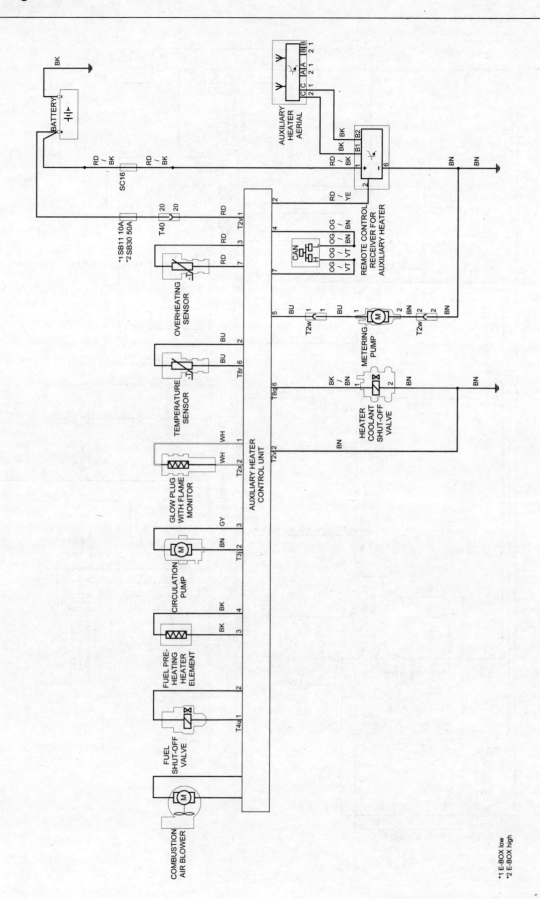

Auxiliary heater

*1 E-BOX low
*2 E-BOX high

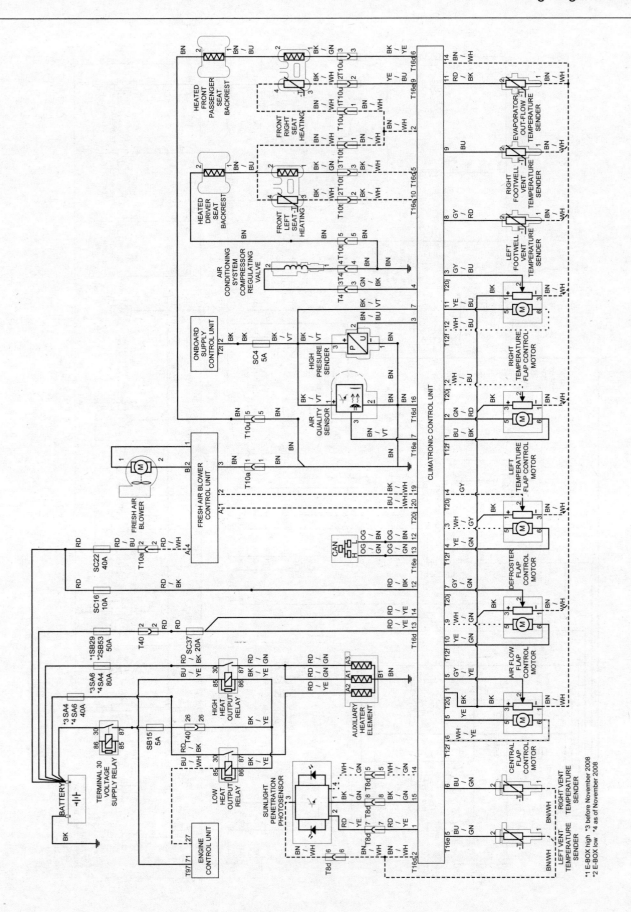

Air conditioning – automatic regulation up to April 2009

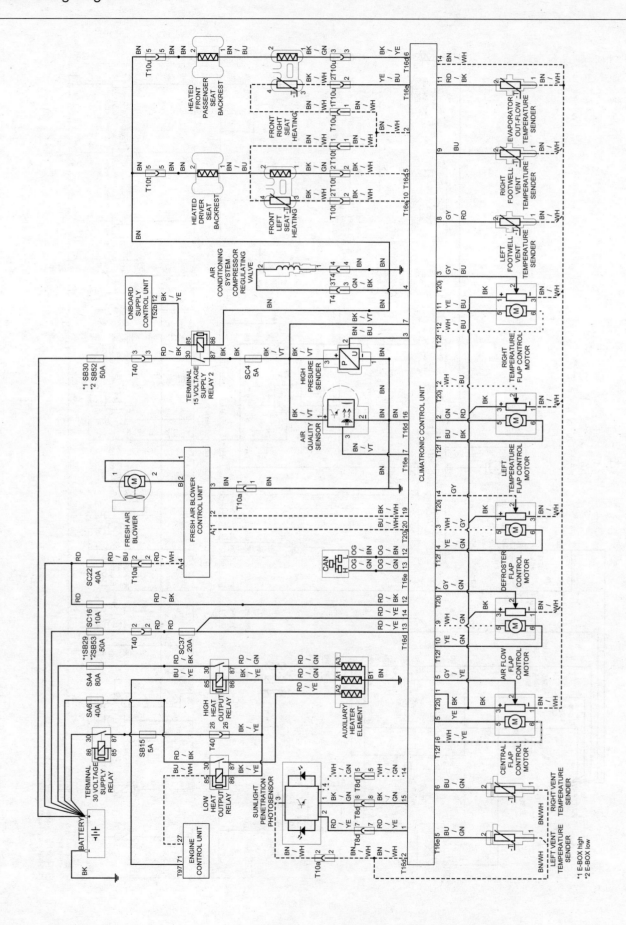

Air conditioning – automatic regulation from May 2009

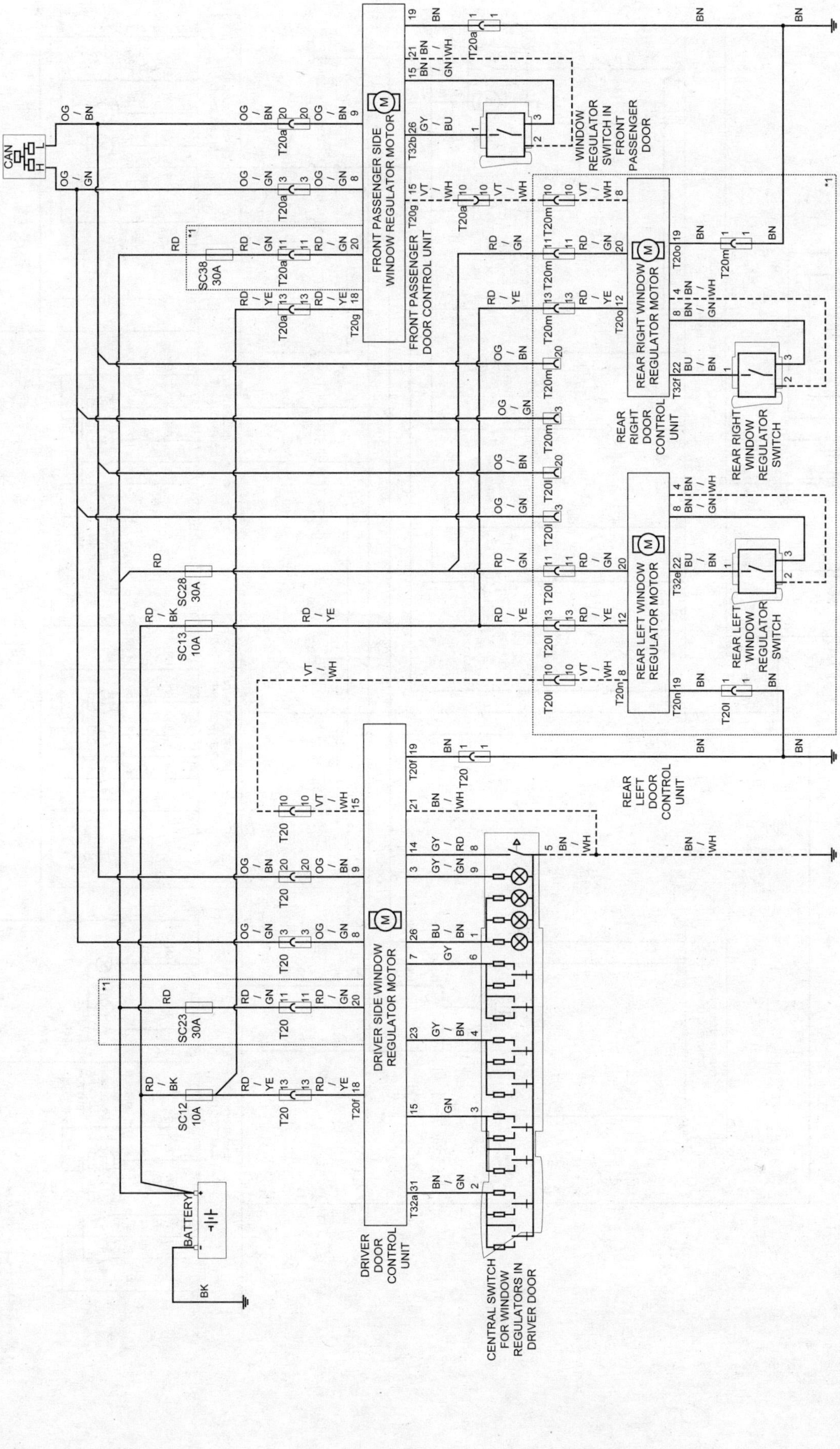

Power windows

*1 For 5-door models only

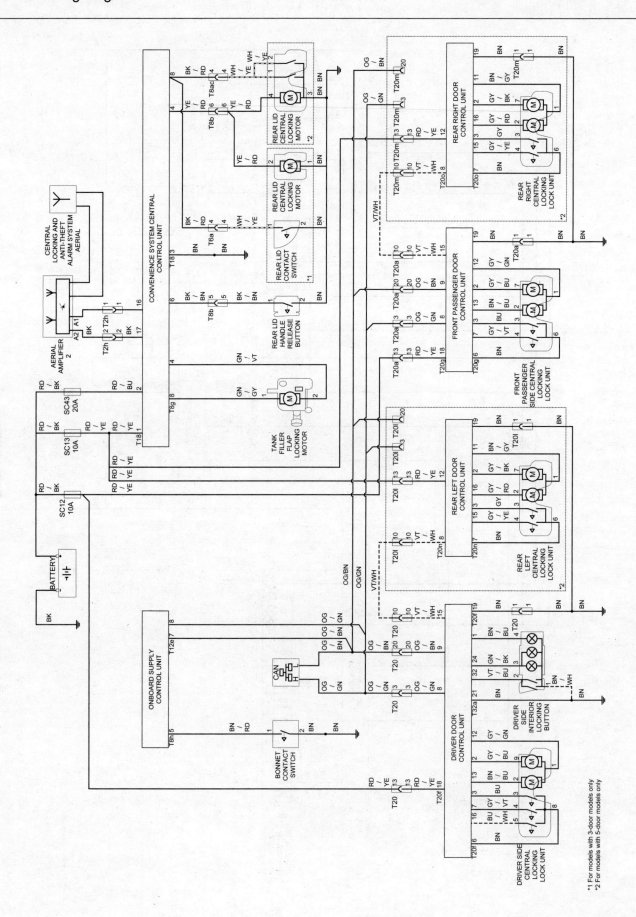

Power door locks up to April 2009

*1 For models with 3-door models only
*2 For models with 5-door models only

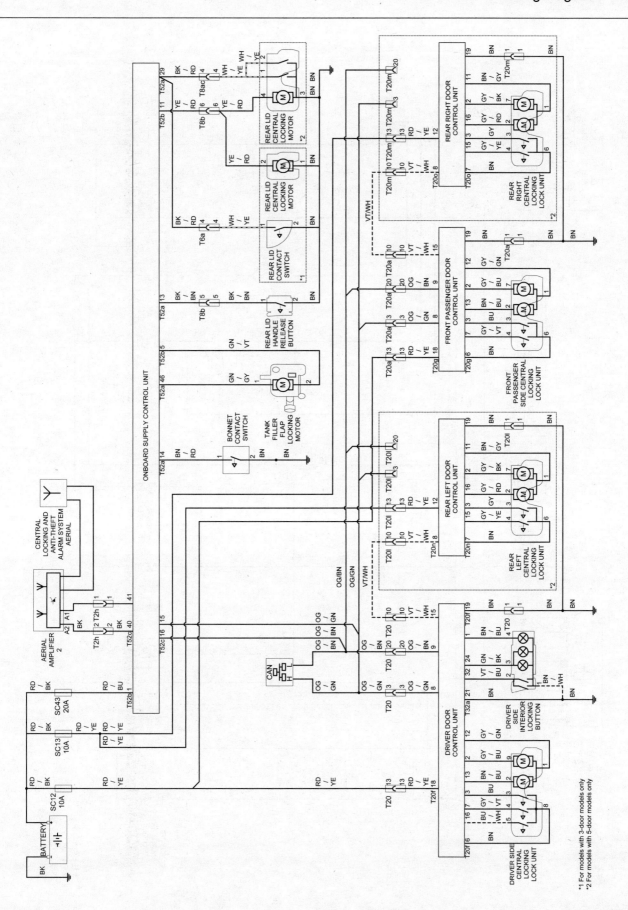

Power door locks from May 2009

*1 For models with 3-door models only
*2 For models with 5-door models only

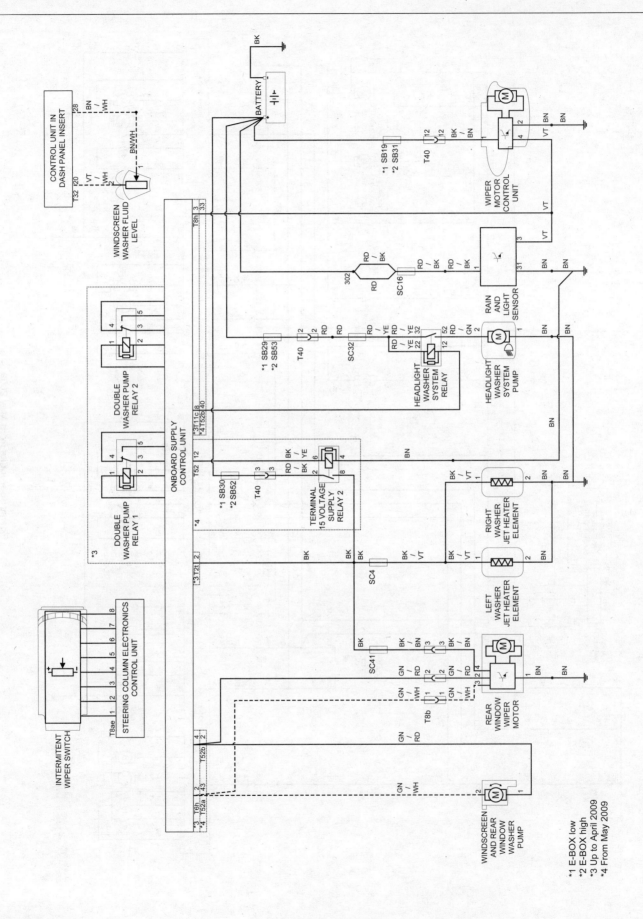

Wiper washer

*1 E-BOX low
*2 E-BOX high
*3 Up to April 2009
*4 From May 2009

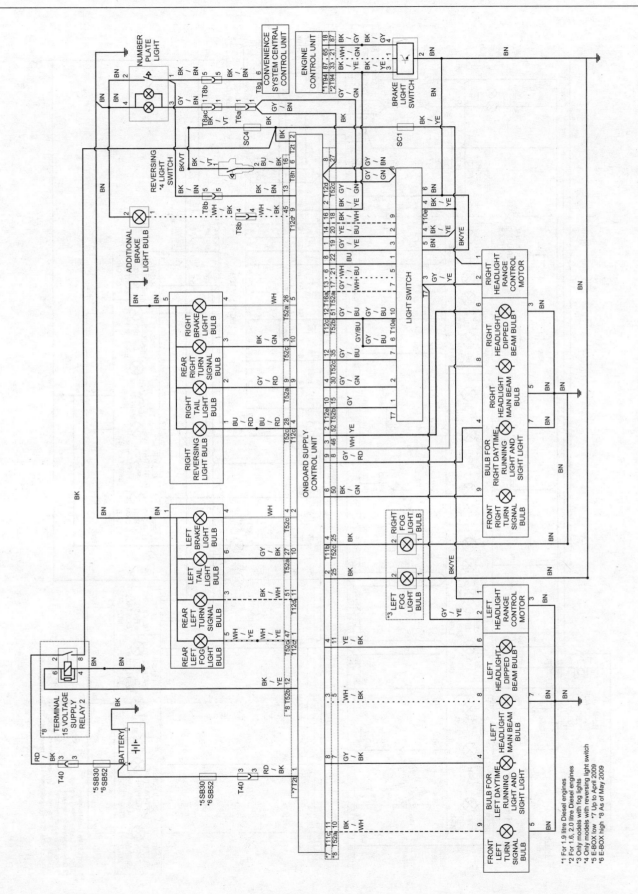

Exterior lighting – 3-door models

*1 For 1.9 litre Diesel engines
*2 For 1.6, 2.0 litre Diesel engines
*3 Only models with fog lights
*4 Only models with reversing light switch
*5 E-BOX low *7 Up to April 2009
*6 E-BOX high *8 As of May 2009

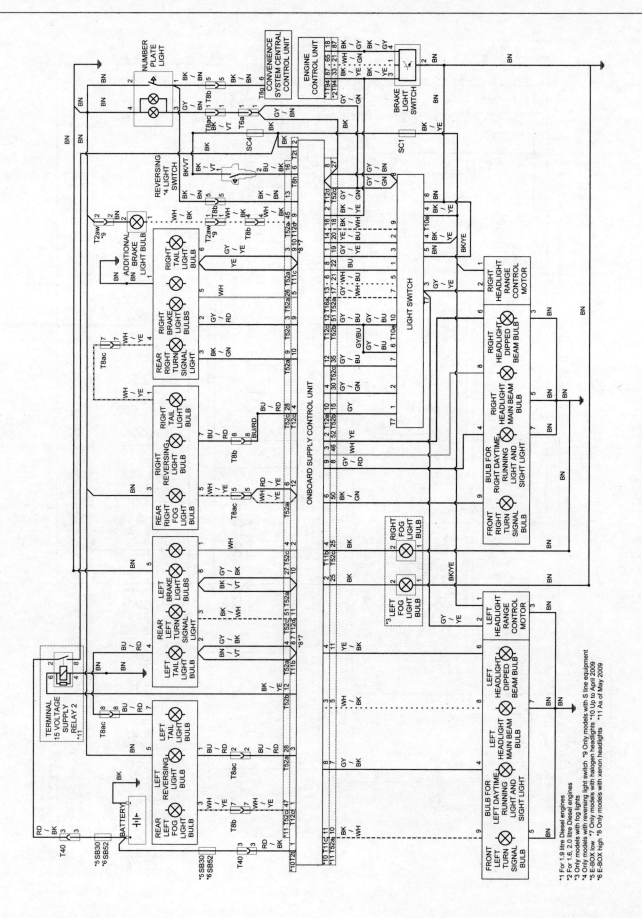

Exterior lighting – 5-door models

*1 For 1.9 litre Diesel engines
*2 For 1.6, 2.0 litre Diesel engines
*3 Only models with fog lights
*4 Only models with reversing light switch *9 Only models with S line equipment
*5 E-BOX low *7 Only models with halogen headlights *10 Up to April 2009
*6 E-BOX high *8 Only models with xenon headlights *11 As of May 2009

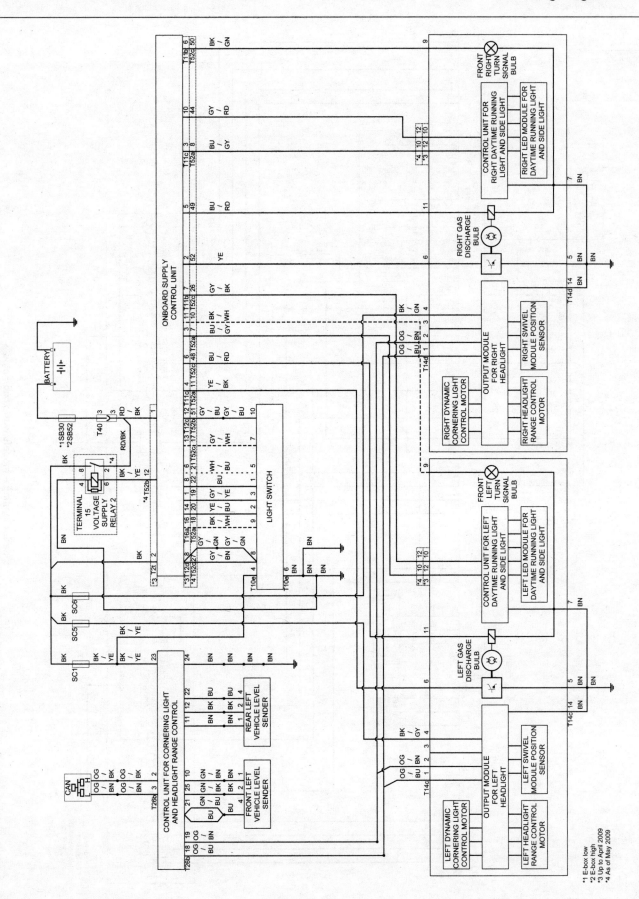

Exterior lighting – models with bi-xenon and cornering light

*1 E-box low
*2 E-box high
*3 Up to April 2009
*4 As of May 2009

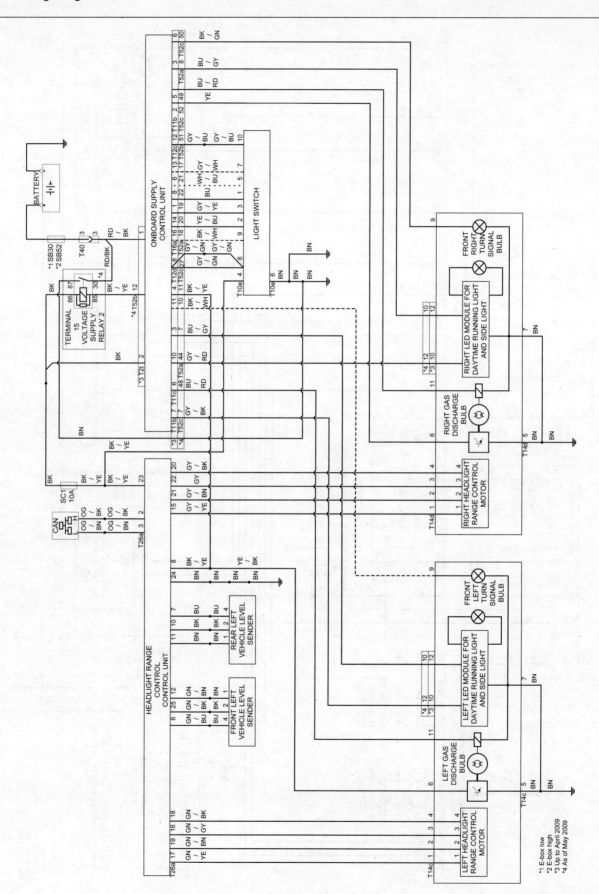

Exterior lighting – models with xenon plus

*1 E-box low
*2 E-box high
*3 Up to April 2009
*4 As of May 2009

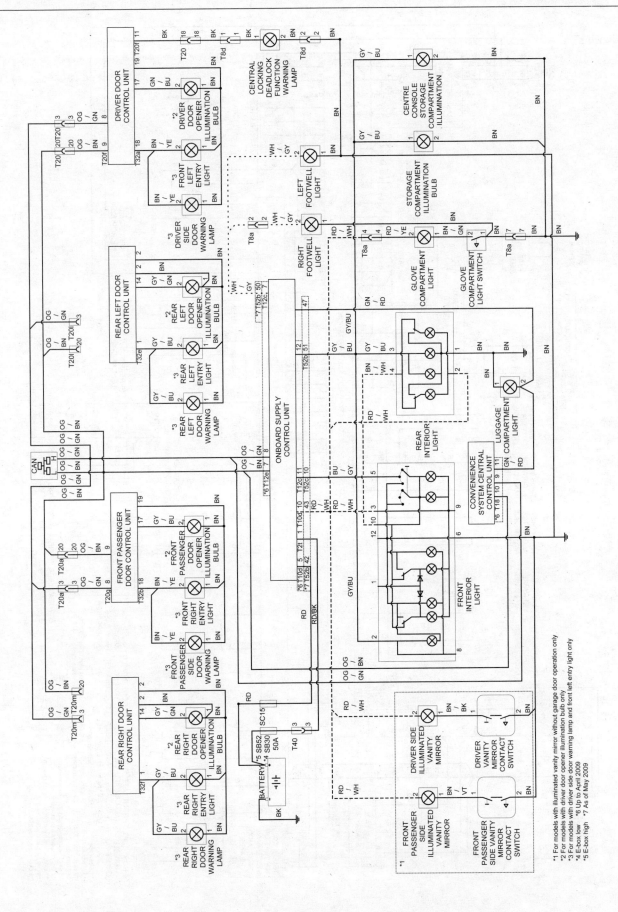

Interior lighting

*1 For models with illuminated vanity mirror without garage door operation only
*2 For models with driver door opener illumination bulb only
*3 For models with driver side door warning lamp and front left entry light only
*4 E-box low *6 Up to April 2009
*5 E-box high *7 As of May 2009

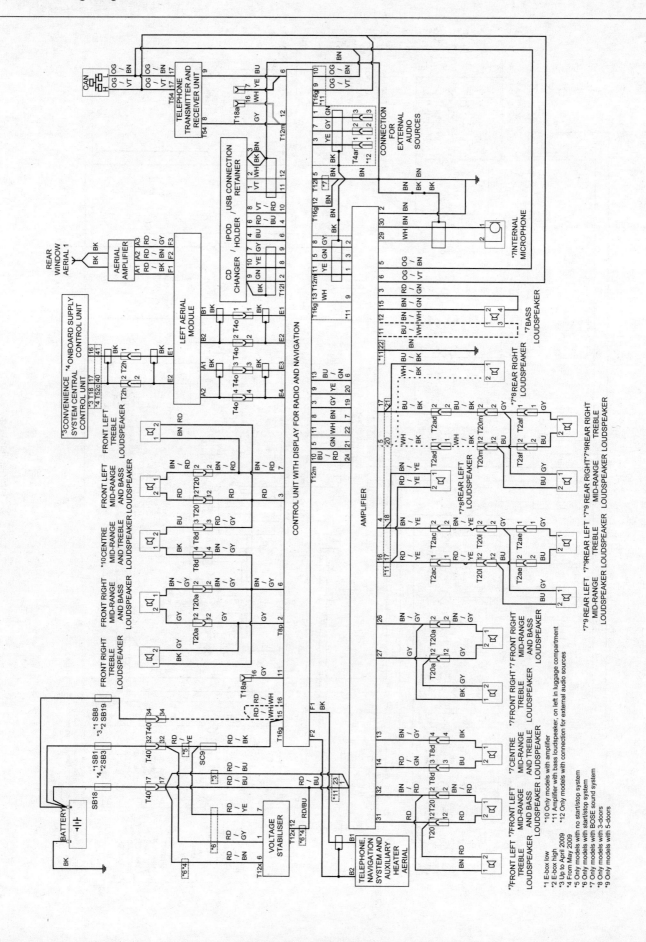

Sound systems – RNS LOW

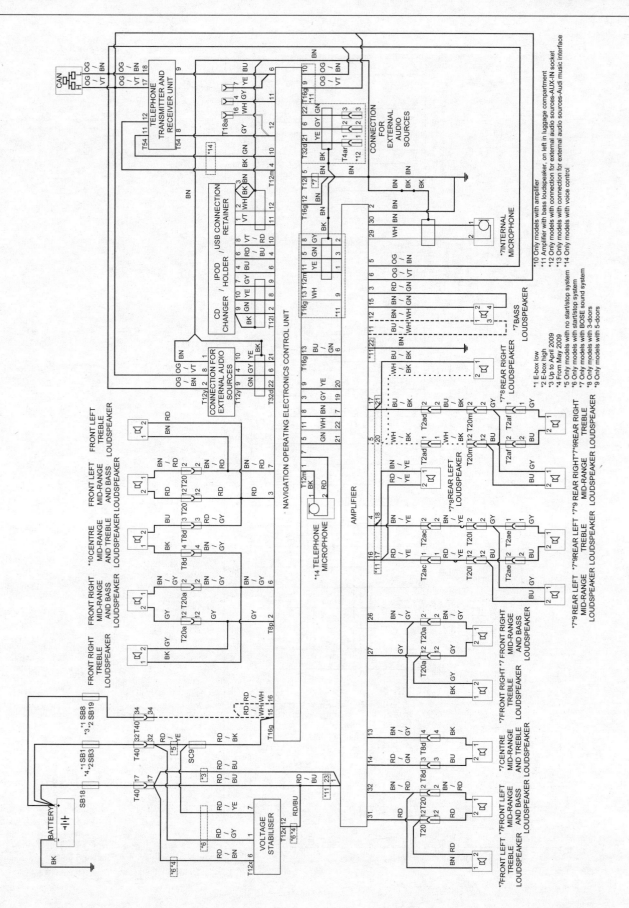

Sound systems – RNS E –part 1

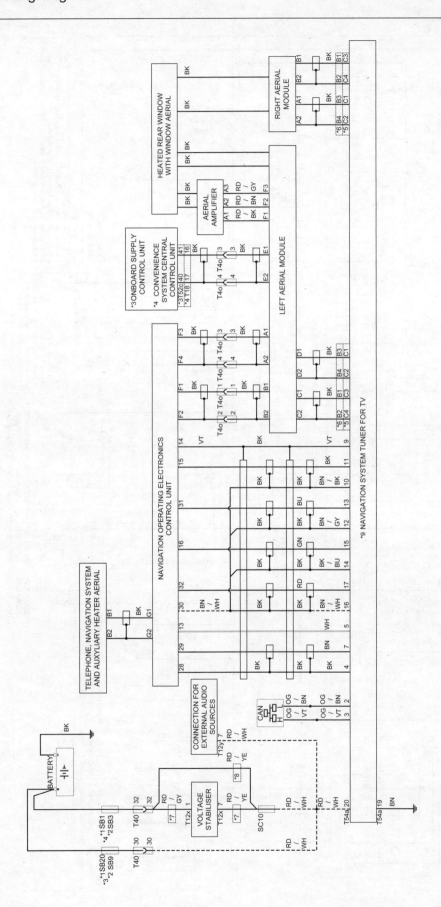

Sound systems – RNS E -part 2 (only models with tv tuner)

*1 E-BOX low
*2 E-BOX high
*3 From May 2009
*4 Up to April 2009
*5 Hybrid tuner
*6 Analogue TV tuner
*7 Only models with start/stop system
*8 Only models with no start/stop system
*9 Only models with TV tuner

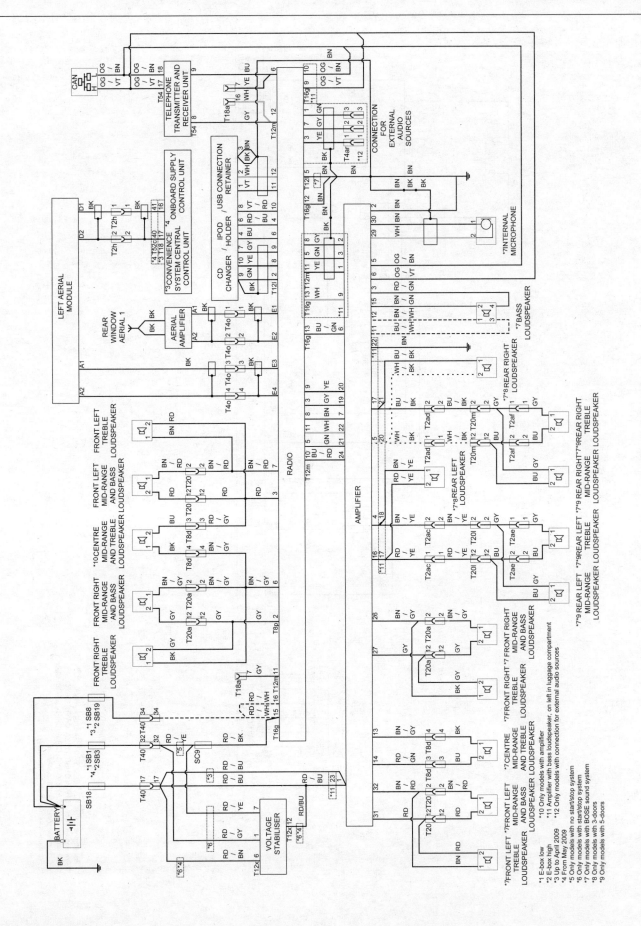

Sound systems – generation II+

*1 E-box low
*2 E-box high
*3 Up to April 2009
*4 From May 2009
*5 Only models with no start/stop system
*6 Only models with start/stop system
*7 Only models with BOSE sound system
*8 Only models with 3-doors
*9 Only models with 5-doors
*10 Only models with amplifier
*11 Amplifier with bass loudspeaker, on left in luggage compartment
*12 Only models with connection for external audio sources

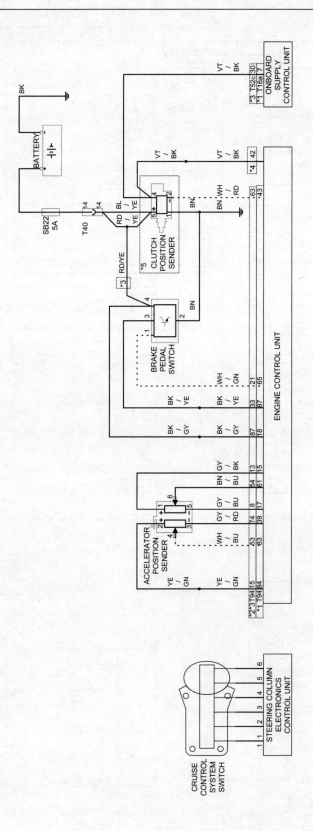

Cruise control

*1 For engine codes AZV, BKD, BMM, BXE, BLS, BMN, BUY
*2 For engine codes CBAB, CBBB, CBBA, CAYB, CAYC
*3 For engine codes CAYB, CAYC, CFFA, CFFB, CFGB, CLJA
*4 Only models with start/stop system
*5 For models with manual gearbox only

Dimensions and weights

Note: All figures and dimensions are approximate and may vary according to model. Refer to manufacturer's data for exact figures.

Overall length
All models . . . .   4203 mm

Overall width
All models (not including mirrors) . . . .   1765 mm
All models (including mirrors) . . . .   1957 mm

Overall height (unladen)
All models . . . .   1421 mm

Wheelbase
All models . . . .   2578 mm

Turning circle
All models . . . .   10.70 m

Weights

Note: The weights below are approximate and are based on 3-door models. For maximum gross weight and kerb weight of 5-door vehicles, add approx 40kg. Refer to manufacturer's documentation for latest information.

Maximum gross vehicle weight:
  1.6 and 2.0 litre models . . . .   1880 kg
  1.9 litre models . . . .   1840 kg
Kerb weight (unladen weight):
  1.6 and 2.0 litre models . . . .   1395 kg
  1.9 litre models . . . .   1370 kg
Maximum front axle weight:
  1.6 and 2.0 litre models . . . .   1035 kg
  1.9 litre models . . . .   1040 kg
Maxiumum rear axle weight:
  1.6 and 2.0 litre models . . . .   1000 kg
  1.9 litre models . . . .   975 kg

Maximum towing weights:

	Unbraked trailer	**Braked trailer**
1.6 and 2.0 litre models	710 kg	1700 kg
1.9 litre models	690 kg	1700 kg

Fuel economy

Although depreciation is still the biggest part of the cost of motoring for most car owners, the cost of fuel is more immediately noticeable. These pages give some tips on how to get the best fuel economy.

Working it out

Manufacturer's figures

Car manufacturers are required by law to provide fuel consumption information on all new vehicles sold. These 'official' figures are obtained by simulating various driving conditions on a rolling road or a test track. Real life conditions are different, so the fuel consumption actually achieved may not bear much resemblance to the quoted figures.

How to calculate it

Many cars now have trip computers which will

display fuel consumption, both instantaneous and average. Refer to the owner's handbook for details of how to use these.

To calculate consumption yourself (and maybe to check that the trip computer is accurate), proceed as follows.

1. Fill up with fuel and note the mileage, or zero the trip recorder.
2. Drive as usual until you need to fill up again.
3. Note the amount of fuel required to refill the tank, and the mileage covered since the previous fill-up.
4. Divide the mileage by the amount of fuel used to obtain the consumption figure.

For example:

Mileage at first fill-up (a) = 27,903
Mileage at second fill-up (b) = 28,346
Mileage covered (b - a) = 443
Fuel required at second fill-up = 48.6 litres

The half-completed changeover to metric units in the UK means that we buy our fuel in litres, measure distances in miles and talk

about fuel consumption in miles per gallon. There are two ways round this: the first is to convert the litres to gallons before doing the calculation (by dividing by 4.546, or see Table 1). So in the example:

48.6 litres ÷ 4.546 = 10.69 gallons
443 miles ÷ 10.69 gallons = 41.4 mpg

The second way is to calculate the consumption in miles per litre, then multiply that figure by 4.546 (or see Table 2).

So in the example, fuel consumption is:

443 miles ÷ 48.6 litres = 9.1 mpl
9.1 mpl x 4.546 = 41.4 mpg

The rest of Europe expresses fuel consumption in litres of fuel required to travel 100 km (l/100 km). For interest, the conversions are given in Table 3. In practice it doesn't matter what units you use, provided you know what your normal consumption is and can spot if it's getting better or worse.

Table 1: conversion of litres to Imperial gallons

litres	1	2	3	4	5	10	20	30	40	50	60	70
gallons	0.22	0.44	0.66	0.88	1.10	2.24	4.49	6.73	8.98	11.22	13.47	15.71

Table 2: conversion of miles per litre to miles per gallon

miles per litre	5	6	7	8	9	10	11	12	13	14
miles per gallon	23	27	32	36	41	46	50	55	59	64

Table 3: conversion of litres per 100 km to miles per gallon

litres per 100 km	4	4.5	5	5.5	6	6.5	7	8	9	10
miles per gallon	71	63	56	51	47	43	40	35	31	28

Maintenance

A well-maintained car uses less fuel and creates less pollution. In particular:

Filters

Change air and fuel filters at the specified intervals.

Oil

Use a good quality oil of the lowest viscosity specified by the vehicle manufacturer (see *Lubricants and fluids*). Check the level often and be careful not to overfill.

Spark plugs

When applicable, renew at the specified intervals.

Tyres

Check tyre pressures regularly. Under-inflated tyres have an increased rolling resistance. It is generally safe to use the higher pressures specified for full load conditions even when not fully laden, but keep an eye on the centre band of tread for signs of wear due to over-inflation.

When buying new tyres, consider the 'fuel saving' models which most manufacturers include in their ranges.

Driving style

Acceleration

Acceleration uses more fuel than driving at a steady speed. The best technique with modern cars is to accelerate reasonably briskly to the desired speed, changing up through the gears as soon as possible without making the engine labour.

Air conditioning

Air conditioning absorbs quite a bit of energy from the engine – typically 3 kW (4 hp) or so. The effect on fuel consumption is at its worst in slow traffic. Switch it off when not required.

Anticipation

Drive smoothly and try to read the traffic flow so as to avoid unnecessary acceleration and braking.

Automatic transmission

When accelerating in an automatic, avoid depressing the throttle so far as to make the transmission hold onto lower gears at higher speeds. Don't use the 'Sport' setting, if applicable.

When stationary with the engine running, select 'N' or 'P'. When moving, keep your left foot away from the brake.

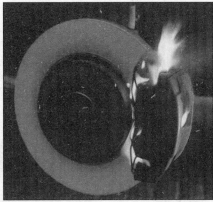

Braking

Braking converts the car's energy of motion into heat – essentially, it is wasted. Obviously some braking is always going to be necessary, but with good anticipation it is surprising how much can be avoided, especially on routes that you know well.

Carshare

Consider sharing lifts to work or to the shops. Even once a week will make a difference.

Electrical loads

Electricity is 'fuel' too; the alternator which charges the battery does so by converting some of the engine's energy of motion into electrical energy. The more electrical accessories are in use, the greater the load on the alternator. Switch off big consumers like the heated rear window when not required.

Freewheeling

Freewheeling (coasting) in neutral with the engine switched off is dangerous. The effort required to operate power-assisted brakes and steering increases when the engine is not running, with a potential lack of control in emergency situations.

In any case, modern fuel injection systems automatically cut off the engine's fuel supply on the overrun (moving and in gear, but with the accelerator pedal released).

Gadgets

Bolt-on devices claiming to save fuel have been around for nearly as long as the motor car itself. Those which worked were rapidly adopted as standard equipment by the vehicle manufacturers. Others worked only in certain situations, or saved fuel only at the expense of unacceptable effects on performance, driveability or the life of engine components.

The most effective fuel saving gadget is the driver's right foot.

Journey planning

Combine (eg) a trip to the supermarket with a visit to the recycling centre and the DIY store, rather than making separate journeys.

When possible choose a travelling time outside rush hours.

Load

The more heavily a car is laden, the greater the energy required to accelerate it to a given speed. Remove heavy items which you don't need to carry.

One load which is often overlooked is the contents of the fuel tank. A tankful of fuel (55 litres / 12 gallons) weighs 45 kg (100 lb) or so. Just half filling it may be worthwhile.

Lost?

At the risk of stating the obvious, if you're going somewhere new, have details of the route to hand. There's not much point in achieving record mpg if you also go miles out of your way.

Parking

If possible, carry out any reversing or turning manoeuvres when you arrive at a parking space so that you can drive straight out when you leave. Manoeuvering when the engine is cold uses a lot more fuel.

Driving around looking for free on-street parking may cost more in fuel than buying a car park ticket.

Premium fuel

Most major oil companies (and some supermarkets) have premium grades of fuel which are several pence a litre dearer than the standard grades. Reports vary, but the consensus seems to be that if these fuels improve economy at all, they do not do so by enough to justify their extra cost.

Roof rack

When loading a roof rack, try to produce a wedge shape with the narrow end at the front. Any cover should be securely fastened – if it flaps it's creating turbulence and absorbing energy.

Remove roof racks and boxes when not in use – they increase air resistance and can create a surprising amount of noise.

Short journeys

The engine is at its least efficient, and wear is highest, during the first few miles after a cold start. Consider walking, cycling or using public transport.

Speed

The engine is at its most efficient when running at a steady speed and load at the rpm where it develops maximum torque. (You can find this figure in the car's handbook.) For most cars this corresponds to between 55 and 65 mph in top gear.

Above the optimum cruising speed, fuel consumption starts to rise quite sharply. A car travelling at 80 mph will typically be using 30% more fuel than at 60 mph.

Supermarket fuel

It may be cheap but is it any good? In the UK all supermarket fuel must meet the relevant British Standard. The major oil companies will say that their branded fuels have better additive packages which may stop carbon and other deposits building up. A reasonable compromise might be to use one tank of branded fuel to three or four from the supermarket.

Switch off when stationary

Switch off the engine if you look like being stationary for more than 30 seconds or so. This is good for the environment as well as for your pocket. Be aware though that frequent restarts are hard on the battery and the starter motor.

Windows

Driving with the windows open increases air turbulence around the vehicle. Closing the windows promotes smooth airflow and

reduced resistance. The faster you go, the more significant this is.

And finally...

Driving techniques associated with good fuel economy tend to involve moderate acceleration and low top speeds. Be considerate to the needs of other road users who may need to make brisker progress; even if you do not agree with them this is not an excuse to be obstructive.

Safety must always take precedence over economy, whether it is a question of accelerating hard to complete an overtaking manoeuvre, killing your speed when confronted with a potential hazard or switching the lights on when it starts to get dark.

Conversion factors

Length (distance)

Inches (in)	x 25.4	= Millimetres (mm)	x 0.0394	= Inches (in)
Feet (ft)	x 0.305	= Metres (m)	x 3.281	= Feet (ft)
Miles	x 1.609	= Kilometres (km)	x 0.621	= Miles

Volume (capacity)

Cubic inches (cu in; in³)	x 16.387	= Cubic centimetres (cc; cm³)	x 0.061	= Cubic inches (cu in; in³)
Imperial pints (Imp pt)	x 0.568	= Litres (l)	x 1.76	= Imperial pints (Imp pt)
Imperial quarts (Imp qt)	x 1.137	= Litres (l)	x 0.88	= Imperial quarts (Imp qt)
Imperial quarts (Imp qt)	x 1.201	= US quarts (US qt)	x 0.833	= Imperial quarts (Imp qt)
US quarts (US qt)	x 0.946	= Litres (l)	x 1.057	= US quarts (US qt)
Imperial gallons (Imp gal)	x 4.546	= Litres (l)	x 0.22	= Imperial gallons (Imp gal)
Imperial gallons (Imp gal)	x 1.201	= US gallons (US gal)	x 0.833	= Imperial gallons (Imp gal)
US gallons (US gal)	x 3.785	= Litres (l)	x 0.264	= US gallons (US gal)

Mass (weight)

Ounces (oz)	x 28.35	= Grams (g)	x 0.035	= Ounces (oz)
Pounds (lb)	x 0.454	= Kilograms (kg)	x 2.205	= Pounds (lb)

Force

Ounces-force (ozf; oz)	x 0.278	= Newtons (N)	x 3.6	= Ounces-force (ozf; oz)
Pounds-force (lbf; lb)	x 4.448	= Newtons (N)	x 0.225	= Pounds-force (lbf; lb)
Newtons (N)	x 0.1	= Kilograms-force (kgf; kg)	x 9.81	= Newtons (N)

Pressure

Pounds-force per square inch (psi; lbf/in²; lb/in²)	x 0.070	= Kilograms-force per square centimetre (kgf/cm²; kg/cm²)	x 14.223	= Pounds-force per square inch (psi; lbf/in²; lb/in²)
Pounds-force per square inch (psi; lbf/in²; lb/in²)	x 0.068	= Atmospheres (atm)	x 14.696	= Pounds-force per square inch (psi; lbf/in²; lb/in²)
Pounds-force per square inch (psi; lbf/in²; lb/in²)	x 0.069	= Bars	x 14.5	= Pounds-force per square inch (psi; lbf/in²; lb/in²)
Pounds-force per square inch (psi; lbf/in²; lb/in²)	x 6.895	= Kilopascals (kPa)	x 0.145	= Pounds-force per square inch (psi; lbf/in²; lb/in²)
Kilopascals (kPa)	x 0.01	= Kilograms-force per square centimetre (kgf/cm²; kg/cm²)	x 98.1	= Kilopascals (kPa)
Millibar (mbar)	x 100	= Pascals (Pa)	x 0.01	= Millibar (mbar)
Millibar (mbar)	x 0.0145	= Pounds-force per square inch (psi; lbf/in²; lb/in²)	x 68.947	= Millibar (mbar)
Millibar (mbar)	x 0.75	= Millimetres of mercury (mmHg)	x 1.333	= Millibar (mbar)
Millibar (mbar)	x 0.401	= Inches of water (inH$_2$O)	x 2.491	= Millibar (mbar)
Millimetres of mercury (mmHg)	x 0.535	= Inches of water (inH$_2$O)	x 1.868	= Millimetres of mercury (mmHg)
Inches of water (inH$_2$O)	x 0.036	= Pounds-force per square inch (psi; lbf/in²; lb/in²)	x 27.68	= Inches of water (inH$_2$O)

Torque (moment of force)

Pounds-force inches (lbf in; lb in)	x 1.152	= Kilograms-force centimetre (kgf cm; kg cm)	x 0.868	= Pounds-force inches (lbf in; lb in)
Pounds-force inches (lbf in; lb in)	x 0.113	= Newton metres (Nm)	x 8.85	= Pounds-force inches (lbf in; lb in)
Pounds-force inches (lbf in; lb in)	x 0.083	= Pounds-force feet (lbf ft; lb ft)	x 12	= Pounds-force inches (lbf in; lb in)
Pounds-force feet (lbf ft; lb ft)	x 0.138	= Kilograms-force metres (kgf m; kg m)	x 7.233	= Pounds-force feet (lbf ft; lb ft)
Pounds-force feet (lbf ft; lb ft)	x 1.356	= Newton metres (Nm)	x 0.738	= Pounds-force feet (lbf ft; lb ft)
Newton metres (Nm)	x 0.102	= Kilograms-force metres (kgf m; kg m)	x 9.804	= Newton metres (Nm)

Power

Horsepower (hp)	x 745.7	= Watts (W)	x 0.0013	= Horsepower (hp)

Velocity (speed)

Miles per hour (miles/hr; mph)	x 1.609	= Kilometres per hour (km/hr; kph)	x 0.621	= Miles per hour (miles/hr; mph)

Fuel consumption*

Miles per gallon, Imperial (mpg)	x 0.354	= Kilometres per litre (km/l)	x 2.825	= Miles per gallon, Imperial (mpg)
Miles per gallon, US (mpg)	x 0.425	= Kilometres per litre (km/l)	x 2.352	= Miles per gallon, US (mpg)

Temperature

Degrees Fahrenheit = (°C x 1.8) + 32   Degrees Celsius (Degrees Centigrade; °C) = (°F - 32) x 0.56

It is common practice to convert from miles per gallon (mpg) to litres/100 kilometres (l/100km), where mpg x l/100 km = 282

Spare parts are available from many sources, including maker's appointed garages, accessory shops, and motor factors. To be sure of obtaining the correct parts, it will sometimes be necessary to quote the vehicle identification number. If possible, it can also be useful to take the old parts along for positive identification. Items such as starter motors and alternators may be available under a service exchange scheme – any parts returned should be clean.

Our advice regarding spare parts is as follows.

Officially appointed garages

This is the best source of parts which are peculiar to your car, and which are not otherwise generally available (eg, badges, interior trim, certain body panels, etc). It is also the only place at which you should buy parts if the car is still under warranty.

Accessory shops

These are very good places to buy materials and components needed for the maintenance of your car (oil, air and fuel filters, light bulbs, drivebelts, greases, brake pads, touch-up paint, etc). Components of this nature sold by a reputable shop are usually of the same standard as those used by the car manufacturer.

Besides components, these shops also sell tools and general accessories, usually have convenient opening hours, charge lower prices, and can often be found close to home. Some accessory shops have parts counters where components needed for almost any repair job can be purchased or ordered.

Motor factors

Good factors will stock all the more important components which wear out comparatively quickly, and can sometimes supply individual components needed for the overhaul of a larger assembly (eg, brake seals and hydraulic parts, bearing shells, pistons, valves). They may also handle work such as cylinder block reboring, crankshaft regrinding, etc.

Engine reconditioners

These specialise in engine overhaul and can also supply components. It is recommended that the establishment is a member of the Federation of Engine Re-Manufacturers, or a similar society.

Tyre and exhaust specialists

These outlets may be independent, or members of a local or national chain. They frequently offer competitive prices when compared with a main dealer or local garage, but it will pay to obtain several quotes before making a decision. When researching prices, also ask what extras may be added – for instance fitting a new valve, balancing the wheel and tyre disposal all both commonly charged on top of the price of a new tyre.

Other sources

Beware of parts or materials obtained from market stalls, car boot sales, on-line auctions or similar outlets. Such items are not invariably sub-standard, but there is little chance of compensation if they do prove unsatisfactory. In the case of safety-critical components such as brake pads, there is the risk not only of financial loss, but also of an accident causing injury or death.

Second-hand components or assemblies obtained from a car breaker can be a good buy in some circumstances, but this sort of purchase is best made by the experienced DIY mechanic.

Modifications are a continuing and unpublicised process in vehicle manufacture, quite apart from major model changes. Spare parts manuals and lists are compiled upon a numerical basis, the individual vehicle identification numbers being essential to correct identification of the component concerned.

When ordering spare parts, always give as much information as possible. Quote the car model, year of manufacture and registration, chassis and engine numbers as appropriate.

The Vehicle Identification Number (VIN) plate is visible from the outside of the vehicle, through the left-hand lower corner of the windscreen, and is also stamped on the top of the right-hand inner wing in the engine compartment (see illustrations).

The Vehicle Data Sticker is located in the spare wheel well accessed through the luggage compartment (see illustration). It contains the VIN, vehicle type, engine power, transmission type, engine and transmission codes, paint number, interior equipment, optional extras, and PR numbers (for maintenance schedule).

The Type plate and factory plate is located at the bottom of the front, left-hand door A-pillar, and is visible with the door open. It contains the gross vehicle weight, front axle weight and rear axle weight.

The Engine Number is stamped into the front of the cylinder block, next to the engine-to-transmission joint. A barcode identification sticker is located on the top of the timing cover or on the right-hand end of the cylinder head (see illustration).

Vehicle Identification Number (VIN) located on the left-hand front edge of the windscreen

Vehicle Identification Number (VIN) located on the top of the right-hand inner wing

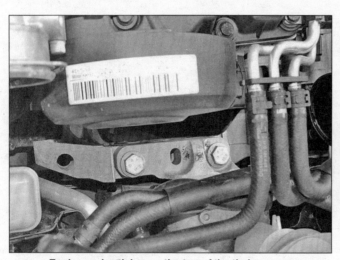

Engine code sticker on the top of the timing cover

Vehicle Data Sticker located in the spare wheel well

Whenever servicing, repair or overhaul work is carried out on the car or its components, observe the following procedures and instructions. This will assist in carrying out the operation efficiently and to a professional standard of workmanship.

Joint mating faces and gaskets

When separating components at their mating faces, never insert screwdrivers or similar implements into the joint between the faces in order to prise them apart. This can cause severe damage which results in oil leaks, coolant leaks, etc upon reassembly. Separation is usually achieved by tapping along the joint with a soft-faced hammer in order to break the seal. However, note that this method may not be suitable where dowels are used for component location.

Where a gasket is used between the mating faces of two components, a new one must be fitted on reassembly; fit it dry unless otherwise stated in the repair procedure. Make sure that the mating faces are clean and dry, with all traces of old gasket removed. When cleaning a joint face, use a tool which is unlikely to score or damage the face, and remove any burrs or nicks with an oilstone or fine file.

Make sure that tapped holes are cleaned with a pipe cleaner, and keep them free of jointing compound, if this is being used, unless specifically instructed otherwise.

Ensure that all orifices, channels or pipes are clear, and blow through them, preferably using compressed air.

Oil seals

Oil seals can be removed by levering them out with a wide flat-bladed screwdriver or similar implement. Alternatively, a number of self-tapping screws may be screwed into the seal, and these used as a purchase for pliers or some similar device in order to pull the seal free.

Whenever an oil seal is removed from its working location, either individually or as part of an assembly, it should be renewed.

The very fine sealing lip of the seal is easily damaged, and will not seal if the surface it contacts is not completely clean and free from scratches, nicks or grooves. If the original sealing surface of the component cannot be restored, and the manufacturer has not made provision for slight relocation of the seal relative to the sealing surface, the component should be renewed.

Protect the lips of the seal from any surface which may damage them in the course of fitting. Use tape or a conical sleeve where possible. Where indicated, lubricate the seal lips with oil before fitting and, on dual-lipped seals, fill the space between the lips with grease.

Unless otherwise stated, oil seals must be fitted with their sealing lips toward the lubricant to be sealed.

Use a tubular drift or block of wood of the appropriate size to install the seal and, if the seal housing is shouldered, drive the seal down to the shoulder. If the seal housing is unshouldered, the seal should be fitted with its face flush with the housing top face (unless otherwise instructed).

Screw threads and fastenings

Seized nuts, bolts and screws are quite a common occurrence where corrosion has set in, and the use of penetrating oil or releasing fluid will often overcome this problem if the offending item is soaked for a while before attempting to release it. The use of an impact driver may also provide a means of releasing such stubborn fastening devices, when used in conjunction with the appropriate screwdriver bit or socket. If none of these methods works, it may be necessary to resort to the careful application of heat, or the use of a hacksaw or nut splitter device. Before resorting to extreme methods, check that you are not dealing with a left-hand thread!

Studs are usually removed by locking two nuts together on the threaded part, and then using a spanner on the lower nut to unscrew the stud. Studs or bolts which have broken off below the surface of the component in which they are mounted can sometimes be removed using a stud extractor.

Always ensure that a blind tapped hole is completely free from oil, grease, water or other fluid before installing the bolt or stud. Failure to do this could cause the housing to crack due to the hydraulic action of the bolt or stud as it is screwed in.

For some screw fastenings, notably cylinder head bolts or nuts, torque wrench settings are no longer specified for the latter stages of tightening, "angle-tightening" being called up instead. Typically, a fairly low torque wrench setting will be applied to the bolts/nuts in the correct sequence, followed by one or more stages of tightening through specified angles.

When checking or retightening a nut or bolt to a specified torque setting, slacken the nut or bolt by a quarter of a turn, and then retighten to the specified setting. However, this should not be attempted where angular tightening has been used.

Locknuts, locktabs and washers

Any fastening which will rotate against a component or housing during tightening should always have a washer between it and the relevant component or housing.

Spring or split washers should always be renewed when they are used to lock a critical component such as a big-end bearing retaining bolt or nut. Locktabs which are folded over to retain a nut or bolt should always be renewed.

Self-locking nuts can be re-used in non-critical areas, providing resistance can be felt when the locking portion passes over the bolt or stud thread. However, it should be noted that self-locking stiffnuts tend to lose their effectiveness after long periods of use, and should then be renewed as a matter of course.

Split pins must always be replaced with new ones of the correct size for the hole.

When thread-locking compound is found on the threads of a fastener which is to be re-used, it should be cleaned off with a wire brush and solvent, and fresh compound applied on reassembly.

Special tools

Some repair procedures in this manual entail the use of special tools such as a press, two or three-legged pullers, spring compressors, etc. Wherever possible, suitable readily-available alternatives to the manufacturer's special tools are described, and are shown in use. In some instances, where no alternative is possible, it has been necessary to resort to the use of a manufacturer's tool, and this has been done for reasons of safety as well as the efficient completion of the repair operation. Unless you are highly-skilled and have a thorough understanding of the procedures described, never attempt to bypass the use of any special tool when the procedure described specifies its use. Not only is there a very great risk of personal injury, but expensive damage could be caused to the components involved.

Environmental considerations

When disposing of used engine oil, brake fluid, antifreeze, etc, give due consideration to any detrimental environmental effects. Do not, for instance, pour any of the above liquids down drains into the general sewage system, or onto the ground to soak away. Many local council refuse tips provide a facility for waste oil disposal, as do some garages. You can find your nearest disposal point by calling the Environment Agency on 08708 506 506 or by visiting www.oilbankline.org.uk.

Note: It is illegal and anti-social to dump oil down the drain. To find the location of your local oil recycling bank, call 08708 506 506 or visit www.oilbankline.org.uk.

The jack supplied with the vehicle tool kit should only be used for changing the roadwheels – see Wheel changing Chapter 0, Section 4. When carrying out any other kind of work, raise the vehicle using a hydraulic (or 'trolley') jack, and always supplement the jack with axle stands positioned under the vehicle jacking points.

When using a hydraulic jack or axle stands, always position the jack head or axle stand head under one of the relevant jacking points.

To raise the front and/or rear of the vehicle, use the jacking/support points at the front and rear ends of the door sills, indicated by the triangular depressions in the sill panel **(see illustration)**. Position a block of wood with a groove cut in it on the jack head to prevent the vehicle weight resting on the sill edge; align the sill edge with the groove in the wood so that the vehicle weight is spread evenly over the surface of the block. Supplement the jack with axle stands (also with slotted blocks of wood) positioned as close as possible to the jacking points **(see illustrations)**.

Do not jack the vehicle under any other part of the sill, sump, floor pan, or any of the steering or suspension components. With the vehicle raised, an axle stand should be positioned beneath the vehicle jack location point on the sill.

 Warning: Never work under, around, or near a raised car, unless it is adequately supported in at least two places.

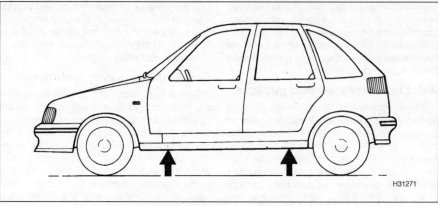

Front and rear jacking points (arrowed)

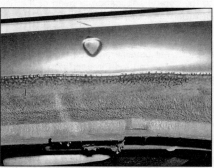

5.3b The jacking points are indicated by an arrow on the sill

5.3c Use an axle stand with a suitable block of wood

Caution: After reconnecting the battery, the safety function of the electric windows will not be re-instated until the windows have been reprogrammed. This could potentially cause severe pinching injuries.

Several of the systems require battery power to be available at all times (permanent live). This is either to ensure their continued operation (such as the clock), or to maintain electronic memory settings, which would otherwise be erased. Whenever the battery is to be disconnected, first note the following points, to ensure there are no unforeseen consequences:

a) *Firstly, on any vehicle with central door locking, it is a wise precaution to remove the key from the ignition, and to keep it with you. This avoids the possibility of the key being locked inside the car, should the central locking engage when the battery is reconnected.*

b) *If a security-coded audio unit is fitted, and the unit and/or the battery is disconnected, the unit will not function until the correct security code has been entered. Therefore, if you do not know the correct security code for the radio/CD unit, do not disconnect either of the battery terminals, or remove the radio/CD unit from the vehicle. The code appears on a code card supplied with*
the car when new. Details for entering the code appear in the vehicle handbook. Should the code have been misplaced or forgotten, on production of proof of ownership, an Audi dealer or in-car entertainment specialist may be able to help.

c) *The engine management system ECU is of the 'self-learning' type, meaning that, as it operates, it adapts to changes in operating conditions, and stores the optimum settings found (this is especially true for idle speed settings). When the battery is disconnected, these 'learned' settings are lost, and the ECU reverts to the base factory settings. When the engine is restarted, it may idle and run roughly until the ECU has 'relearned' the best settings. To further this 'learning' process, take the car for a road test of at least 15 minutes' duration, covering as many engine speeds and loads as possible, and concentrating on the 2000 to 4000 rpm range. On completion, let the engine idle for at least 10 minutes, turning the steering wheel occasionally and switching on high-current-draw equipment such as the heater fan or heated rear window. If the engine does not regain its normal performance, have the system checked for faults by an Audi dealer.*

d) *On vehicles equipped with an original equipment anti-theft alarm system, before disconnecting the battery, de-activate the alarm system; otherwise the alarm will be triggered.*

e) *After the battery has been reconnected, the warning lights for the ESP and electro-mechanical steering will light up and stay on. They will extinguish if you drive briefly in a straight line at a speed of 9 to 13 mph.*

Devices known as 'memory-savers' or 'code-savers' can be used to avoid some of the above problems. Precise details of use vary according to the device used. Typically, it is plugged into the cigarette lighter socket, and is connected by its own wiring to a spare battery; the vehicle battery is then disconnected from the electrical system, leaving the memory-saver to pass sufficient current to maintain audio unit security codes, and other memory values, and also to run permanently-live circuits such as the clock.

⚠ **Warning: Some of these devices allow a considerable amount of current to pass, which can mean that many of the vehicle's systems are still operational when the main battery is disconnected. If a memory-saver is used, ensure that the circuit concerned is actually 'dead' before carrying out any work on it.**

Introduction

A selection of good tools is a fundamental requirement for anyone contemplating the maintenance and repair of a motor vehicle. For the owner who does not possess any, their purchase will prove a considerable expense, offsetting some of the savings made by doing-it-yourself. However, provided that the tools purchased meet the relevant national safety standards and are of good quality, they will last for many years and prove an extremely worthwhile investment.

To help the average owner to decide which tools are needed to carry out the various tasks detailed in this manual, we have compiled three lists of tools under the following headings: *Maintenance and minor repair, Repair and overhaul*, and *Special*. Newcomers to practical mechanics should start off with the *Maintenance and minor repair* tool kit, and confine themselves to the simpler jobs around the vehicle. Then, as confidence and experience grow, more difficult tasks can be undertaken, with extra tools being purchased as, and when, they are needed. In this way, a *Maintenance and minor repair* tool kit can be built up into a *Repair and overhaul* tool kit over a considerable period of time, without any major cash outlays. The experienced do-it-yourselfer will have a tool kit good enough for most repair and overhaul procedures, and will add tools from the *Special* category when it is felt that the expense is justified by the amount of use to which these tools will be put.

Maintenance and minor repair tool kit

The tools given in this list should be considered as a minimum requirement if routine maintenance, servicing and minor repair operations are to be undertaken. We recommend the purchase of combination spanners (ring one end, open-ended the other); although more expensive than open-ended ones, they do give the advantages of both types of spanner.

☐ *Combination spanners:*
 Metric - 8 to 19 mm inclusive
☐ *Adjustable spanner - 35 mm jaw (approx.)*
☐ *Spark plug spanner (with rubber insert) - petrol models*
☐ *Spark plug gap adjustment tool - petrol models*
☐ *Set of feeler gauges*
☐ *Brake bleed nipple spanner*
☐ *Screwdrivers:*
 Flat blade - 100 mm long x 6 mm dia
 Cross blade - 100 mm long x 6 mm dia
 Torx - various sizes (not all vehicles)
☐ *Combination pliers*
☐ *Hacksaw (junior)*
☐ *Tyre pump*
☐ *Tyre pressure gauge*
☐ *Oil can*
☐ *Oil filter removal tool (if applicable)*
☐ *Fine emery cloth*
☐ *Wire brush (small)*
☐ *Funnel (medium size)*
☐ *Sump drain plug key (not all vehicles)*

Repair and overhaul tool kit

These tools are virtually essential for anyone undertaking any major repairs to a motor vehicle, and are additional to those given in the *Maintenance and minor repair* list. Included in this list is a comprehensive set of sockets. Although these are expensive, they will be found invaluable as they are so versatile - particularly if various drives are included in the set. We recommend the half-inch square-drive type, as this can be used with most proprietary torque wrenches.

The tools in this list will sometimes need to be supplemented by tools from the *Special* list:

☐ *Sockets to cover range in previous list (including Torx sockets)*
☐ *Reversible ratchet drive (for use with sockets)*
☐ *Extension piece, 250 mm (for use with sockets)*
☐ *Universal joint (for use with sockets)*
☐ *Flexible handle or sliding T "breaker bar" (for use with sockets)*
☐ *Torque wrench (for use with sockets)*
☐ *Self-locking grips*
☐ *Ball pein hammer*
☐ *Soft-faced mallet (plastic or rubber)*
☐ *Screwdrivers:*
 Flat blade - long & sturdy, short (chubby), and narrow (electrician's) types
 Cross blade – long & sturdy, and short (chubby) types
☐ *Pliers:*
 Long-nosed
 Side cutters (electrician's)
 Circlip (internal and external)
☐ *Cold chisel - 25 mm*
☐ *Scriber*
☐ *Scraper*
☐ *Centre-punch*
☐ *Pin punch*
☐ *Hacksaw*
☐ *Brake hose clamp*
☐ *Brake/clutch bleeding kit*
☐ *Selection of twist drills*
☐ *Steel rule/straight-edge*
☐ *Allen keys (inc. splined/Torx type)*
☐ *Selection of files*
☐ *Wire brush*
☐ *Axle stands*
☐ *Jack (strong trolley or hydraulic type)*
☐ *Light with extension lead*
☐ *Universal electrical multi-meter*

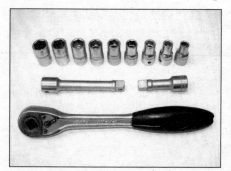

Sockets and reversible ratchet drive

Brake bleeding kit

Torx key, socket and bit

Hose clamp

Angular-tightening gauge

Special tools

The tools in this list are those which are not used regularly, are expensive to buy, or which need to be used in accordance with their manufacturers' instructions. Unless relatively difficult mechanical jobs are undertaken frequently, it will not be economic to buy many of these tools. Where this is the case, you could consider clubbing together with friends (or joining a motorists' club) to make a joint purchase, or borrowing the tools against a deposit from a local garage or tool hire specialist.

The following list contains only those tools and instruments freely available to the public, and not those special tools produced by the vehicle manufacturer specifically for its dealer network. You will find occasional references to these manufacturers' special tools in the text of this manual. Generally, an alternative method of doing the job without the vehicle manufacturers' special tool is given. However, sometimes there is no alternative to using them. Where this is the case and the relevant tool cannot be bought or borrowed, you will have to entrust the work to a dealer.

- ☐ *Angular-tightening gauge*
- ☐ *Valve spring compressor*
- ☐ *Valve grinding tool*
- ☐ *Piston ring compressor*
- ☐ *Piston ring removal/installation tool*
- ☐ *Cylinder bore hone*
- ☐ *Balljoint separator*
- ☐ *Coil spring compressors (where applicable)*
- ☐ *Two/three-legged hub and bearing puller*
- ☐ *Impact screwdriver*
- ☐ *Micrometer and/or vernier calipers*
- ☐ *Dial gauge*
- ☐ *Tachometer*
- ☐ *Fault code reader*
- ☐ *Cylinder compression gauge*
- ☐ *Hand-operated vacuum pump and gauge*
- ☐ *Clutch plate alignment set*
- ☐ *Brake shoe steady spring cup removal tool*
- ☐ *Bush and bearing removal/installation set*
- ☐ *Stud extractors*
- ☐ *Tap and die set*
- ☐ *Lifting tackle*

Buying tools

Reputable motor accessory shops and superstores often offer excellent quality tools at discount prices, so it pays to shop around.

Remember, you don't have to buy the most expensive items on the shelf, but it is always advisable to steer clear of the very cheap tools. Beware of 'bargains' offered on market stalls, on-line or at car boot sales. There are plenty of good tools around at reasonable prices, but always aim to purchase items which meet the relevant national safety standards. If in doubt, ask the proprietor or manager of the shop for advice before making a purchase.

Care and maintenance of tools

Having purchased a reasonable tool kit, it is necessary to keep the tools in a clean and serviceable condition. After use, always wipe off any dirt, grease and metal particles using a clean, dry cloth, before putting the tools away. Never leave them lying around after they have been used. A simple tool rack on the garage or workshop wall for items such as screwdrivers and pliers is a good idea. Store all normal spanners and sockets in a metal box. Any measuring instruments, gauges, meters, etc, must be carefully stored where they cannot be damaged or become rusty.

Take a little care when tools are used. Hammer heads inevitably become marked, and screwdrivers lose the keen edge on their blades from time to time. A little timely attention with emery cloth or a file will soon restore items like this to a good finish.

Working facilities

Not to be forgotten when discussing tools is the workshop itself. If anything more than routine maintenance is to be carried out, a suitable working area becomes essential.

It is appreciated that many an owner-mechanic is forced by circumstances to remove an engine or similar item without the benefit of a garage or workshop. Having done this, any repairs should always be done under the cover of a roof.

Wherever possible, any dismantling should be done on a clean, flat workbench or table at a suitable working height.

Any workbench needs a vice; one with a jaw opening of 100 mm is suitable for most jobs. As mentioned previously, some clean dry storage space is also required for tools, as well as for any lubricants, cleaning fluids, touch-up paints etc, which become necessary.

Another item which may be required, and which has a much more general usage, is an electric drill with a chuck capacity of at least 8 mm. This, together with a good range of twist drills, is virtually essential for fitting accessories.

Last, but not least, always keep a supply of old newspapers and clean, lint-free rags available, and try to keep any working area as clean as possible.

Micrometers

Dial test indicator ("dial gauge")

Oil filter removal tool (strap wrench type)

Compression tester

Bearing puller

This is a guide to getting your vehicle through the MOT test. Obviously it will not be possible to examine the vehicle to the same standard as the professional MOT tester. However, working through the following checks will enable you to identify any problem areas before submitting the vehicle for the test.

It has only been possible to summarise the test requirements here, based on the regulations in force at the time of printing. Test standards are becoming increasingly stringent, although there are some exemptions for older vehicles.

An assistant will be needed to help carry out some of these checks.

The checks have been sub-divided into four categories, as follows:

1 Checks carried out **FROM THE DRIVER'S SEAT**

2 Checks carried out **WITH THE VEHICLE ON THE GROUND**

3 Checks carried out **WITH THE VEHICLE RAISED AND THE WHEELS FREE TO TURN**

4 Checks carried out on **YOUR VEHICLE'S EXHAUST EMISSION SYSTEM**

1 Checks carried out **FROM THE DRIVER'S SEAT**

Handbrake (parking brake)

☐ Test the operation of the handbrake. Excessive travel (too many clicks) indicates incorrect brake or cable adjustment.
☐ Check that the handbrake cannot be released by tapping the lever sideways. Check the security of the lever mountings.

☐ If the parking brake is foot-operated, check that the pedal is secure and without excessive travel, and that the release mechanism operates correctly.
☐ Where applicable, test the operation of the electronic handbrake. The brake should engage and disengage without excessive delay. If the warning light does not extinguish when the brake is disengaged, this could indicate a fault which will need further investigation.

Footbrake

☐ Depress the brake pedal and check that it does not creep down to the floor, indicating a master cylinder fault. Release the pedal,

wait a few seconds, then depress it again. If the pedal travels nearly to the floor before firm resistance is felt, brake adjustment or repair is necessary. If the pedal feels spongy, there is air in the hydraulic system which must be removed by bleeding.

☐ Check that the brake pedal is secure and in good condition. Check also for signs of fluid leaks on the pedal, floor or carpets, which would indicate failed seals in the brake master cylinder.
☐ Check the servo unit (when applicable) by operating the brake pedal several times, then keeping the pedal depressed and starting the engine. As the engine starts, the pedal will move down slightly. If not, the vacuum hose or the servo itself may be faulty.

Steering wheel and column

☐ Examine the steering wheel for fractures or looseness of the hub, spokes or rim.
☐ Move the steering wheel from side to side and then up and down. Check that the steering wheel is not loose on the column, indicating wear or a loose retaining nut. Continue moving the steering wheel as before, but also turn it slightly from left to right.

☐ Check that the steering wheel is not loose on the column, and that there is no abnormal movement of the steering wheel, indicating wear in the column support bearings or couplings.
☐ Check that the ignition lock (where fitted) engages and disengages correctly.
☐ Steering column adjustment mechanisms (where fitted) must be able to lock the column securely in place with no play evident.

Windscreen, mirrors and sunvisor

☐ The windscreen must be free of cracks or other significant damage within the driver's field of view. (Small stone chips are acceptable.) Rear view mirrors must be secure, intact, and capable of being adjusted.

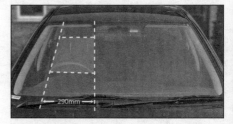

☐ The driver's sunvisor must be capable of being stored in the "up" position.

Seat belts and seats

Note: *The following checks are applicable to all seat belts, front and rear.*

☐ Examine the webbing of all the belts (including rear belts if fitted) for cuts, serious fraying or deterioration. Fasten and unfasten each belt to check the buckles. If applicable, check the retracting mechanism. Check the security of all seat belt mountings accessible from inside the vehicle, ensuring any height adjustable mountings lock securely in place.

☐ Seat belts with pre-tensioners, once activated, have a "flag" or similar showing on the seat belt stalk. This, in itself, is not a reason for test failure.

☐ The front seats themselves must be securely attached and the backrests must lock in the upright position.

Doors

☐ Both front doors must be able to be opened and closed from outside and inside, and must latch securely when closed.

Bonnet and boot/tailgate

☐ The bonnet and boot/tailgate must latch securely when closed.

2 Checks carried out WITH THE VEHICLE ON THE GROUND

Vehicle identification

☐ Number plates must be in good condition, secure and legible, with letters and numbers correctly spaced – spacing at (**A**) should be 33 mm and at (**B**) 11 mm. At the front, digits must be black on a white background and at the rear black on a yellow background. Other background designs (such as honeycomb) are not permitted.

☐ The VIN plate and/or homologation plate must be permanently displayed and legible.

Electrical equipment

☐ Switch on the ignition and check the operation of the horn.

☐ Check the windscreen washers and wipers, examining the wiper blades; renew damaged or perished blades. Also check the operation of the stop-lights.

☐ Check the operation of the sidelights and number plate lights. The lenses and reflectors must be secure, clean and undamaged.

☐ Check the operation and alignment of the headlights. The headlight reflectors must not be tarnished and the lenses must be undamaged.

☐ Switch on the ignition and check the operation of the direction indicators (including the instrument panel tell-tale) and the hazard warning lights. Operation of the sidelights and stop-lights must not affect the indicators - if it does, the cause is usually a bad earth at the rear light cluster. Indicators should flash at a rate of between 60 and 120 times per minute – faster or slower than this could indicate a fault with the flasher unit or a bad earth at one of the light units.

☐ Check the operation of the rear foglight(s), including the warning light on the instrument panel or in the switch.

☐ The warning lights must illuminate in accordance with the manufacturer's design. For most vehicles, the ABS and other warning lights should illuminate when the ignition is switched on, and (if the system is operating properly) extinguish after a few seconds. Refer to the owner's handbook.

Footbrake

☐ Examine the master cylinder, brake pipes and servo unit for leaks, loose mountings, corrosion or other damage. If ABS is fitted, this unit should also be examined for signs of leaks or corrosion.

☐ The fluid reservoir must be secure and the fluid level must be between the upper (**A**) and lower (**B**) markings.

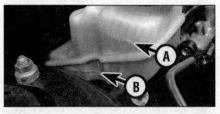

☐ Inspect both front brake flexible hoses for cracks or deterioration of the rubber. Turn the steering from lock to lock, and ensure that the hoses do not contact the wheel, tyre, or any part of the steering or suspension mechanism. With the brake pedal firmly depressed, check the hoses for bulges or leaks under pressure.

Steering and suspension

☐ Have your assistant turn the steering wheel from side to side slightly, up to the point where the steering gear just begins to transmit this movement to the roadwheels. Check for excessive free play between the steering wheel and the steering gear, indicating wear or insecurity of the steering column joints, the column-to-steering gear coupling, or the steering gear itself.

☐ Have your assistant turn the steering wheel more vigorously in each direction, so that the roadwheels just begin to turn. As this is done, examine all the steering joints, linkages, fittings and attachments. Renew any component that shows signs of wear or damage. On vehicles with power steering, check the security and condition of the steering pump, drivebelt and hoses.

☐ Check that the vehicle is standing level, and at approximately the correct ride height.

Shock absorbers

☐ Depress each corner of the vehicle in turn, then release it. The vehicle should rise and then settle in its normal position. If the vehicle continues to rise and fall, the shock absorber is defective. A shock absorber which has seized will also cause the vehicle to fail.

Exhaust system

☐ Start the engine. With your assistant holding a rag over the tailpipe, check the entire system for leaks. Repair or renew leaking sections.

3 Checks carried out **WITH THE VEHICLE RAISED AND THE WHEELS FREE TO TURN**

Jack up the front and rear of the vehicle, and securely support it on axle stands. Position the stands clear of the suspension assemblies. Ensure that the wheels are clear of the ground and that the steering can be turned from lock to lock.

Steering mechanism

☐ Have your assistant turn the steering from lock to lock. Check that the steering turns smoothly, and that no part of the steering mechanism, including a wheel or tyre, fouls any brake hose or pipe or any part of the body structure.
☐ Examine the steering rack rubber gaiters for damage or insecurity of the retaining clips. If power steering is fitted, check for signs of damage or leakage of the fluid hoses, pipes or connections. Also check for excessive stiffness or binding of the steering, a missing split pin or locking device, or severe corrosion of the body structure within 30 cm of any steering component attachment point.

Front and rear suspension and wheel bearings

☐ Starting at the front right-hand side, grasp the roadwheel at the 3 o'clock and 9 o'clock positions and rock gently but firmly. Check for free play or insecurity at the wheel bearings, suspension balljoints, or suspension mount-ings, pivots and attachments.
☐ Now grasp the wheel at the 12 o'clock and 6 o'clock positions and repeat the previous inspection. Spin the wheel, and check for roughness or tightness of the front wheel bearing.

☐ If excess free play is suspected at a component pivot point, this can be confirmed by using a large screwdriver or similar tool and levering between the mounting and the component attachment. This will confirm whether the wear is in the pivot bush, its retaining bolt, or in the mounting itself (the bolt holes can often become elongated).

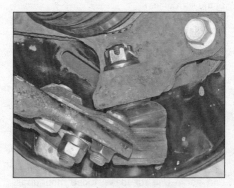

☐ Carry out all the above checks at the other front wheel, and then at both rear wheels.

Springs and shock absorbers

☐ Examine the suspension struts (when applicable) for serious fluid leakage, corrosion, or damage to the casing. Also check the security of the mounting points.
☐ If coil springs are fitted, check that the spring ends locate in their seats, and that the spring is not corroded, cracked or broken.
☐ If leaf springs are fitted, check that all leaves are intact, that the axle is securely attached to each spring, and that there is no deterioration of the spring eye mountings, bushes, and shackles.

☐ The same general checks apply to vehicles fitted with other suspension types, such as torsion bars, hydraulic displacer units, etc. Ensure that all mountings and attachments are secure, that there are no signs of excessive wear, corrosion or damage, and (on hydraulic types) that there are no fluid leaks or damaged pipes.
☐ Inspect the shock absorbers for signs of serious fluid leakage. Check for wear of the mounting bushes or attachments, or damage to the body of the unit.

Driveshafts (fwd vehicles only)

☐ Rotate each front wheel in turn and inspect the constant velocity joint gaiters for splits or damage. Also check that each driveshaft is straight and undamaged.

Braking system

☐ If possible without dismantling, check brake pad wear and disc condition. Ensure that the friction lining material has not worn excessively, (A) and that the discs are not fractured, pitted, scored or badly worn (B).

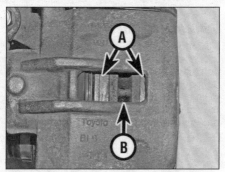

☐ Examine all the rigid brake pipes underneath the vehicle, and the flexible hose(s) at the rear. Look for corrosion, chafing or insecurity of the pipes, and for signs of bulging under pressure, chafing, splits or deterioration of the flexible hoses.
☐ Look for signs of fluid leaks at the brake calipers or on the brake backplates. Repair or renew leaking components.
☐ Slowly spin each wheel, while your assistant depresses and releases the footbrake. Ensure that each brake is operating and does not bind when the pedal is released.

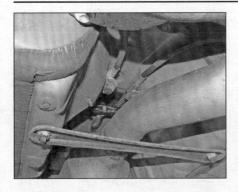

☐ Examine the handbrake mechanism, checking for frayed or broken cables, excessive corrosion, or wear or insecurity of the linkage. Check that the mechanism works on each relevant wheel, and releases fully, without binding.

☐ It is not possible to test brake efficiency without special equipment, but a road test can be carried out later to check that the vehicle pulls up in a straight line.

Fuel and exhaust systems

☐ Inspect the fuel tank (including the filler cap), fuel pipes, hoses and unions. All components must be secure and free from leaks. Locking fuel caps must lock securely and the key must be provided for the MOT test.

☐ Examine the exhaust system over its entire length, checking for any damaged, broken or missing mountings, security of the retaining

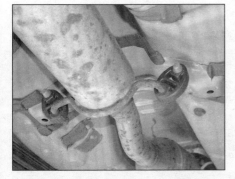

clamps and rust or corrosion.

Wheels and tyres

☐ Examine the sidewalls and tread area of each tyre in turn. Check for cuts, tears, lumps, bulges, separation of the tread, and exposure of the ply or cord due to wear or damage. Check that the tyre bead is correctly seated on the wheel rim, that the valve is sound and properly seated, and that the wheel is not distorted or damaged.

☐ Check that the tyres are of the correct size for the vehicle, that they are of the same size and type on each axle, and that the pressures

are correct.

☐ Check the tyre tread depth. The legal minimum at the time of writing is 1.6 mm over the central three-quarters of the tread width. Abnormal tread wear may indicate incorrect front wheel alignment or wear in steering or suspension components.

☐ If the spare wheel is fitted externally or in a separate carrier beneath the vehicle, check that mountings are secure and free of excessive corrosion.

Body corrosion

☐ Check the condition of the entire vehicle structure for signs of corrosion in load-bearing areas. (These include chassis box sections, side sills, cross-members, pillars, and all suspension, steering, braking system and seat belt mountings and anchorages.) Any corrosion which has seriously reduced the thickness of a load-bearing area (or is within 30 cm of safety-related components such as steering or suspension) is likely to cause the vehicle to fail. In this case professional repairs are likely to be needed.

☐ Damage or corrosion which causes sharp or otherwise dangerous edges to be exposed will also cause the vehicle to fail.

Towbars

☐ Check the condition of mounting points (both beneath the vehicle and within boot/ hatchback areas) for signs of corrosion, ensuring that all fixings are secure and not worn or damaged. There must be no excessive play in detachable tow ball arms or quick-release mechanisms.

4 Checks carried out on YOUR VEHICLE'S EXHAUST EMISSION SYSTEM

Petrol models

☐ The engine should be warmed up, and running well (ignition system in good order, air filter element clean, etc).

☐ Before testing, run the engine at around 2500 rpm for 20 seconds. Let the engine drop to idle, and watch for smoke from the exhaust. If the idle speed is too high, or if dense blue or black smoke emerges for more than 5 seconds, the vehicle will fail. Typically,

blue smoke signifies oil burning (engine wear); black smoke means unburnt fuel (dirty air cleaner element, or other fuel system fault).

☐ An exhaust gas analyser for measuring carbon monoxide (CO) and hydrocarbons (HC) is now needed. If one cannot be hired or borrowed, have a local garage perform the check.

CO emissions (mixture)

☐ The MOT tester has access to the CO limits for all vehicles. The CO level is measured at idle speed, and at 'fast idle' (2500 to 3000 rpm). The following limits are given as a general guide:

At idle speed – Less than 0.5% CO
At 'fast idle' – Less than 0.3% CO
Lambda reading – 0.97 to 1.03

☐ If the CO level is too high, this may point to poor maintenance, a fuel injection system problem, faulty lambda (oxygen) sensor or catalytic converter. Try an injector cleaning treatment, and check the vehicle's ECU for fault codes.

HC emissions

☐ The MOT tester has access to HC limits for all vehicles. The HC level is measured at 'fast idle' (2500 to 3000 rpm). The following limits are given as a general guide:

At 'fast idle' – Less then 200 ppm

☐ Excessive HC emissions are typically caused by oil being burnt (worn engine), or by a blocked crankcase ventilation system ('breather'). If the engine oil is old and thin, an oil change may help. If the engine is running badly, check the vehicle's ECU for fault codes.

Diesel models

☐ The only emission test for diesel engines is measuring exhaust smoke density, using a calibrated smoke meter. The test involves accelerating the engine at least 3 times to its maximum unloaded speed.

Note: *On engines with a timing belt, it is VITAL that the belt is in good condition before the test is carried out.*

☐ With the engine warmed up, it is first purged by running at around 2500 rpm for 20 seconds. A governor check is then carried out, by slowly accelerating the engine to its maximum speed. After this, the smoke meter is connected, and the engine is accelerated quickly to maximum speed three times. If the smoke density is less than the limits given below, the vehicle will pass:

Non-turbo vehicles: 2.5m-1
Turbocharged vehicles: 3.0m-1

☐ If excess smoke is produced, try fitting a new air cleaner element, or using an injector cleaning treatment. If the engine is running badly, where applicable, check the vehicle's ECU for fault codes. Also check the vehicle's EGR system, where applicable. At high mileages, the injectors may require professional attention.

Engine

- ☐ Engine fails to rotate when attempting to start
- ☐ Engine rotates, but will not start
- ☐ Engine difficult to start when cold
- ☐ Engine difficult to start when hot
- ☐ Starter motor noisy or excessively rough in engagement
- ☐ Engine starts, but stops immediately
- ☐ Engine idles erratically
- ☐ Engine misfires at idle speed
- ☐ Engine misfires throughout the driving speed range
- ☐ Engine hesitates on acceleration
- ☐ Engine stalls
- ☐ Engine lacks power
- ☐ Engine backfires
- ☐ Oil pressure warning light illuminated with engine running
- ☐ Engine runs-on after switching off
- ☐ Engine noises
- ☐ Tapping or rattling noises
- ☐ Knocking or thumping noises

Cooling system

- ☐ Overheating
- ☐ Overcooling
- ☐ External coolant leakage
- ☐ Internal coolant leakage
- ☐ Corrosion

Fuel and exhaust systems

- ☐ Excessive fuel consumption
- ☐ Fuel leakage and/or fuel odour

Clutch

- ☐ Pedal travels to floor – no pressure or very little resistance
- ☐ Clutch fails to disengage (unable to select gears)
- ☐ Clutch slips (engine speed increases, with no increase in vehicle speed)
- ☐ Judder as clutch is engaged
- ☐ Noise when depressing or releasing clutch pedal

Manual transmission

- ☐ Noisy in neutral with engine running
- ☐ Noisy in one particular gear
- ☐ Difficulty engaging gears
- ☐ Vibration
- ☐ Jumps out of gear
- ☐ Lubricant leaks

Automatic/DSG transmission

- ☐ Fluid leakage
- ☐ General gear selection problems
- ☐ Transmission fluid brown, or has burned smell
- ☐ Transmission will not downshift (kickdown) with accelerator pedal fully depressed
- ☐ Engine will not start in any gear, or starts in gears other than Park or Neutral
- ☐ Transmission slips, shifts roughly, is noisy, or has no drive in forward or reverse gears

Braking system

- ☐ Vehicle pulls to one side under braking
- ☐ Noise (grinding or high-pitched squeal) when brakes applied)
- ☐ Brakes binding
- ☐ Excessive brake pedal travel
- ☐ Brake pedal feels spongy when depressed
- ☐ Excessive brake pedal effort required stopping vehicle
- ☐ Judder felt through brake pedal or steering wheel when braking
- ☐ Rear wheels locking under normal braking

Driveshafts

- ☐ Clicking or knocking noise on turns (at slow speed on full-lock)

Suspension and steering

- ☐ Vehicle pulls to one side
- ☐ Excessive pitching and/or rolling around corners, or during braking
- ☐ Lack of power assistance
- ☐ Wandering or general instability
- ☐ Excessively stiff steering
- ☐ Excessive play in steering
- ☐ Wheel wobble and vibration
- ☐ Tyre wear excessive

Electrical system

- ☐ Battery will not hold a charge for more than a few days
- ☐ Ignition/no-charge warning light remains illuminated with engine running
- ☐ Ignition/no-charge warning light fails to come on
- ☐ Lights inoperative
- ☐ Instrument readings inaccurate or erratic
- ☐ Horn inoperative, or unsatisfactory in operation
- ☐ Windscreen/tailgate wipers inoperative, or unsatisfactory in operation
- ☐ Windscreen/tailgate washers inoperative, or unsatisfactory in operation
- ☐ Electric windows inoperative, or unsatisfactory in operation
- ☐ Central locking system inoperative, or unsatisfactory in operation

Introduction

The vehicle owner who does his or her own maintenance according to the recommended service schedules should not have to use this section of the manual very often. Modern component reliability is such, that provided those items subject to wear or deterioration are inspected or renewed at the specified intervals, sudden failure is comparatively rare. Faults do not usually just happen as a result of sudden failure, but develop over a period of time. Major mechanical failures in particular are usually preceded by characteristic symptoms over hundreds or even thousands of miles. Those components that do occasionally fail without warning are often small and easily carried in the vehicle.

With any faultfinding, the first step is to decide where to begin investigations. Sometimes this is obvious, but on other occasions, a little detective work will be necessary. The owner who makes half a dozen haphazard adjustments or component renewals may be successful in curing a fault (or its symptoms). However, will be none the wiser if the fault recurs, and ultimately may have spent more time and money than was necessary. A calm and logical approach will be found to be more satisfactory in the long run. Always take into account any warning signs or abnormalities that may have been noticed in the period preceding the fault – power loss, high or low gauge readings, unusual smells, etc – and remember that failure of components such as fuses or spark plugs may only be pointers to some underlying fault.

The pages, which follow, provide an easy-reference guide to the more common problems that may occur during the operation of the vehicle. These problems and their possible causes are grouped under headings denoting various components or systems, such as Engine, Cooling system, etc. The general Chapter, which deals with the problem, is also shown in brackets; refer to the relevant part of that Chapter for system-specific information. Whatever the fault, certain basic principles apply. These are as follows:

Verify the fault. This is simply a matter of being sure that you know what the symptoms are before starting work. This is particularly important if you are investigating a fault for someone else, who may not have described it very accurately.

Do not overlook the obvious. For example, if the vehicle will not start, is there petrol in the tank? (Do not take anyone else's word on this particular point, and do not trust the fuel gauge either!) If an electrical fault is indicated, look for loose or broken wires before digging out the test gear.

Cure the disease, not the symptom. Substituting a flat battery with a fully charged one will get you off the hard shoulder, but if the underlying cause is not attended to, the new battery will go the same way. Similarly, changing oil-fouled spark plugs for a new set will get you moving again, but remember that the reason for the fouling (if it was not simply an incorrect grade of plug) will have to be established and corrected.

Do not take anything for granted. Particularly, do not forget that a new component may itself be defective (especially if it's been rattling around in the boot for months). Also do not leave components out of a fault diagnosis sequence just because they are new or recently fitted. When you do finally diagnose a difficult fault, you will probably realise that all the evidence was there from the start.

Diesel fault diagnosis

The majority of starting problems on small diesel engines are electrical in origin. The mechanic who is familiar with petrol engines but less so with diesel may be inclined to view the diesel's injectors and pump in the same light as the spark plugs and distributor, but this is generally a mistake.

When investigating complaints of difficult starting for someone else, make sure that the correct starting procedure is understood and is being followed. Some drivers are unaware of the significance of the preheating warning light – many modern engines are sufficiently forgiving for this not to matter in mild weather, but with the onset of winter, problems begin.

As a rule of thumb, if the engine is difficult to start but runs well when it has finally got going, the problem is electrical (battery, starter motor or preheating system). If poor performance is combined with difficult starting, the problem is likely to be in the fuel system. The low-pressure (supply) side of the fuel system should be checked before suspecting the injectors and high-pressure pump. The most common fuel supply problem is air getting into the system, and any pipe from the fuel tank forwards must be scrutinised if air leakage is suspected. Normally the pump is the last item to suspect, since unless it has been tampered with, there is no reason for it to be at fault.

Engine

Engine fails to rotate when attempting to start

- [ ] Battery terminal connections loose or corroded *(Weekly checks)*.
- [ ] Battery discharged or faulty (Chapter 5).
- [ ] Broken, loose or disconnected wiring in the starting circuit (Chapter 5).
- [ ] Defective starter solenoid or switch (Chapter 5).
- [ ] Defective starter motor (Chapter 5).
- [ ] Starter pinion or flywheel ring gear teeth loose or broken (Chapters 2A, 2B, 2C and 5).
- [ ] Engine earth strap broken or disconnected (Chapter 5).

Engine rotates, but will not start

- [ ] Fuel tank empty.
- [ ] Battery discharged (engine rotates slowly) (Chapter 5).
- [ ] Battery terminal connections loose or corroded *(Weekly checks)*.
- [ ] Air in fuel system (Chapter 4A and 4B).
- [ ] Major mechanical failure (eg, timing belt) (Chapter 2A, 2B and 2C).

Engine difficult to start when cold

- [ ] Battery discharged (Chapter 5).
- [ ] Battery terminal connections loose or corroded *(Weekly checks)*.
- [ ] Preheating system fault (Chapter 5).
- [ ] Low cylinder compressions (Chapter 2A, 2B, and 2C).

Engine difficult to start when hot

- [ ] Air filter element dirty or clogged (Chapter 1).
- [ ] Low cylinder compressions (Chapter 2A, 2B and 2C).

Starter motor noisy or excessively rough in engagement

- [ ] Starter pinion or flywheel ring gear teeth loose or broken (Chapter 2A, 2B and 2C).
- [ ] Starter motor mounting bolts loose or missing (Chapter 5).
- [ ] Starter motor internal components worn or damaged (Chapter 5).

Engine starts, but stops immediately

- [ ] Faulty injector(s) (Chapter 4A and 4B).
- [ ] Air in fuel system (Chapter 4A and 4B).

Engine idles erratically

- [ ] Air filter element clogged (Chapter 1).
- [ ] Uneven or low cylinder compressions (Chapter 2A, 2B and 2C).
- [ ] Camshaft lobes worn (Chapter 2A, 2B and 2C).
- [ ] Timing belt incorrectly tensioned (Chapter 2A, 2B and 2C).
- [ ] Faulty injector(s) (Chapter 4A and 4B).

Engine misfires at idle speed

- [ ] Faulty injector(s) (Chapter 4A and 4B).
- [ ] Uneven or low cylinder compressions (Chapter 2A, 2B and 2C).
- [ ] Disconnected, leaking, or perished crankcase ventilation hoses (Chapter 4C).

Engine misfires throughout the driving speed range

- [ ] Fuel filter choked (Chapter 1).
- [ ] Fuel pump faulty, or delivery pressure low (Chapter 4A and 4B).
- [ ] Fuel tank vent blocked, or fuel pipes restricted (Chapter 4A and 4B).
- [ ] Faulty injector(s) (Chapter 4A and 4B).
- [ ] Uneven or low cylinder compressions (Chapter 2A, 2B and 2C).

Engine hesitates on acceleration

- [ ] Faulty injector(s) (Chapter 4A and 4B).

Engine stalls

- [ ] Fuel filter choked (Chapter 1).
- [ ] Fuel tank vent blocked, or fuel pipes restricted (Chapter 4A and 4B).
- [ ] Faulty injector(s) (Chapter 4A and 4B).
- [ ] Air in fuel system (Chapter 4A and 4B).

Engine lacks power

- [ ] Timing belt incorrectly fitted or tensioned (Chapter 2A, 2B and 2C).
- [ ] Fuel filter choked (Chapter 1).
- [ ] Uneven or low cylinder compressions (Chapter 2A, 2B and 2C).
- [ ] Brakes binding (Chapter 1 and 9).
- [ ] Clutch slipping (Chapter 6).

Engine backfires

- [ ] Timing belt incorrectly fitted or tensioned (Chapter 2A, 2B and 2C).

Oil pressure warning light illuminated with engine running

- [ ] Low oil level, or incorrect oil grade *(Weekly checks)*.
- [ ] Faulty oil pressure warning light switch (Chapter 2A, 2B and 2C).
- [ ] Worn engine bearings and/or oil pump (Chapter 2A, 2B, 2C and 2D).
- [ ] High engine operating temperature (Chapter 3).
- [ ] Oil pressure relief valve defective (Chapter 2A, 2B and 2C).
- [ ] Oil pick-up strainer clogged (Chapter 2A, 2B and 2C).

Engine runs-on after switching off

- [ ] Excessive carbon build-up in engine (Chapter 2D).
- [ ] High engine operating temperature (Chapter 3).

Engine noises ·

Whistling or wheezing noises

- [ ] Leaking exhaust manifold gasket or pipe-to-manifold joint (Chapter 4C).
- [ ] Leaking vacuum hose (Chapters 4A, 4B and 4C).
- [ ] Blowing cylinder head gasket (Chapter 2A, 2B and 2C).

Tapping or rattling noises

- [ ] Worn valve gear or camshaft (Chapter 2A, 2B and 2C).
- [ ] Ancillary component fault (coolant pump, alternator, etc) – (Chapters 3, 5, etc).

Knocking or thumping noises

- [ ] Worn big-end bearings (regular heavy knocking, perhaps worsening under load) (Chapter 2D).
- [ ] Worn main bearings (rumbling and knocking, perhaps less under load) (Chapter 2D).
- [ ] Piston slap (most noticeable when cold) (Chapter 2D).
- [ ] Ancillary component fault (coolant pump, alternator, etc) – (Chapters 3, 5, etc).

Cooling system

Overheating

- ☐ Insufficient coolant in system (Weekly checks).
- ☐ Thermostat faulty (Chapter 3).
- ☐ Radiator core blocked, or grille restricted (Chapter 3).
- ☐ Electric cooling fan or thermo-switch faulty (Chapter 3).
- ☐ Pressure cap faulty (Chapter 3).
- ☐ Inaccurate temperature gauge sender unit (Chapter 3).
- ☐ Airlock in cooling system Chapter 1.

Overcooling

- ☐ Thermostat faulty (Chapter 3).
- ☐ Inaccurate temperature gauge sender unit (Chapter 3).

External coolant leakage

- ☐ Deteriorated or damaged hoses or hose clips (Chapter 1 and 3).
- ☐ Radiator core or heater matrix leaking (Chapter 3).
- ☐ Pressure cap faulty (Chapter 3).
- ☐ Coolant pump seal leaking (Chapter 3).
- ☐ Boiling due to overheating (Chapter 3).
- ☐ Core plug leaking (Chapter).

Internal coolant leakage

- ☐ Leaking cylinder head gasket (Chapter 2A, 2B and 2C).
- ☐ Cracked cylinder head or cylinder bore (Chapter 2D).

Corrosion

- ☐ Infrequent draining and flushing (Chapter 1).
- ☐ Incorrect coolant mixture or inappropriate coolant type (Chapter or 1).

Fuel and exhaust systems

Excessive fuel consumption

- ☐ Air filter element dirty or clogged (Chapter 1).
- ☐ Faulty injector(s) (Chapter 4A and 4B).
- ☐ Tyres under-inflated (Weekly checks).

Fuel leakage and/or fuel odour

- ☐ Damaged or corroded fuel tank, pipes or connections (Chapter 4A and 4B).
- ☐ Excessive noise or fumes from exhaust system (Chapter 4C)Leaking exhaust system or manifold joints (Chapter 4C).
- ☐ Leaking, corroded or damaged silencers or pipe (Chapter 4C).
- ☐ Broken mountings causing body or suspension contact (Chapter 4C).

Clutch

Pedal travels to floor – no pressure or very little resistance

- ☐ Hydraulic fluid level low/air in hydraulic system (Chapter 6).
- ☐ Broken clutch release bearing or fork (Chapter 6).
- ☐ Broken diaphragm spring in clutch pressure plate (Chapter 6).

Clutch fails to disengage (unable to select gears)

- ☐ Clutch disc sticking on transmission input shaft splines (Chapter 6).
- ☐ Clutch disc sticking to flywheel or pressure plate (Chapter 6).
- ☐ Faulty pressure plate assembly (Chapter 6).
- ☐ Clutch release mechanism worn or incorrectly assembled (Chapter 6).

Clutch slips (engine speed increases, with no increase in vehicle speed)

- ☐ Clutch disc linings excessively worn (Chapter 6).
- ☐ Clutch disc linings contaminated with oil or grease (Chapter 6).
- ☐ Faulty pressure plate or weak diaphragm spring (Chapter 6).

Judder as clutch is engaged

- ☐ Clutch disc linings contaminated with oil or grease (Chapter 6).
- ☐ Clutch disc linings excessively worn (Chapter 6).
- ☐ Faulty or distorted pressure plate or diaphragm spring (Chapter 6).
- ☐ Worn or loose engine or transmission mountings (Chapter 2A, 2B and 2C).
- ☐ Clutch disc hub or transmission input shaft splines worn (Chapter 6).

Noise when depressing or releasing clutch pedal

- ☐ Worn clutch release bearing (Chapter 6).
- ☐ Worn or dry clutch pedal bushes (Chapter 6).
- ☐ Faulty pressure plate assembly (Chapter 6).
- ☐ Pressure plate diaphragm spring broken (Chapter 6).
- ☐ Broken clutch disc cushioning springs (Chapter 6).

Manual transmission

Noisy in neutral with engine running

☐ Input shaft bearings worn (noise apparent with clutch pedal released, but not when depressed) (Chapter 7A).*
☐ Clutch release bearing worn (noise apparent with clutch pedal depressed, possibly less when released) (Chapter 6).

Noisy in one particular gear

☐ Worn, damaged or chipped gear teeth (Chapter 7A).*

Difficulty engaging gears

☐ Clutch fault (Chapter 6).
☐ Worn or damaged gear linkage (Chapter 7A).
☐ Incorrectly adjusted gear linkage (Chapter 7A).
☐ Worn synchroniser units (Chapter 7A).*

Vibration

☐ Lack of oil (Chapter 7A).
☐ Worn bearings (Chapter 7A).*

Jumps out of gear

☐ Worn or damaged gear linkage (Chapter 7A).
☐ Incorrectly adjusted gear linkage (Chapter 7A).
☐ Worn synchroniser units (Chapter 7A).*
☐ Worn selector forks (Chapter 7A).*

Lubricant leaks

☐ Leaking differential output oil seal (Chapter 7A).
☐ Leaking housing joint (Chapter 7A).
☐ *Leaking input shaft oil seal (Chapter 7A).*

Although the corrective action necessary to remedy the symptoms described is beyond the scope of the home mechanic, the above information should be helpful in isolating the cause of the condition. This should enable the owner can communicate clearly with a professional mechanic.

Automatic/DSG transmission

Fluid leakage

Note: *Due to the complexity of the automatic transmission, it is difficult for the home mechanic to properly diagnose and service this unit.*

For problems other than the following, the vehicle should be taken to a dealer service department or automatic transmission specialist.

Do not be too hasty in removing the transmission if a fault is suspected, as most of the testing is carried out with the unit still fitted.

Automatic transmission fluid is usually dark in colour.

Fluid leaks should not be confused with engine oil, which can easily be blown onto the transmission by airflow.To determine the source of a leak, first remove all built-up dirt and grime from the transmission housing and surrounding areas using a degreasing agent, or by steam-cleaning.

Drive the vehicle at low speed, so airflow will not blow the leak far from its source.

Raise and support the vehicle, and determine where the leak is coming from.

General gear selection problems

Chapter deals with checking and adjusting the selector cable on automatic transmissions.

The following are common problems, which may be caused by a poorly adjusted cable:
a) Engine starting in gears other than Park or Neutral.
b) Indicator panel indicating a gear other than the one actually being used.
c) Vehicle moves when in Park or Neutral.
d) Poor gear shift quality or erratic gearchanges.

Transmission fluid brown, or has burned smell

☐ Transmission fluid level low (Chapter 7B).
☐ If the fluid appears to have deteriorated badly it is recommended that it be renewed.

Transmission will not downshift (kickdown) with accelerator pedal fully depressed

☐ Low transmission fluid level (Chapter 7B).
☐ Incorrect selector cable adjustment (Chapter 7B).

Engine will not start in any gear, or starts in gears other than Park or Neutral

☐ Incorrect selector cable adjustment (Chapter 7B).

Transmission slips, shifts roughly, is noisy, or has no drive in forward or reverse gears

There are many probable causes for the above problems, but unless there is a very obvious reason (such as a loose or corroded wiring plug connection on or near the transmission), the car should be taken to a franchise dealer for the fault to be diagnosed.

The transmission control unit incorporates a self-diagnosis facility, and any fault codes can quickly be read and interpreted by a dealer with the proper diagnostic equipment.

Braking system

Vehicle pulls to one side under braking

Note: *Before assuming that a brake problem exists, make sure that the tyres are in good condition and correctly inflated, that the front wheel alignment is correct, and that the vehicle is not loaded with weight in an unequal manner. Apart from checking the condition of all pipe and hose connections, any faults occurring on the anti-lock braking system should be referred to an Audi dealer for diagnosis.*

☐ Worn, defective, damaged or contaminated brake pads on one side (Chapters or 1 and 9).
☐ Seized or partially seized brake caliper piston (Chapters or 1 and 9).
☐ A mixture of brake pad lining materials fitted between sides (Chapters or 1 and 9).
☐ Brake caliper mounting bolts loose (Chapter 9).
☐ Worn or damaged steering or suspension components (Chapters 1 and 10).

Noise (grinding or high-pitched squeal) when brakes applied)

☐ Brake pad friction lining material worn down to metal backing (Chapters or 1 and 9).
☐ Excessive corrosion of brake disc. This may be apparent after the vehicle has been standing for some time (Chapters or 1 and 9).
☐ Foreign object (stone chipping, etc.) trapped between brake disc and shield (Chapters or 1 and 9).

Brakes binding

☐ Seized brake caliper piston(s) (Chapter 9).
☐ Incorrectly adjusted handbrake mechanism (Chapter 9).
☐ Faulty master cylinder (Chapter 9).

Excessive brake pedal travel

☐ Faulty master cylinder (Chapter 9).
☐ Air in hydraulic system (Chapters or 1 and 9).
☐ Faulty vacuum servo unit (Chapter 9).

Brake pedal feels spongy when depressed

☐ Air in hydraulic system (Chapters or 1 and 9).
☐ Deteriorated flexible rubber brake hoses (Chapters or 1 and 9).
☐ Master cylinder mounting nuts loose (Chapter 9).
☐ Faulty master cylinder (Chapter 9).

Excessive brake pedal effort required stopping vehicle

☐ Faulty vacuum servo unit (Chapter 9).
☐ Faulty brake vacuum pump (Chapter 9).
☐ Disconnected, damaged or insecure brake servo vacuum hose (Chapter 9).
☐ Primary or secondary hydraulic circuit failure (Chapter 9).
☐ Seized brake caliper piston(s) (Chapter 9).
☐ Brake pads incorrectly fitted (Chapters or 1 and 9).
☐ Incorrect grade of brake pads fitted (Chapters or 1 and 9).
☐ Brake pads contaminated (Chapters or 1 and 9).

Judder felt through brake pedal or steering wheel when braking

☐ Excessive run-out or distortion of discs (Chapters or 1 and 9).
☐ Brake pad worn (Chapters or 1 and 9).
☐ Brake caliper mounting bolts loose (Chapter 9).
☐ Wear in suspension or steering components or mountings (Chapters or 1 and 10).

Rear wheels locking under normal braking

☐ Rear brake pads contaminated (Chapters or 1 and 9).
☐ ABS system fault (Chapter 9).

Driveshafts

Clicking or knocking noise on turns (at slow speed on full-lock)

☐ Lack of constant velocity joint lubricant, possibly due to damaged gaiter (Chapter 8).

☐ Worn outer constant velocity joint (Chapter 8).
☐ Vibration when accelerating or decelerating (Chapter 8)Worn inner constant velocity joint (Chapter 8).
☐ Bent or distorted driveshaft (Chapter 8).

Suspension and steering

Vehicle pulls to one side

Note: *Before diagnosing suspension or steering faults, be sure that the trouble is not due to incorrect tyre pressures, mixtures of tyre types, or binding brakes.*

☐ Defective tyre *(Weekly checks)*.
☐ Excessive wear in suspension or steering components (Chapters or 1 and 10).
☐ Incorrect front wheel alignment (Chapter 10).
☐ Accident damage to steering or suspension components (Chapter or 1 and 10).

Excessive pitching and/or rolling around corners, or during braking

☐ Defective shock absorbers (Chapters or 1 and 10).
☐ Broken or weak spring and/or suspension component (Chapters or 1 and 10).
☐ Worn or damaged anti-roll bar or mountings (Chapter 10).

Lack of power assistance

☐ Faulty rack-and-pinion steering gear (Chapter 10).

Wandering or general instability

☐ Incorrect front wheel alignment (Chapter 10).
☐ Worn steering or suspension joints, bushes or components (Chapters or 1 and 10).
☐ Roadwheels out of balance (Chapters or 1 and 10).
☐ Faulty or damaged tyre *(Weekly checks)*.
☐ Wheel bolts loose (refer to Chapters or 1 and 10 for correct torque).
☐ Defective shock absorbers (Chapters or 1 and 10).

Excessively stiff steering

☐ Lack of steering gear lubricant (Chapter 10).
☐ Seized track rod end balljoint or suspension balljoint Chapters or 1 and 10).
☐ Incorrect front wheel alignment (Chapter 10).
☐ Steering rack or column bent or damaged (Chapter 10).

Excessive play in steering

☐ Worn steering column intermediate shaft universal joint (Chapter 10).
☐ Worn steering track rod end balljoints (Chapters or 1 and 10).
☐ Worn rack-and-pinion steering gear (Chapter 10).
☐ Worn steering or suspension joints, bushes or components (Chapters or 1 and 10).

Wheel wobble and vibration

☐ Front roadwheels out of balance (vibration felt mainly through the steering wheel) (Chapters or 1 and 10).
☐ Rear roadwheels out of balance (vibration felt throughout the vehicle) (Chapters or 1 and 10).
☐ Roadwheels damaged or distorted (Chapters or 1 and 10).
☐ Faulty or damaged tyre *(Weekly checks)*.
☐ Worn steering or suspension joints, bushes or components (Chapters or 1 and 10).
☐ Wheel bolts loose (Chapter 10).

Tyre wear excessive

Tyres worn on inside or outside edges

☐ Tyres under-inflated (wear on both edges) *(Weekly checks)*.
☐ Incorrect camber or castor angles (wear on one edge only) (Chapter 10).
☐ Worn steering or suspension joints, bushes or components (Chapters or 1 and 10).
☐ Excessively hard cornering.
☐ Accident damage.

Tyre treads exhibit feathered edges

☐ ncorrect toe setting (Chapter 10).

Tyres worn in centre of tread

☐ Tyres over-inflated *(Weekly checks)*.

Tyres worn on inside and outside edges

☐ Tyres under-inflated *(Weekly checks)*.

Tyres worn unevenly

☐ Tyres/wheels out of balance (Chapter, 1 or 10).
☐ Excessive wheel or tyre run-out (Chapter, 1 or 10).
☐ Worn shock absorbers (Chapters or 1 and 10).
☐ Faulty tyre *(Weekly checks)*.

Electrical system

Battery will not hold a charge for more than a few days

Note: *For problems associated with the starting system, refer to the faults listed under 'Engine' earlier in this Section.*

☐ Battery defective internally (Chapter 5).
☐ Battery terminal connections loose or corroded *(Weekly checks)*.
☐ Auxiliary drivebelt worn or incorrectly adjusted (Chapter 1).
☐ Alternator not charging at correct output (Chapter 5).
☐ Alternator or voltage regulator faulty (Chapter 5).
☐ Short-circuit causing continual battery drain (Chapters 5 and 12).

Ignition/no-charge warning light remains illuminated with engine running

☐ Auxiliary drivebelt broken, worn, or incorrectly adjusted (Chapter 1).
☐ Alternator brushes worn, sticking, or dirty (Chapter 5).
☐ Alternator brush springs weak or broken (Chapter 5).
☐ Internal fault in alternator or voltage regulator (Chapter 5).
☐ Broken, disconnected, or loose wiring in charging circuit (Chapter 5).

Electrical system (continued)

Ignition/no-charge warning light fails to come on

- [ ] Warning light LED defective (Chapter 12).
- [ ] Broken, disconnected, or loose wiring in warning light circuit (Chapter 12).
- [ ] Alternator faulty (Chapter 5).

Lights inoperative

- [ ] Bulb blown or LED unit faulty (Chapter 12).
- [ ] Corrosion of bulb or bulbholder contacts (Chapter 12).
- [ ] Blown fuse (Chapter 12).
- [ ] Faulty relay (Chapter 12).
- [ ] Broken, loose, or disconnected wiring (Chapter 12).
- [ ] Faulty switch (Chapter 12).

Instrument readings inaccurate or erratic

Fuel or temperature gauges give no reading

- [ ] Faulty gauge sender unit (Chapters 3, 4A and 4B).
- [ ] Wiring open-circuit (Chapter 12).
- [ ] Faulty gauge (Chapter 12).

Fuel or temperature gauges give continuous maximum reading

- [ ] Faulty gauge sender unit (Chapters 3, 4A and 4B).
- [ ] Wiring short-circuit (Chapter 12).
- [ ] Faulty gauge (Chapter 12).

Horn inoperative, or unsatisfactory in operation

Horn operates all the time

- [ ] Horn push either earthed or stuck down (Chapter 12).
- [ ] Horn cable-to-horn push earthed (Chapter 12).

Horn fails to operate

- [ ] Blown fuse (Chapter 12).
- [ ] Cable or cable connections loose, broken or disconnected (Chapter 12).
- [ ] Faulty horn (Chapter 12).

Horn emits intermittent or unsatisfactory sound

- [ ] Cable connections loose (Chapter 12).
- [ ] Horn mountings loose (Chapter 12).
- [ ] Faulty horn (Chapter 12).

Windscreen/tailgate wipers inoperative, or unsatisfactory in operation

Wipers fail to operate, or operate very slowly

- [ ] Bonnet not closed (built-into the electronic control system) (Chapter 12).
- [ ] Wiper blades stuck to screen, or linkage seized or binding (Weekly checks0,5 and Chapter 12).
- [ ] Blown fuse (Chapter 12).
- [ ] Cable or cable connections loose, broken or disconnected (Chapter 12).
- [ ] Faulty relay (Chapter 12).
- [ ] Faulty wiper motor (Chapter 12).

Wiper blades sweep over too large or too small an area of the glass

- [ ] Wiper arms incorrectly positioned on spindles (Chapter 12).
- [ ] Excessive wear of wiper linkage (Chapter 12).
- [ ] Wiper motor or linkage mountings loose or insecure (Chapter 12).

Wiper blades fail to clean the glass effectively

- [ ] Wiper blade rubbers worn or perished (Weekly checks).
- [ ] Wiper arm tension springs broken, or arm pivots seized (Chapter 12).
- [ ] Insufficient windscreen washer additive to adequately remove road film (Weekly checks).

Windscreen/tailgate washers inoperative, or unsatisfactory in operation

One or more washer jets inoperative

- [ ] Blocked washer jet (Chapter 12).
- [ ] Disconnected, kinked or restricted fluid hose (Chapter 12).
- [ ] Insufficient fluid in washer reservoir (Chapter or 1).

Washer pump fails to operate

- [ ] Broken or disconnected wiring or connections (Chapter 12).
- [ ] Blown fuse (Chapter 12).
- [ ] Faulty washer switch (Chapter 12).
- [ ] Faulty washer pump (Chapter 12).

Electric windows inoperative, or unsatisfactory in operation

Window glass will only move in one direction

- [ ] Faulty switch (Chapter 12).

Window glass slow to move

- [ ] Regulator seized or damaged, or in need of lubrication (Chapter 11).
- [ ] Door internal components or trim fouling regulator (Chapter 11).
- [ ] Faulty motor (Chapter 11).

Window glass fails to move

- [ ] Blown fuse (Chapter 12).
- [ ] Faulty relay (Chapter 12).
- [ ] Broken or disconnected wiring or connections (Chapter 12).
- [ ] Faulty motor (Chapter 11).

Central locking system inoperative, or unsatisfactory in operation

Complete system failure

- [ ] Blown fuse (Chapter 12).
- [ ] Faulty relay (Chapter 12).
- [ ] Broken or disconnected wiring or connections (Chapter 12).
- [ ] Faulty control unit (Chapter 11).

Latch locks but will not unlock, or unlocks but will not lock

- [ ] Faulty control unit (Chapter 11).
- [ ] Broken or disconnected latch operating rods or levers (Chapter 11).
- [ ] Faulty relay (Chapter 12).

One actuator fails to operate

- [ ] Broken or disconnected wiring or connections (Chapter 12).
- [ ] Faulty actuator (Chapter 11).
- [ ] Broken, binding or disconnected latch operating rods or levers (Chapter 11).
- [ ] Fault in door lock (Chapter 11).

A

ABS (Anti-lock brake system) A system, usually electronically controlled, that senses incipient wheel lockup during braking and relieves hydraulic pressure at wheels that are about to skid.

Air bag An inflatable bag hidden in the steering wheel (driver's side) or the dash or glovebox (passenger side). In a head-on collision, the bags inflate, preventing the driver and front passenger from being thrown forward into the steering wheel or windscreen.

Air cleaner A metal or plastic housing, containing a filter element, which removes dust and dirt from the air being drawn into the engine.

Air filter element The actual filter in an air cleaner system, usually manufactured from pleated paper and requiring renewal at regular intervals.

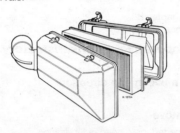

Air filter

Allen key A hexagonal wrench which fits into a recessed hexagonal hole.

Alligator clip A long-nosed spring-loaded metal clip with meshing teeth. Used to make temporary electrical connections.

Alternator A component in the electrical system which converts mechanical energy from a drivebelt into electrical energy to charge the battery and to operate the starting system, ignition system and electrical accessories.

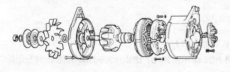

Alternator (exploded view)

Ampere (amp) A unit of measurement for the flow of electric current. One amp is the amount of current produced by one volt acting through a resistance of one ohm.

Anaerobic sealer A substance used to prevent bolts and screws from loosening. Anaerobic means that it does not require oxygen for activation. The Loctite brand is widely used.

Antifreeze A substance (usually ethylene glycol) mixed with water, and added to a vehicle's cooling system, to prevent freezing of the coolant in winter. Antifreeze also contains chemicals to inhibit corrosion and the formation of rust and other deposits that would tend to clog the radiator and coolant passages and reduce cooling efficiency.

Anti-seize compound A coating that reduces the risk of seizing on fasteners that are subjected to high temperatures, such as exhaust manifold bolts and nuts.

Anti-seize compound

Asbestos A natural fibrous mineral with great heat resistance, commonly used in the composition of brake friction materials. Asbestos is a health hazard and the dust created by brake systems should never be inhaled or ingested.

Axle A shaft on which a wheel revolves, or which revolves with a wheel. Also, a solid beam that connects the two wheels at one end of the vehicle. An axle which also transmits power to the wheels is known as a live axle.

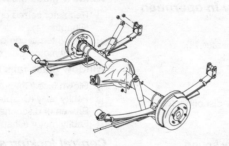

Axle assembly

Axleshaft A single rotating shaft, on either side of the differential, which delivers power from the final drive assembly to the drive wheels. Also called a driveshaft or a halfshaft.

B

Ball bearing An anti-friction bearing consisting of a hardened inner and outer race with hardened steel balls between two races.

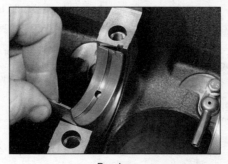

Bearing

Bearing The curved surface on a shaft or in a bore, or the part assembled into either, that permits relative motion between them with minimum wear and friction.

Big-end bearing The bearing in the end of the connecting rod that's attached to the crankshaft.

Bleed nipple A valve on a brake wheel cylinder, caliper or other hydraulic component that is opened to purge the hydraulic system of air. Also called a bleed screw.

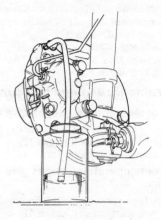

Brake bleeding

Brake bleeding Procedure for removing air from lines of a hydraulic brake system.

Brake disc The component of a disc brake that rotates with the wheels.

Brake drum The component of a drum brake that rotates with the wheels.

Brake linings The friction material which contacts the brake disc or drum to retard the vehicle's speed. The linings are bonded or riveted to the brake pads or shoes.

Brake pads The replaceable friction pads that pinch the brake disc when the brakes are applied. Brake pads consist of a friction material bonded or riveted to a rigid backing plate.

Brake shoe The crescent-shaped carrier to which the brake linings are mounted and which forces the lining against the rotating drum during braking.

Braking systems For more information on braking systems, consult the *Haynes Automotive Brake Manual*.

Breaker bar A long socket wrench handle providing greater leverage.

Bulkhead The insulated partition between the engine and the passenger compartment.

C

Caliper The non-rotating part of a disc-brake assembly that straddles the disc and carries the brake pads. The caliper also contains the hydraulic components that cause the pads to pinch the disc when the brakes are applied. A caliper is also a measuring tool that can be set to measure inside or outside dimensions of an object.

Camshaft A rotating shaft on which a series of cam lobes operate the valve mechanisms. The camshaft may be driven by gears, by sprockets and chain or by sprockets and a belt.

Canister A container in an evaporative emission control system; contains activated charcoal granules to trap vapours from the fuel system.

Canister

Carburettor A device which mixes fuel with air in the proper proportions to provide a desired power output from a spark ignition internal combustion engine.

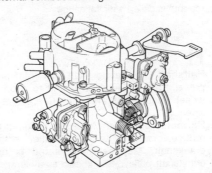

Carburettor

Castellated Resembling the parapets along the top of a castle wall. For example, a castellated balljoint stud nut.

Castellated nut

Castor In wheel alignment, the backward or forward tilt of the steering axis. Castor is positive when the steering axis is inclined rearward at the top.

Catalytic converter A silencer-like device in the exhaust system which converts certain pollutants in the exhaust gases into less harmful substances.

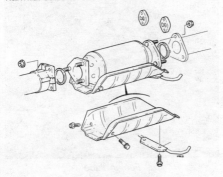

Catalytic converter

Circlip A ring-shaped clip used to prevent endwise movement of cylindrical parts and shafts. An internal circlip is installed in a groove in a housing; an external circlip fits into a groove on the outside of a cylindrical piece such as a shaft.

Clearance The amount of space between two parts. For example, between a piston and a cylinder, between a bearing and a journal, etc.

Coil spring A spiral of elastic steel found in various sizes throughout a vehicle, for example as a springing medium in the suspension and in the valve train.

Compression Reduction in volume, and increase in pressure and temperature, of a gas, caused by squeezing it into a smaller space.

Compression ratio The relationship between cylinder volume when the piston is at top dead centre and cylinder volume when the piston is at bottom dead centre.

Constant velocity (CV) joint A type of universal joint that cancels out vibrations caused by driving power being transmitted through an angle.

Core plug A disc or cup-shaped metal device inserted in a hole in a casting through which core was removed when the casting was formed. Also known as a freeze plug or expansion plug.

Crankcase The lower part of the engine block in which the crankshaft rotates.

Crankshaft The main rotating member, or shaft, running the length of the crankcase, with offset "throws" to which the connecting rods are attached.

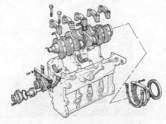

Crankshaft assembly

Crocodile clip See Alligator clip

D

Diagnostic code Code numbers obtained by accessing the diagnostic mode of an engine management computer. This code can be used to determine the area in the system where a malfunction may be located.

Disc brake A brake design incorporating a rotating disc onto which brake pads are squeezed. The resulting friction converts the energy of a moving vehicle into heat.

Double-overhead cam (DOHC) An engine that uses two overhead camshafts, usually one for the intake valves and one for the exhaust valves.

Drivebelt(s) The belt(s) used to drive accessories such as the alternator, water pump, power steering pump, air conditioning compressor, etc. off the crankshaft pulley.

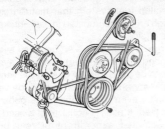

Accessory drivebelts

Driveshaft Any shaft used to transmit motion. Commonly used when referring to the axleshafts on a front wheel drive vehicle.

Driveshaft

Drum brake A type of brake using a drum-shaped metal cylinder attached to the inner surface of the wheel. When the brake pedal is pressed, curved brake shoes with friction linings press against the inside of the drum to slow or stop the vehicle.

Drum brake assembly

E

EGR valve A valve used to introduce exhaust gases into the intake air stream.

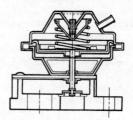

EGR valve

Electronic control unit (ECU) A computer which controls (for instance) ignition and fuel injection systems, or an anti-lock braking system. For more information refer to the *Haynes Automotive Electrical and Electronic Systems Manual*.

Electronic Fuel Injection (EFI) A computer controlled fuel system that distributes fuel through an injector located in each intake port of the engine.

Emergency brake A braking system, independent of the main hydraulic system, that can be used to slow or stop the vehicle if the primary brakes fail, or to hold the vehicle stationary even though the brake pedal isn't depressed. It usually consists of a hand lever that actuates either front or rear brakes mechanically through a series of cables and linkages. Also known as a handbrake or parking brake.

Endfloat The amount of lengthwise movement between two parts. As applied to a crankshaft, the distance that the crankshaft can move forward and back in the cylinder block.

Engine management system (EMS) A computer controlled system which manages the fuel injection and the ignition systems in an integrated fashion.

Exhaust manifold A part with several passages through which exhaust gases leave the engine combustion chambers and enter the exhaust pipe.

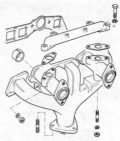

Exhaust manifold

F

Fan clutch A viscous (fluid) drive coupling device which permits variable engine fan speeds in relation to engine speeds.

Feeler blade A thin strip or blade of hardened steel, ground to an exact thickness, used to check or measure clearances between parts.

Feeler blade

Firing order The order in which the engine cylinders fire, or deliver their power strokes, beginning with the number one cylinder.

Flywheel A heavy spinning wheel in which energy is absorbed and stored by means of momentum. On cars, the flywheel is attached to the crankshaft to smooth out firing impulses.

Free play The amount of travel before any action takes place. The "looseness" in a linkage, or an assembly of parts, between the initial application of force and actual movement. For example, the distance the brake pedal moves before the pistons in the master cylinder are actuated.

Fuse An electrical device which protects a circuit against accidental overload. The typical fuse contains a soft piece of metal which is calibrated to melt at a predetermined current flow (expressed as amps) and break the circuit.

Fusible link A circuit protection device consisting of a conductor surrounded by heat-resistant insulation. The conductor is smaller than the wire it protects, so it acts as the weakest link in the circuit. Unlike a blown fuse, a failed fusible link must frequently be cut from the wire for replacement.

G

Gap The distance the spark must travel in jumping from the centre electrode to the side

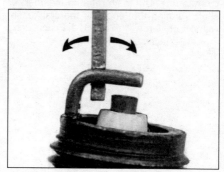

Adjusting spark plug gap

electrode in a spark plug. Also refers to the spacing between the points in a contact breaker assembly in a conventional points-type ignition, or to the distance between the reluctor or rotor and the pickup coil in an electronic ignition.

Gasket Any thin, soft material - usually cork, cardboard, asbestos or soft metal - installed between two metal surfaces to ensure a good seal. For instance, the cylinder head gasket seals the joint between the block and the cylinder head.

Gasket

Gauge An instrument panel display used to monitor engine conditions. A gauge with a movable pointer on a dial or a fixed scale is an analogue gauge. A gauge with a numerical readout is called a digital gauge.

H

Halfshaft A rotating shaft that transmits power from the final drive unit to a drive wheel, usually when referring to a live rear axle.

Harmonic balancer A device designed to reduce torsion or twisting vibration in the crankshaft. May be incorporated in the crankshaft pulley. Also known as a vibration damper.

Hone An abrasive tool for correcting small irregularities or differences in diameter in an engine cylinder, brake cylinder, etc.

Hydraulic tappet A tappet that utilises hydraulic pressure from the engine's lubrication system to maintain zero clearance (constant contact with both camshaft and valve stem). Automatically adjusts to variation in valve stem length. Hydraulic tappets also reduce valve noise.

I

Ignition timing The moment at which the spark plug fires, usually expressed in the number of crankshaft degrees before the piston reaches the top of its stroke.

Inlet manifold A tube or housing with passages through which flows the air-fuel mixture (carburettor vehicles and vehicles with throttle body injection) or air only (port fuel-injected vehicles) to the port openings in the cylinder head.

J

Jump start Starting the engine of a vehicle with a discharged or weak battery by attaching jump leads from the weak battery to a charged or helper battery.

L

Load Sensing Proportioning Valve (LSPV) A brake hydraulic system control valve that works like a proportioning valve, but also takes into consideration the amount of weight carried by the rear axle.

Locknut A nut used to lock an adjustment nut, or other threaded component, in place. For example, a locknut is employed to keep the adjusting nut on the rocker arm in position.

Lockwasher A form of washer designed to prevent an attaching nut from working loose.

M

MacPherson strut A type of front suspension system devised by Earle MacPherson at Ford of England. In its original form, a simple lateral link with the anti-roll bar creates the lower control arm. A long strut - an integral coil spring and shock absorber - is mounted between the body and the steering knuckle. Many modern so-called MacPherson strut systems use a conventional lower A-arm and don't rely on the anti-roll bar for location.

Multimeter An electrical test instrument with the capability to measure voltage, current and resistance.

N

NOx Oxides of Nitrogen. A common toxic pollutant emitted by petrol and diesel engines at higher temperatures.

O

Ohm The unit of electrical resistance. One volt applied to a resistance of one ohm will produce a current of one amp.

Ohmmeter An instrument for measuring electrical resistance.

O-ring A type of sealing ring made of a special rubber-like material; in use, the O-ring is compressed into a groove to provide the sealing action.

O-ring

Overhead cam (ohc) engine An engine with the camshaft(s) located on top of the cylinder head(s).

Overhead valve (ohv) engine An engine with the valves located in the cylinder head, but with the camshaft located in the engine block.

Oxygen sensor A device installed in the engine exhaust manifold, which senses the oxygen content in the exhaust and converts this information into an electric current. Also called a Lambda sensor.

P

Phillips screw A type of screw head having a cross instead of a slot for a corresponding type of screwdriver.

Plastigage A thin strip of plastic thread, available in different sizes, used for measuring clearances. For example, a strip of Plastigage is laid across a bearing journal. The parts are assembled and dismantled; the width of the crushed strip indicates the clearance between journal and bearing.

Plastigage

Propeller shaft The long hollow tube with universal joints at both ends that carries power from the transmission to the differential on front-engined rear wheel drive vehicles.

Proportioning valve A hydraulic control valve which limits the amount of pressure to the rear brakes during panic stops to prevent wheel lock-up.

R

Rack-and-pinion steering A steering system with a pinion gear on the end of the steering shaft that mates with a rack (think of a geared wheel opened up and laid flat). When the steering wheel is turned, the pinion turns, moving the rack to the left or right. This movement is transmitted through the track rods to the steering arms at the wheels.

Radiator A liquid-to-air heat transfer device designed to reduce the temperature of the coolant in an internal combustion engine cooling system.

Refrigerant Any substance used as a heat transfer agent in an air-conditioning system. R-12 has been the principle refrigerant for many years; recently, however, manufacturers have begun using R-134a, a non-CFC substance that is considered less harmful to the ozone in the upper atmosphere.

Rocker arm A lever arm that rocks on a shaft or pivots on a stud. In an overhead valve engine, the rocker arm converts the upward movement of the pushrod into a downward movement to open a valve.

Rotor In a distributor, the rotating device inside the cap that connects the centre electrode and the outer terminals as it turns, distributing the high voltage from the coil secondary winding to the proper spark plug. Also, that part of an alternator which rotates inside the stator. Also, the rotating assembly of a turbocharger, including the compressor wheel, shaft and turbine wheel.

Runout The amount of wobble (in-and-out movement) of a gear or wheel as it's rotated. The amount a shaft rotates "out-of-true." The out-of-round condition of a rotating part.

S

Sealant A liquid or paste used to prevent leakage at a joint. Sometimes used in conjunction with a gasket.

Sealed beam lamp An older headlight design which integrates the reflector, lens and filaments into a hermetically-sealed one-piece unit. When a filament burns out or the lens cracks, the entire unit is simply replaced.

Serpentine drivebelt A single, long, wide accessory drivebelt that's used on some newer vehicles to drive all the accessories, instead of a series of smaller, shorter belts. Serpentine drivebelts are usually tensioned by an automatic tensioner.

Serpentine drivebelt

Shim Thin spacer, commonly used to adjust the clearance or relative positions between two parts. For example, shims inserted into or under bucket tappets control valve clearances. Clearance is adjusted by changing the thickness of the shim.

Slide hammer A special puller that screws into or hooks onto a component such as a shaft or bearing; a heavy sliding handle on the shaft bottoms against the end of the shaft to knock the component free.

Sprocket A tooth or projection on the periphery of a wheel, shaped to engage with a chain or drivebelt. Commonly used to refer to the sprocket wheel itself.

Starter inhibitor switch On vehicles with an automatic transmission, a switch that prevents starting if the vehicle is not in Neutral or Park.

Strut See MacPherson strut.

T

Tappet A cylindrical component which transmits motion from the cam to the valve stem, either directly or via a pushrod and rocker arm. Also called a cam follower.

Thermostat A heat-controlled valve that regulates the flow of coolant between the cylinder block and the radiator, so maintaining optimum engine operating temperature. A thermostat is also used in some air cleaners in which the temperature is regulated.

Thrust bearing The bearing in the clutch assembly that is moved in to the release levers by clutch pedal action to disengage the clutch. Also referred to as a release bearing.

Timing belt A toothed belt which drives the camshaft. Serious engine damage may result if it breaks in service.

Timing chain A chain which drives the camshaft.

Toe-in The amount the front wheels are closer together at the front than at the rear. On rear wheel drive vehicles, a slight amount of toe-in is usually specified to keep the front wheels running parallel on the road by offsetting other forces that tend to spread the wheels apart.

Toe-out The amount the front wheels are closer together at the rear than at the front. On front wheel drive vehicles, a slight amount of toe-out is usually specified.

Tools For full information on choosing and using tools, refer to the *Haynes Automotive Tools Manual.*

Tracer A stripe of a second colour applied to a wire insulator to distinguish that wire from another one with the same colour insulator.

Tune-up A process of accurate and careful adjustments and parts replacement to obtain the best possible engine performance.

Turbocharger A centrifugal device, driven by exhaust gases, that pressurises the intake air. Normally used to increase the power output from a given engine displacement, but can also be used primarily to reduce exhaust emissions (as on VW's "Umwelt" Diesel engine).

U

Universal joint or U-joint A double-pivoted connection for transmitting power from a driving to a driven shaft through an angle. A U-joint consists of two Y-shaped yokes and a cross-shaped member called the spider.

V

Valve A device through which the flow of liquid, gas, vacuum, or loose material in bulk may be started, stopped, or regulated by a movable part that opens, shuts, or partially obstructs one or more ports or passageways. A valve is also the movable part of such a device.

Valve clearance The clearance between the valve tip (the end of the valve stem) and the rocker arm or tappet. The valve clearance is measured when the valve is closed.

Vernier caliper A precision measuring instrument that measures inside and outside dimensions. Not quite as accurate as a micrometer, but more convenient.

Viscosity The thickness of a liquid or its resistance to flow.

Volt A unit for expressing electrical "pressure" in a circuit. One volt that will produce a current of one ampere through a resistance of one ohm.

W

Welding Various processes used to join metal items by heating the areas to be joined to a molten state and fusing them together. For more information refer to the *Haynes Automotive Welding Manual.*

Wiring diagram A drawing portraying the components and wires in a vehicle's electrical system, using standardised symbols. For more information refer to the *Haynes Automotive Electrical and Electronic Systems Manual.*

Note: *References throughout this index are in the form "Chapter number" • "Page number". So, for example, 2C•15 refers to page 15 of Chapter 2C.*

Note: *References throughout this index are in the form "Chapter number" • "Page number". So, for example, 2C•15 refers to page 15 of Chapter 2C.*

Note: *References throughout this index are in the form "Chapter number" • "Page number". So, for example, 2C•15 refers to page 15 of Chapter 2C.*

Preserving Our Motoring Heritage

< The Model J Duesenberg Derham Tourster. Only eight of these magnificent cars were ever built – this is the only example to be found outside the United States of America

Almost every car you've ever loved, loathed or desired is gathered under one roof at the Haynes Motor Museum. Over 300 immaculately presented cars and motorbikes represent every aspect of our motoring heritage, from elegant reminders of bygone days, such as the superb Model J Duesenberg to curiosities like the bug-eyed BMW Isetta. There are also many old friends and flames. Perhaps you remember the 1959 Ford Popular that you did your courting in? The magnificent 'Red Collection' is a spectacle of classic sports cars including AC, Alfa Romeo, Austin Healey, Ferrari, Lamborghini, Maserati, MG, Riley, Porsche and Triumph.

A Perfect Day Out

Each and every vehicle at the Haynes Motor Museum has played its part in the history and culture of Motoring. Today, they make a wonderful spectacle and a great day out for all the family. Bring the kids, bring Mum and Dad, but above all bring your camera to capture those golden memories for ever. You will also find an impressive array of motoring memorabilia, a comfortable 70 seat video cinema and one of the most extensive transport book shops in Britain. The Pit Stop Cafe serves everything from a cup of tea to wholesome, home-made meals or, if you prefer, you can enjoy the large picnic area nestled in the beautiful rural surroundings of Somerset.

John Haynes O.B.E., Founder and Chairman of the museum at the wheel of a Haynes Light 12.

< Graham Hill's Lola Cosworth Formula 1 car next to a 1934 Riley Sports.

The Museum is situated on the A359 Yeovil to Frome road at Sparkford, just off the A303 in Somerset. It is about 40 miles south of Bristol, and 25 minutes drive from the M5 intersection at Taunton.
Open 9.30am - 5.30pm (10.00am - 4.00pm Winter) 7 days a week, *except Christmas Day, Boxing Day and New Years Day*
Special rates available for schools, coach parties and outings Charitable Trust No. 292048